Lecture Notes in Computer S

T0238845

Commenced Publication in 1973
Founding and Former Series Editors:
Gerhard Goos, Juris Hartmanis, and Jan van Leeuwen

Marco Bernardo   Pierpaolo Degano
Gianluigi Zavattaro (Eds.)

Formal Methods for Computational Systems Biology

8th International School on Formal Methods
for the Design of Computer, Communication,
and Software Systems, SFM 2008
Bertinoro, Italy, June 2-7, 2008
Advanced Lectures

 Springer

Volume Editors

Marco Bernardo
Università di Urbino "Carlo Bo"
Istituto di Scienze e Tecnologie dell'Informazione
61029 Urbino, Italy
E-mail: bernardo@sti.uniurb.it

Pierpaolo Degano
Università di Pisa
Dipartimento di Informatica
56127 Pisa, Italy
E-mail: degano@di.unipi.it

Gianluigi Zavattaro
Università di Bologna
Dipartimento di Scienze dell'Informazione
40127 Bologna, Italy
E-mail: zavattar@cs.unibo.it

Library of Congress Control Number: 2008927604

CR Subject Classification (1998): D.2.4, D.2, D.3, F.3, C.3, C.2.4

LNCS Sublibrary: SL 2 – Programming and Software Engineering

ISSN   0302-9743
ISBN-10   3-540-68892-7 Springer Berlin Heidelberg New York
ISBN-13   978-3-540-68892-1 Springer Berlin Heidelberg New York

Springer is a part of Springer Science+Business Media

springer.com

© Springer-Verlag Berlin Heidelberg 2008

Typesetting: Camera-ready by author, data conversion by Scientific Publishing Services, Chennai, India
Printed on acid-free paper   SPIN: 12278602   06/3180   5 4 3 2 1 0

*In Memory of
Nadia Busi*

Preface

This volume presents the set of papers accompanying the lectures of the eighth International School on Formal Methods for the Design of Computer, Communication, and Software Systems (SFM).

This series of schools addresses the use of formal methods in computer science as a prominent approach to the rigorous design of computer, communication, and software systems. The main aim of the SFM series is to offer a good spectrum of current research in foundations as well as applications of formal methods, which can be of help for graduate students and young researchers who intend to approach the field.

SFM 2008 was devoted to formal techniques for computational systems biology and covered several aspects of the field, including computational models, calculi and logics for biological systems, and verification and simulation methods. The school featured not only regular lectures, but also talks given by people involved in the Italian research project on Bio-Inspired Systems and Calculi with Applications (BISCA).

The first part of this volume comprises nine papers based on regular lectures. The paper by Degasperi and Gilmore describes the application of sensitivity analysis techniques to stochastic simulation algorithms. Talcott's paper presents pathway logic, an approach to modeling and analysis of biological processes based on rewriting logic. Fages and Soliman study reaction graphs and activation/inhibition graphs used by biologists through formal methods originating from programming theory. The paper by Maus, John, Röhl, and Uhrmacher discusses categories, abstraction hierarchies, and composition hierarchies playing a role in modeling and simulation for computational biology. Gillespie's paper reviews the theory of stochastic chemical kinetics and several simulation methods that are based on that theory. Păun and Romero-Campero introduce membrane computing, a branch of natural computing aiming to abstract computing models from the structure and functioning of the living cell and the way cells cooperate. The paper by Heiner, Gilbert, and Donaldson illustrates a Petri-net-based framework for modeling and analyzing biochemical pathways, which unifies the qualitative, stochastic, and continuous paradigms. Ciocchetta and Hillston discuss the use of process algebras within systems biology and the related analysis techniques by focussing on Bio-PEPA. Finally, the paper by Dematté, Priami, and Romanel presents BlenX, a new programming language whose original development was thought for biological systems.

The second part of this volume comprises five papers based on BISCA talks. Chiarugi, Degano, Van Klinken, and Marangoni report on experiences in modeling biological cells with process calculi by following a holistic approach. The paper by Barbuti, Caravagna, Maggiolo–Schettini, Milazzo, and Pardini describes the calculus of looping sequences, which is suitable for modeling microbiological

systems and their evolution. Bortolussi and Policriti survey the use of hybrid automata in systems biology through a series of case studies. The paper by Versari
and Gorrieri shows how different compartment semantics useful in biological systems modeling can be obtained by means of a simple and conservative extension
of π-calculus. Finally, Zavattaro's paper uniformly introduces various models for
the representation of biochemical systems recently proposed in the literature.

We believe that this book offers a comprehensive view of what has been done
and what is going on worldwide in the field of formal methods for computational
systems biology. We wish to thank all the speakers and all the participants for
a lively and fruitful school. We also wish to thank the entire staff of the University Residential Center of Bertinoro for the organizational and administrative
support. Finally, we are very grateful to the University of Bologna, which kindly
provided a sponsorship for this event under the International Summer School
Program.

We would like to conclude by remembering our friend and colleague Nadia
Busi. Her most important research contributions were related to the study of
expressiveness problems in concurrency theory, with special emphasis on Petri
nets as well as calculi inspired by coordination languages. In 1998 her doctoral
dissertation "Petri Nets with Inhibitor and Read Arcs: Semantics, Analysis and
Application to Process Calculi" received the EATCS-IT prize for the best Italian
PhD thesis in theoretical computer science. More recently, she became interested
in bio-inspired models of computation. In that field, she developed new classes
of models, such as genetic P systems, and investigated decidability properties
of other formalisms, like brane calculi. She also led the research unit of the
University of Bologna within the BISCA project.

Unfortunately Nadia passed away a few months ago at the age of 39, after
playing – with her usual enthusiasm – a fundamental role in planning the scientific program of SFM 2008. Despite the sadness due to her unexpected death,
we decided to proceed with the organization of the school, because SFM 2008
can be viewed as her last contribution to the scientific community – or maybe
because organizing SFM 2008 gave us a chance to feel Nadia still close to us.
This volume is therefore dedicated to the memory of Nadia Busi.

June 2008

Marco Bernardo
Pierpaolo Degano
Gianluigi Zavattaro

Table of Contents

Sensitivity Analysis of Stochastic Models of Bistable Biochemical Reactions

Andrea Degasperi[1] and Stephen Gilmore[2]

[1] Department of Computing Science, University of Glasgow
[2] Laboratory for Foundations of Computer Science, University of Edinburgh

Abstract. Sensitivity Analysis (SA) provides techniques which can be used to identify the parameters which have the greatest influence on the results obtained from a model. Classical SA methods apply to deterministic simulations of ODE models. We extend these to stochastic simulations and consider the analysis of models with bifurcation points and bistable behaviour. We consider local, global and screening SA methods applied to multiple runs of Gillespie's Stochastic Simulation Algorithm (SSA). We present an example of stochastic sensitivity analysis of a real pathway, the MAPK signalling pathway.

1 Introduction

Reaction-based biochemical models use input parameters such as concentrations and kinetic rate constants to predict the time evolution of a biochemical system. The chemical species involved in the reactions have the role of the output variables of the model. Fig. 1 shows an example with four species.

Sensitivity Analysis (SA) studies the relationships between the inputs and the outputs of models. When we wish to perform SA we choose a time point at which to read the output values. In the case of an ODE model, a selected output (species) has a precise value at a given time. Changing one or more parameters of the model may alter this. In the case of stochastic simulation [1] the output of a selected species at a selected time can be considered to be the collection of the values given by the individual simulation runs. If it is sufficiently large, this set of values will reveal the distribution of the output.

One of the basic SA operations is to compute the difference between the output of a model and the output of the same model with one or more parameters perturbed. This is simple to do with ODE models but not so straightforward when facing stochastic simulation. One simple approach is to take as output the mean of the values coming from the simulations. However, this can lead to a loss of information: by taking the mean we are assuming a normal distribution and we are even neglecting the variance. Another possibility is the use of a distribution distance or *histogram distance* which, with sufficient simulation runs, is able to precisely describe the difference. In [2] this is used to quantify how well an approximate SSA emulates the exact SSA. We use it here with SA to quantify the effect of perturbation of the parameters of a stochastic model.

M. Bernardo, P. Degano, and G. Zavattaro (Eds.): SFM 2008, LNCS 5016, pp. 1–20, 2008.
© Springer-Verlag Berlin Heidelberg 2008

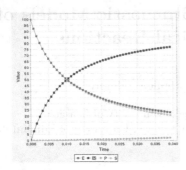
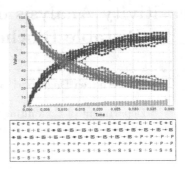

Fig. 1. Examples of time evolution of a biochemical model computed with ODE (on the left) and with SSA (on the right)

Histogram distance is computed as follows:

$$D_k(X,Y) = \sum_{i=1}^{k} \left| \frac{\sum_{j=1}^{|X|} \chi(x_j, I_i)}{|X|} - \frac{\sum_{j=1}^{|Y|} \chi(y_j, I_i)}{|Y|} \right|$$

where X and Y are two sets of numbers, k is the number of histogram columns or intervals which divide the range of the output variable, $|X|$ is the cardinality of the set X (resp. $|Y|$ is the cardinality of the set Y), x_j and y_j are elements of the sets X and Y respectively and the function χ returns 1 if the element x_j belongs to the interval I_i, 0 otherwise. I_i is the i-th interval in the range, which runs from $x_{min} + \frac{(i-1)L}{k}$ to $x_{min} + \frac{iL}{k}$, where $L = x_{max} - x_{min}$.

An interesting measure is then the *self distance*, given by $D_k(X, X')$. This runs the same experiment twice, with the same parameters, and then computes the histogram distance between the results. Perturbations in the parameters which generate values of distances less than or very close to the self distance will be considered not to have an influence, or, at least, we can say that we cannot distinguish any effect arising from this perturbation.

2   Sensitivity Analysis Classifications

According to [3], sensitivity analysis (SA) techniques can be classified as follows.

Local Methods: These concentrate the analysis around a particular point in the parameter space. For example, *local one at a time* and *elementary one at a time* approaches belong to this class.

Screening Methods: These are used to select the most important parameters when the complexity of the model is problematic or the number of parameters intractable. The main idea of these methods is that they should be computationally inexpensive and give the idea of which parameters can be fixed (low importance), even if the information that can be achieved is poor.

They are a tradeoff between information and algorithm complexity. Once the most influential parameters have been identified, it is then possible to apply a more informative and computationally expensive technique.

Global Methods: These techniques try to explore the entire space of the parameters or, at least, explore the subspace that is believed to contain the real value of the parameters and that represents their uncertainty. Usually these are the most computationally expensive, but also the most informative.

2.1   One-At-a-Time Methods

The classical and most widely used SA is the *one-at-a-time* (OAT) approach: a parameter is perturbed (usually by 1%) and the changes in the output measured. Alternatively it is possible to compute the derivative of the output with respect to each parameter to obtain its sensitivity coefficient:

$$S_{ij} = \frac{\delta y_j(\mathbf{p})}{\delta p_i}$$

where $y_j(\mathbf{p})$ is the j-th output of the model which depends on the parameters and p_i is the i-th parameter.

In the study of biochemical systems, OAT methods represent the prevalent practice when analysing ODE models. Other more complex and informative analysis has been proposed [4]. However, none of these are directly applicable to stochastic models whose output is defined as a *probability density function* (pdf) over the number of molecules for each species. The need to consider the entire pdf is very clear in the analysis of bistable systems. These present at a certain time a pdf which is not normal, but instead presents two distinct peaks of likelihood. In this particular context an analysis cannot make any assumptions about the pdf resulting from the model. For this reason SA of stochastic systems is an engaging research question [5] and here we are using histogram distance to quantify the change in the output value:

$$S_i = D(X_n, X_{p_i})$$

where X_n is a *random variable* (r.v.) with nominal pdf $= f(\mathbf{x}, \mathbf{p})$ and X_{p_i} is a r.v. with perturbed pdf $= f(\mathbf{x}, p_1, ..., p_i + \Delta p_i, ..., p_k)$. This distance can instead be divided by Δp_i, leading to a correspondent derivative-based approach.

Together, these approaches can be classified as *local one-at-a-time* (LOAT) SA and are applicable if we assume that varying one parameter at a time affects the output of the model in a proportional way. However, that assumption is often not valid for biological systems making LOAT incapable of giving a complete view of the relationships between parameters and output and also between the parameters themselves. LOAT methods are useful mainly because they can give a first impression of sensitivity indices and because they are computationally inexpensive – an important consideration when dealing with thousands of stochastic simulations.

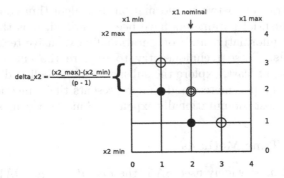

Fig. 2. Example of a grid in the Morris method. In this case we have two parameters ($k = 2$) and a grid level of five ($p = 5$), so the maximum possible combinations are $5^2 = 25$. The black dots are two possible random points, while the circles are other points computed during the algorithm iterations. An efficient implementation should not recompute the point circled twice.

2.2   Morris' Method

Morris' method [3] can be classified as one at a time, because it uses as a basic step the local OAT approach, and global, because the experiment covers the entire space over which the factors are believed to vary. Morris estimates the main effect of a factor by computing a number r of local measures, at different random points $\mathbf{x}_1, ..., \mathbf{x}_r$ in the parameter space, and then taking their average.

When applying this method, a computationally expensive model is assumed, or a model with a large number of factors. The goal is to determine which factors have (a) negligible effects, (b) linear and additive effects, or (c) non-linear interaction effects. This will help to apply later the most appropriate global sensitivity analysis only on the relevant parameters.

The k-dimensional factor vector $\mathbf{x}$ has components x_i that have p values in the set $\{0, 1/(p-1), 2/(p-1), ..., 1\}$. The region of experimentation Ω is then a k-dimensional p-level *grid* (Fig. 2). In practice, the values sampled in Ω are then rescaled to generate the actual values of the parameters as sampled from a specific parameter range. Let Δ be a predetermined multiple of $1/(p-1)$. Then Morris defines the *elementary effect* of the ith factor at a given point $\mathbf{x}$ as:

$$d_i(\mathbf{x}) = \frac{y(x_1, ..., x_i + \Delta, ..., x_k) - y(\mathbf{x})}{\Delta}$$

where $\mathbf{x}$ is any value in Ω selected *such that the perturbed point $\mathbf{x} + \Delta$ is still in Ω*. After sampling r times, the result will be a distribution F_i of elementary effects. The characterisation of this distribution through its mean μ and standard deviation σ gives useful information about the influence of the ith input on the output.

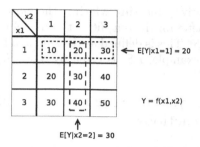

Fig. 3. An example of a possible deterministic model $f(x_1, x_2) = Y$ which depends on the factors x_1 and x_2, together with examples of conditional expectations

2.3 Variance-Based Methods

Variance-based methods use the *variance of the conditional expectation* (VCE) as a measure of the importance of the input factors. The goal in these methods is to estimate the VCE by exploring the space made by all the possible values of the parameters. Applied to ODE-based models, the most well-known techniques are *correlation ratio, Sobol', and Fourier amplitude sensitivity test* (FAST) [3,4,6]. Probability theory states that:

$$V[Y] = V_{\mathbf{x}}[E[Y|\mathbf{x}]] + E_{\mathbf{x}}[V[Y|\mathbf{x}]]. \tag{1}$$

The term $V_{\mathbf{x}}[E[Y|\mathbf{x}]]$ is the variance of the conditional expectation of Y, conditioned on $\mathbf{x}$. This is a suitable measure of the importance of $\mathbf{x}$, identifying the part of the variance of Y due to $\mathbf{x}$. If the variance of Y is matched by the VCE of $\mathbf{x}$ we can say that $\mathbf{x}$ is the only parameter (or set of parameters) which influences Y.

The variance of the conditional expectation is given by:

$$V_{\mathbf{x}}[E[Y|\mathbf{x}]] = \int \left(E[Y|\mathbf{x}] - E[Y]\right)^2 p_{\mathbf{x}}(\mathbf{x}) d\mathbf{x}$$

where $E[Y|\mathbf{x}] = \int y p_{Y|\mathbf{x}}(y) dy$. Here the integral is substituted with the sum over all the possible values of $\mathbf{x}$ sampled from the range of $\mathbf{x}$. A simple example of a deterministic model is shown in Fig. 3.

The parameter space is sampled through the use of a grid. After having collected all the results, the conditional expectations are estimated by fixing a parameter to its possible values in the grid. A complete analysis of the influence of the parameters on the output and on the other parameters is provided but, as can be expected, the algorithm complexity increases exponentially with the grid level and the number of parameters.

Let $S_{\mathbf{x}}$ be the n-th order sensitivity index, with $\mathbf{x} \in \mathbb{N}^n$. This corresponds to the VCE fixing the factors in $\mathbf{x}$ minus the sensitivity indices relative to all the possible combinations of the factors in $\mathbf{x}$. For example, S_{12} is given by $VCE_{12} - S_1 - S_2$ and S_{123} is given by $VCE_{123} - S_{12} - S_{13} - S_{23} - S_1 - S_2 - S_3$. The VCE relative to $\mathbf{x}$, where $\mathbf{x}$ contains all the factors, is nothing but $V[Y]$.

Following [6] the sensitivity measure which is the most suitable to determine the influence of a parameter on the output of the model is the *Total Sensitivity Index* (TSI) or simply TS_i. This is defined as the sum of all the sensitivity indices that contain i in **x**. For example, TS_1 is given by $S_1 + S_{12}$.

3 Sensitivity Analysis of Stochastic Simulations of Biochemical Reactions

In this section we introduce two new sensitivity measures and present them as variants of Morris' method and the variance-based approach respectively. When doing this, we compare these new techniques with their original versions.

From now on, when we refer to results obtained with ODE or deterministic methods, we implicitly intend that they are obtained using a 5/4 Dormand-Prince ODE solver with adaptive step-size. When we refer to results obtained with stochastic simulations, we implicitly intend that we used the original SSA [1], if not otherwise stated.

3.1 The Schlögl Model

The Schlögl model [5,2] is a suitable model to show the differences between usual Local OAT approaches and the one based on histogram distance. It is defined as follows:

Reaction channels	Propensity functions	Stochastic constants	Molecular populations
$A + 2X \xrightarrow{a_1} 3X$	$a_1 = k_1 A X(X-1)/2$	$k_1 = 3 \cdot 10^{-7}$	$X_0 = 247$
$3X \xrightarrow{a_2} A + 2X$	$a_2 = k_2 X(X-1)(X-2)/6$	$k_2 = 1 \cdot 10^{-4}$	$A = 1 \cdot 10^5$
$B \xrightarrow{a_3} X$	$a_3 = k_3 B$	$k_3 = 1 \cdot 10^{-3}$	$B = 2 \cdot 10^5$
$X \xrightarrow{a_4} B$	$a_4 = k_4 X$	$k_4 = 3.5$	

where A and B are kept constant. That is, they are available in sufficient supply that we do not model changes to their molecular populations. The parameter values are set close to a bifurcation point, where a small perturbation in them can lead to completely different results in the ODE time evolution, as can be seen in Fig. 4 (left and centre).

From a single set of parameters the time evolution of the stochastic simulations will follow either one of two possible behaviours, as can be observed in Fig. 4 (right). With the goal of describing the behaviour of this system, ODE models, or the simple average of X from different stochastic simulations could be inappropriate if not misleading. The use of estimated distributions can be considered a more suitable choice.

3.2 Local Methods

Three local one-at-a-time sensitivity analyses have been applied to the Schlögl model: *LOAT (ODE)*, *LOAT (Gillespie Average)* and *LOAT (Gillespie Density)*.

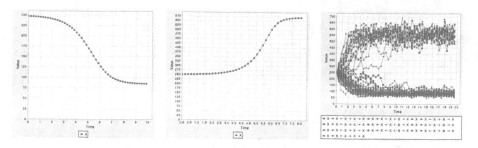

Fig. 4. Left, the time evolution of the output variable X of the Schlögl ODE model obtained with the value of the parameters stated in the text. Centre, the time evolution of X changing only the initial number of molecules of X from 247 to 250: the behaviour seems to completely change. Right, 50 runs of the SSA on the Schlögl model shows the behaviour in a more informative way.

These differ in the way in which the distance is calculated and in the method used to compute the time evolution of the system.

LOAT (ODE): The difference is computed from the output resulting from the ODE models. Performing the analysis more than once will lead to the same result, due to the deterministic nature of the ODEs.

LOAT (Gillespie Average): Many exact SSA simulations are computed here, so the result may change from analysis to analysis, reducing its variation if the number of stochastic simulations increases. The average of the simulations output is used.

LOAT (Gillespie Density): Also in this case, the exact SSA (Gillespie's Direct Method) is used to compute the evolution of the system. In this analysis the histogram distance is used instead of the simple difference of the averages.

Given the difference in the order of magnitude of the parameters of the Schlögl model, we may be more interested in the *relative* perturbation. For this reason we consider the simple output difference a more interesting sensitivity index than the derivative and we will discuss that first.

In Fig. 5 the first significant observation is that the ODE and Gillespie Density procedures share common results. They both show that k_1 produces the same variation as A and that k_3 produces the same variation as B. Indeed, we know that k_1 and A are related, because they could have been considered a single parameter (consider the propensity functions), and this fact has been captured by the analysis. The same reasoning holds for k_3 and B. On the other hand, an important and expected difference appears in the influence of X_0. With ODEs, the output variation induced by the perturbation of X_0 is similar to that of k_1 and k_3, showing high sensitivity. This is due to crossing the bifurcation point. The Gillespie Density method shows instead a low value of histogram distance for the same perturbation, revealing it to be far less influential than k_1. (This latter method can easily be proved to be the correct one by considering Fig. 6,

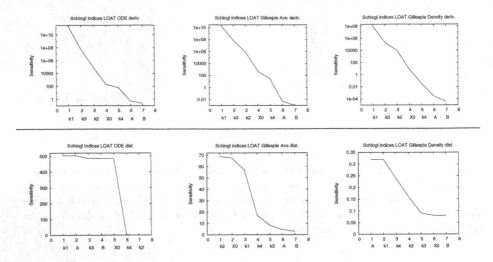

Fig. 5. Results of the three LOAT SA described in the text. The time of the analysis is 20 seconds with a perturbation of 1%. Above the line all results are computed using derivatives (distance divided by the perturbation). Below the line all results are computed using elementary OAT (just distance). The histogram distance is computed with 50 histogram columns and 5000 runs. The histogram self distance for X is 0.068. ODE fractional value 0.001. Results obtained using the simulator Dizzy [7].

where the histograms of the distribution of X at time 20, generated with nominal and perturbed parameter values, nearly coincide. In Fig. 6 can also be observed how the perturbation of k_1 influences the outcome of the stochastic simulations.) Parameter k_3, along with B, has been discovered to be not particularly influential, with a histogram distance close to the self distance.

The Gillespie Average approach seems instead inconsistent, particularly when it shows k_1 and A to have different sensitivities.

To conclude the discussion of the results we can notice how the derivative approach (Fig. 5, above the line) attributes the same order of importance to the parameters in all three cases. However, this is due mainly to their different orders of magnitude and not significant with regard to the sensitivity of the system. It is clear that, at least in this context, a parameter that is estimated to be of the order of 10^{-5} and a parameter that is estimated to be of the order of 10^3 are not directly comparable.

According to the results of this first study we will from now on prefer the simple distance, specifying the relative perturbation in percentage.

3.3 Screening Methods

In this section we apply Morris' method in two different versions: firstly an adapted version of the original algorithm which makes use of the output of ODEs; and secondly a novel modification which uses the information captured by sets of stochastic simulations.

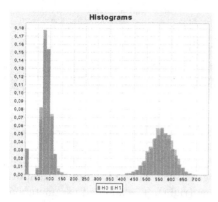 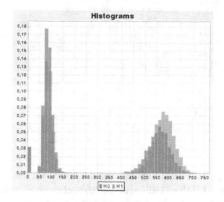

Fig. 6. Values of output X of the stochastic simulations at time 20. On the left with nominal parameter values (H0) and X_0 perturbed by 1% (H1). On the right with nominal parameter values (H0) and k_1 perturbed by 1% (H1). Each histogram is obtained from 5000 samples grouped in 50 columns.

Given our previous experience with LOAT SA we make use of two different *elementary effects*: one being the simple difference of the outputs of ODE models; the other the histogram distance of outputs of stochastic simulations. Moreover we consider the possibility of having multiple outputs:

$$d_{ij}(\mathbf{x}) = y_j(x_1, ..., x_i + \Delta, ..., x_k) - y_j(\mathbf{x})$$
$$d_{ij}(\mathbf{x}) = D(Y_j, Y_j')$$

where in general d_{ij} is the local influence of the ith input on the jth output of the model. Considering a certain fixed time t when the analysis is performed, y_j is the outcome of the output j at that time and $\mathbf{x}$ is the vector of parameters. Y_j is the *random variable* (r.v.) of the outcome of the jth output at time t distributed following the pdf $f(y_j, \mathbf{x})$ and Y_j' is the r.v. of the outcome of the jth output at the same time distributed following the pdf $f(y_j, x_1, ..., x_i + \Delta, ..., x_k)$. $D(Y_j, Y_j')$ is the histogram distance between Y_j and Y_j'.

In order for these two measures to have meaning, we modified slightly the method to generate perturbations which are always comparable. The ranges are chosen as displacement from a nominal value which is proportional ($\pm 10\%$) to that value. In the p-level grid we allow only unitary perturbations (not multiples of $1/(p-1)$ but exactly $1/(p-1)$ every time). This way, every difference corresponds to the same percentage in perturbation with respect to the parameter nominal value which is central in the grid (Fig. 2).

Morris' Methods on the Schlögl Model. The two screening methods have been applied to the Schlögl model. Fig. 7 shows the outcome of the analysis with ODEs used to determine the time evolution of the system. The average elementary effect has the role of ordering the parameters from the most to the least influential. However, the elevated standard deviation of all the parameters

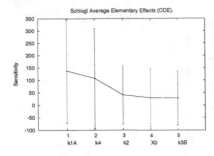 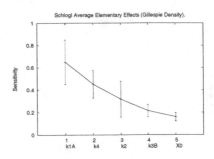

Fig. 7. Result of Morris' method on the Schögl model. Time evolution is computed with ODEs (left) and with stochastic simulations (right). The adopted parameters are 1000 random points for ODE r (40 for stochastic simulations), grid level 5 p, time of the analysis 10s, ±5% from nominal value, ODE fractional value 0.001. Number of stochastic simulations 1000 and number of histogram columns 50. The average histogram self distance of the random points was 0.141 with std. dev. 0.025.

sensitivities makes this classification difficult and reveals that the model is likely to be nonlinear with respect to the parameters and strong dependency between the parameters is also likely to exist.

Fig. 7 shows also Morris' method applied using histogram distance. It is important to bear in mind that all the conclusions are up to the level of precision that is given by the average self distance. Observing Fig. 7 (right) we can at this point say that, with the current approximations, the initial number of molecules of the species X is a factor that appears not to be influencing the value of the species X at time 10 seconds. We can also see that the product k_3B has a weak influence and that this influence does not change particularly as other parameters change (relatively low standard deviation). The other three parameters, k_2, k_4 and k_1A show instead that they have a significant influence, particularly k_1A, and their relative larger standard deviation implies non-linearity and correlations. The reduction of the relative standard deviation in the novel Morris' method helps us to be more confident when stating which factors are the most important and which require to be further analysed.

3.4   Global Methods

We applied variance-based analysis to the Schlögl model, both with the ODE and the stochastic simulation approach. The analysis has been performed considering a subset of three parameters, selected as the most important factors arising from a previous analysis with Morris' method (Fig. 7 on the right). The factors are k_4, k_1A and k_2.

The results of the analysis of the two variance-based approaches are shown in Table 1. We notice that the order of importance of the three parameters is the same, according to the total sensitivity indices. Differences in the first and second order sensitivity indices may be due to the relative weaker importance

Table 1. Variance-based sensitivity analysis of Schlögl model. First-order sensitivity indices relative to the factors k_4 (1), $k_1 A$ (2) and k_2 (3) and other combined effects are shown. The last three rows show the total sensitivity indices. Time of the analysis 10s, grid level 5, fractional step size of ODE method 0.001, number of stochastic simulations 1000, number of histogram columns 50.

	VCE with histogram distance		VCE with ODEs	
index	sensitivity	rank	sensitivity	rank
S_1	0.244	2	21278	2
S_2	0.325	1	30366	1
S_3	0.064	5	4028	5
S_{12}	0.086	4	10033	3
S_{13}	0.008	7	299	7
S_{23}	0.086	3	456	6
S_{123}	0.054	6	8969	4
TS_1	0.392	2	40580	2
TS_2	0.551	1	49826	1
TS_3	0.213	3	13752	3

that k_2 seems to have in the classical analysis. Indeed, sensitivities involving k_2, like S_{13} or S_{23} are weaker in the classical analysis.

4 Sensitivity Analysis of the Mitogen-Activated Protein Kinase (MAPK) Cascades

Mitogen-activated protein kinase (MAPK) cascades [8,9] are signalling pathways which share a particular common structure consisting usually of three levels, where the signal is transmitted from one level to another through the phosphorylation of a kinase. Once activated this phosphorylates the kinase at the next level down the cascade (Fig. 8, left). The MAPK protein that triggers the cell response usually needs to be activated through a two-site phosphorylation. The catalyst for this reaction is a MAPKK (MAPK kinase) molecule and, at the upper level, the same role belongs to a MAPKKK (MAPKK kinase) molecule. The last molecule in this model is the MKP (MAP kinase phosphatase) which dephosphorylates, and so deactivates, the MAPK molecule.

We consider a single level of the MAPK cascade with only one MAPK kinase and without making any distinction between MAPK phosphorylated on tyrosine or theronine. The model consists of a two step double phosphorylation (Fig. 8 on the right). When speaking about this level of the MAPK cascade, we use M, Mp and Mpp as the unphosphorylated, monophosphorylated and biphosphorylated forms of MAPK.

The model of MAPK which we use in this section has been presented in [8] as a system of ODEs which describe the evolution of the concentration of M, Mp and Mpp in time. The rate at which these concentrations change is obtained using assumptions from the Michaelis-Menten kinetics. We use the same set of

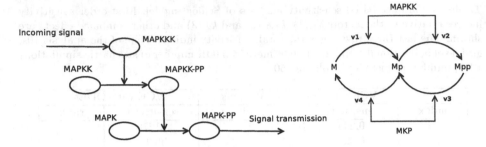

Fig. 8. On the left: structure of a MAPK cascade. At each level, the enzyme that catalyzes the reaction in the next level is activated by a two-site phosphorylation. On the right: model of a level of the MAPK cascade.

equations, but with number of molecules instead of concentrations. This procedure is correct if we assume that the product of the cell volume and the Avogadro number is equal to 1.

The system in Fig. 8 (on the right) is defined by the following enzymatic reactions. Notice how, in the first two lines, phosphorylation and product dissociation are considered a single step, while, in the last two lines, dephosphorylation and product release are two distinct steps.

$$M + MAPKK \overset{k_1,k_{-1}}{\longleftrightarrow} M\text{-}MAPKK \overset{k_2}{\to} Mp + MAPKK$$
$$Mp + MAPKK \overset{k_3,k_{-3}}{\longleftrightarrow} Mp\text{-}MAPKK \overset{k_4}{\to} Mpp$$
$$Mpp + MKP3 \overset{h_1,h_{-1}}{\longleftrightarrow} Mpp\text{-}MKP3 \overset{h_2}{\to} Mp\text{-}MKP3 \overset{h_3,h_{-3}}{\longleftrightarrow} Mp + MKP3$$
$$Mp + MKP3 \overset{h_4,h_{-4}}{\longleftrightarrow} Mp\text{-}MKP3^* \overset{h_5}{\to} M\text{-}MKP3 \overset{h_6,h_{-6}}{\longleftrightarrow} M + MKP3$$

This system can be reduced to only four reactions, under the assumptions of constant number of ATP/ADP molecules and protein-protein complexes at steady-state. These are the resulting reactions and rate equations.

$$M \overset{v_1}{\to} Mp \qquad v_1 = \frac{k_1^{cat} \cdot MAPKK \cdot M/K_{m1}}{(1 + M/K_{m1} + Mp/K_{m2})}$$

$$Mp \overset{v_1}{\to} Mpp \qquad v_2 = \frac{k_2^{cat} \cdot MAPKK \cdot Mp/K_{m2}}{(1 + M/K_{m1} + Mp/K_{m2})}$$

$$Mpp \overset{v_3}{\to} Mp \qquad v_3 = \frac{k_3^{cat} \cdot MKP3 \cdot Mpp/K_{m3}}{(1 + Mpp/K_{m3} + Mp/K_{m4} + M/K_{m5})}$$

$$Mp \overset{v_4}{\to} M \qquad v_4 = \frac{k_4^{cat} \cdot MKP3 \cdot Mp/K_{m4}}{(1 + Mpp/K_{m3} + Mp/K_{m4} + M/K_{m5})}$$

In these expressions $MAPKK$ and $MKP3$ are the total amount of molecules of the two enzymes and are considered constant through time. The nominal

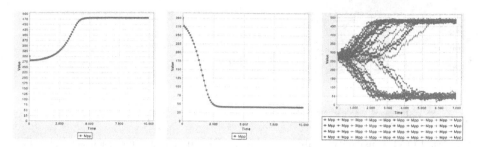

Fig. 9. Left, time evolution of the *Mpp* molecule of the MAPK model computed with ODEs using the nominal parameter values described in the text. Centre, the initial number of molecules of the phosphatase MKP3 is incremented by 5%. Right, 40 runs of the SSA with the nominal parameter values show how the evolution of the system may lead to two different stable systems.

values of the parameters and the relationship with the kinetics of the elementary enzymatic reactions are given below.

$$
\begin{array}{l|l}
k_1^{cat} = k_2 = 0.01 & M_0 = 200 \\
k_2^{cat} = k_4 = 15 & Mp_0 = 0 \\
k_3^{cat} = h_2/(1 + h_2/h_3) = 0.084 & Mpp_0 = 300 \\
k_4^{cat} = h_5 \cdot (1 + h_5/h_6 + h_{-3} \cdot (h_{-4} + h_5)/(h_3 \cdot h_4))^{-1} = 0.06 & MAPKK_0 = 50 \\
& MKP3_0 = 100
\end{array}
$$

$$
\begin{aligned}
K_{m1} &= (k_{-1} + k_2)/k_1 = 50 \\
K_{m2} &= (k_{-3} + k_4)/k_3 = 500 \\
K_{m3} &= (h_{-1} + h_2)/(h_1 + h_1 \cdot h_2/h_3) = 22 \\
K_{m4} &= (h_{-4} + h_5) \cdot (h_4 \cdot (1 + h_5/h_6 + h_{-3} \cdot (h_{-4} + h_5)/(h_3 \cdot h_4)))^{-1} = 18 \\
K_{m5} &= (h_6/h_{-6}) = 78
\end{aligned}
$$

The particularity of these parameter values is that they are close to a bifurcation point. As can be seen in Fig. 9 (left and centre), a small perturbation of an ODE parameter value can lead to a radical change in the behaviour of the time evolution of the double phosphorylated MAPK (Mpp). As with the Schlögl model a set of runs of the SSA shows that the real behaviour of the system with the nominal parameters is a choice between two stable systems. Moreover, thanks to [8], we know that this system with the stated parameters presents three steady-states which we can consider to be three attractors for the stochastic simulations. This situation is confirmed by the graph of the time evolution of *Mpp* in Fig. 9 (right). Although the choice appears to be between two attractors, it is delayed in those runs which are influenced by a central attractor.

4.1   Sensitivity Analysis

In this section we apply both classical SA and the techniques which we developed earlier to the presented MAPK model. We will proceed with a comparison of the methods throughout the analysis. Our choice is to measure the influence of

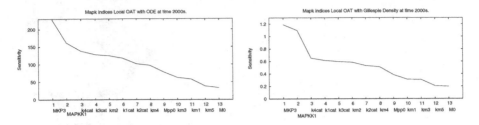

Fig. 10. LOAT sensitivity analysis of the MAPK model at time 2000 seconds. The result of classical analysis is on the left and the result of the analysis based on histogram distance is on the right. ODE time evolution is computed with fractional step size of 0.0001, while we used 10000 stochastic simulations and 50 histogram columns in the SSA runs. The perturbation of each parameter has been by 5%. The histogram self distance is 0.1.

the factors, kinetics and initial number of molecules, on the amount of double phosphorylated MAPK (*Mpp*). To do so, we choose the time of the analysis to be 2000 seconds. This time, as revealed in Fig. 9, is at the core of the choice between the two possible behaviours of the system and is within the limits of our possibilities in terms of computational power when using the SSA.

Local one-at-a-time Analysis. As a first step in the sensitivity analysis of the MAPK model, we performed a LOAT analysis. As we have seen, this consists of the perturbation of one of the factors at a time and in the measurement of the corresponding output change with respect to the original model. We used two different measures: the simple difference of the values of *Mpp* at time 2000 seconds generated using ODE-based results; and the histogram distance between the sets of values of *Mpp* at time 2000 seconds collected using stochastic simulations. With this first and computationally inexpensive analysis, we can have an idea of the relevance of the factors in the immediate surrounding of the factor nominal values. However, we have to bear in mind that without a global analysis we cannot be certain of the implications that may arise from perturbing more than one factor simultaneously. This last point cannot be neglected when trying to assert the influence of a factor on the model.

The results of the local one-at-a-time analysis are shown in Fig. 10. The thirteen factors are listed in the graphs from the most relevant to the least. We can notice that the relative order of importance is not particularly affected by the method used for the analysis. However, with the deterministic approach it appears that just the amount of phosphatase MKP3 is the most relevant factor, while with the stochastic approach, the intuition is that both the amount of kinase MAPKK and phosphatase MKP3 are the most relevant factors, above all the others.

This last statement can be defended, at least in this local analysis, through reference to the histograms generated using the results of the stochastic simulations of the perturbed models. Fig. 11 highlights that the initial amount of MAPKK and MKP3 are both the most influential factors. Moreover, they play

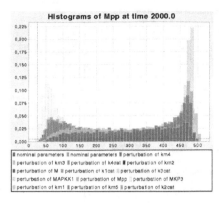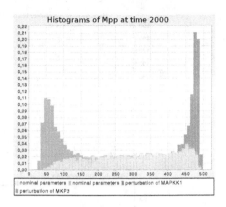

Fig. 11. Histograms which collect the values of *Mpp* obtained using 10000 stochastic simulations. Each histogram is divided into 50 columns. Left, all the histograms resulting from the one-at-a-time (OAT) analysis, one for each factor perturbed. Right, a second OAT analysis with only the histograms relative to the perturbations of the initial amount of MAPKK and MKP3. The histograms labelled with *nominal parameters* are those generated with the values of the parameters stated in the text.

the strongest role in the choice between the two possible stable systems. They have opposite roles, since increasing the amount of one of the two enzymes leads to opposite choices. It is indeed not surprising that the condition of bi-stability is guided by the right proportion in the amount of enzymes that catalyze the reactions.

Screening with Morris' Methods. Before we proceed to a more detailed analysis, we wish to use a screening method to identify and then exclude those factors that are clearly the least influential. Once we have isolated only a small part of most influential factors, we can proceed with the computationally expensive techniques which can provide the most detailed analysis. To do so, we use the techniques we developed earlier based on Morris' method. As we have seen, we consider a range of possible values for each factor and then we sample in the vector space generated by all the possible combinations of values of all the factors. This sampling is done randomly and through the use of a grid. We use here a grid level of five, meaning that each of the thirteen parameters can assume one of five possible values. For each random point selected in the grid of all the possible combinations of values, a LOAT analysis is performed. The indices resulting from that are the *elementary effects* which are local with respect to that random point. Averaging over all these local analyses reveals whether the degree of importance of a parameter is constant or changes when the other factors assume other values. The results of Morris' method applied to the MAPK model are shown in Fig. 12.

Also in this case we compare the results obtained with the deterministic method which uses the time evolution computed with ODE and the stochastic method which uses time evolution computed with SSA. The ODE-based

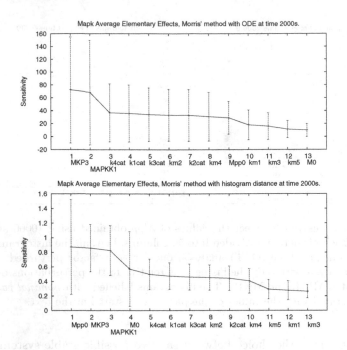

Fig. 12. The result of Morris' method applied to the MAPK model. ODE integration uses a fractional step size of 0.0001. Result obtained with a grid level of 5 and an average over 1000 random points. In the approach based on histogram distance, 1000 runs of SSA, 50 columns and 40 random points have been used and the average histogram distance is 0.15 with standard deviation of 0.061. The parameters vary within ± 10% of their nominal value.

approach highlights that, although the most influential parameters are confirmed to be the initial amount of MAPKK and MKP3, the elementary effects of the factors are extremely variable. In this case it is difficult to say which factors we want to include in the detailed global analysis, if we exclude MAPKK and MKP3. The important standard deviation of the elementary effects is certainly due to a correlation between the factors and the non-linearity of the model output with respect to the parameters.

Before discussing the results obtained with Morris' method based on histogram distance, we need to point out that we were forced to limit the accuracy of the analysis, due to the demanding asymptotic complexity of the algorithms and the computational power available to us. Each experiment is made of 1000 stochastic simulations, number which leads to a relatively high histogram self distance of 0.150, and a standard deviation of 0.061. However, we have already seen in the LOAT analysis that the self distance can be considerable even with the greater precision of 10000 stochastic simulations (self distance of 0.1, see Fig. 10). Therefore, it appears that the point in time where we perform our analysis is particularly unstable, with high stochasticity and indecision from the single runs about which stable system to choose. We can then assume that we have two factors that limit the accuracy of our results: a limited number of stochastic simulations and a strong stochasticity already present in the model.

The results of Morris' method based on histogram distance, shown in Fig. 12, confirm the strongly non-linear dependence in the model and the inconstant influence of the parameters on the amount of double phosphorylated MAPK at time 2000 seconds. On a more positive note, this method appears to achieve a more precise information than the ODE-based analysis. First of all, many parameters have reduced the standard deviation of their elementary effect. We can therefore be more confident when stating that some factors are less influential than others. Moreover, the strong influence which is attributed to the initial amount of the enzymes MAPKK and MKP3 is more clearly evident. Finally, this second analysis assigns a different role to the factors Mpp_0 and M_0. Here, they appear to have a stronger average sensitivity, though this sensitivity may vary considerably (large standard deviation), showing a strong dependence on the value of the other parameters.

Global Analysis with Variance Decomposition. Thanks to the screening which we applied in the previous section, we can now apply a global and more informative method to a reduced set of parameters taken from the factors of the MAPK model. The factors that proved to be the most influential are the initial number of molecules of MAPKK and MKP3, so we investigate their influence as single parameters and their combined effect. For this purpose we used the techniques developed in Section 3.4. Again, a method based on differences of outputs of ODEs and one based on histogram distances of executions of SSA are compared. These measures consider the variance of the output: while the former focuses on the variance of the ODE output, the latter estimates the variance in the distribution approximated by histograms. In both cases, the quantity of the variance that is due to each parameter is identified (Table 2).

In both the approaches, the initial amount of MAPKK and MKP3 present the same level of importance, with the former that is slightly more influential. The difference lies in the importance that is given to the combined effect of the two factors. While with the first approach the combined effect is considerably less than the single effects, with the second approach it appears that the two

Table 2. First and second order sensitivity indices relative to the factors $MAPKK_0$ (1) and $MKP3_0$ (2) of the MAPK model and their combined effect (12), obtained computing the variance of the conditional expectation. The fractional step size used in the ODE integration is 0.0001, the number of stochastic simulations used is 5000 and the number of histogram columns is 50. The parameters vary within $\pm$ 10% of their nominal value.

	Variance-based with ODEs		Variance-based with histogram distance	
index	sensitivity	rank	sensitivity	rank
S_1	15695.65	1	0.350	2
S_2	15308.66	2	0.332	3
S_{12}	5631.88	3	0.811	1

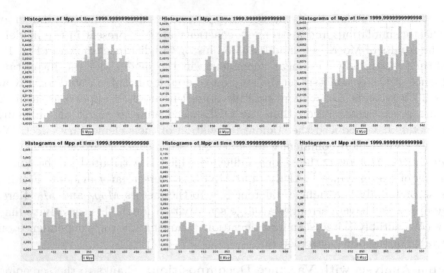

Fig. 13. Distribution of the values of Mpp from 2000 stochastic simulations at time 2000 seconds, with simultaneous perturbation of MAPKK and MKP3. Above, from left to right: number of molecules of the enzymes decreased by 20%, 10% and with their nominal value. Below, from left to right: number of molecules of the enzymes increased by 10%, 20% and 30%.

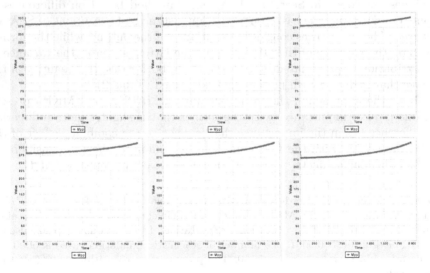

Fig. 14. Time evolution of the double phosphorylated MAPK (Mpp) with ODE for 2000 seconds, with simultaneous perturbation of MAPKK and MKP3. Above, from left to right: number of molecules of the enzymes decreased by 20%, 10% and with their nominal value. Below, from left to right: number of molecules of the enzymes increased by 10%, 20% and 30%.

parameters are more linked. Changing them together leads to a stronger influence with respect to a one-at-a-time change.

The visualisations in Fig. 13 help to prove the connection and reciprocal influence of the factors of this model. In this figure one can see that the combined perturbation of MAPKK and MKP3 leads to a variation of the distribution of the set of values obtained with the stochastic simulations. Although the mean of these values appears to be the same, the distributions seem to pass from a compact and largely Gaussian shaped (on the left) to a more irregular one, which begins to show the two peaks of the bi-stability. This observations can be interpreted as the simple fact that increasing the amount of enzymes accelerates the process, allowing the two stable choices to be reached sooner. Other interesting visualisations are those in Fig. 14, where we can observe that the ODE integration fails to interpret the high stochasticity and indecision present in the system at time 2000 seconds. However, also in this case, incrementing or decreasing the quantity of enzymes accelerates or slows the production of MAPK-PP (Mpp).

5   Conclusions

In this paper we have shown an example of how sensitivity analysis of a model of biochemical reactions can be performed using both deterministic and stochastic approaches. As a first result, we have shown how global analysis such as Morris' method first and the variance decomposition after, are necessary and must be used to identify the relationship between the factors. For example, if we had to rely only on a local analysis, we would just accept the order of importance given in Fig. 10. However, thanks to the further application of a global screening method (Fig. 12), we have been able to state that this order of importance may vary if we change the value of more than a single factor at once. This suggested, if not actually demanded, a further and more informative analysis concerning those factors that seemed the most influential and dependent on the others. In this case, we showed the intuitive relationship between the enzymes MAPKK and MKP3, whose simultaneous increment accelerates the system and whose proportions play the main role in the bi-stability of the system.

As a second but not less important result, the comparison between deterministic and stochastic approaches to sensitivity analyis highlighted how, when dealing with bistable systems near a bifurcation point, it becomes necessary to have a sensitivity analysis tool that takes into account the distribution behind a set of stochastic simulations. Although the analytical analysis of the ODEs is fundamental to identify the bifurcation points and the multiple steady-states, ODE integrations cannot model the uncertainty in the time evolution of the system close to those bifurcation points. In this situation of high stochasticity, a more suitable sensitivity analysis is one that takes into account the variations between sets of stochastic simulations rather than the simple output of a ODE integration. Here, for example, we have seen how a modified version of Morris' method, identified some properties that the deterministic method was not able to capture.

Acknowledgements. Stephen Gilmore is supported by the "Stochastic process algebra for biochemical signalling pathway analysis" (SIGNAL) project funded by the Engineering and Science Research Council (EPSRC) under grant number EP/E031439/1.

References

1. Gillespie, D.T.: Exact stochastic simulation of coupled chemical reactions. Journal of Physical Chemistry 81(25), 2340–2361 (1977)
2. Cao, Y., Petzold, L.: Accuracy limitations and the measurement of errors in the stochastic simulation of chemically reacting systems. J. Comput. Phys. 212(1), 6–24 (2006)
3. Saltelli, A., Chan, K., Scott, E.M. (eds.): Sensitivity Analysis. Wiley, Chichester (2000)
4. Saltelli, A., Ratto, M., Stefano, T., Francesca, C.: Sensitivity analysis for chemical models. Chem Rev 105(7), 2811–2828 (2005)
5. Gunawan, R., Cao, Y., Petzold, L., Doyle, F.J.: Sensitivity analysis of discrete stochastic systems. Biophys J 88(4), 2530–2540 (2005)
6. Chan, K., Saltelli, A., Tarantola, S.: Sensitivity analysis of model output: Variance-based methods make the difference. In: Proceedings of the 1997 Winter Simulation Conference, pp. 261–268 (1997)
7. Ramsey, S., Orrell, D., Bolouri, H.: Dizzy: stochastic simulation of large-scale genetic regulatory networks. J Bioinform Comput Biol 3(2), 415–436 (2005)
8. Markevich, N.I., Hoek, J.B., Kholodenko, B.N.: Signaling switches and bistability arising from multisite phosphorylation in protein kinase cascades. The Journal of Cell Biology 164, 353–359 (2004)
9. Klipp, E., Herwig, R., Kowald, A., Wierling, C., Lehrach, H. (eds.): Systems Biology in practice. Wiley-Vch, Chichester (2005)

Pathway Logic

Carolyn Talcott*

SRI International

333 Ravenswood Avenue, Menlo Park, CA 94025, USA

clt@csl.sri.com

Abstract. Pathway Logic (PL) is an approach to modeling and analysis of biological processes based on rewriting logic. This tutorial describes the use of PL to model signal transduction processes. It begins with a general discussion of Symbolic Systems Biology, followed by some background on rewriting logic and signal transduction. The representation and analysis of a small model Ras and Raf activation is presented in some detail. This is followed by discussion of a curated model of early signaling events in response to Epidermal Growth Factor stimulation.

Keywords: Symbolic systems biology, rewriting logic, signal transduction, Pathway Logic, Epidermal Growth Factor signaling.

1 Symbolic Modeling of Cellular Processes

Biological processes are complex. They exhibit dynamics with a huge range of time scales: microseconds to years. The spatial scales cover 12 orders of magnitude: metabolite to single protein to cell to organ to whole organism. Just considering the cellular level, cells interact with their environemt, both sensing and affecting. They have many behaviors: they can grow, proliferate, migrate, differentiate, or die. Underlying these behaviors are a variety of processes such as gene regulation, signal transduction, and metabolism that interact with one another in complex ways. Genes are regulated by proteins (and other molecular entities) binding to promoter regions. This determines which genes are expressed (turned on) and thus which new proteins are produced. These proteins may in turn regulate the same or other genes. A cell senses its environment by receptors in the membrane that recognize specific types of molecule or condition. This results in *signal transduction* that transmits the information to appropriate components inside the cell. Mechansims underlying the flow of information include modification of protein state, formation of complexes, and change of location. The flow is controlled by mechanisms that activate or inactivate proteins in the signaling path. Metabolism involves both synthesis and degradation of chemicals to generate energy, synthesize protein building blocks (amino acids), and cell structure components amongst other things. Metabolic processes are controlled by enzymes which may in turn be activated or inhibited by signaling processes. Furthermore, metabolites such as glucose play role in controling signal flow.

---

* This work was partially supported by NSF grant IIS-0513857. The development of Pathway Logic was partially supported by grants from NIH NIGMS and NCI.

M. Bernardo, P. Degano, and G. Zavattaro (Eds.): SFM 2008, LNCS 5016, pp. 21–53, 2008.

Oceans of experimental biological data are being generated, from both traditional and emerging high throughput techniques. How can we use this data to develop better models? Important intuitions are captured in mental models that biologists build of biological processes and the cartoons they draw. The trouble is that these models are not amenable to computational analysis. High level statistical models can be developed, for example to discover possible correlations and causal relations, such models may suggest useful insights, but have many limitations such as features that can not be modeled. Low level, detailed kinetic or stochastic models can be developed for small subsystems, but often requires parameter fitting, so that the reaction rates used reflect unknown biological context.

Symbolic systems biology is the *qualitative and quantitative* study of biological processes as integrated systems rather than as isolated parts. Our focus is on modeling causal networks of biomolecular interactions in a logical framework at multiple scales. The aim is to develop formal models that are as close as possible to domain experts (biologists) mental models. Furthermore, it is important to be able to compute with and analyze these complex networks. The latter includes techniques for abstracting and refining the logical models; using simulation and deduction to compute or check postulated properties; and make testable predictions about possible outcomes, using experimental results to update the models.

There are many challenges in developing symbolic systems models. One challenge is choosing the right abstractions. Biological networks (metabolic, protein, or regulatory, for example) are large and diverse. It is important to balance computational complexity against model fidelity and to be able to move between models of different levels of detail, using different formalisms in meaningful ways. Biological networks combine to produce high levels of physiological organization, for example, circadian clock subnetworks are integrated with metabolic, survival, and growth subnetworks. A second challenge is to be able to compose different views or models of different components into integrated system models.

Symbolic/logical models allow one to represent partial information and to model and analyze systems at multiple levels of detail, depending on information available and questions to be studied. Such models are based on formalisms that provide language for representing system states and mechanisms of change such as reactions, well-defined semantics for these languages, and tools for analysis based on the underlying semantics. Of particular interest are symbolic models that are *executable*, that is the model describes system states and provides rules specifying the ways in which the state may change. Such models can be used for simulation of system behavior. In addition properties of processes can be stated in associated logical languages and checked using tools for formal analysis.

Given an executable model such as that described above, the path graph of a given initial state is a graph whose nodes are the reachable states and whose edges are the rules connecting them. Paths through the graph then correspond to possible ways a system can evolve. An execution strategy picks out a particular path among those possible. For such a model, there are many kinds of analysis that can be carried out, including: static analysis, forward simulation, forward search, backward search, model checking, constraint solving, and meta analysis.

Static analysis allows one to examine the structure of the model and to understand how the elements are related and organized (the sort structure). It can be used to infer flow of control and dependencies. Static analysis also provides a means to check for inconsistencies or ill-formed declarations and to look for missing information.

Forward simulation runs the model from a given initial state using a specified strategy either for a fixed number of steps, or until no more rewrites apply. This is extremely fast, and very useful for initial exploration.

Forward search is a breadth-first search of all paths through the transition graph for a given initial state. It will find ALL possible outcomes from a given initial state. Search can also be constrained to find a possibly limited number of states satisfying a given property.

Backward search runs the model backwards. For models satisfying certain constraints, backwards search can answer the question: "From what initial states can we get to this state?". For example it can be used to find all possible precursors to a particular checkpoint.

Model checking expands the collection of properties that can be investigated. Search concerns only properties of individual states. Model-checking tools are based on algorithms to determine if all computations of a system (pathways / sequences of steps) satisfy a given property. For example we can ask if molecule X is never produced before molecule Y has been produced. If not, a pathway that fails to satisfy the property (molecule Y is produced and molecule X is produced before it) is returned. Turning this around, to find a pathway satisfying a property of particular interest, one asserts that no such pathway exists and a counterexample will be one of the desired pathways. An example of another kind of property that can be model checked is: "If we reach a state that satisfies P then do we always later reach a state satisfying Q?"

Constraint solving attempts to find values for a set of variables that satisfy a given set of constraints. Maximal satisfiability (MaxSat) problems are a generalization of constraint satisfaction problems where there may be conflicting constraints, and hence no assignment of values to variables that will satisfy them all. Weights (importance measures) are assigned to constraints and a MaxSat solver finds a solution maximizing the total weight of the satisfied constraints. Many static analysis problems can be formulate as constraint systems. Steady state analyses such as determining possible flows of information or chemicals through a system can be formulated as constraint problems.

Meta analysis allows us to reason about the models themselves. Essential features of models can be abstracted to form families of related models, allowing us to work with uncertainty about reactions. Starting with a base set of known reactions, different instantiations of sets of reactions can be explored. For example, we can search for models where a given path property is true in a given initial state. In addition, rules themselves can be abstracted into families of rules, each family corresponding, for example, to a particular type of reaction, such as activation, inhibition, or translocation. It also allows the knowledge base to be queried as data base, for example finding all rules that involve a given protein (in any or a specified state or location). Finally, using mappings of logics a model can be mapped to another formalism to take advantage of additional tools.

2   A Sampling of Symbolic Modeling Approaches

A variety of formalisms initially developed to model and analyze concurrent computer systems have been used to develop symbolic models of biological systems, including: Petri nets [38,48]; the pi-calculus [34,35] and its stochastic variants [41]; membrane calculi [43,36,28]; statecharts [20,10], life sequence charts [24]; rule-based systems including Rewriting Logic [33,7] and P-systems [37]; and hybrid systems [21]. For a recent review of 'executable specification approaches' see [15]. A series of abstract machines each suited to modeling biological process associated to a different class of macromolecules is presented in [4] giving an nice introduction to the concepts to be modeled.

There are many variants of the Petri net formalism and a variety of languages and tools for specification and analysis of systems using Petri nets. Petri nets model networks of reactions that describe processes as well as process execution. Petri nets have a graphical representation that corresponds naturally to conventional representations of biochemical networks. They have been used to model metabolic pathways and simple genetic networks (e.g., see [22,42,19,26,32,16]). In [29] timed Petri nets are used to model cellular signaling. These studies have been largely concerned with dynamic or kinetic models of biochemistry. In [55] a more abstract and qualitative view is taken, mapping biochemical concepts such as stoichiometry, flux modes, and conservation relations to well-known Petri net theory concepts. Overviews of different Petri net formalisms and their application to modeling biological processes can be found in [18,6].

In contrast to Petri nets in which system state is explicit and processes emerge from rules/transistions that change the state, process calculi model molecular components as as processes. State is implicit in the interactions that processes may participate in. A pi-calculus model for the receptor tyrosine kinase/mitogen-activated protein kinase (RTK/-MAPK) signal transduction pathway is presented in [44]. BioSPI, a tool implementing a stochastic variant of the pi-calculus, has been used to simulate both the time course and probability of biochemical reactions [41].

BioAmbients [43], an adaptation of the Ambients formalism for mobile computations has been developed to model dynamics of biological compartments. BioAmbient type models can be simulated using an extension of the BioSPI tool. A technique for analysis of control and information flow in programs has been applied to analysis of BioAmbient models [36]. This can be used, for example, to show that according to the model a given protein could never appear in a given compartment, or a given complex could never form.

Statecharts naturally express compartmentalization and hierarchical processes as well as flow of control among subprocesses. They have been used to model T-cell activation [23,10]. Life Sequence Charts [8] are an extension of the Message Sequence Charts modeling notation for system design. This approach has been used to model the process of cell fate acquisition during C.elegans vulval development [24].

Like Petri nets, rule-based formalisms model the state of molecular components directly, and state change is specified by rules. Pathway Logic [11,12,49,51] represents biological processes using theories in rewriting logic. System state is represented as an algebraic term, and behavior is specified by rewrite rules. Models can be directtly analysed by execution, search, and model-checking, or by mapping to other formalisms, such as Petri Nets. The remainder of this paper gives more detail about Pathway Logic. P-systems is a multiset rewriting formalism that provides a built in notion of location. A continuous variant of P-systems is used in [40] to model intra-cellular signaling. The model can be used to predict concentration of components, for example phosphorylated Erk, over time by a discrete step approximation method. A simple formalism for representing interaction networks using an algebraic rule-based approach very similar to the Pathway Logic approach is presented in [14,5]. The language has three interpretations: a qualitative binary interpretation much like the Pathway Logic models; a quantitative interpretation in which concentrations and reaction rates are used; and a stochastic interpretation. Queries are expressed in a formal logic called Computation Tree Logic (CTL) and its extensions to model time and quantities. CTL queries can express reachability (find pathways having desired properties), stability, and periodicity. Techniques for learning new rules to achieve a desired system specification are described in [3].

Hybrid systems techniques are important for modeling processes where one wants to capture both continuous and discrete aspects. Models of glucose/insulin metabolism and B. subtilis sporulation are described in [30]. Hybrid system abstraction methods (see [53]) are used to analyze the model, for example to develop parameters for insulin control in diabetic patients. In [17] hybrid system models of the delta-notch system in Drysophila are studied using control theory and hybrid abstraction methods.

Symbolic executable models can be mapped to alternative logical formalisms for analysis. As will be discussed later, certain rewriting logic models can be mapped to Petri Nets for analysis by special purpose, efficient model checkers. In [2] a continuous stochastic logic and the probabilistic symbolic model checker, PRISM, is used to express and check a variety of temporal queries for both transient behaviors and steady state behaviors. Proteins modeled as synchronous concurrent processes, and concentrations are modeled by discrete, abstract quantities. Metabolic or signaling networks can be analyzed using a constraint-based technique that generalizes the well-known flux balance analysis [9] by representing the network as constraints on the reactions, rather than on the reacting components. In [54] this technique is used to compute preferred steady states under different conditions, also represented as constraints. Apart from understanding the steady-state configurations, constraint-based analysis can also be used to identify modules in the network, trace the flow of information in the network, and identify cross talk and conflicts.

3   Pathway Logic Overview

Pathway Logic [11,12,49,52,50,51] is a symbolic systems biology approach to the modeling and analysis of molecular and cellular processes based on rewriting logic [33]. Such formal theories can include both specific facts and general principles relating and categorizing data elements and processes. New data structures for representing biological entities and their relations and properties can easily be defined. Theories concerning different types of information can also be combined using well-understood operations for combining logical theories. A wide range of analytical tools developed for the analysis of computer system specifications is being adapted to carry out new kinds of analysis of experimental data curated into formal theories.

In PL, biological molecules, their states, locations, and their roles in molecular or cellular processes can be modeled at very different levels of abstraction. For example, a complex signaling protein can be modeled either according to an overall state, its post-tranlational modifications, or as a collection of protein functional domains and their internal or external interactions. Similarly biological processes can be represented at different levels of granularity using rewrite rules. Each rule represents a step (at the chosen level of granularity) in a biological process such as metabolism or intra/intercellular signaling. A rule may represent a family of reactions using variables to stand for families of molecular components. Rules express dependencies on biological context; for example, a scaffold needed to hold proteins in position to interact productively.

A collection of rules together with the underlying data type specifications forms a PL knowledge base. Each biological molecule that is declared in a PL rewrite theory has associated metadata linking it to standard database entries, for example HUGO or SwissProt for proteins, along with other information such as category and synonyms. This information is part of the knowledge base. It is important to place the knowledge in a broader context and to be able to integrate it with other knowledge sources. Each rule has associated evidence used to justify the rule, which is also part of the knowledge base.

A PL model is a specification of an initial state (cell components and locations) interpreted in the context of a knowledge base. Such models are executable and can be understood as specifying possible ways a sytem can evolve. Logical inference and analysis techniques are used for simulation to study possible ways a system could evolve, to assemble pathways as answers to queries, and to reason about dynamic assembly of complexes, cascading transmission of signals, feedback-loops, cross talk between subsystems, and larger pathways. Logical and computational reflection are used to transform and further analyze models.

Pathways are not predefined. Instead they are assembled by applying the rules starting from an initial state, searching for a state meeting given conditions. For example, a pathway leading to specific conditions, such as activation of a Ras protein can be generated as the result of a logical query. A subnet (subset of reactions) composed of all possible relevant pathways can also be generated. A subnet consisting of connections to a given set of molecular components can be generated by graph exploration techniques.

PL knowledge is represented and analyzed using Maude [7], a rewriting-logic-based formalism. The Pathway Logic Assistant (PLA) [52] provides an interactive visual representation of PL models. In PLA, models are represented as graphs with nodes for rules and components, and edges connecting reactant components to rules and rules to product components (formally these graphs are Petri Nets). These models can be queried and in silico experiments can be performed to study the effects of perturbations on these networks. Using PLA a biologist can:

- ask for a list of dishes available for study, and modify or create dishes;
- display the network of signaling reactions for a specified model;
- formulate and submit queries to find pathways, for example, activating one protein without activating a second protein, or exhibiting a phenotype signature such as apoptosis;
- compare two pathways;

- find knockouts—proteins whose omission prevents reaching a specified state;
- incrementally explore network connections to given rules or components;
- visualize gene expression data in the context of a network (by coloring the coded proteins according to expression level)

PLA, sample models, tutorial material, papers and presentations are available from the Pathway Logic web site, `http://pl.csl.sri.com/`.

4   Introduction to Formal Executable Specification and Maude

As mentioned in Section 3, Pathway Logic models of biological processes are developed using the Maude system, a formal language and tool set based on rewriting logic. Rewriting logic [33] is a logical formalism that is based on two simple ideas: states of a system are represented as elements of an algebraic data type, and the behavior of a system is given by local transitions between states described by *rewrite rules*. By algebraic data type, we mean a set whose elements are constructed from atomic elements by application of constructors. We represent data elements by terms, where a term can be a variable, a constant, or application of a constructor to a list of terms. For example the natural numbers are constructed from 0 by application of the successor function $s(0), s(s(0)) \ldots$. Functions on data types are defined by equations that allow you to compute the result of applying the function. For example $+$ can be defined by two equations: $n + 0 = n$ and $n + s(m) = s(n + m)$, where n and m are variables standing for arbitrary numbers. One data type might be a subtype (subset) of another. For example the non-zero numbers are a subset of all numbers. Elements of one data type might consist of lists or multisets of elements from another type. For example a system might be represented by a set of pairs such as `{ (A,2)  (B,5)  (C,0) }`.

A rewrite rule has the form $t \Rightarrow t'$ *if* c where t and t' are patterns (terms possibily containing place holder variables) and c is a condition (a boolean term). Such a rule applies to a system in state s if t can be matched to a part of s by supplying the right values for the place holders, and if the condition c holds when supplied with those values. In this case the rule can be applied by replacing the part of s matching t by t' using the matching values for the place holders in t'. The process of application of rewrite rules generates computations (also thought of as deductions). In the case of biological processes these computations correspond to pathways.

Maude is a language and tool based on rewriting logic tt⟨`http://maude.cs.ttuiuc.edu`⟩. Maude provides a high performance rewriting engine featuring matching modulo associativity, commutativity, and identity axioms; and search and model-checking capabilities. Thus, given a specification S of a concurrent system, one can execute S to find one possible behavior; use search to see if a state meeting a given condition can be reached; or model-check S to see if a temporal property is satisfied, and if not to see a computation that is a counter example.

In the following we use a simple example to introduce Maude notation and give some intuition about how to represent and analyze the structure and behavior of concurrent systems using Maude. We call the example *Magic Marbles*. In the world of magic mables, a marble can be plain or have some magical potential. Activator marbles can give positive or negative potential to plain marbles. If a marble with negative potential contacts a marble with positive potential the potential is cancelled and they both become plain. A marbles world consists of a collection (formally a multiset) of marbles interacting according to the laws described above.

We formalize the marbles world in Maude by defining three modules: data types representing marbles are specified in MAGIC-MARBLES-DATA, MAGIC-MARBLES-STATE specifies marbles world states as multisets of marbles, and MAGIC-MARBLES-RULES specifies the rules governing magic marble behavior.

A Maude module begins with the keyword fmod (a functional module, specifying one or more data types) or mod (a system module, with rules specifying system behavior), followed by the module name, and ends with a corresponding keyword endfm, or endm, respectively.

The module MAGIC-MARBLES-DATA begins by declaring a sort Marble, the data type consisting of all marbles, and a subsort (think subset or subtype) PlainMarble, plain marbles. This is followed by an ops declaration naming several specific plain marbles, for example a red marble redM. Next a sort MagicMarble of marbles with magical potential is declared. It is also a subsort of Marble. Magic potential is represented abstractly by a sort Potential. Four different potentials are defined (the second ops declaration):

- +, - represent postive and negative potentials
- *, @ represent the potenial of an activator marble to generate a postive or negative potential respectively.

A marble with potential p is constructed by annotating a plain marble m with p, written [m | p]. The _s in the declaration beginning op `[_|_`] are place holders for the two arguments, the first of sort PlainMarble, the second of sort Potential.

```
fmod MAGIC-MARBLES-DATA is
   sort Marble .
   sort PlainMarble . subsort PlainMarble < Marble .
   ops redM blueM greenM purpleM whiteM blackM
        : -> PlainMarble [ctor] .

   sort MagicMarble .   subsort MagicMarble < Marble .

   sort Potential .
   ops + - * @ : -> Potential [ctor] .
   op `[_|_`] : PlainMarble Potential -> MagicMarble [ctor] .
endfm
```

As examples, we have

- [whiteM | *] a white marble with positive activator potential
- [whiteM | @] a white marble with negative activator potential
- [greenM | +] a green marble with positive potential

The module MAGIC-MARBLES-STATE extends MAGIC-MARBLES-DATA (using the inclusion statement beginning inc) specifying a sort Mix of multisets of marbles.

(A multiset or bag is a collection of elements where the number of occurrences of an given element matters, but the order does not.) The constant none is empty multiset, and multiset union is declared as a binary operator with empty syntax (_ _, that is application of the operator is juxtaposition of the two arguments, much like forming strings by juxtaposing characters). The operator is declared to be associative and commutative with identity none.

```
fmod MAGIC-MARBLES-STATE is
   inc MAGIC-MARBLES-DATA .
sort Mix .
subsort Marble < Mix .
op none : -> Mix [ctor] .
op _ _ : Mix Mix -> Mix [assoc comm id: none] .
endfm
```

Thus redM blueM [whiteM | *] is a mix of three marbles, two plain and one with positive activating potential.

The module MAGIC-MARBLES-RULES specifies how marbles interact using three rules. A rule begins with the key word rl followed by the rule label enclosed in []s. The lefthand side (premiss) and righthand side (conclusion) of a rule are separated by the => sign. The rules labeled plus and minus formalize the informal statements "Activator marbles can give positive or negative potential to plain marbles", "a marble with the * potential is a positive activator", and "a marble with the @ potential is a negative activator." The rule labeled cancel formalizes the statement "when a marble with negative potential contacts a marble with positive potential the potential is cancelled and they both become plain".

```
mod MAGIC-MARBLES-RULES is
   inc MAGIC-MARBLES-STATE .
   vars pm0 pm1 : PlainMarble .
   rl[plus]:   pm0 [ pm1 | *] => [ pm0 | + ] [ pm1 | @ ] .
   rl[minus]:  pm0 [ pm1 | @] => [ pm0 | - ] [ pm1 | * ] .
   rl[cancel]:  [pm0 | +] [ pm1 | -] =>   pm0   pm1 .
endm
```

Note that an activator switches parity when it activates. The variables pm0, pm1 stand for arbitrary plain marbles.

Now we have an executable formal specification of magical marbles. What can we do with it? The simplest thing to do is to pick a starting state and use the rewrite and continue commands to watch it run. The command rew [1] t . rewrites the term t one step. The command cont 1 . continues rewriting one more step. Suppose we have an initial state [whiteM | *] redM blueM with two plain marbles and a postive activator. The rule plus applies to the subterm [whiteM | *] redM matching pm0 to redM and pm1 to whiteM (since the order of multiset elements doesn't matter), and replacing the matched subterm by the corresponding instance of the rules righthand side, [redM | +] [whiteM | @].

```
Maude> rew [1] [whiteM | *] redM blueM .
result Mix: blueM [redM | +] [whiteM | @]
```

Rewriting can be continued by rewriting with the minus rule and then by the cancel rule.

```
Maude> cont 1 .
result Mix: [redM | +] [blueM | -] [whiteM | *]    *** by [minus]
Maude> cont 1 .
result Mix: redM blueM [whiteM | *]                *** by[cancel]
```

This computation could be continued as many steps as you like. There are many other possible computations starting from our initial state, each making different choices of which plain marble to use in the plus step.

The command search [n] istate =>+ pattern searches the states reachable from istate for states matching pattern, stopping when it has found n solutions, or it runs out of states. It starts by finding all states that result from application of one rewrite rule, the finding all states that result from application of one rewrite rule to each of these states, and so on. Using the search command we can ask whether it is possible to make the red and blue marbles simultaneously positive, starting from the our initial state.

```
Maude> search [1] [whiteM | *] redM blueM
            =>+ M:Mix [redM | + ] [blueM | + ] .
Maude> no Solution .
```

The answer is no. If we add another positive activator then getting two positive marbles is easy.

We can make the structure of magic marble states a little more interesting by introducing boxes that can contain marbles, or other boxes, and such that under certain conditions a marble can enter or leave a box. Specifically, only plain marbles can enter or leave a box. For a marble to enter a box, the box must contain a negative activator, while for a marble to leave a box, there must be a postive activator outside the box.

The module BOXED-MARBLES-DATA extends MAGIC-MARBLES-STATE with new sorts BoxId (box identifier) and Box. The subsort declaration Box < Mix says that boxes can appear in mixes. A box has an identifer and contains a mix. For example {B0 | redM blueM} is a box with identifier B0 and contents redM blueM. For convenience we define a constant bMix to be a box with identifier B0 that contains a white positive activator marble, and two nested boxes.

```
fmod BOXED-MARBLES-DATA is
  inc MAGIC-MARBLES-STATE .
  sorts Box BoxId .
  subsort Box < Mix .
  ops B0 B1 B2 : -> BoxId .
  op `{_|_`} : BoxId Mix -> Box [ctor] .

**** sample box mix
  op bMix : -> Mix .
  eq bMix = { B0 | [whiteM | *]
                  {B1 | redM blueM [blackM | @]}
                  {B2 | greenM purpleM [blackM | @]}} .
endfm
```

The module BOXED-MARBLES-RULES gives the rules for moving marbles in and out of boxes.

```
mod BOXED-MARBLES-RULES is
  inc BOXED-MARBLES-DATA .
  inc MAGIC-MARBLES-RULES .

  vars pm0 pm1 : PlainMarble .
  var mx : Mix .
  var bid : BoxId .

  rl[in]:
    { bid | mx [ pm0 | @] } pm1 => { bid | mx [ pm0 | @] pm1 } .
  rl[out]:
    { bid | mx  pm1 } [ pm0 | *] => { bid | mx } [ pm0 | *] pm1 .
endm
```

To reason about location of marbles we define a predicate inBox which, given a mix and a box identifer, checks whether a box with that identifier contains a target mix. It selects a box in the outer mix. If the box has the given identifier it checks whether the box contains the target mix, otherwise it looks for nested boxes and in the rest of the outer mix.

```
op inBox : Mix BoxId Mix -> Bool .
var mx mx0 mx' : Mix .
var bid bid' : BoxId .
eq inBox({bid' | mx} mx', bid,mx0) =
   (if bid == bid' and contains(mx,mx0)
    then true
    else (if inBox(mx',bid,mx0)
          then true
          else inBox(mx,bid,mx0)
          fi) fi) .
eq inBox(mx,bid,mx0) = false [owise] .
```

The term contains(mx,mx0) evaluates to true if every element of mx0 is in mx. For example inBox(bMix,B1,redM) = true and inBox(bMix,B0,whiteM) = false. Suppose we want to know if, in bMix, the marbles in boxes B1 and B2 can change places. This can be answered by searching, using the inBox predicate. There is only one solution, shown below.

```
Maude> search [1] bMix =>+ M:Mix such that
   inBox(M:Mix,B1,greenM purpleM) and inBox(M:Mix,B2,redM blueM) .

Maude> Solution 1 (state 1387)
M:Mix --> {B0 | [whiteM | *]
             {B1 | greenM purpleM [blackM | @]}
             {B2 | redM blueM [blackM | @]}}
```

An alternative to search is to use model checking. A model checker checks properties of the possible computations starting from a given initial state. The properties are

expressed in Linear Temporal Logic (LTL). The module MARBLES-MC defines model
checking states for Magic Marbles and defines a state proposition based the inBox
predicate. The {_} operator encapsulates a mix, thus defining a boundary. Proposi-
tions are defined using the relation, {mx}|= prop, read the mix mx satifies the propo-
sition prop. A predicate on mixes (and other arguments) can easily be turned into
a proposition, by defining a corresponding operator that maps the remaining arguments to the sort Prop. For example, inBoxP(bid,mx0) is the proposition corresponding the predicate inBox(mx,bid,mx0) and {mx} satisfies inBoxP(bid,mx0)
if inBox(mx,bid,mx0).

```
mod MARBLES-MC is
  inc BOXED-MARBLES-RULES .
  inc MODEL-CHECKER .

  op '{_'} : Mix -> State .
  op inBoxP : BoxId Mix -> Prop .

  vars mx  mx0 : Mix .
  var bid : BoxId .
  eq {mx} |= inBoxP(bid,mx0) = inBox(mx,bid,mx0) == true .
endm
```

If P is a state proposition, then the property [] P says that every state in a computation satisfies P and [] ~P says that no state in a computation satisfies P. Thus to see if
a state satisfying P can be reached, we can use the Maude model checker to evaluate
modelCheck({mx}, []~P). If a state can be reached satisfying P, the model checker
will return a counter-example showing the transitions (state and rule label) of a computation containing such a state. For example, we can find a way to move redM from box
B1 to B2 as follows.

```
red modelCheck({bMix}, []~inBoxP(B2,redM)) .
result ModelCheckResult: counterexample(
    {{{B0 | [whiteM | *]
       {B1 | redM blueM [blackM | @]}
       {B2 | greenM purpleM [blackM | @]}}},
     'out}
    {{{B0 | redM [whiteM | *]
       {B1 | blueM [blackM | @]}
       {B2 | greenM purpleM [blackM | @]}}},
     'in}
    {{{B0 | [whiteM | *]
       {B1 | blueM [blackM | @]}
       {B2 | redM greenM purpleM [blackM | @]}}},
    ...}
 ...
```

The first transition applies the out rule to move redM out of box B1. The second transition applies the in rule to move redM into box B2. The ...s indicate that the counter
example continues. This is an artifact of the model checker requirement that counter

examples are infinite. The remainder of the computation is building a loop and can be ignored for our purposes. The above is a reachability question that can also be answered by search, although it is harder to extract the computation it can be done.

5   Signal Transduction: What to Model

We will focus on modeling signal transduction networks. The Wikipedia article on signal transduction   http://en.wikipedia.org/wiki/Signal_transduction contains an excellent overview and is a good place to start reading to learn more.

To illustrate key signaling concepts and modeling ideas, we will use epidermal growth factor receptor (EgfR) signaling, which regulates growth, survival, proliferation, and differentiation in mammalian cells. In particular we will look at the MAPK (Mitogen-Activated Protein Kinase) pathway [46,13,27,25]. Figure 1 shows the cartoon drawing of the MAPK pathway (taken from Wikipedia). The pathway is also often represented as a linear sequence of events:

$$Egf \rightarrow EgfR \rightarrow Grb2 \rightarrow Sos1 \rightarrow Ras \rightarrow Raf1 \rightarrow Mek \rightarrow Erk$$

Here is a biologist style explanation of what this picture or sequence represents. The explanation uses PL terminology, with corresponding names from the figure in parentheses.

"In this canonical pathway, Egf (EGF) binds to the Egf receptor (EgfR) and stimulates its protein tyrosine kinase activity to cause autophosphorylation, thus activating EgfR. Next, the adaptor protein Grb2 (GRB2) and the guanine nucleotide exchange factor Sos1 (SOS) are recruited to the membrane and bind to the activated EgfR. The Sos1-containing EgfR complex activates a Ras family GTPase, and the activated Ras protein activates Raf1, a member of the RAF serine/threonine protein kinase family. Raf1 then activates the protein kinase Mek1/2 (MEK), which then activate Erk1/2 (MAPK)."

Even without understanding the terminology, it should be clear that much of the actual model remains in the mind of the biologist and is not captured by the picture. In the remainder of this section we will look at the steps leading to activation of Ras in some detail, to explain the terms used in the biologists style desription of the pathway, and introduce the concepts and mechanisms that we want to model. A PL model of this pathway is discussed in Section 6, and the full PL model of Egf stimulation is discussed in Section 8.

One of the first things to notice is that a protein may have many names, depending on who is talking about it. The simplest variation is capitalization. PL uses the convention that the name of a protein is capialized like a proper name, while in the figure protein names are all-caps. The numbers in PL names make explicit the fact that there are numbered variants of a protein, for example Sos1 (as opposed to Sos2) or Mek1/2 (meaning eith Mek1 or Mek2). The figure uses a more abstract representation. The figure uses MAPK, which abbreviates Mitogen-Activated Protein Kinase, rather than Erk (or Erk1/2). Sometimes a protein name is an acronym of a name that is related to the proteins function or how it was discovered. For example, Egf abbreviates "Epidermal Growth Factor", indicating that it is a protein involved in signaling related to decisions about growth. EgfR (Epidermal growth factor receptor) is also known as ErbB1 or

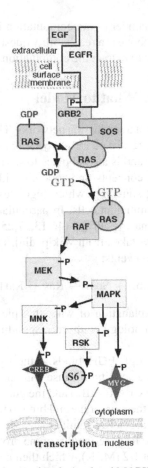

Fig. 1. Cartoon of Egf stimulated MAPK Pathway

HerbB1. Grb2, abbreviates "Growth factor receptor-bound protein 2" and Sos1 abbriv-
iates "Son of sevenless 1" (first discovered in Drysophila and named for its connection
to the tyrosine kinase receptor "sevenless".)

One way to determine if two names refer to the same protein is to link the name to
a database entry that is accepted as a standard (of course there are several standards).
Pathway logic links all protein names to their Swiss-Prot entry. Swiss-Prot is a manually
curated biological database of protein sequences. In addition to the protein sequence,
the Swiss-Prot entry for a protein includes synonyms, literature references, information about function, location, interactions, links to databases containing special purpose
information such a protein functional domains and gene annotations. For example the
SwissProt name for EgfR is EGFR_HUMAN and the SwissProt entry for EgfR can be
found at http://www.expasy.ch/cgi-bin/niceprot.pl?P00533 where
P00533 is the SwissProt accession number.

Adaptor proteins play key roles in signaling pathways. They serve to hold interacting proteins in spatial configurations that make interaction possible. In the case of the

adaptor Grb2, this is represented in the figure by nitches in the Grb2 icon so that it brings EgfR and Sos1 together enabling Sos1 to carry out its function to activate Ras.

GTP (Guanosine triphosphate) is an important molecule in metabolism, protein synthesis, and signal transduction. In our example, binding of GTP activates Ras, and subsequent hydrolysis of the bound GTP to GDP and phosphate inactivates Ras, thus acting as a kind of switch. The switch can be turned on by proteins, such as Sos1, known as *guanine nucleotide exchange factors* (GEFs), and can be turned off by GTPase-activating proteins (GAPs) that accelerate hydrolysis of GTP to GDP (guanosine diphosphate). GEFs act by binding Ras-GDP forcing it to release the bound GDP. Once released from the GEF, Ras quickly binds fresh GTP from the cytosol. Ras is called a GTPase because of its ability to bind and hyrolize GTP.

The notion of location plays an important role in cellular signaling. Proteins need to be co-located to interact. *Compartments* in a cell serve to collect interacting groups of proteins (and other molecular components). Each compartment has a membrane and an interior and compartments may be nested. A cell is itself a compartment. Its membrane is called the *cell membrane* and its interior is called the *cytoplasm*. In the cytoplasm there are many other compartments, most importantly, the nucleus, where the cell's DNA resides. In the figure 1 we can trace the Egf signal from the outside of the cell, through the cell membrane, traversing the cytoplasm and eventually reaching the nucleus. In the process Grb2 and Sos1 are *recruited* from the cytoplasm to the interior of the membrane, to bind to the inner part of EgfR.

Proteins and other molecules are categorized according to their function. A *receptor* is a protein that receives a signal by recognizing and binding to a signaling molecule called a *ligand*. This results in a *complex* in which the two proteins are linked together, likely causing a change in shape and activity of the receptor thus initiating a signaling process. The first step of our example pathway is activation of EgfR. The EgfR protein is a receptor that has three regions: one that sticks outside the cell, one traversing the cell membrane, and one that sticks into the cytoplasm. Thus, it receives signals from outside the cell and transmits them to the inside. In our example, the ligand Egf binds to external portion of Egf and then the Egf-EgfR complex dimerizes (pairs with another Egf-EgfR complex).

A signal is propagated by changes in the *state* of involved proteins. One way to change state is complexing with other proteins. Another important form of state change is *post-translational modification*. This is a change in the chemical structure of a protein after its translation. Phosphorylation, attaching a phospate group to one of the amino acid sites of a protein, is an example of post-translational modification. A *kinase* is a protein that facilitates *phosporylation*. Usually kinases have specific proteins or classes of proteins as targets and act on specific amino acid sites. Dually a *phosphatase* facilitates removal of a phosphate group. Phosphorylation (de-phosphorylation) changes the state of a protein, and is one of the ways that signals get propagated (or blocked). In our example, EgfR is not only a receptor, it is a kinase and capable of phosphorylating other EgfRs. When the Egf-EgfR homo-dimer forms EgfR *authophosphorylates* and becomes active.

Now we can explain why the pathway called the "mitogen-activated protein kinase" (MAPK) pathway. A *mitogen* is a molecule that signals a cell to trigger mitosis and thus commence cell division. A MAPK pathway activates MAPK proteins such as Erk, which propagae the mitotic signal to the nucleus. We note that Mek is a kinase kinase, (also called MAPKK or MAPK Kinase), as it phosphorylates the kinase Erk. Continuing the trend, Raf1 is a kinase kinase kinase also called MAPKKK.

6 Building a Pathway Logic Knowledge Base

Now we describe a small PL knowledge base, SmallKB, that represents initial signaling events in response to Epidermal Growth Factor (Egf) stimulation discussed in Section 5. The full Egf stimulation model is discussed in Section 8.

Recall that a rewriting logic specification has two parts: an equational part specify structure and static properties of system states, and a rules part specifying system behaviors. A Pathway Logic (PL) knowledge base is structured in four layers: (1) sorts and operations, (2) molecular components, (3) rules, and (4) initial states (called dishes). Layers 1, 2, and 4 make up the equational part.

6.1 The Equational Part

The *sorts and operations* layer declares the main sorts, subsort relations, and operators to construct representations of cellular states. The sorts of entities include Chemical, Protein, Complex, and Location (position is cellular compartments), and Cell. These are all subsorts of the sort, Soup, that represents 'liquid' mixtures, as multisets of entities. The sort Modification is used to represent post-translational protein modifications. They can be abstract, to specify that a protein is activated, bound, or phosphorylated, or more specific, for example, phosphorylation at a particular site. Modifications are applied using the operator [_-_]. (Note the similarity to the annotation of marbles with potential in section 4.) For example, the term [Raf1 - act] represents Raf1 in an activated state, and [Hras - GTP] represents the protein Hras in its "on" state (loaded with GTP). (Hras is a specific member of the Ras family.) The term [Gab1 - Yphos] represents Gab1 phosphorylated on a tyrosine site while [Gab1 - phos(Y 627)] represents Gab1 phosphorylated on tyrosine 627. Complex formation is represented by the operation (_:_). For example, the term (Egf : [EgfR - act]) represents the complex resulting from binding of Egf to EgfR and subsequent activation of EgfR. A cell state is represented by a term of the form

                    [cellType | locs] .

The symbol cellType specifies the type of cell, for example Macrophage or Fibroblast. The symbol Cell is used to indicate an unspecified cell type. The symbol locs represents the contents of a cell organized by cellular location. Each location is represented by a term of the form { locName | components } where locName identifies the location, for example CLm for cell membrane, and components stands for the mixture of proteins and other compounds in that location. For example,

        [Cell | {CLm | EgfR PIP2}
                {CLi | [Hras - GDP]   Src}
                {CLc | Gab1 Grb2 Pi3k Plcg Sos1}]) .

represents a generic cell with three locations: the membrane (location tag CLm) contains EgfR and a chemical PIP2 (see below); the inside of the membrane (location tag CLi) contains Hras loaded with GDP and Src; and the cytoplasm (location tag CLc) contains Gab1, Grb2, Pi3k, Plcg, and Sos1.

The *components* layer specifies particular entities (proteins, genes, chemicals) and introduces additional sorts for grouping proteins in families. For example ErbB1L is a subsort of Protein whose elements are ErbB1 (EgfR) ligands. Components are declared as constants, giving their sort and also metadata that gives synonyms and links the component to standard names and database entries, and may provide other information. For example the epidermal growth factor Egf with sort ErbB1L, and metadata giving its HUGO and SwissProt names, its SwissProt accession number, and its *category*. in addition to two synonyms.

```
op Egf : -> ErbB1L [metadata "(\
  (spname EGF_HUMAN)\
  (spnumber P01133)\
  (hugosym EGF)\
  (category Ligand)\
  (synonyms \"Pro-epidermal growth factor precursor, EGF\" \
       \"Contains: Epidermal growth factor, Urogastrone\"))"].
```

Similarly, EgfR is delcared simply to be a protein.

```
op EgfR : -> Protein [metadata "(\
  (spname EGFR_HUMAN)\
  (spnumber P00533)\
  (hugosym EGFR)\
  (category Receptor)\
  (synonyms \"Epidermal growth factor receptor precursor\" \
       \"Receptor tyrosine-protein kinase ErbB-1, ERBB1\"))"].
```

PIP2 is a chemical (a lipid) residing in the membrane. Its phosphorylated form, PIP3, plays an important role in a number of signaling pathways, either directly or through its cleavage products. Chemicals have metadata linking them to the KEGG database entry, where much information can be found.

```
op PIP2 : -> Chemical [metadata "(\
  (category Chemical)\
  (keggcpd C04569)\
  (synonyms \"Phosphatidylinositol-4,5P \" ))"] .
```

The *rules* layer is the heart of a PL KB. It contains rewrite rules specifying individual reaction steps. In the case of signal transduction rules represent processes such as activation, phosphorylation, complex formation, or translocation. The rules layer is discussed in Section 6.2 below.

The *queries* layer specifies initial states (called dishes) to be studied. Initial states are in silico Petri dishes containing a cell and ligands of interest in the supernatant. An initial state is represented by a term of the form

```
                        PD(out cell)
```

where `cell` represents a cell state and `out` represents a soup of ligands and other molecular components in the cells surroundings. In fact a dish can contain many cells, however the current PL analysis tools only treat single cells. For example an initial state to study Ras activation in `SmallKB` is given by the dish term

```
op rasDish   : -> Dish .
eq rasDish =
    PD(Egf [Cell | {CLm | EgfR  PIP2}
                   {CLi | [Hras - GDP]  Src}
                   {CLc | Gab1 Grb2 Pi3k Plcg Sos1}]) .
```

The dish contains `Egf` in the supernatant, and the cell discussed above.

6.2   The Rules Part

PL rules are curated from the literature, and each rule has associated evidence items describing experimental data that serve as evidence for the rule. Discussion of evidence is beyond the scope of this tutorial as it requires some understanding of experimental methods to be meaningful. The rules for the initial response to Egf signaling closely parallel the biologists informal explaination of Figure 1 given in Section 5.

```
rl[1.EgfR.act]:
  ?ErbB1L:ErbB1L
  [CellType:CellType | ct {CLm | clm EgfR}]
  =>
  [CellType:CellType | ct
    {CLm | clm ([EgfR - act] : ?ErbB1L:ErbB1L)} ] .
```

Rule 1 (label `1.EgfR.act`) describes the binding of an ErbB1 ligand to EgfR. The term `?ErbB1L:ErbB1L` is a variable that matches any ErbB1 ligand, for example `Egf`, and `CellType:CellType` is a variable that matches any cell type. `{CLm | clm EgfR}` matches any cell membrane location that contains `EgfR`, since `clm` is a variable that will match the rest of the membrane contents. Thus the left hand side subterm

```
    [CellType:CellType | ct {CLm | clm EgfR}]
```

matches any cell that contains `EgfR` in the cell membrane, since the variable `ct` will match any additional locations. For example, it matches the initial state `rasDish` with

```
  ?ErbB1L:ErbB1L := Egf
  clm := PIP2
ct := {CLi | [Hras - GDP] Src} {CLc | Gab1 Grb2 Pi3k Plcg Sos1}
```

and the result of rewriting `rasDish` with rule 1 is

```
PD([HMEC |
    {CLm | ([EgfR - act] : Egf)  PIP2}
    {CLi | [Hras - GDP]  Src}
    {CLc | Gab1 Grb2 Pi3k Plcg Sos1}]) .
```

which is obtained by instantiating the rules right hand side using the variable bindings from the left hand side match.

Once the receptor is activated it can recruit Grb2 to the membrane interior. This is describe by the rule labeled 5.Grb2.reloc.

```
rl[5.Grb2.reloc]:
  {CLm | clm ([EgfR - act] : ?ErbB1L:ErbB1L)  }
  {CLi | cli                                  }
  {CLc | clc Grb2                             }
  =>
  {CLm | clm ([EgfR - act] : ?ErbB1L:ErbB1L) }
  {CLi | cli [Grb2 - reloc]        }
  {CLc | clc                       } .
```

Notice that on the left, Grb2 is in the CLc location (cytoplasm) while on the right it is in CLi location. The modification reloc makes the change in location explicit. It is not strictly necessary, but makes the changes easier to follow. Continuing the rewriting of rasDish with rule 5.Grb2.reloc we get

```
PD([HMEC |
  {CLm | ([EgfR - act] : Egf)  PIP2}
  {CLi | [Hras - GDP]  Src [Grb2 - reloc]}
  {CLc | Gab1 Pi3k Plcg Sos1}]) .
```

Now Sos1 can be recruited to the membrane complex by binding to Grb2. This is described by rule 13.Sos1.reloc. Note that in this particular representation the complex formation is abstracted to colocation. We could also make the complex explicit if needed for some analysis.

```
rl[13.Sos1.reloc]:
  {CLi | cli [Grb2 - reloc]                  }
  {CLc | clc Sos1                            }
  =>
  {CLi | cli [Grb2 - reloc] [Sos1 - reloc] }
  {CLc | clc                               } .
```

The resulting state is

```
PD([HMEC |
  {CLm | ([EgfR - act] : Egf)  PIP2}
  {CLi | [Hras - GDP]  Src [Grb2 - reloc] [Sos1 - reloc]}
  {CLc | Gab1  Pi3k Plcg }]) .
```

In the next section we will see how to tranform the Maude terms in to a graph representation that makes it easier to visualize and understand reaction networks and their evolution. In particular, a graphical representation of the above three step computation is shown below in Figure 3.

7 Computing with a PL KB

The Pathway Logic Assistant (PLA) provides interactive graphical access to a PL knowledge base. For this purpose, rule sets and computations are represented using Petri nets [39,38,48], which have a natural graphical representation, and additionally, there are very efficient tools for analyzing the Petri net models generated by PLA. (See Section 2 for discussion of other uses of Petri nets in systems biology.)

7.1 PL Petri Nets

Petri Nets were invented to model execution of concurrent processes and thus are nicely suited to modeling signals propagating through a cell. A Pathway Logic Petri net (simply called Petri net, in what follows) can be thought of as graph with two kinds of nodes: rule nodes (shown as squares) and occurrence nodes (shown as ovals). Rule nodes, called transitions in the Petri net community, represent reactions, and occurrence nodes, called places in the Petri net community, represent reactants, products, or modifiers. Occurrences can be thought of as atomic propositions asserting that a protein (in a given state) or other component (small molecule, complex, . . .) occurs in a given compartment. In this view, rules are logical implications.

An occurrence oval is labeled by a string representation of the corresponding Maude term. For example the string representation of `Efg` outside a cell is `Egf-Out` and `Egf:EgfR-act-CLm` is the string representation of `Egf  :  [EgfR - act]` in the cell membrane. The reactants of a rule are the occurrences connected to the rule by arrows from the occurrence to the rule. The products of a rule are the occurrences connected to the rule by arrows from the rule to the occurrence. The modifiers of a rule (enzymes and other components that must be present but are unchanged) are the occurrences connect to the rule by a dashed arrow. For example, the Petri net representation of the rule for recruitment of `Sos1` is shown in Figure 2.

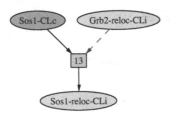

Fig. 2. Petri net transitions for rule 13.Sos1.reloc

The rule is represented by the rectangle labeled `13` (short form of `13.Sos1.reloc`). The reactant `Sos1` in the cytoplasm is represented by the oval labeled `Sos1-CLc` with an arrow from the oval to the rule rectangle. The product `[Sos1 - reloc]` at the membrane interior is represented by the oval labeled `Sos1-reloc-CLi` with an arrow from the rule rectangle to the oval. `[Grb2-reloc]` drives the reaction but is not changed (at our level of representation), thus it is represented by the oval labeled `Grb2-reloc-CLi` with a dashed arrow from the oval to the rule rectangle.

A set of Petri net rules corresponding to the rules of a PL knowledge base is called a transistion knowledge base (TKB). The analog of a PL dish is a PL Petri net state, which specifies which occurrences are present, that is, it specifies the state and location of each molecular component. Given a state, a Petri net rule is enabled if all of its occurrences connected by incoming arrows (reactants and modifiers) are present in the state. When an enabled rule fires, the reactant occurrences are removed from the state and the product occurrences are added. The modifier occurrences are left unchanged.

Corresponding to a PL model, a Petri net model consists of a set of rules (a TKB) and an initial state. To execute a Petri net model one puts tokens on the ovals corresponding to occurrences present in the initial state, and moves tokens as rules become enabled and fired. Figure 3 shows the execution of a Petri net model of the process that recruits Sos1 to the membrane interior.

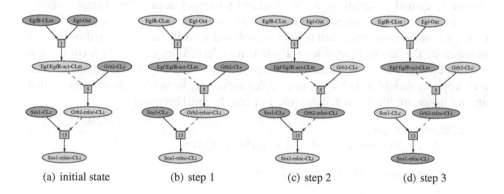

| (a) initial state | (b) step 1 | (c) step 2 | (d) step 3 |

Fig. 3. Execution of the Sos1 recruitment pathway

There are three rules (corresponding to the rewrite rules discussed in Section 6). Darker ovals represent occurrences that are present (marked with a token). Figure 3(a) shows the initial state with Egf-Out, EgfR-CLm, Grb2-CLc, and Sos1-CLc marked as initially present. The only rule enabled is rule 1. Figure 3(b) shows the result of firing rule 1, removing tokens from Egf-Out and EgfR-CLm and adding a token to Egf:EgfR-act-CLm. Now rule 5 is enabled and Figure 3(c) shows the result of firing rule 5. This enables rule 13 and Figure 3(d) shows the final state.

Starting with a PL knowledge base, we convert it to a Petri net TKB, and we convert dishes to occurrence sets, in a way that preserves the possible executions. We can then analyze models by finding subnets relevant to a desired state (goal), finding pathways reaching a goal, compare subnets and/or pathways, finding knockouts (omissions from the initial state that prevent reaching a goal), or exploring a network of rules by incrementally adding connected components and rules to an chosen initial set. This is explained in more detail in the following subsections. Details, including proof that the Petri net representation is equivalent to the rewriting logic represenation, for the questions of interest, can be found in [52].

7.2   Converting a PL KB to a Petri Net TKB

Transformation to Petri net representation accomplishes several things. One is support for graphical representation. Another is making things concrete. The full PL representation allows for rules that express families of reactions and for multiple cells and cell types. In PLA we restrict attention to systems with a single cell and for each variable that stands for a single component, we fix a specific (finite) set of components that can be values of that variable. For example, in the SmallKB knowledge base, there are two proteins that can be values of the variable ?ErbB1L:ErbB1L of sort ErbB1L, namely Egf and Tgfa. Producing a Petri net representation of the Pathway Logic knowledge base proceeds in two steps. The first step is transforms rules to occurrence form, by transforming the dishes or cells appearing in PL rules into occurrence sets. The second step is to instantiate remaining variables with known values.

Formally, an occurrence is a pair consisting of a component (a protein, possibly modified, a small molecule, or a complex) and a location name. For example, <Egf, Out> is an occurrence representing Efg outside a cell and < Egf : [EgfR - act], CLm> is a occurrence representing Egfr complexed with Egf and activated in the cell membrane. The left or right side of a rule is transformed by pairing each component with its location (the name of the enclosing location), dropping the location container, and dropping variables such as ct or clm that serve only to name location contents that are not important for the rule. Thus rule 1 (1.EgfR.act) becomes

```
rl[1.EgfR.act.pn]
    < ?ErbB1L:ErbB1L, Out >  < EgfR , CLm >
    =>
    < ?ErbB1L:ErbB1L : [EgfR - act], CLm >
```

When we instantiate remaining variables, we also convert rules (logical statements) into elements of a data type called PNetTransition. The allows us to compute with and reason about the Petri net rules directly. A single rewrite rule can be given to execute the transitions. A pnet transition term has the form

$$pnTrans(label, iOccs, oOccs, bOccs)$$

where label is a quoted identifier, and iOccs, oOccs bOccs are multisets of occurrences: iOccs are the occurrences required and removed by the transition (connected to the rule by incoming arrows), oOccs are the occurrences produced by the transition (connected to the rule by outgoing arrows), and bOccs are the occurrences required but not removed by the transition (connected to the rule by dashed arrows). As an example, two pnet transitions are obtained by instantiating the occurrence form of rule 1, the first by instantiating the variable ?ErbB1L:ErbB1L with Egf

```
pnTrans('1.EgfR.act,
        < Egf,Out > < EgfR,CLm >,
        < Egf :[EgfR -   act],CLm >,
        none)
```

and the second by instantiating with Tgfa.

```
pnTrans('1.EgfR.act#1,
        < EgfR,CLm > < Tgfa,Out >,
        < Tgfa :[EgfR - act],CLm >,
        none)
```

The transition label is the rule label, suffixed with #1, #2, ... if there are multiple instantiations. Since in rule 1 there are no unchanged occurrences, iOccs is simply the instantiated occurrences from the rule lefthand side, oOccs is the instantiated occurrences from the rule righthand side, and bOccs is none, the empty occurrence set.

As another example, the Sos1 recruitment rule (13.Sos1.reloc) is transformed into the following pnet transition.

```
pnTrans('13.Sos1.reloc,
        < Sos1,CLc >,
        <[Sos1 - reloc],CLi >,
        <[Grb2 - reloc],CLi >)
```

In this case bOccs is <[Grb2 - reloc],CLi > which is necessary for the rule to fire, but not used up.

The process of converting a rule set into a list of pnet transitions uses Maude's meta-level, where rules are represented as data and one can manipulate terms with variables (which are also just data in the meta-level).

7.3   PL PNet Models

Once we have a TKB we can derive models and compute with them, asking for subnets, pathways, knockouts, and making comparisons. A model consists of a pnet transition list (specifying the possible transitions) and a set of occurrences representing the initial (or current) state. It is derived from a dish and a TKB by transforming the dish into a set of occurrences and doing a *forwards collection* in the TKB from the occurrence set to derive the set of transitions the could possible be enabled in a computation starting from the initial state. The idea of the forward collection is to iteratively augment the occurrence set with all occurrences that could be produced by firing enabled transitions (from TKB), without removing the iOccs part of the transition, and add then enabled transitions to the accumulating list of transitions. In a little more detail, the collection process operates on a tuple (tkb,occs,pntl,pending,more?) where tkb is list of possible transistions, occs, is the accumulated occurrence set, pntl is the accumulated transition list. pending is list of tkb elements that are not yet enabled in occs, and more? is a boolean which remembers if any new occs have been added to the accumulated set. Initially the triple is (TKB,dOccs,nil,nil,false) where dOccs is the dish occurrence set, and nil is the empty list. In one pass, each collection step transforms the tuple by removing a transition from tkb and adding it to pntl if the transition is enabled in occs. Otherwise it is added to pending. If there are any occurrences in the transition oOccs part that are not in occs, they are added to occs and the done? becomes true. The pass ends when there are no more transitions in tkb. If more? is true then a new pass is started. Otherwise the accumulated pntl is returned. This can be expressed as a function fwdCollect defined by the following equations.

```
eq fwdCollect(tkb,dish)
    = fwdCollect(tkb,dish2occs(dish),nil,nil,false) .
eq fwdCollect(pnTrans(rid,iOccs,oOccs,bOccs) tkb,
              occs, pntl,pending,more?)
    =
    if contains(occs,union(iOccs,oOccs)) .
    then fwdCollect(tkb, union(occs,oOccs),
            (pntl, pnTrans(rid,iOccs,oOccs,bOccs)),pending,
            (if (oOccs - occs == none) then more? else true fi)
    else fwdCollect(tkb, occs, pntl,
            (pending, pnTrans(rid,iOccs,oOccs,bOccs)),more?)
    fi .
eq fwdCollect(nil,occs,pntl,pending,false) = pntl.
eq fwdCollect(nil,occs,pntl,pending,true) =
        fwdCollect(pending,occs,pntl,nil,false) .
```

This forward collection produces a transition list that is possibly an over approximation. That is, any transition of TKB that becomes enabled in some computation from the initial state will be in the accumulated transition list but, there may be some transitions that do not become enabled in any computation from the initial state. The crucial point is that we don't loose any possible computations by restricting the set of transitions to be considered, and the simple over approximation makes the model derivation feasible.

Figure 4 shows a screen shot of the Petri net model of Raf activation, generated by PLA from the dish rafDish whose occurrence set is rafDishOccs

```
eq rafDishOccs =
    < Egf, Out > < EgfR, CLm >   < PIP2, CLm >
    < [Hras - GDP], CLi> < Src, CLi> < [Ube213 - ubiq], CLi >
    < Cbl, CLc >   < Gabl, CLc >   < Grb2, CLc >   < Pi3k, CLc >
    < Plcg, CLc >   < Sos1, CLc >   < 1433x1, CLc >   < Pak1, CLc >
    < Raf1, CLc >   < PP2a, CLc > .
```

As discussed above, ovals are occurrences, with initial occurrences darker. Rectangles are transitions. Dashed arrows indicate an occurrence that is both input and output. The thumbnail sketch in the upper right shows the full network. The main frame shows a magnified version of the portion of the network in the red rectangle. The view in the main frame can be changed by dragging the red rectangle around in the thumbnail frame. It can also be changed using the scroll bars. The Finder in the lower right allows one to locate occurrences and rules by name, and center the view on the selected node.

PLA provids a simple query language for specifying signaling pathways of interest. A query specifies three sets: goals, avoids, and hides. Goals are a set of occurrences that should appear at the end of a pathway, as they represent properties of a desired state. Avoids are a set of occurrences that should not appear in any state in the execution of the pathway. Hides are a set of rules that should not fire in the pathway. To make a query, goals, avoids, and hides sets can be selected by clicking the occurrence or rule to select, and pressing the corresponding button in the information window that appears. Once query elements have been selected, the user can ask to see the relevant subnet or to find a path. The relevant subnet contains all of rules needed for any (minimal) pathway satisfying the query, while the path is just the first path found by the analysis

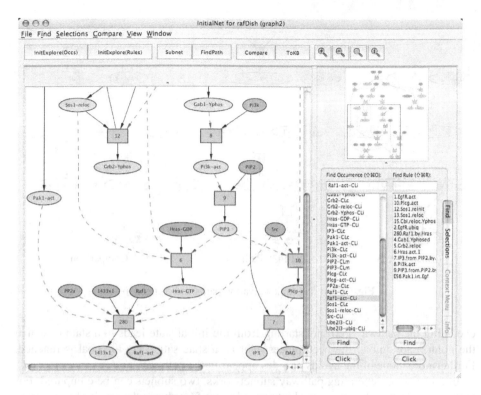

Fig. 4. Raf Activation Model viewed in PLA

tool. The relevant subnet is computed directly from the pnet transitions list, together with the initial state and query elements in a manner similar to the forward collection function above.

The logic underlying the query language is a temporal logic Goal queries are answered by model-checking the assertion that the goal set is not reachable, from the initial state `ioccs` in a transition list `pntl*` from which transitions that produce an avoid or are in the hides set are removed.

```
(pntl*,ioccs) |= []~ goal
```

A pathway satisfying a query is obtained by translating the reduced pnet transition list and query into the language of the LoLA model checker [45,31], asserting that no such pathway exists. If a pathway does exist LoLA returns a list of transitions in the pathway, which PLA converts to a Petri net for display and possibly further analysis. The LoLA model checker is highly optimized for Petri nets, and thus allows use to compute with very large models.

Figure 5 shows pathways in the Raf1 model that recruit `Sos1` (a), and activate `Pi3k` (b), obtained by making `Sos1-reloc-CLi` or `Pi3k-act-CLi` a goal (indicated by coloring the oval green) and using FindPath. The key property of a pathway is that

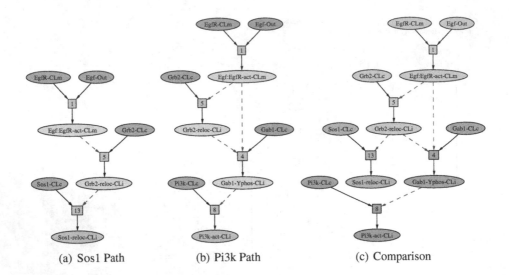

(a) Sos1 Path   (b) Pi3k Path   (c) Comparison

Fig. 5. Sos1 and Pi3k activation paths and comparison

executing the pathway Petri net starting from the initial state leads to a state in which the goal(s) are among the occurrences, that is, a state satisfying the goal is reached. Furthermore, none of the avoids or hides appear in the pathway.

In addition to generating pathway subnetworks, two subnets can be compared. For this, the two networks are merged into one. Figure 5(c) shows the result of comparing the Sos1 and Pi3k pathways. Nodes in both pathways are colored pink, nodes only in the Sos1 pathway are colored cyan, and nodes only in the Pi3k pathway are colored dark lavendar.

The Sos1 and Pi3k pathways are part of the model of Hras activation, and ultimately of Raf activation. Figure 6(a) shows a pathway activating Hras, obtained by specifying Hras-GTP-CLi as a goal. Figure 6(b) shows the Sos1 and Pi3k comparison as a subnet of the Hras activation pathway (nodes only in the Hras path are white).

In principle is it possible to formulate more complex queries, for example expressing that a particular element is a check-point, or that a particular activation state is always eventually reachable. In [1] a study was carried out in which Pathway Logic models were exported to the SAL language [47] and comparison of the effectiveness of several model-checkers in answering temporal logic queries was made. For the large models that we are interested in querying, bounded model checking was able to find counter-examples and thus to generate pathways for goals/avoids queries, but none of the general model checkers was able to check more complex formulas on large models. The special purpose Petri net analysis seems to scale much better, and the goals/avoids queries are easy for the biologists to understand.

The SmallKB and the Ras and Raf1 activation initial states are available as part of the Pathway Logic Demo available from the Pathway Logic web site <http://pl.csl. sri.com/> along with papers, tutorial material and download of the Pathway Logic Assistant tool.

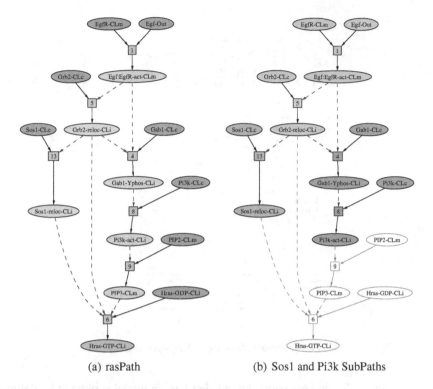

(a) rasPath   (b) Sos1 and Pi3k SubPaths

Fig. 6. Ras activation pathway and Sos1,Pi3k subnets

8   PL Model of Egf Stimulation

As an example of a non-trivial signaling model, we describe a Pathway Logic model that includes all known early responses to Epidermal growth factor (Egf) stimulation. As mentioned in Section 5 Epidermal growth factor receptor (EgfR) signaling regulates growth, survival, proliferation, and differentiation in mammalian cells.

Figure 7 show a cartoon version of molecular components and interactions involved in EfgR signaling. Although the cartoon summarizes a lot of information, the representation is not suited for computational analysis. The PL model of Egf stimulation is based on a PL knowledge base of early response events in adherent cells expressing Egf-receptors. Rules in the knowledge base are based on experimental results and data curated from the published scientific literature. The first step in the construction of the knowledge base was to collect the data: 174 papers were searched for appropriate experiments and the results were listed as 1373 evidence items that contain information about state changes. The evidence items are used to determine the components of a reaction rule. The reaction network assembled from data supporting events that might be downstream of EgfR signaling includes over 370 reactions involving more than 460 occurrences (signaling molecules in different states and locations). These rules were combined with a collection of Common Rules curated from additional experimental data from experiments not specific to Egf stimulation.

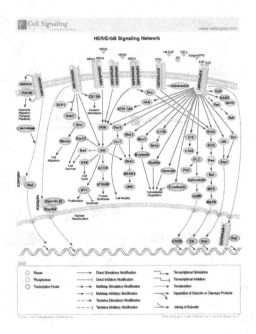

Fig. 7. Cartoon drawing of Egf signaling

As explained in Section 6, given a knowledge base, a model is obtained by defining an initial state—the cellular components (proteins, chemicals, or nucleic acids), their modifications, and locations. For the Egf model, the initial state represents a serum starved, adherent cell expressing EgfR and was curated from published experimental data. An impression of the Pathway Logic Assistant (PLA) rendering of the model as a Petri net is shown in Figure 8 (a). Clearly this is a complex model. PLA can be used to browse the model and to ask for subnets or pathways satisfying goals of interest. For example, the subnet of all reactions relevant to activation of Erk in response to a

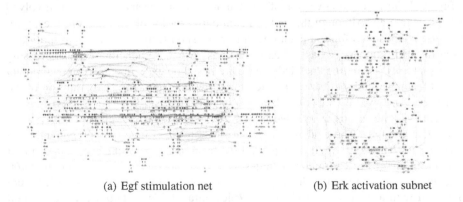

(a) Egf stimulation net   (b) Erk activation subnet

Fig. 8. Model of Egf stimulation

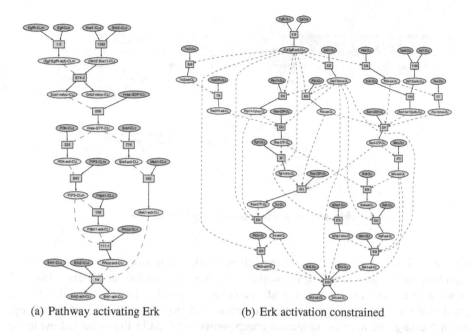

(a) Pathway activating Erk   (b) Erk activation constrained

Fig. 9. Pathways activating Erk

stimulus by Egf is obtained by making Erk1 (and/or Erk2) a goal and asking PLA for the subnet. This is shown in Figure 8 (b).

Unfortunately, there are so many potential paths to Erk activation that the Petri net is still too complicated to comprehend without visualization tools or additional simplifying constraints. The result of asking PLA to find a pathway activating Erk is shown in Figure 9 (a). This pathway is similar to the canonical pathway that extends our Raf activation pathway of Section 7. But, the subnet for Erk activation contains many possible paths that activate Erk. Which is the "correct" path? Currently there is no tool that will produce all paths for individual inspection and further analysis.

Our approach is to use additional biological knowledge to further constrain the network. A list of 85 state changes demonstrated experimentally to occur in response to a short stimulus with Egf was collected as part of the curation process. These occurrences (protein states) were set as goals. This will ensure that the paths used to reach specific chosen goals are consistent with other observed events. In addition, Egf specific rules were given precedence over Common Rules abstracting these rules. The Egf specific rules that contain requirements specific to Egf signaling that must be satisfied before they can fire. This ensures that any pathways found will include events that must happen before Erk is activated. Figure 10 shows the pathway satisfying all of the additional constraints. The existence of the constrained network containing all 85 events observed in response to Egf stimulation is a form of model validation (or more accurately failure of invalidation). Figure 9 (b) shows the path to Erk activation within the constrained

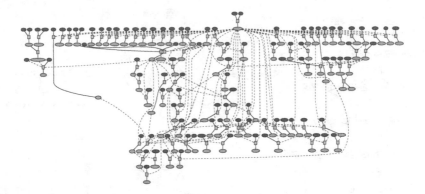

Fig. 10. Constrained model of Egf stimulation

network. This is also a pathway in the full network, but it differs from that found by searching in the unconstrained network, as we have forced the model-checking tool to work in the context of realizing all the other observed events. We see that it is a great deal more complicated than the canonical pathway. This result is not surprising, given the large number of molecular components involved in the collected evidence items.

The constrained path from Egf to Erk contains many unfamiliar events in comparison to the canonical pathway. For example, Rala is required for Src activation in response to Egf, but Sos1 is not required for Hras activation in response to Egf. More generally, models based on a knowledge base such as the curated PL knowledge base demonstrate that the series of events between activation of EgfR by Egf and activation of Erk and other goals may not be as simple as those described in canonical pathways.

9 Conclusion

Pathway Logic is a symbolic systems biology approach to modeling biological processes based on rewriting logic. We have described the use of Pathway Logic to model signal transduction processes, and the use of the Pathway Logic Assistant to browse and analyse these models. Pathway logic can also be used to model and analyze metabolic networks and to interpret experimental data. Future challenges include integration of signaling and metabolic network models, and new abstractions to simplify networks and identify meaningful modules.

Acknowledgements. The author would like to thank the SFM-Bio organizers for inviting this tutorial paper; and the members of the Pathway Logic team for their contributions to the development of modeling techniques and the analysis and visualization tools. Particular thanks to Merrill Knapp, our curator-in-chief, for always being willing to explain the biology, help with illustrations, and give constructive criticisms.

References

1. Apolzan, R.: Rapid prototyping applications of formal reasoning tools to biological cellular signalling networks (2005), http://mcs.une.edu.au/~iop/Data/Papers/

2. Calder, M., Vyshemirsky, V., Gilbert, D., Orton, R.: Analysis of signalling pathways using the PRISM model checker. In: Plotkin, G. (ed.) Proceedings of the Third International Conference on Computational Methods in System Biology (2005)

3. Calzone, L., Chabrier-Rivier, N., Fages, F., Gentils, L., Soliman, S.: Machine learning biomolecular interactions from temporal logic properties. In: Plotkin, G. (ed.) Proceedings of the Third International Conference on Computational Methods in System Biology (2005)

4. Cardelli, L.: Abstract machines of systems biology. In: Priami, C., Merelli, E., Gonzalez, P., Omicini, A. (eds.) Transactions on Computational Systems Biology III. LNCS (LNBI), vol. 3737, pp. 145–168. Springer, Heidelberg (2005)

5. Chabrier-Rivier, N., Chiaverini, M., Danos, V., Fages, F., Schächter, V.: Modeling and querying biomolecular interaction networks. Theoretical Computer Science 351(1), 24–44 (2004)

6. Chaouiya, C.: Petri net modelling of biological networks. Briefings in Bioinformatics 8, 210–219 (2007)

7. Clavel, M., Durán, F., Eker, S., Lincoln, P., Martí-Oliet, N., Meseguer, J., Talcott, C.: All About Maude: A High-Performance Logical Framework. Springer, Heidelberg (2007)

8. Damm, W., Harel, D.: Breathing life into message sequence charts. Formal Methods in System Design 19(1) (2001)

9. Edwards, J.S., Covert, M., Palsson, B.O.: Metabolic modelling of microbes: The flux-balance approach. Environmental Microbiology 4(3), 133–140 (2002)

10. Efroni, S., Harel, D., Cohen, I.R.: Towards rigorous comprehension of biological complexity: Modeling, execution and visualization of thymic t-cell maturation. Genome Research, Special issue on Systems Biology (in press, 2003)

11. Eker, S., Knapp, M., Laderoute, K., Lincoln, P., Meseguer, J., Sonmez, K.: Pathway Logic: Symbolic analysis of biological signaling. In: Proceedings of the Pacific Symposium on Biocomputing, pp. 400–412 (January 2002)

12. Eker, S., Knapp, M., Laderoute, K., Lincoln, P., Talcott, C.: Pathway Logic: Executable models of biological networks. In: Fourth International Workshop on Rewriting Logic and Its Applications. Electronic Notes in Theoretical Computer Science, vol. 71, Elsevier, Amsterdam (2002)

13. Pearson, G., et al.: Mitogen-activated protein (MAP) kinase pathways: regulation and physiological functions. Endocr. Rev, 153–183 (2001)

14. Fages, F., Soliman, S., Chabrier-Rivier, N.: Modelling and querying interaction networks in the biochemical abstract machine BIOCHAM. Journal of Biological Physics and Chemistry 4(2), 64–73 (2004)

15. Fisher, J., Henzinger, T.A.: Executable cell biology. Nature Biotechnology 25(11) (2007)

16. Genrich, H., Küffner, R., Voss, K.: Executable Petri net models for the analysis of metabolic pathways. Software Tools for Technology Transfer 3 (2001)

17. Ghosh, R., Tiwari, A., Tomlin, C.: Automated symbolic reachability analysis with application to delta-notch signaling automata. In: Maler, O., Pnueli, A. (eds.) HSCC 2003. LNCS, vol. 2623, pp. 233–248. Springer, Heidelberg (2003)

18. Gilbert, D., Heiner, M., Lehrack, S.: A unifying framework for modelling and analysing biochemical pathways using petri nets. In: Calder, M., Gilmore, S. (eds.) CMSB 2007. LNCS (LNBI), vol. 4695, pp. 200–216. Springer, Heidelberg (2007)

19. Goss, P.J., Peccoud, J.: Quantitative modeling of stochastic systems in molecular biology using stochastic Petri nets. Proceedings of the National Academy of Science 95, 6750–6755 (1998)

20. Harel, D.: Statecharts: A visual formalism for complex systems. Science of Computer Programming 8, 231–274 (1987)
21. Henzinger, T.A.: The theory of hybrid automata. In: 11th IEEE Symposium on Logic in Computer Science, pp. 278–292 (1996)
22. Hofestädt, R.: A Petri net application to model metabolic processes. Systems Analysis Modelling Simulation 16, 113–122 (1994)
23. Kam, N., Cohen, I.R., Harel, D.: The immune system as a reactive system: Modeling t cell activation with statecharts. In: Visual Languages and Formal Methods (VLFM 2001), pp. 15–22 (2001)
24. Kam, N., Harel, D., Kugler, H., Marelly, R., Pnueli, A., Hubbard, J., Stern, M.: Formal modeling of C.elegans development: A scenario-based approach. In: Priami, C. (ed.) CMSB 2003. LNCS, vol. 2602, pp. 4–20. Springer, Heidelberg (2003)
25. Kolch, W.: Meaningful relationships: The regulation of the Ras/Raf/MEK/ERK pathway by protein interactions. Biochem J. 351, 289–305 (2000)
26. Küffner, R., Zimmer, R., Lengauer, T.: Pathway analysis in metabolic databases via differential metabolic display (DMD). Bioinformatics 16, 825–836 (2000)
27. Kyriakis, J.M., Avruch, J.: Mammalian mitogen-activated protein kinase signal transduction pathways activated by stress and inflammation. Physiol. Rev. 81, 807–869 (2001)
28. Cardelli, L.: Brane calculi interactions of biological membranes. In: Danos, V., Schachter, V. (eds.) CMSB 2004. LNCS (LNBI), vol. 3082, Springer, Heidelberg (2005)
29. Li, C., Ge, Q.W., Nakata, M., Matsuno, H., Miyano, S.: Modelling and simulation of signal transductions in an apoptosis pathway by using timed petri nets. Journal of Bioscience 32, 113–127 (2007)
30. Lincoln, P., Tiwari, A.: Symbolic systems biology: Hybrid modeling and analysis of biological networks. In: Alur, R., Pappas, G.J. (eds.) HSCC 2004. LNCS, vol. 2993, pp. 660–672. Springer, Heidelberg (2004)
31. LoLA: Low Level Petri net Analyzer (2004),
    http://www.informatik.hu-berlin.de/~kschmidt/lola.html
32. Matsuno, H., Doi, A., Nagasaki, M., Miyano, S.: Hybrid Petri net representation of gene regulatory network. In: Pacific Symposium on Biocomputing, vol. 5, pp. 341–352 (2000)
33. Meseguer, J.: Conditional Rewriting Logic as a unified model of concurrency. Theoretical Computer Science 96(1), 73–155 (1992)
34. Milner, R.: Communication and Concurrency. Prentice-Hall, Englewood Cliffs (1989)
35. Milner, R.: Communicating and Mobile Systems: The pi-Calculus. Cambridge University Press, Cambridge (1999)
36. Nielson, F., Nielson, H.R., Priami, C., Rosa, D.: Control flow analysis for bioambients. In: BioConcur (2003)
37. Päun, G.: Membrane Computing. An Introduction. Springer, Heidelberg (2002)
38. Peterson, J.L.: Petri Nets: Properties, analysis, and applications. Prentice-Hall, Englewood Cliffs (1981)
39. Petri, C.A.: Introduction to general net theory. In: Brauer, W. (ed.) Net Theory and Applications. LNCS, vol. 84, pp. 1–19. Springer, Heidelberg (1980)
40. Priami, C., Regev, A., Shapiro, E., Silverman, W.: Application of a stochastic name-passing calculus to representation and simulation of molecular processes. Information Processing Letters 80, 25–31 (2001)
41. Prez-Jimnez, M.J., Romero-Campero, F.J.: Modelling EGFR signalling cascade using continuous membrane systems (simulation). In: Plotkin, G. (ed.) Proceedings of the Third International Conference on Computational Methods in System Biology (2005)
42. Reddy, V.N., Liebmann, M.N., Mavrovouniotis, M.L.: Qualitative analysis of biochemical reaction systems. Computational Biological Medicine 26, 9–24 (1996)

43. Regev, A., Panina, E., Silverman, W., Cardelli, L., Shaprio, E.: Bioambients: An abstraction for biological compartments (2004)
44. Regev, A., Silverman, W., Shapiro, E.: Representation and simulation of biochemical processes using the pi-calculus process algebra. In: Pacific Symposium on Biocomputing, vol. 6, pp. 459–470. World Scientific Press, Singapore (2001)
45. Schmidt, K.: LoLA: A Low Level Analyser. In: Nielsen, M., Simpson, D. (eds.) ICATPN 2000. LNCS, vol. 1825, pp. 465–474. Springer, Heidelberg (2000)
46. Seger, R., Krebs, E.G.: The mapk signaling cascade. FASEB J. 9(9), 726–735 (1995)
47. Shankar, N.: Symbolic analysis of transition systems. In: Proceedings of the International Workshop on Abstract State Machines, Theory and Applications, pp. 287–302. Springer, Heidelberg (2000)
48. Stehr, M.-O.: A rewriting semantics for algebraic nets. In: Girault, C., Valk, R. (eds.) Petri Nets for System Engineering – A Guide to Modelling, Verification, and Applications, Springer, Heidelberg (2000)
49. Talcott, C., Eker, S., Knapp, M., Lincoln, P., Laderoute, K.: Pathway logic modeling of protein functional domains in signal transduction. In: Proceedings of the Pacific Symposium on Biocomputing (January 2004)
50. Talcott, C.: Formal executable models of cell signaling primitives. In: Margaria, T., Philippou, A., Steffen, B. (eds.) 2nd International Symposium On Leveraging Applications of Formal Methods, Verification and Validation ISOLA06, pp. 303–307 (2006)
51. Talcott, C.: Symbolic modeling of signal transduction in pathway logic. In: Perrone, L.F., Wieland, F.P., Liu, J., Lawson, B.G., Nicol, D.M., Fujimoto, R.M. (eds.) 2006 Winter Simulation Conference, pp. 1656–1665 (2006)
52. Talcott, C., Dill, D.L.: Multiple representations of biological processes. Transactions on Computational Systems Biology (2006)
53. Tiwari, A.: Abstractions for hybrid systems. Formal Methods in Systems Design 32(1), 57–83 (2008)
54. Tiwari, A., Talcott, C., Knapp, M., Lincoln, P., Laderoute, K.: Analyzing pathways using sat-based approaches. In: Anai, H., Horimoto, K., Kutsia, T. (eds.) Ab 2007. LNCS, vol. 4545, pp. 155–169. Springer, Heidelberg (2007)
55. Zevedei-Oancea, I., Schuster, S.: Topological analysis of metabolic networks based on Petri net theory. In: Silico Biology, vol. 3, p. 29 (2003)

Formal Cell Biology in Biocham

François Fages and Sylvain Soliman

Projet Contraintes, INRIA Rocquencourt,
BP105, 78153 Le Chesnay Cedex, France
http://contraintes.inria.fr

Abstract. Biologists use diagrams to represent interactions between molecular species, and on the computer, diagrammatic notations are also employed in interactive maps. These diagrams are fundamentally of two types: reaction graphs and activation/inhibition graphs. In this tutorial, we study these graphs with formal methods originating from programming theory. We consider systems of biochemical reactions with kinetic expressions, as written in the Systems Biology Markup Language (SBML), and interpreted in the Biochemical Abstract Machine (Biocham) at different levels of abstraction, by either an asynchronous boolean transition system, a continuous time Markov chain, or a system of Ordinary Differential Equations over molecular concentrations. We show that under general conditions satisfied in practice, the activation/inhibition graph is independent of the precise kinetic expressions, and is computable in linear time in the number of reactions. Then we consider the formalization of the biological properties of systems, as observed in experiments, in temporal logics. We show that these logics are expressive enough to capture semi-qualitative semi-quantitative properties of the boolean and differential semantics of reaction models, and that model-checking techniques can be used to validate a model w.r.t. its temporal specification, complete it, and search for kinetic parameter values. We illustrate this modelling method with examples on the MAPK signalling cascade, and on Kohn's map of the mammalian cell cycle.

1 Introduction

Biologists use diagrams to represent interactions between molecular species, and on the computer, diagrammatic notations like the ones introduced in Kohn's map [1] are also employed in interactive maps like, for instance, MIM[1]. This type of notation encompasses two types of information : interactions (binding, complexation, protein modification, etc.) and regulations (of an interaction or of a transcription).

The Systems Biology Markup Language (SBML) [2] uses a syntax of reaction rules with kinetic expressions to define reaction models in a precise way, and more and more models are described in such a formalism, like in the biomodels.net repository. This type of language is well suited to describe interactions (and

---

[1] http://discover.nci.nih.gov/mim/

M. Bernardo, P. Degano, and G. Zavattaro (Eds.): SFM 2008, LNCS 5016, pp. 54–80, 2008.

in a limited manner their regulations through the notion of *modifiers*) but not directly molecule to molecule activations and inhibitions.

On the other hand, formal influence graphs for activation and inhibition have been introduced in the setting of gene regulatory networks [3] as an abstraction of complex reaction networks. These graphs completely abstract from the precise interactions, especially at post-transcriptional level, and retain only the activation and inhibition effects between genes. In these influence graphs, the existence of a positive circuit (resp. a negative circuit) has been shown to be a necessary condition for multistationarity (resp. oscillations) in different settings [4,5,6,7,8]. There are several tools providing different kinds of analyses for either reaction models or influence graphs. The only formal relationship relating the two seems to be the extraction of the second one from the Jacobian matrix derived from the first one, when equipped with precise kinetic expressions and parameter values.

In this tutorial, we first provide a syntax for denoting objects in the cell, such as molecular compounds and compartments, and for denoting their interaction and transport. We use the rule-based syntax of the biochemical abstract machine Biocham [9,10] which is similar to (and compatible with) the Systems Biology Markup Language (SBML) [2] nowadays supported by a majority of modeling tools [11,12]. Then we present the different semantics of Biocham models which correspond to different abstraction levels: namely the differential, stochastic, discrete and boolean semantics [13,14,15].

Then in section 3 we study the formal relationship between reaction models and activation/inhibition influence graphs. We show that under the general condition of strongly increasing monotonicity of the kinetic expressions, and in absence of both activation and inhibition effects from one molecule to the same target, the influence graph inferred from the stoichiometric coefficients of the reactions, called the syntactical influence graph, is equal to the influence graph defined by the signs of the coefficients of the Jacobian matrix of the differential semantics, called the differential influence graph. Under these conditions, satisfied by mass action law, Michaelis-Menten and Hill kinetics, the influence graph is thus independent of the kinetic expressions for the reactions, and is computable in linear time in the number of reactions. We show that this remarkable property applies to the transcription of Kohn's map of the mammalian cell cycle control [1] into an SBML model of approx. 800 reactions [16]. On this example, the syntactical influence graph is computed in less than a second, and our equivalence theorem shows that this influence graph remains unchanged for any standard kinetics and any parameter values. The same property of independence from the kinetic expressions holds for the influence graph inferred from the MAPK signalling model of Levchenko et al. [17]. This influence graph exhibits positive as well as negative feedbacks that are hidden in the purely directional cascade of the reaction graph [18] and were the subject of a misinterpretation in [19].

In section 4 we show how temporal logics, as introduced for circuit and program verification, can be used for formalizing the biological properties of a system, and automatically check their satisfaction in a given model by model-checking techniques. Furthermore, by turning the temporal language into a specification language, we show how a temporal specification formalizing the biological data can be used to search for kinetic parameter values. We illustrate how these techniques may be useful to the modeler with the same example as above.

Finally we conclude on these achievements in Biocham and on their perspectives for future work.

2 Reaction Models

2.1 Syntax

Following SBML [2] and Biocham [9,10] conventions, a model of a biochemical system is formally a set of reaction rules of the form e for $S => S'$ where S is a set of molecules given with their stoichiometric coefficient, called a *solution*, S' is the transformed solution, and e is a kinetic expression involving the concentrations of molecules. The reaction rules represent biomolecular interactions between chemical or biochemical compounds, ranging from small molecules to proteins and genes.

The syntax of the formal objects involved and their reactions, is given by the following (simplified) grammar:

object   = *molecule* | *molecule* :: *location*
molecule = *name* | *molecule-molecule* | *molecule~{name, . . . ,name}*
reaction = *solution* => *solution* | *kinetics* for *solution* => *solution*
solution = _ | *object* | *number*∗*object* | *solution* + *solution*

The basic object is a molecular compound. Thanks to the : : operator, it can be given a precise location, which is simply a name denoting a (fixed) compartment, such as the nucleus, the cytoplasm, the membrane, etc. The binding operator – is used to represent complexations and other forms of intermolecular bindings. The alteration operator ~ makes it possible to attach to a compound a set of modifications, such as the set of phosphorylated sites of a protein. For instance, A~{p} denotes a phosphorylated form of the compound A, and A~{p}-B denotes its complexation with B.

Reaction rules transform one formal solution into another one. The following abbreviations are used: A =[C]=> B for the catalyzed reaction A+C => C+B, and A <=> B for the reversible reaction equivalent to the two symmetrical reactions A => B and B => A. The constant _ represents the empty solution. It is used for instance in protein *degradation rules*, like A => _, and in *synthesis rules*, like _ =[G]=> A for the synthesis of A by the (activated gene) catalyst G. The other main rule schemas are *(de)complexation rules*, like A + B => A-B for the complexation of A and B, *(de)phosphorylation rules*, like A =[B]=> A~{p} for the phosphorylation of A catalyzed by the kinase B, and *transport rules*, like A::nucleus => A::cytoplasm for the transport of A from the nucleus to the cytoplasm.

Reactions can be given kinetic expressions. For instance,
k∗[A]∗[B] for A=[B]=>A~{p} specifies a mass action law kinetics with parameter k for the reaction. Classical kinetic expressions are the mass action law kinetics

$$k * \prod_{i=1}^{n} x_i{}^{l_i}$$

for a reaction with n reactants x_i, where l_i is the stoichiometric coefficient of x_i as a reactant, Michaelis-Menten kinetics

$$V_m * x_s/(K_m + x_s)$$

for an enzymatic reaction of the form $x_s = [x_e] => x_p$, where[2] $V_m = k * (x_e + x_e * x_s/K_m)$, and Hill's kinetics

$$V_m * x_s{}^n/(K_m{}^n + x_s{}^n)$$

of which Michaelis-Menten kinetics is a special case with $n = 1$. Kinetic expressions can be written either explicitly, allowing any kinetics, or using shortcuts like MA(k) for a Mass Action law with parameter k, or MM(Vm,Km) for a Michaelian kinetics.

Example 1. The Mitogen-Activated Protein Kinase (MAPK) cascades are a well-known example of signal transduction, since they appear in many receptor-mediated signal transduction schemes. They are actively considered in pharmaceutical research, for their applications to cancer therapies. The MAPK/ERK pathway is indeed hyperactivated in 30% of all human cancer tumours [20].

The structure of a MAPK cascade is a sequence of activations of three kinases in the cytosol. The last kinase, MAPK, when activated, has an effect on different substrates in the cytosol but also on gene transcription in the nucleus.

Since this cascade has been studied a lot, mathematical models of it appear in most model repositories, like for instance that of Cellerator [21] or the SBML repository page [2], both coming from [17]. This cascade was also the first example treated by Regev, Silverman and Shapiro [22] in the pi-calculus process algebra which was an initial source of inspiration for our own work.

Our first running example in this paper is the MAPK model without scaffold of Levchenko et al. [17], transcribed in Biocham as follows:

```
declare MEK~parts_of({p1,p2}).
declare MAPK~parts_of({p1,p2}).
parameter(k1, 1).
parameter(k2, 0.4).
(MA(k1), MA(k2)) for RAF + RAFK <=> RAF-RAFK.
parameter(k3, 0.5).
parameter(k4, 0.5).
(MA(k3),MA(k4)) for RAF~{p1} + RAFPH <=> RAF~{p1}-RAFPH.
parameter(k5, 3.3).
parameter(k6, 0.42).
(MA(k5),MA(k6)) for MEK~$P + RAF~{p1} <=> MEK~$P-RAF~{p1}
```

---

[2] $x_e * x_s/K_m$ is the concentration of the enzyme-substrate complex, supposed constant in the Michaelian approximation and $x_e + x_e * x_s/K_m$ is thus the total amount of enzyme.

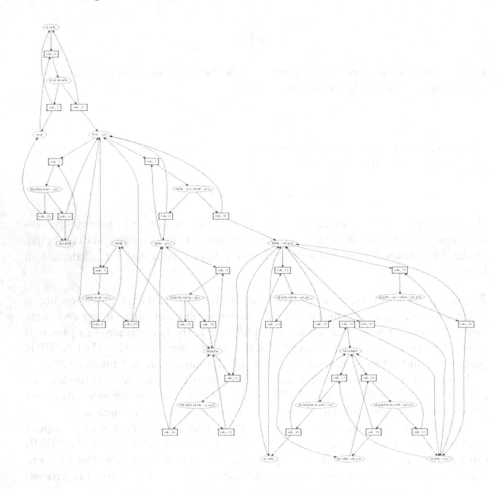

Fig. 1. Reaction (hyper)graph of the MAPK model of[17]

```
                        where p2 not in $P.
parameter(k7, 10).
parameter(k8, 0.8).
(MA(k7),MA(k8)) for MEKPH + MEK~{p1}~$P <=> MEK~{p1}~$P-MEKPH.
parameter(k9, 20).
parameter(k10, 0.7).
(MA(k9),MA(k10)) for MAPK~$P + MEK~{p1,p2} <=> MAPK~$P-MEK~{p1,p2}
                        where p2 not in $P.
parameter(k11, 5).
parameter(k12, 0.4).
(MA(k11),MA(k12)) for MAPKPH + MAPK~{p1}~$P <=> MAPK~{p1}~$P-MAPKPH.
parameter(k13, 0.1).
MA(k13) for RAF-RAFK => RAFK + RAF~{p1}.
parameter(k14, 0.1).
MA(k14) for RAF~{p1}-RAFPH => RAF + RAFPH.
```

```
parameter(k15, 0.1).
parameter(k16, 0.1).
MA(k15) for MEK~{p1}-RAF~{p1} => MEK~{p1,p2} + RAF~{p1}.
MA(k16) for MEK-RAF~{p1} => MEK~{p1} + RAF~{p1}.
parameter(k17, 0.1).
parameter(k18, 0.1).
MA(k17) for MEK~{p1}-MEKPH => MEK + MEKPH.
MA(k18) for MEK~{p1,p2}-MEKPH => MEK~{p1} + MEKPH.
parameter(k19, 0.1).
parameter(k20, 0.1).
MA(k19) for MAPK-MEK~{p1,p2} => MAPK~{p1} + MEK~{p1,p2}.
MA(k20) for MAPK~{p1}-MEK~{p1,p2} => MAPK~{p1,p2} + MEK~{p1,p2}.
parameter(k21, 0.1).
parameter(k22, 0.1).
MA(k21) for MAPK~{p1}-MAPKPH => MAPK + MAPKPH.
MA(k22) for MAPK~{p1,p2}-MAPKPH => MAPK~{p1} + MAPKPH.
present(MAPK,0.3).
present(MAPKPH,0.3).
present(MEK,0.2).
present(MEKPH,0.2).
present(RAF,0.4).
present(RAFK,0.1).
present(RAFPH,0.3).
```

For sake of simplicity, the pattern variables noted $P in the rules have not been described in the syntax. They represent variables bounded by the **declare** statement and that can be constrained in the **where** statement to represent rule schemas, i.e. sets of rules defined by a pattern. The last statements define the initial conditions, i.e. the concentrations of the initially present molecules, the others being set to 0. Figure 1 depicts the reaction (hyper)graph of this model, represented by a bipartite graph where molecules are in circles and reactions in boxes.   □

Example 2. Our second running example in this paper will be the map of Kohn [1] for the mammalian cell cycle control. It has been transcribed in Biocham [16] to serve as a large benchmarking example of approx. 500 species and 800 rules.□

2.2 Differential Semantics

A set of reaction rules $\{e_i \text{ for } S_i => S_i'\}_{i=1,...,n}$ over molecular concentration variables $\{x_1, ..., x_m\}$, can be interpreted under different semantics. The traditional *differential semantics* interpret the rules by the following system of Ordinary Differential Equations (ODE):

$$dx_k/dt = \sum_{i=1}^{n} r_i(x_k) * e_i - \sum_{j=1}^{n} l_j(x_k) * e_j$$

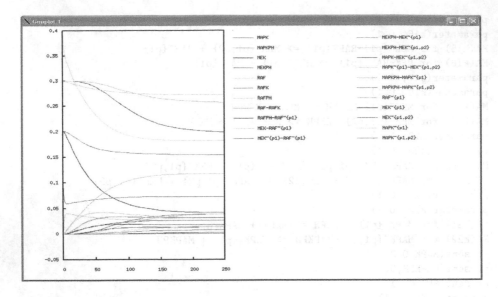

Fig. 2. Simulation result of the ODEs associated to the MAPK cascade

where $r_i(x_k)$ (resp. l_i) is the stoichiometric coefficient of x_k in the right (resp. left) member of rule i.

Example 3. Models based on ordinary differential equations (ODE) like the MAPK cascade of example 1 allow us to reproduce simulation results like the one pictured out in Figure 2, where the concentration of the visualized compounds is represented on the vertical axis, and time on the horizontal axis. It is possible to see from such simulations how the cascade evolves in time. It is possible to change input quantities to check for a significant change in the output of the cascade. Similarly, the sensitivity of the system to the values of the parameters can be checked by running different simulations with different values of the parameters, and this process can of course be automated.   □

2.3   Stochastic Semantics

The most realistic interpretation of biochemical reaction models is provided by the *stochastic semantics*. In that semantics, a reaction model is interpreted as a (continuous time) Markov chain, and the kinetic expressions as transition rates. This interpretation is correct w.r.t. the Master Chemical Equation if we suppose that the reactions happen in a well stirred environment (i.e. "instantaneous" diffusion) with constant pressure, temperature and volume [23].

For a given volume V_k of the location where the compound x_k resides, a concentration C_k for x_k is translated into a molecule number $N_k = \lfloor C_k \times V_k \times N_A \rfloor$, where N_A is Avogadro's number. A state in the stochastic semantics will be a vector of integers indicating the numbers of molecules for each species.

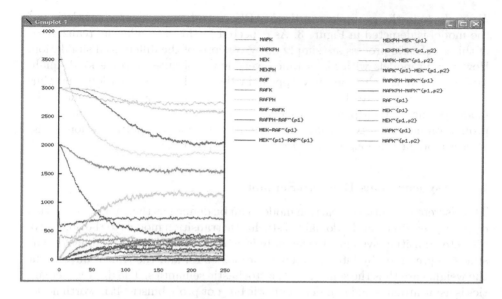

Fig. 3. Stochastic simulation of the MAPK cascade

Formally, given a fixed finite set $\mathcal{M}$ of molecule names, let a *discrete state* be a vector of positive integers of dimension $|\mathcal{M}|$. The universe $\mathcal{S}$ of *stochastic transitions* is the set of triplets (S, S', τ) where S and S' are discrete states and $\tau \in \mathbb{R}^+$ is a weight. The *stochastic transition semantics domain* is the powerset $\mathcal{D}_\mathcal{S} = \mathcal{P}(\mathcal{S})$.

Note first that discrete states have the same mathematical structure as solutions in reaction rules, and can both be represented by $|\mathcal{M}|$-dimensional vectors of positive integers. Note also that in a stochastic transition model $s \in \mathcal{D}_\mathcal{S}$, there can be more than one transition from one state to another one, labelled with different real numbers. We define the *weight* in s of a transition from state S_i to S_j as the sum of the weights $\tau_{ij} = \sum_{(S_i, S_j, \tau) \in s} \tau$.

Now, an element $s \in \mathcal{D}_\mathcal{S}$ of the domain precisely defines a Markov chain where the *probability* p_{ij} of having a transition from state S_i to state S_j is obtained by normalizing the transition weights into $p_{ij} = \frac{\tau_{ij}}{\sum_k \tau_{ik}}$. Then the transition time can be computed as usual. Stochastic simulation techniques like Gillespie's algorithm [24] compute realizations of the processes described by models in the stochastic domain, where random variables range over the probability and the time of transition.

In order to relate the stochastic semantics domain to the syntactical domain of reaction rules, let us consider a reaction rule model $\{e_i \text{ for } l_i \texttt{=>} r_i\}_{i \in I}$, and denote by $S \rightarrow_i S'$ the fact that *rule i fires in state S resulting in state S'*, i.e. if $S \geq l_i$ (pointwise) and $S' = S - l_i + r_i$. In a given state S, the numbers of molecules are fixed integer values and the kinetic expression e_i evaluates into a (positive) real valued *reaction rate*, noted $e_i(S)$. We denote by $\alpha_{\mathcal{RS}} : \mathcal{D}_\mathcal{R} \rightarrow \mathcal{D}_\mathcal{S}$ the function that associates to a reaction model $\{e_i \text{ for } l_i \texttt{=>} r_i\}_{i \in I}$ the *stochastic transition model* $\{(S, S', e_i(S)) \in \mathcal{S} \mid i \in I, \ S \rightarrow_i S'\}$.

Example 4. In the example 1 of the MAPK cascade, a stochastic simulation of the model is depicted in Figure 3. As expected in this example, the realizations of this stochastic process are simply noisy versions of the differential simulation. However, in models with for instance, very few molecules of some kind, qualitatively different behaviors may appear in the stochastic simulation, and thus justify the recourse to that semantics in such cases. A classical example is the model of the lambda phage virus [25] in which a small number of molecules, promotion factors of two genes, can generate an explosive multiplication (lysis) after a more or less long period of passive wait (lysogeny).   □

2.4   Asynchronous Discrete Semantics

The discrete semantics of reaction models can be defined as the trivial abstraction $\alpha_{SD} : \mathcal{D}_S \to \mathcal{D}_D$ from the domain of stochastic transition models to the domain of discrete transition systems, that simply forgets the transition probabilities. The states, represented by integer numbers of molecules, and the transition without the weights are thus the same as in the stochastic semantics. The discrete semantics is asynchronous and non-deterministic but not probabilistic. It is worth noticing that the discrete semantics corresponds to the classical Petri net semantics of reaction models [26,27,28,29]. As a consequence, classical Petri net analysis tools can be used for the analysis of reaction models at this abstraction level. For instance, the elementary mode analysis of metabolic networks [30] has been shown in [31] to be equivalent to the classical analysis of Petri nets by T-invariants. These analyses apply to the discrete semantics of reaction models in all generality.

2.5   Asynchronous Boolean Semantics

The boolean semantics is purely qualitative, and provides somehow the most abstract semantics of reaction models. The rules are interpreted by a (non-deterministic) asynchronous transition system over boolean states representing the absence or presence of molecules. It can be applied to large models for which the kinetic data may be not available such as example 2.

Let a *boolean state* be a vector of booleans of dimension $|\mathcal{M}|$ indicating the presence of each molecule in the state. The universe $\mathcal{B}$ of *boolean transitions* is the set of pairs of boolean states which defines the domain $\mathcal{D}_\mathcal{B} = \mathcal{P}(\mathcal{B})$ of boolean transition models as its powerset.

The boolean semantics of a reaction model can be defined from its discrete transition semantics by the *zero/non-zero abstraction* from the integers to the booleans, and its pointwise extension from discrete states to boolean states, which provides the abstraction function $\alpha_{DB} : \mathcal{D}_D \to \mathcal{D}_\mathcal{B}$ from discrete models to boolean models.

In Biocham however, the boolean semantics of reaction models is computed directly from the syntax of rules, by associating to each reaction rule a set of boolean transition rules that take into account the possible complete consumption or not of the reactants by the reaction [32]. For instance, a reaction rule like A+B=>C+D is interpreted by four boolean transition rules :

1. $A \wedge B \longrightarrow A \wedge B \wedge C \wedge D$
2. $A \wedge B \longrightarrow \neg A \wedge B \wedge C \wedge D$
3. $A \wedge B \longrightarrow A \wedge \neg B \wedge C \wedge D$
4. $A \wedge B \longrightarrow \neg A \wedge \neg B \wedge C \wedge D$

Given a reaction model R, let us denote by S_{BB} the set of boolean transitions obtained by applying these boolean transition rules to each state. The following theorem shows that the Biocham boolean semantics of reaction models *over-approximates* the boolean semantics obtained from the quantitative semantics. The non-existence of a behaviour in the Biocham boolean semantics thus entails its non-existence in the quantitative semantics of the rules whatever the kinetic expressions are.

Theorem 1 ([13]). *For any reaction model R, $\alpha_{DB}(\alpha_{SD}(\alpha_{RS}(R))) \subseteq S_{BB}$.*

It is worth noticing that this property does not hold for the boolean semantics of reaction models that always assume either incomplete consumption, or complete consumption, like in Pathway Logic [33] or in boolean Petri nets [29]. In these formalisms, the correctness of the boolean interpretation w.r.t. a quantitative interpretation is thus left to the modeler who is in charge of explicitly adding reaction rules for the different cases of consumption of the reactants.

Example 5. Figure 4 depicts one boolean simulation of the MAPK model of example 1. In this figure, the horizontal axis represents a logical time axis, where one reaction rule is fired at each time step. Just like the stochastic semantics, there are many possible boolean simulations, but unlike the stochastic semantics, they all have the same probability of realisation.

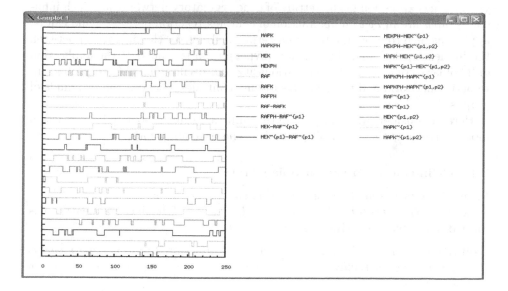

Fig. 4. Boolean simulation of the MAPK cascade

One single boolean simulation is thus not very informative, and we shall rely in section 4 on model-checking techniques to query the set of all possible boolean simulations.

In particular if one behavior is not possible in the boolean semantics, theorem 1 tells us that it is not possible to obtain such a behavior in the stochastic semantics either, whatever the kinetic expressions are.   □

2.6   Hierarchy of Semantics

In [13], the different semantics of Biocham, as well as the syntactical model of reaction rules, are formally related by Galois connections in the framework of abstract interpretation [34,35,36], with the noticeable exception of the differential semantics which does not belong to this hierarchy. These results go beyond the scope of this tutorial, however they establish the formal abstraction relationships between the syntactical, stochastic, discrete and boolean interpretations of reaction rule sets ordered by inclusion. As a consequence, these abstractions can be composed and their commutation with further abstractions (such as for instance the influence graph derived from the reaction model) can be analyzed. On the other hand, the differential semantics is not compatible with the rule set inclusion ordering as the addition of kinetic terms may make them disappear in the differential equations [13].

3   Influence Graphs of Activation and Inhibition

Influence graphs for activation and inhibition have been introduced for the analysis of gene expression in the setting of gene regulatory networks [3]. Such influence graphs are in fact an abstraction of complex reaction networks, and can be applied as such to protein interaction networks. However the distinction between the influence graph and the reaction (hyper)graph is crucial to the application of Thomas's conditions of multistationarity and oscillations [3,6] to protein interaction network, and there has been some confusion between the two kinds of graphs [19].

Here we consider two definitions of the influence graph associated to a reaction model, and show their equivalence under general assumptions.

3.1   Definition from the Jacobian Matrix

In the differential semantics of a reaction rule model $M = \{e_i$ for $l_i => r_i \mid i \in I\}$ we have $\dot{x}_k = dx_k/dt = \sum_{i=1}^{n}(r_i(x_k) - l_i(x_k)) * e_i$. The Jacobian matrix J is formed of the partial derivatives $J_{ij} = \partial \dot{x}_i / \partial x_j$.

Definition 1. *The* differential influence graph *associated to a reaction model is the graph having for vertices the molecular species, and for edge-set the following two kinds of edges:*
   $\{A$ activates $B \mid \partial \dot{x}_B / \partial x_A > 0$ in some point of the space$\}$
   $\cup \{A$ inhibits $B \mid \partial \dot{x}_B / \partial x_A < 0$ in some point of the space$\}$

3.2 Definition from the Stoichiometric Coefficients

Definition 2. *The* syntactical influence graph *associated to a reaction model M is the graph having for vertices the molecular species, and for edges the following set:*

$$\{A \text{ inhibits } B \quad | \ \exists (e_i \text{ for } l_i \Rightarrow r_i) \in M,$$
$$l_i(A) > 0 \text{ and } r_i(B) - l_i(B) < 0\}$$
$$\cup \{A \text{ activates } B \ | \ \exists (e_i \text{ for } l_i \Rightarrow r_i) \in M,$$
$$l_i(A) > 0 \text{ and } r_i(B) - l_i(B) > 0\}$$

In particular, we have the following influences for elementary reactions of complexation, modification, synthesis and degradation:

$$\alpha(\{A + B \Rightarrow C\}) = \{ \quad A \text{ inhibits } B, A \text{ inhibits } A, B \text{ inhibits } A,$$
$$B \text{ inhibits } B, A \text{ activates } C, B \text{ activates } C\}$$
$$\alpha(\{A = [C] \Rightarrow B\}) = \{C \text{ inhibits } A, A \text{ inhibits } A, A \text{ activates } B, C \text{ activates } B\}$$
$$\alpha(\{A = [B] \Rightarrow \_\}) = \{ B \text{ inhibits } A, A \text{ inhibits } A\}$$
$$\alpha(\{\_ = [B] \Rightarrow A\}) = \{ B \text{ activates } A\}$$

The inhibition loops on the reactants are justified by the negative sign in the Jacobian matrix of the differential semantics of such reactions. Unlike the differential influence graph, this graph is clearly trivial to compute by browsing the syntax of the rules:

Proposition 1. *The syntactical influence graph of a reaction model of n rules is computable in $O(n)$ time.*

Example 6. Let us consider the MAPK signalling model of [17]. Figure 1 depicts the reaction graph as a bipartite graph with round boxes for molecules and rectangular boxes for rules. Figure 5 depicts the syntactical influence graph, where activation (resp. inhibition) is materialized by plain (resp. dashed) arrows.

This computed graph reveals the negative feedbacks that are somewhat hidden in a purely directional signalling cascade of reactions. Furthermore, as no molecule is at the same time an activator and an inhibitor of a same molecule, this graph is largely independent of the kinetics of the reactions, as shown by Theorem 3 of next section. It is indeed identical to the differential influence graph for any standard kinetic expressions with any (non zero) kinetic parameter values.

These negative feedbacks, a necessary condition for oscillations [3,7,8], have been formally analyzed in [18] and interpreted as enzyme sequestration in complexes. Furthermore, oscillations in the MAPK cascade model have been shown in [37].

The influence graph also exhibits positive circuits. These are a necessary condition for multistationarity [3,6] that has been observed in the MAPK model, and experimentally in Xenopus oocytes [19]. Note that the absence of circuit in the (directional) reaction graph of MAPK was misinterpreted as a counterexample to Thomas' rule in [19] because of a confusion between both kinds of graphs. □

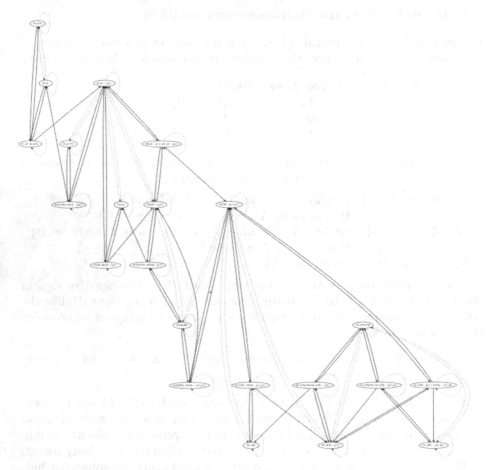

Fig. 5. Influence graph inferred from the MAPK reaction model

Example 7. On the map of Kohn, Example 2, the computation of activation and inhibition influences takes less than one second CPU time (on a PC 1,7GHz) for the complete model, showing the efficiency of the syntactical inference algorithm. The influence graph is composed of 1231 activation edges and 1089 inhibition edges.

Furthermore in this large example no molecule is both an activator and an inhibitor of the same target molecule. Theorem 3 thus entails that the computed influence graph is equal to the differential graph that would be obtained in any kinetic model of Kohn's map for any standard kinetic expressions and for any (non zero) parameter values.

Since there is a lot of kinetic data missing for such a big model, the possibility to nevertheless obtain the exact influence graph without having to estimate parameters or even to choose precise kinetic expressions is quite remarkable, and justifies the use of purely qualitative models for the analysis of feedback circuits.   □

3.3   Over-approximation Theorem

Comparing the differential influence graph and the syntactical influence graph requires that the information in the kinetic expressions and in the reactions be compatible. This motivates the following definition where the first property forbids the presence of purely kinetic inhibitors not represented in the reaction, and the second property enforces that the variables appearing in the kinetic expressions do appear as reactants or enzymes in the reaction.

Definition 3. *In a reaction rule e* for *l=>r, we say that a kinetic expression e is* increasing *iff for all molecules x_k we have*

1. *$\partial e/\partial x_k \geq 0$ in all points of the space,*
2. *$l(x_k) > 0$ whenever $\partial e/\partial x_k > 0$ in some point of the space.*

A reaction model has an increasing kinetics *iff all its reaction rules have an increasing kinetics.*

One can easily check that:

Proposition 2. *Mass action law kinetics for any reaction, as well as Michaelis Menten and Hill kinetics for enzymatic reactions, are increasing.*

On the other hand, negative Hill kinetics of the form $k_1/(k_2+y^n)$ are not increasing. They represent an inhibition by a molecule y not belonging to the reactants, and thus not reflected in the syntax of the reaction.

Theorem 2. *For any reaction model with an increasing kinetics, the differential influence graph is a subgraph of the syntactical influence graph.*

Proof. If (A activates B) belongs to the differential influence graph then $\partial \dot{B}/\partial A > 0$. Hence there exists a term in the differential equation for B, of the form $(r_i(B) - l_i(B)) * e_i$ with $\partial e_i/\partial A$ of the same sign as $r_i(B) - l_i(B)$.

Let us suppose that $r_i(B) - l_i(B) > 0$ then $\partial e_i/\partial A > 0$ and since e_i is increasing we get that $l_i(A) > 0$ and thus that (A activates B) in the syntactical graph. If on the contrary $r_i(B) - l_i(B) < 0$ then $\partial e_i/\partial A < 0$, which is not possible for an increasing kinetics.

If (A inhibits B) is in the differential graph then $\partial \dot{B}/\partial A < 0$. Hence there exists a term in the differential semantics, of the form $(r_i(B) - l_i(B)) * e_i$ with $\partial e_i/\partial A$ of sign opposite to that of $r_i(B) - l_i(B)$.

Let us suppose that $r_i(B) - l_i(B) > 0$ then $\partial e_i/\partial A < 0$, which is not possible for an increasing kinetics. If on the contrary $r_i(B) - l_i(B) < 0$ then $\partial e_i/\partial A > 0$ and since e_i is increasing we get that $l_i(A) > 0$ and thus that (A activates B) is in the syntactical influence graph.

Corollary 1. *For any reaction model with an increasing kinetics, the differential influence graph restricted to the phase space w.r.t. some initial conditions, is a subgraph of the syntactical influence graph.*

Proof. Restricting the points of the phase space to those points that are accessible from some initial states, restricts the number of edges in the differential influence graphs which thus remains a subgraph of the syntactical influence graph.

It is worth noticing that even in the simple case of mass action law kinetics, the differential influence graph may be different from the syntactical influence graph. For instance let x be the following model :

$k_1 * A$ for $A => B$

$k_2 * A$ for $\_ = [A] => A$

In the syntactical influence graph, A *activates* B, A *activates* A and A *inhibits* A, however $\dot{A} = (k_2 - k_1) * A$, hence $\partial \dot{A} / \partial A$ can be made always positive or always negative or always null, resulting in the absence of respectively, A *inhibits* A, A *activates* A or both, in the differential influence graph.

3.4 Equivalence Theorem

Definition 4. *In a reaction rule e `for` $l => r$, a kinetic expression e is strongly increasing iff for all molecules x_k we have*

1. *$\partial e / \partial x_k \geq 0$ in all points of the space,*
2. *$l(x_k) > 0$ iff there exists a point in the space s.t. $\partial e / \partial x_k > 0$*

A reaction model has a strongly increasing kinetics iff all its reaction rules have a strongly increasing kinetics.

Note that *strongly increasing* implies *increasing*.

Proposition 3. *Mass action law kinetics for any reaction, as well as Michaelis Menten and Hill kinetics for enzymatic reactions, are strongly increasing.*

Proof. For the case of Mass action law, the kinetics are of the form:

$$e_i = k_i * \prod_{l=1}^{m} x_l^{l_i(x_l)}$$

with $k_i > 0$ and $l_i(x_l) \geq 0$. We thus have $\partial e_i / \partial x_k = 0$ if $l_i(x_k) = 0$ and $\partial e_i / \partial x_k = k_i * l_i(x_k) * x_k^{l_i(x_k)-1} \prod_{l \neq k} x_l^{l_i(x_l)}$ otherwise, which clearly satisfies (1) and (2).

In the case of Hill kinetics (of which Michaelis Menten is a subcase), we have:

$$e_i = \frac{V_m * x_s^n}{K_m^n + x_s^n}$$

for the reaction $x_s + x_e => x_p + x_e$ and where $V_m = k_2 * x_e^{tot} = k_2 * (x_e + k_1 * x_e * x_s / (k_{-1} + k_2))$ from the steady state approximation. It is obvious that $\partial e_i / \partial x_k = 0$ for all x_k other than x_s and x_e since they do not appear in e_i and one can easily check that with all the constants n, k_1, k_{-1}, k_2 strictly positive, both $\partial e_i / \partial x_e$ and $\partial e_i / \partial x_s$ are greater than 0 at some point in the space.

Lemma 1. *Let M be a reaction model with a strongly increasing kinetics,*

Of (A activates B) is an edge in the syntactical influence graph, and not (A inhibits B), then (A activates B) belongs to the differential influence graph.

If (A inhibits B) is an edge in the syntactical influence graph, and not (A activates B), then (A inhibits B) belongs to the differential influence graph.

Proof. Since $\partial\dot{B}/\partial A = \sum_{i=1}^{n}(r_i(B) - l_i(B)) * \partial e_i/\partial A$ and all e_i are increasing we get that $\partial\dot{B}/\partial A = \sum_{\{i \leq n | l_i(A) > 0\}}(r_i(B) - l_i(B)) * \partial e_i/\partial A$.

Now if (A activates B) is in the syntactical influence graph, but not (A inhibits B), then all rules such that $l_i(A) > 0$ verify $r_i(B) - l_i(B) \geq 0$ and there is at least one rule for which the inequality is strict. We thus get that $\partial\dot{B}/\partial A$ is a sum of positive numbers, amongst which one is such that $r_i(B) - l_i(B) > 0$ and $l_i(A) > 0$ which, since M is strongly increasing, implies that there exists a point in the space for which $\partial e_i/\partial A > 0$. Hence $\partial\dot{B}/\partial A > 0$ at that point, and (A activates B) is thus in the differential influence graph.

For inhibition the same reasoning applies with the opposite sign for the $r_i(B) - l_i(B)$ and thus for the finale partial derivative.

This lemma establishes the following equivalence result:

Theorem 3. *In a reaction model with a strongly increasing kinetics and where no molecule is at the same time an activator and an inhibitor of the same target molecule, the differential and syntactical influence graphs coincide.*

This theorem shows that for standard kinetic expressions, the syntactical influences coincide with the differential influences based on the signs of the coefficients in the Jacobian matrix, when no molecule is at the same time an activator and an inhibitor of the same molecule. The theorem thus provides a linear time algorithm for computing the differential influences in these cases, simply by computing the syntactical influences. It shows also that the differential influence graph is independent of the kinetic expressions.

Corollary 2. *The differential influence graph of a reaction model of n rules with a strongly increasing kinetics is computable in time $O(n)$ if no molecule is at the same time an activator and an inhibitor.*

Corollary 3. *The differential influence graph of a reaction model is independent of the kinetic expressions as long as they are strongly increasing, if no molecule is at the same time an activator and an inhibitor.*

4   Biological Properties Formalized in Temporal Logic

Temporal logics and model-checking algorithms [38] have proved useful to respectively express biological properties of complex biochemical systems and automatically verify their satisfaction in both qualitative and quantitative models, i.e. in boolean [33,32,16], discrete [39,40], stochastic [41,42] and continuous models [14,43,32]. This approach relies on a logical paradigm for systems biology that consists in making the following identifications [44]:

biological model = transition system
biological property = temporal logic formulae
biological validation = model-checking

Having a formal language not only for describing models, i.e. transition systems by either process calculi [22,45,46,47,48], rules [33,10,9], Petri nets [26,29], etc..., but also for formalizing the biological properties of the system known from biological experiments under various conditions, opens a whole avenue of research for designing automated reasoning tools inspired from circuit and program verification to help the modeler [15].

The temporal logics CTL (*Computation Tree Logic*), LTL (*Linear Time Logic*) and PLTL (*Probabilistic LTL*) with numerical constraints are used in the three semantics of reaction models, respectively, in the boolean semantics, the differential semantics and the stochastic semantics.

4.1 Temporal Logics CTL*, CTL, LTL and PLTL

The *Computation Tree Logic* CTL* [38] is an extension of classical logic that allows reasoning about an infinite tree of state transitions. It uses operators about branches (non-deterministic choices) and time (state transitions). Two path quantifiers A and E are thus introduced to handle non-determinism: $A\phi$ meaning that ϕ is true on all branches, and $E\phi$ that it is true on at least one branch. The time operators are F, G, X, U and W; $X\phi$ meaning ϕ is true at the next transition, $G\phi$ that ϕ is always true, $F\phi$ that ϕ is eventually true, $\phi\ U\ \psi$ meaning ϕ is always true until ψ becomes true, and $\phi\ W\ \psi$ meaning ϕ is always true until ψ might become true. In this logic, $F\phi$ is equivalent to *true U* ϕ, $\phi\ W\ \psi$ to $(\phi\ U\ \psi)|G\phi$. We have the following duality properties: $!(E(\phi)) = A(!\phi)$, $!(F(\phi)) = G(!\phi)$, $!(\phi\ U\ \psi) = (!\psi\ W\ !\phi)$ where $!$ denotes negation.

Formally, a *Kripke structure* (see for instance [38]) is a couple $K = (S, R)$ where S is a set of states in which atomic formulas can be evaluated, and $R \subseteq S \times S$ is the transition relation between states, supposed to be total (i.e. $\forall s \in S, \exists s' \in S$ s.t. $(s, s') \in R$). A path in K, starting from state s_0 is an infinite sequence of states $\pi = s_0, s_1, \cdots$ such that $(s_i, s_{i+1}) \in R$ for all $i \geq 0$. We denote by π^k the path $s_k, s_{k+1}, \cdots$. Table 4.1 recalls the inductive definition of the truth value of an LTL formula in a state s or on a path π, in a given Kripke structure K.

The computation Tree Logic CTL is the fragment of CTL* where each temporal operator must be preceded by a path operator, and each path operator has to be immediately followed by a temporal operator.

The Linear Time Logic LTL is the fragment of CTL* without path quantifiers, and where a formula is true in a Kripke structure if it is true on all paths.

The Probabilistic Computation Tree Logic PCTL quantifies the different paths by replacing the E and A modalities of CTL by probabilities.

4.2 Qualitative Biological Properties in CTL

As shown in [32], CTL is sufficiently expressive for formalizing qualitative biological properties, such as :

Table 1. Inductive definition of the truth value of a propositional CTL* formula in a state s or a path π, in a given Kripke structure K

$s \models \alpha$	iff α is a propositional formula true in state s,
$s \models E\psi$	iff there exists a path π starting from s s.t. $\pi \models \psi$,
$s \models A\psi$	iff for all paths π starting from s, $\pi \models \psi$,
$\pi \models \phi$	iff $s \models \phi$ where s is the first state of π,
$\pi \models X\psi$	iff $\pi^1 \models \psi$,
$\pi \models \psi\ U\ \psi'$	iff there exists $k \geq 0$ s.t. $\pi^k \models \psi'$ and $\pi^j \models \psi$ for all $0 \leq j < k$.
$\pi \models \psi\ W\ \psi'$	iff either for all $k \geq 0$, $\pi^k \models \psi$.
	or there exists $k \geq 0$ s.t. $\pi^k \models \psi\&\psi'$ and for all $0 \leq j < k$, $\pi^j \models \psi$.
$\pi \models !\psi$	iff $\pi \not\models \psi$,
$\pi \models \psi\ \&\ \psi'$	iff $\pi \models \psi$ and $\pi \models \psi'$,
$\pi \models \psi\ \vert\ \psi'$	iff $\pi \models \psi$ or $\pi \models \psi'$,
$\pi \models \psi \Rightarrow \psi'$	iff $\pi \models \psi'$ or $\pi \not\models \psi$,

- reachability where `reachable(P)` stands for $EF(P)$;
- steady states where `steady(P)` stands for $EG(P)$;
- stable states where `stable(P)` stands for $AG(P)$;
- checkpoints where `checkpoint(Q,P)` stands for $!E(!Q\ U\ P)$;
- oscillations where `oscil(P)` stands for $AG(EF\ !P \wedge EF\ P)$.
- and `loop(P,Q)` stands for $AG((P \Rightarrow EF\ Q) \wedge (Q \Rightarrow EF\ P))$.

Without strong fairness assumption, it is worth noting that the last two abbreviations are actually necessary but not sufficient conditions for oscillations. The correct formula for oscillations is indeed a CTL* formula that cannot be expressed in CTL: $EG(F\ !P \wedge F\ P)$.

In Biocham, these abbreviations can be used inside CTL formulae. For instance, the formula `reachable(steady(P))` expresses that the steady state denoted by formula P is reachable, or the formula `AG(!P -> checkpoint(Q,P))` expresses that Q is a checkpoint for P not only in the initial state but in all reachable states.

Such boolean CTL specification can also be used to complete or revise a model with machine learning algorithms. In [14], a model revision algorithm is described with the ability to not only add rules to, but also remove rules from a model in order to satisfy a CTL specification.

Example 8. In our running example of the MAPK cascade, one can use Biocham to enumerate, for instance, all simple reachability, stability, checkpoints and oscillation properties that are true in the model. This generates 112 CTL properties that can be taken as a specification. Then the model can be automatically reduced by deleting rules that do not change the satisfaction of the specification. In this model, 20 rules are left and 10 rules are deleted, essentially reverse reaction rules that do not change the specification of the cascade at this boolean abstraction level.

```
biocham: reduce_model.
1: deleting RAF-RAFK=>RAF+RAFK
2: deleting RAFPH-RAF~{p1}=>RAFPH+RAF~{p1}
3: deleting MEK-RAF~{p1}=>MEK+RAF~{p1}
4: deleting MEKPH-MEK~{p1}=>MEKPH+MEK~{p1}
5: deleting MAPK-MEK~{p1,p2}=>MAPK+MEK~{p1,p2}
6: deleting MAPKPH-MAPK~{p1}=>MAPKPH+MAPK~{p1}
7: deleting MEK~{p1}-RAF~{p1}=>MEK~{p1}+RAF~{p1}
8: deleting MEKPH-MEK~{p1,p2}=>MEKPH+MEK~{p1,p2}
9: deleting MAPK~{p1}-MEK~{p1,p2}=>MAPK~{p1}+MEK~{p1,p2}
10: deleting MAPKPH-MAPK~{p1,p2}=>MAPKPH+MAPK~{p1,p2}
```

Furthermore, temporal specifications can be used to correct a model automatically, with the model revision algorithm described in [14] for adding and removing rules in order to satisfy the temporal formulas. For instance, in the original model, if we delete one useful rule, the rule, or another model revision, can be automatically found to satisfy the specification:

```
biocham: delete_rules(RAF~{p1}+RAFPH=>RAF~{p1}-RAFPH).
RAFPH+RAF~{p1}=>RAFPH-RAF~{p1}
biocham: check_all.
The specification is not satisfied.
This formula is the first not verified: Ai(oscil(RAF))
biocham: learn_one_addition(elementary_interaction_rules).
Rules tested: 2027
Possible rules to add: 1
RAFPH+RAF~{p1}=>RAFPH-RAF~{p1}
```

In this example, the deleted rule is recovered from the temporal specification and no other choice is possible for the given pattern of elementary rules to search for. Note that this pattern generates 2027 rules to check, and that this number can be drastically reduced by integrating in the pattern type information such as protein function kinase or phosphatase to restrict the search [49,13].   □

Example 9. In example 2 of Kohn's map with 800 reaction rules over 500 molecular compounds, simple CTL properties have been model-checked in Biocham in a few seconds [16] using the symbolic model-checker NuSMV [50]. This shows the efficiency of model-checking techniques for querying all possible behaviors of a reaction model under the boolean semantics. Omissions in Kohn's map, such as for instance the absence of synthesis for cyclin B, can be immediately detected by the absence of possibility to get oscillations for cyclin B, unlike cyclin A for instance.

4.3   Quantitative Biological Properties Formalized in LTL with Constraints over the Reals

LTL with Constraints Over the Reals. A version of LTL with constraints over the reals, called Constraint-LTL, is used in Biocham [14] to express temporal properties about molecular concentrations. A similar approach is used in the DARPA BioSpice project [43]. Constraint-LTL considers first-order atomic formulae with equality, inequality and arithmetic operators ranging over real values of concentrations and of their derivatives. For instance F([A]>10) expresses that the concentration of A eventually gets above the threshold value 10. G([A]+[B]<[C]) expresses that the concentration of C is always greater than the sum of the concentrations of A and B. Oscillation properties, abbreviated as oscil(M,K), are defined as a change of sign of the derivative of M at least K times: F((d[M]/dt > 0) & F((d[M]/dt < 0) & F((d[M]/dt > 0)...))) The abbreviated formula oscil(M,K,V) adds the constraint that the maximum concentration of M must be above the threshold V in at least K oscillations.

In this context, the Kripke structures in which the LTL formula are interpreted are linear Kripke structures which represent either an experimental data time series or a simulation trace, both completed with loops on terminal states. For instance, in a model described by a system of ordinary differential equations (ODE), and under the hypothesis that the initial state is completely defined, numerical integration methods (such as Runge-Kutta or Rosenbrock method for stiff systems) provide a discrete simulation trace. This trace constitutes a linear Kripke structure in which Constraint-LTL formulae can be interpreted. Since constraints refer not only to concentrations, but also to their derivatives, traces of the form

$$(< t_0, \boldsymbol{x}_0, d\boldsymbol{x}_0/dt, d^2\boldsymbol{x}_0/dt^2 >, < t_1, \boldsymbol{x}_1, d\boldsymbol{x}_1/dt, d^2\boldsymbol{x}_1/dt^2 >, ...)$$

are considered, where at each time point t_i, the trace associates the concentration values $\boldsymbol{x}_i$ to the variables, and the values of their first and second derivatives $d\boldsymbol{x}_i/dt$ and $d^2\boldsymbol{x}_i/dt^2$.

It is worth noting that in adaptive step size integration methods of ODE systems, the step size $t_{i+1} - t_i$ is not constant and is determined through an estimation of the error made by the discretization.

Constraint-LTL Model-Checking Algorithm. Let us assume a finite linear Kripke structure, i.e. a finite chain of states containing a loop on the last state. For these structures, the standard model-checking algorithms [38] can be easily adapted to Constraint-LTL as follows:

Algorithm 1 (Constraint-LTL model-checking). *[14,43]*

1. *label each edge with the atomic sub-formulae of ϕ that are true at this point;*
2. *add sub-formulae of the form $X\phi$ to the immediate predecessors of points labeled with ϕ;*
3. *add sub-formulae of the form $\phi_1 \ U \ \phi_2$ to the points preceding a point labeled with ϕ_2 as long as ϕ_1 holds;*
4. *add sub-formulae of the form $\phi_1 \ W \ \phi_2$ to the last state if it is labeled by ϕ_1, and to the predecessors of the points labeled by $\phi_1 \ W \ \phi_2$ as long as ϕ_1 holds and add sub-formulae of the form $\phi_1 \ W \ \phi_2$ to the points preceding a point labeled with $\phi_1 \wedge \phi_2$ as long as ϕ_1 holds;*
5. *return the edges labeled by ϕ.*

In particular, given an ODE model and a temporal property ϕ to verify within a finite time horizon, the computation of a finite simulation trace by numerical integration provides a linear Kripke structure where the terminal state is completed with a loop. Note that the notion of *next state* (operator X) refers to the state of the following time point in a discretized trace, and thus does not necessarily imply real time neighborhood. The rationale of this algorithm is that the numerical trace contains enough relevant points, and in particular those where the derivatives change abruptly, to correctly evaluate temporal logic formulae. This has been very well verified in practice with various examples of published mathematical models [14].

In [51], the model checking algorithm for constraint LTL is generalized to a constraint LTL solving algorithm with the capability to compute domains of real valued variables (such as thresholds) for which a constraint LTL formula is true. This is used for the analysis of numerical data time series in temporal logic and the automatic generation of a temporal specification of some pattern from biological experiment data time series.

Search of Kinetic Parameter Values from Constraint-LTL Properties. One can use constraint LTL model-checking to design a *generate and test* algorithm for finding parameter values such that a given LTL specification is satisfied.

A set of parameters, together with intervals of possible values and a precision parameter, are input to an enumeration algorithm. All value combinations are then scanned with a step size corresponding to the given precision, until the specification is satisfied.

Example 10. In the example 1 of the MAPK model, this parameter search algorithm can be used, for instance, to increase the overshoot for the complexation RAF-RAFK observed in the simulation of figure 2 as follows:

```
biocham: add_ltl(F([RAF-RAFK]>0.05)).
biocham: check_ltl.
F([RAF-RAFK]>0.05) is false.
biocham: search_parameters([k1], [(0,10)], 40, 20).
First values found that make F([RAF-RAFK]>0.05) true:
parameter(k1,1.75).
Search time: 2.96 s
```

The resulting simulation with the new value found for the complexation parameter k1=1.75 is depicted in figure 6.

This search procedure actually replicates and automates part of what the modeler currently does by hand: trying different parameter values, between bounds that are thought reasonable, or computed by other methods such as bifurcation diagrams, in order to obtain behaviors in accordance with the experimental knowledge. Biocham provides a way to explore much faster this parameter space, once the effort for formalizing the expected behavior in LTL is done. The main novel feature of this method is its capability to express and combine in LTL both

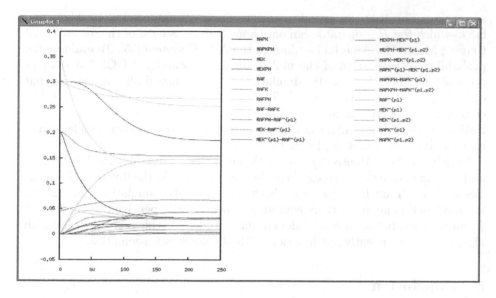

Fig. 6. Simulation result of the MAP cascade with new parameter value inferred for increasing the overshoot on `RAF-RAFK`

qualitative and quantitative constraints on the expected behavior of the model. In [52] it is used for exploring the conditions of entrainment in period of the cell cycle by the circadian cycle in a coupled model of these cycles.

The computational complexity of the parameter values scanning grows linearly in the number of combinations of parameter values to try, that is in $O(d^n)$ where n is the number of parameter values to find and d the number of values to try for each parameter. The difficulty to use other search algorithms better than generate-and-test (such as local search or simulated annealing for instance) comes from the criterion of satisfaction of LTL formulae which is naturally boolean and for which it is not obvious to define a multi-valued measure of satisfaction.

4.4   Probabilistic Model-Checking

For the stochastic semantics, it is natural to consider the PCTL logic [53] which basically replaces the path operators of CTL, E and A, by the operator $P_{\bowtie p}$. This operator represents a constraint $\bowtie_p$ on the probability that the formula under $P_{\bowtie p}$ is true. For instance, $A(\psi\ U\ \psi')$ becomes $P_{\geq 1}(\psi\ U\ \psi')$, i.e. the probability that $\psi\ U\ \psi'$ is realized is 1. The atomic formulae considered here are first-order formulae with arithmetic constraints, ranging on integers representing numbers of molecules.

However, he existing probabilistic model-checking tools, like that of PRISM [54], do not handle well highly non-deterministic examples, nor those where variables have a large domain as it is the case in BIOCHAM models' stochastic semantics.. This led us to actually consider the PLTL fragment of PCTL formulae in which the $P_{\bowtie_p}$ operator can only appear once as head of the formula, and to use a Monte-Carlo method as done in the APMC system [55]. To evaluate the probability of realization of the underlying LTL formula, BIOCHAM samples a certain number of stochastic simulations using standard algorithms like that of Gillespie [24] or of Gibson [56]. The outer probability is then estimated by counting. It is worth noting that this method provides a real estimate of realization of the LTL formula, whereas PCTL expresses the boolean satisfaction of a probability constraint ($\bowtie_p$) over the formula.

In principle, the Monte-Carlo algorithm can thus be used for model-checking and kinetic parameter learning along the same lines as in the differential semantics and constraint-LTL. However, both the stochastic simulation process and the model-checking process are computationally more expensive than in the differential semantics by several orders of magnitude. For this reason, such search algorithms are currently not practical with the stochastic semantics.

5   Conclusion

Systems biology can benefit from formal methods originating from programming theory in many ways. By formalizing the different semantics of a reaction model, we have shown that, to a large extent, the influence graph of a reaction model is independent of the kinetic parameters and kinetic expressions, and that it can be computed in linear time simply from the syntax of the reactions. This happens for strongly increasing kinetics such as classical mass action law, Michaelis-Menten and Hill kinetics, when no molecule is at the same time an activator and an inhibitor of a same target molecule. The inference of the syntactical influence graph from a reaction model has been implemented in Biocham, and applied to various models. On a transcription of Kohn's map into approx. 800 reaction rules, this implementation shows that no molecule is at the same time an activator and an inhibitor of a same molecule, and therefore, our equivalence theorem states that the differential influence graph would be the same for any standard kinetics with any parameter values. On the MAPK signalling cascade that does not contain any feedback reaction, the implementation does reveal both positive and negative feedback circuits in the influence graph, which has been a source of confusion for the correct application of Thomas' rules. Furthermore, in this example again, no molecule is at the same time an activator and an inhibitor of another molecule, showing the independence of the influence graph from the kinetics.

By formalizing the biological properties observed in experiments, in temporal logic, we have illustrated the expressivity of these logics in this context, and we have shown that classical as well as new model-checking techniques can be applied for validating reaction models w.r.t. temporal specifications. The beauty of this approach is that it deals not only with the boolean semantics but also with the differential semantics (and stochastic semantics) of reaction models. Furthermore, such semi-qualitative semi-quantitative temporal specifications can be also used for searching parameter values, in a complementary fashion to classical mathematical methods such as bifurcation diagrams. The improvement of this method by the definition of a measure of satisfaction of a temporal formula with constraints, and a gradient descent analog, are currently under investigation.

Acknowledgements. The material presented in this tutorial has been developed with colleagues since 2001. We are especially grateful to Laurence Calzone, Nathalie Chabrier-Rivier, Aurélien Rizk, and all those who have contributed to the development of Biocham at one stage or another. The first author thanks his successive students of the University of Paris for their reactions to his lectures on this topic. This work benefited from support of the ARC CPBIO (02-04) and ARC MOCA (05-07) http://contraintes.inria.fr/cpbio and moca, INRA Agrobi Insight   (07-09)   http://contraintes.inria.fr/~heitzler/INSIGHT/Home.html, European Union FP6 Strep projects APrIL2 (04-07) http://www.aprill.org/, TEMPO (06-09) http://www.chrono-tempo.org, and network of excellence REWERSE (04-08) http://www.rewerse.net.

References

1. Kohn, K.W.: Molecular interaction map of the mammalian cell cycle control and DNA repair systems. Molecular Biology of the Cell 10, 2703–2734 (1999)
2. Hucka, M., et al.: The systems biology markup language (SBML): A medium for representation and exchange of biochemical network models. Bioinformatics 19, 524–531 (2003)
3. Thomas, R., Gathoye, A.M., Lambert, L.: A complex control circuit: regulation of immunity in temperate bacteriophages. European Journal of Biochemistry 71, 211–227 (1976)
4. Kaufman, M., Soulé, C., Thomas, R.: A new necessary condition on interaction graphs for multistationarity. Journal of Theoretical Biology 248, 675–685 (2007)
5. Soulé, C.: Mathematical approaches to differentiation and gene regulation. C.R. Biologies 329, 13–20 (2006)
6. Soulé, C.: Graphic requirements for multistationarity. ComplexUs 1, 123–133 (2003)
7. Snoussi, E.: Necessary conditions for multistationarity and stable periodicity. J. Biol. Syst. 6, 3–9 (1998)
8. Gouzé, J.L.: Positive and negative circuits in dynamical systems. J. Biol. Syst. 6, 11–15 (1998)
9. Calzone, L., Fages, F., Soliman, S.: BIOCHAM: An environment for modeling biological systems and formalizing experimental knowledge. BioInformatics 22, 1805–1807 (2006)
10. Fages, F., Soliman, S., Chabrier-Rivier, N.: Modelling and querying interaction networks in the biochemical abstract machine BIOCHAM. Journal of Biological Physics and Chemistry 4, 64–73 (2004)
11. Hlavacek, W.S., Faeder, J.R., Blinov, M.L., Posner, R.G., Hucka, M., Fontana, W.: Rules for modeling signal-transduction systems. Science STKE 344, 6 (2006)
12. Soliman, S., Fages, F.: CMBSlib: a library for comparing formalisms and models of biological systems. In: Danos, V., Schachter, V. (eds.) CMSB 2004. LNCS (LNBI), vol. 3082, pp. 231–235. Springer, Heidelberg (2005)

13. Fages, F., Soliman, S.: Abstract interpretation and types for systems biology. In: Theoretical Computer Science (to appear, 2008)
14. Calzone, L., Chabrier-Rivier, N., Fages, F., Soliman, S.: Machine learning biochemical networks from temporal logic properties. In: Priami, C., Plotkin, G. (eds.) Transactions on Computational Systems Biology VI. LNCS (LNBI), vol. 4220, pp. 68–94. Springer, Heidelberg (2006)
15. Fages, F.: From syntax to semantics in systems biology - towards automated reasoning tools. Transactions on Computational Systems Biology IV 3939, 68–70 (2006)
16. Chabrier-Rivier, N., Chiaverini, M., Danos, V., Fages, F., Schächter, V.: Modeling and querying biochemical interaction networks. Theoretical Computer Science 325, 25–44 (2004)
17. Levchenko, A., Bruck, J., Sternberg, P.W.: Scaffold proteins biphasically affect the levels of mitogen-activated protein kinase signaling and reduce its threshold properties. PNAS 97, 5818–5823 (2000)
18. Ventura, A.C., Sepulchre, J.A., Merajver, S.D.: A hidden feedback in signaling cascades is revealed. In: PLoS Computational Biology (to appear, 2008)
19. Markevich, N.I., Hoek, J.B., Kholodenko, B.N.: Signaling switches and bistability arising from multisite phosphorylation in protein kinase cascades. Journal of Cell Biology 164, 353–359 (2005)
20. Kolch, W., Kotwaliwale, A., Vass, K., Janosch, P.: The role of raf kinases in malignant transformation. In: Expert Reviews in Molecular Medicine, vol. 25, Cambridge University Press, Cambridge (2002)
21. Shapiro, B.E., Levchenko, A., Meyerowitz, E.M., Wold, B.J., Mjolsness, E.D.: Cellerator: extending a computer algebra system to include biochemical arrows for signal transduction simulations. Bioinformatics 19, 677–678 (2003)
22. Regev, A., Silverman, W., Shapiro, E.Y.: Representation and simulation of biochemical processes using the pi-calculus process algebra. In: Proceedings of the sixth Pacific Symposium of Biocomputing, pp. 459–470 (2001)
23. Gillespie, D.T.: Exact stochastic simulation of coupled chemical reactions. Journal of Physical Chemistry 81, 2340–2361 (1977)
24. Gillespie, D.T.: General method for numerically simulating stochastic time evolution of coupled chemical-reactions. Journal of Computational Physics 22, 403–434 (1976)
25. Gibson, M.A., Bruck, J.: A probabilistic model of a prokaryotic gene and its regulation. In: Bolouri, H., Bower, J. (eds.) Computational Methods in Molecular Biology: From Genotype to Phenotype, MIT press, Cambridge (2000)
26. Reddy, V.N., Mavrovouniotis, M.L., Liebman, M.N.: Petri net representations in metabolic pathways. In: Hunter, L., Searls, D.B., Shavlik, J.W. (eds.) Proceedings of the 1st International Conference on Intelligent Systems for Molecular Biology (ISMB, pp. 328–336. AAAI Press, Menlo Park (1993)
27. Sackmann, A., Heiner, M., Koch, I.: Application of petri net based analysis techniques to signal transduction pathways. BMC Bioinformatics 7 (2006)
28. Chaouiya, C.: Petri net modelling of biological networks. Briefings in Bioinformatics (2007)
29. Gilbert, D., Heiner, M., Lehrack, S.: A unifying framework for modelling and analysing biochemical pathways using petri nets. In: Calder, M., Gilmore, S. (eds.) CMSB 2007. LNCS (LNBI), vol. 4695, Springer, Heidelberg (2007)
30. Schuster, S., Pfeiffer, T., Moldenhauer, F., et al.: Exploring the pathway structure of metabolism: decomposition into subnetworks and application to mycoplasma pneumoniae. Bioinformatics 18, 51–61 (2002)

31. Zevedei-Oancea, I., Schuster, S.: Topological analysis of metabolic networks based on petri net theory. Silico Biology 3 (2003)
32. Chabrier, N., Fages, F.: Symbolic model cheking of biochemical networks. In: Priami, C. (ed.) CMSB 2003. LNCS, vol. 2602, pp. 149–162. Springer, Heidelberg (2003)
33. Eker, S., Knapp, M., Laderoute, K., Lincoln, P., Meseguer, J., Sönmez, M.K.: Pathway logic: Symbolic analysis of biological signaling. In: Proceedings of the seventh Pacific Symposium on Biocomputing, pp. 400–412 (2002)
34. Cousot, P., Cousot, R.: Abstract interpretation: A unified lattice model for static analysis of programs by construction or approximation of fixpoints. In: POPL 1977: Proceedings of the 6th ACM Symposium on Principles of Programming Languages, Los Angeles, pp. 238–252. ACM Press, New York (1977)
35. Cousot, P.: Constructive design of a hierarchy of semantics of a transition system by abstract interpretation. Theoretical Computer Science 277, 47–103 (2002)
36. Cousot, P.: Types as abstract interpretation. In: POP 1997: Proceedings of the 24th ACM Symposium on Principles of Programming Languages, pp. 316–331. ACM Press, New York (1997)
37. Qiao, L., Nachbar, R.B., Kevrekidis, I.G., Shvartsman, S.Y.: Bistability and oscillations in the huang-ferrell model of mapk signaling. PLoS Computational Biology 3, 1819–1826 (2007)
38. Clarke, E.M., Grumberg, O., Peled, D.A.: Model Checking. MIT Press, Cambridge (1999)
39. Bernot, G., Comet, J.P., Richard, A., Guespin, J.: A fruitful application of formal methods to biological regulatory networks: Extending thomas' asynchronous logical approach with temporal logic. Journal of Theoretical Biology 229, 339–347 (2004)
40. Batt, G., Bergamini, D., de Jong, H., Garavel, H., Mateescu, R.: Model checking genetic regulatory networks using gna and cadp. In: Graf, S., Mounier, L. (eds.) SPIN 2004. LNCS, vol. 2989, Springer, Heidelberg (2004)
41. Calder, M., Vyshemirsky, V., Gilbert, D., Orton, R.: Analysis of signalling pathways using the continuous time markow chains. In: Priami, C., Plotkin, G. (eds.) Transactions on Computational Systems Biology VI. LNCS (LNBI), vol. 4220, pp. 44–67. Springer, Heidelberg (2006)
42. Heath, J., Kwiatkowska, M., Norman, G., Parker, D., Tymchyshyn, O.: Probabilistic model checking of complex biological pathways. In: Priami, C. (ed.) CMSB 2006. LNCS (LNBI), vol. 4210, pp. 32–47. Springer, Heidelberg (2006)
43. Antoniotti, M., Policriti, A., Ugel, N., Mishra, B.: Model building and model checking for biochemical processes. Cell Biochemistry and Biophysics 38, 271–286 (2003)
44. Fages, F.: Temporal logic constraints in the biochemical abstract machine biocham (invited talk). In: Hill, P.M. (ed.) LOPSTR 2005. LNCS, vol. 3901, Springer, Heidelberg (2006)
45. Cardelli, L.: Brane calculi - interactions of biological membranes. In: Danos, V., Schachter, V. (eds.) CMSB 2004. LNCS (LNBI), vol. 3082, pp. 257–280. Springer, Heidelberg (2005)
46. Regev, A., Panina, E.M., Silverman, W., Cardelli, L., Shapiro, E.: Bioambients: An abstraction for biological compartments. Theoretical Computer Science 325, 141–167 (2004)
47. Danos, V., Laneve, C.: Formal molecular biology. Theoretical Computer Science 325, 69–110 (2004)
48. Phillips, A., Cardelli, L.: A correct abstract machine for the stochastic pi-calculus. Transactions on Computational Systems Biology Special issue of BioConcur (to appear, 2004)

49. Fages, F., Soliman, S.: Type inference in systems biology. In: Priami, C. (ed.) CMSB 2006. LNCS (LNBI), vol. 4210, Springer, Heidelberg (2006)
50. Cimatti, A., Clarke, E., Enrico Giunchiglia, F.G., Pistore, M., Roveri, M., Sebastiani, R., Tacchella, A.: Nusmv 2: An opensource tool for symbolic model checking. In: Brinksma, E., Larsen, K.G. (eds.) CAV 2002. LNCS, vol. 2404, Springer, Heidelberg (2002)
51. Fages, F., Rizk, A.: On the analysis of numerical data time series in temporal logic. In: Calder, M., Gilmore, S. (eds.) CMSB 2007. LNCS (LNBI), vol. 4695, pp. 48–63. Springer, Heidelberg (2007)
52. Fages, F., Soliman, S.: Model revision from temporal logic properties in systems biology. In: Probabilistic Inductive Logic Programming. LNCS, vol. 4911, pp. 287–304. Springer, Heidelberg (2008)
53. Hansson, H., Jonsson, B.: A logic for reasoning about time and reliability. Formal Aspects of Computing 6, 512–535 (1994)
54. Kwiatkowska, M.Z., Norman, G., Parker, D.: Prism 2.0: A tool for probabilistic model checking. In: st International Conference on Quantitative Evaluation of Systems (QEST 2004), pp. 322–323. IEEE Computer Society, Los Alamitos (2004)
55. Hérault, T., Lassaigne, R., Magniette, F., Peyronnet, S.: Approximate probabilistic model checking. In: Steffen, B., Levi, G. (eds.) VMCAI 2004. LNCS, vol. 2937, pp. 73–84. Springer, Heidelberg (2004)
56. Gibson, M.A., Bruck, J.: Efficient exact stochastic simulation of chemical systems with many species and many channels. Journal of Physical Chemistry 104, 1876–1889 (2000)

Hierarchical Modeling for Computational Biology

Carsten Maus, Mathias John, Mathias Röhl, and Adelinde M. Uhrmacher

University of Rostock
Albert-Einstein-Str. 21
D-18059 Rostock, Germany
lin@informatik.uni-rostock.de

Abstract. Diverse hierarchies play a role in modeling and simulation for computational biology, e.g. categories, abstraction hierarchies, and composition hierarchies. Composition hierarchies seem a natural and straightforward focus for our
exploration. What are model components and the requirements for a composite
approach? How far do they support the quest for building blocks in computational
biology? Modeling formalisms provide different means for composing a model.
We will illuminate this with DEVS (Discrete event systems specification) and the
π calculus. Whereas in DEVS distinctions are emphasized, e.g. between a system
and its environment, between properties attributed to a system and the system
itself, these distinctions become fluent in the compact description of the π calculus. However, both share the problem that in order to support a comfortable
modeling, a series of extensions have been developed which also influence their
possibility to support a hierarchical modeling. Thus, not individual formalisms
but two families of formalisms and how they support a composite modeling will
be presented. In computational biology one type of composite model deserves a
closer inspection, as it brings together the wish to compose models and the need
to describe a system at different levels in a unique manner, i.e. multi-level models.

Keywords: hierarchical models, DEVS, pi calculus, model components, multi-
level modeling.

1 Introduction

The goal of Computational Biology is to analyze the behavior and interrelationships of
functional biological systems. Modeling and simulation is on its way to be established
as one of the core tools in cell biological studies, which also inspires the development
and use of different modeling and simulation methods.

As biological systems are governed by the laws of chemistry and physics, simulation approaches from these domains are also viable for the simulation of cell biological
models. Nevertheless, the size of these models often limits their applicability. This led
to numerous abstractions: from the actual physical processes, described by quantum
mechanics, over approaches that abstract to entire atoms (*molecular dynamics*), toward
approaches that only consider molecules, compartments, or cells [1]. Simulation algorithms for a sub-molecular scale rely on natural laws that are of continuous nature [2].
At the level of molecules, approaches abstract from the natural laws by assuming that
the molecules move randomly (i.e., Brownian Motion). Turning from single molecules

M. Bernardo, P. Degano, and G. Zavattaro (Eds.): SFM 2008, LNCS 5016, pp. 81–124, 2008.

to concentrations of molecules, a system can be described using ODEs. However, this deterministic continuous simulation is inadequate for models with small numbers of molecules, where stochastic effects play a role. The stochastic effects that occur can be expressed by the Chemical Master Equation (CME), which accurately models the system behavior as a probability distribution of a chemical system's state, depending on the current time. To compute this formula is extremely hard, if not impossible for most practical cases. In [3], Gillespie introduced a stochastic simulation algorithm (SSA) whose outcome exactly samples the chemical master equation. The algorithm assumes that the system under study is in thermal equilibrium, i.e. all molecules are randomly distributed in a uniform manner.

Obviously, each of the modeling and simulation approaches comes along with specific abstractions, assumptions, and constraints, which influence its suitability for a particular case study. Abstractions are essential in modeling, as each model is an abstraction of the system it describes [4]. To save space and time and to improve clarity by concentrating on relevant aspects of behavior, the abstraction of a model might be increased, e.g. by aggregating state variables, spatial and temporal variable scales, or components, or by omitting components, variables, and interactions. Abstractions, assumptions, and constraints are closely inter-related. However, in only few cases this relation is made explicit, e.g. that a less abstract model will lead to a relaxation of assumptions. Widely agreed upon representations of assumptions are lacking, which hampers also a semantically meaningful reuse of models [5] and motivates current approaches like MIRIAM [6].

For understanding the functioning of a whole cell or an entire organ, one abstraction level will likely not suffice. Hybrid modeling approaches combine continuous and discrete perspectives on systems under study [7], and qualitative scales are combined with quantitative ones [8,9]. Those can also be found in the area of computational biology, e.g. [10,11]. Many utilize parallel composition to describe the system as a community of concurrent sub-systems each of which might or might not be described at different levels of abstractions [12], or some might use sequential composition to structure the behavior of the system e.g. with STATE CHARTS [13]. A system being composed of sub-systems, traditionally complements the network perspective and the functional perception of dynamic systems in modeling and simulation. This composition hierarchy, i.e. the parallel composition, is what is typically meant when speaking of a model hierarchy, thus it is the pre-dominant form of hierarchy when it comes to modeling and simulation in general. In computational biology, it is also gaining ground [14,15] and thus competing with another hierarchical concept that has traditionally been associated with biology: categories. Categories [16] are meant to reduce our cognitive effort in dealing with complexity, by providing some structuring. The same can be said for hierarchies in general: "whether nature is truly organized hiearchically is moot. Men's perception of nature is hierarchical." [17].

2   Setting the Context

Statements like "Explanation of observed behavior is not possible with reference solely to the spatial-temporal scale at which the observation was made" [18, p.267] and "behavior at any level is explained in terms of the level below, and its significance is found in the level above" [17, p.127] emphasize the role of hierarchical modeling. For the area of theoretical biology the fundamental importance of hierarchies has been stated early [19], being also reflected in a series of edited books about hierarchy theory coupled with a discussion about reductionism versus holism, e.g. [20,21,22]. Hierarchies are ubiquitous, from atomic and molecular processes up to the systematic classification of living species and large individual populations. Hierarchies form a cognitive means for separating more important elements from less important ones and impose an ordering on elements such that some elements are tagged with a higher rank than others. Thereby, a hierarchy structures knowledge about the relationship between elements of a system and helps reducing the level of detail [23]. Based on [24], we distinguish, according to the role in simulation models, different kinds of hierarchies:

Representation. The higher level forms a representation of the lower level and hides this detailed realization from the user. Icons in VIMS (Visual Interactive Modeling Systems) are an example for abstracting away technical details and hiding them behind an icon. Thereby, these approaches follow the information seeking mantra of [25]: "Overview first, zoom and filter, then details-on-demand".

Classification. Classification is another way of structuring the knowledge about a given system. Categories shall provide the maximum of information with as little cognitive effort as possible [26]. As the later is context dependent, it is not surprising that for many areas, e.g. biology, different opposing methods to construct categories exist [27]. "The objective criterion for being in the same category is having common properties. But there is no objectivist criterion for which properties are to count." [16, p.186]. Categories are the pendant of classes in object-oriented approaches [28]. Already Simula, the first object-oriented programming language, supported the definition of classes and inheritance. Consequently, with establishing object-oriented approaches in modeling and simulation also the use of classes and inheritance have entered state of the art modeling, reflected in developments like e.g. DEVS/SES for discrete systems [29], and, even more visible, MODELICA for continuous systems [30]. In addition, categories in the form of ontologies are starting to play a role for reusing models. Particularly, for a semantically valid reuse and composition of models [31], the annotation of model components with meta-data becomes necessary. Objectives, assumptions, and constraints for each component need to be represented [5], open question are what information to represent and how to represent it for an automatic composition. Due to the many online ontologies in medicine and biology, computational biology has a head start in specifying this meta-data, e.g. [6].

Refinement. Refinement hierarchies structure the space by relating models due to abstraction, or reduction. Typically refinement refers in modeling to adding step-wise more details to a model, and thus is essential in generating (more complex) models. With refinement the relation between alternative, differently detailed models is explored, the intention is to be able to replace one model by another model of the same system. Whereas in programming one starts with a model and refines it in terms of programming, in modeling the opposite direction is often also of interest, i.e., how to develop a more simple and behavior equivalent model? Aggregation of components, moving from quantitative to qualitative scales, or reducing the model are means to achieve a more abstract model. For the purpose of model reduction e.g. sensitivity analysis are exploited [32]: "Perfection is achieved, not when there is nothing more to add, but when there is nothing left to take away" (Antoine de Saint Exupery). Independent whether a model shall be simplified, or more detail added to it, if refinement rules are made explicit they support reasoning about the relation between different models, model parts, and their interactions. This can help ensuring correctness and reliability of large simulation models, e.g. [33], and opens one avenue for combining simulation and verification for a better understanding of dynamic system [34].

Composition. Containment of elements within another element, the "part of"-relation forms probably the most well known type of hierarchy exploited in dynamic systems modeling. It complements the network and functional view [35]. Composition reduces the scope of single models and allows to construct models top-down or bottom up. In computational biology, particularly in synthetic biology, researchers are increasingly concerned with "the definition, description and characterization of the basic biological parts, as well as standard conditions that support the use of parts in combination and overall system operation" [14, p.450]. Whereas compositionality is currently mostly exploited for model description and construction, it gains importance for analyzing dynamic systems as well [36].

In the scope of this paper we will concentrate on composition, although some of the other forms of hierarchical modeling will creep into our exploration of hierarchical modeling in biology sporadically. As already stated, defining a system as being composed of other system, or a model being composed of other models is well established as a means for complexity reduction in systems theory and modeling and simulation. However, in the last 10 years the term "components" and "component-based design" has received a more concrete meaning, due to developments in the area of software components [37] which are also reflected in the area of model components [38]. A component should be a replaceable part of a system and be usable in unforseen contexts for different purposes [37]. Components provide a certain functionality, expressed by a well-defined interface and realized by an implementation [38]. Interfaces should contain as much information, as is needed to use an implementation solely via its interface [39]. In a composition, analysis should be done based on interfaces. An interface may be seen as a model of an implementation. Thus, for simulation model components, an interface is a model of a model. Composition of model parts that were developed independently of each other combine two hierarchical relations: (i) refinement relation between interfaces and implementations and (ii) part-of relations between a composite and its parts. Figure 1 visualizes both hierarchical relations in the context of compositions.

The main challenge for compositional approaches is summarized in the term compositionality. Compositionality requires that the meaning of a composition can be derived solely from the semantic descriptions of the parts together with the rules of combination [40]. Parts have compositional properties if the semantics of a composition can be derived from the semantics of the used components [37]. Generally, we would assume that the less composed a model is the more abstract it is, however, this might not be true in all cases (cf. Figure 2).

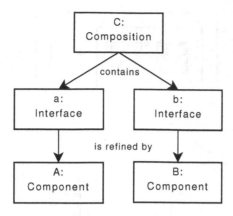

Fig. 1. Composition based on interfaces

Composition hierarchies, that are formed by the "is part of", and abstraction hierarchies do not necessarily coincide, nor are they necessarily entirely independent. One type of model is just defined by a specific combination of composition and refinement, i.e. multi-level models. Multi-level models combine micro and macro models within one model, so they do not substitute one macro model by a micro model but combine both to form a part of the system. This implies that a model describes one system at population and individual level. As micro and macro level do not refer to two separate sub-systems, they do not form two loosely coupled components. The individuals at micro level make up (part of) the population at macro level. Obviously the behavior at micro level will have an effect on the macro level, but also vice versa the dynamics at macro level influence the behavior at micro level. Higher levels place constraints on the behavior at lower levels, and also the behavior of the higher level is consistent with lower level behavior [17]. Downward causation [41] and upward causation link both organizational levels in biology. The question how to put both levels into relation is still controversially discussed: Are micro and macro complementary or incommensurable [42]?

As soon as explicit structures are introduced into modeling the question arises whether and how these structures can be changed. Referring to the composition hierarchy, is it possible that new components are generated, that components are deleted, and that new hierarchical levels are introduced, to allow a hierarchical tree structure to grow in breadth and in depth? This possibility is particularly desirable when modeling biological systems [43], as phenomena like succession, metamorphosis, or cell differentiation ask for a structuring of the temporal plane. Variable structure models are models that contain in their own description the possibility to change their own behavior, interaction, and composition pattern. But which entity is responsible for changing the structure of whom, what information and what communication is required? Solutions have to tackle the question how much autonomy and control [44] are assigned to the different sub-models, or "sed quis custodiet ipsos custodes?" [45].

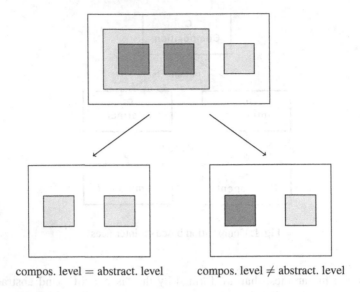

compos. level = abstract. level   compos. level ≠ abstract. level

Fig. 2. Composition and abstraction. Different shades of gray mean different abstraction levels.

2.1 Outline

Compositional hierarchies seem a natural and straightforward focus for our exploration of hierarchical modeling formalisms in computational biology. Thereby, the focus will be on two rather different modeling approaches, one state-oriented, i.e. DEVS, another process-oriented, i.e. the π calculus. We will first discuss DEVS and two extensions that address specific requirements of biological systems, i.e. ρ-DEVS and ML-DEVS. Afterwards stochastic π and extensions that add structure to stochastic π, i.e. BETA-BINDERS, BIOAMBIENTS, and SPICO will be presented and the question will be pursued whether and how they support a hierarchical modeling. Hierarchical component-based modeling is based on the availability of model components and suggests a reuse of model components. Steps towards a component-based design of models will conclude our exploration.

3   Hierarchies in DEVS

The Discrete Event Systems Specification (DEVS) is a modeling formalism originally introduced in the 1970s by B. P. Zeigler [46]. DEVS models consist of atomic and of coupled submodels. The first ones are the active ones, defined by states, state transition and output functions of the model, whereas the latter ones serve only as passive containers for other models and route the incoming and outgoing messages. This modular composition leads automatically to tree-like hierarchies where the root and nodes of the tree reflect coupled models and leafs atomic models (see Figure 3).

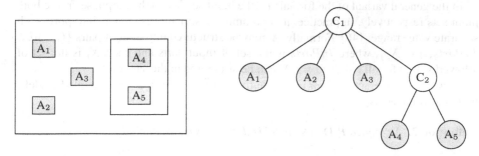

Fig. 3. Tree-like model structure of DEVS. C_i: coupled models, A_i: atomic models. Model interfaces and their couplings are not shown.

3.1 DEVS Basics

Systems modeled with DEVS have a continuous time base but events take place at discrete time points, i.e. DEVS is a classical discrete event formalism. We will start here with a variant of DEVS called parallel DEVS (P-DEVS) [47], which has a few additional features compared to the original DEVS formalism of Zeigler [46]. In the following, we will use DEVS and P-DEVS as synonyms.

Definition 1. *An atomic P-DEVS model is defined as a structure:*

$$\langle X, Y, S, ta, \delta_{ext}, \delta_{int}, \delta_{con}, \lambda \rangle$$

where

X — *is the structured set of inputs*
Y — *is the structured set of outputs*
S — *is the structured set of states*
$ta : S \to \mathcal{R}^{\geq 0} \cup \{\infty\}$ *is the time advance function*
$\delta_{ext} : Q \times X^b \to S$ *is the external state transition function, with*
   $Q = \{(s, e) : s \in S, 0 \leq e < ta(s)\}$ *state set including elapsed time*
$\delta_{int} : S \to S$ *is the internal state transition function*
$\delta_{con} : S \times X^b \to S$ *is the confluent transition function*
$\lambda : S \to Y$ *is the output function*

State transitions can be triggered either by the δ_{int} function, which is called when a specific time interval associated with the current state ($ta(s)$) has been elapsed, or by the δ_{ext} function, which is called if an external message from another model component arrives. Additionally, δ_{con} can also change the model's state. It is called if an internal and external event coincide. For communication, DEVS models are equipped with sets of allowed input and output events. The output generating function λ is called just right before the internal transition function.

In the general variant of the formalism, the input set X and the output set Y are both plain sets respectively. In practice, it is common to structure X and Y into ports with separate value ranges [46]. Formally, X may be structured into a set of pairs $\{(i, v)|i \in InPorts, v \in X_i\}$, where $InPorts$ is the set of input ports and each X_i is the set of allowed values for all $i \in InPorts$. Y can be structured in the same way.

How models interact via their in- and output ports, is specified in the coupled models, which are defined as follows:

Definition 2. *A coupled P-*DEVS *model is defined as a structure:*

$$\langle X, Y, D, M_i, I_i, Z_{i,j} \rangle$$

where

X	*is the structured set of inputs*
Y	*is the structured set of outputs*
D	*is the name set of components*
M_i	*is the structured set of components*
I_i	*is the set of influencers of each component*
$Z_{i,j}$	*is the input output translation function*

Now let's have a look at some examples how DEVS models of biological systems can look like and where limitations appear.

Modeling Biological Systems with DEVS. As the modular structure of DEVS models leads to a strict separation of the individual submodels, intuitively membranes come into mind which separate different cells, organelles, and compartments from each other as well. The model interfaces, i.e. input and output ports, can represent the permeability of the membrane or transport proteins for special molecules. Receptors on the surface of the membrane for catching a signal can also be modeled by input ports. The schematic model structure of a simple cell compartment model is shown in Figure 4. The mitochondrion in the model (the "power plant" of cells) has one input port and one output port for glucose input and ATP output respectively (Figure 5). In real cells only the major products of glucose degradation in the cytoplasm by glycolysis enter the mitochondria and not glucose itself, but modeling is always simplification and for the example here this is a suitable assumption. If a glucose molecule reaches the mitochondrion, the δ_{ext} function is called and the glucose depot variable (#glucose) will be incremented. Afterwards, the main state (phase) of the model changes from the idle phase to the working phase. The working phase needs a specific time (timeToNextATP) to metabolize one glucose to an equivalent of 38 ATP molecules and sending this event through the output port to other model components. This time is not static but dynamically calculated by the function *metabolizeDuration* which is dependent on the glucose amount. The mitochondrion model is just a very small example, but it shows how biological processes can be modeled with DEVS.

Other examples, which the DEVS modeling formalism could be suitable for, are cell to cell influences. Interactions between different cells in a tissue are determined by their

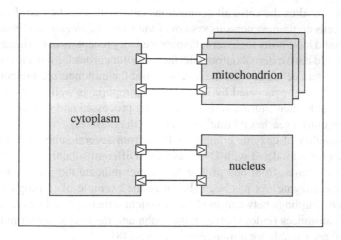

Fig. 4. Structure of a simple cell compartment model. From the mitochondrion model more than one instance exists. The connected small white squares indicate coupled input and output ports.

```
1    X = {glucosIn}
2
3    Y = {atpOut}
4
5    S = { (phase, #glucose, timeToNextATP) |
6             phase ∈ (idle, working),
7             #glucose ∈ N,
8             timeToNextATP ∈ R+ }
9
10   δ_ext =
11        #glucose++;
12        timeToNextATP = metabolizeDuration(#glucose);
13        phase = working
14
15   δ_int =
16        if (#glucose > 0) then
17           #glucose--
18           timeToNextATP = metabolizeDuration(#glucose);
19           phase = working
20        else
21           phase = idle
22
23   δ_con = δ_int; δ_ext
24
25   λ = atpOut("ATP")
26
27   ta = case phase of
28        idle: ∞
29        working: timeToNextATP
30        end case
```

Fig. 5. Atomic model of a mitochondrion. The input port receives glucose shuttling events and the output port releases ATP. State changes are triggered by the δ functions.

neighborhood and thus the cell-cell connections can be clearly defined. In a model of the only 203 cells containing nervous system of the worm *C. elegans* for example, some cell models could have ports for external inputs (sensory receptors in the head) and other sub-models could have external output interfaces (motoneurons for muscle stimulation). The nervous system cells between the receptors and the motoneurons are connected by synapses, which can be modeled by input and output ports as well. A stimulation of a receptor cell would then cause a signal that can be processed and forwarded from one cell to another until it reaches its final destination (the muscles).

The functionality of enzyme complexes built from several subunits like ATP synthases can be nicely modeled with DEVS as well. Different subunits are connected via ports and the messages from one protein to another indicate the proton flow through channels of the enzyme. As has been shown in the example of tryptophan synthase, due to explicit couplings between models, co-valent structures and processes like the tunneling of substances (indole between the alpha and the beta sub-unit in the case of the trytophan) are suitable for a modeling in DEVS [48].

3.2 Dynamically Structured Models

Structural dynamics can be found in biology very frequently. Beginning at the level of molecular dynamics over cell growth up to individuals in an ecosystem. Unfortunately, a classical DEVS model structure is fixed, that means, its composition and couplings of submodels cannot change during simulation. Such a restriction of the formalism consequentially hampers the modeling of dynamic systems with changing communication partners and reactions. In hierarchical modeling formalisms typically two principal possibilities exist to introduce structural changes. Either the composite model is responsible to generate new components and to define new couplings, as e.g. done in [43], or components are responsible for generating new components and changing their own structure, thereby, structural changes are introduced bottom up. Pursuing the first approach, [49] introduces a controller into coupled DEVS models, which initiate structural changes top down. DYNDEVS and ρ-DEVS, both extensions of the DEVS formalism, support adding and removing of model components and couplings dynamically during simulation buttom up.

The DYNDEVS [50] formalism has been developed for describing models whose description entails the possibility to change their own state and behavior pattern. Therefore, model and network transitions, which map the current state of a model into a set of models the model belongs to, have been introduced. Thereby, sequences of models are produced. The idea of DYNDEVS is that models are interpreted as a set of models that are successively generating themselves by model transitions. Each element of the set represents an incarnation of the model and describes a phase of the evolving modeled dynamic system. The formalism supports models which adapt their own interaction structure and their own behavior. The reflective nature of DYNDEVS has been inspired by the work of Nadia Busi on mobile nets [51,52].

DYNDEVS, as other variable structure variants of DEVS before, assumes a static set of ports. This is not surprising, as in systems theory the distinction between system and environment, and maintaining this distinction, is traditionally emphasized. A system seems more likely to change its composition, its interaction structure and its behavior pattern, than its interface to its environment, although it might change its communication partners [50]. However, some systems are characterized just by that: a plasticity of their interface with which systems signalize significant changes to the external world. These phenomena can be found e.g. in the molecular biological domain, where enzymes and proteins change their interface and thereby restrict the type of possible interaction partners. This motivated the development of a further extension, i.e. ρ-DEVS [53].

Definition 3. *An atomic ρ-DEVS model is the structure $\langle m_{init}, \mathcal{M}, X_{sc}, Y_{sc} \rangle$ with $m_{init} \in \mathcal{M}$ the initial model, X_{sc}, Y_{sc} ports to communicate structural changes, and $\mathcal{M}$ a a set of elements with the following structure:*

$$\langle X, Y, S, s_0, \delta_{int}, \delta_{ext}, \delta_{con}, \rho_\alpha, \lambda_\rho, \lambda, ta \rangle$$

where

X, Y *structured sets of inputs and outputs*
S *structured set of states*
$s_0 \in S$ *initial state*
$\delta_{int} : S \to S$ *internal transition function*
$\delta_{ext} : Q \times X^b \to S$ *external transition function, with*
     $Q = \{(s, e) : s \in S, 0 \leq e < ta(s)\}$ *state set including elapsed time*
$\delta_{con} : S \times X^b \to S$ *the confluent transition function*
$\lambda : S \to Y$ *the output function*
$ta : S \to \mathcal{R}^{\geq 0} \cup \{\infty\}$ *the time advance function*
$\rho_\lambda : S \to Y_{sc}$ *scheduled structural changes*
$\rho_\alpha : S \times X_{sc} \to \mathcal{M}$ *model transition*

and $\mathcal{M}$ is the least set for which the following reachability property holds $\forall n \in \mathcal{M}$:

$$n = m_{init} \vee \exists m_0 = m_{init}, \ldots, m_i = n \wedge \rho_\alpha(s^{m_k}) = s^{m_{k+1}} \text{ with}$$
$$i > 0; k = 0, \ldots, i - 1; s^{m_k} \in S^{m_k}; s^{m_{k+1}} \in S^{m_{k+1}}; m_0, \ldots, m_i \in \mathcal{M}.$$

ρ-DEVS defines inputs, outputs, and states, i.e. X, Y, S, as structured sets. These are structured according to a set of variable names, that, in the case of input and output, denote the *ports* by which inputs are received and outputs are launched. As in DYNDEVS, the model transition ρ_α does not interfere with other transitions. It preserves the values of variables which are common to the states of two successive model incarnations and assigns "default initial" values to the "new" variables as it has been done in DYNDEVS (see [50]). X^b denotes a bag of inputs, as several inputs might arrive concurrently, n and m_k etc. denote incarnations of the model set $\mathcal{M}$. Input and output ports in ρ-DEVS are becoming part of the incarnations and thus can be changed via model transition. In addition, a special type of port has been introduced. The role of ρ_λ is to fill the port for structural changes, Y_{sc}, that shall occur at the level of the network model. This information will be accessed by the network transition function ρ_n of the parent coupled model. As other models might induce structural changes that have an effect on the model incarnation, also an input port X_{sc} has been introduced for these types of requests. This input is considered in applying ρ_α and determining the new model incarnation. Both, structural output ports and structural input ports, allow a structural change to transverse up and down the model hierarchy.

To support the hierarchical and modular modeling, a network structure is introduced in ρ-DEVS. A structural change means a change of interaction and composition structure as in DYNDEVS. In addition, ports can change and multi-couplings are introduced (see Definition 5).

Definition 4. *A reflective, higher order network, a ρ-NDEVS, is a structure $\langle n_{init}, \mathcal{N}, X_{sc}, Y_{sc} \rangle$ with $n_{init} \in \mathcal{N}$ the start configuration, X_{sc}, Y_{sc} ports to communicate structural changes, and $\mathcal{N}$ a set with elements of the following structure:*

$$\langle X, Y, C, MC, \rho_N, \rho_\lambda \rangle$$

where

X	*set of structured inputs*
Y	*set of structured outputs*
C	*set of components which are of type ρ-DEVS*
MC	*set of multi-couplings*
$\rho_N : \mathbf{S}^n \times X_{sc} \to \mathcal{N}$	*network transition*
$\rho_\lambda : \mathbf{S}^n \to Y_{sc}$	*structural output function*

with $\mathbf{S}^n = \times_{d \in C} \oplus_{d \in C} Y_{sc}^d$ and $\mathcal{N}$ is the least set for which the following reachability property holds $\forall n \in \mathcal{N}$:

$$n = n_{init} \vee \exists n_0 = n_{init}, \dots, n_i = n \wedge \rho_\alpha(s^{n_k}) = s^{n_{k+1}} \text{ with}$$
$$i > 0; k = 0, \dots, i-1; s^{n_k} \in S^{n_k}; s^{n_{k+1}} \in S^{n_{k+1}}; n_0, \dots, n_i \in \mathcal{N}.$$

In addition, similar to the definition in DYNDEVS, the ρ-NDEVS has to satisfy the following constraint: The application of ρ_N preserves the state and structure of models which belong to the composition of the "old" network and the "new" one. C is the set of components. Components which are newly created are initialized. The initial state of a component is given by the model n_{init} being in its initial state s_{init} [50]. The outputs Y_{sc}^d of the components in C form the quasi-state the structural output function ρ_λ and the network transition ρ_N are based upon. The structural output function defines, given the component's structural outputs, what shall be made available to the coupled model further up, and the network transition takes this information as well as structural input information X_{sc} into account to determine the next network incarnation.

Another specific feature introduced in ρ-DEVS are *multi-couplings*. The idea behind multi-couplings is to make use of the information of the components' available ports and allow a dynamic coupling between models. In this definition, the names of ports become central. Couplings are defined as 1:n, n:1, or n:m relationships between sets of components. Taking part in these couplings is based on the availability of ports.

Definition 5. *A multicoupling* $mc \in MC$ *is defined as a tuple:*

$$mc = \langle \{(C_{src}.port)|C_{src} \in C\},$$
$$\{(C_{tar}.port)|C_{tar} \in C\},$$
$$select \rangle$$
$$with \; select : 2^C \rightarrow 2^C.$$

As couplings are directed, we distinguish between the components that form the source and the target of events, i.e. between C_{scr} and C_{tar}. The existence of ports, i.e. *port*, implies the existence of couplings. The function select determines how the values are distributed. If more than one input port is linked to an output port in regular DEVS, each output will be cloned and sent to all connected input ports. This standard strategy is meaningful if information shall be broadcasted, however, it is not a good strategy for consumable resources like molecules. For the latter, a random selection strategy can be utilized.

For example, we combine the output port of the cytoplasm model from section 3.1 responsible for delivering glucose, i.e. cyt.glucoseOut, with all mitochondria models which accept glucose over an input port, i.e. m.glucoseIn (see Figure 4), and assign a random strategy. In the moment a glucose molecule is launched via the output port, cyt.glucoseOut, one of the mitochondria models will be chosen randomly as its addressee. If the mitochondrion model would be equipped with a dynamic port removal, e.g. if the glucose amount inside the mitochondrion reaches a certain threshold, the multi-coupling would automatically connect only the models with an existing input port glucoseIn to the cytoplasm model:

mc = $\langle$ { (cytoplasm.glucoseOut, m.glucoseIn) |
m $\in \{mitochondrion_1, \dots, mitochondrion_n\}\}$, ranSelOne $\rangle$.

The feature of dynamic structure is essential for modeling cell division and death as shown in Figure 6. After certain time a cell divides into two equal daughter cells which is realized by dynamically adding a new cell model instance. As the two cells are neighbors in a tissue from now on, they can communicate with each other over dynamically added port couplings. These two cells can divide again resulting in a tissue consisting of four cells. If a cell dies after certain time or if an external "kill" event arrives, the model instance including all couplings will be removed which changes the overall model structure again.

Another example of dynamic coupling is depicted in Figure 7. Two different proteins A and B can associate to build a protein complex AB. The backward reaction (dissociation of AB) is also possible and leads to the reversible chemical reaction equation:

$$A + B \; \underset{k_{-1}}{\overset{k_1}{\rightleftharpoons}} \; AB$$

As the speed of a chemical reaction is not only dependent on the reaction rate constant k_i, but also on the concentration (amount per volume) of the involved species, the association and dissociation events are triggered by an extra atomic model (*react*) which holds the current number of *free* and *bound* molecules to calculate the next

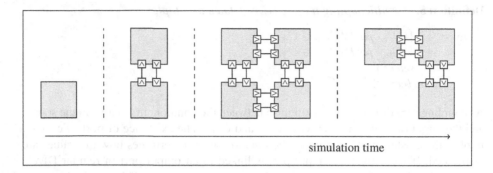

Fig. 6. Dynamic structures in a growth and death model (cell division and apoptosis) during simulation. After certain time cells can divide into daughter cells connected over interfaces for communication. A model instance including all connections will be removed if a cell dies (most right model structure transition).

time of a reaction. All instances of *A* are coupled with the output port *aOut* of the *react* model, but due to the random selection function only one coupling is selected to route a "bind" message when the next time for an association reaction has come. At this moment the addressee changes its state from *free* to *bound*, removes its input port *freeIn* and adds the ports *boundIn* and *bOut*. Now presenting the *bOut* port, this *A* molecule is dynamically coupled with a randomly chosen molecule *B*. The backward reaction is triggered by sending an "unbind" event from the *react* model to a bound protein *A* model (existing *boundIn* port) which causes a state change and the removal of the *bOut* port resulting in the de-coupling of *A* and *B*. Biochemical reactions are a good example for changing interfaces, however it is not clear whether the metaphor of reactive systems, that is emphasized by DEVS as it is emphasized by STATE CHARTS are the most suitable metaphor for this type of systems (see section 4.1).

DEVS is often re-cited as one of the archetypes for composite modeling, its ideas of a modular, hierarchical construction of models being put forward at the beginning of the 1980s has meanwhile been adapted by a wide variety of modeling approaches, including continuous ones like Modelica [30] and recent ones like SysML [54]. However, particularly also in the area of biological modeling its rigid structure revealed also some disadvantages. So it also served as an example what efforts are required to integrate dynamic composition, interaction, and behavior pattern and to allow for changing interfaces. Variable structure models lend structure to the temporal dimension in describing systems. As the relation of bi-simulation has been shown to hold between the original DEVS formalism and its variable structure variants the question arises what benefit to expect from such formalisms and consequently tools. Mostly, it is less the question *whether* a formalism is able to express certain phenomena, but *how* easily this can be done [55,56]. Thus, whereas the extension typically reduces the readability of the formalism, it should increase the readability of the model, as we will also discuss in our next section.

```
1   C = {react, A₁ ... Aₙ, B₁ ... Bₙ}
2
3   MC = { (react.aOut, A.freeIn, ranSelOne),
4          (react.abOut, A.boundIn, ranSelOne),
5          (A.bOut, B.aIn, ranSelOne) }
```

```
1   Y = {aOut, abOut}
2
3   S = { (#A, #B, #AB, timeToNextAss, timeToNextDiss) |
4           #A ∈ N,
5           #B ∈ N,
6           #AB ∈ N,
7           timeToNextAss ∈ R+,
8           timeToNextDiss ∈ R+ }
9
10  δᵢₙₜ =
11       if (timeToNextAss < timeToNextDiss) then
12          #A--; #B--; #AB++;
13       else
14          #A++; #B++; #AB--;
15       timeToNextAss = toTime(#A × #B × k₁);
16       timeToNextDiss = toTime(#AB × k₋₁);
17
18  λ =
19       if (timeToNextAss < timeToNextDiss) then
20          aOut("bind");
21       else
22          abOut("unbind");
23
24  ta = min(timeToNextAss, timeToNextDiss)
```

```
1   X = {freeIn, boundIn}
2
3   Y = {bOut}
4
5   S = {phase ∈ (free, bound)}
6
7   δₑₓₜ =
8        if (freeIn) then
9           phase = bound;
10          removeInPort(freeIn);
11          addInPort(boundIn);
12          addOutPort(bOut);
13       else if (boundIn) then
14          phase = free;
15          addInPort(freeIn);
16          removeInPort(boundIn);
17          removePort(bOut);
18
19  ta = ∞
```

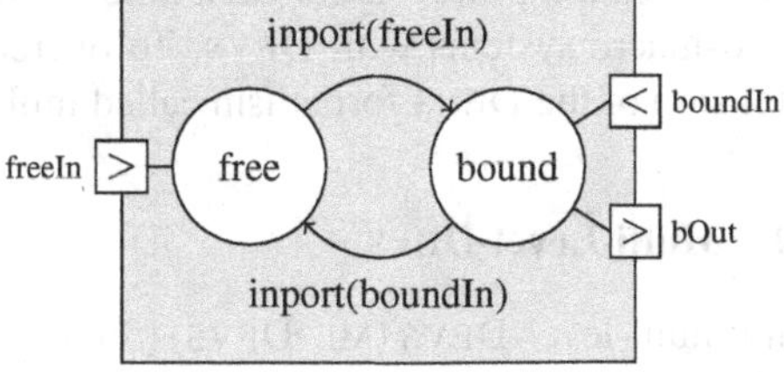

Fig. 7. Biochemical reaction of two proteins A and B to a complex AB. (top) Coupled model with component and multicoupling definitions. (middle) Atomic model responsible for the reactions. (bottom) Atomic model of protein A including a statechart-like representation of its states, their transitions and existing ports. Structured sets and functions without relevance or functionality are not shown.

3.3   Micro-Macro Modeling with DEVS

Modeling a system at different organizational levels requires to take population and individuals, the downward and upward causation between micro and macro level, and the interaction pattern between the individuals into account. This is not a trivial matter, as also problems in synchronizing the activities of macro and micro level arise (particularly if we are working in the discrete-event field) – therefore the few approaches that support this type of multi-level modeling, assume a discrete stepwise progress during simulation, e.g. [57], or use another form of composing models [43].

Although DEVS models show a well-defined hierarchy due to the straightforward modular composition of coupled and atomic models, the behavior of coupled models is completely determined by their sub-components and the way they are coupled with each other. When events depend on the overall state of the system, the passive state-less fate of coupled models burdens the modeling significantly. The biochemical reaction from the previous section (Figure 7), where the reaction rates depend on the concentration of involved species, is a typical example of such a system. The DEVS formalism requires to describe these "high-level" macro properties of the entire coupled model with an atomic model at the same composition level as the other sub-components. Composition hierarchy and organization hierarchy disagree.

Furthermore downward and upward causation between macro and micro have to be realized by sending events asynchronously. This mode of communication is entirely appropriate for independent components reacting to external events, but not for tieing micro and macro levels which influence each other within the same system. In addition, since there is normally a 1:n relation of macro to micro models, one atomic model (macro level) has to interact with all other atomic models (micro) including special communication protocols for each model which forms a further obstacle for modeling micro-macro systems with DEVS. To overcome these problems we developed a new extension of the DEVS formalism called multi-level-DEVS.

3.4   Multi-Level-DEVS

With multi-level-DEVS (ML-DEVS) [58] coupled models can have a state and behavior of their own so that the macro level does not appear as a seperate unit of the coupled model. Moreover, it's possible to define explicitly how the macro level affects the micro level and vice versa (downward and upward causation) by information propagation and activating events.

- **Downward Information Propagation:**
  Obviously, one means to propagate information from macro to micro level is to exchange events between models. However, this is rather tedious, e.g. in case the dynamics of a micro model has to take the global state into consideration. Therefore, we will adopt the idea of value couplings. Information at macro level is mapped to specific port names. Each micro model may access macro variables by defining input ports with corresponding names.

- **Upward Information Propagation:**
  In the opposite direction, the macro level needs access to crucial information at the micro level. For this purpose, we equip micro models with the ability to change their ports and to thereby signalize crucial state changes to the outside world. Upward causation is supported, as the macro model has an overview of the number of micro models being in a particular state – i.e., exhibiting a particular set of ports – and to take this into account when updating the state at macro level.
- **Downward Activation:**
  The macro level can directly activate its components by sending them events – thereby, it becomes possible to synchronously let several micro models interact, which is of particular interest when modeling chemical reactions.
- **Upward Activation:**
  The dynamics at macro level can be activated by the dynamics at micro level, e.g. if the number of components being in a certain state (signalized by their ports) surpasses a certain threshold. Therefore, a form of invariant is defined at macro level, whose violation initiates a transition at macro level. This is inspired by the ideas of hybrid state automata, where the discrete state changes are triggered at the moment the continuous dynamics lead to threshold crossing.

Now let us have a look at the ML-DEVS formalism. Let $X, Y, S = (V; S_1, \ldots, S_n)$ be structured sets with $V = \{v_1, \ldots, v_n\}$ (see [46, p.124]). The input ports of the structured set X may now also hold information handed down via value coupling (see Definition 6 of the coupled ML-DEVS model). Furthermore, let $\mathcal{P}$ be the set of available port names.

Definition 6. *An atomic* ML-DEVS *model is defined as a structure:*

$$\langle X, Y, S, s_{init}, p, \delta, \lambda, ta \rangle$$

where

X	*the structured set of inputs*
Y	*the structured set of outputs*
S	*the structured set of states*
$s_{init} \in S$	*the start state*
$p : S \to 2^{\mathcal{P}}$	*selects the ports available in a given state*
$\delta : X \times Q \to S$	*state transition function*
$\lambda : S \to Y$	*output function*
$ta : S \to \mathcal{R}^{\geq 0} \cup \{\infty\}$	*time advance function*

Atomic ML-DEVS models do no longer consist of internal, external and confluent transition functions, only one transition function δ exists. The main reason for this is the clarity of the formalism. Moreover, the distinction between internal and external state transitions is partly rendered meaningless by the fact that δ_{int} may now rely on macro variables, which are accessed over value-coupled ports. With a single state transition function, one may now decide which transitions have to be distinguished for the model at hand. Since the elapsed time and the inputs at all ports are accessible, the modeler can define what to do under which circumstances. As in regular DEVS, the λ function is invoked just before an internal or confluent event happens. This situation is recognized by the simulator. A time advance function ta is given that associates a duration with each state. Additionally, an atomic model has a function $p : S \rightarrow 2^{\mathcal{P}}$, which defines the ports the model exhibits in a given state.

The definition of a coupled model is based on the definition of an atomic ML-DEVS model. Similar to this, a coupled ML-DEVS model has structured input and output sets X and Y and a state set S. The input ports might hold events or information that was handed down via value coupling from its superordinate coupled model. A λ function produces outputs for the output ports. Similar to coupled models in DEVS, a set C of components is defined.

Definition 7. *A coupled* ML-DEVS *model is formally defined as a structure:*

$$\langle X, Y, S, s_{init}, p, C, MC, \delta, \lambda_{down}, v_{down}, sc, act, \lambda, ta \rangle$$

where

C	*set of sub-models which are of type atomic* ML-DEVS *or coupled* ML-DEVS
MC	*set of multi-couplings,* $\{m \mid m : 2^{\mathcal{P}} \rightarrow 2^{\mathcal{P}}\}$
$\delta : X \times Q \times 2^{C \times \mathcal{P}} \rightarrow S$	*state transition function*
$\lambda_{down} : S \rightarrow 2^{\cup_{c \in C}(X_C \times C \times \mathcal{P})}$	*downward output function*
$v_{down} : V_S \rightarrow \mathcal{P}$	*value coupling downward*
$sc : S \rightarrow 2^C \times 2^{MC}$	*structural change function*
$act_{up} : S \times 2^{C \times \mathcal{P}} \rightarrow \{true, false\}$	*activation function*

Moreover, the following has to hold:

- If a port is an output port, it cannot be an input port:
  $\forall p \in \mathcal{P} : (\exists m \in MC \wedge P \in 2^{\mathcal{P}} : p \in P \wedge m(P) \neq \emptyset) \implies (\nexists m' \in MC \wedge P' \in 2^{\mathcal{P}} : p \in m(P'))$
- Value coupling is defined on ports that are no input ports:
  $\forall v_S \in V_S : (\nexists m \in MC \wedge P \in 2^{\mathcal{P}} : v_{down}(v_S) \in m(P))$

All other elements of the tuple are defined as for atomic ML-DEVS models (Definition 6). The dependencies between macro and micro level could easily lead to an algebraic loop. This is prevented by the simulator [58], which defines the execution semantics of ML-DEVS.

Like in ρ-DEVS, we equipped the coupled models with the possibility to define multi-couplings (see Definition 5 in section 3.2). The transition function δ at macro level takes the state, the information about the model's components and multi-couplings into account when calculating the new state. Again, the function p associates a set of ports with each state. The structural change function sc defines the set of components and multi-couplings for the coupled model's current state. Changes within component structures are initiated top-down. Thus, the macro model is responsible for creating and removing its components and the to change the interaction pattern between them. This differs from the solution that has been realized in ρ-DEVS. However, in ML-DEVS, the coupled model is equipped with a state and a behavior of its own, an ability, which can also be exploited for initiating structural changes. Downward and upward causation are realized in ML-DEVS as follows:

- **Downward information:**
  The downward causation at information level is realized by the function v_{down}, which couples state variables of the coupled model to input ports of its sub-models. Thereby, each relevant variable at macro level is directly accessible by the micro models via their input ports. This implies that the input ports of the micro models are never "empty", because value-coupled information is always accessible.
- **Upward information:**
  The information propagation from micro to macro level is realized by changing ports. The macro model can access the information which ports are available and does so in its δ function to determine the next state at macro level. Each model can change its ports via the function p and thus can signalize important information to other micro models and the macro level.
- **Downward activation:**
  The downward activation is done by the λ_{down} function, which allows to synchronously trigger a number of micro models by sending them events. This does not require a coupling between macro and micro models, as a coupled model may directly access the ports of its components.
- **Upward activation:**
  Changes at the micro level can initiate changes at the macro level. The activation constraint act_{up} guards that the invariants at macro level are fulfilled, otherwise the invocation of the macro model's δ function is triggered. This leads to a new state with a possibly new set of components and multi-couplings.

Regarding the example of section 3.2 again (Figure 7), with ML-DEVS now it's possible to describe the macro level information and behaviour as part of the coupled model (Figure 8). The port selection function p allows to specify which ports are available in the different model states. For example the protein A's output port $bOut$ is available only if it's in the *bound* state. The change from the *unbound* to this state is triggered by the coupled macro model which generates activation events by the λ_{down} function. Therefore, an input port (*macroIn*) has to be available but no explicit coupling from macro level to the protein A model is needed. In addition, a macro level variable (*temp*) has been introduced for depicting the way how value couplings are defined (v_{down} function). Protein B models, which are not shown in the figure, have access to the systems temperature over their input port *tempInput*. The information can be used e.g. to decide if the binding-site for protein A, i.e. input port aIn, is no longer available due to a temperature increase. The example shows some simplifications with respect to the model readability in comparison to the example model of Figure 7. However, for modeling ordinary biochemical reactions, no DEVS variant seems overly suited. Only if the species of biochemical reactions show rich internal dynamics, as e.g. the temperature dependance of protein B, DEVS's reactive systems view appears fitting.

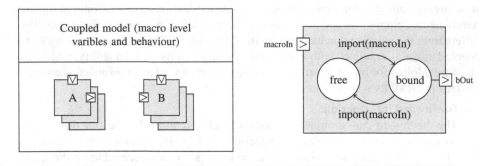

```
1   S = { (timeToNextAss, timeToNextDiss, temp) |
2           timeToNextAss ∈ R+,
3           timeToNextDiss ∈ R+,
4           temp ∈ R+ }
5
6   C = {A₁...Aₙ, B₁...Bₙ}
7
8   MC = { (A.bOut, B.aIn, ranSelOne) }
9
10  δ = #A = count(A,no port bOut);
11      #B = count(B,port aIn);
12      #AB = count(A,port bOut);
13      timeToNextAss = toTime(#A × #B × k₁);
14      timeToNextDiss = toTime(#AB × k₋₁);
15
16  sc = (C,MC)
17
18  λ_down =
19      if (timeToNextAss < timeToNextDiss) then
20      ( "bind", pick(A,no port bOut), macroIn );
21      else
22      ( "unbind", pick(A,port bOut), macroIn );
23
24  v_down = (temp, B, tempInput)
25
26  ta = min(timeToNextAss, timeToNextDiss)
```

Fig. 8. Biochemical reaction example modeled with ML-DEVS. (top) Statechart-like representation of the coupled model and protein A atomic model. (bottom) Description of the coupled model. Structured sets and functions without relevance or functionality are not shown.

4   Hierarchies in the π Calculus

Originally the π calculus [59] was designed for checking communication models. Therefore, only the pure course of action is of interest such that the formalism does not include any notion of time. This makes it rather unpractical for simulation. However, in 1995 Priami introduced an extension to the π calculus, called stochastic π [60], which associates stochastic rates to the described events. Additionally, he defined stochastic semantics for this extension such that it is possible to use stochastic π models directly as an input for Gillespie's Stochastic Simulation Algorithm [3], a widely used method for simulating basic stochastic interactions of molecules. With this step, the way of the π calculus into systems biology was paved and carried on by Regev and Shapiro with their work in 2004 [61] where they described how to model basic and also more complex biochemical reactions in stochastic π. However, for the modeling of complex reaction networks, as they usually occur in systems biology, it became necessary to add more structure to the very lean theoretical framework of the π calculus. Thus, extensions like SPiCO [62], BETA-BINDERS [63] and BIOAMBIENTS [64] introduced a more entity based view. With BIOAMBIENTS even complete hierarchies can be integrated into the π models which shall be the main topic of this section. However, before stressing this point, a basic introduction to the π calculus and its application for the modeling of biochemical reaction networks is given.

4.1 π Calculus Basics

Looking at a π calculus model is like reading a communication protocol; only the very essential communication procedures, i.e. sending and receiving, are of interest. The course of action is given by processes that run in parallel and synchronize on common channels. In the π calculus everything is referenced by name. Therefore, for channels and processes infinite sets of names C and P are given. Channels are introduced with the ν operator and have a certain scope depending on where they are established. Each communication has two partners, the sender and the receiver. They exchange messages that can either be empty or hold a channel name. The sending of a channel extends its scope, such that the receiver can now use it for further communication. Processes can have multiple, mutually exclusive communication options at a time that are given by summations. If more than one option is possible the choice of which communication occurs is non-deterministic. By using the polyadic extension of the π calculus it is also possible to transfer multiple channel names at a time and to use channel names as parameters of processes (see Table 1). For further reading on the theoretical foundations of the π calculus, e.g. its formal semantics, see [59].

Mapping a Simple Reaction Network. With this theoretical framework of communicating processes it is possible to model different biochemical reactions. Lets consider a very simple reaction network with two reactions (see fig. 9). Our model shall be divided into three parts: channel definitions, process definitions and an initial process. In the first part, a channel is introduced for each reaction with a corresponding name (here the ν operator is omitted to denote that the channels' scope is global). This is followed

Table 1. π calculus syntax (polyadic version)

Process	$P ::=$	$P_1 \parallel P_2$	Parallel Composition
		$(\nu\, c).P$	ν Operator
		$\sum_i S_i$	Summation
		$A(\tilde{x})$	Application
Summation	$S ::=$	$x!(\tilde{y}).P$	Send
		$x?(\tilde{y}).P$	Receive
Definition	$D ::=$	$A(\tilde{y}) = P$	

by a process definition for each involved species. Thereby, a species is characterized by its capability of taking part in reactions. E.g. chlorine can either react with sodium to common salt or with hydrogen to hydrochloric acid. Thus, for chlorine a summation is defined with two summands such that it can either receive on $nacl$ or on hcl. Since $Na()$ and $H()$ form the sending parts on these channels, $Cl()$ can either react with sodium or with hydrogen and receives either the $toNa$ or the toH channel respectively. After communicating the involved species turn into their bound states. Following the ideas of Regev and Shapiro [61], the exchanged channels can now be used as back-bones to perform the decay, i.e. the reverse reaction, of the generated complex. Thus, after communicating on $toCl$ the complex forming parts turn from their bound to their initial state (see fig. 11). The specification of the model is completed, by introducing the initial process, which defines the starting solution, i.e. how many elements of each species are initially in the modeled system.

Instead of using a common backbone channel it is also possible to introduce a separate process that describes the chemical behavior of the resulting complex. This is due to the fact that complexes often show totally different behavior compared to their parts. To implement this sort of reaction, one reactant proceeds with the resulting molecule while the other completely vanishes (see fig. 10).

Although the reaction network is entirely implemented, the model is still not complete. Still missing are the reaction rates. As already mentioned, the original π calculus does not support any notion of time and thus reaction constants, that base on time, cannot be included. This is were the stochastic π extension comes into play. It provides the ability to attach stochastic rates to the channels that represent reaction constants. Since for each reaction a channel is introduced, it is possible to assign the reaction constants to the reactions, e.g. $Na() = (\nu\ toCl : r_{-1})\ldots$, where r_{-1} represents the stochastic decay rate of $NaCl$. How to transfer reaction constants into stochastic rates can be read in e.g. [65]. The now completed model can be directly simulated with the SSA. Notice that the stochastic π calculus is well-suited as an input language for the SSA because of the following reasons:

1. The SSA presumes that only two particles can react at a time. This presumption is supported by the π syntax where communication can only happen between two processes.

$$nacl : \mathrm{Na^+ + Cl^-} \underset{k_{-1}}{\overset{k_1}{\rightleftharpoons}} \mathrm{NaCl}$$

$$hcl : \ \mathrm{H^+ + Cl^-} \underset{k_{-2}}{\overset{k_2}{\rightleftharpoons}} \mathrm{HCl}$$

Fig. 9. A simple chemical system with two reactions – reaction rates above and underneath the arrows for forth and back reaction respectively

...

Process Definitions

$Na() = nacl!(). NaCl()$

$H() = hcl!(). HCl()$

$Cl() = nacl?() + hcl?()$

...

Fig. 10. Complexes as separate processes – further definition of $NaCl()$ and $HCl()$ is required

Channel Definitions

$nacl$

hcl

Process Definitions

$Na() = (\nu\, toCl). nacl!(toCl). NaBound(toCl)$

$NaBound(free) = free?(). Na()$

$H() = (\nu\, toCl). hcl!(). HBound(toCl)$

$HBound(free) = free?(). H()$

$Cl() = nacl?(toNa). ClBound(toNa) + hcl?(toH). ClBound(toH)$

$Cl(decay) = decay!(). Cl()$

Initial Process

$(Na() \,|...|\, Na() \,|\, H() \,|...|\, H() \,|\, Cl() \,|...|\, Cl())$

Fig. 11. A π model for a chemical system with two reactions

2. The SSA works with integer numbers of molecules instead of concentrations. This is also true for stochastic π where an integer number of processes run in parallel, representing the elements of a system.
3. The SSA uses the same stochastic rates that are attached to the stochastic π channels.

Although, the prerequisite that every reaction must have exactly two reactants seems to hamper the applicability of the π calculus to the modeling of complex biological systems, e.g. in comparison to process algebras like PEPA [66], it is absolutely possible to represent sophisticated reaction patterns, like e.g. gene expression or cooperative binding, as it is shown in [65]. Whereas composition is one of the basic ingredients of the π calculus, this does not imply an explicit hierarchical modeling. This lack of explicit structures, everything being fluent in π, is addressed in various extensions.

4.2 π Calculus Extensions

Because of the rather abstract view of communicating processes, different extensions of the π calculus exist that aim to add more structure into models. In what follows, these extensions are shortly discussed.

Table 2. SPICO syntax – sending and receiving extended with functional symbols

Process	$P ::= P_1 \parallel P_2$	Parallel Composition
	$\mid (\nu c).P$	ν Operator
	$\mid \sum_i S_i$	Summation
	$\mid A(\tilde{x})$	Application
Summation	$S ::= x!f(\tilde{y}).P$	Send
	$\mid x?f(\tilde{y}).P$	Receive
Definition	$D ::= A(\tilde{y}) = P$	

SPICO. SPICO [62] adds more structure to the π calculus by emphasizing the notion of concurrent objects. Therefore, it considers the communication of π processes as calls of object methods. To establish this view, SPICO extends the sending and receiving actions with functional symbols (see Table 2). Two processes can only communicate if their sending and receiving pattern match. Thus, channels can rather be seen as references to objects. As usual, these objects provide different methods that are addressed with the corresponding functional symbol.

The functional symbols can become very handy when entities with multiple functionality are modeled. In Biology, this situation occurs for example in the case of overlapping binding sites (see [62]). These complexes consist of two binding sites that allow for only one ligand to bind at a time – if one site is occupied it blocks its peer and in the moment that the ligand departs both sites are free again. In this scenario each binding site needs to provide the functionality of getting blocked and unblocked by its partner. Following the introducing example of how to model chemical reactions in the π calculus, it would be necessary for the sites to share four channels, a block and an unblock channel for each site. However, with SPICO it is sufficient to create two channels, since only a reference from each site to its peer is needed. Depending on their state, the sites then provide the block and unblock function when necessary (see fig. 12).

The advantage of saving two channels does not seem too striking but consider the case that an entity provides multiple functions. Still only one channel would be needed

...

Process Definitions

$Free(me, peer) = me?bind().\,peer!block().\,Bound(me, peer) +$
$\qquad\qquad\qquad me?block().\,Blocked(me, peer)$
$Bound(me, peer) = me?depart().\,peer!unblock().\,Free(me, peer)$
$Blocked(me, peer) = me?unblock().\,Free(me, peer)$

...

Initializing Process

$(\nu\, s : r_s).\,(\nu\, s' : r_{s'}).\,(Free(s, s') \mid Free(s', s) \mid Ligand() \mid...\mid Ligand())$

Fig. 12. Overlapping sites in SPICO – instead of four only two channels are needed, $Ligand()$ is to be defined [62]

for implementing such complex behavior. This is even more valuable when modeling entity connections that change over time. In that case the exchanged channels have to be modified dynamically. A good biological example for such a scenario is the DNA transcription, where a molecule called Polymerase moves along the DNA and reads out each molecule of the strand individually.

To amplify the object-oriented view even more the methodology of inheritance is integrated. Therefore, similar to other π based modeling tools like BioSPi [67], SPiCO lets the user implement separate modules that are parametrized with channels. As a new feature, these modules can be extended with additional processes. Thus, it is possible to define rather generic species that are refined for specific modeling scenarios. As shown in [68] this is a very useful feature when modeling complex biological systems.

BETA-BINDERS. The basic idea of BETA-BINDERS is to wrap basic π processes P into boxes called bio-processes BP (see Table 3). To the bio-processes beta-binders B are assigned which are sets of elementary beta-binders. Elementary beta-binders have the form $\beta(x, \Gamma)$ where x is the corresponding channel name for the inner π processes and Γ is a type. Types are sets of names. Communication over two elementary beta-binders of two different bio-processes can happen if their type sets overlap, i.e. their intersection is not empty. Thus, in BETA-BINDERS two kinds of communication exist, the usual one as know from stochastic π and the one of two bio-processes over their beta-binders (see fig. 13). The inner π processes of a bio-process can modify its elementary beta-binders by the actions *hide, unhide* and *expose*. While the first ones enable and disable the communication on an elementary beta-binder the latter one adds a completely new one to the bio-process. Additionally to the operators, BETA-BINDERS provides *join* and *split*-functions that merge and divide bio-processes and can be flexibly defined by users. For more information see [63].

The basic idea of BETA-BINDERS can be best depicted by an example. Many intra-cellular reactions are catalyzed by enzymes that bind to substrates and convert them into products. To control the activity of enzymes, inhibitors exist that block their binding sites. In BETA-BINDERS this scenario can be modeled by defining bio-processes for

Table 3. BETA-BINDERS syntax – boxes called bio-processes BP wrap π processes P and provide sets of elementary beta-binders B that represent the communication capabilities of BP

Process	$P ::=$	$P_1 \parallel P_2$	Parallel Composition
	$\mid$	$(\nu\, c).P$	ν Operator
	$\mid$	$\sum_i S_i$	Summation
Summation	$S ::=$	$x!(y).P$	Send
	$\mid$	$x?(y).P$	Receive
	$\mid$	$hide(x)$	Hide Channel
	$\mid$	$unhide(x)$	Reverse Hiding
	$\mid$	$expose(x)$	Reveal Channel
Bio-Process	$BP ::=$	$BP_1 \parallel BP_2$	Parallel Composition
	$\mid$	$B\,[P]$	Single Box

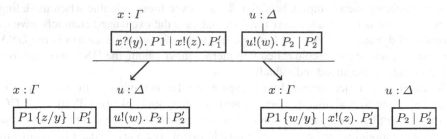

Fig. 13. Communication in BETA-BINDERS – two different reductions (communications) are possible; left: the π processes in the left bio-process communicate directly over x; right: the bio-processes communicate over the beta-binders x and u, which means that the intersection set of their types Γ and Δ is not empty

$$x : \{f, g\} \qquad z : \{g\} \qquad\qquad x^h : \{f, g\} \qquad z^h : \{g\}$$

$$\boxed{Enzyme} \quad \boxed{Inhibitor} \xrightarrow{\ join\ } \boxed{Enzyme \mid Inhibitor}$$

$$x : \{f, g\} \qquad y : \{f\} \qquad\qquad x^h : \{f, g\} \qquad y^h : \{f\}$$

$$\boxed{Enzyme} \quad \boxed{Substrate} \xrightarrow{\ join\ } \boxed{Enzyme \mid Substrate}$$

Fig. 14. Example model in BETA-BINDERS [63] – because of the type set of its beta-binder, *Enzyme* can either communicate with *Substrate* or with *Inhibitor*. Either way, it forms a complex with the respective communication partner by a *join* transition that has only hidden binders due to the fact that it shall not take part in any reaction.

the substrate, the enzyme and the inhibitor (see fig. 14). Since their beta-binders include overlapping type sets, *Enzyme* can either bind to *Substrate* or to *Inhibitor*. In any case, the binding is achieved by merging (*join*) the respective bio-processes and hiding their elementary beta-binders, which represents the inability of the molecules to undergo further bindings. Consequently, their splitting would result in either an *Enzyme* and a *Product* or an *Enzyme* and an *Inhibitor*.

BIOAMBIENTS. Similar to BETA-BINDERS, BIOAMBIENTS wraps π processes into boxes, which in this case are called ambients. Yet, the main difference is that ambients can not only contain π processes but also other ambients, i.e. they can be nested. To fully exploit this feature, BIOAMBIENTS comes with a whole set of new constructs (see Table 4). On one hand these regard the direction of interaction. *p2c* and *c2p* communication describe the sending and receiving from an ambient to its nested ambients and vice-versa. The *local* and *s2s* constructs define the synchronization in a single ambient of either π processes or ambients. On the other hand they regard the motion capability of ambients. An ambient can enter another ambient if accepted (*enter*/*accept*), or it can leave the surrounding ambient (*exit*/*expel*). Additionally, two ambients can merge (*merge+*/*merge−*).

Table 4. BIOAMBIENTS syntax – π processes that can be wrapped by ambients $[P]$, communicate into different directions δ and move between ambients

Process	$P ::=$	$P_1 \parallel P_2$	Parallel Composition
		$(\nu\, c).P$	ν Operator
		$\sum_i S_i$	Summation
		$[P]$	Ambient
Summation	$S ::=$	$\delta\, x!(y).P$	Send with Direction
		$\delta\, x?(y).P$	Receive with Direction
		$enter\ x.P$	Enter
		$accept\ x.P$	Accept
		$exit\ x.P$	Exit
		$expel\ x.P$	Expel
		$merge +\ x.P$	Merge+
		$merge -\ x.P$	Merge-
Direction	$\delta ::=$	$local$	Processes in Ambient
		$s2s$	Ambients in Ambient
		$p2c$	Ambient to Nested Ambient
		$c2p$	Nested Ambient to Ambient

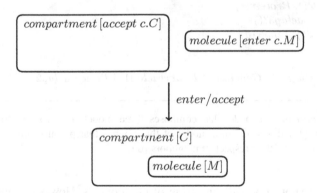

Fig. 15. Example model in BIOAMBIENTS- a molecule enters a cell by $enter/accept$ on channel c

The focus of BIOAMBIENTS is mainly to reflect biological compartments. This can best be shown by an example: the penetration of a molecule, e.g. a protein, into a compartment. To implement this in BIOAMBIENTS, two ambients are defined: *molecule* and *compartment*. Whereas the ambient *molecule* provides the action *enter* on channel c, *compartment* provides an *accept* on the same channel such that after synchronizing the ambient *compartment* contains the ambient *molecule* (see fig. 15).

4.3   Micro-Macro Modeling with the π Calculus

As discussed in Section 2, components are an essential ingredient for building hierarchical models and therefore also for micro-macro modeling. On first sight, the basic

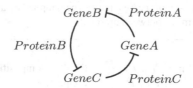

Fig. 16. Concept of *Repressilator* - genes produce proteins that inhibit the protein production of their neighbors

---

Channel Definitions

$a : r_a$

$b : r_b$

$c : r_c$

$delay1 : r_{d1}$

$delay2 : r_{d2}$

$delay3 : r_{d3}$

Process Definitions

$Gene(a,b) = delay1?().\ (Protein(b)\ |\ Gene(a,b))$
$\qquad\qquad + a?().\ delay2?().\ Gene(a,b)$
$Protein(b) = b!().\ Protein(b)$
$\qquad\qquad + delay3?()$
$Timer(d) = d!().\ Timer(d)$

Initial Process

$(Gene(a,b)\ |\ Gene(b,c)\ |\ Gene(c,a)\ |\ Timer(delay1)\ |\ Timer(delay2)\ |\ Timer(delay3))$

Fig. 17. *Repressilator* - a model that composes three model parts (parametric processes), *Gene()*, *Protein()* and *Timer*, to a model of three genes that produce proteins that inhibit the production process of their respective neighbors [69]

π calculus seems not to provide any form of components. However, parametric processes are the starting point for their introduction. This is because parametric processes define a clear interface in form of their parametric channels. Thus, one can implement and compose separate model parts. To depict this concept, an example is given in Table 17. It describes a well-known phenomenon in cell-biology, which is called *Repressilator*. It consists of a certain amount of genes, that each encodes for a specific protein. The only role the produced proteins play is to inhibit the protein production of the respective neighbored gene (see fig. 16). To model this in stochastic π three parametric processes are defined, *Gene*, *Protein*, and *Timer*. The latter process is just a technical add-on to time the decay of complexes. Each of the parametric processes can be parametrized with different channels, such that they can be used to describe multiple elements of the system, e.g. *Gene* for three different genes.

However, the parametric process itself cannot be seen as a complete component. What is missing in general, is the possibility to determine entity borders. This is very obvious in case of the parametric process $P(x_1, x_2) = x_1!(). (R(x_1, x_2) \parallel Q(x_2))$ which could either describe an entity that consists of two parallel processes, like e.g. the $Na\text{-}Cl$ complex, or an entity which produces another one and by doing so it turns into another state, like e.g. a gene that produces a protein and then automatically blocks. Thus, with parametric processes only, no clear separation between entities and their environment can be achieved. Yet for the π calculus, the notion of components has been completed by a syntactical add-on which is provided by modeling tools, like BioSPi, namely the module. As already mentioned, modules define a clear interface by channel parameters that are applied to their inner parametric processes. Additionally, they do not allow any inner process to proceed with a process which is not internally defined. Hence, modules are closed and therefore they can be implemented separately, parameterized and applied to different modeling scenarios which is a very useful option when modeling large systems.

As described above, SPiCO additionally extends the concept of modules by the methodology of inheritance. In SPiCO modules can be defined and then extended by additional processes and thus additional behavior. Notice, that SPiCO modules still fulfill the component prerequisite of closure because also in the process of extending modules inner processes can only precede with processes that are defined internally. However, in SPiCO the concept of classification, which is discussed in Section 2 as a special sort of hierarchy, can be mapped. A module that extends another one can be considered to be in a *is a* relation with the extended one. Such a hierarchy could be: β-catenin *is a* protein *is a* molecule which could be implemented in SPiCO by defining a module called *molecule* and then extending it by a module called *protein* which is itself extended by the module *beta − catenin*. In a modeling scenario where multiple proteins are involved, the *protein* could then be extended more than once (see fig. 18).

Although, well-established on a syntactical level, modules can not considered to be full components in the sense of modeling because they are not transfered down to the execution. In any case, they are translated into normal π processes for simulation. In contrast, BETA-BINDERS introduces with its bio-processes components to the execution level. Bio-processes are considered to be components because they separate their inner processes from the outside. Additionally, beta-binders are explicit interfaces of bio-processes that define with their type sets different connectivity relations, i.e. $1 : 1$,

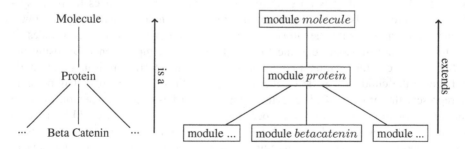

Fig. 18. Inheritance in SPiCO – the *is a* relation between elements is represented by extending modules

$1 : n$, $n : 1$ and $n : m$, depending on how the declared type sets overlap. Another important concept regarding BETA-BINDERS is the notion of variable interfaces, which is implemented by the actions *hide*, *unhide* and *expose*, that allow for the dynamic modification of beta-binder availability. By this means, bio-processes provide the complete methodology of components, which is also known e.g. from DEVS, and an essential prerequisite for introducing hierarchies. Yet, the BETA-BINDERS concept does not support the definition of hierarchies because its components (bio-processes) cannot be nested. However, its compositional model structure is highly flexible because with the *join* and *split* functions components can be added or removed from the system. Thus, BETA-BINDERS seems to be a good language for compositional modeling but cannot be used for implementing hierarchies and is therefore not applicable to micro-macro modeling.

A complete hierarchical framework is provided by BIOAMBIENTS. It supports the concept of components as well as hierarchies. In detail: the ambients of BIOAMBIENTS fulfill all requirements of components. On one hand, they wrap π processes into boxes such that elements can be clearly distinguished from their environment. On the other hand, they define clear interfaces which are defined by the inner π processes. Since BIOAMBIENTS uses the π calculus to describe its interfaces, the communication structure between its components is highly dynamic. After every communication step, interfaces, i.e. channels, are made available or unavailable. By this means, very dynamic systems can be described in a very elegant way. However, one drawback of using stochastic π as the interface language is that it is not possible to easily define different kinds of connectivity relations, since it is restricted to $1 : 1$-communication.

BIOAMBIENTS allows for the nesting of ambients such that it completely supports hierarchical modeling on multiple levels. Thereby the inner π processes of an ambient represent the macro level for the nested ambients, that are the micro level. In Section 2 the different causations are discussed that are necessary for multilevel modeling. In BIOAMBIENTS, these are realized with the different communication directions, i.e. $p2c$-communication represents the downward and $c2p$-communication the upward causation. $s2s$-communication describes the interactions of components that are on the same hierarchical level whereas *local*-communication is restricted to processes within one component.

The hierarchical structures of BIOAMBIENTS can be modified in multiple ways (see fig. 19). As usual, it is possible to easily add and remove nodes from the system (and therefore also from the hierarchy) by the means of basic π calculus operations. Furthermore, with the $merge + /merge-$-pair one can melt two nodes of the tree structure to model e.g. the fusion of two cell compartments. By using the $enter/accept$-communication a complete subtree is transferred from its parent node to become the child of a node on the same level. With this construct it is possible to represent the process of phagocytosis which describes a cell's ingestion of some part of its environment. Its reverse operation is $exit/expel$ which could be used to abstract a cell's ejection of molecules. Thus, BIOAMBIENTS provides an extensive set for modifying hierarchical structures and is thus well-suited for micro-macro modeling.

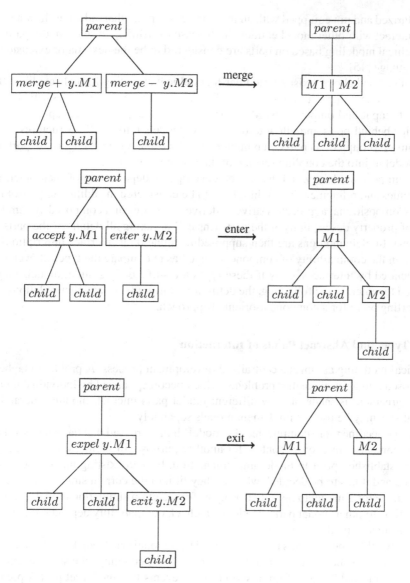

Fig. 19. Modification of hierarchical structures in BIOAMBIENTS by $merge +$ /$merge-$, $enter/accept$, and $exit/expel$

5   Components and Hierarchies

A prevalent challenge of modeling and simulation is to define a model in a way that it can be reused by someone else than the original developer himself [70]. Standard exchange formats like SBML do currently not support to exchange model components, but focus on the exchange of whole simulation models. Model structures are not modularized and not equipped with an interface description that indicates, how a model may interact with other model entities. In the case of SBML, reuse of model parts and hierarchical modeling based on ports are considered to be the next major extensions of the language [15].

As discussed above, existing modular-hierarchical modeling formalisms like DEVS allow to define composition hierarchies. The interface of a model is described by the set of its input and output ports. Modular-hierarchical approaches encapsulate model behavior behind ports and allow to decompose models into smaller structures, which may only be coupled via ports. Sub models may be exchanged as long as the ports of a sub model fit into the coupling scheme of the surrounding model.

To compose models, which have been developed independently of each other, type hierarchies and refinement hierarchies have to be considered in addition to part-of relations. Compositional approaches strive to derive properties of a composed system from a set of property descriptions of the parts (instead of taking all details of the parts into account). Implementations are then supposed to refine their interface descriptions. To decide on the compatibility of components, one has to compare the types of events that are declared by interfaces. Only if these types are sufficiently similar, models may be coupled together. In the following, the definition of event types and their relations form the starting point for a component-oriented approach.

5.1 Types and Abstract Points of Interaction

Classical modeling assumes a centralized development process. A problem maybe decomposed into a set of smaller problems, which become realized by individual models. If an agreement is made on how different model parts interact, modular-hierarchical formalisms may be used to implement models separately.

Things become more complicated if a model shall be reused that has been developed by someone else, in another context for another purpose. In such cases contracts cannot be established prior to model implementation. Instead existing models need to be checked and it has to be decided, whether they fit into the current simulation model. A prerequisite for a model to be suited as a part for a certain simulation model is that it is compatible to other model parts. Methods to check compatibility depend on how types of ports are specified.

In DEVS the type of events to be exchanged by a model (via a port) is defined as a set. Coupled system specifications require for port-to-port couplings the set of events that a source port could sent to form a subset of the events that the target port is prepared to receive [46, p.130]. This requirement ensures that a source port only sends events that are acceptable by the target port. This has a direct correspondence to type systems, which require for directed communication channels that the sending port to be a sub type of the receiving port [71]. Sub-type relations formalize under which conditions one type can be substituted by another type.

In modeling and simulation tools, types of model components are usually defined based on the programming language used, e.g. Java [72,73]. Thereby, type definitions are bound to a particular type system, e.g. that of a Java. Attempts to increase interoperability of systems, such as the web service architecture [74], utilize XML to abstract from tool-specific and programming-specific representations. Data descriptions based on XML are generally considered to be robust, extensible, and well suited to represent complex data structures [75].

XML Schema Definition (XSD) allows to constrain the content of elements and attributes by type and value range assignments. Standardized by the W3C [76], XSD is written itself in XML and supports structuring of definitions into namespaces. XSD comes with built-in simple data types and allows to combine these to construct complex types. Of particular interest for a decoupled modeling process is the ability to either define types locally or to import existing type definitions via URI-based references.

XSD is compatible to specifications that go beyond the syntactical dimension of types. SAWSDL, which stands for Semantic Annotations for WSDL [77], is a standard for semantic annotations of type definitions. With SAWSDL an XSD type definition may refer to a concept of an ontology to declare what entity is meant to be represented by the type.

Example 1. Figure 20 lists the *XML Schema Definition* of two complex types. The concrete type ATP is derived from the abstract type Molecule. Each molecule is required to have a unique identifier. ATP is defined as a special kind of molecule. The attribute modelReference holds a reference to the ATP entry of KEGG. This semantic annotation provides the information that the type named "ATP" represents the molecule ATP. Glucose may be derived from Molecule in the same manner.

With XSD types can be specified in documents, which are separated from the actual model definitions. Thereby type definitions become independent of modeling formalisms and simulation tools. Schema matching approaches may be used to decide on the compatibility of types [78].

```
<?xml version="1.0"?>
<xs:schema xmlns:xs="http://www.w3.org/2001/XMLSchema"
 xmlns="unihro/cbio/molecules"
 targetNamespace="unihro/cbio/molecules"
 xmlns:sawsdl="http://www.w3.org/2002/ws/sawsdl/spec/sawsdl#">
  <xs:complexType name="Molecule" abstract="true">
    <xs:sequence>
      <xs:element name="id" type="xs:integer" minOccurs="1"/>
      <xs:element name="mul" type="xs:integer"/>
    </xs:sequence>
  </xs:complexType>
<xs:complexType name="ATP" sawsdl:modelReference=
    "http://www.genome.jp/dbget-bin/www_bget?cpd:C00002">
  <xs:complexContent>
    <xs:extension base="Molecule">
    </xs:extension>
  </xs:complexContent>
</xs:complexType>
<xs:complexType name="Glucose" ...
</xs:schema>
```

Fig. 20. Type definition in XSD with reference to semantics

5.2   Interfaces, Implementations, and Refinement

Interface definition languages for software and services allow to group atomic points of interaction into more complex structures. In the area of programming languages and UML these composite points of interaction are called interfaces and group method declarations. The idea behind interfaces is to extract certain patterns of interaction (at least the structural part thereof) from implementations. Interfaces are separate units of definition that may be referenced by different implementations and function as contracts between implementations.

Roles and Composite Points of Interaction. A component usually exhibits a set of interfaces and requires another set of interfaces to be provided by models it has to interact with as part of a larger simulation model. For the purpose of discrete-event modeling, method-oriented interfaces do not fit well to modeling formalisms that are based on event ports. Therefore, SysML, a modeling language based on UML, allows to define composite *flowports* that group asynchronous interaction capabilities [54].

Similar to SysML, we group event-based interaction capabilities in so called roles. Based on type definitions in XSD, roles may be separated from model definitions and reside in own XML documents – similar to interfaces defined in the Web Service Description Language (WSDL) [79].

Example 2. Figure 21 shows the definition of a role, which the cytoplasm may play when interacting with a mitochondrion. The role describes the interaction potential of the cytoplasm as the ability to send Glucose and receive ATP. The document defining the role imports the type definitions listed above.

Roles extract interface information with respect to a certain abstraction from a model definition. A role declares a set of directed event ports, which have a logical relation.

Example 3. If the cytoplasm model is supposed to interact with other types of models, e.g. with the nucleus for getting a transcription of the DNA, according roles have to be

```
<description
    xmlns="http://www.informatik.uni−rostock.de/cosa/role"
            xmlns:cell="unihro/cbio/cell">
  <id>cell:EnergyReq</id>
  <types>
    <import namespace="unihro/cbio/types"/>
  </types>
  <role xmlns:types="unihro/cbio/types">
    <eventport name="atp" isInput="true" type="types:ATP"/>
    <eventport name="gly" isInput="false" type="types:Glucose"/>
  </role>
</description>
```

Fig. 21. Definition of a role based on imported types

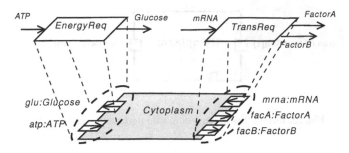

Fig. 22. Assembling atomic interaction capabilities in roles

introduced. Figure 22 visualizes how the interface of the cytoplasm model may be split up into two roles: EnergyReq for interacting with mitochondria and TransReq for interacting with the nucleus.

Interfaces. For reusing a model all interaction capabilities have to be described unambiguously. Interfaces are used to combine a set of roles, each describing a certain aspect of the model's overall communication potential. As types announce "atomic" interaction capabilities, roles announce complex ones. By composite ports, an interface declares that it may be coupled several times in the same manner with different models.

For exploiting the potential of e.g. multiple connectivity of a port, a model component needs to be customizable to fit into a particular composition context. Therefore, parametrization of model components is needed, such that a component represents a whole class of models, which are suited for a set of similar contexts.

Example 4. An interface definition for the cytoplasm model is depicted in Figure 23. The interface possess two composite ports. The first port is named "trans" and typed by the role TransReq. The second port bears the name "energy" and is of type EnergyReq. Whereas "trans" has to be connected exactly once the number of connections to port "energy" may range from one up to an arbitrary number (indicated by the symbol *).

The parameter with name "mito" and type int allows to configure a cytoplasm component to a certain number of connections to mitochondria.

Composite ports and parameters form the basic ingredients of an interface description for model components. If a model should be reused in a new context, the concepts underlying a model definition need to be considered [80]. As simulation models abstract from certain properties, their reuse depends on the assumptions, simplifications, and constraints made in the model. The conceptual dimension of models is usually described in semi-structured data and needs to be evaluated by humans. An example for an interface description is listed in Figure 24.

As XML documents, interfaces are described platform-independent, maybe stored in databases, and can be analyzed for compatibility based on type definitions in XSD.

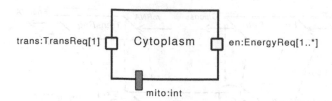

Fig. 23. Interface with two composite ports and a parameter

```
<interface
    xmlns="http://www.informatik.uni-rostock.de/cosa/publici"
           xmlns:cyto="unihro/cbio/cytoplasm"
           xmlns:cell="unihro/cbio/cell">
  <id>cyto:interface</id>
  <profile>
    <name>Cytoplasm</name>
    <application_domain>Cell simulation</application_domain>
    <description>Simple model of the a cell's
        cytoplasm</description>
    <objective>Represent all cell activities except that of the
        nucleus and the mitochondria</objective>
    <key_abstractions>May only be coupled to a nucleus and a set
        of mitochondria.</key_abstractions>
    <author>Mathias Roehl</author>
  </profile>
  <param name="mito" type="http://www.w3.org/2001/XMLSchema:int"
        value="1" description="number of mitochondria this model
        should be coupled to"/>
  <port minMultiplicity="1" maxMultiplicity="*">
    <name>en</name>
    <type>cell:EnergyReq</type>
  </port>
  <impl>cyto:impl</impl>
</interface>
```

Fig. 24. Definition of a model interface in XML

Refinement. Public interface descriptions serve as contracts between model components. To be of any value, properties declared in an interface has to be fulfilled by the implementation. Via reference to roles an interface declares a set of directed event ports. Its implementation has to provide these ports. Model implementations are not allowed direct dependencies to other model implementations.

Ports need need to be associated with the declared interaction capabilities. A difficulty arises from the multiplicities of complex ports. If a port may be connected multiple times, name clashes might occur that have to be resolved.

Example 5. The two complex ports offered by the cytoplasm interface are both typed by a role. All three atomic ports of the role TransReq can be directly mapped to

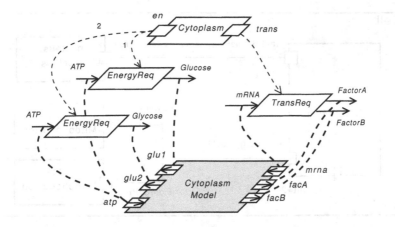

Fig. 25. Binding of abstract interaction points to ports of an implementation

an implementation port. In contrast, the port "en" may be connected multiple times according to the role `EnergyReq`. For each of the multiplicities separate bindings have to be defined. One possibility is to bind different multiplicities of the output channel of type `Glucose` to different output ports of the implementation model, such that each mitochondrion can be addressed individually. As it is not relevant for the cytoplasm model from whom ATP is received, both the first and the second input channel of type `ATP` are bound to the same implementation port. Figure 25 visualizes the binding of abstract to concrete ports with bold dashed lines.

Based on port binding, refinement can now be formulated. A model refines an interface if for all multiplicities of all declared interaction capabilities implementation ports exists that are bound to them. To summarize, an interface contains a set of composite ports. Composite ports reference roles, each of which comprises a set of event ports. Looking at the composition of models, composite ports declare the provisions and requirements of a model. At the time of composition ports have to be connected with compatible counterparts.

5.3 Composition Hierarchies

Couplings connect composite ports of one model component to compatible ports of another component. Communication between components is only allowed along these connections. For the purpose of simulation, all connections have to be associated with a precise meaning, i.e. they have to be mapped to atomic communication channels. To this end, each connection needs to define to which position, in the range of multiplicities of a port, it refers.

Example 6. Figure 26 shows a simple example for using composite structures to specify compositions of model components. A cell is defined as the composite component `Cell` that contains and connects model components of type `Cytoplasm`, `Nucleus`, and `Mitchondrion`. The cytoplasm and the nucleus are connected via their

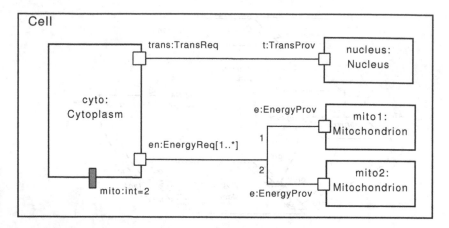

Fig. 26. Composite structure of a cell

`TransReq` and `TransProv` port respectively. Both `Mitochondrion` instances become connected to the cytoplasm at a different position within the multiplicity of the port "en". The cytoplasm's parameter "mito" is accordingly set to 2.

To support the hierarchical construction of models a component may itself refer to other components as sub components, contain connections, and thereby become a composite component. Consequently, connections fall into two different classes. On the one hand, it is possible to connect compatible ports of sub components. On the other hand, connections may delegate ports of the same type between a component and a port of its sub components. Nevertheless, for a composition to be complete all required ports of all components need eventually to be connected to compatible counterparts.

Example 7. The Cell may itself be modeled as a component, which provides two parameters and is equipped with a composite port to interact with other cells. The latter requires the definition of a new role and another implementation of the cytoplasm model, as the cytoplasm needs to interact accordingly. Figure 27 depicts the hierarchical relation between the interface of a cell and its implementation as a composite component. For using the cell component, values have to be assigned to the parameters. The parameter "mito" prescribes the number of mitochondrion components to use inside the cell and the parameter "nex" determines the number of connections to other cell components. The implied structure at the atomic interaction level for the parameter values "mito"=10 and "nex"=1 is shown in Figure 28.

For using a component within a certain composition, the component has to be connected via its ports. At the level of a cell, the `Cytoplasm` and `Mitochondrion` component are black boxes except their published ports. Besides the references to the published ports and parameters, the cell makes no further assumptions about the implementation of its sub components. Compositions abstract from internal details of the parts being composed. Furthermore, component implementations are hidden. The knowledge of a component ends at its borders. A component can interact with its environment only

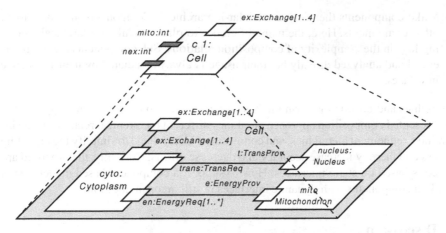

Fig. 27. Hierarchical composition structures

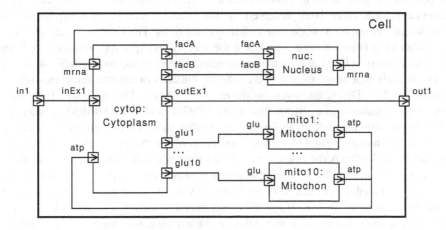

Fig. 28. Resulting model structure

via its ports. Thereby, direct dependencies between components and their contexts of use are eliminated and components may be developed independently of each other. The presented approach to composition builds upon the following concepts:

- Define the type of events to be exchanged between models in a platform-independent manner and put these definitions in separate XML documents, such that they can be stored, queried, and retrieved from public databases.
- Group atomic interaction capabilities in role descriptions, which represent patterns of interaction (currently merely the static part) and let interfaces refer to roles to announce composite ports. Interfaces allow to
  - offer a role multiple times to different interaction partners,
  - reuse interaction capabilities for different model components,
  - use different styles of connection by explicit port bindings, and to
  - realize configuration points to adjust a component to a specific usage context.

– Make components themselves modular-hierarchical. Components may be part of other components. Here, the main difference to plain modular-hierarchical modeling lays in the complexity of composition relations. Sub components are not referenced and analyzed directly but their usage is always mediated by their respective interfaces.

Hierarchies and abstraction form the basic prerequisites to compositional approaches. The presented composition approach combines different hierarchical relations (type hierarchies, refinement hierarchies, and composition hierarchies) to simplify the modeling process and thereby increase accuracy and decrease efforts. Currently, the proposed approach is based on static interfaces. How to support a component-based model design based on components with dynamic interfaces is still an open question.

6   Discussion

Our focus has been on the compositional hierarchy in modeling biological systems. Two different approaches have been presented, i.e. DEVS and π calculus. In being applied in the biological realm, both encountered various extensions. The rigid hierarchical structure of DEVS has been softened, whereas in the π calculus explicit structures have been added. Reasons to soften the hierarchical structures were to support variable structure models, models that allow to describe changing patterns of interaction, composition, behavior, i.e. DYNDEVS, and even interfaces, i.e. ρ-DEVS. The more structured versions of the π calculus, i.e. BETA-BINDERS, SPiCO, and BIOAMBIENTS, inherited the flexibility from the underlying formalism. Among them BIOAMBIENTS is the only one supporting a composition hierarchy. The origin of DEVS lies in the 70s and in systems theory, and reflects the discussions of that time about hierarchical organizations of dynamic systems and the crucial distinction between system and environment. The concepts introduced, e.g. a clear interface between system and environment, reappear in recent approaches like SysML. However, its set-based definition appears bulky in comparison to the more recent and lean π calculus. In any case, the extensions tend to burden formalisms even if they lighten the modeling effort. Components are the building blocks for this type of hierarchical modeling. Components require an interface and they need to be operationally closed. For reuse it is beneficial to treat interfaces as separate units, this is supported by formalisms like BETA-BINDERS, DEVS, and DYNDEVS. The flexibility of the interface as realized in BIOAMBIENTS and ρ-DEVS hampers such a separate treatment of interfaces. However, they support a plasticity that is characteristic for many biological systems. BIOAMBIENTS as well as ML-DEVS support in addition to the flexible interface another feature that is of importance in describing biological systems, to combine micro and macro modeling of a system within one model and thus to explicitly support downward and upward causation.

Acknowledgments

This research is supported by the DFG (German Research Foundation) as part of the research projects DIERMOSIS and DIEM OSIRIS.

References

1. Vaidehi, N., Goddard III, W.: Atomic level simulation models for biological systems. In: Bower, J., Bolouri, H. (eds.) Computational Models of Molecular and Cellular Interaction, pp. 161–188. MIT Press, Cambridge (2001)
2. Takahashi, K., Nanda, S., Arjunan, V., Tomita, M.: Space in systems biology of signaling pathways: towards intracellular molecular crowding in silico. FEBS letters 579(8), 1783–1788 (2005)
3. Gillespie, D.T.: A general method for numerically simulating the stochastic time evolution of coupled chemical reactions. Journal of Computational Physics 22(4), 403–434 (1976)
4. Fishwick, P.A.: Role of process abstraction in simulation. IEEE Trans. Syst. Man Cybern. 18(1), 18–39 (1988)
5. Overstreet, C.M., Nance, R.E., Balci, O.: Issues in enhancing model reuse. In: International Conference on Grand Challenges for Modeling and Simulation, San Antonio, Texas, USA, January 27-31 (2002)
6. Le Novère, N., Finney, A., Hucka, M., Bhalla, U.S., Campagne, F., Collado-Vides, J., Crampin, E.J., Halstead, M., Klipp, E., Mendes, P., Nielsen, P., Sauro, H., Shapiro, B., Snoep, J.L., Spence, H.D., Wanner, B.L.: Minimum information requested in the annotation of biochemical models (miriam). Nature Biotechnology 23(12), 1509–1515 (2005)
7. Alur, R., Grosu, R., Hur, Y., Kumar, V., Lee, I.: Modular Specification of Hybrid Systems in CHARON. In: HSCC 2000: Proceedings of the Third International Workshop on Hybrid Systems: Computation and Control, pp. 6–19. Springer, Heidelberg (2000)
8. Fishwick, P.A., Zeigler, B.P.: A Multimodel Methodology for Qualitative Model Engineering. Modeling and Computer Simulation 2(1), 52–81 (1992)
9. Berleant, D., Kuipers, B.: Qualitative and Quantitative Simulation: Bridging the Gap. Artificial Intelligence 95(2), 215–255 (1997)
10. de Jong, H., Page, M., Hernandez, C., Geiselmann, J.: Qualitative simulation of genetic regulatory networks: Method and application. In: IJCAI, pp. 67–73 (2001)
11. Antoniotti, M., Mishra, B., Piazza, C., Policriti, A., Simeoni, M.: Modeling cellular behavior with hybrid automata: Bisimulation and collapsing. In: Priami, C. (ed.) CMSB 2003. LNCS, vol. 2602, pp. 57–74. Springer, Heidelberg (2003)
12. Takahashi, K., Kaizu, K., Hu, B., Tomita, M.: A multi-algorithm, multi-timescale method for cell simulation. Bioinformatics 20(4), 538–546 (2004)
13. Fisher, J., Piterman, N., Hubbard, E., Stern, M., Harel, D.: Computational insights into C. elegans vulval development. Proc. Natl. Acad. Sci. 6(102), 1951–1956 (2005)
14. Endy, D.: Foundations for engineering biology. Nature 438, 449–453 (2005)
15. Hoops, S.: Hierarchical modeling. In: Result of the SBML Composition Workshop 2007. University of Connecticut Health Center, Farmington, CT, USA (September 2007), http://sbml.org/index.php/Events/Other_Events/SBML_Composition_Workshop_2007/Hierarchical_Modeling
16. Lakoff, G.: Women, Fire and dangerous things. University of Chicago Press (1987)
17. Webster, J.: Hierarchical organization of ecosystems. In: Halfon, E. (ed.) Theoretical Systems Ecology, pp. 119–129. Academic Press, London (1979)
18. Wiegert, R.: Holism and reductionism in ecology: Hyptohesis, scale and systems models. Oikos 53, 267–269 (1988)
19. Bertalanffy, L.v.: General systems theory. George Braziller (1968)
20. Whyte, L.L., Wilson, A., Wilson, D. (eds.): Hierarchical Structures. Elsevier, Amsterdam (1969)
21. Pattee, H. (ed.): Hierarchy Theory. George Braziller (1973)

22. Ayla, F.J., Dobzhansky, T. (eds.): Studies in the philosophy of biology. University of California Press (1974)
23. Chwif, L., Barretto, M.R.P., Paul, R.J.: On simulation model complexity. In: WSC 2000: Proceedings of the 32nd conference on Winter simulation. Society for Computer Simulation International, San Diego, CA, USA, pp. 449–455 (2000)
24. Luna, J.J.: Hierarchical relation in simulation models. In: WSC 1993: Proceedings of the 25th conference on Winter simulation, pp. 132–137. ACM, New York (1993)
25. Shneiderman, B.: Designing the User Interface: Strategies for Effective Human-Computer Interaction, 3rd edn. Addison-Wesley, Reading (1997)
26. Rosch, E.: Principles of categorization. In: Rosch, E., Lloyd, B. (eds.) Cognition and categorization, pp. 27–48, Lawrence Earlbaum (1978)
27. Mayr, E.: Biological classification: toward a synthesis of opposing methodologies. In: Sober, E. (ed.) Conceptual issues in Evoutionary biology, pp. 646–662. MIT Press, Cambridge (1984)
28. Wegner, P.: Concepts and paradigms of object-oriented programming. OOPS Messenger 1(1), 7–87 (1990)
29. Zeigler, B.P., Sarjoughian, H.S.: Implications of M&S foundations for the V&V of large scale complex simulation models. In: Proceedings of the Foundations for V&V in the 21st Century Workshop, Laurel, MD (2002)
30. Fritzon, P.: Principles of object-oriented modeling and simulation with modelica 2.1. Wiley, Chichester (2003)
31. Tolk, A.: What comes after the semantic web – pads implications for the dynamic web. In: PADS 2006: Proceedings of the 20th Workshop on Principles of Advanced and Distributed Simulation, p. 55. IEEE Computer Society, Washington (2006)
32. Degenring, D., Frömel, C., Dikta, G., Takors, R.: Sensitivity analysis for the reduction of complex metabolism models. Journal of Process Control 14(7), 729–745 (2004)
33. Boström, P., Morel, L., Walden, M.: Stepwise development of simulink models using the refinement calculus framework. In: Jones, C.B., Liu, Z., Woodcock, J. (eds.) ICTAC 2007. LNCS, vol. 4711, pp. 79–93. Springer, Heidelberg (2007)
34. Nicol, D., Priami, C., Nielson, H., Uhrmacher, A. (eds.): Simulation and Verification of Dynamic Systems. Dagstuhl Seminar Proceedings 0161 (2006) ISSN 1862-4405
35. Klir, G.: Architecture of Systems Problem Solving. Plenum Press (1985)
36. Sauro, H., Uhrmacher, A., Harel, D., Kwiatkowska, M., Hucka, M., Mendes, P., Shaffer, C., Stroembaeck, L., Tyson, J.: Challenges for modeling and simulation in computational biology. In: Proc. of the Winter Simulation Conference, IEEE/ACM (2006)
37. Szyperski, C.: Component software: beyond object-oriented programming, 2nd edn. ACM Press/Addison-Wesley Publishing Co (2002)
38. Verbraeck, A.: Component-based distributed simulations: the way forward? In: PADS '04: Proceedings of the eighteenth workshop on Parallel and distributed simulation, New York, NY, USA, ACM Press (2004) 141–148
39. de Alfaro, L., Henzinger, T.A.: Interface-based design. In: Broy, M., Gruenbauer, J., Harel, D., Hoare, C.A.R. (eds.) Engineering Theories of Software-intensive Systems. NATO Science Series: Mathematics, Physics, and Chemistry, vol. 195, pp. 83–104 (2005)
40. Janssen, T.M.V.: Compositionality (with an appendix by B. Partee). In: van Benthem, J., ter Meulen, A. (eds.) Handbook of Logic and Language, pp. 417–473. Elsevier, Amsterdam (1997)
41. Cambell, D.: Downward causation. In: Ayla, F., Dobzhansky, T. (eds.) Studies in the philosophy of biology, pp. 179–186. University of California Press (1974)
42. Tilly, C.: Micro, macro, or megrim? In: Schlumbohm, J. (ed.) Mikrogeschichte - Makrogeschichte: komplementär oder inkommensurabel? Göttinger Gespräche zur Geschichtswissenschaft, vol. 7, Wallstein Verlag (1998)

43. Uhrmacher, A.M.: Reasoning about changing structure, a modeling concept for ecological systems. Applied Artificial Intelligence 9(2), 157–180 (1995)
44. Goguen, J., Varela, F.: Systems and distinctions. duality and complementarity. International journal of general systems 5, 31–43 (1979)
45. Heylighen, F.R.E., Demeyere, F. (eds.): Self-Steering and Cognition in Complex Systems – Towards a New Cybernetics, pp. 107–113. Gordon Breach Science (1990)
46. Zeigler, B.P., Praehofer, H., Kim, T.G.: Theory of Modeling and Simulation. Academic Press, London (2000)
47. Chow, A.C., Zeigler, B.P.: Parallel devs: a parallel, hierarchical, modular, modeling formalism. In: WSC 1994: Proceedings of the 26th conference on Winter simulation. Society for Computer Simulation International, San Diego, CA, USA, pp. 716–722 (1994)
48. Degenring, D., Röhl, M., Uhrmacher, A.M.: Discrete event, multi-level simulation of metabolite channeling. Biosystems 75(1-3), 29–41 (2004)
49. Barros, F.: Modeling Formalism for Dynamic Structure Systems. ACM Transactions on Modeling and Computer Simulation 7(4), 501–514 (1997)
50. Uhrmacher, A.: Dynamic Structures in Modeling and Simulation - A Reflective Approach. ACM Transactions on Modeling and Simulation 11(2), 206–232 (2001)
51. Asperti, A., Busi, N.: Mobile petri nets. Technical Report UBLCS-96-10, University of Bologna (1996)
52. Busi, N.: Mobile nets. In: Ciancarini, P., Fantechi, A., Gorrieri, R. (eds.) FMOODS. IFIP Conference Proceedings, vol. 139, Kluwer Academic Publishers, Dordrecht (1999)
53. Uhrmacher, A., Himmelspach, J., Röhl, M., Ewald, R.: Introducing variable ports and multi-couplings for cell biological modeling in devs. In: Proc. of the 2006 Winter Simulation Conference, pp. 832–840 (2006)
54. OMG.: Systems modeling language (OMG SysML^{TM}) v1.0. OMG Available Specification, Document Number: formal/07-09-01 (September 2007)
55. Kuttler, C., Uhrmacher, A.: Multi-level modeling in systems biology by discrete event approaches. IT Themenheft Systems Biology (2006)
56. Ewald, R., Maus, C., Rolfs, A., Uhrmacher, A.M.: Discrete event modelling and simulation in systems biology. Journal of Simulation 1(2), 81–96 (2007)
57. Möhring, M.: Social science multilevel simulation with mimose. In: Social Science Microsimulation [Dagstuhl Seminar, May, 1995], London, UK, pp. 123–137. Springer, Heidelberg (1996)
58. Uhrmacher, A.M., Ewald, R., John, M., Maus, C., Jeschke, M., Biermann, S.: Combining micro and macro-modeling in devs for computational biology. In: Proc. of the 2007 Winter Simulation Conference (2007)
59. Milner, R.: Communicating and Mobile Systems: the Pi-Calculus. Cambridge University Press, Cambridge (1999)
60. Priami, C.: Stochastic pi-Calculus. The Computer Journal 38(7), 578–589 (1995)
61. Regev, A., Shapiro, E.: The π-calculus as an abstraction for biomolecular systems. In: Ciobanu, Gabriel Rozenberg, G. (eds.) Modeling in Molecular Biology, Springer, Heidelberg (2004)
62. Kuttler, C., Lhoussaine, C., Niehren, J.: A stochastic pi calculus for concurrent objects. In: Algebraic Biology, pp. 232–246. Springer, Heidelberg (2007)
63. Degano, P., Prandi, D., Priami, C., Quaglia, P.: Beta-binders for biological quantitative experiments. Electronic Notes in Theoretical Computer Science 164(3), 101–117 (2006)
64. Regev, A., Panina, E.M., Silverman, W., Cardelli, L., Shapiro, E.: BioAmbients: an abstraction for biological compartments. Theor. Comput. Sci. 325(1), 141–167 (2004)
65. Kuttler, C., Niehren, J.: Gene Regulation in the Pi Calculus: Simulating Cooperativity at the Lambda Switch. In: Priami, C., Ingólfsdóttir, A., Mishra, B., Riis Nielson, H. (eds.) Transactions on Computational Systems Biology VII. LNCS (LNBI), vol. 4230, pp. 24–55. Springer, Heidelberg (2006)

66. Hillston, J.: Process algebras for quantitative analysis. In: Logic in Computer Science. Proceedings. 20th Annual IEEE Symposium on. LICS 2005, pp. 239–248 (2005)
67. Regev, A., Silverman, W., Shapiro, E.: Representation and simulation of biochemical processes using the pi-calculus process algebra. In: Proceedings of the Pacific Symposium of Biocomputing 2001, pp. 459–470 (2001)
68. Kuttler, C.: Modeling Bacterial Gene Expression in a Stochastic Pi-Calculus with Concurrent Objects. PhD thesis, University of Lille 1 (2007)
69. Phillips, A., Cardelli, L.: Efficient, correct simulation of biological processes in the stochastic pi-calculus. In: Computational Methods in Systems Biology, pp. 184–199. Springer, Heidelberg (2007)
70. Davis, P.K., Anderson, R.H.: Improving the composability of DoD models and simulations. JDMS 1(1), 5–17 (2004)
71. Pierce, B.C.: Types and programming languages. MIT Press, Cambridge (2002)
72. Zeigler, B.P., Sarjoughian, H.S.: Introduction to DEVS modeling and simulation with JAVA: Developing component-based simulation models. Arizona Cneter for Integrative Modleing and Simulation, University of Arizona and Arizona State University, Tucson, Arizona, USA (January 2005)
73. Brooks, C., Lee, E.A., Liu, X., Neuendorffer, S., Zhao, Y., Zheng, H.: Heterogeneous concurrent modeling and design in java (volume 1: Introduction to ptolemy ii). Technical Report UCB/EECS-2007-7, EECS Department, University of California, Berkeley (January 2007)
74. W3C: Web services architecture W3C Working Group Note February 11 (2004),
    http://www.w3.org/TR/2004/NOTE-ws-arch-20040211/
75. Harold, E.R.: Processing XML with Java. Pearson Education, London (2002)
76. W3C: XML Schema part 0: Primer 2nd edn W3C Recommendation (October 28, 2004),
    http://www.w3.org/TR/2004/REC-xmlschema-0-20041028/
77. W3C: Semantic annotations for WSDL (2006) W3C Working Draft (September 28, 2006),
    http://www.w3.org/TR/2006/WD-sawsdl-20060928/
78. Röhl, M., Morgenstern, S.: Composing simulation models using interface definitions based on web service descriptions. In: Proceedings of the 2007 Winter Simulation Conference, pp. 815–822 (2007)
79. W3C: Web services description language (WSDL) version 2.0 part 1: Core language (2006) W3C Candidate Recommendation (March 27, 2006),
    http://www.w3.org/TR/2006/CR-wsdl20-20060327
80. Tolk, A., Muguira, J.: The level of conceptual interoperability model. In: Fall Simulation Interoperability Workshop (SISO), Orlando (September 2003)

Simulation Methods in Systems Biology

Daniel T. Gillespie

Dan T Gillespie Consulting,
30504 Cordoba Pl., Castaic, California 91384 USA
GillespieDT@mailaps.org

Abstract. This chapter reviews the theory of stochastic chemical kinetics and several simulation methods that are based on that theory. An
effort is made to delineate the logical connections among the major elements of the theory, such as the chemical master equation, the stochastic
simulation algorithm, tau-leaping, the chemical Langevin equation, the
chemical Fokker-Planck equation, and the deterministic reaction rate
equation. Focused presentations are given of two approximate simulation strategies that aim to improve simulation efficiency for systems
with "multiscale" complications of the kind that are often encountered
in cellular systems: The first, *explicit tau-leaping*, deals with systems
that have a wide range of molecular populations. The second, the *slow-
scale stochastic simulation algorithm*, is designed for systems that have
a wide range of reaction rates. The latter procedure is shown to provide a stochastic generalization of the Michaelis-Menten analysis of the
enzyme-substrate reaction set.

Keywords: stochastic chemical kinetics, master equation, stochastic
simulation algorithm, tau-leaping, Langevin equation, Fokker-Planck
equation, multiscale, stiff systems, slow-scale stochastic simulation algorithm, Michaelis-Menten, enzyme-substrate reaction.

1   Introduction

The dynamics of cellular chemical systems can sometimes (but not always) be
approximated by assuming that the reactant molecules are "stirred" to such an
extent that their positions become randomized and need not be tracked in detail.
When that is so, the state of the system can be defined by the instantaneous
molecular populations of the various chemical species. This chapter discusses
some of the ways in which such systems can be numerically simulated. The focus
will be on simulation methods that take explicit account of the discreteness
and stochasticity that is always present at the molecular level, and which is
sometimes important in cellular systems, where the molecular populations of
some key species can be small.

We begin in Sec. 2 by reviewing the theory of *stochastic chemical kinetics*,
which provides the rational basis for all the simulation methods that will be
discussed. We derive the chemical master equation and the stochastic simulation algorithm, and then show how a series of well defined approximations leads

M. Bernardo, P. Degano, and G. Zavattaro (Eds.): SFM 2008, LNCS 5016, pp. 125–167, 2008.
© Springer-Verlag Berlin Heidelberg 2008

successively to tau-leaping, the chemical Langevin and Fokker-Planck equations, and finally the traditional deterministic description in terms of ordinary differential equations. In Sec. 3 we consider some practical issues involved in implementing the *explicit tau-leaping* simulation method; this procedure, encompassing as it does Langevin leaping and the deterministic reaction rate equation, accommodates systems with a wide range of molecular populations. In Sec. 4 we present the *slow-scale stochastic simulation algorithm*, which is designed for systems that have a wide range of reaction rates. In Sec. 5 we show how application of the slow-scale stochastic simulation algorithm to the *enzyme-substrate* reaction set yields a stochastic generalization of the deterministic Michaelis-Menten theory. We conclude in Sec. 6 with some brief comments on future directions for research.

2   Foundations of Stochastic Chemical Kinetics

The theory of stochastic chemical kinetics has been reviewed in several recent articles [1,2,3], and the reader may consult any of those for further details and for references to the original literature. We consider a system of molecules of N chemical species $\{S_1, \ldots, S_N\}$, which interact through M *elemental* reaction channels $\{R_1, \ldots, R_M\}$. An elemental reaction is one that occurs essentially instantaneously. In practice, there are only two types of elemental reaction: *unimolecular*, in which a single molecule changes form; and *bimolecular*, in which two molecules collide and a chemical change occurs as a result. All other types of reaction (trimolecular, reversible, etc.) are made up of a series of two or more elemental reactions.

The ideal way to simulate the time evolution of a chemical system would be to use *molecular dynamics*, in which the exact positions and velocities of all the molecules in the system are tracked. Molecular dynamics thus simulates every molecular collision that occurs in the system, both the "reactive" collisions that lead to bimolecular reactions, and the "non-reactive" collisions in which the two colliding molecules simply bounce off each other without undergoing any chemical change. But this highly detailed computational approach is unfeasible for nearly all real systems.

2.1   The Well-Stirred Condition and the Propensity Functions

A great simplification occurs if successive reactive collisions tend to be separated in time by very many non-reactive collisions. This might occur naturally, in which case we would say the system is self-stirring, or it might occur through exogenous stirring or shaking. Either way, the net effect is a randomization of the velocities and the positions of the molecules: the velocities acquire a Maxwell-Boltzmann distribution appropriate to the system temperature T, and the positions become randomly uniform over the containing volume Ω. In what follows, we will be exclusively concerned with such *well-stirred* systems. Whereas specifying the state of a general chemical system requires giving the instantaneous position, velocity, and species of each molecule in the system, specifying the state of a well-stirred system is enormously easier: We need only specify the vector $\mathbf{X}(t) = (X_1(t), \ldots, X_N(t))$, where $X_i(t)$ is the number of S_i molecules contained in Ω at time t.

For a well-stirred system, each reaction channel R_j can be characterized mathematically by two quantities: The first is its *state-change vector* $\boldsymbol{\nu}_j = (\nu_{1j}, \ldots, \nu_{Nj})$, where ν_{ij} is defined to be the change in the S_i molecular population caused by one R_j reaction event; thus, an R_j reaction induces the state change $\mathbf{x} \to \mathbf{x} + \boldsymbol{\nu}_j$. The other defining quantity for reaction R_j is its *propensity function* a_j. It is defined by the statement

$a_j(\mathbf{x})\, dt \equiv$ the *probability*, given $\mathbf{X}(t) = \mathbf{x},$ that one R_j reaction will occur

inside Ω in the next *infinitesimal* time interval $[t, t + dt)$.   (1)

(We view dt as a real variable that is distinct from, and independent of, t; the domain of definition of dt is the interval $[0, \varepsilon]$, where ε is arbitrarily close to 0.)

The definition (1) can be viewed as the *fundamental premise* of stochastic chemical kinetics, because everything else in the theory follows from it. But the validity of (1) cannot simply be assumed or postulated mathematically; rather, it must be grounded in physical theory. This requires finding the specific physical conditions under which functions a_j having the property (1) exist, and then determining the forms of those functions. This effort typically focuses on identifying for each R_j a *reaction probability rate constant* c_j, which is defined so that $c_j dt$ gives the probability that a randomly chosen combination of R_j reactant molecules will react accordingly in the next dt. Then we can use the addition law of probability theory to compute the probability (1) as the sum of $c_j dt$ over all distinct combinations of R_j reactant molecules in the current state $\mathbf{x} = (x_1, \ldots, x_N)$. This leads to the following general forms for the propensity functions of the basic elemental reaction types:

$$S_1 \xrightarrow{c_j} \text{products:} \quad a_j(\mathbf{x}) = c_j x_1, \tag{2a}$$

$$S_1 + S_2 \xrightarrow{c_j} \text{products:} \quad a_j(\mathbf{x}) = c_j x_1 x_2, \tag{2b}$$

$$2S_1 \xrightarrow{c_j} \text{products:} \quad a_j(\mathbf{x}) = c_j \tfrac{1}{2} x_1 (x_1 - 1) . \tag{2c}$$

The forms of c_j will be highly reaction specific. For the unimolecular reaction (2a), c_j might be quantum mechanical in origin. For the bimolecular reactions (2b) and (2c), c_j will typically be the product of the probability that a randomly chosen pair of reactant molecules will collide in the next dt, times the probability such a collision will produce an R_j reaction [4]. The collision factor will generally be inversely proportional to Ω, reflecting the fact that two molecules will have a harder time finding each other in a larger container. Model theoretical derivations of the collision probability factor can be given for *well-stirred* molecules moving either ballistically (as in a dilute gas) or diffusively (as in a solution). In what follows, we shall simply assume that the propensity functions $a_j(\mathbf{x})$, like the state-change vectors $\boldsymbol{\nu}_j$, are all given.

2.2 The Chemical Master Equation

The probabilistic nature of (1) implies that the most we can hope to predict about the system is the *probability* $P(\mathbf{x}, t \mid \mathbf{x}_0, t_0)$ of finding $\mathbf{X}(t) = \mathbf{x}$, given that $\mathbf{X}(t_0) = \mathbf{x}_0$ for $t_0 \leqslant t$. We can derive a time-evolution equation for P by using the laws of probability to write $P(\mathbf{x}, t + dt \mid \mathbf{x}_0, t_0)$ as the sum of the probabilities of all the mutually exclusive ways in which the system could evolve from state $\mathbf{x}_0$ at time t_0 to state $\mathbf{x}$ at time $t + dt$, via *specified* states at time t:

$$P(\mathbf{x}, t + dt \mid \mathbf{x}_0, t_0) = P(\mathbf{x}, t \mid \mathbf{x}_0, t_0) \times \left[1 - \sum_{j=1}^{M} (a_j(\mathbf{x})dt) \right]$$
$$+ \sum_{j=1}^{M} P(\mathbf{x} - \boldsymbol{\nu}_j, t \mid \mathbf{x}_0, t_0) \times (a_j(\mathbf{x} - \boldsymbol{\nu}_j)dt) \ .$$

The first term on the right is the probability that the system is already in state $\mathbf{x}$ at time t, and then no reaction of any kind occurs in $[t, t + dt)$. The generic second term is the probability that the system is one R_j reaction removed from state $\mathbf{x}$ at time t, and then one R_j reaction occurs in $[t, t + dt)$. That these $M + 1$ routes to state $\mathbf{x}$ at time $t + dt$ are mutually exclusive and collectively exhaustive is ensured by taking dt to be so small that the probability of more than one reaction occurring in $[t, t + dt)$ is negligibly small. Subtracting $P(\mathbf{x}, t \mid \mathbf{x}_0, t_0)$ from both sides of the above equation, dividing through by dt, and then taking the limit $dt \to 0$, we obtain the *chemical master equation* (CME):

$$\frac{\partial P(\mathbf{x}, t \mid \mathbf{x}_0, t_0)}{\partial t} = \sum_{j=1}^{M} [a_j(\mathbf{x} - \boldsymbol{\nu}_j)P(\mathbf{x} - \boldsymbol{\nu}_j, t \mid \mathbf{x}_0, t_0) - a_j(\mathbf{x})P(\mathbf{x}, t \mid \mathbf{x}_0, t_0)] \ .$$

$$(3)$$

In principle, the CME completely determines the function $P(\mathbf{x}, t \mid \mathbf{x}_0, t_0)$. But in practice, this equation is usually very difficult, if not impossible, to solve. One might hope to learn something from the CME about the behavior of *averages*, like $\langle f(\mathbf{X}(t)) \rangle \equiv \sum_{\mathbf{x}} f(\mathbf{x})P(\mathbf{x}, t \mid \mathbf{x}_0, t_0)$, but this too turns out to be difficult if any of the reaction channels are bimolecular. For example, by multiplying (3) by $\mathbf{x}$ and then summing over $\mathbf{x}$, we can derive the relation

$$\frac{d \langle \mathbf{X}(t) \rangle}{dt} = \sum_{j=1}^{M} \boldsymbol{\nu}_j \langle a_j(\mathbf{X}(t)) \rangle \ . \tag{4}$$

If all the reactions were unimolecular, the propensity functions would all be linear in $\mathbf{x}$ and we would have $\langle a_j(\mathbf{X}(t)) \rangle = a_j(\langle \mathbf{X}(t) \rangle)$. Equation (4) would then be a closed ordinary differential equation for the first moment $\langle \mathbf{X}(t) \rangle$. But if, as is usually the case, any reaction is bimolecular, the right hand side of (4) will contain at least one second moment of the form $\langle X_i(t)X_{i'}(t) \rangle$, and (4) would then be merely the first of an infinite, open-ended set of equations for all the moments.

In the hypothetical case in which there are *no fluctuations*, i.e., if $\mathbf{X}(t)$ were a deterministic or *sure* process, we would have $\langle f(\mathbf{X}(t)) \rangle = f(\mathbf{X}(t))$ for all functions f. Equation (4) would then reduce to

$$\frac{d\mathbf{X}(t)}{dt} = \sum_{j=1}^{M} \boldsymbol{\nu}_j a_j(\mathbf{X}(t)) . \tag{5}$$

This is the *reaction rate equation* (RRE) of traditional deterministic chemical kinetics – a set of N coupled first-order ordinary differential equations for the molecular populations $X_i(t)$, which are here continuous sure variables. (The RRE is more commonly encountered written in terms of the concentration variable, $\mathbf{Z}(t) = \mathbf{X}(t)/\Omega$, but that simple scalar transformation is inconsequential for our purposes here.) Although this line of reasoning shows that the deterministic RRE (5) would be valid if all fluctuations could be ignored, it does not tell us how or why the fluctuations might ever be ignorable. One of the aims of this section will be to show how the RRE (5) follows from (1) through a series of physically transparent approximating assumptions.

2.3   The Stochastic Simulation Algorithm

An alternate approach to describing the behavior of the system is to construct a *numerical realization* of $\mathbf{X}(t)$, i.e., a simulated trajectory of $\mathbf{X}(t)$-versus-t. This is *not* the same as solving the CME numerically; however, much the same effect can be achieved by either histogramming or averaging the results of many realizations. The key to constructing a simulated trajectory of $\mathbf{X}(t)$ is not the CME or the function $P(\mathbf{x}, t \,|\, \mathbf{x}_0, t_0)$, but rather another probability function, $p(\tau, j \,|\, \mathbf{x}, t)$, which is defined as follows:

$p(\tau, j \,|\, \mathbf{x}, t)\, d\tau \equiv$ the probability, given $\mathbf{X}(t) = \mathbf{x}$, that the *next*

reaction in the system will occur in the infinitesimal time

interval $[t + \tau, t + \tau + d\tau)$, *and* will be an R_j reaction . (6)

Formally, this function is the joint probability density function of the two random variables "time to the next reaction" (τ) and "index of the next reaction" (j), given that the system is in state $\mathbf{x}$ at the current time t.

To derive an analytical expression for $p(\tau, j \,|\, \mathbf{x}, t)$, we begin by introducing yet another probability function, $P_0(\tau \,|\, \mathbf{x}, t)$, which is defined as the probability, given $\mathbf{X}(t) = \mathbf{x}$, that no reaction of any kind occurs in the time interval $[t, \, t + \tau)$. By the definition (1) and the laws of probability theory, this function must satisfy

$$P_0(\tau + d\tau \,|\, \mathbf{x}, t) = P_0(\tau \,|\, \mathbf{x}, t) \times \left[1 - \sum_{j'=1}^{M} (a_{j'}(\mathbf{x}) d\tau) \right] ,$$

since the right side gives the probability that no reaction occurs in $[t, \, t + \tau)$ and then no reaction occurs in $[t + \tau, \, t + \tau + d\tau)$ (as usual we take the infinitesimal time span $d\tau$ to be so small that it can contain no more than one reaction). A simple rearrangement of this equation and passage to the limit $d\tau \rightarrow 0$ results in the differential equation

$$\frac{dP_0(\tau \,|\, \mathbf{x}, t)}{d\tau} = -a_0(\mathbf{x})\, P_0(\tau \,|\, \mathbf{x}, t) \ ,$$

where we have defined

$$a_0(\mathbf{x}) \equiv \sum_{j'=1}^{M} a_{j'}(\mathbf{x}) \ . \tag{7}$$

The solution to this differential equation for the initial condition $P_0(0 \,|\, \mathbf{x}, t) = 1$ is

$$P_0(\tau \,|\, \mathbf{x}, t) = \exp\left(-a_0(\mathbf{x})\,\tau\right) \ .$$

Now we observe that the probability defined in (6) can be written

$$p(\tau, j \,|\, \mathbf{x}, t)\, d\tau = P_0(\tau \,|\, \mathbf{x}, t) \times (a_j(\mathbf{x})d\tau) \ ,$$

since the right side gives the probability that no reactions occur in $[t,\, t + \tau)$ and then one R_j reaction occurs in $[t + \tau, t + \tau + d\tau)$. When we insert the above formula for $P_0(\tau \,|\, \mathbf{x}, t)$ into this last equation and cancel the $d\tau$'s, we obtain

$$p(\tau, j \,|\, \mathbf{x}, t) = a_j(\mathbf{x})\, \exp\left(-a_0(\mathbf{x})\,\tau\right) \ . \tag{8}$$

Writing this result in the form

$$p(\tau, j \,|\, \mathbf{x}, t) = a_0(\mathbf{x})\, \exp\left(-a_0(\mathbf{x})\,\tau\right) \times \frac{a_j(\mathbf{x})}{a_0(\mathbf{x})}$$

shows that τ is the exponential random variable with mean (and standard deviation) $1/a_0(\mathbf{x})$, while j is a statistically independent integer random variable with point probabilities $a_j(\mathbf{x})/a_0(\mathbf{x})$.

There are several exact Monte Carlo methods for generating samples of such random variables. For example, application of the classic "inversion" generating method (see, e.g., Chapter 1 of [5]) yields the following procedure: Draw two random numbers r_1 and r_2 from the uniform distribution in the unit-interval and take

$$\tau = \frac{1}{a_0(\mathbf{x})} \ln\left(\frac{1}{r_1}\right) \ , \tag{9a}$$

$$j = \text{ the smallest integer satisfying } \sum_{j'=1}^{j} a_{j'}(\mathbf{x}) > r_2\, a_0(\mathbf{x}) \ . \tag{9b}$$

Using these generating formulas gives the following so-called *direct method* of implementing the *stochastic simulation algorithm* (SSA):

1. Initialize the time $t = t_0$ and the system's state $\mathbf{x} = \mathbf{x}_0$.
2. With the system in state $\mathbf{x}$ at time t, evaluate all the $a_j(\mathbf{x})$ and their sum $a_0(\mathbf{x})$.

3. Generate values for τ and j using Eqs. (9).
4. Effect the next reaction by replacing $t \leftarrow t + \tau$ and $\mathbf{x} \leftarrow \mathbf{x} + \boldsymbol{\nu}_j$.
5. Record $(\mathbf{x}, t)$ as desired. Return to Step 2, or else stop.

The $\mathbf{X}(t)$ trajectory that is produced by the SSA might be thought of as a stochastic version of the trajectory that would be obtained by numerically solving the RRE (5). But note that the time step τ in the SSA is exact, and is not a finite approximation to some infinitesimal dt as is the time step in most numerical ODE solvers. If it is found that every SSA-generated trajectory is practically indistinguishable from the RRE trajectory, then we may conclude that microscale randomness is negligible for this system. But if the SSA trajectories are found to deviate significantly from the RRE trajectory, or from each other, then we must conclude that microscale randomness is not negligible, and the deterministic RRE does not provide an accurate description of the system's true behavior. Figure 1 shows two SSA-generated trajectories for the simple reaction $S_1 \rightarrow \emptyset$, and compares those trajectories to the predictions of the CME and the RRE.

The CME and the SSA are logically equivalent to each other, since each is derived without approximation from premise (1). But even when the CME is intractable, the SSA is straightforward to implement. In fact, as a numerical procedure, the SSA is even simpler than procedures that are typically used to numerically solve the RRE (5). The catch is that the SSA is often very slow. The source of this slowness can be traced to the factor $1/a_0(\mathbf{x})$ in (9a) for the time-step τ; that factor can be very small if at least one reactant species is present in large numbers, and that is nearly always the case for real systems.

Besides the direct method just described, other implementations of the SSA are the first reaction method, the next reaction method, the first family method, the modified direct method, and the sorting direct method. Reference [3] describes these methods briefly and gives references to the original papers. The next reaction, modified direct, and sorting direct methods are especially noteworthy, since they give significant speedups over the other methods while remaining exact. But as procedures that simulate every reaction event one at a time, none of these will be fast enough for most practical applications. This prompts us to consider the possibility of giving up some of the exactness of the SSA in return for greater simulation speed.

2.4   Tau-Leaping

One approximate accelerated simulation strategy is *tau-leaping*. It steps the system ahead in time by a *pre-selected* interval τ which may encompass more than one reaction event. The key to doing this properly is the Poisson random variable with mean m, which we denote by $\mathcal{P}(m)$. One way of defining that integer-valued random variable is as follows: $\mathcal{P}(a\tau)$ is the *number of events* that will occur in a time τ, given that the $\mathcal{P}(a\tau)$ of an event occurring in any infinitesimal time dt is $a\,dt$ where a is a nonnegative real *constant*.

Suppose the system is in state $\mathbf{x}$ at time t. And suppose we choose a time τ that is small enough to satisfy the *Leap Condition*, which is this: Each a_j

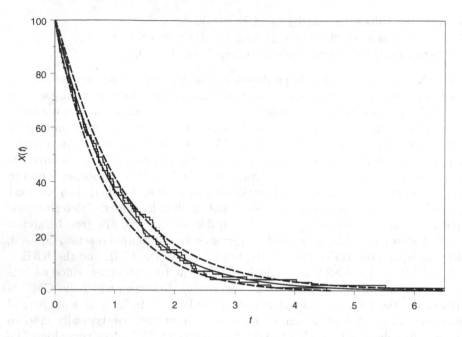

Fig. 1. Trajectories of $X_1(t)$-versus-t for the simple reaction $S_1 \xrightarrow{c_1} \emptyset$, with $c_1 = 1$ and $X_1(0) = 100$. The center solid curve is the solution $X_1(t) = 100 \cdot e^{-t}$ of the RRE for this system, $dX_1/dt = -X_1$. The CME can be solved exactly for this system (but for very few other systems), and its solution shows $X_1(t)$ to be the *binomial* random variable with mean $100 \cdot e^{-t}$ and standard deviation $10 \cdot \sqrt{e^{-t} \cdot (1 - e^{-t})}$. The resulting "one-standard deviation envelope" is shown in the figure by the two dashed lines. The SSA for this reaction decrements x_1 by 1 at each reaction, with the time to the next reaction in state x_1 being computed as $\tau = (1/x_1) \ln(1/r)$. Two independent SSA realizations, which were made using different seeds for the unit-interval uniform random numbers r, are shown as the step-curves. There will always be exact agreement between the mean of the CME and the solution of the RRE if all the propensity functions are linear in the species populations, as is the case here. Otherwise the two will not be exactly equal, but the difference between them will nearly always be very small of the populations are even moderately large.

will remain approximately constant at its value $a_j(\mathbf{x})$ during the time interval $[t, t + \tau]$. Satisfaction of this condition is secured in practice by requiring that, for every $j = 1, \ldots, M$, $|\Delta_\tau a_j(\mathbf{x})/a_j(\mathbf{x})|$, the absolute fractional change in a_j during the next time τ, will not exceed some sufficiently small ε. When the Leap Condition is satisfied, R_j will (approximately) have probability $a_j(\mathbf{x}) \, dt$ of firing in every dt subinterval of $[t, t + \tau]$. So by definition, *the number of times R_j will fire* in $[t, t+\tau]$ is (approximately) the Poisson random variable $\mathcal{P}(a_j(\mathbf{x}) \tau)$. Since each firing of R_j changes the system state by $\boldsymbol{\nu}_j$, then the state at time $t + \tau$ can be computed from the state $\mathbf{x}$ at time t by the formula

$$\mathbf{X}(t + \tau) \doteq \mathbf{x} + \sum_{j=1}^{M} \mathcal{P}_j(a_j(\mathbf{x})\tau) \, \boldsymbol{\nu}_j \, . \tag{10}$$

Equation (10) is called the *tau-leaping formula*. Its accuracy depends solely on how well the Leap Condition is satisfied (i.e., on how small we choose the control parameter ε). If we can find a τ that is at once *small enough* to satisfy the Leap Condition sufficiently well, yet nevertheless *large enough* that many reactions will fire during time $[t, t + \tau]$, then tau-leaping can give a faster simulation than the SSA. This turns out to be possible for many systems.

2.5   The Chemical Langevin and Fokker-Planck Equations

In Section 3 we will consider some practical issues that must be resolved in order for the tau-leaping strategy to be efficiently implemented. For now though, we want to show that two well established theorems of probability theory allow the tau-leaping formula (10) to be further approximated in a way that is both useful and illuminating. The first theorem we will need deals with $\mathcal{N}(m, \sigma^2)$, the normal (or Gaussian) random variable with mean m and variance σ^2. It says that

$$\mathcal{N}(m, \sigma^2) = m + \sigma\mathcal{N}(0, 1) . \tag{11}$$

The second theorem says that the Poisson random variable $\mathcal{P}(m)$ with mean m also has variance m, and when $m \gg 1$, it can be well approximated by a *normal* random variable with the same mean and variance:

$$\mathcal{P}(m) \approx \mathcal{N}(m, m) \quad \text{if } m \gg 1 . \tag{12}$$

So, with the system in state $\mathbf{x}$ at time t, suppose we can find a τ that is *small* enough that the Leap Condition is satisfied, i.e., for some $\varepsilon \ll 1$,

$$|\Delta_\tau a_j(\mathbf{x})/a_j(\mathbf{x})| \leqslant \varepsilon \quad \text{for all } j = 1, \dots, M , \tag{13}$$

and yet is also *large* enough that

$$a_j(\mathbf{x})\tau \gg 1 \quad \text{for all } j = 1, \dots, M . \tag{14}$$

It turns out that these two conditions will simultaneously be satisfied for most systems *if the reactant populations are sufficiently large*. Assuming these conditions are satisfied, then condition (13) permits us to invoke the tau-leaping formula (10). And condition (14) then allows us to invoke theorem (12) to approximate $\mathcal{P}_j(a_j(\mathbf{x})\tau)$ in (10) by a *normal* random variable with the same mean and variance:

$$\mathbf{X}(t + \tau) \doteq \mathbf{x} + \sum_{j=1}^{M} \mathcal{N}_j\left(a_j(\mathbf{x})\tau, a_j(\mathbf{x})\tau\right) \boldsymbol{\nu}_j .$$

Invoking theorem (11), this can also be written

$$\mathbf{X}(t + \tau) \doteq \mathbf{x} + \sum_{j=1}^{M} \left[a_j(\mathbf{x})\tau + \sqrt{a_j(\mathbf{x})\tau}\, \mathcal{N}_j(0, 1)\right] \boldsymbol{\nu}_j ,$$

which in turn can be rearranged to

$$\mathbf{X}(t+\tau) \doteq \mathbf{x} + \sum_{j=1}^{M} \boldsymbol{\nu}_j \, a_j \, (\mathbf{x}) \, \tau + \sum_{j=1}^{M} \boldsymbol{\nu}_j \, \sqrt{a_j \, (\mathbf{x})} \, \mathcal{N}_j(0,1) \, \sqrt{\tau} \ . \tag{15}$$

Equation (15) has two names: the *Langevin leaping formula* and the "standard form" *chemical Langevin equation* (CLE). When the latter name is used, the time increment τ is regarded as a "macroscopic dt". Equation (15) evidently expresses the increment in the state in the small time τ as the sum of two terms: the first term, which is non-random and proportional to τ, is called the *drift* term; the second term, which is random and proportional to $\sqrt{\tau}$, is called the *diffusion* term. Since τ is "small" then $\tau \ll \sqrt{\tau}$, so the drift term will always be very much smaller than the diffusion term. The reason we cannot just drop the drift term from (15) is that the diffusion term also contains as a factor a zero-mean normal random number, which will be as often positive as negative; therefore, over a *long series of successive τ-intervals*, the state change caused by the "tortoise-like" drift term will be comparable to the state change caused by the "hare-like" diffusion term.

It can be shown that the seemingly arbitrary mathematical structure of (15), which has the deterministic term proportional to τ and the stochastic term proportional to $\sqrt{\tau}$ and a zero-mean normal random variable, is the *only self-consistent form* that the increment of a "continuous, past-forgetting" process can have if the increment has a finite mean and variance [6,7]. All continuous Markov processes are governed by Langevin equations with those features. In most science and engineering applications of Langevin equations, the coefficient of τ in the drift term is inferred from a phenomenological macroscopic rate equation, and the coefficient of $\mathcal{N}_j(0,1)\sqrt{\tau}$ in the diffusion term is then chosen to secure some preconceived thermodynamic property. So it is noteworthy that the *chemical* Langevin equation (15) has *not* been obtained here using such *ad hoc* reasoning; instead, it has been logically deduced from the propensity function hypothesis (1) under conditions that allow specific approximations to be made. Of course, in circumstances where conditions (13) and (14) cannot both be met, the CLE will have no claim to legitimacy.

In the theory of continuous Markov processes, it can be shown that the CLE (15) can also be written in the form [6,7,8]

$$\frac{d\mathbf{X}(t)}{dt} \doteq \sum_{j=1}^{M} \boldsymbol{\nu}_j \, a_j \, (\mathbf{X}(t)) + \sum_{j=1}^{M} \boldsymbol{\nu}_j \, \sqrt{a_j \, (\mathbf{X}(t))} \, \Gamma_j(t) \ . \tag{16}$$

This equation is known as the "white noise form" CLE. The $\Gamma_j(t)$'s here are statistically independent *Gaussian white noise* processes that satisfy $\langle \Gamma_j(t) \, \Gamma_{j'}(t') \rangle = \delta_{jj'} \, \delta(t-t')$, where the first delta function is Kronecker's and the second is Dirac's. The CLE (16) has the canonical form of what mathematicians call a "stochastic differential equation."

Another result of continuous Markov process theory is that the time evolution of $\mathbf{X}(t)$ prescribed by (15) [or (16)] induces a time evolution in the probability density function $P(\mathbf{x}, t \mid \mathbf{x}_0, t_0)$ of $\mathbf{X}(t)$ that is described by the partial differential [7,8,9]

$$
\begin{aligned}
\frac{\partial P(\mathbf{x}, t \mid \mathbf{x}_0, t_0)}{\partial t} \doteq & -\sum_{i=1}^{N} \frac{\partial}{\partial x_i} \left[\left(\sum_{j=1}^{M} \nu_{ij} a_j(\mathbf{x}) \right) P(\mathbf{x}, t \mid \mathbf{x}_0, t_0) \right] \\
& + \frac{1}{2} \sum_{i=1}^{N} \frac{\partial^2}{\partial x_i^2} \left[\left(\sum_{j=1}^{M} \nu_{ij}^2 a_j(\mathbf{x}) \right) P(\mathbf{x}, t \mid \mathbf{x}_0, t_0) \right] \\
& + \sum_{\substack{i,i'=1 \\ (i<i')}}^{N} \frac{\partial^2}{\partial x_i \partial x_{i'}} \left[\left(\sum_{j=1}^{M} \nu_{ij} \nu_{i'j} a_j(\mathbf{x}) \right) P(\mathbf{x}, t \mid \mathbf{x}_0, t_0) \right] .
\end{aligned}
\tag{17}
$$

This equation is called the *chemical Fokker-Planck equation* (CFPE). The *jump* Markov process governed by the master equation (3) has now been *approximated* by the *continuous* Markov process that is governed by the Langevin equation (15) [or (16)] and the Fokker-Planck equation (17). The transition from a discrete (integer) valued process $\mathbf{X}(t)$ to a continuous (real) valued process $\mathbf{X}(t)$ happened when we approximated the integer-valued Poisson random variables in the tau-leaping formula (10) by the real-valued normal random variables in the Langevin leaping formula (15).

Equations (16) and (17) may appear to be complicated and intimidating, so it is worth emphasizing that the logical content of those two equations is completely captured by (15). And (15) in turn is just a straightforward approximation of the tau-leaping formula (10) that is justified whenever τ satisfies, in addition to the Leap Condition (13), the condition (14).

2.6   The Thermodynamic Limit and the Reaction Rate Equation

We are now in a position to derive the traditional deterministic RRE (5) *within the context of stochastic chemical kinetics*. In practice, most chemical systems contain huge numbers of molecules, and are thus well on their way to the so-called *thermodynamic limit*, in which the species populations X_i and the system volume Ω all approach infinity in such a way that the species concentrations X_i/Ω remain constant. The large molecular populations of such systems usually mean that their dynamical behavior is well described by the CLE (15) [or (16)]. An inspection of the CLE (16) shows that its deterministic drift term is *linear* in the propensity functions, while its stochastic diffusion term is proportional to the *square root* of the propensity functions. Now, it can be shown that in the thermodynamic limit, *all propensity functions grow in direct proportion to the size of the system*. For a unimolecular propensity function of the form $c_j x_i$ this is obvious, since c_j is independent of the size of the system. For a bimolecular propensity function of the form $c_j x_i x_{i'}$ this follows because c_j is inversely proportional to the system volume Ω, and that offsets one of the two population variables. Therefore, as the thermodynamic limit is approached, the drift term in the CLE (16) grows like the system size, while the diffusion term grows more slowly as the *square root* of the system size. This establishes the well known rule-of-thumb in chemical kinetics that *relative fluctuations in a macroscopic chemically reacting system typically scale as the inverse square root of the system size.* In the full thermodynamic limit, the diffusion term in the CLE (16) becomes vanishingly small compared to the drift term, and the CLE then reduces to the RRE (5).

2.7 The Broad View

The logical relationships among the various assumptions, approximations and equations of stochastic chemical kinetics are summarized in Fig. 2.

We conclude this overview of stochastic chemical kinetics by noting that there are many systems in biochemistry for which the potential number N of molecular species is much larger than the total number of reactant molecules in the system (e.g., proteins with many binding sites), and the potential number M of reaction channels is much larger than the number of reaction events that will be simulated. For such systems, it will not be feasible to enumerate all the potential species and reaction channels in the way we have tacitly assumed. There are two general ways of dealing with this difficulty.

One is to proceed along the lines of an adaptation of the SSA devised by Lok and Brent [10]: Species and reactions are introduced into the SSA program only when they become needed, and removed whenever they become not needed. This tactic will usually keep the numbers of active species and reactions at manageable levels, and can make possible the simulation of many systems that could otherwise not be simulated. This tactic also brings to light a practical advantage that the discrete, stochastic approach to chemical kinetics has over the traditional continuous, deterministic approach: When using the RRE, *all* potential species and reactions come into play after the very first timestep, and that can make for an unmanageably large number of ODEs in the circumstances just described.

A different way of dealing with the problem of astronomically large numbers of potential species and reactions is to move closer to a molecular dynamics approach, and track the position of every key molecule. Doing that would also avoid the sometimes unacceptable limitations imposed by the well-stirred assumption. But the cost of doing this is substantial, since one has to accurately simulate the physical motion of every important molecule in the system. That task can be simplified somewhat by assuming that those molecules move about by "hopping" from one "spatial lattice point" to another, but the physical fidelity of that approximation can be difficult to assess.

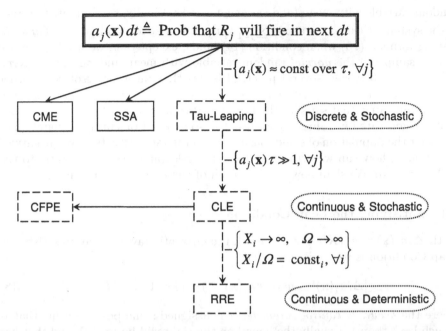

Fig. 2. *The logical structure of stochastic chemical kinetics.* Everything follows from the fundamental premise at the top via the laws of probability theory, but the premise itself must be grounded in physical theory. Inference routes that are exact are shown by solid arrows. Inference routes that are approximate are shown by dashed arrows, with the condition justifying the approximation indicated in braces immediately to the right. Solid outlined boxes are exact results: the *chemical master equation* (CME) and the *stochastic simulation algorithm* (SSA). Dashed outlined boxes are approximate results: the *tau-leaping formula*, the *chemical Langevin equation* (CLE), the *chemical Fokker-Planck equation* (CFPE), and the *reaction rate equation* (RRE). The condition justifying the arguments leading from the fundamental premise to tau-leaping is called the Leap Condition, and the condition justifying the arguments leading from the CLE to the RRE is called the thermodynamic limit. The top-to-bottom progression from discrete-stochastic to continuous-stochastic to continuous-deterministic is typically realized as the molecular populations of all the reactant species is made larger and larger.

3 Implementing Explicit Tau-Leaping and Langevin Leaping

Besides playing the theoretical role of a conceptual bridge between the CME/SSA and the RRE, tau-leaping also provides a faster way to stochastically simulate a chemical system than the SSA, albeit at the cost of some accuracy. Applying the tau-leaping formula (10) might seem at first sight to be straightforward: With the system in state $\mathbf{x}$ at time t, we first pick a value for τ that satisfies the Leap Condition (no propensity function will change appreciably in the next τ). Then, for each $j = 1, \ldots, M$, we generate a sample k_j of $\mathcal{P}\left(a_j(\mathbf{x})\tau\right)$, the Poisson random variable with mean (and variance) $a_j(\mathbf{x})\tau$. Finally, we compute the state of the system at time $t+\tau$ as $\mathbf{x}+\sum_{j=1}^{M} k_j \boldsymbol{\nu}_j$. Likewise for applying the *Langevin* leaping formula (15) when condition (14) holds, except then we would generate k_j as a sample of the *normal* random variable with mean and variance $a_j(\mathbf{x})\tau$.

There are, however, several practical issues that must be resolved in order to carry out this strategy efficiently: First, how can we estimate in advance the *largest* value of τ that satisfies the Leap Condition? Second, how can we ensure that the generated k_j values do not result in some reactions firing so many times in τ that the population of some consumed reactant species gets driven negative? And finally, how can we arrange it so that tau-leaping segues efficiently to the SSA as $\tau \to 0$? We shall now consider each of these questions in turn.

3.1 Satisfying the Leap Condition

With $\Delta_\tau a_j(\mathbf{x}) \equiv a_j\left(\mathbf{X}(t+\tau)\right) - a_j(\mathbf{x})$, the currently favored way to satisfy the Leap Condition is to choose τ so that

$$|\Delta_\tau a_j(\mathbf{x})| \leqslant \max\left(\varepsilon\, a_j(\mathbf{x}), c_j\right) \quad (j=1,\ldots,M) , \tag{18}$$

where the *accuracy control parameter* ε is assigned some positive value that is "much less" than 1. Usually the bound on the right will be $\varepsilon\, a_j(\mathbf{x})$, and that has the effect of bounding the absolute fractional change in each a_j by ε. Smaller values of ε will result in a better satisfaction of the Leap Condition. But since molecular populations cannot change by less than 1, the smallest possible non-zero change in any of the basic propensity functions in (2) is c_j; therefore, we take care in (18) not to insist that any propensity function should change by an amount less than that.

But $|\Delta_\tau a_j(\mathbf{x})|$ is a random variable, so its value cannot be predicted with certainty. How then should we go about imposing the bound (18)? Since simply rejecting values of τ that produce leaps that violate (18) runs the risk of biasing the generated random numbers, we propose to simply apply the bound to *both the mean and the standard deviation* of $|\Delta_\tau a_j(\mathbf{x})|$; those two quantities can be reasonably well estimated so long as τ is not too large. Of course, this tactic does not result in a "hard" bound, since it will produce values of $|\Delta_\tau a_j(\mathbf{x})|$ that occasionally violate (18). But that should not really pose a problem, since the value assigned to ε is largely arbitrary; i.e., there is no magic value of ε for which condition (18) will absolutely secure the mandate of the Leap Condition that no propensity function will change "noticeably" in time τ. The real goal here is to bound the changes in all the propensity functions in a reasonably *uniform* way, and the procedure just described should do that. We note in passing that the original presentation of the tau-leaping method in [11] deviated from the procedure just described in two ways: First, only the mean (and not the standard deviation) of $|\Delta_\tau a_j(\mathbf{x})|$ was bounded; this defect was corrected in [12]. Second, the bound on the right of (18) was taken to be $\varepsilon\, a_0(\mathbf{x})$, where $a_0(\mathbf{x})$ is the sum of all the propensity functions (7); this gave a too generous bound for small-valued propensity functions, and it was changed in [13].

3.2   A Tau-Selection Strategy

A direct imposition of the bound (18) leads to a procedure for computing the largest $\tau = \tau(\varepsilon, \mathbf{x})$ satisfying that bound whose computational complexity is of the order of the *square* of the number of reaction channels M. We describe here a faster procedure that is only of order M [13]. This faster procedure is "indirect" in that it actually bounds the *population* changes in time τ, $\Delta_\tau x_i \equiv X_i(t+\tau) - x_i$, according to

$$|\Delta_\tau x_i| \leqslant \max\left(\varepsilon_i x_i, 1\right) \quad \forall i \in I_{\mathrm{rs}} . \tag{19}$$

Here, I_{rs} denotes the set of indices of all *reactant species*; those are the only species whose population changes we need be concerned with, since a change in the population of a non-reactant species will not affect the value of any propensity function. The trick in using (19) instead of (18) is to choose the functions $\varepsilon_i \equiv \varepsilon_i(\varepsilon, x_i)$ in (19) in such a way that satisfaction of (18) will automatically follow. This can be done in the following way. Before the simulation begins, determine by inspecting the forms of all the reactions $R_1, \ldots, R_M$ the following quantity for all $i \in I_{\mathrm{rs}}$:

$$HOR(i) \equiv \underline{h}\text{ighest } \underline{o}\text{rder of } \underline{r}\text{eaction in which } S_i \text{ appears as a reactant} . \tag{20}$$

For example, if S_1 were a reactant only in the reaction $S_1 \to S_2$, we would have $HOR(1) = 1$. But if S_1 also appeared in the reaction $S_1 + S_3 \to S_4$, we would have $HOR(1) = 2$. With the values of $HOR(i)$ all ascertained, we then set the functions $\varepsilon_i(\varepsilon, x_i)$ for each reactant species S_i as follows:

$$\text{If } HOR(i) = 1, \text{ set } \varepsilon_i = \varepsilon . \tag{21a}$$

If $HOR(i) = 2$, set $\varepsilon_i = \varepsilon/2$, *except* if any reaction requires

$$\text{two } S_i \text{ reactant molecules set } \varepsilon_i = \varepsilon/\left(2 + (x_i - 1)^{-1}\right) . \tag{21b}$$

To see that this way of defining $\varepsilon_i(\varepsilon, x_i)$ results in condition (19) guaranteeing condition (18), we reason as follows: If $HOR(i) = 1$, we will have for one or more j's, $a_j = c_j x_i$. Then $\Delta_\tau a_j = c_j \Delta_\tau x_i$, so $\Delta_\tau a_j/a_j = \Delta_\tau x_i/x_i$. Therefore, if we bound $\Delta_\tau x_i/x_i$ by ε, we will also bound $\Delta_\tau a_j/a_j$ by ε. If $HOR(1) = HOR(2) = 2$, reflecting that for some j, $a_j = c_j x_1 x_2$, then we will have $\Delta_\tau a_j \doteq c_j x_2 \Delta_\tau x_1 + c_j x_1 \Delta_\tau x_2$, and thus $\Delta_\tau a_j/a_j \doteq \Delta_\tau x_1/x_1 + \Delta_\tau x_2/x_2$. Therefore, if we bound each of the two terms on the right side of this last equation by $\varepsilon/2$, then we will bound $\Delta_\tau a_j/a_j$ by ε. Finally, if $HOR(i) = 2$ because $a_j = \frac{1}{2} x_i(x_i - 1)$, then $\Delta_\tau a_j \doteq \frac{1}{2} c_j(x_i - 1)\Delta_\tau x_i + \frac{1}{2} c_j x_i \Delta_\tau x_i$; thus $\Delta_\tau a_j/a_j \doteq (\Delta_\tau x_i/x_i)\left(2 + (x_i - 1)^{-1}\right)$. So if we bound $\Delta_\tau x_i/x_i$ by $\varepsilon/\left(2 + (x_i - 1)^{-1}\right)$, then we will bound $\Delta_\tau a_j/a_j$ by ε. Similar formulas for ε_i can be derived for idealized tri-molecular reactions [13].

With the forms of the functions $\varepsilon_i(\varepsilon, x_i)$ determined, we must next figure out how to find the *largest* τ that satisfies condition (19). As mentioned earlier, we will take this to be the largest τ for which the *mean* and the *standard deviation* of $|\Delta_\tau x_i|$ both satisfy (19). Now, the basic tau-leaping formula (10) tells us that

$$\Delta_\tau x_i = \sum_j \nu_{ij} \mathcal{P}_j\left(a_j \tau\right) .$$

Since the random variables $\mathcal{P}_j(a_j\tau)$ in this formula are statistically independent with means $a_j\tau$ and variances $a_j\tau$, then by a well-known theorem in statistics the mean and variance of this linear combination can be computed as

$$\langle \Delta_\tau x_i \rangle = \sum_j \nu_{ij}(a_j\tau), \ \text{var}\{\Delta_\tau x_i\} = \sum_j \nu_{ij}^2(a_j\tau) \ .$$

The condition "$|\Delta_\tau x_i| \leqslant \max\{\varepsilon_i x_i, 1\}$" will therefore be satisfied, at least by our criterion, if and only if

$$\left| \sum_j \nu_{ij} a_j \tau \right| \leqslant \max\{\varepsilon_i x_i, 1\} \quad \text{and} \quad \sqrt{\sum_j \nu_{ij}^2 a_j \tau} \leqslant \max\{\varepsilon_i x_i, 1\} \ . \tag{22}$$

Solving these two inequalities for τ is straightforward, and gives

$$\tau = \min_{i \in I_{rs}} \left\{ \frac{\max\{\varepsilon_i x_i, 1\}}{\left| \sum_j \nu_{ij} a_j(\mathbf{x}) \right|}, \frac{\max\{\varepsilon_i x_i, 1\}^2}{\sum_j \nu_{ij}^2 a_j(\mathbf{x})} \right\} \ . \tag{23}$$

3.3 Avoiding Negative Populations

Now that we have a way to estimate the largest value of τ that satisfies the Leap Condition, we turn to the problem of how to avoid producing negative molecular populations. If the population of a consumed reactant species becomes small, it might get "overdrawn" in a leap and go negative. This was a common problem with the original formulation of tau-leaping [11], and it was widely attributed at the time to the fact that the Poisson random variable $\mathcal{P}(m)$ is unbounded. But in fact, the most common cause of negative population values with the original tau-leaping algorithm was its tactic of bounding $|\Delta_\tau a_j(\mathbf{x})|$ by $\varepsilon a_0(\mathbf{x})$. Doing that allowed small-valued propensity functions to change by too large an amount during τ, and some of them would occasionally go negative. Changing the bound from $\varepsilon a_0(\mathbf{x})$ to $\max(\varepsilon\, a_j(\mathbf{x}), c_j)$ greatly reduces the number of "negatives". (Taking a broader view, a change in the value $a_j(\mathbf{x})$ from positive to negative should *always* be regarded as a "noticeable" change, and therefore should not be allowed by any implementation of the Leap Condition.) But the improved bounding strategy we are now using does have a weakness: Since each propensity function change gets estimated *separately*, no attention is paid to the possibility that two or more different reactions with a *common* consumed reactant might, acting together, inadvertently overdraw that reactant.

To keep that from happening, we introduce a second tau-leaping control parameter (in addition to ε) which we call n_c [14]. Using this parameter, we classify any R_j as *critical* if it is within n_c firings of exhausting any of its reactants. For example, if $n_c = 10$, then the reaction $S_1 \to S_2$ would be classified as critical if $1 \leqslant x_1 \leqslant 10$. We call any reaction that does *not* meet this criterion *non-critical.* Our strategy will be to implement the tau-leaping procedure in such a way that, during any leap, there will *at most one* firing of a *critical* reaction. That will make it impossible for any *critical* reaction to overdraw any of its reactants.

And since the only reactions that are in danger of making such an overdraw will be critical, provided n_c is chosen large enough, then the negativity problem is essentially solved. In more practical terms, if a negative population *is* encountered during a tau-leaping simulation run, that should be taken as a sign that the simulation run should be started over with either a smaller value for ε or a larger value for n_c.

To ensure that there will be no more than one critical reaction occurring during a leap, we proceed as follows. For the *non-critical* reactions R_j, whose indices j make up (by definition) the set J_{ncr}, we compute using (23) the largest leap time τ' that is consistent with the Leap Condition (except if there are *no* non-critical reactions we set $\tau' = \infty$):

$$\tau' = \min_{i \in I_{rs}} \left\{ \frac{\max\{\varepsilon_i x_i, 1\}}{\left| \sum_{j \in J_{ncr}} \nu_{ij}\, a_j(\mathbf{x}) \right|}, \frac{\max\{\varepsilon_i x_i, 1\}^2}{\sum_{j \in J_{ncr}} \nu_{ij}^2\, a_j(\mathbf{x})} \right\} . \tag{24}$$

The restriction in (24) of the j-sums to the non-critical reactions makes τ' the maximum leap time *if no critical reaction fires*. Next we focus on the *critical* reactions R_j, whose indices j make up (by definition) the set J_{cr}. For leaps no larger than τ', the propensity functions of the critical reactions will not be much affected by any firings of the non-critical reactions. So to a good approximation, we can use the SSA to determine the time τ'' when the next *critical* reaction would fire, and the index j_c of that reaction (except if there are *no* critical reactions we set $\tau'' = \infty$). To do this, we first compute

$$a_{0c}(\mathbf{x}) \equiv \sum_{j \in J_{cr}} a_j(\mathbf{x}) . \tag{25}$$

Then we draw two unit-interval uniform random number r_1 and r_2 and compute

$$\tau'' = \frac{1}{a_{0c}(\mathbf{x})} \ln\left(\frac{1}{r_1}\right) , \tag{26}$$

$$j_c = \text{smallest integer satisfying} \sum_{j \in J_{cr}}^{j_c} a_{j'}(\mathbf{x}) \geqslant r_2 a_{0c}(\mathbf{x}) . \tag{27}$$

Having computed τ' and τ'', we now take the *actual* leap time τ to be the *smaller* of the two. The state at time $t + \tau$ is then computed, at least tentatively, from the tau-leaping formula (10), but applied to the *non-critical* reactions only; i.e.,

$$\mathbf{X}(t + \tau) \doteq \mathbf{x} + \sum_{j \in J_{ncr}} \mathcal{P}_j\left(a_j(\mathbf{x})\tau\right) \boldsymbol{\nu}_j . \tag{28}$$

If $\tau = \tau' < \tau''$, then no critical reactions will have fired during the leap, so (28) accurately estimates the state change in time τ. But if $\tau = \tau'' \leqslant \tau'$, then the critical reaction with index j_c in (27) will have fired *once* (but no *other* critical reaction will have fired), so we include its effect simply by making the adjustment

$$\mathbf{X}(t + \tau) \leftarrow \mathbf{X}(t + \tau) + \boldsymbol{\nu}_{j_c} . \tag{29}$$

3.4   The Tau-Leaping Procedure

In summary then, the *explicit tau-leaping simulation algorithm* goes as follows:

1. Choose values for ε and n_c. For each *reactant* species S_i, determine the functions $\varepsilon_i(\varepsilon, x_i)$ according to the rules (21). Initialize $t \leftarrow 0$ and $\mathbf{x} \leftarrow \mathbf{x}_0$.
2. In state $\mathbf{x}$ at time t, evaluate all the $a_j(\mathbf{x})$. Classify as *critical* any R_j for which $a_j(\mathbf{x}) > 0$ and which is within n_c firings of exhausting any reactant. Classify all other R_j *non-critical*.
3. Compute τ' using (24) (except if there are no non-critical reactions take $\tau' = \infty$). This is the maximum leap time allowed by the Leap Condition for the *non-critical* reactions.
4. Compute τ'' using (26) (except if there are no critical reactions take $\tau'' = \infty$). This is the time to the next *critical* reaction.
5. Take $\tau = \min(\tau', \tau'')$. Compute $\mathbf{X}(t+\tau)$ using (28). This gives the new state of the system if no critical reaction fired during the leap.
6. If $\tau'' \leqslant \tau'$, compute j_c from (27) and replace $\mathbf{X}(t+\tau) \leftarrow \mathbf{X}(t+\tau) + \boldsymbol{\nu}_{j_c}$.
7. Update $\mathbf{x} \leftarrow \mathbf{X}(t+\tau)$ and $t \leftarrow t+\tau$. Return to Step 2, or else stop.

In using this algorithm, a periodic check should be made to see if any negative populations have been generated. If negative populations are found, this should be taken as a sign that *either ε has been set too large or n_c has been set too small*. The simulation should then be aborted and started over with those control parameters adjusted accordingly. Of course, one should not assume that the *absence* of negative populations assures that the current value of the control parameters are okay. Judgment is needed in setting those parameters.

3.5   An Example

Figures 3 and 4 compare simulations of a model reaction set made using the SSA and the explicit tau-leaping algorithm. The tau-leaping run in Fig. 4 evidently approximates the exact SSA run in Fig. 3 extremely well, yet it ran about ten times faster. See the figure captions for details.

3.6   Segueing to the SSA, Langevin Leaping, and the RRE

An examination of the above tau-leaping algorithm will reveal that if *all* reactions have been classified as *critical*, which will happen if either n_c is taken very large or if many reactant populations have become very small, then *the algorithm reduces to the SSA*. This is very convenient. For, although the bare tau-leaping formula (10) does become exact, and therefore equivalent to the SSA, in the limit $\tau \to 0$, it also becomes *infinitely inefficient* in that limit. That's because with τ so small that $a_j(\mathbf{x})\tau \ll 1$ for all j, the M Poisson random numbers in (10) will usually all be zero, meaning that no reactions at all fire during the leap. Only occasionally will some reaction fire once, but rarely will more than one firing occur. Clearly it would be more efficient in that circumstance to use the SSA, which is exact and always gives one reaction per step. Earlier versions of

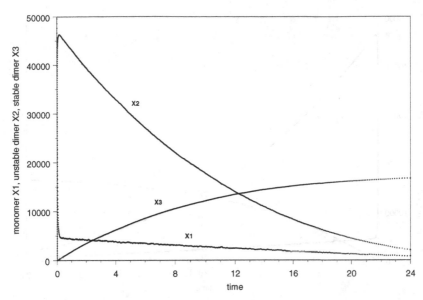

Fig. 3. An exact *SSA* simulation of the reaction set $S_1 \xrightarrow{c_1} \emptyset$, $2\,S_1 \underset{c_3}{\overset{c_2}{\rightleftharpoons}} S_2$, and $S_2 \xrightarrow{c_4} S_3$. The parameter values are $c_1 = 1$, $c_2 = 0.002$, $c_3 = 0.5$ and $c_4 = 0.04$, and the $t = 0$ populations are $X_1 = 100,000$ and $X_2 = X_3 = 0$. We can think of S_1 as a "decaying monomer", S_2 as an "unstable dimer", and S_3 as a "stable dimer". An initial fast transient due to reaction R_2 brings X_1 down to around 5000, and X_2 up to about 47,000. Thereafter the populations evolve more slowly, although with evident fluctuations. The populations were plotted out here after every 500 reaction events. There were a total of 517,067 reactions simulated by the time all the S_1 and S_2 molecules were gone.

the tau-leaping algorithm explicitly checked to make sure that τ is comfortably larger than $1/a_0(\mathbf{x})$, the average size of τ produced by the SSA formula (9a), and if that were not so tau-leaping would revert to the SSA. But this precaution appears to be unnecessary when using the tau-leaping algorithm described above.

Also important is the limit at the other extreme, where tau-leaping segues first to the CLE and then to the RRE. These transitions practically always occur as the molecular populations of the reactant species grow larger. All reaction channels then become non-critical, and the means $a_j(\mathbf{x})\,\tau$ of the Poisson random variables in (28), which give the expected number of firings of each R_j, become large compared to 1. Those Poisson random variables can then be well approximated by *normal* random variables with the same means and variances, and the tau-leaping formula becomes the Langevin leaping formula. For even larger populations the standard deviations of the normal random variables become negligibly small compared to their means, so they can be approximated by *sure* numbers, which results in the RRE. But *all of these transitions will*

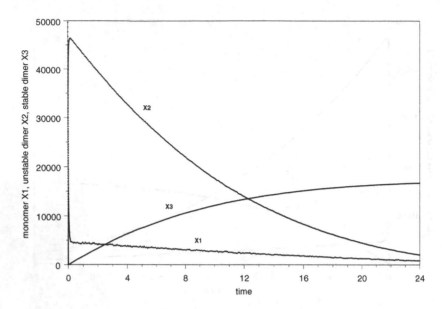

Fig. 4. An approximate *explicit tau-leaping* simulation run of the same reaction set as in Fig. 3. The *control parameters* used here were $\varepsilon = 0.04$ and $n_c = 10$. The species populations here were plotted after every leap, and 905 leaps in all were taken, in contrast to the over half million reaction steps that were taken in Fig. 3. This tau-leaping run was over 10 times faster than the SSA run. The initial transient evidently caused no problems for the method. The only noticeable difference from the SSA plot is that the slowly decreasing X_1 trajectory is slightly noisier here than in the SSA plot. This is a manifestation of *stiffness* (see Sec. 4). The problem is not serious for these parameter values, but it could easily become serious for other parameter values.

happen smoothly and automatically if one writes the Poisson random number generator appropriately: When a call is received by the generator for a Poisson random number with mean and variance $a_j(\mathbf{x})\,\tau$, if that number is "very large" (perhaps $> 10^3$) the generator should return a *normal* random number with that mean and variance, and if $a_j(\mathbf{x})\,\tau$ is "very very large" (perhaps $> 10^8$) the generator should return the *sure* number $a_j(\mathbf{x})\,\tau$. If the Poisson random number generator is written in this way, then if it should happen that *all* the $a_j(\mathbf{x})\,\tau$ are "very large" we will automatically be doing Langevin leaping, and if *all* the $a_j(\mathbf{x})\,\tau$ are "very very large" we will automatically be using the Euler method for numerically solving the RRE (5). But there is no need for us to be aware of which (if any) of those regimes we happen to be in at any moment, nor to have any concern if the firing numbers of some reactions are *Poisson* while others are *normal* while still others are *sure*.

The explicit tau-leaping algorithm as implemented here evidently includes the exact-but-slow SSA at one extreme, and the fast-but-approximate RRE at the other extreme, so the algorithm is actually a fairly robust simulation procedure for stochastic chemical kinetics. Since the SSA is typically required for small molecular populations, while the RRE is usually acceptable only for very large molecular populations, then the explicit tau-leaping algorithm can fairly be said to be "multiscale" with respect to *species populations*.

But the explicit tau-leaping algorithm does have a significant limitation: The Leap Condition will always restrict the size of τ to the time scale of the *fastest* reactions in the system. Therefore, for systems with a very wide range of time scales, for example *stiff* systems, explicit tau-leaping will seem unduly slow. There are two approaches to this problem, both of which are still under active development. One is *implicit tau-leaping* [15,16], which is a stochastic adaptation of the implicit Euler method for ODEs. The other is the *slow-scale SSA*, which is a stochastic adaptation of the rapid (or partial) equilibrium method for ODEs. We shall describe the slow-scale SSA in the next section.

4   The Slow-Scale SSA

Many chemically reacting systems of practical interest, especially cellular systems, consist of a mixture of "fast" reactions that occur very frequently and "slow" reactions that occur only rarely. Perhaps the simplest example of that kind of system is the reaction set

$$S_1 \underset{c_2}{\overset{c_1}{\rightleftharpoons}} S_2 \overset{c_3}{\longrightarrow} S_3 \tag{30}$$

when the rate constants are such that reactions R_1 and R_2 are "fast" and reaction R_3 is "slow" in the sense just defined. In simulating such systems, the SSA will spend most of its time simulating the fast reactions. If those fast reactions are in some sense not as important as the slow ones, this will be an inefficient allocation of computational resources. In the case of reactions (30) for instance, the fact that R_1 and R_2 undo each other tends to make those two reactions uninteresting, whereas the creation of an S_3 molecule might well be an event of some significance. So the question arises, can the simulation of systems like this be made more efficient?

4.1   Stiffness

In the deterministic world of ODEs, the problem we have just described is known as the problem of "dynamical stiffness". A set of ODEs that evolve on a wide range of time scales, with the fastest mode being stable, is said to be *stiff*. Much attention has been devoted to stiff ODEs over the past decades because they arise in many contexts, and several effective ways of dealing with stiff ODEs have been devised [17].

It turns out that stiffness is just as much a problem in a stochastic context [15], but the situation there is less well understood. Among the complicating issues: Do "fast" and "slow" apply to *reactions*, or to *species*, or to both? Exactly how are these terms to be defined operationally? Since the fast and slow components of a system are typically interconnected (if they aren't then there is no problem), can those components be teased apart for analysis without seriously distorting their combined effects?

We describe here one way of dealing with stiff stochastic chemical systems called the *slow-scale stochastic simulation algorithm* (ssSSA) [18]. The ssSSA consists of, first, a procedure for identifying fast and slow reactions and species in circumstances where the fast reactions are relatively unimportant; and second, an approximate procedure derived from the fundamental premise (1) for skipping over the fast reactions and simulating only the slow ones. All this is accomplished through a series of carefully prescribed steps, which we shall now describe. For more details and references to original papers and related works, see [18,19,20,3].

4.2   Fast and Slow Reactions, Fast and Slow Species

The first step in the ssSSA is to make a provisional partitioning of the *reactions* into fast and slow subsets, $\{R_1^f, \ldots, R_{M_f}^f\}$ and $\{R_1^s, \ldots, R_{M_s}^s\}$. The criterion for making this partitioning is somewhat vague: The propensity function $a_j^f(\mathbf{x})$ of each fast reaction R_j^f should *usually* be very much larger than the propensity function $a_j^s(\mathbf{x})$ of any slow reaction R_j^s. The qualifier "usually" is needed because the value of a propensity function depends on the current state $\mathbf{x}$, so a propensity function can be very large in some regions of state space and very small in other regions. It is therefore impossible to know whether a propensity function will be large or small "usually" unless we already have a good idea of how the system behaves. But the partitioning we adopt here is only *provisional*. It will later be subjected to a test that will determine whether or not it is acceptable.

The second step is to partition the *species* into fast and slow subsets. The criterion for doing this is unambiguous: Any species whose population *gets changed* by at least one fast reaction is classified as fast, and all other species are classified as slow. This leads to a partitioning of the state vector into fast and slow components: $\mathbf{X}(t) = (\mathbf{X}^f(t), \mathbf{X}^s(t))$, where $\mathbf{X}^f(t) = (X_1^f(t), \ldots, X_{N_f}^f(t))$ and $\mathbf{X}^s(t) = (X_1^s(t), \ldots, X_{N_s}^s(t))$.

Some points to note: (a) With both the species and the reactions now grouped into fast and slow subsets and re-indexed accordingly, the state change vector components ν_{ij} acquire superscripts, $\nu_{ij}^{\sigma\rho}$, where $\sigma = (f,s)$ tells whether index i is for a fast or slow *species*, and $\rho = (f,s)$ tells whether index j is for a fast or slow *reaction*. (b) A slow species cannot get changed by a fast reaction ($\nu_{ij}^{sf} \equiv 0$), but a fast species can get changed by a slow reaction. (c) All propensity functions can depend on *both* fast and slow species populations; i.e., in general $a_j^f(\mathbf{x}) = a_j^f(\mathbf{x}^f, \mathbf{x}^s)$ and $a_j^s(\mathbf{x}) = a_j^s(\mathbf{x}^f, \mathbf{x}^s)$. (d) The population of a fast species need not be large. (e) It is possible for there to be no slow species, in which case $\mathbf{x}^f = \mathbf{x}$; however, there must always be at least one slow reaction.

4.3   The Virtual Fast Process

The third step in the ssSSA is to define the *virtual fast process*, $\hat{\mathbf{X}}^f(t)$, as the fast species populations evolving under *only* the fast reactions. That is, $\hat{\mathbf{X}}^f(t)$ is $\mathbf{X}^f(t)$

with all the slow reactions switched off. $\hat{\mathbf{X}}^f(t)$ is a fictitious process, in contrast to the real fast process $\mathbf{X}^f(t)$ which consists of the same fast variables evolving under *all* the reactions. The master equation for $\mathbf{X}^f(t)$ will be non-Markovian, and no easier to solve than the (Markovian) master equation for the full process $\mathbf{X}(t)$. But the master equation for $\hat{\mathbf{X}}^f(t)$ will be Markovian, and usually much simpler than that for $\mathbf{X}(t)$; it determines the function $\hat{P}(\mathbf{x}^f, t \mid \mathbf{x}_0, t_0)$, the probability that $\hat{\mathbf{X}}^f(t) = \mathbf{x}^f$ given that $\mathbf{X}(t_0) = \mathbf{x}_0$. We will not actually need to compute $\hat{P}(\mathbf{x}^f, t \mid \mathbf{x}_0, t_0)$ for arbitrary t. But we will need to estimate some properties of

$$\lim_{t \to \infty} \hat{P}(\mathbf{x}^f, t \mid \mathbf{x}_0, t_0) \equiv \hat{P}(\mathbf{x}^f, \infty \mid \mathbf{x}_0) \ . \tag{31}$$

This function, which defines the *asymptotic virtual fast process* $\hat{\mathbf{X}}^f(\infty)$, can in principle be found by solving the (purely algebraic) *stationary* master equation for $\hat{\mathbf{X}}^f(t)$ [cf. (3)]:

$$0 = \sum_{j=1}^{M_f} \left\{ a_j^f(\mathbf{x}^f - \boldsymbol{\nu}_j^f, \mathbf{x}_0^s) \hat{P}(\mathbf{x}^f - \boldsymbol{\nu}_j^f, \infty \mid \mathbf{x}_0) - a_j^f(\mathbf{x}^f, \mathbf{x}_0^s) \hat{P}(\mathbf{x}^f, \infty \mid \mathbf{x}_0) \right\} \ . \tag{32}$$

4.4 The Stochastic Stiffness Conditions

The fourth step in the ssSSA is to verify that the partitioning of the reactions that was done in the first step is acceptable. The partitioning is deemed acceptable if and only if two conditions are satisfied: First, $\hat{\mathbf{X}}^f(t)$ must be "stable", in that $\hat{\mathbf{X}}^f(t \to \infty)$ must *exist*, or equivalently, the function (31) must exist. Second, $\hat{\mathbf{X}}^f(t)$ must approximately attain its limiting form $\hat{\mathbf{X}}^f(\infty)$ *in a time that is small compared to the expected time to the next slow reaction*. In effect, these two conditions are simply demanding that the full process $\mathbf{X}(t)$ be *stiff*: It should have *well-separated* fast and slow modes, and the *fast* mode should be *stable*. If these conditions are not satisfied, and cannot be satisfied by a different choice of fast and slow reactions in the first step, then we should conclude that the fast reactions are *not* less important than the slow ones, and therefore should not be skipped over. Verifying the satisfaction of these two stochastic stiffness conditions can be a challenging task, but it has been successfully done for several simple systems, as we shall see below.

4.5 The Slow Scale Approximation Lemma

The foregoing four steps basically set the stage for the following lemma, which gives the main enabling result for the ssSSA [18]:

   Slow Scale Approximation Lemma. With $\mathbf{X}(t) = (\mathbf{x}^f, \mathbf{x}^s)$, let Δ_s be a time increment that is *large* compared to the time it takes for $\hat{\mathbf{X}}^f(t) \to \hat{\mathbf{X}}^f(\infty)$, yet *small* compared to the expected time to the *next slow* reaction. (The existence of such a Δ_s is guaranteed by the satisfaction of the stochastic stiffness conditions in the fourth step.) Then the probability that the slow reaction R_j^s will fire in $[t, t + \Delta_s)$ is *approximately* $\bar{a}_j^s(\mathbf{x}^f, \mathbf{x}^s) \times \Delta_s$, where

$$\bar{a}_j^s(\mathbf{x}^f, \mathbf{x}^s) = \left\langle a_j^s\left(\hat{\mathbf{X}}^f(\infty), \mathbf{x}^s\right)\right\rangle \equiv \sum_{\mathbf{y}^f} \hat{P}(\mathbf{y}^f, \infty \mid \mathbf{x}^f, \mathbf{x}^s)\, a_j^s(\mathbf{y}^f, \mathbf{x}^s) . \tag{33}$$

Before we prove this lemma, let us make clear its significance. Recall that for a "true" infinitesimal dt, $a_j^s(\mathbf{x}^f, \mathbf{x}^s) \times dt$ gives, by definition, the probability that reaction R_j^s will fire in the next dt. Now, the time increment Δ_s, although large on the "fast" timescale, is *very small* on the "slow" timescale; thus, on the time scale of the slow reactions, Δ_s can be regarded as an "infinitesimal". According to the lemma, if we multiply Δ_s by the function $\bar{a}_j^s(\mathbf{x}^f, \mathbf{x}^s)$ that is defined in (33), we get the probability that R_j^s will fire in the next Δ_s. Therefore, $\bar{a}_j^s(\mathbf{x}^f, \mathbf{x}^s)$ has the *defining attribute* of the propensity function for R_j^s *on the timescale of the slow reactions*. So, if we are content to simulate the system on the timescale of the slow reactions, we can forget about the fast reactions and just simulate the slow ones, provided of course we use the propensity functions $\bar{a}_j^s(\mathbf{x}^f, \mathbf{x}^s)$. The trick, of course, is to evaluate those functions according to (33), either exactly or to an acceptable approximation. Before we consider that matter, though, let us prove the slow scale approximation lemma. The proof turns out to be remarkably straightforward:

Proof of lemma: Let $[t', t' + dt')$ be a "true" infinitesimal subinterval of the "macroscopic" infinitesimal time interval $[t, t + \Delta_s)$. The probability that R_j^s will fire in $[t', t' + dt')$ is, by definition,

$$a_j^s\left(\mathbf{X}^f(t'), \mathbf{X}^s(t')\right) dt' \approx a_j^s\left(\hat{\mathbf{X}}^f(t'), \mathbf{x}^s\right) dt' . \tag{34}$$

The last step follows because it is very unlikely that any *slow* reaction will fire anywhere in the full interval $[t, t + \Delta_s)$, so $\mathbf{X}^f(t')$ can be well approximated there by $\hat{\mathbf{X}}^f(t')$, and $\mathbf{X}^s(t')$ can be well approximated by $\mathbf{x}^s$. Since there is a negligibly small probability of more than one R_j^s reaction firing in $[t, t + \Delta_s)$, we can invoke the addition law of probability for mutually exclusive events to compute

$$\text{Prob}\left\{R_j^s \text{ will fire in } [t, t + \Delta_s)\right\} \approx \int_t^{t+\Delta_s} a_j^s\left(\hat{\mathbf{X}}^f(t'), \mathbf{x}^s\right) dt' , \tag{35a}$$

$$\approx \left\{\frac{1}{\Delta_s} \int_t^{t+\Delta_s} a_j^s\left(\hat{\mathbf{X}}^f(t'), \mathbf{x}^s\right) dt'\right\} \Delta_s , \tag{35b}$$

$$\approx \left\{\sum_{\mathbf{y}^f} \hat{P}(\mathbf{y}^f, \infty \mid \mathbf{x}^f, \mathbf{x}^s)\, a_j^s(\mathbf{y}^f, \mathbf{x}^s)\right\} \Delta_s . \tag{35c}$$

The quantity in braces in (35b) is, since Δ_s is very large on the time scale of the *fast* reactions, the *temporal average* of $a_j^s\left(\hat{\mathbf{X}}^f(t'), \mathbf{x}^s\right)$. In proceeding to (35c), we are choosing to evaluate that temporal average as the *ensemble average*,

$\left\langle a_j^s \left(\hat{\mathbf{X}}^f(\infty), \mathbf{x}^s \right) \right\rangle$. This is a tactic that is ubiquitously employed in statistical physics. It can be justified for any stable jump stochastic process $Y(t)$ by the following chain of reasoning: Letting $t_k = (T/K)k$ for $k = 0, 1, \ldots, K$,

$$\lim_{T \to \infty} \frac{1}{T} \int_0^T Y(t)dt = \lim_{T \to \infty} \frac{1}{T} \lim_{K \to \infty} \sum_{k=0}^{K-1} Y(t_k)(t_{k+1} - t_k)$$

$$= \lim_{T,K \to \infty} \frac{1}{T} \sum_{k=0}^{K-1} Y(t_k) \left(\frac{T}{K} \right) = \lim_{K \to \infty} \frac{1}{K} \sum_{k=1}^{K} Y(\infty)_k = \sum_y P(y, \infty) y , \quad (36)$$

where $Y(\infty)_k$ is a sample value of $Y(\infty)$, and $P(y, \infty) = \mathrm{Prob}\{Y(\infty) = y\}$. With (35c), the lemma is established.

4.6 Strategy of the ssSSA

The strategy of the ssSSA is to simulate *only the slow reactions* with the SSA, but using their slow-scale propensity functions (33). If there is a comfortable separation between the fast and slow timescales, the Slow Scale Approximation Lemma tells us that this procedure should give an accurate picture of how the *slow* species populations evolve.

For the *fast* species, the situation is a little convoluted. The fast species populations are governed mainly by the fast reactions. But when we use the ssSSA, we will no longer be simulating the fast reactions; therefore, we will no longer have the ability to track the "true" populations of the fast species. This loss of precise information about the populations of the fast species is the price we must inevitably pay for skipping over the fast reactions. But there is a way we can simulate how the fast species populations would appear on the timescale of the slow reactions: After the occurrence of each slow reaction, if we simply *wait* for a time that is infinitesimally small on the timescale of the slow reactions, yet large enough for the relaxation $\hat{\mathbf{X}}^f(t) \to \hat{\mathbf{X}}^f(\infty)$ to take place, then measuring the populations of the fast species would be equivalent to drawing a *random sample* $\mathbf{y}^f$ from the probability function $\hat{P}(\mathbf{y}^f, \infty \mid \mathbf{x}^f, \mathbf{x}^s)$. So this is what the ssSSA does for the fast variables: After effecting each slow reaction, the ssSSA in effect "pauses imperceptibly" to allow the fast species populations to "relax", and then it simulates their values by Monte Carlo sampling the random variable $\hat{\mathbf{X}}^f(\infty)$.

It is important to understand, though, that any *errors* we might make in generating values for the fast species populations will *not* affect the subsequent accuracy of the ssSSA simulation. That's because we never make use of those generated values to evaluate any propensity functions. More specifically, we don't need to know $\mathbf{x}^f$ to evaluate the *fast* reaction propensity functions $a_j^f(\mathbf{x}^f, \mathbf{x}^s)$, because we do not simulate the fast reactions. And we don't need to know $\mathbf{x}^f$ to evaluate the propensity functions of any of the *slow* reactions, because (as will be seen more clearly the examples that follow) their propensity functions $\bar{a}_j^s(\mathbf{x}^f, \mathbf{x}^s)$ in (33) depend only on properties of $\mathbf{x}^f$ that are *conserved* by the fast reactions. The only reason for generating "relaxed" values of the fast variables is to indicate how those populations would appear if they were plotted on the timescale of the slow reactions. If such a visualization of the fast variables is not needed – i.e., if all we are interested in are the populations of the slow species – then the step of generating relaxed values for the fast species populations can be omitted without any impairment to the simulation.

The key steps in implementing the ssSSA are therefore as follows:

(i) In state $(\mathbf{x}^f, \mathbf{x}^s)$ at time t, evaluate $\bar{a}_j^s(\mathbf{x}^f, \mathbf{x}^s) = \left\langle a_j^s\left(\hat{\mathbf{X}}^f(\infty), \mathbf{x}^s\right)\right\rangle$ according to (33) for each *slow* reaction R_j^s. This is the hard part. If each slow reaction has no more than one fast reactant species molecule, then this formula simplifies to $\bar{a}_j^s(\mathbf{x}^f, \mathbf{x}^s) = a_j^s\left(\left\langle \hat{\mathbf{X}}^f(\infty)\right\rangle, \mathbf{x}^s\right)$, and all we will need is the first moment of $\hat{\mathbf{X}}^f(\infty)$. But if any slow reaction involves two fast reactant species molecules, we will also need the second moment of $\hat{\mathbf{X}}^f(\infty)$. Approximations may have to be made to compute these moments. For instance, in many cases it has been found acceptable to approximate the first moment $\left\langle \hat{\mathbf{X}}^f(\infty)\right\rangle$ by the stationary solution of the RRE for the virtual fast process.

(ii) Compute the time τ to the next *slow* reaction, and the index j of that reaction, by applying the SSA procedure in (9) to the slow reactions only, using their effective propensity functions $\bar{a}_j^s(\mathbf{x}^f, \mathbf{x}^s)$.

(iii) Implement the next slow reaction by updating $t \leftarrow t + \tau$ and $\mathbf{x} \leftarrow \mathbf{x} + \boldsymbol{\nu}_j^s$.

(iv) Finally, "relax" the *fast* variables by replacing $\mathbf{x}^f$ with a sample $\mathbf{y}^f$ of the probability function $\hat{P}(\mathbf{y}^f, \infty \mid \mathbf{x}^f, \mathbf{x}^s)$. Approximations may be required to do this. But note that any approximation errors in *this* step will have *no effect* on the accuracy of the simulation. If $\hat{P}(\mathbf{y}^f, \infty \mid \mathbf{x}^f, \mathbf{x}^s)$ cannot be computed exactly, it will sometimes be acceptable to approximate it as a normal random variable; that would require estimating only the first and second moments of $\hat{\mathbf{X}}^f(\infty)$.

4.7   An Example

For an illustrative example, let us apply the ssSSA to the reaction set (30). We start by (provisionally) taking R_1 and R_2 to be fast reactions and R_3 a slow reaction. Since species S_1 and S_2 *get changed* by fast reactions, then they will be fast species, whereas S_3, which does not get changed by any fast reaction, will be a slow species. The fast process is thus $\mathbf{X}^f(t) = (X_1(t), X_2(t))$, and the slow process is $\mathbf{X}^s(t) = X_3(t)$. The *virtual* fast process is therefore $\hat{\mathbf{X}}^f(t) = \left(\hat{X}_1(t), \hat{X}_2(t)\right)$, with $\hat{X}_1(t)$ and $\hat{X}_2(t)$ evolving *only* through the fast reactions, $S_1 \underset{c_2}{\overset{c_1}{\rightleftharpoons}} S_2$. For these two reactions, we evidently have the *conservation relation* $\hat{X}_1(t) + \hat{X}_2(t) = x_{12}$. It implies that the virtual fast process $\hat{\mathbf{X}}^f(t)$ has only one independent variable. We can choose that independent variable to be $\hat{X}_2(t)$, and then compute $\hat{X}_1(t)$ as $x_{12} - \hat{X}_2(t)$. The propensity functions for the fast reactions relative to $\hat{X}_2(t)$ take the forms $a_1(x_2) = c_1(x_{12} - x_2)$ and $a_2(x_2) = c_2 x_2$. The associated state-change vectors are $\nu_1 = +1$ and $\nu_2 = -1$. The steady-state or "equilibrium" master equation (32), which determines the probability function for $\hat{X}_2(\infty)$, reads

$$0 = \sum_{j=1}^{2} \left\{ a_j(x_2 - \nu_j)\hat{P}_2(x_2 - \nu_j, \infty \,|\, x_{12}) - a_j(x_2)\hat{P}_2(x_2, \infty \,|\, x_{12}) \right\} . \qquad (37)$$

After substituting into this equation the aforementioned propensity functions and state change vectors, it is not hard to show that this equation implies

$$c_2(x_2 + 1)\hat{P}_2(x_2 + 1, \infty \,|\, x_{12}) = c_1(x_{12} - x_2)\hat{P}_2(x_2, \infty \,|\, x_{12}), \quad \forall x_2 . \qquad (38)$$

The physical sense of this "detailed balance" relation can be seen by multiplying it through by dt: the asymptotic probability of having $x_2 + 1$ S_2 molecules and then losing one of them in the next dt is equal to the asymptotic probability of having x_2 S_2 molecules and then gaining a new one in the next dt. Equation (38) implies the following *recursion relation* for the function $\hat{P}_2(x_2, \infty \,|\, x_{12})$:

$$\hat{P}_2(x_2 + 1, \infty \,|\, x_{12}) = \frac{c_1(x_{12} - x_2)}{c_2(x_2 + 1)} \hat{P}_2(x_2, \infty \,|\, x_{12}), \quad x_2 = 0, \ldots, x_{12} - 1 . \qquad (39)$$

Iterating this recursion relation and then normalizing the result gives

$$\hat{P}_2(x_2, \infty \,|\, x_{12}) = \frac{x_{12}!}{x_2!(x_{12} - x_2)!} \left(\frac{c_1}{c_1 + c_2}\right)^{x_2} \left(\frac{c_2}{c_1 + c_2}\right)^{x_{12} - x_2} , \qquad (40)$$

as can easily be verified by direct substitution into the recursion relation (39). This probability function has the canonical form of the *binomial* distribution; more specifically, it implies that $\hat{X}_2(\infty)$ is the binomial random variable with parameters $c_1/(c_1 + c_2)$ and x_{12}. Thus, the asymptotic virtual fast process $\hat{\mathbf{X}}^{\mathrm{f}}(\infty)$ is exactly known for this problem:

$$\hat{X}_2(\infty) = \mathcal{B}\left(\frac{c_1}{c_1 + c_2}, x_{12}\right), \quad \hat{X}_1(\infty) = x_{12} - \hat{X}_2(\infty) . \qquad (41)$$

Since $\langle \mathcal{B}(p, N) \rangle = pN$, then the slow-scale propensity function for reaction R_3 is

$$\bar{a}_3(\mathbf{x}) \equiv c_3 \left\langle \hat{X}_2(\infty) \right\rangle = \frac{c_3 c_1 x_{12}}{c_1 + c_2} . \qquad (42)$$

Now we must determine under what conditions our initial *provisional* choice of fast and slow reactions is acceptable. More specifically, we must determine under what conditions $\hat{X}_2(t)$ will relax to $\hat{X}_2(\infty)$ in a time that is small compared to the expected time to the next slow (R_3) reaction. Only if this is so will the Slow Scale Approximation Lemma apply. The relaxation time for the process $\hat{X}_2(t)$ turns out to be $1/(c_1 + c_2)$. One way to verify this result is to note that, since the propensity functions for this virtual fast process are linear in x_2, then the *mean* of $\hat{X}_2(t)$ will satisfy the RRE for $\hat{X}_2(t)$; thus,

$$\frac{d\left\langle \hat{X}_2(t) \right\rangle}{dt} = c_1 \left(x_{12} - \left\langle \hat{X}_2(t) \right\rangle \right) - c_2 \left\langle \hat{X}_2(t) \right\rangle . \qquad (43)$$

It is not hard to show that the solution $\left\langle \hat{X}_2(t) \right\rangle$ of this simple ODE approaches its $t = \infty$ limit $c_1 x_{12}/(c_1 + c_2)$ exponentially with characteristic time $1/(c_1 + c_2)$. As for the expected time to the next R_3 reaction, it can be estimated as the reciprocal of the effective propensity function (42) for that reaction. Thus, the criterion for the ssSSA to be applicable is that $1/(c_1 + c_2)$ should be very much less than $(c_1 + c_2)/c_3 c_1 x_{12}$, or

$$(c_1 + c_2)^2 \gg c_3 c_1 x_{12} \ . \tag{44}$$

This condition can always be satisfied by making c_2 sufficiently large compared to c_3. And this is intuitively just what we should expect: If in the reaction set (30) each S_2 molecule is very much more likely to change into an S_1 molecule than an S_3 molecule, then the two reactions R_1 and R_2 will fire much more frequently than reaction R_3. That circumstance will allow R_1 and R_2 to reach equilibrium well before the next R_3 reaction is likely to occur. And that is essentially all that the proof of the Slow-Scale Approximation Lemma requires. Furthermore, the stronger the inequality (44) is (i.e., the "stiffer" the system is), the more accurate will the ssSSA simulation be. Notice that, since the combined number x_{12} of S_1 and S_2 molecules steadily decreases as reactions (30) proceed, then if condition (44) is satisfied at the beginning of a simulation run, it will necessarily be satisfied for the duration of the run.

So, assuming condition (44) is satisfied, here is how the ssSSA simulation of the reaction set (30) would proceed:

1. In state $\mathbf{x} = \left(\mathbf{x}^{\mathrm{f}}, \mathbf{x}^{\mathrm{s}}\right) = ((x_1, x_2), x_3)$ at time t, and with $x_{12} = x_1 + x_2$, evaluate the slow-scale R_3 propensity function $\bar{a}_3(\mathbf{x})$ in (42).

2. Draw a unit-interval uniform random number r, and compute the time to the next R_3 reaction, $\tau = (1/\bar{a}_3(\mathbf{x})) \ln (1/r)$.

3. Advance to the time of the next R_3 reaction by replacing $t \leftarrow t + \tau$, and actualize that reaction by replacing $x_2 \leftarrow x_2 - 1$ and $x_3 \leftarrow x_3 + 1$. Then update $x_{12} \leftarrow x_1 + x_2$ (or equivalently, $x_{12} \leftarrow x_{12} - 1$).

4. "Relax" the fast variables by first setting x_2 equal to a random sample of the binomial random variable $\mathcal{B}(c_1/(c_1 + c_2), x_{12})$, and then setting $x_1 = x_{12} - x_2$.

5. Record (t, x_1, x_2, x_3) if desired. Return to 1, or else stop.

Figures 5, 6, 7 and 8 show comparison runs of the SSA and the above ssSSA procedure for two different sets of rate constants. The SSA plots (in Figs. 5 and 7) were plotted out only after the occurrence of each R_3 reaction – i.e. on the slow timescale – in order to make a fair comparison with the ssSSA plots (in Figs. 6 and 8). See the figure captions for details. In both examples the ssSSA results are statistically indistinguishable from the SSA results, but were obtained in orders of magnitude shorter times. And the ssSSA had no problems when the fast species had low population numbers (Fig. 8).

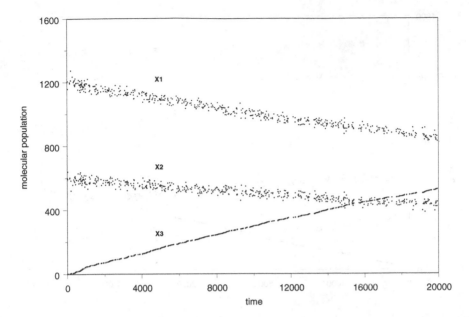

Fig. 5. An exact SSA simulation of reactions (30), $S_1 \underset{c_2}{\overset{c_1}{\rightleftharpoons}} S_2 \overset{c_3}{\longrightarrow} S_3$, for the parameter values $c_1 = 1$, $c_2 = 2$, and $c_3 = 5 \times 10^{-5}$. A point was plotted out immediately after the occurrence of each (slow) R_3 reaction. Over 40 million reactions in all were simulated in the time span shown, so between successive R_3 reactions there were, on average, about 76,000 R_1 and R_2 reactions.

4.8   The ssSSA in More Complicated Situations

Reaction set (30) is probably the simplest of all stiff chemical systems, so it is not surprising that for it we can analytically calculate everything the ssSSA needs to know about the asymptotic virtual fast process $\hat{\mathbf{X}}^f(\infty)$ without making any approximations. But we will not be able to do that for most systems.

In situations where one cannot conveniently develop reasonably accurate analytical approximations for $\hat{\mathbf{X}}^f(\infty)$, one can try a variation on the ssSSA called the *nested SSA* (nSSA) [21]. The nSSA essentially estimates the slow-scale propensity functions $\bar{a}^s_j(\mathbf{x}^f, \mathbf{x}^s)$ by computing the *temporal* average in (35b) instead of the *ensemble* average in (35c). More specifically, the nSSA uses the SSA to numerically construct a *realization* $\hat{\mathbf{x}}^f(t')$ of the virtual fast process $\hat{\mathbf{X}}^f(t')$ from time $t' = t$, when that process has the value $\mathbf{x}^f$, to time $t' = t + T_f$, where T_f is chosen to be larger the relaxation time of $\hat{\mathbf{X}}^f(t')$. One estimates the slow-scale propensity functions by numerically evaluating the integrals

$$\bar{a}^s_j(\mathbf{x}^f, \mathbf{x}^s) \approx \frac{1}{T_f} \int_t^{t+T_f} a^s_j \left(\hat{\mathbf{x}}^f(t'), \mathbf{x}^s \right) dt' , \tag{45}$$

and then one takes the "relaxed sample" of $\hat{\mathbf{X}}^f(\infty)$ to be $\hat{\mathbf{x}}^f(t + T_f)$. Since these two estimates will be exact only in the limit $T_f \to \infty$, the trick is to determine

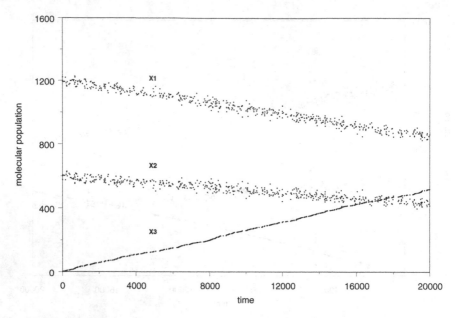

Fig. 6. An approximate ssSSA simulation of the reactions in Fig. 5. Here only the slow reactions are simulated, and there were 521 of them in all. For this simple system, all of the procedures of the ssSSA can be carried out exactly, but the accuracy of the simulation still depends on how well the stiffness condition (44) is satisfied. For these parameter values, condition (44) is initially satisfied by two orders of magnitude, and that figure improves as the reaction proceeds. This ssSSA plot, which is made on the timescale of the slow reaction R_3, is statistically indistinguishable from the SSA plot in Fig. 5. But whereas the SSA run took 20 minutes of computer time to execute, this ssSSA run took less than a second.

the smallest value of T_f that gives sufficiently accurate results. And of course, the stiffness condition must still be satisfied, since it is assumed by (35b). Here that condition essentially amounts to requiring that T_f be small compared to the average time to the next slow reaction.

For systems with virtual fast processes that are only a little more complicated than that for reactions (30), it is usually possible to get accurate results with the ssSSA by making suitable *approximations* in calculating the needed properties of the asymptotic virtual fast process. One example of this is worked out in [18], where analytical approximations are developed for applying the ssSSA to the reaction set that was simulated in Figs. 3 and 4, except the values of the reaction rate constants are changed to make the reactions $2S_1 \rightleftharpoons S_2$ "fast" and the other two reactions "slow". In a test run, the ssSSA results were statistically indistinguishable from the SSA results on the time scale of the slow reactions. But whereas the compute time was 17 minutes for the exact SSA, it was less than a second for the ssSSA. If the explicit tau-leaping procedure had been applied to this "stiffer" situation, a much smaller gain in simulation speed would have been achieved because the Leap Condition would restrict the leaps to the timescale of the fast reactions.

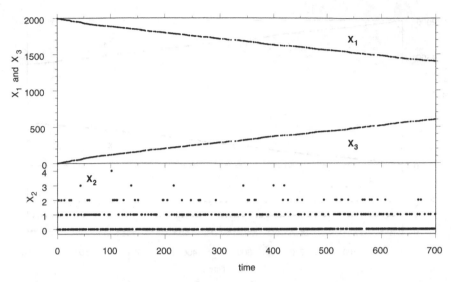

Fig. 7. An exact SSA simulation run of the same reactions (30) as in Fig. 5, but with different reaction rates: $c_1 = 10$, $c_2 = 4 \times 10^4$ and $c_3 = 2$. These values cause the S_2 population to be very small – usually 0 and rarely greater than 3. Over 23 million reactions were simulated in the time span shown. The S_1 and S_3 populations in the upper box were plotted out after the occurrence of each R_3 reaction. However, the S_2 population in the lower box was plotted out at equal time intervals of $\Delta t = 1.167$, a value chosen to give approximately the same number of plot points. If the S_2 population had been plotted out immediately after each R_3 reaction, the density of dots along the $X_2 = 1$ and $X_2 = 2$ lines would be slightly but noticeably heavier than shown here, while the density of dots along the $X_2 = 0$ line would be slightly lighter. The reason is that an R_3 reaction will be n times more likely to occur in the next dt when there are n S_2 molecules than when there is one S_2 molecule, so plotting the fast species populations *immediately* after a slow reaction will give a biased picture of the fast species populations on the slow timescale. Such a bias is actually present in the trajectory of the other fast species S_1, but it is not noticeable at its larger population level.

Another example of a successful approximate implementation of the ssSSA is to the simple enzyme-substrate reaction set. We shall describe how this is done, and how it relates to the well known Michaelis-Menten treatment of that problem, in the next section.

5 Applying the ssSSA to the Enzyme-Substrate Reaction Set

The simple enzyme-substrate reaction set is

$$E + S \underset{c_2}{\overset{c_1}{\rightleftharpoons}} ES \overset{c_3}{\longrightarrow} E + P \ , \tag{46}$$

where E is an enzyme molecule, S a substrate molecule, ES an enzyme-substrate complex, and P a product molecule. The traditional deterministic analysis of this

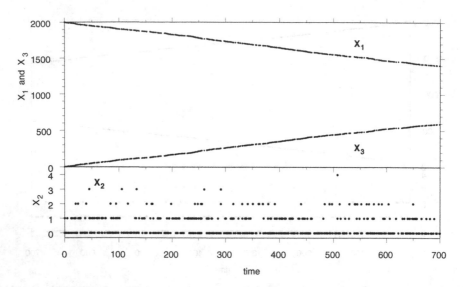

Fig. 8. An ssSSA simulation of the same reactions that were simulated in Fig. 7. Condition (44) is satisfied initially by over four orders of magnitude, and that figure becomes more favorable as the reactions proceed. These trajectories are evidently statistically indistinguishable from those in exact SSA run, showing that there is no requirement by the ssSSA for the population of the fast species to be "large". The simulation time speed up was not measured, but it is roughly commensurate with the fact that the SSA run in Fig. 7 simulated over 23 million reactions, while this ssSSA run simulated only 587 reactions.

reaction set gives rise the famous Michaelis-Menten formula for the "rate v" at which product is formed. An analysis using the ssSSA has been given in [19], under the stiffness condition that reactions R_1 and R_2 are "fast" and reaction R_3 is "slow". That analysis effectively generalizes the deterministic Michaelis-Menten result to a stochastic context. Since the enzyme-substrate reaction set (46) is so important in cellular chemistry, we shall now show how the ssSSA deals with it.

5.1   The Step-by-Step Analysis

We start by (provisionally) taking R_1 and R_2 to be the fast reactions and R_3 a slow reaction. Since species E, S and ES get changed by a fast reaction, they will be fast species, while P will be a slow species; thus, the fast process is $\mathbf{X}^f(t) = (X_E(t), X_S(t), X_{ES}(t))$ and the slow process is $\mathbf{X}^s(t) = X_P(t)$. The *virtual* fast process is therefore $\hat{\mathbf{X}}^f(t) = \left(\hat{X}_E(t), \hat{X}_S(t), \hat{X}_{ES}(t) \right)$ evolving under *only* the fast reactions $E + S \underset{c_2}{\overset{c_1}{\rightleftharpoons}} ES$. We observe that this virtual fast process obeys *two conservation relations*:

$$\hat{X}_E(t) + \hat{X}_{ES}(t) = x_{E*}, \quad \hat{X}_S(t) + \hat{X}_{ES}(t) = x_{S*} . \tag{47}$$

The first expresses the conservation of enzyme units, and the second the conservation of substrate units. (Note that the real fast process $\mathbf{X}^f(t)$ obeys the first conservation relation but not the second.) Because of these two conservation relations, the virtual fast process has only one independent variable. We shall choose that independent variable to be $\hat{X}_{ES}(t)$, and then let it determine $\hat{X}_E(t)$ and $\hat{X}_S(t)$ through the conservation relations. The propensity functions for the two fast reactions relative to $\hat{X}_{ES}(t)$ are

$$a_1(x_{ES}) = c_1(x_{E^*} - x_{ES})(x_{S^*} - x_{ES}), \quad a_2(x_{ES}) = c_2 x_{ES} , \tag{48}$$

and the associated state-change vectors are

$$\nu_1 = +1, \quad \nu_2 = -1 . \tag{49}$$

The asymptotic master equation for $\hat{X}_{ES}(t)$ reads

$$0 = \sum_{j=1}^{2} \left\{ a_j(x_{ES} - \nu_j)\hat{P}(x_{ES} - \nu_j, \infty \,|\, x_{E^*}, x_{S^*}) - a_j(x_{ES})\hat{P}(x_{ES}, \infty \,|\, x_{E^*}, x_{S^*}) \right\} \tag{50}$$

where $\hat{P}(x_{ES}, \infty \,|\, x_{E^*}, x_{S^*})$ is the probability that $\hat{X}_{ES}(\infty)$ will equal x_{ES}, given that there are x_{E^*} (bound or unbound) enzyme units and x_{S^*} (bound or unbound) substrate units. After substituting into this equation the propensity functions (48) and the state change vectors (49), one can show that it implies

$$c_2(x_{ES} + 1)\hat{P}(x_{ES} + 1, \infty \,|\, x_{E^*}, x_{S^*})$$
$$= c_1(x_{E^*} - x_{ES})(x_{S^*} - x_{ES})\hat{P}(x_{ES}, \infty \,|\, x_{E^*}, x_{S^*}), \quad \forall x_{ES} . \tag{51}$$

This "detailed balance relation" in turn implies that $\hat{P}(x_{ES}, \infty \,|\, x_{E^*}, x_{S^*})$ satisfies the recursion relation

$$\hat{P}(x_{ES} + 1, \infty \,|\, x_{E^*}, x_{S^*}) = \frac{c_1(x_{E^*} - x_{ES})(x_{S^*} - x_{ES})}{c_2(x_{ES} + 1)}\hat{P}(x_{ES}, \infty \,|\, x_{E^*}, x_{S^*})$$
$$(x_{ES} = 0, 1, \ldots, x_{ES}^{\max} - 1) , \tag{52}$$

where the maximum possible number of enzyme-substrate units is

$$x_{ES}^{\max} \equiv \min(x_{E^*}, x_{S^*}) . \tag{53}$$

In principle, $\hat{P}(x_{ES})$ can be computed from the recursion relation (52), with $\hat{P}(0)$ being chosen to make $\sum_{x_E=0}^{x_{ES}^{\max}} \hat{P}(x_{ES}) = 1$. But an analytical iteration of (52) does not lead to a tractable formula, as it does for (39). Therefore, we have to find some way to estimate the mean $\left\langle \hat{X}_{ES}(\infty) \right\rangle$ of that probability function, in order to estimate

$$\bar{a}_3(\mathbf{x}) = c_3 \left\langle \hat{X}_{ES}(\infty) \right\rangle . \tag{54}$$

And we have to find a way to generate random samples of $\hat{P}(x_{ES})$, so that we can get "relaxed" values for the fast species. Following [19], we take a two-pronged approach to these tasks, depending on whether $x_{ES}^{\max}$ in (53) is "small" or "large".

For *small* $x_{\mathrm{ES}}^{\max}$, it is feasible to iterate the recursion (52) *numerically* to obtain exact values for $\hat{P}(x_{\mathrm{ES}}, \infty \,|\, x_{\mathrm{E}^*}, x_{\mathrm{S}^*})$. With those values in hand, we can straightforwardly evaluate $\bar{a}_3(\mathbf{x})$ numerically as

$$\left\langle \hat{X}_{\mathrm{ES}}(\infty) \right\rangle = \sum_{x_{\mathrm{ES}}=0}^{x_{\mathrm{ES}}^{\max}} x_{\mathrm{ES}} \hat{P}(x_{\mathrm{ES}}, \infty \,|\, x_{\mathrm{E}^*}, x_{\mathrm{S}^*}) \ . \tag{55}$$

And we can generate a "relaxed" value of X_{ES} by using the standard "inversion" Monte Carlo procedure of drawing a unit-interval uniform random number r and taking X_{ES} to be the *smallest integer* satisfying

$$\sum_{x_{\mathrm{ES}}=0}^{X_{\mathrm{ES}}} \hat{P}(x_{\mathrm{ES}}, \infty \,|\, x_{\mathrm{E}^*}, x_{\mathrm{S}^*}) \geqslant r \ . \tag{56}$$

The relaxed values of the other two fast species are then obtained from the conservation relations (47):

$$X_{\mathrm{E}} = x_{\mathrm{E}^*} - X_{\mathrm{ES}}, \ \ X_S = x_{\mathrm{S}^*} - X_{\mathrm{ES}} \ . \tag{57}$$

The Appendix of [19] describes these computations in more detail.

For *large* $x_{\mathrm{ES}}^{\max}$, a numerical iteration of the recursion (52) would take too much time. But tests have shown [19] that in this circumstance, the mean $\left\langle \hat{X}_{\mathrm{ES}}(\infty) \right\rangle$ in (55) can be well-approximated by the asymptotic (stationary) solution $\bar{x}_{\mathrm{ES}}$ of the RRE for $\hat{X}_{\mathrm{ES}}(t)$ [cf. (5)]:

$$0 = \sum_{j=1}^{2} \nu_j a_j(\bar{x}_{\mathrm{ES}}) \ . \tag{58}$$

With formulas (48) and (49), this equation reads

$$c_1(x_{\mathrm{E}^*} - \bar{x}_{\mathrm{ES}})(x_{\mathrm{S}^*} - \bar{x}_{\mathrm{ES}}) - c_2 \bar{x}_{\mathrm{ES}} = 0 \ . \tag{59}$$

This is a simple quadratic in $\bar{x}_{\mathrm{ES}}$, and its solution is

$$\bar{x}_{\mathrm{ES}} = \frac{1}{2} \left\{ \left(x_{\mathrm{E}^*} + x_{\mathrm{S}^*} + \frac{c_2}{c_1} \right) - \sqrt{\left(x_{\mathrm{E}^*} + x_{\mathrm{S}^*} + \frac{c_2}{c_1} \right)^2 - 4 x_{\mathrm{E}^*} x_{\mathrm{S}^*}} \right\} \ . \tag{60}$$

So, for large $x_{\mathrm{ES}}^{\max}$, we evaluate $\bar{a}_3(\mathbf{x}) = c_3 \left\langle \hat{X}_{\mathrm{ES}}(\infty) \right\rangle$ by simply approximating

$$\left\langle \hat{X}_{\mathrm{ES}}(\infty) \right\rangle \approx \bar{x}_{\mathrm{ES}} \ . \tag{61}$$

To generate a random sample from $\hat{P}(x_{\mathrm{ES}}, \infty \,|\, x_{\mathrm{E}^*}, x_{\mathrm{S}^*})$ for estimating the "relaxed" values of the fast variables, we can take some comfort in the fact that any errors we make in doing that will *not* affect the subsequent accuracy of the simulation. With that in mind, we simply approximate $\hat{P}(x_{ES}, \infty \mid x_{E^*}, x_{S^*})$ by a *normal* probability density function whose mean is as given in (61). For the variance of this approximating normal, we use the value obtained by fitting the (single) peak in the function defined by the recursion relation (52) with a Gaussian form, and then taking $\mathrm{var}\left\{\hat{X}_{ES}(\infty)\right\}$ to be the variance of the fitted Gaussian. The details of how this is done are spelled out in [19] (see also [5], Sec. 6.4.C). The resulting formula is

$$\mathrm{var}\left\{\hat{X}_{ES}(\infty)\right\} \approx \frac{(c_2/c_1)\tilde{x}_{ES}}{-2\tilde{x}_{ES} + (x_{E^*} + x_{S^*} + 2) + (c_2/c_1)} \ . \tag{62}$$

Here, $\tilde{x}_{ES}$ locates the maximum of the function defined by the recursion relation (52), and is given by

$$\tilde{x}_{ES} = \frac{1}{2}\left(x_{E^*} + x_{S^*} + \frac{c_2}{c_1} + 2\right)$$
$$- \frac{1}{2}\sqrt{\left(x_{E^*} + x_{S^*} + \frac{c_2}{c_1} + 2\right)^2 - 4(x_{E^*} + 1)(x_{S^*} + 1)} \ . \tag{63}$$

5.2   Checking the Stiffness Condition

One of the strengths of the ssSSA is that it gives us a rational criterion for determining when it can be applied. The criterion is that relaxation time of the virtual fast process should be small compared to the expected time to the next slow reaction. In this case, that criterion leads to the specific condition

$$-2c_1\tilde{x}_{ES} + c_1(x_{E^*} + x_{S^*} + 2) + c_2 \gg c_3\tilde{x}_{ES} \ . \tag{64}$$

Here, the quantity on the right is the reciprocal of the estimated time to the next R_3 reaction, and the quantity on the left is the reciprocal of the estimated relaxation time of the process $\hat{X}_{ES}(t)$. For details on how the latter estimate is made, see [18] and [19].

An inspection of condition (64) shows that it will inevitably be satisfied if c_2 is sufficiently large compared to c_3. The physical interpretation of that is easily understood: When $c_2 \gg c_3$, an ES molecule will decay much more frequently to $E + S$ than to $E + P$. So between two successive R_3 firings there will typically be many firings of R_1 and R_2. That will allow reactions R_1 and R_2 to come to an approximate equilibrium well before the next R_3 reaction occurs. And that is the key condition required by our proof of the Slow-Scale Approximation Lemma, which provides the logical basis for the ssSSA in (33).

5.3   The Simulation Procedure

The recipe for applying the ssSSA to the enzyme-substrate reaction set (46) therefore goes as follows – all of course under the assumption that condition (64) is satisfied:

1. In state $\mathbf{x} = (\mathbf{x}^f, \mathbf{x}^s) = ((x_E, x_S, x_{ES}), x_P)$ at time t, and with $x_{E^*} = x_E + x_{ES}$, $x_{S^*} = x_S + x_{ES}$, and $x_{ES}^{max} = \min(x_{E^*}, x_{S^*})$, evaluate $\bar{a}_3(\mathbf{x}) = c_3 \left\langle \hat{X}_{ES}(\infty) \right\rangle$. For this, compute $\left\langle \hat{X}_{ES}(\infty) \right\rangle$ from (55) if x_{ES}^{max} is "small", or from (61) otherwise.

2. Draw a unit-interval uniform random number r, and compute the time to the next R_3 reaction, $\tau = (1/\bar{a}_3(\mathbf{x})) \ln(1/r)$.

3. Advance to the time of the next R_3 reaction by replacing $t \leftarrow t + \tau$. Actualize that reaction by replacing $x_{ES} \leftarrow x_{ES} - 1$, $x_E \leftarrow x_E + 1$, $x_P \leftarrow x_P + 1$. Then update $x_{S^*} \leftarrow x_S + x_{ES}$ (or equivalently, $x_{S^*} \leftarrow x_{S^*} - 1$) and also $x_{ES}^{max} \leftarrow \min(x_{E^*}, x_{S^*})$.

4. Relax the *fast* variables by first taking x_{ES} to be a random sample of $\hat{P}(x_{ES}, \infty \mid x_{E^*}, x_{S^*})$, and then taking $x_E = x_{E^*} - x_{ES}$ and $x_S = x_{S^*} - x_{ES}$. In generating the value for x_{ES}, use the exact method (56) if x_{ES}^{max} is "small"; otherwise, take x_{ES} to be a sample of the *normal* random variable with mean (61) and variance (62), rounded to the nearest integer in $[0, x_{ES}^{max}]$.

5. Record $(t, x_E, x_S, x_{ES}, x_P)$ if desired. Return to step 1, or else stop.

It may well be possible to devise more efficient procedures for estimating $\bar{a}_3(\mathbf{x})$ in step 1, and for generating the relaxed fast variables in step 4. The main message here is the overall strategy of the ssSSA approach to the reaction set (46), and why we can expect this approach to give accurate results whenever $c_2 \gg c_3$.

5.4 Examples

Figures 9, 10, 11 and 12 compare results obtained with the exact SSA and the approximate ssSSA for two different sets of rate constants and initial populations. In both cases, the SSA and ssSSA results are seen to be statistically indistinguishable, and the speedup of the latter over the former is substantial. Notice in particular that the ssSSA has no problems with fast initial transients (see Figs. 9 and 10), or with fast species that have very low populations (see Figs. 11 and 12).

5.5 Connection to Michaelis-Menten

How is the foregoing ssSSA approach to the enzyme-substrate reaction set related to the famous Michaelis-Menten approach? The most obvious advantage of the ssSSA approach is that it accurately captures all the discreteness and stochasticity of reactions (46) on the timescale of the slow reaction R_3. But to see that the two approaches essentially agree otherwise, we need to quickly review the conventional derivation of the Michaelis-Menten formula.

The goal of the Michaelis-Menten approach is to estimate the supposedly deterministic rate

$$v \equiv c_3 X_{ES} \tag{65}$$

at which product molecules are being formed by reactions (46). If we were content to express v in terms of the enzyme-substrate complex population X_{ES}, then (65)

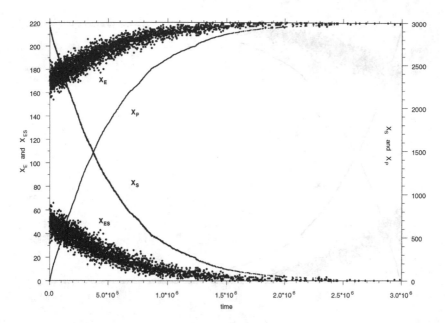

Fig. 9. An exact SSA simulation of the enzyme-substrate reaction set (46), $E + S \overset{c_1}{\underset{c_2}{\rightleftharpoons}}$ $ES \overset{c_3}{\longrightarrow} E + P$, with rate constants $c_1 = c_3 = 10^{-4}$ and $c_2 = 1$. At time $t = 0$ there were 220 free enzyme molecules ($X_E = 220$), 3000 free substrate molecules ($X_S = 3000$), and no enzyme-substrate complex or product molecules ($X_{ES} = X_P = 0$). The E and SE populations refer to the left scale, while the S and P populations refer to the right scale. The populations of the species were plotted out immediately after each R_3 reaction. Over 58 million reactions in all were simulated here, of which only 3000 were R_3 reactions, so between successive R_3 reactions there were an average of 19,300 R_1 and R_2 reactions.

would suffice. But X_{ES} is usually difficult to measure, and as is illustrated in Figs. 9 and 11, X_{ES} fluctuates because of reactions R_1 and R_2. So the Michaelis-Menten approach makes an *assumption*. More specifically, it makes *either* the "partial (or rapid) equilibrium" assumption that R_1 and R_2 are in equilibrium with each other,

$$c_1 X_E X_S = c_2 X_{ES} , \tag{66}$$

or it makes the "quasi-steady-state" assumption that the population of the enzyme-substrate complex is constant in time,

$$dX_{ES}/dt = c_1 X_E X_S - c_2 X_{ES} - c_3 X_{ES} = 0 . \tag{67}$$

For the case $c_3 \ll c_2$ of interest here, these two assumptions are indistinguishable, because the third term in (67) is negligibly small compared to the second term.

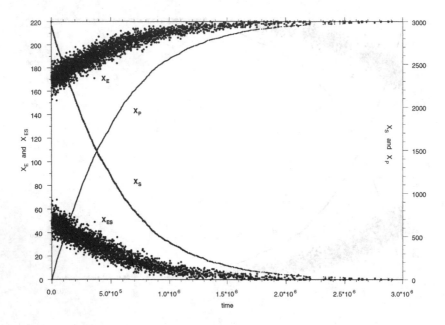

Fig. 10. An approximate ssSSA run of the same enzyme-substrate reactions that were simulated exactly in Fig. 9. The stiffness condition (64) is initially satisfied by a factor of 260, and that figure improves as the reactions proceed. Only the R_3 reactions were simulated here – there were 3000 of them in all. This plot is statistically indistinguishable from the plot in Fig. 9, but the ssSSA program that generated it ran over 950 times faster than the SSA program that generated the plot in Fig. 9. Notice the ssSSA had no problem with the initial fast transient that brought the free enzyme population down from 220 to around 170.

Using assumption (66), the problematic enzyme-substrate complex population can be expressed in terms of the free enzyme and free substrate populations as

$$X_{ES} = \frac{c_1}{c_2} X_E X_S. \tag{68}$$

By substituting this into (65) we get a formula for v in terms of X_E and X_S. But a glance at Fig. 9 shows that X_E is just as problematic a variable as X_{ES}. A more convenient variable than X_E would be the *total* enzyme population, $x_{E^*} = X_E + X_{ES}$ in (47), which stays constant. Using it to eliminate X_E from (68) gives

$$X_{ES} = \frac{c_1}{c_2} \left(x_{E^*} - X_{ES} \right) X_S \ . \tag{69}$$

Solving this equation for X_{ES} gives

$$X_{ES} = \frac{x_{E^*} X_S}{(c_2/c_1) + X_S} \ , \tag{70}$$

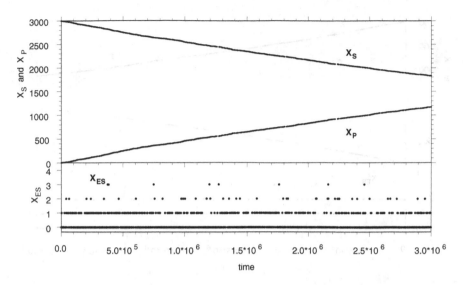

Fig. 11. Another exact SSA simulation of the enzyme-substrate reaction set (46), but using different rate constants ($c_1 = 10^{-4}$, $c_2 = 6$, and $c_3 = 10^{-3}$) and a different total number of enzyme units (10 instead of 220). The initial populations were $X_E = 10$, $X_S = 3000$, and $X_{ES} = X_P = 0$. The populations of the E, S, and P species were plotted out immediately after each R_3 reaction, but the population of ES was plotted out at equal time intervals, for reasons explained in the caption of Fig. 7. A total of 13.7 million reaction events in all were simulated here; only 1,172 of those were R_3 events. For this choice of rate constants, the ES population is usually 0 or 1, and rarely more than 3.

and substituting this into (65) gives the famous *Michaelis-Menten formula* for the rate of production of product molecules:

$$v = \frac{c_3 x_{E^*} X_S}{(c_2/c_1) + X_S} \equiv v_{MM} \ . \tag{71}$$

But further reflection on (71) leads to the realization that having the variable X_S in this formula is almost as unsatisfactory as having either of the variables X_E or X_{ES}. That's because the values of *all three* of those "fast" variables are rapidly changing due to the fast reactions R_1 and R_2. And if we stop simulating R_1 and R_2, as we clearly do in the Michaelis-Menten approach, we can no longer claim to know the values of *any* of those fast species populations. But this problem can easily be remedied by recognizing that reactions R_1 and R_2 do *not* change the *total* substrate population, $x_{S^*} = X_S + X_{ES}$ in (47). Using it to eliminate X_S from (70) gives

$$X_{ES} = \frac{x_{E^*}(x_{S^*} - X_{ES})}{(c_2/c_1) + (x_{S^*} - X_{ES})} \ . \tag{72}$$

Upon solving this (quadratic) equation in X_{ES}, we find that

$$X_{ES} = \bar{x}_{ES} \ , \tag{73}$$

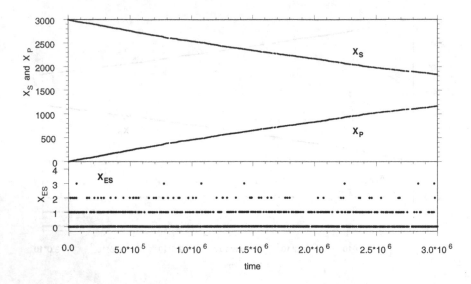

Fig. 12. An approximate ssSSA run of the same reactions that were simulated exactly in Fig. 11. The stiffness condition (64) is initially satisfied by about four orders of magnitude, and that figure improves as the reactions proceed. Only the R_3 reactions were simulated here; there were 1,165 of them. This plot is statistically indistinguishable from the plot in Fig. 11, but the compute time here was faster by a factor of about 400.

where $\bar{x}_{ES}$ is defined in (60). Formula (73) is equivalent to the Michaelis-Menten formula (70) since they are derived from the same assumptions. But whereas (70) expresses X_{ES} in terms of x_{E^*} and X_S, (73) expresses X_{ES} in terms of x_{E^*} and x_{S^*}. Equation (73) thus has the advantage that it does not require knowing the essentially unknowable fast species population X_S.

When we substitute (73) into formula (65) we get

$$v = c_3 \bar{x}_{ES} \ , \tag{74}$$

and here at last we have the connection with the ssSSA: Comparing (74) with (61) and (54), we see that v is the "large x_{ES}^{max}" approximation to $\bar{a}_3(\mathbf{x})$. Thus, the Michaelis-Menten rate is essentially the ssSSA's slow-scale propensity function for reaction R_3 when the molecular populations are "not too small". Or, from the other point of view, for not too small molecular populations the ssSSA's $\bar{a}_3(\mathbf{x})$ is given by the standard Michaelis-Menten formula, written however in terms of the *total* substrate population instead of the *free* substrate population.

This quantitative connection between the ssSSA treatment of the enzyme-substrate reaction set (46) and the traditional Michaelis-Menten treatment is reassuring. But these considerations also reveal that the ssSSA treatment provides a firmer basis for understanding and simulating reactions (46): Whereas the Michaelis-Menten analysis proceeds from an *assumption*, in the form of either the rapid equilibrium assumption or the quasi-steady-state assumption, the ssSSA proceeds from a *proven result*, in the form of the Slow Scale Approximation

Lemma. That lemma, whose proof begins with a straightforward application of the addition law of probability in (35a), shows that the ssSSA will be valid whenever the relaxation time of reactions R_1 and R_2 is small compared to the expected time between successive firings of reaction R_3. This criterion is difficult even to articulate in the context of the ODE formalism of the Michaelis-Menten approach, because in that formalism all reactions happen *concurrently*, and there is no notion of a "time between successive firings of reaction R_3". But the fact that the Michaelis-Menten result emerges naturally within the ssSSA when large numbers of molecules are involved shows that it can be considered "established" *without* having to make any ad hoc assumptions like (66) or (67).

6 Looking Ahead

There are many ways to improve and extend the ideas and techniques described in this chapter. Ways of combining explicit and implicit tau-leaping have been devised [22], but could no doubt be improved. And ways of efficiently applying the ssSSA to more complicated systems need to be developed.

Taking a broader view, the propensity function formalism needs to be extended, where possible, to bimolecular reactions that do not assume that the reactant molecules move about as either well-stirred dilute gas molecules or as well-stirred diffusing molecules. Enlightenment is needed on how propensity functions are affected by the finite sizes of the reactant molecules [23], and by crowding from larger inert molecules. There is a need to develop efficient methods for simulating systems in which the natural motions of the molecules do not adequately "stir" the system between successive occurrences of bimolecular reactions. Are such spatially inhomogeneous systems best simulated by dividing the volume Ω into smaller, spatially homogeneous subvolumes that diffusively share molecules with neighboring subvolumes? Or should such systems instead be simulated by adopting an approach closer to molecular dynamics, in which the positions of key reactant molecules are tracked in detail?

It seems likely to this writer that progress on these difficult issues will be made faster and more reliably by initially focusing on specific, simple, experimentally inspired models, rather than by trying to develop general simulation schemes for simulating all types of systems under all possible conditions.

Acknowledgements. I am pleased to thank the following individuals for their help and collaboration in striving for an understanding of the issues discussed in this chapter: Linda Petzold, Yang Cao, Muruhan Rathinam, Sotiria Lampoudi, Hong Li, and John Doyle. I am also happy to thank Carol Gillespie for programming and graphing all of the computer simulations reported in the figures. Financial support for this writing was provided by the University of California under Consulting Agreement 054281A20 with the Computer Science Department at Santa Barbara; and by the California Institute of Technology, through

Consulting Agreement 102-1080890 with the Control and Dynamical Systems Department pursuant to NIH Grant R01 GM078992 from the National Institute of General Medical Sciences, and through Contract 82-1083250 pursuant to NIH Grant R01 EB007511.

References

1. Gillespie, D.: Stochastic chemical kinetics. In: Yip, S. (ed.) Handbook of Materials Modeling, pp. 1735–1752. Springer, Heidelberg (2005)
2. Gillespie, D., Petzold, L.: Numerical simulation for biochemical kinetics. In: Szallasi, Z., Stelling, J., Periwal, V. (eds.) System Modeling in Cellular Biology, pp. 331–353. MIT Press, Cambridge (2006)
3. Gillespie, D.: Stochastic simulation of chemical kinetics. Ann. Rev. Phys. Chem. 58, 35–55 (2007)
4. Gillespie, D.: A rigorous derivation of the chemical master equation. Physica A 188, 404–425 (1992)
5. Gillespie, D.: Markov Processes: An Introduction for Physical Scientists. Academic (1992)
6. Gillespie, D.: The mathematics of Brownian motion and Johnson noise. Am. J. Phys. 64, 225–240 (1996)
7. Gillespie, D.: The multivariate Langevin and Fokker-Planck equations. Am. J. Phys. 64, 1246–1257 (1996)
8. Gillespie, D.: The chemical Langevin equation. J. Chem. Phys. 113, 297–306 (2000)
9. Gillespie, D.: The chemical Langevin and Fokker-Planck equations for the reversible isomerization reaction. J. Phys. Chem. A 106, 5063–5071 (2002)
10. Lok, L., Brent, R.: Automatic generation of cellular reaction networks with Moleculizer 1. 0. Nature Biotechnology 23, 131–136 (2005)
11. Gillespie, D.: Approximate accelerated stochastic simulation of chemically reacting systems. J. Chem. Phys. 115, 1716–1733 (2001)
12. Gillespie, D., Petzold, L.: Improved leap-size selection for accelerated stochastic simulation. J. Chem. Phys. 119, 8229–8234 (2003)
13. Cao, Y., Gillespie, D., Petzold, L.: Efficient step size selection for the tau-leaping simulation method. J. Chem. Phys. 124, 044109 (2006)
14. Cao, Y., Gillespie, D., Petzold, L.: Avoiding negative populations in explicit Poisson tau-leaping. J. Chem. Phys. 123, 054104 (2005)
15. Rathinam, M., Petzold, L., Cao, Y., Gillespie, D.: Stiffness in stochastic chemically reacting systems: The implicit tau-leaping method. J. Chem. Phys. 119, 12784–12794 (2003)
16. Rathinam, M., Petzold, L., Cao, Y., Gillespie, D.: Consistency and stability of tau-leaping schemes for chemical reaction systems. Multiscale Model. Simul. 4, 867–895 (2005)
17. Ascher, M., Petzold, L.: Computer Methods for Ordinary Differential Equations and Differential Algebraic Equations. In: SIAM (1998)
18. Cao, Y., Gillespie, D., Petzold, L.: The slow-scale stochastic simulation algorithm. J. Chem. Phys. 122, 014116 (2005)
19. Cao, Y., Gillespie, D., Petzold, L.: Accelerated stochastic simulation of the stiff enzyme-substrate reaction. J. Chem. Phys. 123, 144917 (2005)

20. Gillespie, D., Petzold, L., Cao, Y.: Comment on Nested stochastic simulation algorithm for chemical kinetic systems with disparate rates. (J. Chem. Phys. 123, 0194107 (2005)); J. Chem. Phys. 126, 0137101 (2007)
21. Liu, E.W., Vanden-Eijnden, D., Nested, E.: stochastic simulation algorithm for chemical kinetic systems with disparate rates. J. Chem. Phys. 123, 194107 (2005)
22. Cao, Y., Gillespie, D., Petzold, L.: Adaptive explicit-implicit tau-leaping with automatic tau-selection. J. Chem. Phys. 126, 224101 (2007)
23. Gillespie, D., Lampoudi, S., Petzold, L.: Effect of reactant size on discrete stochastic chemical kinetics. J. Chem. Phys. 126, 034302 (2007)

Membrane Computing as a Modeling Framework.
Cellular Systems Case Studies

Gheorghe Păun[1] and Francisco José Romero-Campero[2]

[1] Institute of Mathematics of the Romanian Academy
PO Box 1-764, 014700 Bucureşti, Romania
`george.paun@imar.ro, gpaun@us.es`
[2] Automated Scheduling, Optimisation and Planning Research Group
School of Computer Science and Information Technology
University of Nottingham, Jubilee Campus, Nottingham, NG8 1BB, UK
`fxc@cs.nott.ac.uk`

Abstract. Membrane computing is a branch of natural computing aiming to abstract computing models from the structure and functioning of the living cell, and from the way cells cooperate in tissues, organs, or other populations of cells. This research area developed very fast, both at the theoretical level and in what concerns the applications. After a very short description of the domain, we mention here the main areas where membrane computing was used as a framework for devising models (biology and bio-medicine, linguistics, economics, computer science, etc.), then we discuss in a certain detail the possibility of using membrane computing as a high level computational modeling framework for addressing structural and dynamical aspects of cellular systems. We close with a comprehensive bibliography of membrane computing applications.

1   Introduction

Membrane computing is a branch of natural computing, the broad area of research concerned with computation taking place in nature and with human-designed computing inspired by nature. Membrane computing abstracts computing models from the architecture and the functioning of living cells, as well as from the organization of cells in tissues, organs (brain included) or other higher order structures such as colonies of cells (e.g., bacteria).

Membrane computing was initiated in 1998 (with the seminal paper published in 2000) and the literature of this area has grown very fast (already in 2003, Thompson Institute for Scientific Information, ISI, has qualified the initial paper as "fast breaking" and the domain as "emergent research front in computer science" – see `http://esi-topics.com`). Details, in particular, many downloadable papers, including pre-proceedings of yearly workshops and brainstorming weeks on membrane computing, can be found at `http://psystems.disco.unimib.it`.

The initial goal was to learn from cell biology something possibly useful to computer science, and the area quickly developed in this direction. Several classes

M. Bernardo, P. Degano, and G. Zavattaro (Eds.): SFM 2008, LNCS 5016, pp. 168–214, 2008.
© Springer-Verlag Berlin Heidelberg 2008

of computing models – called *P systems* – were defined in this context, inspired from biological facts or motivated from mathematical or computer science points of view. In the last few years, a number of applications were reported in several areas – biology, bio-medicine, linguistics, computer graphics, economics, approximate optimization, cryptography, etc. Several software products for simulating P systems and attempts of implementing P systems on a dedicated hardware were reported; also an attempt towards an implementation in bio-chemical terms is in progress.

After very briefly presenting the basic ideas of membrane computing (main types of P systems, main categories of results), we enumerate the domains where membrane computing was used as a modeling framework; then we pass to presenting P systems as a high level computational modeling framework which integrates the structural and dynamical aspects of cellular systems in a comprehensive and relevant way while providing the required formalization to perform mathematical and computational analysis. Several case studies are discussed in some detail.

The paper ends with a comprehensive bibliography, with papers clustered according to the area of applications; at the beginning of the bibliography we also provide several titles of a general interest, giving basic information about membrane computing.

2 A Quick Description of Membrane Computing

The main ingredients of a P system are (i) *the membrane structure*, delimiting compartments where (ii) *multisets of objects* evolve according to (iii) *(reaction) rules* of a bio-chemical inspiration. The rules can process both objects and membranes. Thus, membrane computing can be defined as a framework for devising cell-like or tissue-like computing models which process multisets in compartments defined by means of membranes. These models are (in general) distributed and parallel. When a P system is considered as a computing device, hence it is investigated in terms of (theoretical) computer science, the main issues studied concern the *computing power* (in comparison with standard models from computability theory, especially Turing machines/Chomsky grammars and their restrictions) and the *computing efficiency* (the possibility of using parallelism for solving computationally hard problems in a feasible time). Computationally and mathematically oriented ways of using the rules and of defining the result of a computation are considered in this case. When a P system is constructed as a model of a bio-chemical process, it is examined in terms of dynamical systems, with the evolution in time being the issue of interest, not a specific output.

At this moment, there are three main types of P systems: (i) cell-like P systems, (ii) tissue-like P systems, and (iii) neural-like P systems.

The first type imitates the (eukaryotic) cell, and its basic ingredient is the *membrane structure*, a hierarchical arrangement of membranes (understood as three dimensional vesicles), i.e., delimiting compartments where multisets of objects are placed; the objects are in general described by symbols from a given alphabet, but also string-objects can be considered; rules for evolving these objects are provided, also localized, acting in specified compartments or on specified membranes. The most common types of rules are multiset rewriting rules (similar to chemical reactions) and transport rules, e.g., symport or antiport rules, inspired by biological processes. The objects not only evolve, but they also pass through membranes (we say that they are "communicated" among compartments). The rules can have several forms, and their use can be controlled in various ways: promoters, inhibitors, priorities, etc. Also the hierarchy of membranes can evolve, e.g., by creating and destroying membranes, by division, by bio-like operations of exocytosis, endocytosis, phagocytosis, and so on.

In tissue-like P systems, several one-membrane cells are considered as evolving in a common environment. They contain multisets of objects, while also the environment contains objects. Certain cells can communicate directly (channels are provided between them) and all cells can communicate through the environment. The channels can be given in advance or they can be dynamically established – this latter case appears in so-called *population P systems*. In the case when the cells are simple, of a limited capacity (as the number of objects they contain or of rules they can use), we obtain the notion of *P colony*.

Finally, there are two types of neural-like P systems. One is similar to tissue-like P system in that the cells (neurons) are placed in the nodes of an arbitrary graph and they contain multisets of objects, but they also have a *state* which controls the evolution. Another variant was recently introduced, under the name of *spiking neural P systems*, where one uses only one type of objects, the *spike*, and the main information one works with is the distance between consecutive spikes.

From a theoretical point of view, P systems are both powerful (most classes are Turing complete, even when using ingredients of a reduced complexity – a small number of membranes, rules of simple forms, ways of controlling the use of rules directly inspired from biology are sufficient for generating/accepting all sets of numbers or languages generated by Turing machines) and efficient (many classes of P systems, especially those with enhanced parallelism, can solve computationally hard problems – typically **NP**-complete problems, but also harder problems, e.g., **PSPACE**-complete problems – in feasible time – typically polynomial). Then, as a modeling framework, membrane computing is rather adequate for handling discrete (biological) processes, having many attractive features: easy understandability, scalability and programmability, inherent compartmentalization and non-linearity, etc.

The cell-like P systems were introduced first and their theory is now very well developed; tissue-like P systems have also attracted a considerable interest, while the neural-like systems, mainly under the form of spiking neural P systems, were only recently investigated. Correspondingly, most applications use cell-like P systems, several of them also involve tissue-like P systems, but very few research efforts were paid to using spiking neural P systems in applications (although several suggestions from "classic" neural computing are obvious – for instance, trying applications to pattern recognition).

3   Applications of Membrane Computing

As it is natural, membrane computing was first and much more intensively used as a modeling framework for addressing biological processes. In this respect, P systems can be seen as models approaching reality at the micro level, where "reactants" and "reactions" can be known individually, opposed to the macro approach (e.g., by means of differential equations), which deals with populations of reactants which can be considered infinite (large enough to be better approximated by infinity rather than by finite, discrete sets). We have mentioned above several attractive features of P systems as models of biological processes: inherent compartmentalization, easy extensibility, direct understandability (by the biologist), easy programmability, non-linear behavior. P systems are particularly suitable, if not the "obligatory", in the cases when we have to deal with a reduced number of object or with slow reactions – and this is the case in a large number of biological processes, especially related to networks of pathway controls, genetic processes, protein interactions.

It should be noted here that many of the reported applications in biology and bio-medicine are of a *postdiction* type: one takes a biological process, as described already in biological publications, one writes a membrane computing model of it, then one writes a program or one takes a program existing in the literature (for instance, at the membrane computing P page), and one simulates the model by means of this program, comparing the results with those already known from literature (based on differential equations models or on experimental results). There also are a few papers of a *prediction* type, involving biological research hypotheses and thus returning really new information to biologist, not yet known through other means. Of course, this latter direction of research is of much more interest, but the former one is still useful/necessary, because it checks the models and the programs, thus validating the tools for prediction applications.

Similar from many points of view to the bio-chemical reality is the economic reality (e.g., at the market level), where compartments can be defined where various "objects" (good, parts of goods, money, working time, contracts, and so on and so forth) "react" according to well-specified rules. There also is an important difference between bio-chemistry and economic interaction: in the latter case, the behavior of agents is not purely probabilistically controlled, e.g., depending on the multiplicity of "reactants" (stoichiometry), but the psychological factor is also important. Anyway, this direction of research needs further efforts, but it is much favored by the fact that multi-agent computer based approaches (simulations) are more and more used in economics, somewhat contrasted to the fact that "exact" methods, e.g., of the kind provided by the classic operational research, seem to be less applicable to non-trivial, complex economic phenomena.

It was also used in economics the language of membrane computing, the mathematical and the graphical one. This is much more visible in the applications to linguistics.

The applications to computer science are rather diverse. A good example is that of computer graphics: some papers are rather practical (somewhat complementing the applications of Lindenmayer systems in computer graphics, one add

membrane distribution to known approaches, with good results in terms of efficiency), many others are of a theoretical type (P systems with two-dimensional
objects or generating in well specified ways picture languages, mainly arrays).
Whether or not the second direction of research may be considered as dealing
with "real" applications is debatable in this moment, that is why only a few
titles of this kind are mentioned.

Similar discussions can be made in what concerns applications in sort-
ing/ranking, cryptography, modelling/simulating circuits, parallel architectures,
etc. They mainly show the great expressivity power of P systems, their versa-
tility, but the results of the mentioned papers are not yet of a direct practical
interest in computer science.

A promising exception to the previous remark is the use of membrane computing ideas in evolutionary computing. The so-called membrane algorithms introduced by T.Y. Nishida and much investigated by L. Huang and his collaborators,
seem to be rather efficient and useful, both in terms of the convergence speed,
the quality of the provided solutions, and the average and the worst solutions
(which proves that such approaches are reliable and effort-saving).

We have ended with a short list of papers dealing with "other applications" (such as simulating ambient calculus or other well-know models and
paradigms from computer science), but we have not included papers from the
large literature dealing with polynomial (often even linear) solutions to computationally hard problems (typically, **NP**-complete, but also **PSPACE**-complete
problems). The bibliography from `http://psystems.disco.unimib.it,`
`http://ppage.psystems.eu` contains many papers (and PhD theses) with this
subject, as well as further titles pertaining to all sections of the paper bibliography.

4   Looking for Cell Models

We pass now to discussing in more details and illustrating the issue of using P
systems as models for cell systems, starting with a general presentation of the
related efforts and directions of research.

The complexity and apparent messiness of interactions in cellular systems
makes necessary the development of models able to provide a better understanding of their dynamics and properties. The use of models is intrinsic to any
scientific activity. A model is an abstraction of the *real world* onto a mathemat-
ical/computational formalism which highlights some key features while ignoring
others that are assumed to be irrelevant. Therefore, a model should not be seen
or presented as a representation of the truth, but instead as a statement of our
current knowledge of the phenomenon under research. A model is even useful
when proved to disagree with real data, since it shows that our current hypotheses do not match the reality and it helps experimentalists to decide which
experiments are necessary to advance understanding.

Although biologists are familiar with modeling, quantitative computational
mathematical models have lain outside the mainstream due to the lack of

techniques from both experimental and theoretical/computational sides. Nonetheless, at the end of the last century extraordinary advances were achieved in both computer science and biology reaching the point where each one can benefit from the other one. In this respect, a new field is emerging which integrates biology, mathematics and computer science, *systems biology*. Systems biology constitutes a purely interdisciplinary field aiming to merge classical biology, computer science and mathematics. Ideally it will produce a new generation of scientists able to understand and apply concepts, techniques and sources of inspirations coming from any of the three classical fields enumerate above into any of the others.

The new advances in cellular biology have made possible the enumeration of the components of cellular systems on a large scale. Initially, a reductionist approach was taken with the aim of understanding the functioning of cells by identifying and characterizing each one of their individual constituents. This approach did not produce the expected knowledge uncovering the fact that the functioning of cellular systems arises as an emergent process from the interactions between their different components. The young field of systems biology presents a systemic methodology whose goal is to deepen the understanding of cellular level dynamics as emergent properties arising over time from the interactions between different systems made of molecular entities. Systems biology focuses on the nature of the interactions and links that connect cellular systems and the functional states of the networks that result from the assembly of such links. Due to the complexity of these connections and to the huge amount of data produced by experimentalists computational/ mathematical modeling, simulation and analysis are essential techniques in this field.

In a cell system biology model it is desirable to have at least four properties: relevance, understandability, extensibility and computability [22].

• Relevance: A model must be relevant capturing the essential features of the phenomenon investigated. It should present a unifying specification of the different components that constitute the system, the interactions between them, their dynamic behavior as well as the physical structure of the system itself.

• Understandability: The abstract formalisms used to model cellular systems should correspond well to the informal concepts and ideas from molecular biology. A model should provide a better and integrated understanding of the real cellular system instead of producing a complicated and hard to decipher formalism.

• Extensibility: In a cellular model we should be able to identify easily its different components so they can be rearranged, duplicated, composed, etc. in an easy way to produce other models. Models of cellular systems should also be extensible to higher levels of organizations, like colonies, tissues, organs, organism, etc. Our knowledge of cellular systems continues to expand and change. In order to handle this continuous supply of new discoveries a model should be adapted easily to incorporate new information.

• Computability and Mathematical tractability: It should be possible to implement a model in a computer so that we can realize it to study the dynamics of the system by manipulating experimental conditions in the model without having to perform complex and costly experiments. The computability of the model also allows us to apply analytical techniques on it to infer qualitative and quantitative properties of the system in an automatic way. In this respect, the model should be mathematically tractable.

Our research towards using P systems as a computational/mathematical modeling framework for the specification and analysis of cell system biology aims to produce a high level formalism which integrates the structural and dynamical aspects of cellular systems in a comprehensive and relevant way while providing the required formalization to perform mathematical and computational analysis. To this aim, we introduce stochastic P systems as a modeling framework for cell systems biology models, with a detailed methodology for the specification of the components of cellular systems and of the most important molecular interactions in living cells. Then we propose the analysis of P system models using the probabilistic model checker PRISM. The lac operon regulation system is studied as a case study to illustrate this modeling approach.

5   Related and Previous Work

Modeling of cellular systems is currently subject to very intensive research. There are multiple approaches ranging from graphical representations to sophisticated computational and mathematical formalisms. Here we cannot present an exhaustive enumeration of the different modeling methodologies and will only discuss roughly those modeling approaches closely related to the work presented in this paper.

5.1   Ordinary Differential Equations

Ordinary differential equations (ODEs) constitute the most widely used approach in modeling molecular interaction networks in cellular systems. Writing and solving numerically a system of ODEs describing a reaction network can be largely automated. Each molecular species is assigned a continuous variable which represents its concentration. For each molecular species, a differential equation is written to describe its concentration change over time due to the reactions with other species in the system. The rate of each reaction is represented using a *kinetic law*, which commonly depends on one or more rate constants. *Exponential decay law, mass action law, Michaelis-Menten dynamics* and *Hill dynamics* are the most widely used kinetic laws. In this respect models based on ODEs are referred to as *macroscopic* since they do not represent mechanistic aspects of the interactions between molecules they focused on the modeling of the macroscopic effect of the molecular interactions using specific kinetic laws.

Although, ODEs have been used successfully to model kinetics of conventional macroscopic chemical reactions the realization of a reaction network as a system of ODEs is based on two assumptions:

1. First, cells are assumed to be well stirred and homogeneous volumes. Whether or not this is a good approximation depends on the time and space scales involved. In bacteria molecular diffusion is sufficiently fast to mix compounds. The time needed for a protein to diffuse throughout a bacterium size volume is a few seconds. Therefore if we are interested in transcription/translation processes (minutes), cell cycle (hours), circadian rhythms (one day), etc. the well stirred volume assumption is justified in bacteria. This is not the case in eukaryotic cells where the volume is considerably bigger and it is structured in different compartments.

2. The second basic assumption is that chemical concentrations vary continuously over time in a deterministic way. This assumption is valid if the number of molecules of each specifies in the reaction volume (the cell or the subcellular compartment) are sufficiently large and the reactions are fast.

Therefore in cellular systems with low number of molecules and slow molecular interactions the application of the classical macroscopic and deterministic approach based on ODEs is questionable. Instead *mesoscopic, discrete* and *stochastic* approaches are more suitable [11]. In this last approach the most relevant individual parts of the system are taken into account but details like position and momenta are neglected. One focuses on the number of individual components of the system, the statistics of the events and how often they take place. The mesoscopic approach is more tractable than the microscopic approach while keeping more relevant information than the macroscopic approach.

5.2   Computational Modeling

The complexity of mesoscopic, discrete and stochastic models makes necessary the use of computers to help to analyze them. Until recently the majority of computational models were implemented in custom programs and published as statements of the underlying mathematical model. No computational formalism was explicitly used to model and simulate cellular systems. Nevertheless, to be useful a computational model must be presented within a well defined, consistent and formal framework. Following this line, recently several formal computational frameworks has been proposed to model cellular systems. Here we will only discuss briefly Petri nets and process algebra as they are closely related to P systems.

- **Petri Nets** are a mathematical and computational tool for modeling and analysis of discrete event systems typically with a concurrent behavior. They offer a formal way to represent the structure of the interactions in a discrete event system, simulate its behavior, and prove certain properties of the system [20]. Roughly speaking a Petri net is a directed graph formed by two kinds of nodes called places and transitions. Directed edges, called arcs, connect places to transitions, and transitions to places. A non-negative integer number of tokens is assigned to each place. Tokens move from one place to another one connected to it through a transition when this transition fires.

A system of interacting molecules can be modeled using Petri nets by representing each molecular species as a different place and each biochemical transformation as a different transition. The number of tokens inside a place is used to specify the number of molecules of the corresponding molecular species [20]. Within this framework only qualitative analysis can be performed, in order to be able to develop quantitative analysis *Stochastic Petri Nets (SPN)* were introduce in [12]. In SPNs each transition is associated with a rate parameter used to compute a time delay following an negative exponential distribution. Then transitions fire according to these time delays.

- **Process algebra** is a family of formalisms for the description of interactions, communications, and synchronization between a collection of concurrent processes. Algebraic laws are provided allowing process descriptions to be manipulated and analyzed. The π-calculus is one of the most widely used process algebras in cellular modeling. It was introduced as a formal language to describe mobile concurrent processes that interact through communication channels [16]. It is now a widely accepted model for interacting systems with dynamically evolving communication topology. The π-calculus has a simple semantics and a tractable algebraic theory. Starting with atomic actions and simpler processes, complex processes can be constructed in specific ways.

  In the π-calculus formalism a system of interacting molecular entities is modeled by a system of interacting processes which communicate through complementary communication channels. Each molecular species or domain is represented by a different process. The number of copies of each process is used to specified the number of molecules. Molecular interactions are described using complementary communication channels [22].

Although these computational frameworks captures some of the information regarding cellular systems and their components, none fully integrates the dynamics and structural details of the systems. One of the main points which is neglected is the key role played by membranes and compartmentalization in the structure and functioning of living cells. There have been several attempts in specifying and simulating membranes and compartments in the process algebra [5,21]. Nevertheless, it has been discussed that the models developed using process algebra can be obscure, non intuitive and difficult to understand [22]. In this work we aim to develop a formal modeling framework based on P systems which explicitly represent in a relevant and comprehensible manner the key role played by membranes.

6   Stochastic P Systems for Cell Systems Biology Models

Let us stress once again that P systems, according to the original motivation, were not intended to provide a comprehensive and accurate model of the living cell, rather, to explore the computational nature of various features of biological membranes. Although most research in P systems concentrates on computational powers, recently they have been used to model biological phenomena within the framework of computational systems biology presenting models of oscillatory systems [8], signal transduction [17], gene regulation control [24], quorum sensing [23] and metapopulations [18].

6.1 P System Specifications and Models

In order to develop a modeling framework based on P systems a variant has been proposed to formalize the specification of cellular systems, the parameters associated with a specification and the models obtained from specifications by instantiating their parameters with specific values [18].

In what follows the main definitions used in this work are presented. First, we introduce *P system specifications* which will constitute the main structure used to analyze particular cellular systems. A set of *parameters* is identified from the components of a P system specification. Then, the basic definition of P system specifications is extended to introduce *P system models*. Given a possible sets of values for the parameters of a P system specification, a P system model is obtained by instantiating the set of parameters using the given parameter values.

Definition 1 (P system Specification)
A P system specification is a construct:

$$\Pi = ((\Sigma_{obj}, \Sigma_{str}), L, \mu, M_1, M_2, \ldots, M_n, (R_{l_1}^{obj}, R_{l_1}^{str}), \ldots, (R_{l_m}^{obj}, R_{l_m}^{str}))$$

where:

- $(\Sigma_{obj}, \Sigma_{str})$ *are finite alphabets of symbols. The symbols from Σ_{obj} represent individual objects whereas the symbols from Σ_{str} represent objects that can be arranged to form strings.*
- $L = \{l_1, \ldots, l_m\}$ *is a finite alphabet of symbols representing labels for the compartments and identifying compartment types[1].*
- μ *is a membrane structure containing $n \geq 1$ membranes identified in a one to one manner with values in $\{1, \ldots, n\}$ and labeled with elements from L.*
- $M_i = (l_i, w_i, s_i)$, *for each $1 \leq i \leq n$, is the initial configuration of membrane i with $l_i \in L$, the label of this membrane, $w_i \in \Sigma_{obj}^*$ a finite multiset of individual objects and s_i a finite set of strings over Σ_{str}. A multiset of objects, obj is represented as $obj = o_1 + o_2 + \cdots + o_m$ with $o_1, \ldots, o_m \in \Sigma_{obj}$. Strings are represented as follows $\langle s_1.s_2.\cdots.s_i \rangle$ where $s_1, \ldots, s_i \in \Sigma_{str}$.*
- $(R_{l_t}^{obj}, R_{l_t}^{str})$ *are finite sets of rewriting rules associated with compartments of the type represented by the label $l_t \in L$. More specifically:*

  - *The rules in $R_{l_t}^{obj} = \{r_1^{obj,l_t}, \ldots, r_{k_{obj,l_t}}^{obj,l_t}\}$, for each $1 \leq t \leq m$, are multiset rewriting rules of the following form:*

$$r_j^{obj,l_t} : obj_1 [obj_2]_l \xrightarrow{c_j^{obj,l_t}} obj_1' [obj_2']_l$$

---

[1] Compartments with the same label will be considered of the same type and thus the same set of rules will be associated with them.

with $obj_1, obj_2, obj_1', obj_2'$ some finite multisets of objects from Σ_{obj} and l a label from L. These rules are multiset rewriting rules that operate on both sides of membranes, that is, a multiset obj_1 placed outside a membrane labeled by l and a multiset obj_2 placed inside the same membrane can be simultaneously replaced with a multiset obj_1' and a multiset obj_2', respectively.

- The rules in $R_{l_t}^{str} = \{ r_1^{str,l_t}, \ldots, r_{k_{str,l_t}}^{str,l_t} \}$, for each $1 \leq t \leq m$, are rewriting rules on multisets of strings and objects of the following form:

$$r_j^{str,l_t} : [\, obj + str \,]_l \xrightarrow{c_j^{str,l_t}} [\, obj' + str_1'; str_2' + \cdots + str_s' \,]_l$$

with obj, obj' multisets of objects over Σ_{obj} and $str, str_1', \ldots, str_s'$ strings over Σ_{str}. These rules operate on both multisets of objects and strings. The objects obj are replaced by the objects obj'. Simultaneously a substring str is replaced by str_1' whereas the strings $str_2' + \cdots + str_s'$ are produced to form part of the content of the compartment.

Note that a constant, c_j^{obj,l_t} or c_j^{str,l_t}, is associated specifically with each rule. This constant will be referred to as stochastic constant and will be used to compute the propensity of the rule.

Definition 2 (Parameters)

Given a P system specification $\Pi = ((\Sigma_{obj}, \Sigma_{str}), L, \mu, M_1, \ldots, M_n,$ $(R_{l_1}^{obj}, R_{l_1}^{str}), \ldots, (R_{l_m}^{obj}, R_{l_m}^{str}))$ the set of parameters $\mathcal{P}(\Pi) = (\mathcal{M}_0(\Pi), \mathcal{C}(\Pi))$ consists of:

1. The initial multisets $\mathcal{M}_0(\Pi) = (M_1, \ldots, M_n)$ associated with the compartments.
2. The stochastic constants $\mathcal{C}(\Pi) = (c_j^{obj,l_t}, c_{j'}^{str,l_t})$ for $1 \leq j \leq k_{obj,l_t}$, $1 \leq j' \leq k_{str,l_t}$ and $1 \leq t \leq m$, associated with the rewriting rules in $(R_{l_1}^{obj}, R_{l_1}^{str}), \ldots, (R_{l_m}^{obj}, R_{l_m}^{str})$.

Definition 3 (P system Model)

Let Π be a P system specification with parameters $\mathcal{P}(\Pi) = (\mathcal{M}_0(\Pi), \mathcal{C}(\Pi))$ and $(\mathbb{M}_0, \mathbb{C})$ a family of possible values for the initial multisets $\mathcal{M}_0(\Pi)$ and for the stochastic constants $\mathcal{C}(\Pi)$. A family of P system models, $\mathcal{F}(\Pi; \mathbb{M}_0, \mathbb{C})$, is obtained from Π and $(\mathbb{M}_0, \mathbb{C})$ by instantiating the parameters $\mathcal{P}(\Pi)$ using values from $\mathbb{M}_0$ and $\mathbb{C}$.

Hence given $(\mathbb{M}_0, \mathbb{C})$ sets of possible values for the parameters $\mathcal{P}(\Pi)$ specific values $(M_1^0, \ldots, M_n^0) \in \mathbb{M}_0$ and $(c_{j,0}^{obj,l_t}, c_{j',0}^{str,l_t}) \in \mathbb{C}$ can be selected to obtain a P system model $(\Pi; (M_1^0, \ldots, M_n^0), (c_{j,0}^{obj,l_t}, c_{j',0}^{str,l_t})) \in \mathcal{F}(\Pi; \mathbb{M}_0, \mathbb{C})$. In this way a family of P system models $\mathcal{F}(\Pi; \mathbb{M}_0, \mathbb{C})$ sharing the same P system specification can be used to study the behavior of a particular cellular system specified by Π under the different initial conditions collected in $\mathbb{M}_0$ and study the sensitivity of the system for the different rule constants in $\mathbb{C}$.

6.2   Stochastic P Systems and Gillespie's Kinetics Theory

At the microscopic level of functioning of cellular processes the interactions between molecules follow the laws of physics. A fundamental result of theoretical statistical physics is the famous $\sqrt{n}$ law, which states that the noise in a system is inversely proportional to the square root of the number of particles. Therefore, systems with a low number of molecules show high fluctuations and the application of the classical deterministic and continuous approaches is questionable. Mesoscopic, discrete and stochastic approaches are more accurate under these circumstances. In this subsection we present a stochastic extension of the original membrane computing framework using Gillespie's kinetics theory.

In the original approach of membrane computing P systems evolve in a non deterministic and maximally parallel manner. All the objects in every membrane that can evolve according to any rule must evolve. This produces a semi-quantitative framework that takes into account the discrete character of the molecular population and the role played by membranes in the structure and functioning of living cells. Although such coarse abstraction has been proved to achieve some success [2,3], this approach fails to model quantitative aspects that are key to the functioning of many cellular systems. Specifically the non deterministic and maximally parallel approach produces the following two inaccuracies:

1. Reactions do not occur at a correct rate.
2. All time steps are equal and do not represent the time evolution of the real cellular system.

These two problems are interdependent and must be addressed when devising a relevant modeling framework for cellular systems as it has been done in other computational approaches [12,22].

In the field of membrane computing, the discrete aspect of the different components as well as the distributed and compartmentalized character of the structure, where the computation takes place, are fundamental. This is not the case with the non deterministic and maximal parallel semantics as have been studied in different variants [7,10]. In this section the original approach will be replaced with a strategy based on Gillespie's theory of stochastic kinetics [11].

To provide P systems with a stochastic extension a constant c is associated with each rule. This constant depends only on the physical properties of the molecules involved in the reaction described by the rule and on other physical parameters of the system like temperature. It is used to compute the propensity of each rule which in turn determines the probability and time needed to apply the rule.

The starting point consists of treating each compartment, delimited by a membrane, as a well mixed and fixed volume where the classical *Gillespie algorithm* is applied. Given the state of a compartment i, $M_i = (l_i, w_i, s_i)$, and the sets of rules associated with it, $R_{l_i}^{obj}$ and $R_{l_i}^{str}$, the next rule to be applied and its waiting time is computed according to Gillespie algorithm:

1. Compute for each rule r_j associated with the compartment its propensity, $a_j(M_i)$, by multiplying the stochastic constant associated specifically with the rule by the number of distinct possible combinations of the objects and substring present on the left-side of the rule with respect to the current contents of the membranes involved in the rule.
2. Compute the sum of all propensities:

$$a_0(M_i) = \sum_{r_j \in (R_{l_i}^{obj} \cup R_{l_i}^{str})} a_j(M_i)$$

3. Draw two random numbers r_1 and r_2 from the uniform distribution in the unit-interval, and select τ_i and j_i according to

$$\tau_i = \frac{1}{a_0(M_i)} \ln\left(\frac{1}{r_1}\right)$$

$$j_i = \text{the smallest integer satisfying } \sum_{j=1}^{j_i} a_j(\mathbf{x}) > r_2 a_0(M_i)$$

This discrete-event simulation algorithm, usually referred to as Gillespie algorithm or SSA (Stochastic Simulation Algorithm), has the nice properties that it simulates every reaction event and is exact in the sense that it generates exact independent realizations of the underlying stochastic kinetic model. Nevertheless, it should be emphasized that Gillespie algorithm was developed for a single, well mixed and fixed volume or compartment. In contrast, in P systems we have a hierarchical structure defining different compartments with specific rules. In what follows we present an adaptation of the Gillespie algorithm that can be applied in the hierarchical and compartmentalized structure of a P system model. This will be referred to as *Multi-compartmental Gillespie algorithm*.

Next, a detailed specification of this algorithm is presented:

- **Initialization**
  - set time of the simulation $t = 0$;
  - for each membrane i compute a triple (τ_i, j_i, i) by using the procedure described before; construct a list containing all such triples;
  - sort this list of triples (τ_i, j_i, i) in increasing order according to τ_i;
- **Iteration**
  - extract the first triple, $(\tau_{i_0}, j_{i_0}, i_0)$ from the list;
  - set time of the simulation $t = t + \tau_{i_0}$;
  - update the waiting time for the rest of the triples in the list by subtracting τ_{i_0};
  - apply the rule $r_{j_{i_0}}$ in membrane i_0 only once changing the number of objects and sites in the membranes affected by the application of the rule;
  - for each membrane i' affected by the application of the rule remove the corresponding triple $(\tau_{i'}, j_{i'}, i')$ from the list;

o for each membrane i' affected by the application of the rule $r_{j_{i_0}}$ re-run the Gillespie algorithm for the new context in i' to obtain $(\tau'_{i'}, j'_{i'}, i')$, the next rule $r_{j'_{i'}}$, to be used inside membrane i' and its waiting time $\tau'_{i'}$;

o add the new triples $(\tau'_{i'}, j'_{i'}, i')$ in the list and sort this list according to each waiting time and iterate the process.

• **Termination**
  o Terminate simulation when time of the simulation t reaches or exceeds a preset maximal time of simulation.

It is worth noting that this is a local algorithm in the sense that all computations only consider the content and rules of a single compartment. The only remaining global computation is the location of the index of the smallest waiting time, which could be improved by keeping all reaction times in an *indexed priority queue*. The advantage of having local computations is that the algorithm is easily implemented in an event-driven object-oriented programming style, such an implementation could be multithreaded on a hyper-threading machine and would also lend itself to full message-passing implementation on a parallel computing cluster.

There exists a different well established approach to modeling cell systems in membrane computing, based on the so called *Metabolic Algorithm* [4]. This algorithm keeps maximal parallelism as the strategy for the evolution of their models. Nonetheless they use rules of the form $a \to a$, called *transparent rules*, that have no effect on the state of the system, in order to bound the number of applied rules that actually change the system. Specific functions, called *reaction maps*, defined ad hoc, are also associated with rules to represent the reactions rates. By doing this the first of the two problems presented before is somehow solved; nevertheless the real evolution time of the system is not treated in this approach. Finally, the *Metabolic Algorithm* is deterministic and so its applicability in certain cell systems suffers from the same drawbacks as other deterministic approaches like ODEs. The relationship between this approach and ODEs has been studied in [9].

Another stochastic approach in P systems has been proposed in [18], dynamical probabilistic P systems. This approach also keeps maximal parallelism and uses transparent rules to bound the number of effective rule applications. The non determinism is replaced by a probabilistic strategy which associates probabilities with the rules depending on the content of membranes. Nevertheless, this approach does not represent the real evolution time of the system as in the metabolic algorithm.

7   P System Specifications of Cellular Systems

Most modelling approaches in systems biology are formalisms coming from different sources of inspirations not related to biology. For example, the π-calculus was introduced to specify mobile concurrent processes that interact through communication channels [16]. In contrast, P systems are inspired directly from the functioning and structure of the living cell. Therefore, the concepts in P systems are more similar to those used in molecular cell biology than the abstractions of other formalisms. This feature of P systems is key to produce relevant, comprehensive and integrative specifications of the different cellular components.

In this section, we present some principles for the specification of cellular systems in P systems. More specifically we will describe some ideas of how to describe cellular regions and compartments, protein-protein interactions and gene expression control.

7.1 Specification of Cellular Compartments

As mentioned previously, membranes play a key role in the functioning and structural organization of both prokaryotic and eukaryotic cells. The key differential feature of P systems with respect to other discrete, mesoscopic and stochastic approaches is the so called *membrane structure* which provides an explicit description of the compartmentalization in the structural organization of cells. The specification of compartmentalization has been addressed in P systems in different systems, for instance selective uptake of molecules from the environment [24], signalling at the cell surface [6] and colonies of interacting bacteria which communicate by sending and receiving diffusing signals [23].

In the specification of compartments in cellular systems it is necessary to consider two distinct and relevant regions:

1. The compartment surface where a set of proteins, which control the movement of molecules and detect signals, are located.
2. The lumen or aqueous interior space where a characteristic complement of proteins interact to carry out specific functions.

In our P system modeling framework, membranes are used to define the relevant regions in cellular systems. Therefore they do not always correspond with real cell membranes although normally they do. According to this idea, in this work two different membranes will be used to specify the two relevant regions associated with a cellular compartment:

1. A first membrane will represent the compartment surface. In the region defined by this membrane the objects describing molecules associated with the compartment surface will be located. The processes involving molecular transport and cell signalling will be represented by rules which will also be associated with this region.
2. A second membrane will describe the aqueous interior of the compartment and thus it will be embedded inside the previous one. The multiset of objects and strings specifying the proteins and other molecules located in the lumen of the compartment will be placed in the region defined by this membrane. The rules describing the molecular interactions taking place inside the compartment are also associated with this membrane.

In cases where the compartment surface does not play a crucial role the first membrane is omitted and only one membrane defining the compartment interior is used.

7.2   Specification of Protein-Protein Interactions

Large and complex networks of interacting molecular entities are responsible for most of the information processing within living cells. Here we aim to provide a comprehensive and relevant P system modeling schema for the most important protein-protein interactions that take place in living cells. More specifically we will focuss on the formation and dissociation of complexes and on the fundamental processes of communication and transport between different compartments in cellular systems.

The theoretical and experimental description of protein-protein interactions is related to the field of chemical kinetics. A primary objective in this area is to determine the propensity or probability of a protein interaction, in order to describe the rate at which reactants are transformed into products. In this section every P system schema for protein-protein interactions is presented together with the propensities associated with each rule. These propensities are computed according to Gillespie's theory of stochastic kinetics [11].

• **Transformation and Degradation:** A molecule a can react to produce another molecule b or it can be degraded by the cell machinery.

In P system specifications, transformation and degradation are represented using the rewriting rules in the schema (1). In these rules the object a is replaced with the object b or is simply removed in the case of degradation. The compartment type where the molecules are transformed or degraded is also specified using square brackets with a label l. A constant c is associated with the rule so that its propensity [2] can be computed.

$$r_1 : [\, a\,]_l \xrightarrow{c} [\, b\,]_l \qquad prop(r_i) = c \cdot |a| \quad i = 1, 2$$
$$r_2 : [\, a\,]_l \xrightarrow{c} [\ \ ]_l \tag{1}$$

• **Complex Formation and Dissociation:** Two molecules, a and b, can collide and stick to produce a complex c. Once a complex has been formed it can dissociate back into its components, d and e which could have changed as a consequence of the interaction.

In biochemistry, these reactions are referred to as complex formation, more specifically heterodimer formation when $a \neq b$ and homodimer formation when $a = b$; and complex dissociation. In P system specifications, complex formation and dissociation reactions are specified using the rewriting rules in the schema (2) which take the name of the reactions they represent. In the complex formation rule, r_{cf}, the objects a and b, representing the corresponding molecules, are replaced with the object c, representing the complex. In the same manner, in the complex dissociation rule, r_{cd}, the object c is replaced with the objects d

---

[2] In this work $|a|$ will be used to represent the number of molecules a.

and e. The compartment type in which the reactions take place is specified using square brackets and a label l.

$$r_{cf} : [\, a + b\,]_l \xrightarrow{c_{cf}} [\, c\,]_l \quad prop(r_{cf}) = \begin{cases} c_{cf} \cdot |a||b| & \text{if } a \neq b \\ c_{cf} \cdot \dfrac{|a|(|a| - 1)}{2} & \text{if } a = b \end{cases}$$

$$r_{cd} : [\, c\,]_l \xrightarrow{c_{cd}} [\, d + e\,]_l \quad prop(r_{cd}) = c_{cd} \cdot |c| \tag{2}$$

- **Diffusion in and out:** Small molecules can readily move by simple passive diffusion across membranes without the aid of transport proteins and without the consumption of any metabolic energy.

  The rewriting rules in (3) constitute a P system specification for diffusion in and out of a compartment. This compartment is represented by square brackets with a label l. For diffusion in the object a is moved from the compartment surrounding compartment l inside the region defined by it. Viceversa for the case of diffusion out from compartment l.

$$r_1 : a\, [\ ]_l \xrightarrow{c_{in}} [\, a\,]_l \quad prop(r_1) = c_{in}|a|$$

$$r_2 : [\, a\,]_l \xrightarrow{c_{out}} a\, [\ ]_l \quad prop(r_2) = c_{out}|a| \tag{3}$$

- **Binding and Debinding:** One of the key steps in the process of converting signals into cellular responses, *signal transduction*, is the binding of signalling molecules to structurally complementary sites on the extracellular or membrane-spanning domains of receptors leading to their activation.

  In P system specifications, the binding and debinding of a ligand to its receptor, located on the cell surface, is specified using the rewriting rules in (4). For the binding rule, the object a representing the ligand is placed outside the compartment representing the cell surface, square brackets with label l. The receptor is specified using the object b placed inside the square brackets. These two objects are replaced with the object c, the complex receptor-ligand, inside the square brackets which represent the compartment surface. The debinding reaction is specified by replacing the object c, inside the square brackets, with the object d, representing the ligand, outside the square brackets and the object e, representing the free receptor, inside them.

$$r_1 : a\, [\, b\,]_l \xrightarrow{c_{lb}} [\, c\,]_l \quad prop(r_1) = c_{lb}|a||b|$$

$$r_2 : [\, c\,]_l \xrightarrow{c_{ld}} d\, [\, e\,]_l \quad prop(r_2) = c_{ld}|c| \tag{4}$$

The P system schema representing binding and debinding reactions has been mainly used to model signalling at the cell surface [6,17]. Nevertheless, this schema is not limited to representing receptor activation. It can also be used to specify selective uptake (binding) of certain substances from the environment and delivering of substances to the environment (debinding) by specific transport proteins located on the cell surface [24].

• **Recruitment and Releasing:** Binding of a ligand to its receptor produces a conformational change in the cytosolic domains of the receptor that triggers the recruitment of some cytoplasmic proteins. These proteins are subsequently transformed and released back into the cytoplasm which ultimately induces specific cellular responses.

The rules in (5) model recruitment and releasing in P system specifications. The compartment from where or to where the proteins are recruited or released is specified using square brackets with a label l. In the recruitment rule, r_{rt} the active receptor is represented by the object a placed outside the compartment l where the object b represents the protein that is recruited. These objects are replaced with the object c outside compartment l specifying the formation of the complex formed by the active receptor and the recruited protein.

Conversely, in the releasing rule, r_{rl}, the object c outside compartment l is replaced with the objects d outside and the object e inside the compartment.

$$r_{rt} : a\,[\,b\,]_l \xrightarrow{c_{rt}} c\,[\,]_l \quad prop(r_{rt}) = c_{rt}|a||b|$$
$$r_{rl} : c\,[\,]_l \xrightarrow{c_{rl}} d\,[\,e\,]_l \quad prop(r_{rl}) = c_{rl}|c| \tag{5}$$

This P system specification has been used in signal transduction systems [6,17] and to describe processes involving uptake (recruitment) of certain substances from the cytoplasm and the delivering of some substances to the cytoplasm (releasing) by specific transport proteins located on the cell surface [24].

7.3 Specification of Gene Regulation

Living cells can sense very complex environmental and internal signals through some of the molecular interactions described previously. Cells respond to these signals by producing appropriate proteins codified in specific genes. The rate of production of these proteins is regulated by special proteins called *transcription factors* which bind to genes. There are, basically, two different types of transcription factors, *activators* and *repressors*. Although both types bind to genes they have opposite effects. Activators increase the rate of transcription of genes whereas repressors produce a decrease in the rate of transcription of the genes to which they bind. Cells use transcription factors as an internal representation of the environmental and internal state of the cell.

The interaction between transcription factors and genes leading to a change in the rate of production of certain proteins are described by *transcription networks*. In this section, P system specification schemas for transcription networks in prokraryotes are presented. For simplicity only prokaryotes will be considered. In spite of the differences between gene regulation control in prokaryotes and eukaryotes the same fundamental principles and mechanisms still apply in both cases [19].

The *central dogma* of molecular cell biology states that the necessary information for the production of proteins is contained in stretches of DNA called genes. Transcription of a gene is the process by which a protein called *RNA polymerase* produces the mRNA that corresponds to a gene's coding sequence. This mRNA is then translated into a protein or gene product, by *ribosomes*, complexes made of specific proteins and ribosomal RNA. This picture is much more complex than it first appears since *transcription factors*, which are also proteins encoded in certain genes, acts as regulators in the transcription rate of genes by binding to specific regions or sites of the DNA. These genes can codify in turn other transcription factors or other proteins produced to carry out specific tasks. This provides a feedback pathway by which genes can regulate the expression of other genes and, in this manner, the production of the proteins encoded by them. In this work two different approaches to the specification of transcription networks and gene regulation processes will be discussed.

In the first approach individual objects will be used to specify proteins, transcription factors and genes. Rewriting rules on multisets of objects will describe the interactions between the different components of transcription networks. In the second approach a much more detailed description of the interactions will be developed using objects to represent proteins and transcription factors and strings to represent genes, operons[3] and mRNA. Rewriting rules on multisets of objects and strings will provide a more mechanistic description of the processes that take place in transcription networks.

Specification of Transcription Networks Using Objects. In a simplistic approach processes like transcription and translation can be abstracted as individual reactions. In this case, genes and operons will be specified as individual objects which produce in a single step their complementary mRNA also represented by a single object. The production of a protein from the mRNA is also described in a single step. Finally, the processes involved in gene expression control, like binding and debinding of transcription factors, are also specified using rewriting rules on multisets of objects.

• **Transcription and Translation:** In the P system specification schema in (6) the objects *gene*, *rna* and *prot* specify the stretch of DNA consisting of the gene, its complementary mRNA, and its gene product or protein, respectively. The transcription of the gene into its complementary mRNA is described by the rewriting rule, r_{tc}. According to this rule in the compartments of the type represented by the label l, the object *gene* is replaced with the objects *gene* and *rna*. In this manner, when the rule is applied, the object *gene* remains in the compartment and an object *rna* representing the mRNA is produced.

$$r_{tc} : [\, gene \,]_l \xrightarrow{c_{tc}} [\, gene + rna \,]_l \quad prop(r_{tc}) = c_{tc}|gene|$$
$$r_{tl} : [\, rna \,]_l \xrightarrow{c_{tl}} [\, rna + prot \,]_l \quad prop(r_{tl}) = c_{tl}|rna| \tag{6}$$

In a similar way translation is described by the single rewriting rule r_{tl}, according to which the object *rna* is replaced with the objects *rna* and *prot*. The application of this rule does not consume the object *rna* but it produces an object *prot* representing the translated protein.

---

[3] An operon is a group of genes physically linked on the chromosome and under the control of the same promoters. In an operon, the linked genes give rise to a single mRNA molecule that is translated into the different gene products.

• **Binding and Debinding of Transcription Factors to Genes:** The processes of binding and debinding of a transcription factor to a gene can be described by similar rules to the ones used to specify complex formation and dissociation. The P system specification schema in (7) constitutes the specification of these processes through rewriting rules on multisets of objects.

Rule r_{gon} describes the binding of a transcription factor, Tf, to a gene, specified by the object $gene$. According to this rule in compartments of the type l an object Tf and an object $gene$ can be replaced with an object Tf–$gene$, which represents the situation when the transcription factor is bound to the gene. The reverse process, the debinding of a transcription factor from a gene, is described through the rule r_{goff}. When this rule is applied in compartments of the type l the object Tf–$gene$ is replaced by the objects $gene$ and Tf.

$$
\begin{aligned}
r_{gon} &: [\, Tf + gene\,]_l \xrightarrow{c_{gon}} [\, Tf\text{–}gene\,]_l \quad prop(r_{gon}) = c_{gon}|Tf||gene| \\
r_{goff} &: [\, Tf\text{–}gene\,]_l \xrightarrow{c_{goff}} [\, Tf + gene\,]_l \quad prop(r_{goff}) = c_{goff}|Tf\text{–}gene|
\end{aligned}
\tag{7}
$$

Specification of Transcription Networks Using Strings. The use of individual objects to represent the complex structure of genes in the DNA and RNA and the use of single rules to describe the complex processes of transcription and translation is widely used. Nevertheless, transcription networks present some crucial features that questions the applicability of this approach. For instance, in prokaryotes, genes codifying proteins involved in similar tasks are arranged together in a piece of DNA called operon so that they are transcribed in a single strand of mRNA. The order in which these genes are placed in operons is relevant, as it determines the order in which they are transcribed, and thus the order in which their protein products become available. Therefore, it is necessary to specify genes using linear structures like strings if one wants to produce relevant models of transcription networks. Another important fact that is overlooked in approaches describing transcription and translation as individual processes is that in prokaryotes shortly after transcription has started and before it is over ribosomes can bind to the growing mRNA and start translation. Furthermore, there can be many processes of transcription and translation going on at the same time. Summing up, transcription and translation are concurrent and parallel processes that are difficult to specify using individual objects and single step rules.

Finally, another problem that arises from the use of single step rules for the description of transcription networks is the difference in the time scales of their processes. While protein-protein interactions take seconds, transcription and translation may need half an hour to complete. This difference in the time scales produces a difference of many orders of magnitude in the stochastic constants associated with the corresponding rules. When this is the case the applicability of Gillespie's theory of stochastic kinetics is questionable as the difference among the stochastic constants distorts appreciably the evolution of the system. In this section this problem is solved by decomposing the processes of transcription and translation into simpler interactions whose time scales are similar to those of protein-protein interactions.

In what follows we propose the use of strings to represent the linear structure of strands of DNA and RNA and the use of rewriting rules on multisets of objects and strings to describe the binding and debinding of transcription factors to genes and the processes of transcription and translation as concurrent and parallel processes. A typical representation of a gene as a string in presented below where each substring represent a relevant region or site in the gene

$$\langle\, op\,.\,site_{ini}\,.\,site_{mid}\,.\,\cdots\,.\,site_{mid}\,.\,site_{ter}\,\rangle$$

• **Binding and Debinding of Transcription Factors to Specific Sites on the DNA:** Transcription factors bind to specific regions of the genes called operators. These sites are normally located around the region where the RNAP binds to start transcription. The binding of a transcription factor to an operator produces a change in the conformation of that region increasing or decreasing the rate at which RNAP starts the transcription.

The P system specification schema in (8) describes the binding and debinding of a transcription factor represented by the object Tf to an operator specified by the substring $\langle op \rangle$. Specifically, rule r_{tfb} describes the binding of the transcription factor. The effect of this rule consists of the consumption of an object Tf and the rewriting of the substring $\langle op \rangle$ representing the free operator with the substring $\langle op' \rangle$ representing the operator occupied by the transcription factor. The reverse process is described in rule r_{tfd}. An application of this rule produces an object Tf and the replacement of the substring $\langle op' \rangle$ with the substring $\langle op \rangle$.

$$
\begin{aligned}
r_{tfb} &: [\, Tf + \langle op \rangle\,]_l \xrightarrow{c_{tfb}} [\, \langle op' \rangle\,]_l \quad prop(r_{tfb}) = c_{on}|Tf||\langle op \rangle| \\
r_{tfd} &: [\, \langle op' \rangle\,]_l \xrightarrow{c_{tfd}} [\, Tf + \langle op \rangle\,]_l \quad prop(r_{tfd}) = c_{off}|\langle op' \rangle|
\end{aligned}
\qquad (8)
$$

The constants c_{tfb} and c_{tfd} represent the affinity between the transcription factor and the operator.

• **Transcription:** To carry out transcription, RNAP performs several distinct steps, namely, transcription initiation, mRNA elongation and transcription termination. In what follows a detailed description of the P system schemas used to specify these stages is presented.

– First the RNA polymerase, described by the object RNAP, recognizes and binds reversibly to a specific site at the beginning of the gene, called the *promoter*, represented by the substring $\langle prom \rangle$. The rewriting rules on multisets of objects and strings in (9) describe the binding and debinding of the RNAP to and from the promoter.

The binding of the RNAP to the promoter is described in rule r_{rb}. An application of this rule in a compartment of the type specified by the label l consumes an object RNAP and replaces $\langle prom \rangle$ with $\langle prom.RNAP \rangle$ in a string which contains $\langle prom \rangle$ as substring. This produces the insertion of the object RNAP after $\langle prom \rangle$ describing the binding of the RNAP to the promoter of the gene.

The debinding of the RNAP from the promoter is specified in rule r_{rd}. According to this rule in a compartment of type l the substring $\langle prom.RNAP \rangle$ is rewritten with the substring $\langle prom \rangle$ and an object RNAP is produced. An application of this rule produces the removal of the object RNAP from the string where $\langle prom \rangle$ is located, representing the dropping of the RNAP from the promoter.

$$r_{rb} : [\, \text{RNAP} + \langle prom \rangle \,]_l \xrightarrow{c_{rb}} [\, \langle prom.\text{RNAP} \rangle \,]_l$$
$$prop(r_{rb}) = c_{on}|\text{RNAP}||\langle prom \rangle|$$

$$r_{rd} : [\, \langle prom.\text{RNAP} \rangle \,]_l \xrightarrow{c_{rd}} r[\, \text{RNAP} + \langle prom \rangle \,]_l$$
$$prop(r_{rd}) = c_{rd}|\langle prom.\text{RNAP} \rangle| \tag{9}$$

– Transcription initiation is described by the rewriting rule on strings in (10). This rule specifies the melting of the double strand of the DNA and the transcription of the first nucleotides. These nucleotides are represented by the substring $\langle site_{ini} \rangle$. The complementary ribonucleotides are represented by the substring $\langle \overline{site}_{ini} \rangle$ which mark the beginning of the nascent (growing) mRNA. The effect of an application of the rule r_{ti} in a compartment of type l consists of the replacement of the substring $\langle \text{RNAP}.site_{ini} \rangle$ with the substring $\langle site_{ini}.\overline{site}_{ini}.\text{RNAP} \rangle$ in the string representing the gene.

$$r_{ti} : [\, \langle \text{RNAP}.site_{ini} \rangle \,]_l \xrightarrow{c_{ti}} [\, \langle site_{ini}.\overline{site}_{ini}.\text{RNAP} \rangle \,]_l$$
$$prop(r_{ti}) = c_{ini}|\langle \text{RNAP}.site_{ini} \rangle| \tag{10}$$

Note that after an application of rule r_{ti} the substring $\langle prom \rangle$ is free so another object RNAP can bind to it. In this manner we can represent the binding of an RNAP to the promoter of a gene which is currently being transcribed. That is, we can describe different processes of transcription taking place at the same time.

– During the stage of strand elongation, RNAP moves along the template DNA adding nucleotides to the nascent (growing) RNA chain. Although, the growing mRNA hangs from the RNA polymerase and is not part of the DNA; in our specification, the substring representing the growing mRNA is part of the string which represents the DNA. Nevertheless, different symbols will be used to specify DNA sites and RNA sites so the growing mRNA can be easily identified.

The rewriting rule r_{el} in (11) describes the process of mRNA elongation. The substring $\langle \overline{site}_{ini}.w.\text{RNAP}.site_{mid} \rangle$ represents the situation when RNAP with a partially formed chain of mRNA, $\langle \overline{site}_{ini}.w \rangle$, is ready to transcribe the next site in the DNA, $\langle site_{mid} \rangle$.

The addition of newly transcribed nucleotides is achieved by adding the substring $\langle \overline{site}_{mid} \rangle$ to the substring representing the growing mRNA, $\langle \overline{site}_{ini}.w \rangle$. The movement of the RNA polymerase along the DNA leaving behind transcribed sites is described by moving the substring $\langle site_{mid} \rangle$ from immediately ahead of the symbol RNAP to the end of the growing mRNA represented by the substring $\langle \overline{site}_{ini} \rangle$. All this is achieved by rewriting the substring $\langle \overline{site}_{ini}.w.\text{RNAP}.site_{mid} \rangle$ with the substring $\langle site_{mid}.\overline{site}_{ini}.w.\overline{site}_{mid}\text{RNAP} \rangle$.

$$r_{el} : [\, \langle \overline{site}_{ini}.w.\text{RNAP}.site_{mid} \rangle \,]_l \xrightarrow{c_{el}} [\, \langle site_{mid}.\overline{site}_{ini}.w.\overline{site}_{mid}\text{RNAP} \rangle \,]_l$$

$$prop(r_{el}) = c_{el}|\langle \overline{site}_{ini}.w.\text{RNAP}.site_{mid} \rangle| \tag{11}$$

– The last stage in RNA synthesis is transcription termination. When the RNAP reaches specific termination sites in the DNA a completed RNA molecule is released and the RNAP dissociates from the gene. Rule r_{ter} in (12) describes this process. The situation when the RNAP with a growing mRNA reaches a termination site is represented by the substring $\langle \overline{site}_{ini}.w.\text{RNAP}.site_{ter} \rangle$. The dissociation of the RNA polymerase from the DNA is described by rewriting the substring $\langle \overline{site}_{ini}.w.\text{RNAP}.site_{ter} \rangle$ with $\langle site_{ter} \rangle$. The release of the RNA polymerase is specified by the production of an object RNAP. Finally, the release of a completed mRNA is represented by the production of a new string $\langle \overline{site}_{ini}.w.\overline{site}_{ter} \rangle$.

$$r_{ter} : [\, \langle \overline{site}_{ini}.w.\text{RNAP}.site_{ter} \rangle \,]_l \xrightarrow{c_{ter}} [\, \text{RNAP} + \langle site_{ter} \rangle;\ \langle \overline{site}_{ini}.w.\overline{site}_{ter} \rangle \,]_l$$

$$prop(r_{ter}) = c_{ter} | \langle \overline{site}_{ini}.w.\text{RNAP}.site_{ter} \rangle |$$

(12)

• **Translation:** Translation is the whole process by which the nucleotide sequence of an mRNA is used to order and join the amino acids in a polypeptide chain to synthesize a protein. Ribosomes direct the formation of proteins. Similarly to transcription, the complex process of translation can be divided into three stages, initiation, elongation and termination.

– In prokaryotes, shortly after RNAP starts transcription and before it is over, ribosomes bind to specific sites in the growing mRNA called *ribosome binding sites* (RBS) to start translation. Rule r_{tli} describes translation initiation. In this rule the RBS is specified using the substring $\langle \overline{site}_{ini} \rangle$ and ribosomes are represented using the object Rib. An application of this rule in a compartment of type l consumes an object Rib and rewrites the substring $\langle \overline{site}_{ini} \rangle$ with $\langle \overline{site}_{ini}.\text{Rib} \rangle$.

$$r_{tli} : [\, \text{Rib} + \langle \overline{site}_{ini} \rangle \,]_l \xrightarrow{c_{tli}} [\, \langle \overline{site}_{ini}.\text{Rib} \rangle \,]_l$$
$$prop(r_{tli}) = c_{tli} | \text{Rib} || \langle \overline{site}_{ini} \rangle |$$

(13)

Note that in our approach transcription and translation are specified as concurrent and parallel processes since rules representing translation initiation can be applied before rules describing transcription termination.

– Ribosomes direct elongation of the polypeptide sequence forming a protein by moving along a mRNA chain. In our approach we overlook the growing sequence of amino acids and only specify the movement of ribosomes along the mRNA as we focus on the release of the protein once translation is finished.

The rule in (14) describes a step of elongation. The translocation of a ribosome along the mRNA is achieved by rewriting the substring $\langle \text{Rib}.\overline{site}_{mid} \rangle$ with the substring $\langle \overline{site}_{mid}.\text{Rib} \rangle$.

$$r_{tle} : [\, \langle \text{Rib}.\overline{site}_{mid} \rangle \,]_l \xrightarrow{c_{tle}} [\, \langle \overline{site}_{mid}.\text{Rib} \rangle \,]_l$$
$$prop(r_{tle}) = c_{tle} | \langle \text{Rib}.\overline{site}_{mid} \rangle |$$

(14)

– In translation termination ribosomes dissociate from a mRNA and release a completed polypeptide chain forming a protein when they reach specific sites marking termination points. This last process is described by the rule r_{tlt} in (15).

The situation when a ribosome reaches a termination site is represented by the substring $\langle \text{Rib}.\overline{site}_{ter} \rangle$. The dissociation of the ribosome from the mRNA and the release of the protein are described by rewriting the substring $\langle \text{Rib}.\overline{site}_{ter} \rangle$ with the substring $\langle \overline{site}_{ter} \rangle$ in the string representing the mRNA and the production of an object Rib and Prot specifying a free ribosome and a newly produced protein, respectively.

$$r_{tlt} : [\, \langle \text{Rib}.\overline{site}_{ter} \rangle \,]_l \xrightarrow{c_{tlt}} [\, \text{Rib} + \text{Prot} + \langle \overline{site}_{ter} \rangle \,]_l$$
$$prop(r_{tlt}) = c_{tlt} |\langle \text{Rib}.\overline{site}_{ter} \rangle| \tag{15}$$

8 Analysis of P System Models Using PRISM

Most research in systems biology focuses on the development of models of biological systems accurately enough such as to be able to reveal new properties that can be difficult or impossible to discover through direct lab experiments. One key question is what one can do with a model, other than simple simulation. Is it enough just to realize many simulations of a model to obtain novel knowledge on the system under study? This question has been considered in detail for deterministic models where a rich theory has been produced to analyze systems of differential equations. However, this is not the case for stochastic models, as such systems defy conventional intuition and consequently are harder to conceive. The field is widely open for theoretical advances that help us to reason about systems in greater detail and with finer precision.

There are several attempts in this direction which consists of applying model checking tools to computational models of cellular systems [13]. There are previous studies investigating the use of model checking on P system [1,15]. In this section we will propose the use of a probabilistic symbolic model checking approach based on PRISM (Probabilistic and Symbolic Model Checker) [14].

Model checking is a well established and widely used formal method for verifying the correctness of real life systems. *Probabilistic model checking* is a probabilistic variant of the classical model checking augmented with quantitative information regarding the likelihood that transitions occur and the times at which they do so. One of the major advantages of probabilistic model checking is that it is an exhaustive approach, that is, all possible behaviors of the system are analyzed. Analytical methods based on probabilistic model checking consists of three different steps:

1. First, one must design a precise mathematical model of the system which is to be analyzed. In this work, P system models will be used as the formal description required in this step.
2. Once the formal model is built, one has to translate it into the specific language of the probabilistic model checker, PRISM in this case.
3. Finally, some properties of the model must be identified and expressed formally using temporal logic. This allows the probabilistic model checker to analyze these properties in an automatic way against the constructed model.

The fundamental components of the PRISM language are *modules*, *variables* and *commands*. A model is composed of a number of modules which can interact with each other. A module contains a number of local variables and commands. The values of these variables at any given time constitute the state of the module. The space of reachable states is computed using specified ranges for each variable and their initial values. The global state of the whole model is determined by the local state of all modules.

The behavior of each module is described by a set of commands. A predicate is associated with each command to determine when the command is applicable. The application of a command updates the values of the variables in the module describing a transition of the module. The application of commands is driven by some probabilistic information assign to them using specific expressions.

Once a probabilistic model has been specified and constructed in PRISM, one needs to identify one or more *properties* of the model to be analyzed by the model checker. This is done using temporal logic. One key feature of PRISM is the use of rewards associated with states and transitions. This allows to express reward-based properties which are quantitative in nature. Rewards associated with states, *cumulated rewards*, are incremented in proportion to the time spent in the state, while rewards associated with transitions *impulse rewards* are incremented each time the transition is taken.

Translation of P system Models into PRISM

As mentioned before in order to perform model checking analysis on a P system model it is necessary to translate it into the PRISM language. The three essential components of a P system are a membrane structure consisting of a number of membranes that can interact with each other, multisets of objects[4] and rewriting rules associated with membranes. These components can easily be mapped into the components of the PRISM language using modules to represent membranes, variables to describe objects and commands to specify rules. A detailed description of how to specify P systems models in the PRISM language is presented in what follows.

• Membrane structure: Recall that each membrane is uniquely identified with an identifier i. Therefore, for each membrane i a module with name `compartment_i` will be introduced in the model.

• Alphabet and initial multisets: For each object *obj* that can be present inside the compartment defined by membrane i a local variable `obj_i` will be declared in module `compartment_i`. The initial value of this variable is determined by the initial multiset associated with membrane i. The value range of the variables representing objects will be determined experimentally or it will be derived from the literature. In order to specify these ranges two constants will be declared `upb_obj_i` and `lob_obj_i`.

• Rewriting rules: Commands are used in PRISM to describe the rewriting rules of a P system. Given a rule of the form:

$$r_j^{l_i} : obj_1 \, [\, obj_2 \,]_l \xrightarrow{c_j^{l_i}} obj_1' \, [\, obj_2' \,]_l$$

---

[4] Strings are not easily represented in PRISM and will not be considered in this work.

with $obj_1 = o_1^1 + \cdots + o_{n_1}^1, obj_2 = o_1^2 + \cdots + o_{n_2}^2, obj_1' = oo_1^1 + \cdots + oo_{m_1}^1, obj_2' = oo_1^2 + \cdots + oo_{m_2}^2$ some finite multisets and $c_j^{l_i}$ the stochastic constant associated with the rule. Assuming that the label of membrane i is l and that it is embedded inside membrane k the objects in the rule are specified as follows. The variables o_1_1_k, ..., o_n_1_1_k, oo_1_1_k, ..., oo_m_1_1_k specify the objects from obj_1 and obj_1' in module compartment_k. The objects o_1_2_i, ..., o_n_2_2_i and oo_1_2_i, oo_m_2_2_i represent the objects from obj_2 and obj_2' in module compartment_i. The stochastic constants associated with the rules are specified using PRISM constants.

In general, rules need two membranes to interact in a synchronized way to exchange objects. Therefore when a rule affects two different compartments, the two modules representing them will synchronize the application of two different commands by using a label which identifies the rule r_j_l_i.

The command in module compartment_i describing the effect of an application of rule $r_j^{l_i}$ in compartment i will be:

```
[ r_j_l_i ] o_1_2_i > 0 & ... & o_n_2_2_i > 0 &
            oo_1_2_i < upb_oo_1_2_i & ... &
            oo_m_2_2_i < upb_oo_m_2_2_i - >
              c_j_l_i * o_1_2_i * ... * o_n_2_2_i :
                (o_1_2_i' = o_1_2_i - 1) & ... &
                (o_n_2_2_i' = o_n_2_2_i - 1) &
                (oo_1_2_i' = oo_1_2_i + 1) & ... &
                (oo_m_2_2_i' = oo_m_2_2_i + 1);
```

The command in module compartment_k describing the effect of an application of rule $r_j^{l_i}$ in compartment k will be:

```
[ r_j_l_i ] o_1_1_k > 0 & ... & o_n_1_1_k > 0 &
            oo_1_1_k < upb_oo_1_1_k & ... &
            oo_m_1_1_k < upb_oo_m_1_1_k - >
              o_1_1_k * ... * o_n_1_1_k :
                (o_1_1_k' = o_1_1_k - 1) & ... &
                (o_n_1_1_k' = o_n_1_1_k - 1) &
                (oo_1_1_k' = oo_1_1_k + 1) & ... &
                (oo_m_1_1_k' = oo_m_1_1_k + 1);
```

Observe that these two commands are applied when the guards hold, that is, if and only if there are some reactants in the corresponding membranes and the products have not reached the upper bounds determined experimentally. Also note that the rate of this transition is the product of the individual rates:

```
(c_j_l_i * o_1_2_i * ... * o_n_2_2_i) (o_1_1_k * ... * o_n_1_1_k)
```

When this transition is performed the local variables representing the reactants are decreased by one and the variables representing the products are increased by one.

Some Specifications of P System Properties in PRISM

The first step when analyzing a model in PRISM is to associate the appropriate rewards with the corresponding states and transitions. A typical analysis consists of the study of the evolution over time of the number of objects or molecules and the number of applications of rules. Therefore, two different lists of rewards will be used. The first list will associate with each state a reward representing the number of a particular object. A constant `obj` is used to identify which object is being tracked at the moment. In a similar manner a list of rewards will be used to associated with each transition a reward of 1 representing that the rule has been applied once. A constant `rule` is used to identify which rule is being analyzed.

```
rewards "molecules"             rewards "rules"
obj = 1 : = o1_i;               [ r_1_env ] rule = 1 : 1;
:                               :
obj = n : on_i ;                [ r_14_cyto ] rule = 19 : 1;
endrewards                      endrewards
```

Once the corresponding rewards have been associated with particular states and transitions one can use PRISM to model check some properties of the system. The type of properties analyzed in this section are only intended to illustrate how to use PRISM to study the behavior of P system models. We do not intend to cover all possible properties, not even the most common ones, that can be checked in PRISM as the properties to study depend very much on the model being analyzed.

A typical analysis, when dealing with stochastic models, is to compute the expected number of molecules over time. This can be studied in PRISM using instantaneous reward properties where a constant `time` indicates the time instant for which the expected number of molecules is computed, see below left. PRISM also allows to reason about the evolution of P system models as a consequence of the applications of different rules. One can compute the expected number of applications of the different rules within T units of time using cumulative reward properties, see below right.

```
R = ? [ I = time ]              R = ? [ C <= T ]
```

Another important type of quantitative property which can be computed using PRISM is the expected time for an event to take place. This can be done with reachability reward properties. For instance the property specified below can be used to compute the expected time for the number of objects `o1_i` to get over a threshold `Th`.

```
R = ? [ F o1_i > Th ]
```

PRISM allows us to reason about the probability that a certain type of behavior is observed at specific times during the evolution of our stochastic models. This is done by using the operator `P` and a path property which can use the temporal operators next `X`, until `U` and bounded until `U time`. For instance the property below computes the probability of `o1_i` getting over a threshold `Th` within the first T units of time of the evolution of the model.

$$P = ? [\text{true U} <= T \text{ o1\_i} > Th]$$

Finally, PRISM allows us to reason about the *long run, equilibrium* or *steady state* behavior of our models. In this case the operator S is used. For example the probability of the number of objects o1_i to be between the values o1_up and o1_down in the long run can be computed using the following expression:

$$S = ? [\text{o1\_i} < \text{o1\_up \& o1\_i} > \text{o1\_down}]$$

9   The Lac Operon System, a Case Study

In this section the lac operon regulation system in *Escherichia coli* (*E. coli*) is used as a case study to illustrate the general principles presented in this paper. Here we present a summary of the model developed in [24]. Gene expression is highly regulated in order to produce the necessary proteinic machinery to respond to environmental changes. At a given time a particular cell only synthesizes those proteins necessary for its survival under the specific conditions of that time. Gene expression is primarily regulated by mechanisms that control transcription initiation.

The lac operon is a group of three genes, lacZ, lacY and lacA physically linked together in an operon. These genes codify β-galactosidase, LacY and LacA, proteins involved in the metabolism and transport of lactose. The lac operon has a dual, positive and negative, regulation system that allows *E. coli* to uptake and consume lactose only in the absence of glucose [19].

9.1   A P System Specification of the Lac Operon

Our P system specification of the lac operon regulation system consists of the following construct:

$$\Pi_{lac} = ((\Sigma_{lac}^{obj}, \Sigma_{lac}^{str}), \{e, s, c\}, [\ [\ [\ ]_3\ ]_2\ ]_1, M_1, M_2, M_3, ((R_e^{obj}, \emptyset), (R_s^{obj}, \emptyset), (R_c^{obj}, R_c^{str}))$$

– <u>Specification of the molecular entities</u>: In our P system specification, Π_{lac}, each protein and proteinic complex is represented by an individual object in the alphabet Σ_{lac}^{obj}. As discussed in section 7.3 the specification of operons as strings is more accurate than as individual objects. Following this idea the lac operon is represented by the following string whose components define the relevant sites for the regulation of the operon. These sites are represented by the symbols in Σ_{lac}^{str}.

$$\langle \text{cap.op.} \overbrace{\text{lacZ}_s.\text{lacZ}_m \cdots \text{lacZ}_m.\text{lacZ}_e}^{30} . \overbrace{\text{lacY}_s.\text{lacY}_m \cdots \text{lacY}_m.\text{lacY}_e}^{12} . \overbrace{\text{lacA}_s.\text{lacA}_m \cdots \text{lacA}_m.\text{lacA}_e}^{6} \rangle$$

– <u>Specification of the relevant regions</u>: In the lac operon regulation system the cell surface plays a crucial role since the proteins involved in the selective uptake of glucose and lactose are located in this region of the system. According to section 7.1 two membranes are used to specify an *E. coli* bacterium in our P systems specification Π_{lac}. Specifically, membrane 2 with label s is introduced to describe the cell surface and membrane 3 embedded in the previous one with label c specifies the cytoplasm. Moreover, in the lac operon system the growing media is also a relevant region as bacteria response differently according to its conditions (presence or absence of glucose/lactose). Therefore, membrane 1 labeled by e is used to describe the growing media or environment. Figure 1 depicts a graphical representation of the membrane structure in Π_{lac}.

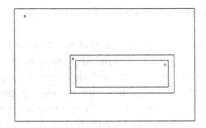

Fig. 1. Membrane structure in the lac operon regulation system

– Specification of the molecular interactions:

The molecular interactions in the regulation system of the lac operon are specified using the rewriting rules in $((R_e^{obj}, \emptyset), (R_s^{obj}, \emptyset), (R_c^{obj}, R_c^{str}))$. Here we only present a few rules to illustrate our approach. For a complete specification of the molecular interactions in the lac operon see [24].

The uptake of glucose, Gluc, and lactose, Lact, from the environment by the proteins LacY and EIICB~P located on the cell surface, membrane labeled by s, is specified by the binding rules $r_4, r_8 \in R_e^{obj}$. The delivering to the cytoplasm of the sugars is described by the releasing rules $r_6, r_9 \in R_s^{obj}$.

r_4: Gluc [EIICB~P]$_s$ $\overset{c_4}{\to}$ [EIICB~P–Gluc]$_s$

r_6: EIICB~P–Gluc [ ]$_c$ $\overset{c_6}{\to}$ EIICB [Gluc~P]$_c$

r_8: Lact [LacY]$_s$ $\overset{c_8}{\to}$ [Lact-LacY]$_s$

r_9: Lact-LacY [ ]$_c$ $\overset{c_9}{\to}$ LacY [Lact]$_c$

Glucose uptake needs a phosphate group from EIICB~P. This protein is phosphorylated by EIIA~P which is in turn is involved in the production of the activator cAMP according to the recruitment and releasing rules $r_{19} \in R_c^{obj}$ and $r_{20} \in R_s^{obj}$. As a consequence of these rules in the presence of glucose EIIA~P will be utilized in the glucose transport system and it will not be available to produce the activator.

r_{19}: AC-EIIA~P [ATP]$_c$ $\overset{c_{19}}{\to}$ AC~P-EIIA~P-ATP [ ]$_c$

r_{20}: AC–EIIA~P-ATP [ ]$_c$ $\overset{c_{20}}{\to}$ AC~P–EIIA~P [cAMP]$_c$

When lactose is transported inside the cytoplasm it interacts with β-galactosidase producing as a byproduct allolactose, Allolact. Allolactose binds to the repressor, LacI, forming a complex, rule $r_{15} \in R_c^{obj}$. This changes the repressor making it incapable of binding to the operator of the operon.

r_{15}: [LacI + Allolact]$_c$ $\overset{c_{15}}{\rightarrow}$ [LacI-Allolact]$_c$

The mechanism by which LacI represses the transcription of the lac operon is by reversibly binding to a specific site called operator. This site is represented by the substring $\langle$ op $\rangle$. This process is represented by the rewriting rules on multiset of objects and strings $r_{25}, r_{26} \in R_c^{str}$.

r_{25}: [LacI + $\langle$ op $\rangle$]$_c$ $\overset{c_{25}}{\rightarrow}$ [$\langle$ op^{LacI} $\rangle$]$_c$
r_{26}: [$\langle$ op^{LacI} $\rangle$]$_c$ $\overset{c_{26}}{\rightarrow}$ [LacI + $\langle$ op $\rangle$]$_c$

The activator CRP-cAMP$_2$ binds to another specific site represented by the substring $\langle$ cap $\rangle$ according to similar transcription factor binding and debinding rules. The RNAP recognizes with different affinities the unoccupied and occupied sites showing a higher transcription initiation rate in the latter case. This is represented in the rules $r_{29}, r_{30} \in R_c^{str}$. Note that there is a 40 fold increase between c_{29} and c_{30}.

r_{29}: [RNAP + $\langle$ cap $\rangle$]$_c$ $\overset{c_{29}}{\rightarrow}$ [$\langle$ cap.RNAP $\rangle$]$_c$, $c_{29} = 5 \times 10^{-4} molec^{-1} sec^{-1}$
r_{30}: [RNAP + $\langle$ cap$^{CRP-cAMP_2}$ $\rangle$]$_c$ $\overset{c_{30}}{\rightarrow}$ [$\langle$ cap$^{CRP-cAMP_2}$. RNAP $\rangle$]$_c$,
$\qquad c_{30} = 0.02 molec^{-1} sec^{-1}$

An example of transcription elongation rule in the lac operon is $r_{36} \in R_c^{str}$. Here the RNAP transcribes a specific site of the lacY gene and attaches the corresponding ribonucleotides $\overline{lacY}_m$ to the growing mRNA , $\langle$ $\overline{op}.w$ $\rangle$.

r_{36}: [$\langle$ $\overline{op}.w$. RNAP. lacY$_m$ $\rangle$]$_c$ $\overset{c_{36}}{\rightarrow}$ [$\langle$ lacY$_m.\overline{op}.w.\overline{lacY}_m$.RNAP $\rangle$]$_c$

The transcription of the lac operon terminates when the RNAP reaches the transcription termination site represented by the string $\langle$ lacA$_e$ $\rangle$. Rule $r_{40} \in R_c^{str}$ specifies the dissociation of the RNAP from the operon and the releasing of a complete mRNA strand, $\langle$ $\overline{op}.w.\overline{lacA}_e$ $\rangle$.

r_{40}: [$\langle$ $\overline{op}.w$.RNAP.lacA$_e$ $\rangle$]$_c$ $\overset{c_{40}}{\rightarrow}$ [RNAP + $\langle$ lacA$_e$ $\rangle$; $\langle$ $\overline{op}.w.\overline{lacA}_e$ $\rangle$]$_c$

Examples of translation initiation and elongation are rules $r_{41} \in R_c^{str}$ and $r_{45} \in R_c^{str}$ respectively. Note that the rewriting rule on multiset of objects and strings r_{41} describes the recognition by a ribosome of the RBS for lacZ. The rules r_{45} specifies the movement along the mRNA of ribosomes.

r_{41}: [Rib + $\langle$ $\overline{lacZ}_s$ $\rangle$]$_c$ $\overset{c_{41}}{\rightarrow}$ [$\langle$ Rib.$\overline{lacZ}_s$ $\rangle$]$_c$
r_{45}: [$\langle$ Rib.$\overline{lacZ}_m$ $\rangle$]$_c$ $\overset{c_{45}}{\rightarrow}$ [$\langle$ $\overline{lacZ}_m$.Rib $\rangle$]$_c$

Finally translation finishes when ribosomes reach termination sites in the mRNA. For instance, rule $r_{46} \in R_c^{str}$, represents translation termination for lacZ when a ribosome reaches the termination site $\overline{lacZ}_e$ and releases a molecule β-galactosidase, the protein codified by the lacZ gene.

r_{46}: [$\langle$ Rib.$\overline{lacZ}_e$ $\rangle$]$_c$ $\overset{c_{46}}{\rightarrow}$ [β−Galac + Rib + $\langle$ $\overline{lacZ}_e$ $\rangle$]$_c$

9.2 P System Models of the Lac Operon

A family of P system models based on our specification Π_{lac} is introduced to study the behavior of the lac operon regulation system under different initial conditions. The parameters of Π_{lac}, $\mathcal{P}(\Pi_{lac}) = (\mathcal{M}_0(\Pi_{lac}), \mathcal{C}(\Pi_{lac}))$ consists of the initial multisets associated with the environment M_1, cell surface M_2 and cytoplasm M_3 and the stochastic constants associated with the rewriting rules $\mathcal{C}(\Pi_{lac})$. Since we are interested in the behavior of the lac operon system under different environmental conditions specific values $\mathcal{C}^0$, M_2^0 and M_3^0 will be given to $\mathcal{C}(\Pi_{lac})$, M_2 and M_3 [24]. In contrast we will vary the values given to M_1 to represent different conditions. More specifically, we will study our system in the presence of lactose and absence of glucose, $M_1^1 = (e, Lact^{3000}, \emptyset)$ and presence of lactose and glucose $M_1^2 = (e, Lact^{3000} + Glucose^{3000}, \emptyset)$. Our study will be performed by running simulation using the algorithm introduced in section 6.2.

– Presence of lactose: This case is represented by the P system model $(\Pi_{lac}; (M_1^1, M_2^0, M_3^0), \mathcal{C}^0)$. Under this condition our simulation showed that the state of the promoter of the lac operon is $\langle$ cap$^{CRP-cAMP_2}.op \rangle$. Since lactose is in the media allolactose will appear in the cytoplasm and inutilize the repressor LacI. The absence of glucose in the media will allow AC–EIIA∼P to synthesize the activator cAMP which will interact with the protein CRP and bind to the promoter of the lac operon to increasing transcription initiation by RNAP. This configuration of the promoter yields a full transcription of the operon by many RNAPs, Figure 2 top left, which in turn produces a massive number of the proteins encoded in the operon, for instance LacY, Figure 2 top right.

– Presence of lactose and glucose: This situation is represented by the P system model $(\Pi_{lac}; (M_1^2, M_2^0, M_3^0), \mathcal{C}^0)$. The state of the promoter in this case is $\langle$cap.op$\rangle$ which corresponds with a low transcription of the lac operon in spite of the presence of lactose, this phenomenon is referred to as *catabolite repression*. The presence of lactose in the media excludes the repressors but the presence of glucose in the media represses the synthesis of the activator which produces a non-repressed non-activated operon. Under these conditions only a few RNAP will be active transcribing the operon, Figure 2 bottom left, and only after a delay which corresponds to the time necessary to consume glucose, the proteins codified in the operon are produced, Figure 2 bottom right.

9.3 An Analysis of Gene Expression Using P Systems and PRISM

As it can be seen in the results obtained when modeling the lac operon system gene expression shows a considerable level of noise. In this section in order to illustrate the use of P system models and PRISM to study the stochasticity in cellular systems we will use the abstract gene regulation system in Figure 3. This simple model consists only of rewriting rules on multisets of objects modeling transcription, translation and the interactions between a transcription factor and a gene.

We start by checking the average time the gene is occupied by a transcription factor for different affinities, $\frac{c_6}{c_5}$, and number of transcription factors. This can be

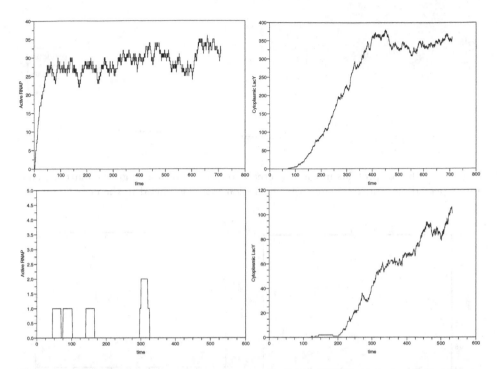

Fig. 2. Number of RNAP transcribing the operon (left) and LacY molecules (right) in the presence of lactose and absence of glucose (top) and in the presence of lactose and glucose (bottom)

P System Rules	PRISM Specification
	module compartment
	gene : [0 .. 1] init 0;
	rna : [0 .. uprna] init 0;
$r_1 : [\,gene\,]_c \xrightarrow{c_1} [\,gene + rna\,]_c$	prot : [0 .. upprot] init 0;
$r_2 : [\,rna\,]_c \xrightarrow{c_2} [\,rna + prot\,]_c$	[r1] gene = 0 & rna < uprna ->
$r_3 : [\,rna\,]_c \xrightarrow{c_3} [\,\,]_c$	c_1 : (rna' = rna + 1);
$r_4 : [\,prot\,]_c \xrightarrow{c_4} [\,\,]_c$	[r2] rna > 0 & prot < upprot ->
$r_5 : [\,Tf + gene\,]_c \xrightarrow{c_5} [\,Tf\text{-}gene\,]_c$	c_2*rna : (prot' = prot + 1);
$r_6 : [\,Tf\text{-}gene\,]_c \xrightarrow{c_6} [\,Tf + gene\,]_c$	[r3] rna > 0 -> c_3*rna : (rna' = rna - 1;)
	[r4] prot > 0 -> c_4*prot : (prot' = prot - 1);
	[r5] Tf > 0 & gene = 0 -> c_5*Tf : (gene' = 1);
	[r6] gene = 1 -> c_6 : (gene' = 0);
	endmodule

Fig. 3. P System rules and PRISM specification for an abstract gene regulation system

done in PRISM by associating a reward of one to every state in which the gene is occupied and using a cumulative reward query. Our results, Figure 4 right, show that for affinities between 10^{12} to 10^9 M fewer than five transcription factors are enough to occupy the gene almost all the time. For an affinity of 10^8 M the

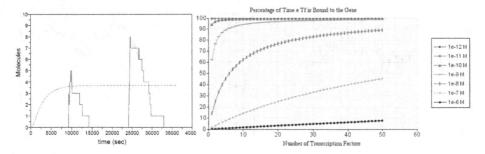

Fig. 4. Number of proteins in the expected evolution and in a single simulation (left) and expected percentage of time a transcription factor is bound to the gene (right)

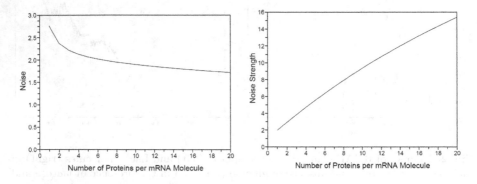

Fig. 5. Noise (left) and noise strength (right) in translational bursting

system is able to discriminate more precisely between only a few transcription factors, fewer than ten, and many, more than thirty. In the first case the gene is occupied less than half of the time whereas for the second case the gene is occupy most of the time. For affinities of the order of $10^7 - 10^6$ M the gene is seldom occupied even when more than fifty transcription factors are present in the system.

We also study the expected number of proteins produced when a very low transcription rate is considered, $c_1 = 10^{-4}sec^{-1}$, Figure 4 left. Note that the expected number of proteins in the long run is three. Nevertheless, when running a single simulation we observe sporadic bursts in the number of protein reaching high peaks. This phenomenon is known as *translation bursting* and is due to a high translation efficiency or expected number of proteins produce by a single molecule of mRNA. Using PRISM we checked that this value is equal to $\frac{c_2}{c_3}$. For different expected number of proteins produced by a molecule of mRNA we study the noise in the system, $\eta = \frac{\sigma}{\mu}$ [5] and the noise strength $\phi = \frac{\sigma^2}{\mu}$. These values were computed using PRISM. Our results show that although high translation efficiencies produce a slight decrease in the level of noise, Figure 5 left,

---

[5] σ represents the standard deviation and μ the expected value.

they produce a considerable increase in the noise strength, Figure 5 right. This analysis highlights the important of posttranscriptional regulation, a mechanism that is widely overlooked in gene regulation modeling.

10   Conclusions

Modeling in systems biology is subject to very intensive research. Nevertheless, most modeling approaches proposed so far do not present a unifying framework for the specification of the structural components of the cell together with the description of their dynamical interactions. In this work, we have presented P systems as a high level computational modeling framework which integrates the structural and dynamical aspects of cellular systems in a comprehensive and relevant way while providing the required formalization to perform mathematical and computational analysis. The non deterministic and maximally parallel original strategy has been replaced by an adaption of Gillespie algorithm to the multicompartmental structure of P systems in order to develop a stochastic and quantitative framework.

We have discussed a methodology to specify compartments using membranes; molecular entities as objects or strings depending on the relevance of the internal structure and the most important molecular interactions as rewriting rules on multisets of objects and strings. Our modeling framework is not restricted to the simple generation of simulations of our models. We have taken the first steps towards the development of techniques to analyze P system models based on probabilistic and symbolic model checking.

Finally, our work has uncovered several open problems and future lines of research in the use of P systems as a modeling framework in systems biology.

1. The adaption of Gillespie algorithm to a multicompartmental structure has produced a local algorithm easily implemented in an event-driven object-oriented programming style. Such an implementation could be multithreaded on a hyper-threading machine and would also lend itself to full message-passing implementation on a parallel computing cluster. In spite of this no such implementation has been addressed yet.
2. One of the key advantages of P systems with respect to other modeling approaches is the explicit specification of the structural components of cellular systems, more precisely of compartments. In this respect, it is worth noting that up to now P systems have overlooked a key component of the structure of living cells, the cytoskeleton, a dense network of protein filaments that permeate the cytosol and mechanically support membranes and proteins. It is also involved in a great variety of processes like molecular transport, cell division, cell mobility, etc.
3. Regarding membrane interactions in cellular systems we have not investigated important processes where membranes are crucial like cell division, cell adhesion, biofilm formation, etc. The specification and simulation of this type of processes remain an open problem and a future direction to explore.

4. Finally, although very easy to understand P systems present a current limitation to the transparency and utility of the specifications and models designed within their framework. The P system abstractions are purely textual and so far lack of a graphical formal representation for the visualization of the modeled systems.

Summing up, P systems constitute a reliable formal framework for the specification, simulation and analysis of cell systems biology models presenting many challenging future directions.

Acknowledgement

The work of Gh.P. was supported by project BioMAT 2-CEx06-11-97/19.09.06 and project CellSim PC-1284.

General Membrane Computing References

1. G. Ciobanu, Gh. Păun, M.J. Pérez-Jiménez, eds.: *Applications of Membrane Computing*. Springer, 2006 (**AMC 2006** in references below).
2. M. Ionescu, Gh. Păun, T. Yokomori: Spiking neural P systems. *Fundamenta Informaticae*, 71, 2-3 (2006), 279–308.
3. Gh. Păun: Computing with membranes. *Journal of Computer and System Sciences*, 61, 1 (2000), 108–143 (first circulated as Turku Center for Computer Science-TUCS Report 208, November 1998, www.tucs.fi).
4. Gh. Păun: *Computing with Membranes: An Introduction*. Springer, 2002.
5. Gh. Păun: Membrane computing. Main ideas, basic results, applications. In *Molecular Computational Models: Unconventional Approaches* (M. Gheorghe, ed.), Idea Group Publ., London, 2004, 1–31.
6. Gh. Păun: Introduction to membrane computing. In *Proc. Brainstorming Workshop on Uncertainty in Membrane Computing*, Palma de Mallorca, Nov. 2004, 17–65.
7. Gh. Păun, M.J. Pérez-Jiménez: Membrane computing. Brief introduction, recent results and applications. *BioSystems*, 85, 1 (2006), 11–22.
8. M.J. Pérez-Jiménez: An approach to computational complexity in membrane computing. In *Membrane Computing, 5th International Workshop, WMC 2004, Milan, Italy, June 2004, Revised, Selected and Invited Papers*, LNCS 3365, Springer, 2005, 85–109.
9. P Systems Web Page: http://psystems.disco.unimib.it.

Applications to Biology and Bio-medicine

1. S. Aguzzolli, I.I. Ardelean, D. Besozzi, B. Gerla, C. Manara: P systems under uncertainty: The case of transmembrane proteins. In *Proc. Brainstorming Workshop on Uncertainty in Membrane Computing*, Palma de Mallorca, 2004, 107–118.

2. I.I. Ardelean: Biological roots and applications of P systems. Further suggestions. In *Membrane Computing, WMC2006, Leiden, Revised, Selected and Invited Papers*, LNCS 4361, Springer, 2006, 1–17.

3. I.I. Ardelean, D. Besozzi: On modeling ion fluxes across biological membranes with P systems. In *Proc. Third Brainstorming Week on Membrane Computing*, Sevilla, 2005, RGNC Report 01/2005, 35–42.

4. I.A. Ardelean, D. Besozzi: Some notes on the interplay between P systems and chemotaxis in bacteria. In *Proc. Fourth Brainstorming Week on Membrane Computing*, Sevilla, 2006, RGNC Report 02/2006, 41–48.

5. I.I. Ardelean, D. Besozzi, M.H. Garzon, G. Mauri, S. Roy: P system models for mechanosensitive channels. In **AMC 2006**, 43–82.

6. I. Ardelean, M. Cavaliere: Playing with a probabilistic P system simulator: Mathematical and biological problems. *New Generation Computing*, 22, 4 (2004), 311–329.

7. I.I. Ardelean, M. Cavaliere: Modelling biological processes by using a probabilistic P system software. *Natural Computing*, 2, 2 (2003), 173–197.

8. J. Auld, L. Bianco, G. Ciobanu, M. Gheorghe, D. Pescini, F.J. Romero-Campero: Population P systems – A model for the behaviour of systems of bio-entities. In *Pre-proc. WMC7*, Leiden, The Netherlands, 2006, 15–20.

9. R. Barbuti, A. Maggiolo-Schettini, P. Milazzo, A. Troina: The calculus of looping sequences for modeling biological membranes. In *Membrane Computing. Eight Workshop on Membrane Computing, WMC2007, Thessaloniki, Greece, June 2007. Revised, Selected and Invited Papers*, LNCS 4860, Springer, 2007.

10. F. Bernardini: *Membrane Systems for Molecular Computing and Biological Modelling*. PhD Thesis, Univ. Sheffield, Anglia, 2006.

11. F. Bernardini, M. Gheorghe, N. Krasnogor: Quorum sensing P systems. *Theoretical Computer Sci.*, 371, 1-2 (2007), 20–33.

12. F. Bernardini, M. Gheorghe, N. Krasnogor, R.C. Muniyandi, M.J. Pérez-Jiménez, F.J. Romero-Campero: On P systems as a modelling tool for biological systems. In *Membrane Computing, International Workshop, WMC6, Vienna, Austria, 2005, Selected and Invited Papers*, LNCS 3850, Springer, 2006, 114–133.

13. F. Bernardini, M. Gheorghe, N. Krasnogor, M.J. Pérez-Jiménez, F.J. Romero-Campero: Modelling vibrio fischeri's behaviour using P systems. Submitted 2005.

14. F. Bernardini, V. Manca: Dynamical aspects of P systems. *BioSystems*, 70, 2 (2003), 85–93.

15. F. Bernardini, F.J. Romero-Campero, M. Gheorghe, M.J. Pérez-Jiménez: A modeling approach based on P systems with bounded parallelism. In *Membrane Computing, 7th International Workshop, WMC 2006, Leiden, The Netherlands, July 2006, Revised, Selected and Invited Papers*, LNCS 4361, Springer, 2006, 49–65.

16. D. Besozzi: *Computational and Modelling Power of P Systems*. PhD Thesis, Univ. degli Studi di Milano, Italy, 2004.

17. D. Besozzi, I.I. Ardelean, G. Mauri: The potential of P systems for modeling the activity of mechanosensitive channels in E. Coli. In *Pre-proc. WMC 2003*, Tarragona, GRLMC Report 28/03, 84–102.

18. D. Besozzi, P. Cazzaniga, D. Pescini, G. Mauri: Seasonal variance in P systems models for metapopulations. *Progress in Natural Science*, 17, 4 (2007), 392–400.

19. D. Besozzi, G. Ciobanu: A P system description of the sodium-potassium pump. In *Membrane Computing, 5th International Workshop, WMC 2004, Milan, Italy, June 2004, Revised, Selected and Invited Papers*, LNCS 3365, Springer, 2005, 210–223.

20. L. Bianco: Psim – A computational platform for metabolic P systems. In *Membrane Computing. Eight Workshop on Membrane Computing, WMC2007, Thessaloniki, Greece, June 2007. Revised, Selected and Invited Papers*, LNCS 4860, Springer, 2007.

21. L. Bianco, F. Fontana, G. Franco, V. Manca: P systems for biological dynamics. In **AMC 2006**, 83–128.

22. L. Bianco, F. Fontana, V. Manca: P systems with reaction maps. *Intern. J. Found. Computer Sci.*, 17, 1 (2006), 27–48.

23. L. Bianco, F. Fontana, V. Manca: Computation of biochemical dynamics using MP systems. *Computational Methods in Systems Biology*, Intern. Conference, Trento, 2006, poster.

24. L. Bianco, V. Manca: Metabolic algorithms and signal transduction dynamical networks. In *Proc. Brainstorming Workshop on Uncertainty in Membrane Computing*, Palma de Mallorca, 2004, 119–120.

25. L. Bianco, V. Manca: Symbolic generation and representation of complex oscillations. *Intern. J. Computer Math.*, 83, 7 (2006), 549–568.

26. L. Bianco, D. Pescini, P. Siepmann, N, Krasnogor, F.J. Romero-Campero, M. Gheorghe: Towards a P systems Pseudomonas quorum sensing model. In *Membrane Computing, 7th International Workshop, WMC 2006, Leiden, The Netherlands, July 2006, Revised, Selected and Invited Papers*, LNCS 4361, Springer, 2006, 197–214.

27. M. Cavaliere: Modelling biological processes in P systems. Handling imprecision and constructing new models. In *Proc. Brainstorming Workshop on Uncertainty in Membrane Computing*, Palma de Mallorca, 2004, 143–144.

28. M. Cavaliere, I.I. Ardelean: Modelling respiration in bacteria and respiration/photosynthesis interaction in Cyanobacteria by using a P system simulator. In **AMC 2006**, 129–158.

29. M. Cavaliere, S. Sedwards: Membrane systems with peripheral proteins: transport and evolution. *Technical Report* 04/2006, Centre for Computational and Systems Biology, Trento, 2006.

30. M. Cavaliere, S. Sedwards: Modelling cellular processes using membrane systems with peripheral and integral proteins. *Computational Methods in Systems Biology*, Intern. Conference, Trento, 2006, LNBI 4210, Springer, 2006, 108–126.

31. M. Cavaliere, S. Sedwards: Decision problems in membrane systems with peripheral proteins, transport and evolution. *Technical Report* 12/2006, Centre for Computational and Systems Biology, Trento, 2006.

32. P. Cazzaniga, D. Pescini, D. Besozzi, E. Martegani, G. Mauri: Stochastic modelling and simulations of the Ras/cAMP/PKA pathway in the yeast Saccharomyces cerevisiae. *Proc. CMBS 2007.*

33. P. Cazzaniga, D. Pescini, D. Besozzi, G. Mauri: Tau leaping stochastic simulation method in P systems. In *Membrane Computing, 7th International Workshop, WMC 2006, Leiden, The Netherlands, July 2006, Revised, Selected and Invited Papers*, LNCS 4361, Springer, 2006, 298–313.

34. P. Cazzaniga, D. Pescini, F.J. Romero-Campero, D. Besozzi, G. Mauri: Stochastic approaches in P systems for simulating biological systems. In *Proc. Brainstorming Week on Membrane Computing 2006*, Fenix Editora, Sevilla, 2006, 145–164.

35. S. Cheruku, A. Păun, F.J. Romero-Campero, M.J. Pérez-Jiménez, O.H. Ibarra: Simulating FAS-induced apoptosis by using P systems. *Progress in Natural Science*, 17, 4 (2007), 424–431.

36. G. Ciobanu: Modeling cell-mediated immunity by means of P systems. In **AMC 2006**, 159–180.

37. D.V. Corne, P. Frisco: Dynamics of HIV infection studied with cellular automata and conformon-P systems. *BioSystems*, 2007.

38. S. Dunn, P. Stivers: P system models of bistable, enzyme driven chemical reaction networks. In *Bio-Inspired Modeling of Cognitive Tasks, Proc. IWINAC 2007*, Mar Menor, 2007, LNCS 4527, 203–213.

39. F. Fontana, L. Bianco, V. Manca: P systems and the modeling of biochemical oscillations. In *Membrane Computing, International Workshop, WMC6, Vienna, Austria, 2005, Selected and Invited Papers*, LNCS 3850, Springer, 2006, 199–208.

40. G. Franco, N. Jonoska, B. Osborn, A. Plaas: Knee joint injury and repair modeled by membrane systems. *BioSystems*, 2007.

41. G. Franco, V. Manca: A membrane system for the leukocyte selective recruitment. In *Membrane Computing. Intern. Workshop, WMC2003, Tarragona*, LNCS 2933, Springer, 2004, 181–190.

42. R. Freund, T. Gschwandtner: P systems for modelling biological processes in living cells. Submitted 2006.

43. P. Frisco, D.W. Corne: Advances in modeling the dynamics of HIV infection with conformon-P systems. In *Membrane Computing. Eight Workshop on Membrane Computing, WMC2007, Thessaloniki, Greece, June 2007. Revised, Selected and Invited Papers*, LNCS 4860, Springer, 2007.

44. M. Gheorghe: P systems – a new computational approach in systems biology. In *Pre-proceedings of BIC-TA 2006. Volume of Membrane Computing Section*, 7–14.

45. M.A. Gutiérrez-Naranjo, M.J. Pérez-Jiménez, A. Riscos-Núñez, F.J. Romero-Campero: A membrane computing view on tumours. *Progress in Natural Science*, 17, 4 (2007), 449–457.

46. M.A. Gutiérrez-Naranjo, M.J. Pérez-Jiménez, F.J. Romero-Campero: Simulating avascular tumors with membrane systems. In *Proc. Third Brainstorming Week on Membrane Computing*, Sevilla, 2005, RGNC Report 01/2005, 185–196.

47. T. Hinze, S. Hayat, T. Lenser, N. Matsumaru, P. Dittrich: Hill kinetics meets P systems. A case study on gene regulatory networks as computing agents in silico and in vivo. In *Membrane Computing. Eight Workshop on Membrane Computing, WMC2007, Thessaloniki, Greece, June 2007. Revised, Selected and Invited Papers*, LNCS 4860, Springer, 2007.

48. T. Hinze, T. Lenser, P. Dittrich: A protein substructure based P system for description and analysis of cell signalling network. In *Membrane Computing, WMC2006, Leiden, Revised, Selected and Invited Papers*, LNCS 4361, Springer, 2006, 409–423.

49. D. Jackson, M. Gheorghe, M. Holcombe, F. Bernardini: An agent-based behavioural model of Monomorium pharaonis colonies. In *Membrane Computing. Intern. Workshop, WMC2003, Tarragona*, LNCS 2933, Springer, 2004, 232–239.

50. N. Krasnogor, M. Gheorghe, G. Terrazas, S. Diggle, P. Williams, M. Camara: An appealing computational mechanism drawn from bacterial quorum sensing. *Bulletin of the EATCS*, 85 (2005), 135–148.

51. V. Manca: Topics and problems in metabolic P systems. In *Proc. Brainstorming Week on Membrane Computing 2006*, Fenix Editora, Sevilla, 2006, Vol. 2, 173–184.

52. V. Manca: MP systems approaches to biochemical dynamics: biological rhythms and oscillations. In *Membrane Computing, WMC2006, Leiden, Revised, Selected and Invited Papers*, LNCS 4361, Springer, 2006, 86–99.

53. V. Manca: Metabolic P systems for biochemical dynamics. *Progress in Natural Science*, 17, 4 (2007), 384–391.

54. V. Manca, L. Bianco, F. Fontana: Evolution and oscillation in P systems. Applications to biological phenomena. In *Membrane Computing. International Workshop WMC5, Milano, Italy, 2004*, LNCS 3365, Springer, 2005, 63–84.

55. S. Marcus: Bridging P systems and genomics: A preliminary approach. In *Membrane Computing, International Workshop, WMC-CdeA 2002. Curtea de Argeş, Romania, August 2002, Revised Papers*, LNCS 2597, Springer, 2003, 371–376.

56. E. Martegani, R. Tisi, F. Belotti, S. Colombo, C. Paiardi, J. Winderickx, P. Cazzaniga, D. Besozzi, G. Mauri: Identification of an intracellular signalling complex for ras/camp pathway in yeast: experimental evidences and modelling. *ISSY 25 Conf.*, Hanassari, Espo, Finland, 2006.

57. I. Nepomuceno, J.A. Nepomuceno, F.J. Romero-Campero: A tool for working with the SBML format in P systems modelling biological processes. In *Proc. Third Brainstorming Week on Membrane Computing*, Sevilla, 2005, RGNC Report 01/2005, 219–228.

58. T.Y. Nishida: Simulation of photosynthesis by a K-subset transforming system with membranes. *Fundamenta Informaticae*, 49, 1-3 (2002), 249–259.

59. T.Y. Nishida: A membrane computing model of photosynthesis. In **AMC 2006**, 181–202.

60. A. Păun, M.J. Pérez-Jiménez, F.J. Romero-Campero: Modeling signal transduction using P systems. In *Membrane Computing, WMC2006, Leiden, Revised, Selected and Invited Papers*, LNCS 4361, Springer, 2006, 100–122.

61. M.J. Pérez-Jiménez: P systems-based modelling of cellular signalling pathways. In *Pre-proc. WMC7, 2006*, Leiden, The Netherlands, 54–73.
62. M.J. Pérez-Jiménez, F.J. Romero-Campero: Modelling EGFR signalling network using continuous membrane systems. In *Third Workshop on Computational Methods in Systems Biology*, Edinburgh, 2005.
63. M.J. Pérez-Jiménez, F.J. Romero-Campero: A study of the robustness of the EGFR signalling cascade using continuous membrane systems. In *Proc. IWINAC 2005*, La Palma de Gran Canaria, LNCS 3561, Springer, 2005, vol. I, 268–278.
64. D. Pescini, D. Besozzi, G. Mauri: Investigating local evolutions in dynamical probabilistic P systems. In *Proc. SYNASC 05*, IEEE Press, 2005, 440–447.
65. D. Pescini, D. Besozzi, C. Zandron, G. Mauri: Analysis and simulation of dynamics in probabilistic P systems. In *Proc. DNA11*, UWO, London, Ontario, 2005, LNCS 3892, Springer, 2006, 236–247.
66. A. Profir, N. Barbacari, C. Zelinschi: Gene regulatory network modelling by means of membrane systems. In *Pre-proc. WMC6*, Vienna, July 2005, 162–178.
67. A. Profir, E. Boian, N. Barbacari, E. Guţuleac, C. Zelinschi: Modelling molecular genetic triggers by means of P transducers. In *Pre-proc. WMC2004*, Milano, Italy, 360–362.
68. Y. Pu, Y. Yu, X. Dong: Simulation of biomolecular processes by using stochastic P systems. In *Proc. Workshop on High Performance Computing in the Life Sciences*, Ouro Preto, Brasil, October 2006.
69. F.J. Romero-Campero: *P Systems, a Computational Modelling Framework for Systems Biology*. PhD Thesis, Univ. Sevilla, 2008.
70. A. Romero-Jiménez, M.A. Gutiérrez-Naranjo, M.J. Pérez-Jiménez: Graphical modelling of higher plants using P systems. In *Membrane Computing, WMC2006, Leiden, The Netherlands, Revised, Selected and Invited Papers*, LNCS 4361, Springer, 2006, 496–507.
71. F.J. Romero-Campero, M. Gheorghe, G. Ciobanu, J. Auld, M.J. Pérez-Jiménez: Cellular modelling using P systems and process algebra. *Progress in Natural Science*, 17, 4 (2007), 375–383.
72. I. Stamatopoulou, M. Gheorghe, P. Kefalas: Modelling of dynamic configuration of biology-inspired multi-agent systems with communicating X-machines and population P systems. In *Membrane Computing. Eight Workshop on Membrane Computing, WMC2007, Thessaloniki, Greece, June 2007. Revised, Selected and Invited Papers*, LNCS 4860, Springer, 2007.
73. Y. Suzuki, S. Ogishima, H. Tanaka: Modeling the p53 signaling network by using P systems. In *Pre-proceedings of Workshop on Membrane Computing, WMC2003*, Tarragona, GRLMC Report 28/03, 449–454.
74. Y. Suzuki, H. Tanaka: Abstract rewriting systems on multisets, ARMS, and their application for modelling complex behaviours. In *Brainstorming Week on Membrane Computing*, Tarragona, February 2003, TR 26/03, URV, 2003, 313–331.
75. Y. Suzuki, H. Tanaka: Modeling p53 signalins pathways by using multiset processing. In **AMC 2006**, 203–214.

76. G. Terrazas, N. Krasnogor, M. Gheorghe, F. Bernardini, S. Diggle, M. Camara: An environment aware P system model of quorum sensing. In *Proc. New Computational Paradigms. First Conf. on Computability in Europe, CiE2005, Amsterdam*, LNCS 3536, Springer, 2005, 479–485.

77. M. Umeki, Y. Suzuki: Direct simulation of the Oregonator model by using a class of P systems. In *Membrane Computing. Eight Workshop on Membrane Computing, WMC2007, Thessaloniki, Greece, June 2007. Revised, Selected and Invited Papers*, LNCS 4860, Springer, 2007.

Applications to Linguistics

1. G. Bel Enguix: Preliminaries about some possible applications of P systems to linguistics. In *Membrane Computing, WMC-CdeA2002, Curtea de Argeş, Romania, August 2002, Revised Papers*, LNCS 2597, Springer, 2003, 74–89.

2. G. Bel Enguix: Analyzing P systems structure. Working, predictions and some linguistic suggestions. In *Proc. Workshop on Membrane Computing, Milan, Italy*, 2004, 138–150.

3. G. Bel Enguix: Unstable P systems. Applications to linguistics. In *Membrane Computing, 5th International Workshop, WMC 2004, Milan, Italy, June 2004, Revised, Selected and Invited Papers*, LNCS 3365, Springer, 2005, 190–209.

4. G. Bel-Enguix, R. Gramatovici: Active P automata and natural language processing. In *Membrane Computing. Intern. Workshop, WMC2003, Tarragona*, LNCS 2933, Springer, 2004, 31–42.

5. G. Bel Enguix, M.D. Jiménez-López: Biosyntax. An overview. *Fundamenta Informaticae*, 64, 1-4 (2005), 17–28.

6. G. Bel Enguix, M.D. Jiménez-López: Modelling parallel conversations with P systems. *Proc. SYNASC 05*, IEEE Press, 2005, 395–398.

7. G. Bel Enguix, M.D. Jiménez-López: Linguistic membrane systems and applications. In **AMC 2006**, 347–388.

8. G. Bel Enguix, M.D. Jiménez-López: Dynamic meaning membrane systems: An application to the description of semantic change. *Fundamenta Informaticae*, 76, 3 (2007), 219-237.

9. R. Gramatovici, G. Bel Enguix: Parsing with P automata. In **AMC 2006**, 389–410.

Applications to Economics

1. J. Bartosik: Paun's systems in modeling of human resource management. *Proc. Second Conf. Tools and Methods of Data Transformation*, WSU Kielce, 2004.

2. J. Bartosik: Heaps of pieces and Paun's systems. *Proc. Second Conf. Tools and Methods of Data Transformation*, WSU Kielce, 2004.

3. J. Bartosik: Membrany dynamicsne w modelowaniu systemow ekonomicznych. *Conf. Bad. Oper. i Syst.*, 2006.

4. J. Bartosik, W. Korczynski: Systemy membranowe jako modele hierarchicznych struktur zarzadzania. *Mat. Pokonferencyjne Ekonomia, Informatyka, Zarzadzanie. Teoria i Praktyka*, Wydzial Zarzadzania AGH, Tom II, AGH 2002.

5. F. Bernardini, M. Gheorghe, M. Margenstern, S. Verlan: Producer/consumer in membrane systems and Petri nets. *CiE 2007.*

6. R. Freund, M. Oswald, T. Schirk: How a membrane agent buys goods in a membrane store. *Progress in Natural Science*, 17, 4 (2007), 442–448.

7. W. Korczynski: Transformacje systemow Pauna jako model przeksztalcen systemowych. *Raport z Badan Grantu W2/2003*, WSU Kielce, 2004.

8. W. Korczynski: On a model of economic systems. *Second Conf. Tools and Methods of Data Transformation*, WSU Kielce, 2004.

9. W. Korczynski: Păun's systems and accounting. *Pre-proc. Sixth Workshop on Membrane Computing*, Vienna, Austria, July 2005, 461–464.

10. W. Korczynski, G. Wawrzola, S. Wawrzola: On a reconstruction problem for membrane systems. *Second Conf. Tools and Methods of Data Transformation*, WSU Kielce, 2004.

11. M. Oswald: Independent agents in a globalized world modelled by tissue P systems. In *Workshop on Artificial Life and Robotics*, 2006.

12. Gh. Păun, R. Păun: Membrane computing as a framework for modeling economic processes. In *Proc. SYNASC 05*, Timişoara, Romania, IEEE Press, 2005, 11–18.

13. Gh. Păun, R. Păun: A membrane computing approach to economic modeling: The producer-retailer interactions and investments. *Analiză şi Prospectivă Economică (Economic Analysis and Forecasting)*, Part I: 3, 1 (2006), 30–37, Part II: 4, 2 (2006), 47–54.

14. Gh. Păun, R. Păun: Membrane computing models for economics. An invitation-survey. *Studii şi Cercetări de Calcul Economic şi Cibernetică Economică (Economic Studies and Research)*, 2007.

Applications to Computer Science
Sorting and Ranking

1. A. Alhazov, D. Sburlan: Static sorting algorithms for P systems. In *Preproceedings of Workshop on Membrane Computing, WMC2003*, Tarragona, GRLMC Report 28/03, 17–40.

2. A. Alhazov, D. Sburlan: Static sorting P systems. In **AMC 2006**, 215–252.

3. J.J. Arulanandhan: Implementing bead-sort with P systems. In *Proc. Unconventional Models of Computation Conf. 2002*, LNCS 2509, Springer, 2002, 115–125.

4. M. Ionescu, D. Sburlan: Some applications of spiking neural P systems. In *Pre-proc. Eight Workshop on Membrane Computing, WMC2007*, Thessaloniki, Greece, June 2007, 383–394.

Simulating Circuits and Parallel Architectures

1. A. Binder, R. Freund, G. Lojka, M. Oswald: Applications of membrane systems in distributed systems. *Progress in Natural Science*, 17, 4 (2007), 401–410.
2. M. Cavaliere, V. Deufemia: Specifying dynamic software architectures by using membrane systems. In *Proc. Third Brainstorming Week on Membrane Computing*, Sevilla, 2005, RGNC Report 01/2005, 87–106.
3. R. Ceterchi, M. Pérez-Jiménez: Simulating shuffle-exchange networks with P systems. In *Proc. Second Brainstorming Week on Membrane Computing*, Sevilla, 2004, RGNC Report 01/2004, 117–129.
4. R. Ceterchi, M. Pérez-Jiménez: A perfect shuffle algorithm for reduction processes and its simulation with P systems. In *Proc ICCC, Oradea*, Ed. Univ. Oradea, 2004, 92–98.
5. R. Ceterchi, M.J. Pérez-Jiménez: Simulating parallel architectures with P systems. In *Proc. Fourth Workshop on Membrane Computing, Milan, Italy*, 2004, 184–185.
6. R. Ceterchi, M.J. Pérez-Jiménez, A.I. Tomescu: Simulating the bitonic sort on a 2D-mesh with P systems. In *Membrane Computing. Eight Workshop on Membrane Computing, WMC2007, Thessaloniki, Greece, June 2007. Revised, Selected and Invited Papers*, LNCS 4860, Springer, 2007.
7. R. Ceterchi, D. Sburlan: Simulating Boolean circuits with P systems. In *Membrane Computing. Intern. Workshop, WMC2003, Tarragona*, LNCS 2933, Springer, 2004, 104–122.
8. A. Leporati, C. Zandron, G. Mauri: Simulating the Fredkin gate with energy-based P systems. *J. Univ. Computer Science*, 10, 5 (2004), 600–619.
9. A. Leporati, C. Zandron, G. Mauri: Reversible P systems to simulate Fredkin circuits. *Fundamenta Informaticae*, 74, 4 (2006), 529–548.
10. D. Sburlan: From cells to software architecture. A P system outlook of computational design. *Third Workshop on Mathematical Modelling of Environmental and Life Sciences Problems*, Constanţa, 2004.
11. I. Stamatopoulou, P. Kefalas, M. Gheorghe: OPERAS$_{CC}$ – An instance of a formal framework for MAS modelling based on population P systems. In *Membrane Computing. Eight Workshop on Membrane Computing, WMC2007, Thessaloniki, Greece, June 2007. Revised, Selected and Invited Papers*, LNCS 4860, Springer, 2007.
12. K. Ueda, N. Kato: LNMtal – a language model with links and membranes. In *Membrane Computing. 5th Intern Workshop, WMC2004. Milan, Italy, June 2004. Revised Selected and Invited Papers*, LNCS 3365, Springer, 2005, 110–125.

Computer Graphics, Picture Languages

1. R. Ceterchi, R. Gramatovici, N. Jonoska: P systems for tiling rectangular pictures. In *Membrane Computing. Intern. Workshop, WMC2003, Tarragona*, LNCS 2933, Springer, 2004, 88–103.

2. R. Ceterchi, R. Gramatovici, N. Jonoska, K.G. Subramanian: Tissue-like P systems with active membranes for picture generation. *Fundamenta Informaticae*, 56, 4 (2003), 311–328.

3. K.S. Dersanambika, K. Krithivasan: Contextual array P systems. *Intern. J. Computer Math.*, 81, 8 (2004), 955–969.

4. K.S. Dersanambika, K. Krithivasan, K.G. Subramanian: P systems generating hexagonal picture languages. In *Pre-proceedings of Workshop on Membrane Computing, WMC2003*, Tarragona, GRLMC Report 28/03, 209–221.

5. R. Freund, M. Oswald, A. Păun: P systems generating trees. In *Membrane Computing. 5th Intern. Workshop, WMC2004, Milan, Italy, June 2004. Revised Selected and Invited Papers*, LNCS 3365, Springer, 2005, 309–219.

6. A. Georgiou, M. Gheorghe: P systems used in plant graphics. In *Pre-proceedings of Workshop on Membrane Computing, WMC2003*, Tarragona, GRLMC Report 28/03, 266–272.

7. A. Georgiou, M. Gheorghe, F. Bernardini: Membrane-based devices used in computer graphics. In **AMC 2006**, 253–282.

8. S. N. Krishna, K. Krithivasan, R. Rama: P systems with picture objects. *Acta Cybernetica*, 15, 1 (2001), 53–74.

9. R. Rama, H. Ramesh: On generating trees by P systems. *Proc. SYNASC 05, Timişoara, Romania*, IEEE Press, 2005, 462–466.

10. A. Romero-Jiménez, M.A. Gutiérrez-Naranjo, M.J. Pérez-Jiménez: The growth of branching structures with P systems. In *Proc. Fourth Brainstorming Week on Membrane Computing*, Sevilla, 2006, RGNC Report 02/2006, Vol. II, 253–266.

11. K.G. Subramanian, S. Hemalatha, C. Sri Hari Nagore: On image generation by sequential/parallel rewriting P systems. In *Proc. Intern. Conf. on Signal Processing, Communications and Networking*, Anna University, Chennai, IEEE & IETE, 2007, 70–73.

12. K.G. Subramanian, R. Saravanan, K. Rangarajan: Array P systems and basic puzzle grammars. *National Conf. in Intelligent Optimization Modeling*, Gandhigram Rural Institute-Deemed University, India, March 2006.

Cryptography

1. A. Atanasiu: Authentication of messages using P systems. In *Membrane Computing, International Workshop, WMC-CdeA 2002. Curtea de Argeş, Romania, August 2002, Revised Papers*, LNCS 2597, Springer, 2003, 33–42.

2. S.N. Krishna, R. Rama: Breaking DES using P systems. *Theoretical Computer Sci.*, 299, 1-3 (2003), 495–508.

3. O. Michel, F. Jacquemard: An analysis of a public key protocol with membranes. In **AMC 2006**, 283–302.

4. A. Obtulowicz: On P systems with active membranes solving integer factorization problem in a polynomial time. In *Multiset Processing*, LNCS 2236, Springer, 2001, 257–286.

5. A. Obtulowicz: Membrane computing and one-way functions. *Intern. J. Found. Computer Sci.*, 12, 4 (2001), 551–558.

Optimization

1. L. Huang: *Research on Membrane Computing. Optimization Methods.* PhD Thesis, Institute of Advanced Process Control, Zhejiang University, China, 2007.
2. L. Huang, X.-X. He, N. Wang, Y. Xie: P systems based multi-objective optimization algorithm. *Progress in Natural Science*, 17, 4 (2007), 458–464.
3. L. Huang, I.H. Suh: Design of controllers for marine Diesel engine by membrane computing. *Intern. J. Innovative Computing, Information and Control*, 2007.
4. L. Huang, L. Sun, N. Wang, X.M. Jin: Multiobjective optimization of simulated moving bed by tissue P system. *Chinese J. Chemical Engineering*, 15, 5 (2007), 683–690.
5. L. Huang, N. Wang: An optimization algorithms inspired by membrane computing. In *Proc. ICNC 2006*, LNCS 4222, Springer, 2006, 49–55.
6. L. Huang, N. Wang: Multiobjective optimization for controllers. *Acta Automatica Sinica*, 2007.
7. L. Huang, N. Wang: A variant of P systems for optimization. *Neurocomputing*, 2007.
8. L. Huang, N. Wang: An extension of membrane computing – a type of evolutionary computing. *J. Central South Univ., China*, 2007.
9. T.Y. Nishida: An application of P systems – A new algorithm for NP-complete optimization problems. In *Proceedings of the 8th World Multi-Conference on Systems, Cybernetics and Informatics*, vol. V, 2004, 109–112.
10. T.Y. Nishida: Membrane algorithm – an approximate algorithm for NP-complete optimization problems exploiting P systems. In *Membrane Computing, International Workshop, WMC6, Vienna, Austria, 2005, Selected and Invited Papers*, LNCS 3850, Springer, 2006, 55–66.
11. T.Y. Nishida: Membrane algorithms. Approximate algorithms for NP-complete optimization problems. In **AMC 2006**, 303–314.
12. T.Y. Nishida: Membrane algorithm with Brownian subalgorithm and genetic subalgorithm. *Intern. J. Found. Computer Sci.*, 18, 6 (2007), 1353–1360.
13. D. Zaharie, G. Ciobanu: Distributed evolutionary algorithms inspired by membranes in solving continuous optimization problems. In *Membrane Computing, WMC2006, Leiden, The Netherlands. Revised, Selected and Invited Papers*, LNCS 4361, Springer, 2006, 536–554.

Others

1. B. Aman, G. Ciobanu: Translating mobile ambients into P systems. In *Proc. MeCBIC 2006*, Veneţia, 2006.
2. B. Aman, G. Ciobanu: On the relationship between P systems and mobile ambients. *FML Technical Report*, http://iit.iit.tuiasi.ro/TR/, 2006.
3. A. Atanasiu: Arithmetic with membranes. In *Pre-proc. Workshop on Multiset Processing*, Curtea de Argeş, Romania, TR 140, CDMTCS, Univ. Auckland, 2000, 1–17.

4. M. Gheorghe: P systems – A modelling language. In *Pre-Proc. Unconventional Programming Paradigms, UPP04*, Le Mont Saint-Michel, September 2004, 23–27.
5. M.A. Gutiérrez-Naranjo, V. Rogozhin: Deductive databases and P systems. *Computer Science J. of Moldova*, 12, 1 (2004), 80–88.
6. I. Petre, L. Petre: Mobile ambients and P systems. *J. Univ. Computer Science*, 5, 9 (1999), 588–598.
7. Z. Qi, C. Fu, S. Shi, J. You: The P system based model for mobile transactions. In *Fourth Intern. Conf. on Computer and Information Theory*, CIT2004, 534–539.
8. Z. Qi, R. Rao, G. Xue, J. You: A new formal model based on P systems for mobile transactions. In *Proc. IEEE Intern. Conf. on Services Computing*, SCC2004, 16–22.
9. V. Rogozhin, E. Boian: Simulation of mobile ambients by P systems. Part 1, *Pre-proceedings of Workshop on Membrane Computing, WMC2003*, Tarragona, GRLMC Report 28/03, 404–427. Part 2, *Proc. Second Brainstorming Week on Membrane Computing*, Sevilla, 2004, RNGC Report 01/2004, 431–442.
10. V. Rogojin, E. Boian: Simulation of mobile ambients by tissue P systems with a dynamic network of membranes. In *Proc. ICCC, Oradea*, Ed. Univ. Oradea, 2004, 377–382.
11. Y. Suzuki, Y. Fujiwara, J. Takabayashi, H. Tanaka: Artificial life applications of a class of P systems: Abstract rewriting systems on multisets. In *Multiset Processing*, LNCS 2236, Springer, 2001, 299–346.
12. Y. Suzuki, H. Tanaka: Artificial life and P systems. In *Pre-proc. Workshop on Multiset Processing*, Curtea de Argeş, Romania, TR 140, CDMTCS, Univ. Auckland, 2000, 265–285.

References

1. Andrei, O., Ciobanu, G., Lucanu, D.: Executable specification of P systems. In: Mauri, G., Păun, G., Jesús Pérez-Jímenez, M., Rozenberg, G., Salomaa, A. (eds.) WMC 2004. LNCS, vol. 3365, pp. 126–145. Springer, Heidelberg (2005)
2. Ardelean, I.I., Cavaliere, M.: Modelling biological processes by using a probabilistic P system software. Natural Computing 2(2), 173–197 (2003)
3. Besozzi, D., Ciobanu, G.: A P systems description of the sodium-potassium pump. In: Mauri, G., Păun, G., Jesús Pérez-Jímenez, M., Rozenberg, G., Salomaa, A. (eds.) WMC 2004. LNCS, vol. 3365, pp. 210–223. Springer, Heidelberg (2005)
4. Bianco, L., Fontana, F., Manca, V.: P systems with reaction maps. International Journal of Foundations of Computer Science 17(1), 27–48 (2006)
5. Cardelli, L.: Brane calculi: Interactions of biological membranes. In: Danos, V., Schachter, V. (eds.) CMSB 2004. LNCS (LNBI), vol. 3082, pp. 257–278. Springer, Heidelberg (2005)
6. Cheruku, S., Paun, A., Romero-Campero, F.J., Pérez-Jiménez, M.J., Ibarra, O.H.: Simulating fas-induced apoptosis by using P systems. Progress in Natural Science 17(4), 424–431 (2007)

7. Ciobanu, G., Pan, L., Păun, G.: P systems with minimal parallelism. Theoretical Computer Science 378(1), 117–130 (2007)
8. Fontana, F., Bianco, L., Manca, V.: P systems and the modelling of biochemical oscillations. In: Freund, R., Păun, G., Rozenberg, G., Salomaa, A. (eds.) WMC 2005. LNCS, vol. 3850, pp. 199–208. Springer, Heidelberg (2006)
9. Fontana, F., Manca, V.: Discrete solutions to differential equations by metabolic P systems. Theoretical Computer Science 372(2-3), 165–182 (2007)
10. Freund, R.: P systems working in the sequential mode on arrays and strings. International Journal of Foundations of Computer Science 16(4), 663–682 (2005)
11. Gillespie, D.T.: Stochastic simulation of chemical kinetics. Annu. Rev. Phys. Chem. 58, 35–55 (2007)
12. Goss, P.J., Peccoud, J.: Quantitative modelling of stochastic system in molecular biology by using stochastic petri nets. Proc. Natl. Acad. Sci. USA 95, 6750–6755 (1998)
13. Heath, J., Kwiatkowska, M.Z., Norman, G., Parker, D., Tymchyshyn, O.: Probabilistic model checking of complex biological pathways. Theoretical Computer Science 391(3), 239–257 (2008)
14. Kwiatkowska, M., Norman, G., Parker, D.: Stochastic model checking. In: Bernardo, M., Hillston, J. (eds.) SFM 2007. LNCS, vol. 4486, pp. 220–270. Springer, Heidelberg (2007)
15. Li, C., Dang, Z., Ibarra, O.H., Yen, H.-C.: Signaling p systems and verification problems. In: Caires, L., Italiano, G.F., Monteiro, L., Palamidessi, C., Yung, M. (eds.) ICALP 2005. LNCS, vol. 3580, pp. 1462–1473. Springer, Heidelberg (2005)
16. Milner, R.: Communication and Mobile Systems: The π-calculus. Cambridge University Press, Cambridge (1999)
17. Pérez-Jiménez, M.J., Romero-Campero, F.J.: P systems, a new computational modelling tool for systems biology. In: Transactions on Computational Systems Biology VI, pp. 176–197 (2006)
18. Pescini, D., Besozzi, D., Mauri, G., Zandron, C.: Dynamical probabilistic p systems. International Journal of Foundations of Computer Science 17(1), 183–195 (2006)
19. Ptashne, M., Gann, A.: Genes and Signals. Cold Spring Harbor Laboratory Press (2002)
20. Reddy, V., Liebman, M., Maverovouniotis, M.: Qualitative analysis of biochemical reaction systems. Computers in Biology and Medicine 26(1), 9–24 (1996)
21. Regev, A., Panina, E., Silvermann, W., Cardelli, L., Shapiro, E.: Bioambients: an abstraction for biological compartments. Theoretical Computer Science 325, 141–167 (2004)
22. Regev, A., Shapiro, E.: The π-calculus as an abstraction for biomolecular systems. In: Modelling in Molecular Biology, pp. 1–50. Springer, Berlin (2004)
23. Romero-Campero, F.J., Pérez-Jiménez, M.J.: A model of the quorum sensing system in vibrio fischeri using P systems. Artificial Life 14(1), 95–109 (2008)
24. Romero-Campero, F.J., Pérez-Jiménez, M.J.: Modelling gene expression control using P systems: The lac operon, a case study. BioSystems 91(3), 438–457 (2008)

Petri Nets for Systems and Synthetic Biology

Monika Heiner[1], David Gilbert[2], and Robin Donaldson[2]

[1] Department of Computer Science, Brandenburg University of Technology
Postbox 10 13 44, 03013 Cottbus, Germany
monika.heiner@tu-cottbus.de
[2] Bioinformatics Research Centre, University of Glasgow
Glasgow G12 8QQ, Scotland, UK
drg@brc.dcs.gla.ac.uk, radonald@brc.dcs.gla.ac.uk

Abstract. We give a description of a Petri net-based framework for modelling and analysing biochemical pathways, which unifies the qualitative, stochastic and continuous paradigms. Each perspective adds its contribution to the understanding of the system, thus the three approaches do not compete, but complement each other. We illustrate our approach by applying it to an extended model of the three stage cascade, which forms the core of the ERK signal transduction pathway. Consequently our focus is on transient behaviour analysis. We demonstrate how qualitative descriptions are abstractions over stochastic or continuous descriptions, and show that the stochastic and continuous models approximate each other. Although our framework is based on Petri nets, it can be applied more widely to other formalisms which are used to model and analyse biochemical networks.

1 Motivation

Biochemical reaction systems have by their very nature three distinctive characteristics. (1) They are inherently bipartite, i.e. they consist of two types of game players, the species and their interactions. (2) They are inherently concurrent, i.e. several interactions can usually happen independently and in parallel. (3) They are inherently stochastic, i.e. the timing behaviour of the interactions is governed by stochastic laws. So it seems to be a natural choice to model and analyse them with a formal method, which shares exactly these distinctive characteristics: stochastic Petri nets.

However, due to the computational efforts required to analyse stochastic models, two abstractions are more popular: qualitative models, abstracting away from any time dependencies, and continuous models, commonly used to approximate stochastic behaviour by a deterministic one. We describe an overall framework to unify these three paradigms, providing a family of related models with high analytical power.

The advantages of using Petri nets as a kind of umbrella formalism are seen in the following:

M. Bernardo, P. Degano, and G. Zavattaro (Eds.): SFM 2008, LNCS 5016, pp. 215–264, 2008.
© Springer-Verlag Berlin Heidelberg 2008

- intuitive and executable modelling style,
- true concurrency (partial order) semantics, which may be lessened to inter-leaving semantics to simplify analyses,
- mathematically founded analysis techniques based on formal semantics,
- coverage of structural and behavioural properties as well as their relations,
- integration of qualitative and quantitative analysis techniques,
- reliable tool support.

This chapter can be considered as a tutorial in the step-wise modelling and analysis of larger biochemical networks as well as in the structured design of systems of ordinary differential equations (ODEs). The qualitative model is introduced as a supplementary intermediate step, at least from the viewpoint of the biochemist accustomed to quantitative modelling only, and serves mainly for model validation since this cannot be performed on the continuous level, and is generally much harder to do on the stochastic level. Having successfully validated the qualitative model, the quantitative models are derived from the qualitative one by assigning stochastic or deterministic rate functions to all reactions in the network. Thus the quantitative models preserve the structure of the qualitative one, and the stochastic Petri net describes a system of stochastic reaction rate equations (RREs), and continuous Petri net is nothing else than a structured description of ODEs.

systems biology: modelling as formal knowledge representation

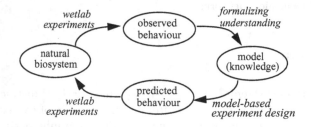

synthetic biology: modelling for system construction

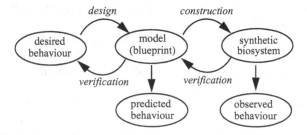

Fig. 1. The role of formal models in systems biology and synthetic biology

This framework is equally helpful in the setting of systems biology as well as synthetic biology, see Figure 1. In systems biology, models help us in formalising our understanding of what has been created by natural evolution. So first of all, models serve as an unambiguous representation of the acquired knowledge and help to design new wetlab experiments to sharpen our comprehension.

In synthetic biology, models help us to make the engineering of biology easier and more reliable. Models serve as blueprints for novel synthetic biological systems. Their employment is highly recommended to guide the design and construction in order to ensure that the behaviour of the synthetic biological systems is reliable and robust under a variety of conditions.

Formal models open the door to mathematically founded analyses for model validation and verification. This paper demonstrates typical analysis techniques, with special emphasis on transient behaviour analysis. We show how to systematically derive and interpret the partial order run of the signal response behaviour, and how to employ model checking to investigate related properties in the qualitative, stochastic and continuous paradigms. All analysis techniques are introduced through a running example. To be self-contained, we give the formal definitions of the most relevant notions, which are Petri net specific.

This paper is organised as follows. In the following section we outline our framework, discussing the special contributions of the three individual analysis approaches, and examining their interrelations. Next we provide an overview of the biochemical context and introduce our running example. We then present the individual approaches and discuss mutually related properties in all three paradigms in the following order: we start off with the qualitative approach, which is conceptually the easiest, and does not rely on knowledge of kinetic information, but describes the network topology and presence of the species. We then demonstrate how the validated qualitative model can be transformed into the stochastic representation by addition of stochastic firing rate information. Next, the continuous model is derived from the qualitative or stochastic model by considering only deterministic firing rates. Suitable sets of initial conditions for all three models are constructed by qualitative analysis. Finally, we refer to related work, before concluding with a summary and outlook regarding further research directions.

2   Overview of the Framework

In the following we describe our overall framework, illustrated in Figure 2, that relates the three major ways of modelling and analysing biochemical networks described in this paper: qualitative, stochastic and continuous.

The most abstract representation of a biochemical network is *qualitative* and is minimally described by its topology, usually as a bipartite directed graph with nodes representing biochemical entities or reactions, or in Petri net terminology *places* and *transitions* (see Figures 4 – 6). Arcs can be annotated with stoichiometric information, whereby the default stoichiometric value of 1 is usually omitted.

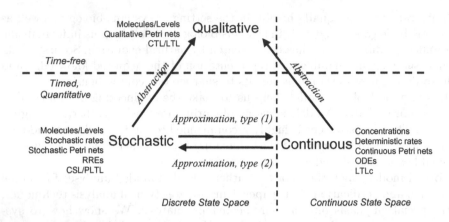

Fig. 2. Conceptual framework

The qualitative description can be further enhanced by the abstract representation of discrete quantities of species, achieved in Petri nets by the use of tokens at places. These can represent the number of molecules, or the level of concentration, of a species. The standard semantics for these qualitative Petri nets (QPN) does not associate a time with transitions or the sojourn of tokens at places, and thus these descriptions are time-free. The qualitative analysis considers however all possible behaviour of the system under any timing. The behaviour of such a net forms a discrete state space, which can be analysed in the bounded case, for example, by a branching time temporal logic, one instance of which is Computational Tree Logic (CTL), see [CGP01].

Timed information can be added to the qualitative description in two ways – stochastic and continuous. The stochastic Petri net (SPN) description preserves the discrete state description, but in addition associates a probabilistically distributed firing rate (waiting time) with each reaction. All reactions, which occur in the QPN, can still occur in the SPN, but their likelihood depends on the probability distribution of the associated firing rates. Special behavioural properties can be expressed using e.g. Continuous Stochastic Logic (CSL), see [PNK06], a probabilistic counterpart of CTL, or Probabilistic Linear-time Temporal Logic (PLTL), see [MC2], a probabilistic counterpart to LTL [Pnu81]. The QPN is an abstraction of the SPN, sharing the same state space and transition relation with the stochastic model, with the probabilistic information removed. All qualitative properties valid in the QPN are also valid in the SPN, and vice versa.

The continuous model replaces the discrete values of species with continuous values, and hence is not able to describe the behaviour of species at the level of individual molecules, but only the overall behaviour via concentrations. We can regard the discrete description of concentration levels as abstracting over the continuous description of concentrations. Timed information is introduced by the association of a particular deterministic rate information with each transition, permitting the continuous model to be represented as a set of ordinary differential equations (ODEs). The concentration of a particular species in such a model will have the same value at each point of time for repeated experiments. The state space of such models is continuous and linear. So it has to be analysed by a linear time temporal logic (LTL), for example, Linear Temporal Logic with constraints (LTLc) in the manner of [CCRFS06], or PLTL [MC2].

The stochastic and continuous models are mutually related by approximation. The stochastic description can be used as the basis for deriving a continuous Petri net (CPN) model by approximating rate information. Specifically, the probabilistically distributed reaction firing in the SPN is replaced by a particular average firing rate over the continuous token flow of the CPN. This is achieved by approximation over hazard (propensity) functions of type (1), described in more detail in section 5.1. In turn, the stochastic model can be derived from the continuous model by approximation, reading the tokens as concentration levels, as introduced in [CVGO06]. Formally, this is achieved by a hazard function of type (2), see again section 5.1.

It is well-known that time assumptions generally impose constraints on behaviour. The qualitative and stochastic models consider all possible behaviours under any timing, whereas the continuous model is constrained by its inherent determinism to consider a subset. This may be too restrictive when modelling biochemical systems, which by their very nature exhibit variability in their behaviour.

3   Biochemical Context

We have chosen a model of the mitogen-activated protein kinase (MAPK) cascade published in [LBS00] as a running case study. This is the core of the ubiquitous ERK/MAPK pathway that can, for example, convey cell division and differentiation signals from the cell membrane to the nucleus. The model does not describe the receptor and the biochemical entities and actions immediately downstream from the receptor. Instead the description starts at the RasGTP complex which acts as a kinase to phosphorylate Raf, which phosphorylates MAPK/ERK Kinase (MEK), which in turn phosphorylates Extracellular signal Regulated Kinase (ERK). This cascade (RasGTP $\rightarrow$ Raf $\rightarrow$ MEK $\rightarrow$ ERK) of protein interactions controls cell differentiation, the effect being dependent upon the activity of ERK. We consider RasGTP as the input signal and ERKPP (activated ERK) as the output signal.

The scheme in Figure 3 describes the typical modular structure for such a signalling cascade, compare [CKS07]. Each layer corresponds to a distinct protein species. The protein Raf in the first layer is only singly phosphorylated. The proteins in the two other layers, MEK and ERK respectively, can be singly as well as doubly phosphorylated. In each layer, forward reactions are catalysed by kinases and reverse reactions by phosphatases (Phosphatase1, Phosphatase2, Phosphatase3). The kinases in the MEK and ERK layers are the phosphorylated forms of the proteins in the previous layer. Each phosphorylation/dephosphorylation step applies mass action kinetics according to the following pattern: $A + E \rightleftharpoons AE \rightarrow B + E$, taking into account the mechanism by which the enzyme acts, namely by forming a complex with the substrate, modifying the substrate to form the product, and a disassociation occurring to release the product.

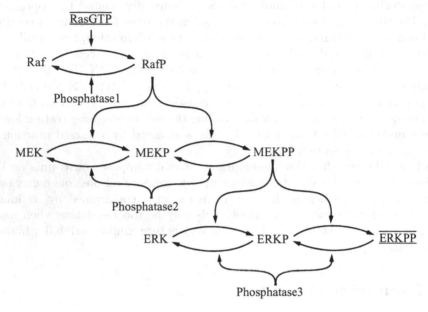

Fig. 3. The general scheme of the considered signalling pathway: a three-stage double phosphorylation cascade. Each phosphorylation/dephosphorylation step applies the mass action kinetics pattern $A + E \rightleftharpoons AE \rightarrow B + E$. We consider RasGTP as the input signal and ERKPP as the output signal.

4   The Qualitative Approach

4.1   Qualitative Modelling

To allow formal reasoning of the general scheme of a signal transduction cascade, which is given in Figure 3 in an informal way, we are going to derive a corresponding Petri net. Petri nets enjoy formal semantics amenable to mathematically sound analysis techniques. The first two definitions introduce the standard notion of place/transition Petri nets, which represents the basic class in the ample family of Petri net models.

Definition 1 (Petri net, Syntax). *A Petri net is a quadruple $\mathcal{N} = (P, T, f, m_0)$, where*

– *P and T are finite, non empty, and disjoint sets. P is the set of places (in the figures represented by circles). T is the set of transitions (in the figures represented by rectangles).*

– $f : ((P \times T) \cup (T \times P)) \to \mathbb{N}_0$ *defines the set of directed* arcs, *weighted by nonnegative integer values.*

– $m_0 : P \to \mathbb{N}_0$ *gives the* initial marking.

Thus, Petri nets (or nets for short) are weighted, directed, bipartite graphs. The idea to use Petri nets for the representation of biochemical networks is rather intuitive and has been mentioned by Carl Adam Petri himself in one of his internal research reports on interpretation of net theory in the seventies. It has also been used as the very first introductory example in [Mur89], and we follow that idea in this tutorial, compare Figure 4.

Places usually model passive system components like conditions, species or any kind of chemical compounds, e.g. proteins or proteins complexes, playing the role of precursors or products. Transitions stand for active system components like atomic actions or any kind of chemical reactions, e.g. association, disassociation, phosphorylation, or dephosphorylation, transforming precursors into products.

The arcs go from precursors to reactions (ingoing arcs), and from reactions to products (outgoing arcs). In other words, the preplaces of a transition correspond to the reaction's precursors, and its postplaces to the reaction's products. Enzymes establish side conditions and are connected in both directions with the reaction they catalyse; we get a read arc.

Arc weights may be read as the multiplicity of the arc, reflecting known stoichiometries. Thus, the (pseudo) arc weight 0 stands for the absence of an arc. The arc weight 1 is the default value and is usually not given explicitly.

A place carries an arbitrary number of *tokens*, represented as black dots or a natural number. The number zero is the default value and usually not given explicitly. Tokens can be interpreted as the available amount of a given species in number of molecules or moles, or any abstract, i.e. discrete concentration level.

In the most abstract way, a concentration can be thought of as being 'high' or 'low' (present or absent). Generalizing this Boolean approach, any continuous concentration range can be divided into a finite number of equally sized subranges (equivalence classes), so that the concentrations within can be considered to be equivalent. The current number of tokens on a place will then specify the current level of the species' concentration, e.g. the absence of tokens specifies level 0. In the following, when speaking in terms of level semantics, we always give the highest level number.

A particular arrangement of tokens over the places of the net is called a marking, modelling a system state. In this paper, the notions *marking* and *state* are used interchangeably.

We introduce the following notions and notations. $m(p)$ yields the number of tokens on place p in the marking m. A place p with $m(p) = 0$ is called *clean (empty, unmarked)* in m, otherwise it is called *marked* (non-clean). A set of places is called clean if all its places are clean, otherwise marked. The preset of a node $x \in P \cup T$ is defined as $^\bullet x := \{y \in P \cup T | f(y, x) \neq 0\}$, and its postset as $x^\bullet := \{y \in P \cup T | f(x, y) \neq 0\}$. Altogether we get four types of sets:

- $\bullet t$, the preplaces of a transition t, consisting of the reaction's precursors,
- $t \bullet$, the postplaces of a transition t, consisting of the reaction's products,
- $\bullet p$, the pretransitions of a place p, consisting of all reactions producing this species,
- $p \bullet$, the posttransitions of a place p, consisting of all reactions consuming this species.

We extend both notions to a set of nodes $X \subseteq P \cup T$ and define the set of all prenodes $\bullet X := \bigcup_{x \in X} \bullet x$, and the set of all postnodes $X^\bullet := \bigcup_{x \in X} x^\bullet$. See Figure 11 for an illustration of these notations.

Petri Net, Semantics. Up to now we have introduced the static aspects of a Petri net only. The behaviour of a net is defined by the firing rule, which consists of two parts: the precondition and the firing itself.

Definition 2 (Firing rule). *Let* $\mathcal{N} = (P, T, f, m_0)$ *be a Petri net.*

- *A transition* t *is* enabled *in a marking* m, *written as* $m[t\rangle$, *if* $\forall p \in \bullet t : m(p) \geq f(p, t)$, *else* disabled.
- *A transition* t, *which is enabled in* m, *may* fire.
- *When* t *in* m *fires, a new marking* m' *is reached, written as* $m[t\rangle m'$, *with* $\forall p \in P : m'(p) = m(p) - f(p, t) + f(t, p)$.
- *The firing happens atomically and does not consume any time.*

Please note, a transition is never forced to fire. Figuratively, the firing of a transition moves tokens from its preplaces to its postplaces, while possibly changing the number of tokens, compare Figure 4. Generally, the firing of a transition changes the formerly current marking to a new reachable one, where some transitions are not enabled anymore while others get enabled. The repeated firing of transitions establishes the behaviour of the net.

The whole net behaviour consists of all possible partially ordered firing sequences (partial order semantics), or all possible totally ordered firing sequences (interleaving semantics), respectively.

Every marking is defined by the given token situation in all places $m \in \mathbb{N}_0^{|P|}$, whereby $|P|$ denotes the number of places in the Petri net. All markings, which can be reached from a given marking m by any firing sequence of arbitrary length, constitute the *set of reachable markings* $[m\rangle$. The set of markings $[m_0\rangle$ reachable from the initial marking is said to be the *state space* of a given system.

All notions introduced in the following in this section refer to a place/transition Petri net according to Definitions 1 and 2.

Running Example. In this modelling spirit we are now able to create a Petri net for our running example. We start with building blocks for some typical chemical reaction equations as shown in Figure 5. We get the Petri net in Figure 6 for our running example by composing these building blocks according to the scheme of Figure 3. As we will see later, this net structure corresponds exactly to the set of ordinary differential equations given in [LBS00]. Thus, the net can

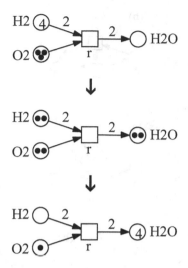

Fig. 4. The Petri net for the well known chemical reaction r: $2H_2 + O_2 \rightarrow 2H_2O$ and three of its markings (states), connected each by a firing of the transition r. The transition is not enabled anymore in the marking reached after these two single firing steps.

equally be derived by SBML import and automatic layout, manually improved from this ODE model.

Reversible reactions have to be modelled explicitly by two opposite transitions. However in order to retain the elegant graph structure of Figure 6, we use macro transitions, each of which stands here for a reversible reaction. The entire (flattened) place/transition Petri net consists of 22 places and 30 transitions, where $r1, r2, \ldots$ stand for reaction (transition) labels.

We associate a discrete concentration with each of the 22 species. In the qualitative analysis we apply Boolean semantics where the concentrations can be thought of as being "high" or "low" (above or below a certain threshold). This results into a two level model, and we extend this to a multi-level model in the quantitative analysis, where each discrete level stands for an equivalence class of possibly infinitely many concentrations. Then places can be read as integer variables.

4.2   Qualitative Analysis

A preliminary step will usually execute the net, which allows us to experience the model behaviour by following the token flow[1]. Having established initial confidence in the model by playing the token game, the system needs to be formally analysed. Formal analyses are exhaustive, opposite to the token game, which exemplifies the net behaviour.

---

[1] If the reader would like to give it a try, just download our Petri net tool [Sno08].

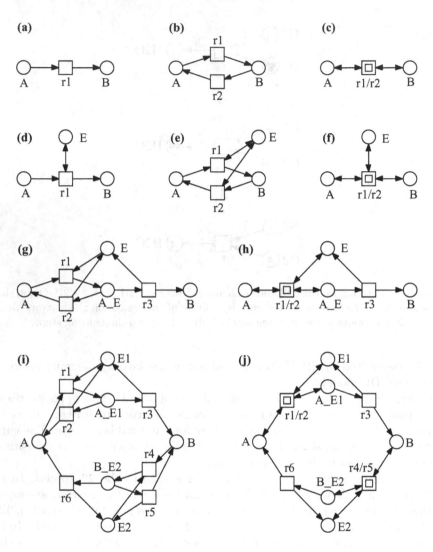

Fig. 5. The Petri net components for some typical basic structures of biochemical reaction networks. (a) simple reaction $A \rightarrow B$; (b) reversible reaction $A \rightleftharpoons B$; (c) hierarchical notation of (b); (d) simple enzymatic reaction, Michaelis-Menten kinetics; (e) reversible enzymatic reaction, Michaelis-Menten kinetics; (f) hierarchical notation of (e); (g) enzymatic reaction, mass action kinetics, $A + E \rightleftharpoons A\_E \rightarrow B + E$; (h) hierarchical notation of (g); (i) two enzymatic reactions, mass action kinetics, building a cycle; (j) hierarchical notation of (i). Two concentric squares are macro transitions, allowing the design of hierarchical net models. They are used here as shortcuts for reversible reactions. Two opposite arcs denote read arcs, see (d) and (e), establishing side conditions for a transition's firing.

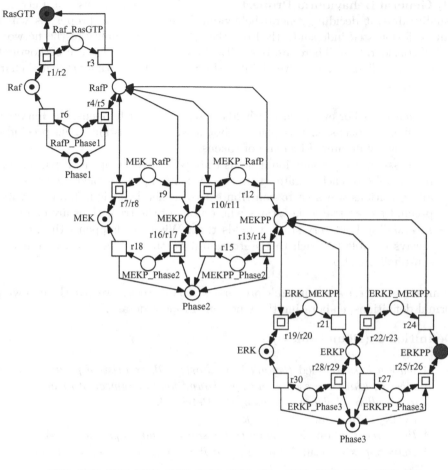

PUR	ORD	HOM	NBM	CSV	SCF	CON	SC	FT0	TF0	FP0	PF0	NC
Y	Y	Y	Y	N	N	Y	Y	N	N	N	N	nES
DTP	CPI	CTI	SCTI	SB	k-B	1-B	DCF	DSt	DTr	LIV	REV	
Y	Y	Y	N	Y	Y	Y	N	0	N	Y	Y	

Fig. 6. The bipartite graph for the extended ERK pathway model according to the scheme in Figure 3. Places (circles) stand for species (proteins, protein complexes). Protein complexes are indicated by an underscore "_" between the constituent protein names. The suffixes P or PP indicate phosphorylated or doubly phosphorylated forms respectively. The name *Phase* serves as shortcut for *Phosphatase*. The species that are read as input/output signals are given in grey. Transitions (squares) stand for irreversible reactions, while macro transitions (two concentric squares) specify reversible reactions, compare Figure 5. The initial state is systematically constructed using standard Petri net analysis techniques. At the bottom the two-line result vector as produced by Charlie [Cha08] is given. Properties of interest in this vector for this biochemical network are explained in the text.

(0) General Behavioural Properties. The first step in analysing a Petri net usually aims at deciding general behavioural properties, i.e. properties which can be formulated independently from the special functionality of the network under consideration. There are basically three of them, which are orthogonal: boundedness, liveness, and reversibility [Mur89]. We start with an informal characterisation of the key issues.

– *boundedness* For every place it holds that: Whatever happens, the maximal number of tokens on this place is bounded by a constant. This precludes overflow by unlimited increase of tokens.
– *liveness* For every transition it holds that: Whatever happens, it will always be possible to reach a state where this transition gets enabled. In a live net, all transitions are able to contribute to the net behaviour forever, which precludes dead states, i.e. states where none of the transitions are enabled.
– *reversibility* For every state it holds that: Whatever happens, the net will always be able to reach this state again. So the net has the capability of self-reinitialization.

In most cases these are requirable properties. To be precise, we give the following formal definitions, elaborating these notions in more details.

Definition 3 (Boundedness)

– *A place p is k-bounded (bounded for short) if there exists a positive integer number k, which represents an upper bound for the number of tokens on this place in all reachable markings of the Petri net:*
  $\exists k \in \mathbb{N}_0 : \forall m \in [m_0\rangle : m(p) \leq k$.
– *A Petri net is k-bounded (bounded for short) if all its places are k-bounded.*
– *A Petri net is* structurally bounded *if it is bounded in any initial marking.*

Definition 4 (Liveness of a transition)

– *A transition t is* dead *in the marking m if it is not enabled in any marking m' reachable from m:*
  $\nexists m' \in [m\rangle : m'[t\rangle$.
– *A transition t is* live *if it is not dead in any marking reachable from m_0.*

Definition 5 (Liveness of a Petri net)

– *A marking m is* dead *if there is no transition which is enabled in m.*
– *A Petri net is* deadlock-free (weakly live) *if there are no reachable dead markings.*
– *A Petri net is* live (strongly live) *if each transition is live.*

Definition 6 (Reversibility). *A Petri net is* reversible *if the initial marking can be reached again from each reachable marking: $\forall m \in [m_0\rangle : m_0 \in [m\rangle$.*

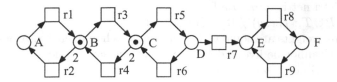

Fig. 7. A net to illustrate the general behavioural properties. The place A is 0-bounded, place B is 1-bounded and all other places are 2-bounded, so the net is 2-bounded. The transitions r1 and r2 in the leftmost cycle are dead at the initial marking. The transitions r8 and r9 in the rightmost cycle are live. All other transitions are not live; so the net is weakly live. The net is not reversible, because there is no counteraction to the token decrease by firing of r4. There are dynamic conflicts, e.g. in the initial marking between r4 and r5.

Finally we introduce the general behavioural property *dynamic conflict*, which refers to a marking enabling two transitions, but the firing of one transition disables the other one. The occurrence of dynamic conflicts causes alternative (branching) system behaviour, whereby the decision between these alternatives is taken nondeterministically. See Figure 7 for an illustration of these behavioural properties.

Running Example. Our net enjoys the three orthogonal general properties of a qualitative Petri net: it is bounded, even structural bounded (SB), live (LIV), and reversible (REV).

Boundedness can always be decided in a static way, i.e. without construction of the state space, while the remaining behavioural properties generally require dynamic analysis techniques, i.e. the explicit construction of the partial or full state space. However as we will see later, freedom of dead states (DSt) can still be decided in a static way for our running example.

The essential steps of the systematic analysis procedure for our running example are given in more detail as follows. They represent a typical pattern how to proceed. So they may be taken as a recipe how to analyse your own system.

(1) Structural Properties. The following structural properties are elementary graph properties and reflect the modelling approach. They can be read as preliminary consistency checks to preclude production faults in drawing the net. Remarkably, certain combinations of structural properties allow conclusions on behavioural properties; some examples of such conclusions will be mentioned. The list follows the order as used in the two-line result vector produced by our qualitative analysis tool Charlie [Cha08], compare Figure 6.

PUR. A Petri net is *pure* if
$$\forall x, y \in P \cup T : f(x, y) \neq 0 \Rightarrow f(y, x) = 0,$$
i.e. there are no two nodes, connected in both directions. This precludes read arcs. Then the net structure is fully represented by the incidence matrix, which is used for the calculation of the P- and T-invariants, see step (2).

ORD. A Petri net is *ordinary* if
$\forall x, y \in P \cup T : f(x, y) \neq 0 \Rightarrow f(x, y) = 1$,
i.e. all arc weights are equal to 1. This includes homogeneity. A non-ordinary
Petri net cannot be live and 1-bounded at the same time.

HOM. A Petri net is *homogeneous* if
$\forall p \in P : t, t' \in p^\bullet \Rightarrow f(p, t) = f(p, t')$,
i.e. all outgoing arcs of a given place have the same multiplicity.

NBM. A net has *non-blocking multiplicity* if
$\forall p \in P : {}^\bullet p \neq \emptyset \wedge min\{f(t, p) | \forall t \in {}^\bullet p\} \geq max\{f(p, t) | \forall t \in p^\bullet\}$,
i.e. an input place causes blocking multiplicity. Otherwise, it must hold for
each place: the minimum of the multiplicities of the incoming arcs is not less
than the maximum of the multiplicities of the outgoing arcs.

CSV. A Petri net is *conservative* if
$\forall t \in T : \sum_{p \in {}^\bullet t} f(p, t) = \sum_{p \in t^\bullet} f(t, p)$,
i.e. all transitions add exactly as many tokens to their postplaces as they sub-
tract from their preplaces, or briefly, all transitions fire token-preservingly.
A conservative Petri net is structurally bounded.

SCF. A Petri net is *static conflict free* if
$\forall t, t' \in T : t \neq t' \Rightarrow {}^\bullet t \cap {}^\bullet t' = \emptyset$,
i.e. there are no two transitions sharing a preplace. Transitions involved in
a static conflict compete for the tokens on shared preplaces. Thus, static
conflicts indicate situations where dynamic conflicts, i.e. nondeterministic
choices, may occur in the system behaviour. However, it depends on the
token situation whether a conflict does actually occur dynamically. There is
no nondeterminism in SCF nets.

CON. A Petri net is *connected* if it holds for every two nodes a and b that there
is an undirected path between a and b. Disconnected parts of a Petri net
cannot influence each other, so they can usually be analysed separately. In
the following we consider only connected Petri nets.

SC. A Petri net is *strongly connected* if it holds for every two nodes a and
b that there is a directed path from a to b. Strong connectedness involves
connectedness and the absence of boundary nodes. It is a necessary condition
for a Petri net to be live and bounded at the same time.

FT0, TF0, FP0, PF0. A node $x \in P \cup T$ is called *boundary node* if
${}^\bullet x = \emptyset \vee x^\bullet = \emptyset$. Boundary nodes exist in four types:
  – input transition - a transition without preplaces (${}^\bullet t = \emptyset$, shortly FT0),
  – output transition - a transition without postplaces ($t^\bullet = \emptyset$, shortly TF0),
  – input place - a place without pretransitions (${}^\bullet p = \emptyset$, shortly FP0),
  – output place - a place without posttransitions ($p^\bullet = \emptyset$, shortly PF0).
A net with boundary nodes cannot be bounded and live at the same time.
For example, an input transition is always enabled, so its postplaces are
unbounded, while input places preclude liveness. Boundary nodes model
interconnections of an open system with its environment. A net without
boundary nodes is self-contained, i.e. a closed system. It needs a non-clean
initial marking to become live.

Definition 7 (Net structure classes)

- *A Petri net is called* State Machine *(SM) if*
    $$\forall t \in T : |{}^\bullet t| = |t^\bullet| \leq 1,$$
    i.e. there are neither forward branching nor backward branching transitions.
- *A Petri net is called* Synchronization Graph *(SG) if*
    $$\forall p \in P : |{}^\bullet p| = |p^\bullet| \leq 1,$$
    i.e. there are neither forward branching nor backward branching places.
- *A Petri net is called* Extended Free Choice *(EFC) if*
    $$\forall p, q \in P : p^\bullet \cap q^\bullet = \emptyset \vee p^\bullet = q^\bullet,$$
    i.e. transitions in conflict have identical sets of preplaces.
- *A Petri net is called* Extended Simple *(ES) if*
    $$\forall p, q \in P : p^\bullet \cap q^\bullet = \emptyset \vee p^\bullet \subseteq q^\bullet \vee q^\bullet \subseteq p^\bullet,$$
    i.e. every transition is involved in one conflict at most.

Please note, these definitions refer to the net structure only, neglecting any arc multiplicities. However, these net classes are especially helpful in the setting of ordinary nets. SM and SG [2] are dual notions; a SM net can be converted into an SG net by exchanging places and transitions, and vice versa. Both net classes are properly included in the EFC net class, which again is properly included in the ES net class.

SM nets are conservative, and thus the prototype of bounded models; they correspond to the well-known notion of finite state automata. SG nets are free of static conflicts, and therefore of nondeterminism. In EFC nets, transitions in conflict are always together enabled or disabled; so there is always a free choice between them in dynamic conflict situations. EFC nets have the pleasant property of monotonously live, i.e. if they are live in the marking m, then they remain live for any other marking m' with $m' \geq m$. In ES nets, the conflict relation is transitive: if $t1$ and $t2$ are in conflict, and $t2$ and $t3$ are in conflict, then $t1$ and $t3$ are in conflict too. ES nets have the distinguished property to be live independent of time, i.e. if they are live, then they remain live under any timing [Sta89].

All these structural properties do not depend on the initial marking. Most of these properties can be locally decided in the graph structure. Connectedness and strong connectedness need to consider the global graph structure, which can be done using standard graph algorithms.

Running Example. The net is pure and ordinary, therefore homogeneous as well, but not conservative. There are static conflicts. The net structure does not comply to any of the introduced net structure classes, so it is said to be *not Extended Simple* (nES). The net is strongly connected, which includes connectedness and absence of boundary nodes, and thus self-contained, i.e. a closed system. Therefore, in order to make the net live, we have to construct an initial marking, see step (3) below.

---

[2] We use *synchronisation graph* instead of the more popular term *marked graph*, which might cause confusion.

(2) Static Decision of Marking-independent Behavioural Properties.
To open the door to analysis techniques based on linear algebra, we represent
the net structure by a matrix, called incidence matrix in the Petri net community, and stoichiometric matrix in systems biology. We briefly recall the essential
technical terms.

Definition 8 (P-invariants, T-invariants)

- *The* incidence matrix *of $\mathcal{N}$ is a matrix $\mathbb{C} : P \times T \to \mathbb{Z}$, indexed by P and
  T, such that $\mathbb{C}(p,t) = f(t,p) - f(p,t)$.*
- *A* place vector (transition vector) *is a vector $x : P \to \mathbb{Z}$, indexed by P
  ($y : T \to \mathbb{Z}$, indexed by T).*
- *A* place vector (transition vector) *is called a* P-invariant (T-invariant) *if it
  is a nontrivial nonnegative integer solution of the linear equation system
  $x \cdot \mathbb{C} = 0$ ($\mathbb{C} \cdot y = 0$).*
- *The set of nodes corresponding to an invariant's nonzero entries are called
  the* support *of this invariant x, written as $supp(x)$.*
- *An invariant x is called* minimal *if $\nexists$ invariant $z : supp(z) \subset supp(x)$, i.e.
  its support does not contain the support of any other invariant z, and the
  greatest common divisor of all nonzero entries of x is 1.*
- *A net is* covered by P-invariants, shortly CPI, *(covered by T-invariants, shortly
  CTI) if every place (transition) belongs to a P-invariant (T-invariant).*

CPI causes structural boundedness (SB), i.e. boundedness for any initial marking. CTI is a necessary condition for bounded nets to be live. But maybe even
more importantly, invariants are a beneficial technique in model validation, and
the challenge is to check all invariants for their biological plausibility. Therefore,
let's elaborate these notions more carefully, compare also Figure 8.

The *incidence matrix* of a Petri net is an integer matrix $\mathbb{C}$ with a row for each
place and a column for each transition. A matrix entry $\mathbb{C}(p,t)$ gives the token
change on place p by the firing of transition t. Thus, a preplace of t, which is
not a postplace of t, has a negative entry, while a postplace of t, which is not a
preplace of t, has a positive entry, each corresponding to the arc multiplicities.
The entry for a place, which is preplace as well as postplace of a transition,
gives the difference of the multiplicities of the transition's outgoing arc minus
the transition's ingoing arc. In this case we lose information; the non-ordinary
net structure cannot be reconstructed uniquely out of the incidence matrix.

The columns of $\mathbb{C}$ are place vectors, i.e. vectors with as many entries as there
are places, describing the token change on a marking by the firing of the transition defining the column index. The rows of $\mathbb{C}$ are transition vectors, i.e. vectors
with as many entries as there are transitions, describing the influence of all
transitions on the tokens in the place, defining the row index. For stoichiometric
reaction networks, e.g. metabolic networks, the incidence matrix coincides with
the stoichiometric matrix.

A *P-invariant* x is a nonzero and nonnegative integer place vector such that
$x \cdot \mathbb{C} = 0$; in words, for each transition it holds that: multiplying the P-invariant
with the transition's column vector yields zero. Thus, the total effect of each

transition on the P-invariant is zero, which explains its interpretation as a token conservation component. A P-invariant stands for a set of places over which the weighted sum of tokens is constant and independent of any firing, i.e. for any markings m_1, m_2, which are reachable by the firing of transitions, it holds that $x \cdot m_1 = x \cdot m_2$. In the context of metabolic networks, P-invariants reflect substrate conservations, while in signal transduction networks P-invariants often correspond to the several states of a given species (protein or protein complex). A place belonging to a P-invariant is obviously bounded.

Analogously, a *T-invariant* y is a nonzero and nonnegative integer transition vector such that $\mathbb{C} \cdot y = 0$; in words, for each place it holds that: multiplying the place's row with the T-invariant yields zero. Thus, the total effect of the T-invariant on a marking is zero. A T-invariant has two interpretations in the given biochemical context.

- The entries of a T-invariant specify a multiset of transitions which by their partially ordered firing reproduce a given marking, i.e. basically occurring one after the other. This partial order sequence of the T-invariant's transitions may contribute to a deeper understanding of the net behaviour. A T-invariant is called *feasible* if such a behaviour is actually possible in the given marking situation.
- The entries of a T-invariant may also be read as the relative firing rates of transitions, all of them occurring permanently and concurrently. This activity level corresponds to the steady state behaviour.

The two transitions modelling the two directions of a reversible reaction always make a minimal T-invariant; thus they are called *trivial T-invariants*. A net which is covered by nontrivial T-invariants is said to be *strongly covered by T-invariants* (SCTI). Transitions not covered by nontrivial T-invariants are candidates for model reduction, e.g. if the model analysis is concerned with steady state analysis only.

The set x_i of all minimal P-invariants (T-invariants) of a given net is unique and represents a generating system for all P-invariants (T-invariants). All invari-

r1: $2\,A \xrightarrow{E} 2\,B$
r2/3: $A \rightleftharpoons B$

	r1	r2	r3
A	−2	−1	1
B	2	1	−1
E	0	0	0

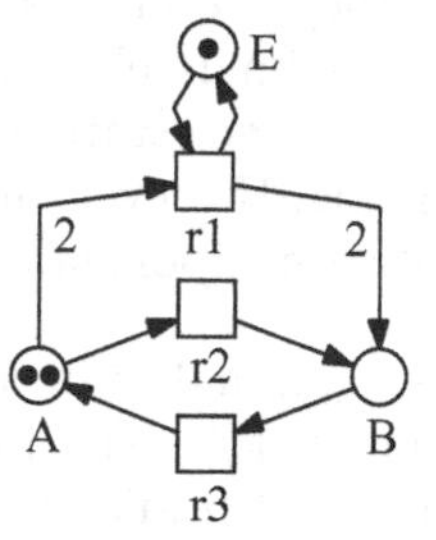

$x_1 = (1,1,0) = (\text{A, B})$,
$x_2 = (0,0,1) = (\text{E})$

$y_1 = (1,0,2) = (\text{r1}, 2 \cdot \text{r3})$,
$y_2 = (0,1,1) = (\text{r2, r3})$

$y_3 = (1,1,3) = y_1 + y_2$

Fig. 8. Two reaction equations with the corresponding Petri net, its incidence matrix, and the minimal P-invariants x_1, x_2, and the minimal T-invariants y_1, y_2, and a non-minimal T-invariant y_3. The invariants are given in the standard vector notation as well as in a shorthand notation, listing the nonzero entries only. The net is not pure; the incidence matrix does not reflect the dependency of r1 on E.

ants x can be computed as nonnegative linear combinations: $n \cdot x = \sum (a_i \cdot x_i)$, with $n, a_i \in \mathbb{N}_0$, i.e., the allowed operations are addition, multiplication by a natural number, and division by a common divisor.

Technically, we need to solve a homogenous linear equation system over natural numbers (nonnegative integers). This restriction of the data space establishes – from a mathematical point of view – a challenge, so there is no closed formula to compute the solutions. However there are algorithms – actually, a class of algorithms – constructing the solution (to be precise: the generating system for the solution space) by systematically considering all possible candidates.

This algorithm class has been repetitively re-invented over the years. So, these algorithms come along with different names; but if you take a closer look, you will always encounter the same underlying idea. All these versions may be classified as "positive Gauss elimination"; the incidence matrix is systematically transformed to a zero matrix by suitable matrix operations.

However, there are net structures where we get the invariants almost for free. For ordinary state machines it holds:

- each (minimal) cycle is a (minimal) T-invariant;
- for strongly connected state machines, the reverse direction holds also: each (minimal) T-invariant corresponds to a (minimal) cycle;
- all places of a strongly connected state machine form a minimal P-invariant.

Likewise, for ordinary synchronisation graphs it holds:

- each (minimal) cycle is a (minimal) P-invariant;
- for strongly connected synchronisation graphs, the reverse direction holds also: each (minimal) P-invariant corresponds to a (minimal) cycle;
- all transitions of a strongly connected synchronisation graph form a minimal T-invariant.

A minimal P-invariant (T-invariant) defines a connected subnet, consisting of its support, its pre- and posttransitions (pre- and postplaces), and all arcs in between. There are no structural limitations for such subnets induced by minimal invariants, compare Figure 9, but they are always connected, however not necessarily strongly connected. These minimal self-contained subnets may be read as a decomposition into token preserving or state repeating modules, which should have an enclosed biological meaning. However, minimal invariants generally overlap, and in the worst-case there are exponentially many of them.

Running Example. There are seven minimal P-invariants covering the net (CPI), and consequently the net is bounded for any initial marking (SB). All these P-invariants x_i contain only entries of 0 and 1, permitting a shorthand specification by just giving the names of the places involved.

Each P-invariant stands for a reasonable conservation rule, the species preserved being given by the first name in the invariant. Due to the chosen naming convention, this particular name also appears in all the other place names of the same P-invariant.

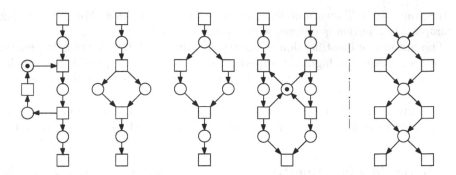

Fig. 9. The four nets on the left are each covered by one minimal T-invariants. Invariants can contain any structures (from left to right): cycles, forward/backward branching transitions, forward branching places, backward branching places. Generally, invariants overlap, and in the worst-case there are exponentially many of them; the net on the far-right has 2^4 T-invariants.

$x_1 = (\textbf{RasGTP}, \text{Raf\_RasGTP})$
$x_2 = (\textbf{Raf}, \text{Raf\_RasGTP}, \text{RafP}, \text{RafP\_Phase1}, \text{MEK\_RafP}, \text{MEKP\_RafP})$
$x_3 = (\textbf{MEK}, \text{MEK\_RafP}, \text{MEKP\_RafP}, \text{MEKP\_Phase2}, \text{MEKPP\_Phase2},$
$\qquad \text{ERK\_MEKPP}, \text{ERKP\_MEKPP}, \text{MEKPP}, \text{MEKP})$
$x_4 = (\textbf{ERK}, \text{ERK\_MEKPP}, \text{ERKP\_MEKPP}, \text{ERKP}, \text{ERKPP\_Phase3},$
$\qquad \text{ERKP\_Phase3}, \text{ERK\_PP})$
$x_5 = (\textbf{Phase1}, \text{RafP\_Phase1})$
$x_6 = (\textbf{Phase2}, \text{MEKP\_Phase2}, \text{MEKPP\_Phase2})$
$x_7 = (\textbf{Phase3}, \text{ERKP\_Phase3}, \text{ERKPP\_Phase3})$

The net under consideration is also covered by T-invariants (CTI), however not strongly covered (SCTI). Besides the expected ten trivial T-invariants for the ten reversible reactions, there are five nontrivial, but obvious minimal T-invariants, each corresponding to one of the five phosphorylation/dephosphorylation cycles in the network structure:

$y_1 = (\text{r1}, \text{r3}, \text{r4}, \text{r6}),$
$y_2 = (\text{r7}, \text{r9}, \text{r16}, \text{r18}),$
$y_3 = (\text{r10}, \text{r12}, \text{r13}, \text{r15}),$
$y_4 = (\text{r19}, \text{r21}, \text{r28}, \text{r30}),$
$y_5 = (\text{r22}, \text{r24}, \text{r25}, \text{r27}).$

The interesting net behaviour, demonstrating how input signals finally cause output signals, is contained in a nonnegative linear combination of all five nontrivial T-invariants,

$$y_{1-5} = y_1 + y_2 + y_3 + y_4 + y_5,$$

which is called an I/O T-invariant in the following. The I/O T-invariant is systematically constructed by starting with the two minimal T-invariants, involving the input and output signal, which define disconnected subnetworks. Then we add minimal sets of minimal T-invariants to get a connected subnet, which corresponds to a T-invariant feasible in the initial marking. For our running example, the solution is unique, which is not generally the case.

The automatic identification of nontrivial minimal T-invariants is in general useful as a method to highlight important parts of a network, and hence aids its comprehension by biochemists, especially when the entire network is too complex to easily comprehend.

P/T-invariants relate only to the structure, i.e. they are valid independently of the initial marking. In order to proceed we first need to generate an initial marking.

(3) Initial Marking Construction. For a systematic construction of the initial marking, we consider the following criteria.

- Each P-invariant needs at least one token.
- All (nontrivial) T-invariants should be feasible, meaning, the transitions, making up the T-invariant's multi-set can actually be fired in an appropriate (partial) order.
- Additionally, it is common sense to look for a minimal marking (as few tokens as possible), which guarantees the required behaviour.
- Within a P-invariant, choose the species with the most *inactive* or the *monomeric* state.

Running Example. Taking all these criteria together, the initial marking on hand is: RasGTP, MEK, ERK, Phase1, Phase2 and Phase3 get each one token, while all remaining places are empty. With this initial marking, the net is covered by 1-P-invariants (exactly one token in each P-invariant), therefore the net is 1-bounded (indicated as 1-B in the analysis result vector, compare Figure 6). That is in perfect accordance with the understanding that in signal transduction networks a P-invariant comprises all the different states of one species. Obviously, each species can be only in one state at any time.

Generalising this reasoning to a multi-level concept, we could assign n tokens to each place representing the most inactive state, in order to indicate the highest concentration level for them in the initial state. The "abstract" mass conservation within each P-invariant would then be n tokens, which could be distributed fairly freely over the P-invariant's places during the behaviour of the model. This results in a dramatic increase of the state space, as we will later see, while not improving the qualitative reasoning.

We check the I/O T-invariant for feasibility in the constructed initial marking, which then involves the feasibility of all trivial T-invariants. In order to preserve all the concurrency information we have, we construct a new net which describes the behaviour of our system net under investigation. We obtain an *infinite partial order run*, the beginning of which is given as labelled condition/event net in Figure 10. Here, transitions represent events, labelled by the name of the reaction taking place, while places stand for binary conditions, labelled by the name of the species, set or reset by the event, respectively. We get this run by unfolding the behaviour of the subnet induced by the T-invariant. This run can be characterized in a shorthand notation by the following set of partially ordered words

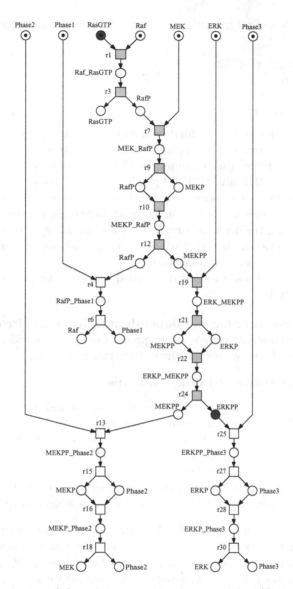

Fig. 10. The beginning of the infinite partial order run of the I/O T-invariant $y_{1-5} = y_1 + y_2 + y_3 + y_4 + y_5$ of the place/transition Petri net given in Figure 6. We get this run by unfolding the behaviour of the subnet induced by the T-invariant, whereby any concurrency is preserved. Here, transitions represent events, labelled by the name of the reaction taking place, while places stand for binary conditions, labelled by the name of the species, set or reset by the event, respectively. The highlighted set of transitions and places is the required minimal sequence of events to produce the output signal ERKPP. We get a totally ordered sequence of events for our running example. Generally, this sequence will be partially ordered only.

out of the alphabet of all transition labels T (";" stands for "sequentiality", "||" for "concurrency"):

>(r1; r3; r7; r9; r10; r12;
>>((r4; r6) ||
>>((r19; r21; r22; r24);
>>>((r13; r15; r16; r18) || (r25; r27; r28; r30))))).

This partial order run gives further insight into the dynamic behaviour of the network, which may not be apparent from the standard net representation, e.g. we are able to follow the (minimal) producing process of the proteins RafP, MEKP, MEKPP, ERKP and ERKPP (highlighted in Figure 10), and we notice the clear independence, i.e. concurrency of the dephosphorylation in all three levels. The entire run describes the whole network behaviour triggered by the input signal, i.e. including the dephosphorylation. This unfolding is completely defined by the net structure, the initial marking and the multiset of firing transitions. Thus it can be constructed automatically.

Having established and justified our initial marking, we proceed to the next steps of the analysis.

(4) Static Decision of Marking-dependent Behavioural Properties. The following advanced structural Petri net properties can be decided by combinatorial algorithms. First, we need to introduce two new notions.

Definition 9 (Structural deadlocks, traps)

- *A nonempty set of places $D \subseteq P$ is called* structural deadlock (co-trap) *if* $\bullet D \subseteq D \bullet$ *(the set of pretransitions is contained in the set of posttransitions), i.e. every transition which fires tokens onto a place in this structural deadlock set, also has a preplace in this set.*
- *A set of places $Q \subseteq P$ is called* trap *if* $Q \bullet \subseteq \bullet Q$ *(the set of posttransitions is contained in of pretransitions), i.e. every transition which subtracts tokens from a place of the trap set, also has a postplace in this set.*

Pretransitions of a structural deadlock [3] cannot fire if the structural deadlock is clean. Therefore, a structural deadlock cannot get tokens again as soon as it is clean, and then all its posttransitions $t \in D \bullet$ are dead. A Petri net without structural deadlocks is live, while a system in a dead state has a clean structural deadlock.

Posttransitions of a trap always return tokens to the trap. Therefore, once a trap contains tokens, it cannot become clean again. There can be a decrease of the total token amount within a trap, but not down to zero.

An input place p establishes a structural deadlock $D = \{p\}$ on its own, and an output place q, a trap $Q = \{q\}$. If each transition has a preplace, then $P \bullet = T$,

---

[3] The notion *structural deadlock* has nothing in common with the famous deadlock phenomenon of concurrent processes. The Petri net community has been quite creative in trying to avoid this name clash (co-trap, siphon, tube). However, none of these terms got widely accepted.

and if each transition has a postplace, then $^\bullet P = T$. Therefore, in a net without boundary transitions, the whole set of places is a structural deadlock as well as a trap. If D and D' are structural deadlocks (traps), then $D \cup D'$ is also a structural deadlock (trap).

A structural deadlock (trap) is *minimal* if it does not properly contain a structural deadlock (nonempty trap). The network, defined by a minimal structural deadlock (trap), is strongly connected. A trap is *maximal* if it is not a proper subset of a trap. Every structural deadlock includes a unique maximal trap with respect to set inclusion (which may be empty).

The support of a P-invariant is structural deadlock and trap at the same time. But caution: not every place set which is a structural deadlock as well as a trap is a P-invariant. Even more, a P-invariant may properly contain a structural deadlock. Of special interest are often those minimal deadlocks (traps), which are not at the same time a P-invariant, for which we introduce the notion *proper deadlock (trap)*. See also Figure 11 for an example to illustrate these two notions of structural deadlock and trap.

Structural deadlock and trap are closely related but contrasting notions. When they come on their own, we get usually deficient behaviour. However, both notions have the power to complement each other perfectly.

Definition 10 (Deadlock trap property)
A Petri net satisfies the deadlock trap property (DTP) if

- *every deadlock includes an initially marked trap,*
  To optimize computational effort this can be translated into:
- *the maximal trap in every minimal deadlock is initially marked.*

This is only possible if there are no input places. An input place establishes a structural deadlock on its own, in which the maximal trap is empty, and therefore not marked. The DTP can still be decided by structural reasoning only. Its importance becomes clear by the following theorems.

Theorem 1 (Relations between structural and behavioural properties)

1. *A net without structural deadlocks is live.*
2. *$ORD \wedge DTP \Rightarrow$ no dead states*
3. *$ORD \wedge ES \wedge DTP \Rightarrow$ live*
4. *$ORD \wedge EFC \wedge DTP \Leftrightarrow$ live*

The first theorem occasionally helps to decide liveness of unbounded nets. The last theorem is also known as *Commoner's theorem*, published in 1972. Theorems 2-4 have been generalized to non-ordinary nets by requiring homogeneity and non-blocking multiplicity [Sta90]. The proof for ordinary Petri nets can be found in [DE95].

Running Example. The Deadlock Trap Property holds, but no special net structure class is given, therefore we know now that the net is weakly live, i.e. there is no dead state (DSt). Please note, for our given net we are not able to decide liveness by structural reasoning only.

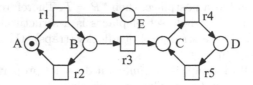

structural deadlock:

•$\{A, B\} \subseteq \{A, B\}$•

pretransitions: •$\{A, B\} = \{r1, r2\}$

posttransitions: $\{A, B\}$• $= \{r1, r2, r3\}$

trap:

$\{C, D, E\}$• $\subseteq$ •$\{C, D, E\}$

posttransitions: $\{C, D, E\}$• $= \{r4, r5\}$

pretransitions: •$\{C, D, E\} = \{r1, r3, r4, r5\}$

Fig. 11. The token on place A can rotate in the left cycle by repeated firing of r1 and r2. Each round produces an additional token on place E, making this place unbounded. This cycle can be terminated by firing of transition r3, which brings the circulating token from the left to the right side of the Petri net. The place set $\{A, B\}$ cannot get tokens again as soon as it got clean. Thus, it is a (proper) structural deadlock. On the contrary, the place set $\{C, D, E\}$ cannot become clean again as soon as it got a token. The repeated firing of r4 and r5 reduces the total token number, but cannot remove all of them. Thus, the place set $\{C, D, E\}$ is a (proper) trap.

(5) Dynamic Decision of Behavioural Properties. In order to decide liveness and reversibility we need to construct the state space. This could be done according the partial order semantics or the interleaving semantics. To keep things simple in this introductory tutorial we consider here the interleaving semantics only, which brings us to the reachability graph.

Definition 11 (Reachability graph). *Let* $\mathcal{N} = (P, T, f, m_0)$ *be a Petri net. The* reachability graph *of* $\mathcal{N}$ *is the graph* $\mathcal{RG}(\mathcal{N}) = (V_{\mathcal{N}}, E_{\mathcal{N}})$, *where*

- $V_{\mathcal{N}} := [m_0\rangle$ *is the set of nodes,*
- $E_{\mathcal{N}} := \{ (m, t, m') \mid m, m' \in [m_0\rangle, t \in T : m[t\rangle m' \}$ *is the set of arcs.*

The nodes of a reachability graph represent all possible states (markings) of the net. The arcs in between are labelled by single transitions, the firing of which causes the related state change, compare Figure 12. The reachability graph gives us a finite automaton representation of all possible single step firing sequences. Consequently, concurrent behaviour is described by enumerating all interleaving firing sequences; so the reachability graph reflects the behaviour of the net according to the interleaving semantics.

The reachability graph is finite for bounded nets only. A branching node in the reachability graph, i.e. a node with more than one successor, reflects either alternative or concurrent behaviour. The difference is not locally decidable anymore in the reachability graph. For 1-bounded ordinary state machines, net structure and reachability graph are isomorphic.

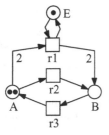
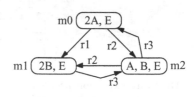

Fig. 12. A Petri net (left) and its reachability graph (right). The states are given in a shorthand notation. In state m0, transitions r1 and r2 are in a dynamic conflict; the firing of one transition disables the other one. In state m2, transitions r2 and r3 are concurrently enabled; they can fire independently, i.e. in any order. In both cases we get a branching node in the reachability graph.

Reachability graphs tend to be huge. In the worst-case the state space grows faster than any primitive recursive function[4], basically for two reasons: concurrency is resolved by all interleaving sequences, see Figure 13, and the tokens in over-populated P-invariant can distribute themselves fairly arbitrarily, see Figure 14. The state space explosion motivates the static analyses, as discussed in the preceding analysis steps. If we succeed in constructing the complete reachability graph, we are able to decide behavioural Petri net properties.

- A Petri net is k-bounded iff there is no node in the reachability graph with a token number larger than k in any place.
- A Petri net is reversible iff the reachability graph is strongly connected.
- A Petri net is deadlock-free iff the reachability graph does not contain terminal nodes, i.e., nodes without outgoing arcs.
- In order to decide liveness, we partition the reachability graph into strongly connected components (SCC), i.e. maximal sets of strongly connected nodes. A SCC is called terminal if no other SCC is reachable in the partitioned graph. A transition is live iff it is included in all terminal SCCs of the partitioned reachability graph. A Petri net is live iff this holds for all transitions.

The occurrence of dynamic conflicts is checked at best during the construction of the reachability graph, because branching nodes do not necessarily mean alternative system behaviour.

Running Example. We already know that the net is bounded, so the reachability graph has to be finite. It comprises in the Boolean token interpretation 118 states out of 2^{22} theoretically possible ones; see Table 1 for some samples of the size of the state space in the integer token semantics (discrete concentration levels). Independently of the size, the reachability graph we get forms one strongly connected component. Therefore, the Petri net is reversible, i.e. each system state

---

[4] To be precise: the dependence of the size of a reachability graph on the size of the net cannot be bounded by a primitive recursive function [PW03].

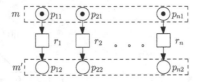

Fig. 13. State explosion problem 1. There are $n!$ interleaving sequences from m (all places p_{*1} carry a token) to m' (all places p_{*2} carry a token), causing $2^n - 2$ intermediate states.

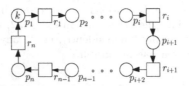

Fig. 14. State explosion problem 2. The k tokens are bound to circulate within the given cycle. They can arbitrarily distribute themselves on the n places, forming a P-invariant. There are $(n + k - 1)!/[(n - 1)! \, k!]$ possibilities for this distribution (combinations with repetition). Each distribution defines a state.

is always reachable again. Further, each transition (reaction) appears at least once in this strongly connected component, therefore the net is live. There are dynamic conflicts, e.g. between r2 and r3 in all states, where Raf_RasGTP is marked.

Moreover, from the viewpoint of the qualitative model, all of these states of the reachability graph's only strongly connected component are equivalent, and each could be taken as an initial state resulting in exactly the same total (discrete) system behaviour. This prediction will be confirmed by the observations gained during quantitative analyses, see Sections 5.2 and 6.2.

This concludes the analysis of *general* behavioural net properties, i.e. of properties we can speak about in syntactic terms only, without any semantic knowledge. The next step consists in a closer look at *special* behavioural net properties, reflecting the expected special functionality of the network.

Table 1. State explosion in the running example

levels	IDD data structure[a] number of nodes	reachability graph number of states
1	52	118
4	115	$2.4 \cdot 10^4$
8	269	$6.1 \cdot 10^6$
40	3,697	$4.7 \cdot 10^{14}$
80	13,472	$5.6 \cdot 10^{18}$
120	29,347	$1.7 \cdot 10^{21}$

[a] This computational experiment has been performed with idd-ctl, a model checker based on interval decision diagrams (IDD).

(6) Model Checking of Special Behavioural Properties. Temporal logic is particularly helpful in expressing special behavioural properties of the expected transient behaviour, whose truth can be determined via model checking. It is an unambiguous language, providing a flexible formalism which considers the validity of propositions in relation to the execution of the model. Model checking generally requires boundedness. If the net is 1-bounded, there exists a particularly rich choice of model checkers, which get their efficiency by exploiting sophisticated data structures and algorithms.

One of the widely used temporal logics is the *Computational Tree Logic* (CTL). It works on the computational tree, which we get by unwinding the reachability graph, compare Figure 15. Thus, CTL represents a branching time logic with interleaving semantics.

The application of this analysis approach requires an understanding of temporal logics. Here, we restrict ourselves to an informal introduction into CTL. CTL - as any temporal logic - is an extension of a classical (propositional) logic. The atomic propositions consist of statements on the current token situation in a given place. In the case of 1-bounded models, places can be read as Boolean variables, with allows propositions such as $RafP$ instead of $m(RafP) = 1$. Likewise, places are read as integer variables for k-bounded models, $k \neq 1$.

Propositions can be combined to composed propositions using the standard logical operators: $\neg$ (negation), $\wedge$ (conjunction), $\vee$ (disjunction), and $\rightarrow$ (implication), e.g. $RafP \wedge ERKP$.

The truth value of a proposition may change by the execution of the net; e.g. the proposition $RafP$ does not hold in the initial state, but there are reachable states where Raf is phosphorylated, so $RafP$ holds in these states. Such temporal relations between propositions are expressed by the additionally available temporal operators.

In CTL there are basically four of them (ne**X**t, **F**inally, **G**lobally, **U**ntil), which come in two versions (**E** for Existence, **A** for All), making together eight operators. Let $\phi_{[1,2]}$ be an arbitrary temporal-logic formulae. Then, the following formulae hold in state m,

- **EX** ϕ : if there is a state reachable by one step where ϕ holds.
- **EF** ϕ : if there is a path where ϕ holds finally, i.e., at some point.
- **EG** ϕ : if there is a path where ϕ holds globally, i.e., forever.
- **E** $(\phi_1 \; \mathbf{U} \; \phi_2)$: if there is a path where ϕ_1 holds until ϕ_2 holds.

The other four operators, which we get by replacing the **E**xistence operator by the **A**ll operator, are defined likewise by extending the requirement *"there is a path"* to *"for all paths it holds that"*. A formula holds in a net if it holds in its initial state. See Figure 16 for a graphical illustration of the eight temporal operators.

Running Example. We confine ourselves here to two CTL properties, checking the generalizability of the insights gained by the partial order run of the I/O T-invariant. Recall that places are interpreted as Boolean variables in order to simplify notation.

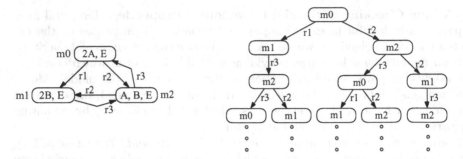

Fig. 15. Unwinding the reachability graph (left) into an infinite computation tree (right). The root of the computation tree is the initial state of the reachability graph.

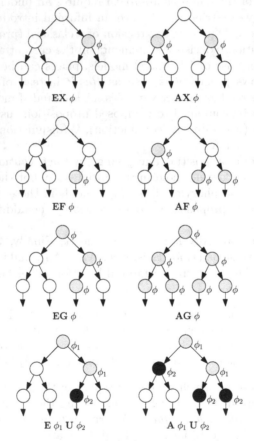

Fig. 16. The eight CTL operators and their semantics in the computation tree, which we get by unwinding the reachability graph, compare Figure 15. The two path quantifiers **E**, **A** relate to the branching structure in the computation tree: **E** - for some computation path (left column), **A** - for all computation paths (right column).

Property Q1: The signal sequence predicted by the partial order run of the I/O T-invariant is the only possible one. In other words, starting at the initial state, it is necessary to pass through states RafP, MEKP, MEKPP and ERKP in order to reach ERKPP.

$$\neg \, [\, \mathbf{E} \, (\, \neg \, \text{RafP} \qquad \mathbf{U} \, \text{MEKP} \,) \, \vee \, \mathbf{E} \, (\, \neg \, \text{MEKP} \, \mathbf{U} \, \text{MEKPP} \,) \, \vee$$
$$\mathbf{E} \, (\, \neg \, \text{MEKPP} \, \mathbf{U} \, \text{ERKP} \,) \, \vee \, \mathbf{E} \, (\, \neg \, \text{ERKP} \, \mathbf{U} \, \text{ERKPP} \,) \, \,]$$

Property Q2: Dephosphorylation takes place independently. E.g., the duration of the phosphorylated state of ERK is independent of the duration of the phosphorylated states of MEK and Raf.

$$(\, \mathbf{EF} \, [\, \text{Raf} \wedge (\, \text{ERKP} \vee \text{ERKPP} \,) \,] \, \wedge \, \mathbf{EF} \, [\, \text{RafP} \wedge (\, \text{ERKP} \vee \text{ERKPP} \,) \,] \, \wedge$$
$$\mathbf{EF} \, [\, \text{MEK} \wedge (\, \text{ERKP} \vee \text{ERKPP} \,) \,] \, \wedge$$
$$\mathbf{EF} \, [\, (\, \text{MEKP} \vee \text{MEKPP} \,) \wedge (\, \text{ERKP} \vee \text{ERKPP} \,) \,] \,)$$

Temporal logic is an extremely powerful and flexible language to describe special properties, however needs some experience to get accustomed to it. Applying this analysis technique requires seasoned understanding of the network under investigation, combined with the skill to correctly express the expected behaviour in temporal logics.

In subsequent sections we will see how to employ the same technique in a quantitative setting. We will use Q1 as a basis to illustrate how the stochastic and continuous approaches provide complementary views of the system behaviour.

4.3   Summary

To summarize the preceding validation steps, the model has passed the following validation criteria.

- **validation criterion 0** All expected structural properties hold, and all expected general behavioural properties hold.
- **validation criterion 1** The net is CPI, and there are no minimal P-invariant without biological interpretation.
- **validation criterion 2** The net is CTI, and there are no minimal T-invariant without biological interpretation. Most importantly, there is no known biological behaviour without a corresponding, not necessarily minimal, T-invariant.
- **validation criterion 3** All expected special behavioural properties expressed as temporal-logic formulae hold.

One of the benefits of using the qualitative approach is that systems can be modelled and analysed without any quantitative parameters. In doing so, all possible behaviour under any timing is considered. Moreover the qualitative step helps in identifying suitable initial markings and potential quantitative analysis techniques. Now we are ready for a more sophisticated quantitative analysis of our model.

5   The Stochastic Approach

5.1   Stochastic Modelling

As with a qualitative Petri net, a stochastic Petri net maintains a discrete number of tokens on its places. But contrary to the time-free case, a firing rate (waiting time) is associated with each transition t, which are random variables $X_t \in [0, \infty)$, defined by probability distributions. Therefore, all reaction times can theoretically still occur, but the likelihood depends on the probability distribution. Consequently, the system behaviour is described by the same discrete state space, and all the different execution runs of the underlying qualitative Petri net can still take place. This allows the use of the same powerful analysis techniques for stochastic Petri nets as already applied for qualitative Petri nets.

For better understanding we describe the general procedure of a particular simulation run for a stochastic Petri net. Each transition gets its own local timer. When a particular transition becomes enabled, meaning that sufficient tokens arrive on its preplaces, then the local timer is set to an initial value, which is computed at this time point by means of the corresponding probability distribution. In general, this value will be different for each simulation run. The local timer is then decremented at a constant speed, and the transition will fire when the timer reaches zero. If there is more than one enabled transition, a race for the next firing will take place.

Technically, various probability distributions can be chosen to determine the random values for the local timers. Biochemical systems are the prototype for exponentially distributed reactions. Thus, for our purposes, the firing rates of all transitions follow an exponential distribution, which can be described by a single parameter λ, and each transition needs only its particular, generally marking-dependent parameter λ to specify its local time behaviour. The following definition summarises this informal introduction.

Definition 12 (Stochastic Petri net, Syntax). *A biochemically interpreted stochastic Petri net is a quintuple* $\mathcal{SPN}_{Bio} = (P, T, f, v, m_0)$, *where*

- *P and T are finite, non empty, and disjoint sets. P is the set of places, and T is the set of transitions.*
- *$f : ((P \times T) \cup (T \times P)) \to \mathbb{N}_0$ defines the set of directed arcs, weighted by nonnegative integer values.*
- *$v : T \to H$ is a function, which assigns a stochastic hazard function h_t to each transition t, whereby*
  $H := \bigcup_{t \in T} \left\{ h_t \mid h_t : \mathbb{N}_0^{|{}^{\bullet}t|} \to \mathbb{R}^+ \right\}$ *is the set of all stochastic hazard functions, and $v(t) = h_t$ for all transitions $t \in T$.*
- *$m_0 : P \to \mathbb{N}_0$ gives the initial marking.*

The stochastic hazard function h_t defines the marking-dependent transition rate $\lambda_t(m)$ for the transition t. The domain of h_t is restricted to the set of preplaces of t to enforce a close relation between network structure and hazard functions. Therefore $\lambda_t(m)$ actually depends only on a sub-marking.

Stochastic Petri Net, Semantics. Transitions become enabled as usual, i.e. if all preplaces are sufficiently marked. However there is a time, which has to elapse, before an enabled transition $t \in T$ fires. The transition's waiting time is an exponentially distributed random variable X_t with the *probability density function*:

$$f_{X_t}(\tau) = \lambda_t(m) \cdot e^{(-\lambda_t(m) \cdot \tau)}, \qquad \tau \geq 0.$$

The firing itself does not consume time and again follows the standard firing rule of qualitative Petri nets. The semantics of a stochastic Petri net (with exponentially distributed reaction times for all transitions) is described by a continuous time Markov chain (CTMC). The CTMC of a stochastic Petri net without parallel transitions is isomorphic to the reachability graph of the underlying qualitative Petri net, while the arcs between the states are now labelled by the transition rates. For more details see [MBC+95], [BK02].

Based on this general $\mathcal{SPN}_{Bio}$ definition, specialised biochemically interpreted stochastic Petri nets can be defined by specifying the required kind of stochastic hazard function more precisely. We give two examples, reading the tokens as molecules or as concentration levels. The *stochastic mass-action hazard function* tailors the general $\mathcal{SPN}_{Bio}$ definition to biochemical mass-action networks, where tokens correspond to molecules:

$$h_t := c_t \cdot \prod_{p \in {}^\bullet t} \binom{m(p)}{f(p,t)}, \tag{1}$$

where c_t is the transition-specific stochastic rate constant, and $m(p)$ is the current number of tokens on the preplace p of transition t. The binomial coefficient describes the number of unordered combinations of the $f(p,t)$ molecules, required for the reaction, out of the $m(p)$ available ones.

Tokens can also be read as concentration levels, as introduced in [CVGO06]. The current concentration of each species is given as an abstract level. We assume the maximum molar concentration is M, and the amount of different levels is $N+1$. Then the abstract values $0, \ldots, N$ represent the concentration intervals 0, $(0, 1 * M/N]$, $(1 * M/N, 2 * M/N]$, $\ldots$, $(N - 1 * M/N, N * M/N]$. Each of these (finitely many) discrete levels stands for an equivalence class of (infinitely many) continuous states. The *stochastic level hazard function* tailors the general $\mathcal{SPN}_{Bio}$ definition to biochemical mass-action networks, where tokens correspond to concentration levels; for ordinary nets we get:

$$h_t := k_t \cdot N \cdot \prod_{p \in {}^\bullet t} \left(\frac{m(p)}{N}\right), \tag{2}$$

where k_t is the transition-specific deterministic rate constant, and N the number of the highest level. The transformation rules between the stochastic and deterministic rate constants are well-understood, see e.g. [Wil06]. In practice, kinetic rates are taken from literature, textbooks, etc. or determined from biochemical experiments. A hazard function (2) is the means whereby the continuous model (see the framework in Figure 2 and Section 6) can be approximated by the stochastic model; this can generally be achieved by a limited number of levels – see Section 5.2.

We only consider here the level semantics. Since the continuous concentrations of proteins in our running example are all in the same range (0.1...0.4 mMol in 0.1 steps), we employ a model with only 4, and a second version with 8 levels, compare Figure 17.

The corresponding CTMCs (and reachability graphs) comprise 24,065 states for the 4 level version and 6,110,643 states for the 8 level version, compare Table 1.

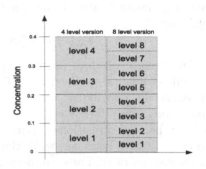

Fig. 17. The partitioning of the concentration scale into discrete levels

5.2   Stochastic Analysis

Due to the isomorphy of the reachability graph and the CTMC, all qualitative analysis results obtained in Section 4 are still valid. The influence of time does not restrict the possible system behaviour. Specifically it holds that the CTMC of our case study is reversible, which ensures ergodicity; i.e. we could start the system in any of the reachable states, always resulting in the same CTMC with the same steady state probability distribution.

Additionally, probabilistic analyses of the transient and steady state behaviour are now available. Generally, this can be done in an analytical as well as in a simulative manner. The analytical approach works on the CTMC, which therefore has to be finite. Consequently, the net to be analysed has to be bounded. On the contrary, the simulative approach works also for systems with infinite state space or state space beyond the current limits of exact analyses, and for systems with complex dynamics as semi-Markov processes or generalized semi-Markov processes.

In order to use the probabilistic model checker PRISM [PNK06] for the analytical approach, we encode the running example in its modelling language. We follow the technique proposed in [DDS04], which is more natural for Petri nets than the one proposed in [CVGO06] for algebraic models. This translation requires knowledge of the boundedness degree of all species involved, which we acquire by the structural analysis technique of P-invariants.

In the following the reader is assumed to be familiar with related standard techniques and terminology.

(1) Equivalence Check by Transient Analysis. We start with transient analysis to prove the sufficient equivalence between the stochastic model in the level semantics and the corresponding continuous model, justifying the interpretation of the properties gained by the stochastic model also in terms of the continuous one. PRISM permits the analysis of the transient behaviour of the stochastic model; e.g., the concentration of RafP at time t is given by:

$$C_{RafP}(t) = \frac{0.1}{s} \cdot \underbrace{\sum_{i=1}^{4s} \left(i \cdot P(L_{RafP}(t) = i) \right)}_{expected\ value\ of\ L_{RafP}(t)} .$$

The random variable $L_{RafP}(t)$ stands for the level of RafP at time t. We set s to 1 for the 4 level version, and to 2 for the 8 level version. The factor $\frac{0.1}{s}$ calibrates the expected value for a given level to the concentration scale. In the 4 level version a single level (token) represents 0.1 mMol and 0.05 mMol in the 8 level version. Figure 18 shows the simulation results for the species MEK and RasGTP in the time interval [0..100] according to the continuous and the stochastic models respectively. These results confirm that 4 levels are sufficiently adequate to approximate the continuous model, and that 8 levels are preferable if the computational expenses are acceptable.

(2) Analytical Stochastic Model Checking. In Section 4.2 we employed CTL to express behavioural properties. Since we have now a stochastic model, we apply Continuous Stochastic Logic (CSL), which replaces the path quantifiers (**E**, **A**) in CTL by the probability operator $\mathbf{P}_{\bowtie p}$, whereby $\bowtie p$ specifies the probability of the given formula. For example, introducing in CSL the abbreviation $\mathbf{F}\,\phi$ for $true\,\mathbf{U}\,\phi$, the CTL formula $\mathbf{EF}\,\phi$ becomes the CSL formula $\mathbf{P}_{\geq 0}[\,\mathbf{F}\,\phi\,]$, and $\mathbf{AF}\,\phi$ becomes $\mathbf{P}_{\geq 1}[\,\mathbf{F}\,\phi\,]$.

We give two properties related to the partial order run of the I/O T-invariant, see Section 4.2 and qualitative property Q1 therein, from which we expect a consecutive increase of RafP, MEKPP and ERKPP. Both properties are expressed as so-called experiments, which are analysed varying the parameter L over all levels, i.e. 0 to N. For the sake of efficiency, we restrict the **U** operator to 100 time steps. Note that places are read as integer variables in the following.

Property S1a: What is the probability of the concentration of RafP increasing, when starting in a state where the level is for the first time at L (the latter side condition is specified by the filter given in braces)?

$$\mathbf{P}_{=?}\,[\,(\,\text{RafP} = \text{L}\,)\,\mathbf{U}^{<=100}\,(\,\text{RafP} > \text{L}\,)\,\{\,\text{RafP} = \text{L}\,\}\,]$$

The results indicate, see Figure 19(a), that it is absolutely certain that the concentration of RafP increases from level 0 and likewise there is no increase from level N; this behaviour has already been determined by the qualitative analysis. Furthermore, an increase in RafP is very likely in the lower levels, increase and decrease are almost equally likely in the intermediate levels, while in the higher levels, but obviously not in the highest, an increase is rather unlikely (but not impossible). In summary this means that the total mass, circulating within the first layer of the signalling cascade, is unlikely to be accumulated in the activated form. We need this understanding to interpret the results for the next property.

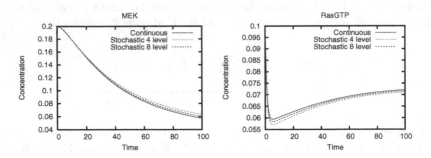

Fig. 18. Comparison of the concentration traces

Property S2a: What is the probability that, given the initial concentrations of RafP, MEKPP and ERKPP being zero, the concentration of RafP rises above some level L while the concentrations of MEKPP and ERKPP remain at zero, i.e. RafP is the first species to react?

$$\mathbf{P}_{=?} \, [\, (\, (\, MEKPP = 0 \,) \wedge (\, ERKPP = 0 \,) \,) \, \mathbf{U}^{<=100} \, (\, RafP > L \,)$$
$$\{ \, (\, MEKPP = 0 \,) \wedge (\, ERKPP = 0 \,) \, \wedge (\, RafP = 0 \,) \, \} \,]$$

The results indicate, see Figure 19(b), that the likelihood of the concentration of RafP rising, while those of MEKPP and ERKPP are zero, is very high in the bottom half of the levels, and quite high in the lower levels of the upper half. The decrease of the likelihood in the higher levels is explained by property S1. Property S2 is related to the qualitative property Q1 (Section 4.2), and the continuous property C1 (Section 6.2) – the concentration of RafP rises before those of MEKPP and ERKPP.

Due to the computational efforts of analytical stochastic model checking, we are only able to treat properties over a stochastic model with 4 or at most 8 levels. This restricts the kind of properties that we can prove; e.g., in order to check increases of MEKPP and ERKPP – as suggested by the qualitative property Q1 and done above for RafP in the stochastic properties S1 and S2 – we would need 50 or 200 levels respectively.

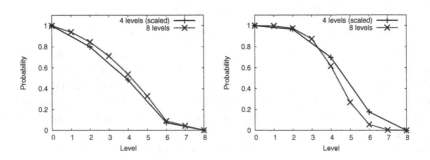

Fig. 19. Probability of the accumulation of RafP. (a) property S1. (b) property S2.

Analytical stochastic model checking becomes more and more impractical with increasing size of the state space. In order to avoid the enormous computational power required for larger state spaces, the time-dependent stochastic behaviour can be simulated by dedicated algorithms, and evaluated by simulative stochastic model checking, see next step, or approximated by a deterministic continuous behaviour, see Section 6.

(3) Simulative Stochastic Model Checking. This approach of Monte Carlo sampling handles large state spaces through approximating results by analysing only a subset of the state space – a set of finite outputs from a stochastic simulation algorithm (SSA), e.g. Gillespie's exact SSA [Gil77].

The type of logic now suitable for describing properties changes from branching time (e.g., CSL operating over CTMC) to linear time. A linear time logic operates in-turn over sets of linear paths through the state space, equivalent to operating on simulation outputs. A given property holds if it holds in all paths. Consequently, there are no path quantifiers in LTL.

We apply PLTL, a probabilistic linear time temporal logic [MC2]. This logic extends standard LTL to a stochastic setting, with a $\mathbf{P}_{\bowtie p}$ operator, such as in CSL, and a filter construct, $\{\phi\}$, defining the initial state of the property. However, PLTL does not have the ability to embed probability operators or perform steady state analysis.

The semantics is defined over sets of linear traces of temporal behaviour, in this case by stochastic simulation runs. Each trace is evaluated to a Boolean truth value, and the probability of a property holding true is computed by the fraction of true values in the set over the whole set. Please note, the choice of simulator and simulation parameters used to compute the sequence of states can affect the semantics of the PLTL property and the correctness of the result.

This approach to model checking incorporates two approximations. The truth value of a single trace is approximated by operating over a finite sequence of states only; and the probability of the property is approximated through sampling a finite number of traces (a subset of the model's behaviours) only.

PLTL could be considered as a linear time counterpart to CSL, and can easily be used to formalise the visual evaluation of diagrams as generated by deterministic/stochastic simulation runs or by recording experimental time series. We repeat properties S1a and S2a. Notice that the properties no longer require time bounds on temporal operators.

Property S1s: What is the probability of the concentration of RafP increasing, when starting in a state where the level is for the first time at L (the latter side condition is specified by the filter given in braces)?

$$\mathbf{P}_{=?} \left[\, (\, \text{RafP} \; = \; L \,) \, \mathbf{U} \, (\, \text{RafP} > L \,) \, \{ \, \text{RafP} = L \, \} \, \right]$$

We check this property using 100 simulation traces from Gillespie's algorithm with a simulation time of 300s as input to the PLTL model checker MC2 [MC2].

This property can be assessed with far greater numbers of tokens than possible in the analytical approach. We highlight the efficiency of the simulative approach

Table 2. Example figures for MC2 model checking of property S1 at varying number of levels/molecules

Levels	MC Time[a]	Simulation Output Size
4	10 s [b]	750 KB
8	15 s [b]	1.5 MB
40	1.5 minutes [b]	7.5 MB
400	1 minute [c]	80 MB
4,000	30 minutes [c]	900 MB

[a] Both Gillespie simulation and MC2 checking.
[b] Computation on a standard workstation.
[c] Distributed computation on a computer cluster comprising 45 Sun X2200 servers each with 2 dual core processors (180 CPU cores).

in Table 5.2 providing the time taken at varying numbers of tokens to perform model checking.

We extend the analysis of property S1 up to 4,000 molecules, shown in Figure 20, and observe that when increasing the number of molecules, the behaviour of the pathway tends towards the deterministic behaviour. The deterministic behaviour states that the protein RafP will always increase (property probability 1) until it reaches its maximum concentration value of around 0.1182 $mMol$. With increasing molecules, the maximum possible number of molecules in the stochastic behaviour of RafP tends towards the deterministic maximum (vertical line). The stochastic behaviour is seen to tend towards a probability of 0.5 in its possible concentration range, due to the stochastic nature where there is always a possibility of the protein decreasing or increasing when at a certain concentration.

Property S2s: What is the probability that, given the initial concentrations of RafP, MEKPP and ERKPP being zero, the concentration of RafP rises above some level L while the concentrations of MEKPP and ERKPP remain at zero, i.e. RafP is the first species to react?

$$\mathbf{P}_{=?} \left[\left(\left(MEKPP = 0 \right) \wedge \left(ERKPP = 0 \right) \right) \mathbf{U} \left(RafP > L \right) \right.$$
$$\left. \left\{ \left(MEKPP = 0 \right) \wedge \left(ERKPP = 0 \right) \wedge \left(RafP = 0 \right) \right\} \right]$$

To perform the analysis, we use the same simulation time (300s) and number of runs (100) as per S1s. Similarly, we extend this analysis up to 4,000 molecules, shown in Figure 21, and again note that the stochastic behaviour begins to approximate the deterministic behaviour. In the deterministic behaviour, only at the initial state of the system are RafP, MEKPP and ERKPP all zero, hence a probability of 1 at this state and probability of 0 elsewhere. With increasing molecules, the stochastic behaviour becomes less curved and more step-like, tending towards the vertical line in the deterministic behaviour.

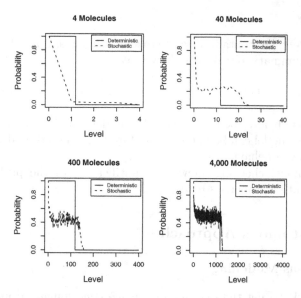

Fig. 20. Simulative stochastic model checking for property S1 at a varying number of molecules; 4, 40, 400 and 4,000. This shows a progression towards the deterministic behaviour as the number of molecules increases.

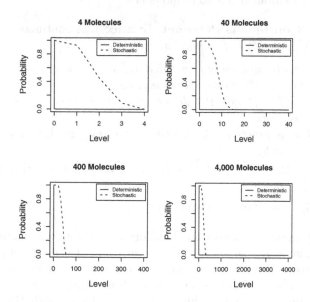

Fig. 21. Simulative stochastic model checking for property S2 at a varying number of molecules; 4, 40, 400 and 4,000. This shows a progression towards the deterministic behaviour as the number of molecules increases.

5.3 Summary

The stochastic Petri net contains discrete tokens and transitions which fire probabilistically. In summary, our results show that

1. Transient analysis helps to decide on the number of tokens to adequately describe the system.
2. The stochastic behaviour tends towards the deterministic behaviour. Thus the stochastic model can be approximated by a continuous model, representing the averaged behaviour only.
3. Stochastic model checking allows a quantification of the probabilities at which qualitative properties hold.

6 The Continuous Approach

6.1 Continuous Modelling

In a continuous Petri net the marking of a place is no longer an integer, but a positive real number, called token value, which we are going to interpret as the concentration of the species modelled by the place. The instantaneous firing of a transition is carried out like a continuous flow.

Definition 13 (Continuous Petri net, Syntax). *A continuous Petri net is a quintuple $\mathcal{CON}_{Bio} = (P, T, f, v, m_0)$, where*

- *P and T are finite, non empty, and disjoint sets. P is the set of continuous places. T is the set of continuous transitions.*
- *$f : ((P \times T) \cup (T \times P)) \to \mathbb{R}_0^+$ defines the set of directed arcs, weighted by nonnegative real values.*
- *$v : T \to H$ is a function which assigns a firing rate function h_t to each transition t, whereby*
  $H := \bigcup_{t \in T} \left\{ h_t | h_t : \mathbb{R}^{|{}^\bullet t|} \to \mathbb{R} \right\}$ is the set of all firing rate functions, and
  $v(t) = h_t$ for all transitions $t \in T$.
- *$m_0 : P \to \mathbb{R}_0^+$ gives the initial marking.*

The firing rate function h_t defines the marking-dependent continuous transition rate for the transition t. The domain of h_t is restricted to the set of preplaces of t to enforce a close relation between network structure and firing rate functions. Therefore $h_t(m)$ actually depends only on a sub-marking.

Technically, any mathematical function in compliance with this restriction is allowed for h_t. However, often special kinetic patterns are applied, whereby Michaelis-Menten and mass-action kinetics seem to be the most popular ones.

Please note, a firing rate may also be negative, in which case the reaction takes place in the reverse direction. This feature is commonly used to model reversible reactions by just one transition, where positive firing rates correspond to the forward direction, and negative ones to the backward direction.

Continuous Petri Net, Semantics. Each continuous marking is a place vector $m \in \left(\mathbf{R}_0^+\right)^{|P|}$, and $m(p)$ yields again the marking on place p, which is now a real number. A continuous transition t is enabled in m, if $\forall p \in {}^\bullet t : m(p) > 0$. Due to the influence of time, a continuous transition is forced to fire as soon as possible.

The semantics of a continuous Petri net is defined by a system of ODEs, whereby one equation describes the continuous change over time on the token value of a given place by the continuous increase of its pretransitions' flow and the continuous decrease of its posttransitions' flow, i.e., each place p subject to changes gets its own equation:

$$\frac{dm\,(p)}{dt} = \sum_{t \in {}^\bullet p} f\,(t,p)\,v\,(t) - \sum_{t \in p^\bullet} f\,(p,t)\,v\,(t),$$

Each equation corresponds basically to a line in the incidence matrix, whereby now the matrix elements consist of the rate functions multiplied by the arc weight, if any.

In other words, the continuous Petri net becomes the structured description of the corresponding ODEs. Due to the explicit structure we expect to get descriptions which are less error prone compared to those ones created manually from the scratch. In fact, writing down a system of ODEs by designing continuous Petri nets instead of just using a text editor might be compared to high-level instead of assembler programming.

For our running case study, we derive the continuous model from the qualitative Petri net by associating a *mass action rate* with each transition in the network.

We can likewise derive the continuous Petri net from the stochastic Petri net by approximating over the hazard function of type (1), see for instance [Wil06]. In both cases, we obtain a *continuous Petri net*, preserving the structure of the qualitative one, see our framework in Figure 2.

The complete system of nonlinear ODEs generated from the continuous Petri net of our running example is given in [GHL07a], Appendix C.

The initial concentrations as suggested by the qualitative analysis correspond to those given in [LBS00], when mapping nonzero values to 1. For reasons of better comparability we have also considered more precise initial concentrations, where the presence of a species is encoded by biologically motivated real values varying between 0.1 and 0.4 in steps of 0.1.

6.2   Continuous Analysis

As soon as there are transitions with more than one preplace, we get a non-linear system, which calls for a numerical treatment of the system on hand. In order to simulate the continuous Petri net, exactly the same algorithms are employed as for numerical differential equation solvers.

In the following the reader is assumed to be familiar with related standard techniques and terminology.

(1) **Steady State Analysis.** Since there are 22 species, there are 2^{22}, i.e. 4,194,304 possible initial states in the qualitative Petri net (Boolean token interpretation). Of these, 118 were identified by the reachability graph analysis (Section 4.2) to form one strongly connected component, and thus to be "good" initial states. These are 'sensible' initial states from the point of view of biochemistry in that in all these 118 cases, and in none of the other 4,194,186 states, each protein species is in a high initial concentration in only one of the following states: uncomplexed, complexed, unphosphorylated or phosphorylated. These conditions relate exactly to the 1-P-invariant interpretation given in our initial marking construction procedure in Section 4.2.

We then compute the steady state of the set of species for each possible initial state, using the MatLab ODE solver ode45, which is based on an explicit Runge-Kutta formula, the Dormand-Prince pair [DP80], with 350 time steps.

In Figure 22 (a) we reproduce the computed behaviour of MEK for all 118 good initial states, showing that despite differences in the concentrations at early time points, the steady state concentration is the same in all 118 states. We also reproduce two arbitrary chosen simulations of the model, compare Figure 23. The equivalence of the final states, compared with the difference in some intermediate states is clearly illustrated in these figures.

In summary, our results show that all of the 'good' 118 states result in the same set of steady state values for the 22 species in the pathway, within the bounds of computational error of the ODE solver. In [GHL07b] it is also shown that none of the remaining possible initial states results in a steady state close to that generated by the 118 markings in the reachability graph. See Table 4 in [GHL07a], Appendix C for the steady state concentrations of the 22 species.

This is an interesting result, because the net considered here is not covered by the class of net structures discussed in [ADLS06] with the unique steady state property.

(2) **Continuous Model Checking of the Transient Behaviour.** Corresponding to the partial order run of the I/O T-invariant, see Section 4.2, we expect a consecutive increase of RafP, MEKPP, ERKPP, which we get confirmed by the transient behaviour analysis, compare Figure 22 (b). To formalise the visual evaluation of the diagram we use the continuous linear logic LTLc [CCRFS06] and PLTL [MC2] in a deterministic setting. Both are interpreted over the continuous simulation trace of ODEs.

The following three queries confirm together the claim of the expected propagation sequence. In the queries we have to refer to absolute values. The steady state values are obtained from the steady state analysis in the previous section; these are 0.12 mMol for RafP, 0.008 mMol for MEKPP and 0.002 mMol for ERKPP, all of them being zero in the initial state. If a species' concentration is above half of its steady state value, we call this concentration level significant. Note that in order to simplify the notation, places are interpreted as real variables in the following.

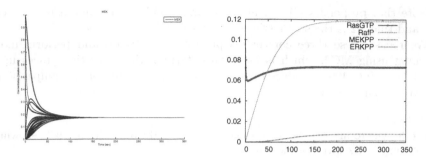

Fig. 22. (a) Steady state analysis of MEK for all 118 'good' states. (b) Continuous transient analysis of the phosphorylated species RasP, MEKPP, ERKPP, triggered by RasGTP.

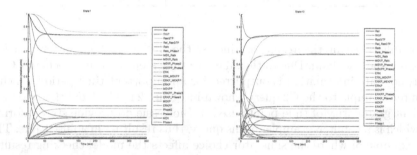

Fig. 23. Dynamic behaviour for state 1 (left) and state 10 (right). State 1 corresponds to the initial marking suggested by Section 4.2.

Property C1: The concentration of RafP rises to a significant level, while the concentrations of MEKPP and ERKPP remain close to zero; i.e. RafP is really the first species to react.

$$((MEKPP < 0.001) \wedge (ERKPP < 0.0002))\ \mathbf{U}\ (RafP > 0.06)$$

Property C2: if the concentration of RafP is at a significant concentration level and that of ERKPP is close to zero, then both species remain in these states until the concentration of MEKPP becomes significant; i.e. MEKPP is the second species to react.

$$((RafP > 0.06) \wedge (ERKPP < 0.0002)) \Rightarrow$$
$$((RafP > 0.06) \wedge (ERKPP < 0.0002))\ \mathbf{U}\ (MEKPP > 0.004)$$

Property C3: if the concentrations of RafP and MEKPP are significant, they remain so, until the concentration of ERKPP becomes significant; i.e. ERKPP is the third species to react.

$$((RafP > 0.06) \wedge (MEKPP > 0.004)) \Rightarrow$$
$$((RafP > 0.06) \wedge (MEKPP > 0.004))\ \mathbf{U}\ (ERKPP > 0.0005)$$

Note that properties C1, C2 and C3 correspond to the qualitative property Q1, and that S2 is the stochastic counterpart of C1.

We recast these three continuous properties to PLTL and perform model checking using MC2, which is fed with deterministic simulation traces up to simulation time 400s, produced with the BioNessie simulator. A comparison of the MC2 results to the Biocham results is summarised in Table 3.

Table 3. The results for the replication of C1, C2 and C3 queries in MC2, showing a discrepancy in C2 with the Biocham results

Query	Biocham	BioNessie & MC2
C1	true	true
C2	true	false
C3	true	true

The difference in the results is due to the different ODE solvers used in BioNessie and Biocham. Due to the adaptive time steps used in Biocham's ODE solver, no state information is outputted for an important time period which is a counter-example to the C2 query, shown in Figure 24. The fixed time step and sufficient granularity of time points used in BioNessie do provide state information which is a counter-example to this query, thus resulting in a false value. This is an example of where the simulator choice affects the model checking result.

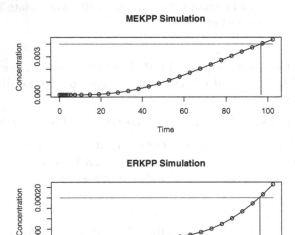

Fig. 24. The output of Biocham simulation showing that it does not output a state in the time period where ERKPP (bottom) > 0.0002 before MEKPP (top) > 0.004, which is a counter example to C2.

6.3 Summary

The continuous Petri net contains tokens with a continuous value and continuous firing of transitions. In summary, our results show that

1. All of the 118 good states identified by the reachability graph of the validated qualitative Petri net result in the same set of steady state values for the 22 species in the pathway.
2. None of the remaining possible initial states of the qualitative Petri net in the Boolean semantics results in a final steady state close to that generated by the good initial markings in the reachability graph.
3. Model checking this Petri net, which contains only a single deterministic behaviour, is akin to analysing the average behaviour of the system. We have shown that the properties as derived from the partial order run of the qualitative model also hold in the average behaviour.

7 Tools

The running example in its interpretation as the three Petri net models have been done using Snoopy [Sno08], a tool to design and animate or simulate hierarchical graphs, among them the qualitative, stochastic and continuous Petri nets as used in this chapter. Snoopy provides export to various analysis tools as well as Systems Biology Markup Language (SBML) [HFS⁺03] import and export [HRS08].

The qualitative analyses have been made with the Petri net analysis tool Charlie [Cha08]. Charlie's result vector is inspired by the Integrated Net Analyser INA [SR99], the analysis tool we have used for about 20 years. The exploration of the state space growth for increasing level numbers has been done with idd-ctl, a CTL model checker and reachability analyser utilising interval decision diagrams for concise state space representations [Tov06]. The Model Checking Kit [SSE03] has been used for qualitative model checking of 1-bounded models.

The quantitative analyses have been done using Snoopy's build-in simulation algorithms for stochastic and continuous Petri nets, and by BioNessie [Bio08], an SBML-based simulation and analysis tool for biochemical networks. Additionally, MATLAB [SR97] was used to produce the steady state analysis of all initial states in the continuous model.

We employed PRISM [PNK06] for probabilistic model checking of branching time logic, MC2 [MC2], a model checker by Monte Carlo sampling, for probabilistic and continuous model checking of linear time logic, and Biocham [CCRFS06] for LTLc-based continuous model checking.

More Petri nets tools and related material can be found on the Petri Nets World's web page: http://www.informatik.uni-hamburg.de/TGI/PetriNets/.

8 Further Reading and Related Work

Petri nets, as we understand them today, have been initiated by concepts proposed by Carl Adam Petri in his Ph.D. thesis in 1962 [Pet62]. The first substantial results making up the still growing body of Petri net theory appeared around 1970. Initial textbooks devoted to Petri nets were issued in the beginning of the eighties. General introductions into Petri net theory can be found, for example, in [Mur89], [Rei82], [Sta90]; for a comprehensive textbook covering extended free choice nets see specifically [DE95]. An excellent textbook for theoretical issues is [PW03], which however is in German. The text [DJ01] might be useful, if you just want to get the general flavour in reasonable time.

Petri nets have been employed for technical and administrative systems in numerous application domains since the mid-seventies. The employment in systems biology has been first published in [Hof94], [RML93]. Recent surveys on applying Petri nets for biochemical networks are [Cha07] and [Mat06], offering a rich choice of further reading pointers, among them numerous case studies applying Petri nets to biochemical networks. Besides the net classes introduced in this chapter, coloured Petri nets, duration and interval time Petri nets as well as hybrid Petri nets in various extensions have been employed.

Stochastic Petri nets are an established concept for performance and dependability analysis of technical systems, see [MBC+95], [BK02], recently extended by probabilistic model checking [DDS04]. An excellent textbook for numerical solution of Markov chains is [Ste94]. An overview on stochastic issues for systems biology is given in [Wil06]. The approximation of continuous behaviour by the discretisation of species' concentrations by a finite number of levels has been proposed in [CVGO06]. The application of stochastic Petri nets to biochemical networks was first proposed in [GP98], where they were applied to a gene regulatory network. Further case studies are discussed in [SPB01], [WMS05], [ST05], [SSW05], [Cur06]. A precise definition of biochemically interpreted stochastic Petri nets has been introduced in [GHL07b].

A comprehensive survey on timed Petri net concepts, among them continuous and hybrid Petri nets, however not stochastic Petri nets, in the context of technical systems can be found in [DA05]. See [MFD+03] for cases studies employing hybrid Petri nets to model and analyse biochemical pathways. A precise definition of biochemically interpreted continuous Petri nets has been introduced in [GH06].

P- and T-invariants are well-known concepts of Petri net theory since the very beginning [Lau73]. There are corresponding notions in systems biology, called chemical moieties, elementary modes and extreme pathways, which are elaborated in the setting of biochemical networks in [Pal06]. For biochemical systems without reversible reactions, the notions T-invariants, elementary modes and extreme pathways coincide. The validation of biochemical networks by means of T-invariants is demonstrated in [HK04].

Model checking has been very popular for the verification of technical systems since the eighties. A good starting point for qualitative model checking (CTL, LTL) is [CGP01]. For biochemical networks, qualitative model checking (Boolean semantics) has been introduced in [EKL+02], [CF03], and analytical stochastic model checking in [CVGO06], [HKN+06]. CSL, the stochastic counterpart to CTL, has been originally introduced in [AAB00], and extended in

[CBK03]. PRISM [PNK06] provides an efficient numerical implementation for CSL model checking, also exploiting symbolic representations. Approximative model checking of CSL using discrete event simulation of probabilistic models has been proposed in [YS02] and implemented in the tool Ymer [YKNP06]. The simulative stochastic model checker MC2 has been inspired by the idea of approximative LTL checking of deterministic simulation runs, proposed in [APUM03], [CCRFS06], [FR07].

The Biocham approach [CCRFS06], as it stands now, restricts itself to a branching time Boolean semantics for qualitative models, while we consider the more general case of integer semantics, which may collapse to the Boolean one. Petri net based model checking also supports the partial order semantics. To analyse continuous models, Biocham provides LTLc, which we used for continuous model checking of the transient behaviour. Meanwhile, this step is facilitated substantially by the extension introduced in [FR07], which permits the inference of the variable values fulfilling a given temporal property from a (set of) continuous simulation run(s).

Finally, there is a lot of activity relating stochastic and continuous models – see [TSB04] for a review. Most work has ignored analysis but instead focussed on simulation, at the molecular, inherently stochastic, level and the population (continuous) level using differential equations, possibly stochastic, e.g. [AME04], [Kie02] and [SK05].

The relation between systems of ordinary differential equations and the net structure of the underlying Petri nets are discussed in [ADLS06].

The systematic qualitative analysis of a metabolic network is demonstrated in [KH08], following basically the same outline as used in section 4.2. How to combine qualitative and quantitative analysis techniques is elaborated in [HDG08] for another signal transduction network and in [GHR⁺08] for a gene transduction network.

9   Summary

In this paper we have described an overall framework that relates the three major ways of modelling biochemical networks – qualitative, stochastic and continuous – and illustrated this in the context of Petri nets. In doing so we have given a precise definition of biochemically interpreted stochastic and continuous Petri nets. We have shown that the qualitative time-free description is the most basic, with discrete values representing numbers of molecules or levels of concentrations. The qualitative description abstracts over two timed, quantitative models. In the stochastic description, discrete values for the amounts of species are retained, but a stochastic rate is associated with each reaction. The continuous model describes amounts of species using continuous values and associates a deterministic rate with each reaction. These two time-dependent models can be mutually approximated by hazard functions belonging to the stochastic world.

We have illustrated our framework by considering qualitative, stochastic and continuous Petri net descriptions of the ERK signalling pathway, based on the model from [LBS00]. We have focussed on analysis techniques available in each of these three paradigms, in order to illustrate their complementarity. Timing diagrams as produced by numerical simulation techniques are much harder to assess in term of plausibility. That is why we start with qualitative analyses to increase our confidence in the model structure. Our special emphasis has been on model checking, which is especially useful for transient behaviour analysis, and we have demonstrated this by discussing related properties in the qualitative, stochastic and continuous paradigms. Although our framework is based on Petri nets, it can be applied more widely to other formalisms which are used to model and analyse biochemical networks.

The models developed over the three paradigms share the same structure, so they should share some properties too. However, the interrelationships between these models are not properly understood, yet.

Acknowledgements. The running case study has been partly carried out by Sebastian Lehrack during his study stay at the Bioinformatics Research Centre of the University of Glasgow. This stay was supported by the Max Gruenebaum Foundation [MGF] and the UK Department of Trade and Industry Beacon Bioscience Programme.

We would like to thank Rainer Breitling, Richard Orton and Xu Gu for the constructive discussions as well as Vladislav Vyshermirsky for his support in the computational experiments.

References

[AAB00]   Singhal, V., Aziz, A., Sanwal, K., Brayton, R.: Model checking continuous time Markov chains. ACM Trans. on Computational Logic 1(1), 162–170 (2000)

[ADLS06]   Angeli, D., De Leenheer, P., Sontag, E.D.: On the structural monotonicity of chemical reaction networks. In: Proc. 45th IEEE Conference on Decision and Control, pp. 7–12 (2006)

[AME04]   Adalsteinsson, D., McMillen, D., Elston, T.C.: Biochemical network stochastic simulator (bionetS): software for stochastic modeling of biochemical networks. BMC Bioinformatics 5, 24 (2004)

[APUM03]   Antoniotti, M., Policriti, A., Ugel, N., Mishra, B.: Model building and model checking for biochemical processes. Cell Biochemistry and Biophysics 38, 271–286 (2003)

[Bio08]   BioNessie website. A biochemical pathway simulation and analysis tool. University of Glasgow (2008), http://www.bionessie.org

[BK02]   Bause, F., Kritzinger, P.S.: Stochastic Petri Nets. Vieweg (2002)

[CBK03]   Hermanns, H., Baier, C., Haverkort, B., Katoen, J.-P.: Model-checking algorithms for continuous-time markov chains. IEEE Trans. on Software Engineering 29(6), 524–541 (2003)

[CCRFS06]   Calzone, L., Chabrier-Rivier, N., Fages, F., Soliman, S.: Machine learning biochemical networks from temporal logic properties. In: Priami, C., Plotkin, G. (eds.) Transactions on Computational Systems Biology VI. LNCS (LNBI), vol. 4220, pp. 68–94. Springer, Heidelberg (2006)

[CF03]   Chabrier, N., Fages, F.: Symbolic model checking of biochemical net-
            works. In: Priami, C. (ed.) CMSB 2003. LNCS, vol. 2602, pp. 149–162.
            Springer, Heidelberg (2003)
[CGP01]   Clarke, E.M., Grumberg, O., Peled, D.A.: Model checking. MIT Press,
            Cambridge (2001) (third printing)
[Cha07]   Chaouiya, C.: Petri net modelling of biological networks. Briefings in
            Bioinformatics 8(4), 210–219 (2007)
[Cha08]   Charlie Website. A Tool for the Analysis of Place/Transition Nets.
            BTU Cottbus (2008), http://www-dssz.informatik.tu-cottbus.de/
            software/charlie/charlie.html
[CKS07]   Chickarmane, V., Kholodenko, B.N., Sauro, H.M.: Oscillatory dynamics
            arising from competitive inhibition and multisite phosphorylation. Jour-
            nal of Theoretical Biology 244(1), 68–76 (2007)
[Cur06]   Curry, E.: Stochastic Simulation of the Entrained Circadian Rhythm.
            Master thesis, School of Informatics, Univ. of Edinburgh (2006)
[CVGO06]   Calder, M., Vyshemirsky, V., Gilbert, D., Orton, R.: Analysis of sig-
            nalling pathways using continuous time Markov chains. In: Priami, C.,
            Plotkin, G. (eds.) Transactions on Computational Systems Biology VI.
            LNCS (LNBI), vol. 4220, pp. 44–67. Springer, Heidelberg (2006)
[DA05]   David, R., Alla, H.: Discrete, Continuous, and Hybrid Petri Nets.
            Springer, Heidelberg (2005)
[DDS04]   D'Aprile, D., Donatelli, S., Sproston, J.: CSL model checking for the
            GreatSPN tool. In: Aykanat, C., Dayar, T., Körpeoğlu, İ. (eds.) ISCIS
            2004. LNCS, vol. 3280, Springer, Heidelberg (2004)
[DE95]   Desel, J., Esparza, J.: Free Choice Petri Nets. Cambridge University
            Press, New York (1995)
[DJ01]   Desel, J., Juhás, G.: What is a Petri Net? In: Ehrig, H., Juhás, G., Pad-
            berg, J., Rozenberg, G. (eds.) APN 2001. LNCS, vol. 2128, pp. 1–25.
            Springer, Heidelberg (2001)
[DP80]   Dormand, J.R., Prince, P.J.: A family of embedded runge-kutta formulae.
            J. Comp. Appl. Math. 6, 1–22 (1980)
[EKL+02]   Eker, S., Knapp, M., Laderoute, K., Lincoln, P., Meseguer, J., Sonmez,
            K.: Pathway logic: Symbolic analysis of biological signaling. In: Proc.
            Seventh Pacific Symposium on Biocomputing, pp. 400–412 (2002)
[FR07]   Fages, F., Rizk, A.: On the analysis of numerical data time series in
            temporal logic. In: Calder, M., Gilmore, S. (eds.) CMSB 2007. LNCS
            (LNBI), vol. 4695, pp. 48–63. Springer, Heidelberg (2007)
[GH06]   Gilbert, D., Heiner, M.: From Petri nets to differential equations - an
            integrative approach for biochemical network analysis. In: Donatelli, S.,
            Thiagarajan, P.S. (eds.) ICATPN 2006. LNCS, vol. 4024, pp. 181–200.
            Springer, Heidelberg (2006)
[GHL07a]   Gilbert, D., Heiner, M., Lehrack, S.: A unifying framework for modelling
            and analysing biochemical pathways using Petri nets. In: TR I-02, CS
            Dep., BTU Cottbus (2007)
[GHL07b]   Gilbert, D., Heiner, M., Lehrack, S.: A unifying framework for modelling
            and analysing biochemical pathways using Petri nets. In: Calder, M.,
            Gilmore, S. (eds.) CMSB 2007. LNCS (LNBI), vol. 4695, pp. 200–216.
            Springer, Heidelberg (2007)

[GHR+08]   Gilbert, D., Heiner, M., Rosser, S., Fulton, R., Gu, X., Trybiło, M.: A Case Study in Model-driven Synthetic Biology. In: 2nd IFIP Conference on Biologically Inspired Collaborative Computing (BICC), IFIP WCC 2008, Milano (to appear, 2008)

[Gil77]   Gillespie, D.T.: Exact stochastic simulation of coupled chemical reactions. The Journal of Physical Chemistry 81(25), 2340–2361 (1977)

[GP98]   Goss, P.J.E., Peccoud, J.: Quantitative modeling of stochastic systems in molecular biology by using stochastic Petri nets. Proc. Natl. Acad. Sci., USA, 95, 2340–2361 (1998)

[HDG08]   Heiner, M., Donaldson, R., Gilbert, D.: Petri Nets for Systems Biology. In: Iyengar, M.S. (ed.) Symbolic Systems Biology: Theory and Methods, Jones and Bartlett Publishers, Inc (to appear, 2008)

[HFS+03]   Hucka, M., Finney, A., Sauro, H.M., Bolouri, H., Doyle, J.C., Kitano, H. et al.: The systems biology markup language (SBML): A medium for representation and exchange of biochemical network models. J. Bioinformatics 19, 524–531 (2003)

[HK04]   Heiner, M., Koch, I.: Petri Net Based Model Validation in Systems Biology. In: Cortadella, J., Reisig, W. (eds.) ICATPN 2004. LNCS, vol. 3099, pp. 216–237. Springer, Heidelberg (2004)

[HKN+06]   Heath, J., Kwiatkowska, M., Norman, G., Parker, D., Tymchyshyn, O.: Probabilistic model checking of complex biological pathways. In: Priami, C. (ed.) CMSB 2006. LNCS (LNBI), vol. 4210, pp. 32–47. Springer, Heidelberg (2006)

[Hof94]   Hofestädt, R.: A Petri net application of metabolic processes. Journal of System Analysis, Modeling and Simulation 16, 113–122 (1994)

[HRS08]   Heiner, M., Richter, R., Schwarick, M.: Snoopy - A Tool to Design and Animate/Simulate Graph-Based Formalisms. In: Proc. PNTAP 2008, ACM, New York (to appear, 2008)

[KH08]   Koch, I., Heiner, M.: Petri Nets. In: Junker, B.H., Schreiber, F. (eds.) Biological Network Analysis, 7, pp. 139–179. Wiley Book Series on Bioinformatics (2008)

[Kie02]   Kierzek, A.M.: STOCKS: STOChastic kinetic simulations of biochemical systems with gillespie algorithm. Bioinformatics 18(3), 470–481 (2002)

[Lau73]   Lautenbach, K.: Exact Liveness Conditions of a Petri Net Class (in German). Technical report, GMD Report 82, Bonn (1973)

[LBS00]   Levchenko, A., Bruck, J., Sternberg, P.W.: Scaffold proteins biphasically affect the levels of mitogen-activated protein kinase signaling and reduce its threshold properties. Proc. Natl. Acad. Sci. USA 97(11), 5818–5823 (2000)

[Mat06]   Li, C., Miyano, S., Matsuno, H.: Petri net based descriptions for systematic understanding of biological pathways. IEICE Trans. Fundam. Electron. Commun. Comput. Sci. E89-A(11), 3166–3174 (2006)

[MBC+95]   Ajmone Marsan, M., Balbo, G., Conte, G., Donatelli, S., Franceschinis, G.: Modelling with Generalized Stochastic Petri Nets, 2nd edn. Wiley Series in Parallel Computing. John Wiley and Sons, Chichester (1995)

[MC2]   MC2 Website. MC2 - PLTL model checker. University of Glasgow (2008), http://www.brc.dcs.gla.ac.uk/software/mc2/

[MFD+03]   Matsuno, H., Fujita, S., Doi, A., Nagasaki, M., Miyano, S.: Towards Pathway Modelling and Simulation. In: van der Aalst, W.M.P., Best, E. (eds.) ICATPN 2003. LNCS, vol. 2679, pp. 3–22. Springer, Heidelberg (2003)

[MGF]   Max-Gruenebaum-Foundation,
            http://www.max-gruenebaum-stiftung.de
[Mur89]   Murata, T.: Petri nets: Properties, analysis and applications. Proc.of the
            IEEE 77(4), 541–580 (1989)
[Pal06]   Palsson, B.O.: Systems Biology: Properties of Reconstructed Networks.
            Cambridge University Press, Cambridge (2006)
[Pet62]   Petri, C.A.: Communication with Automata (in German). Schriften des
            Instituts für Instrumentelle Mathematik, Bonn (1962)
[PNK06]   Parker, D., Norman, G., Kwiatkowska, M.: PRISM 3.0.beta1 Users' Guide
            (2006)
[Pnu81]   Pnueli, A.: The temporal semantics of concurrent programs. Theor. Com-
            put. Sci. 13, 45–60 (1981)
[PW03]   Priese, L., Wimmel, H.: Theoretcial Informatics - Petri Nets (in German).
            Springer, Heidelberg (2003)
[Rei82]   Reisig, W.: Petri nets; An introduction. Springer, Heidelberg (1982)
[RML93]   Reddy, V.N., Mavrovouniotis, M.L., Liebman, M.L.: Petri Net Represen-
            tations in Metabolic Pathways. In: Proc. of the Int. Conf. on Intelligent
            Systems for Molecular Biology (1993)
[SK05]   Salis, H., Kaznessis, Y.: Accurate hybrid stochastic simulation of a system
            of coupled chemical or biochemical reactions. J. Chem. Phys. 122 (2005)
[Sno08]   Snoopy Website. A Tool to Design and Animate/Simulate Graphs.
            BTU Cottbus (2008), http://www-dssz.informatik.tu-cottbus.de/
            software/snoopy.html
[SPB01]   Srivastava, R., Peterson, M.S., Bentley, W.E.: Stochastic kinetic analysis
            of the *escherichia coli* stress circuit using σ^{32}-targeted antisense. Biotech-
            nology and Bioengineering 75(1), 120–129 (2001)
[SR97]   Shampine, L.F., Reichelt, M.W.: The MATLAB ODE Suite. SIAM Jour-
            nal on Scientific Computing 18, 1–22 (1997)
[SR99]   Starke, P.H., Roch, S.: INA - The Intergrated Net Analyzer. Humboldt
            University Berlin (1999), www.informatik.hu-berlin.de/ starke/
            ina.html
[SSE03]   Schröter, C., Schwoon, S., Esparza, J.: The Model Checking Kit. In: van
            der Aalst, W.M.P., Best, E. (eds.) ICATPN 2003. LNCS, vol. 2679, pp.
            463–472. Springer, Heidelberg (2003)
[SSW05]   Shaw, O.J., Steggles, L.J., Wipat, A.: Automatic parameterisation of
            stochastic Petri net models of biological networks. CS-TR-909, School
            of CS, Univ. of Newcastle upon Tyne (2005)
[ST05]   Schulz-Trieglaff, O.: Modelling the randomness in biological systems.
            Master thesis, School of Informatics, University of Edinburgh (2005)
[Sta89]   Starke, P.H.: Some Properties of Timed Nets under the Earliest Firing
            Rule. In: Rozenberg, G. (ed.) APN 1989. LNCS, vol. 424, pp. 418–432.
            Springer, Heidelberg (1990)
[Sta90]   Starke, P.H.: Analysis of Petri Net Models (in German). B.G. Teubner,
            Stuttgart, Stuttgart (1990)
[Ste94]   Stewart, W.J.: Introduction to the Numerical Solution of Markov Chains.
            Princeton University Press, Princeton (1994)
[Tov06]   Tovchigrechko, A.: Model checking using interval decision diagrams. PhD
            thesis, BTU Cottbus, Dep. of CS, (submitted 2006)
[TSB04]   Turner, T.E., Schnell, S., Burrage, K.: Stochastic approaches for mod-
            elling in vivo reactions. Comp. Biology and Chemistry 28(3), 165–178
            (2004)

[Wil06]   Wilkinson, D.J.: Stochastic Modelling for System Biology, 1st edn. CRC Press, New York (2006)

[WMS05]   Sujathab, A., Marwan, W., Starostzik, C.: Reconstructing the regulatory network controlling commitment and sporulation in Physarum polycephalum based on hierarchical Petri net modeling and simulation. J. of Theoretical Biology 236(4), 349–365 (2005)

[YKNP06]   Younes, H., Kwiatkowska, M., Norman, G., Parker, D.: Numerical vs. statistical probabilistic model checking. STTT 8(3), 216–228 (2006)

[YS02]   Younes, H.L.S., Simmons, R.G.: Probabilistic verification of descrete event systems using acceptance sampling. In: Brinksma, E., Larsen, K.G. (eds.) CAV 2002. LNCS, vol. 2404, pp. 223–235. Springer, Heidelberg (2002)

Remark. This paper is a substantially extended version of [GHL07b]. The complete model specifications are given in the appendix of [GHL07a]. The data files of the running example in its three versions and the analysis results are available at www-dssz.informatik.tu-cottbus.de/examples/levchenko.

Process Algebras in Systems Biology

Federica Ciocchetta and Jane Hillston

Laboratory for Foundations of Computer Science,
The University of Edinburgh, Edinburgh EH9 3JZ, Scotland
{fciocche,jeh}@inf.ed.ac.uk

Abstract. In this chapter we introduce process algebras, a class of formal modelling techniques developed in theoretical computer science, and discuss their use within systems biology. These formalisms have a number of attractive features which make them ideal candidates to be intermediate, formal, compositional representations of biological systems. As we will show, when modelling is carried out at a suitable level of abstraction, the constructed model can be amenable to analysis using a variety of different approaches, encompassing both individuals-based stochastic simulation and population-based ordinary differential equations. We focus particularly on Bio-PEPA, a recently defined extension of the PEPA stochastic process algebra, which has features to capture both stoichiometry and general kinetic laws. We present the definition of the language, some equivalence relations and the mappings to underlying mathematical models for analysis. We demonstrate the use of Bio-PEPA on two biological examples.

1   Introduction

In recent years there has been increasing interest in the application of process algebras in the modelling and analysis of biological systems [60,26,28,58,19,49,14]. Process algebras have some interesting properties that make them particularly useful in describing biological systems. First of all, they offer *compositionality*, i.e. the possibility of defining the whole system starting from the definition of its subcomponents. Secondly, process algebras give a formal representation of the system avoiding ambiguity. Thirdly, biological systems can be abstracted by concurrent systems described by process algebras: species may be seen as processes that can interact with each other and reactions may be modelled using actions. Finally, different kinds of analysis can be performed on a process algebra model. These analyses provide conceptual tools which are complementary to established techniques: it is possible to detect and correct potential inaccuracies, to validate the model and to predict its possible behaviours.

The original work on process algebra modelling of biochemical pathways by Regev *et al.* was based on the abstraction *"processes as molecules"* [60]. This abstraction has proven to be fruitful and highly influential with most of the subsequent work based on the same abstraction. However, it is not without its drawbacks. It takes an inherently individual-based view of the system (i.e. views

M. Bernardo, P. Degano, and G. Zavattaro (Eds.): SFM 2008, LNCS 5016, pp. 265–312, 2008.

the system at the level of individual molecules) which has the consequence that the state space, under all but the smallest examples, will be prohibitively large and amenable only to analysis via simulation.

In recent years Calder *et al.* [14,15] have been experimenting with alternative abstractions using the stochastic process algebra, PEPA, which was originally defined for performance analysis of computer systems [42]. Two different approaches have been proposed: one based on reagents (the so-called *reagent-centric view*) and another based on pathways (*pathway-centric view*). In both cases the species concentrations are discretized into levels, each level abstracting an interval of concentration values. In the reagent-centric view the PEPA sequential components represent the different concentration levels of the species. In this approach the abstraction is *"processes as species"* and not *"processes as molecules"*. In the pathway-centric approach adopts an alternative abstract view: the processes represent sub-pathways. Here multiple copies of components represent levels of concentration. The two views have been shown to be equivalent[15].

Even though PEPA and other stochastic process algebras have proved useful in studying signalling pathways, they do not readily allow us to represent all the features of biological networks. The main difficulties are the definition of *stoichiometric coefficients* (i.e. the coefficients used to show the quantitative relationships of the reactants and products in a biochemical reaction) and the representation of *kinetic laws*. Concerning stoichiometry, in the reagent-centric view of PEPA stoichiometry is not represented explicitly. Furthermore, in other process algebras it is not possible to render interactions with more than two reactants as biochemical interactions are abstracted by pairwise communications. This is justified by appeal to Gillespie's stochastic simulation algorithm which, in the original version, assumes elementary (i.e. monomolecular and bimolecular) reactions. However, it is often convenient to model at a more abstract level, where reactions involving more than two species are common (e.g. Michaelis-Menten). In terms of kinetic laws, PEPA and other process algebras consider elementary reactions with constant rates (*mass-action* kinetic laws). The problem of extending to the domain of kinetic laws beyond basic mass-action (hereafter called *general kinetic laws*) is particularly relevant, as these kinds of reactions are frequently found in the literature as abstractions of complex situations whose details are unknown. Reducing all reactions to the elementary steps is complex and often impractical. In the case of process algebras such as π-calculus the assumption of elementary reactions is motivated by the fact that they rely on Gillespie's stochastic simulation for analysis. Some recent works have extended the approach of Gillespie to deal with complex reactions [1,17] but these extensions are yet to be reflected in the work using process algebras. Previous work concerning the use of general kinetic laws in process algebras and formal methods was presented in [9,20]. These are discussed in Section 2.3.

In this chapter we give a tutorial introduction to Bio-PEPA, a new language for the modelling and analysis of biochemical networks. A preliminary version of the language was proposed in [22], with full details presented in [23]. Here, in addition to defining the language we illustrate its use with a number of examples.

Bio-PEPA is based on the reagent-centric view in PEPA, modified in order to represent explicitly some features of biochemical models, such as stoichiometry and the role of the different species in a given reaction. A major feature of Bio-PEPA is the introduction of functional rates to express general kinetic laws. Each action type represents a reaction in the model and is associated with a functional rate.

The idea underlying our work is represented schematically in the diagram in Fig. 1. The context of application is biochemical networks. Broadly speaking, biochemical networks consist of some chemical species, which interact with each other through chemical reactions. The dynamics of reaction are described in terms of some kinetic laws. The biochemical networks can be obtained from databases such as *KEGG* [46,45] and *BioModels Database* [8,56][1]. From the biological model, we develop the Bio-PEPA specification of the system. This is an *intermediate, formal, compositional* representation of the biological model. At this point we can apply different kinds of analysis, including stochastic simulation [36], analysis based on ordinary differential equations, numerical solution of continuous time Markov chains (CTMC) and stochastic model checking using PRISM [61,40]. It is worth noting that each of these analyses can help in understanding the system. The choice of one or more methods depends on the context of application [68]. There exist some relations between the different kinds of analysis. It is well-known that the results of stochastic simulations tend to the ODEs solution when the number of elements is relatively high. Similarly, it is shown in [35] that the numerical solution of the CTMC with levels (derived from the PEPA pathway-centric view) tends to the solution of the ODEs when the number of levels increases.

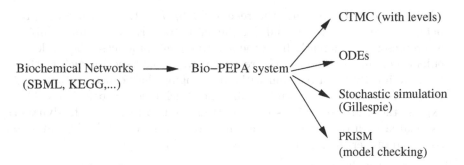

Fig. 1. Schema of the Bio-PEPA framework

The rest of the chapter is organised as follows. In the next section we outline our modelling domain, biochemical networks, and discuss the development of process algebras and their use to model biological systems. The recent development of Bio-PEPA has been informed by earlier work using the PEPA process

---

[1] The *BioModels Database* is a collection of SBML models. SBML is a widely used XML-based format for representing models of biochemical reaction networks.

algebra so this work is also briefly presented. In Section 3 we give a detailed account of Bio-PEPA; its syntax, semantics, equivalence relations and analysis techniques. The use of the language is illustrated in Section 4, in which the translation of two biological models into Bio-PEPA and their subsequent analysis is described. Finally, in Section 5 we present some conclusions and future perspectives.

2   Background

In this section we outline the application domain of this tutorial before giving an introduction to process algebras. Subsequent sections will focus on one particular process algebra, Bio-PEPA, but here we aim to give a broad overview of the class of formalisms known as process algebras.

2.1   Application Domain: Biochemical Networks

The application domain of this tutorial concerns biochemical networks, such as those collected in the Biomodels Database [56] and KEGG [46].

A biochemical system $\mathcal{M}$ is composed of:

1. a set of *compartments* **C**. These represent the locations of the various species;
2. *a set of chemical species* **S**. These species may be genes, proteins, etc.;
3. *a set of reactions* **R**. We consider *irreversible reactions*. Reversible reactions are decomposed as a pair of forward and inverse reactions.

   The general form of an irreversible reaction j is given by:

$$\kappa_{1j}A_1+\kappa_{2j}A_2+....+\kappa_{n_jj}A_{n_j} \xrightarrow{E_1,E_2,...I_1,I_2,...;f_j} \kappa'_{1j}B_1+\kappa'_{2j}B_2+....+\kappa'_{m_jj}B_{m_j} \tag{1}$$

   where A_h, $h = 1,...,n_j$, are the reactants, B_l, $l = 1,...,m_j$, are the products, E_v are the enzymes and I_u, the inhibitors. Enzymes and inhibitors are represented differently from the reactants and products. Their role is to enhance or inhibit the reaction, respectively. We call species such as these, that are involved in a reaction without changing their concentration, *modifiers*. The parameters κ_{hj} and κ'_{lj} are the stoichiometric coefficients. These express the degree to which species participate in a reaction. The dynamics associated with the reaction is described by a kinetic law f_j, depending on some parameters and on the concentrations of some species.

The best known kinetic law is *mass-action*: the rate of the reaction is proportional to the product of the reactants' concentrations. In published models it is common to find *general kinetic laws*, which describe approximations of sequences of reactions. They are useful when it is difficult to derive certain information from the experiments, e.g. the reaction rates of elementary steps, or when there are different time-scales for the reactions. Generally these laws are valid under some conditions, such as the *quasi-steady-state assumption (QSSA)*. This describes the situation where one or more reaction steps may be considered faster than the others and so the intermediate elements can be considered to be constant. There is a long list of kinetic laws; for details see [65].

2.2 Overview of Process Algebras

Process algebras are calculi that were originally motivated by problems associated with concurrent computer systems [51,43]. The objective was to specify and formally reason about such systems. In subsequent years process algebras have been used extensively to describe complex systems characterized by *concurrency*, *communication, synchronization* and *nondeterminism*. Process algebras offer several attractive features. The most important of these are *compositionality*, the ability to model a system as the interaction of its subsystems, *formality*, the ability to give a precise meaning to all terms in the language, and *abstraction*, the ability to build up complex models from detailed components but disregarding internal behaviour when it is appropriate to do so.

The most widely known process algebras are Milner's Calculus of Communicating Systems (CCS) [51] and Hoare's Communicating Sequential Processes (CSP) [43]. Process algebras are typically defined by a simple syntax and semantics. The semantics may be given by axioms or inference rules expressed in an operational way [57]. A system is defined as a collection of agents which execute atomic actions. Some operators are introduced for combining the primitives. For instance in CCS the main operators are:

prefix $a.P$, after action a the agent becomes a P
parallel composition $P \mid Q$, agents P and Q proceed in parallel
choice $P + Q$, the agent behaves as P or Q
restriction $P \backslash M$, the set of actions M may not occur
relabelling $P[a_1/a_0, ..]$, in this agent label a_1 is renamed a_0
the null agent 0, this agent cannot act (deadlock)

One of the main features of process algebras is the possibility to express communication between two processes. In some cases, such as CCS [51] and the π-calculus [52], a communication between two parallel processes is enabled when one process can perform an action a (receive) and the other process can perform the complementary action $\bar{a}$ (send). So the actions must be complementary (input-output) and share the same name (a in the case considered). The resulting communication has the distinguished label τ, which indicates an internal (invisible) action. A distinguishing feature of π-calculus with respect to CCS is the possibility to represent *name-passing*: communicating processes can exchange names over channels and consequently they may change their interaction topology.

The communication mechanism in CSP is different from the one described above as there is no notion of complementary actions. In CSP, two agents communicate by simultaneously executing actions with the same label. Since during the communication the joint action remains visible to the environment, it can be reused by other concurrent processes so that more than two processes can be involved in the communication (*multiway synchronisation*).

The analysis of the behaviours of the model, represented in a formal language, is generally produced through a *Labelled Transition System (LTS)* derived from the operational semantics. This may be regarded as a *derivative tree* or *graph* in which language terms form the nodes and transitions are the arcs. This structure is a useful tool for reasoning about agents and the systems they represent: two agents are considered to be equivalent if they are observed to perform exactly the same actions and the resulting agents are also equivalent. Strong and weak forms of equivalence are defined depending on whether the internal actions of an agent are deemed to be observable.

In CCS and CSP, since the objective is qualitative analysis rather than quantitative, time and uncertainty are abstracted away. In the last two decades, various suggestions for incorporating time and probability into these formalisms have been investigated (see [54] for an overview of process algebras with time). For example, Temporal CCS (TCCS) [53] extends CCS with *fixed delays* and *wait-for synchronisation* (asynchronous waiting). Note that most of the timed extensions, including TCCS, retain the assumption that actions are instantaneous and regard time progression as orthogonal to the activity of the system. Probabilistic extensions of process algebras, such as PCCS [44], allow uncertainty to be quantified using a probabilistic choice combinator. In this case a probability is associated with each possible outcome of a choice.

In the early 1990s several stochastic extensions of process algebra (*stochastic process algebras* or SPAs), were introduced. The motivation for SPA was performance modelling and quantification, in the form of random variables characterising the duration of actions, was added to models. In most cases, the random variables are assumed to be exponentially distributed and a rate is added to each prefix to represent the parameter of the exponential distribution that describes the dynamic behaviour of the associated action. A *race condition* is then assumed to resolve conflicts: all the activities that are enabled in a given state compete and the fastest one succeeds. The choice of the exponential distribution means that each process algebra model is associated with a continuous time Markov chain (CTMC) [42]. It is then possible to carry out performance analysis based on this underlying mathematical model. Some examples of SPA are TIPP [38], EMPA[2] [4,5], PEPA [42], SPADE[3] [67] and Stochastic π-calculus [59].

2.3   Process Algebras in Systems Biology

Recently, as a response to the need to model the dynamics of complex biological systems, there have been several applications of process calculi in systems biology [60,62,28,58,27,18,19,14]. These techniques are appropriate for formally describing and analysing a biological system as a whole and for reasoning about protein/gene interactions. Indeed, there is a strong correspondence between concurrent systems described by process algebras and biological ones: biological entities may be abstracted as processes that can interact with each other and reactions may be modelled as actions.

Process calculi have several properties that make them useful for studying biological systems:

---

[2] Originally called simply MPA.
[3] Originally called CCS+.

- they allow the formal specification of the system;
- they offer different levels of abstraction for the same biological system;
- they can make interactions explicit, in particular biological elements may be seen as entities that interact and evolve;
- they support modularity and compositionality;
- they provide well-established techniques for reasoning about possible behaviours. They may be used not only for the simulation of the system, but also for the verification of formal properties and for behavioural comparison through equivalences.

Several process calculi have been proposed in biology. Each of them has different properties able to render different aspects of biological phenomena. They may be divided into two main categories:

- calculi defined originally in computer science and then applied in biology, such as the biochemical stochastic π-calculus [60], CCS-R [28] and PEPA [42];
- calculi defined specifically by observing biological structures and phenomena, such as BioAmbients [19], Brane Calculi [18], κ-calculus [27], and Beta-binders [58].

One of the first process algebras used in systems biology is the biochemical π-calculus [60], a variant of the π-calculus defined to model biological systems. The underlying idea of application of the π-calculus to biology is the *molecule-as-computation* abstraction [63,60]: each biological entity and interaction is associated with an agent specification in the calculus. Specifically, molecules are modelled as processes, interaction capabilities as channels, interactions as communications between processes, modifications as state and channel changes and, finally, compartments and membranes as restrictions. Two stochastic simulation tools based on Gillespie [36] have been defined (BIOSPI [6] and SPIM [66]), various applications have been shown [50,26,49,21] and some modified versions have been proposed (e.g. SPICO[48] and Sp@ [69]).

CCS-R [28] is a variant of CCS with new elements which allow the capture of reversibility. The interactions are described in terms of binary synchronised communications, similarly to π-calculus. It was motivated by modelling reversible reactions in biochemistry. The successor of CSS-R is the Reversible CCS (RCCS) [31]. This calculus allows processes to backtrack if this is in agreement with a notion of casual equivalence defined in the paper.

Beta-binders [58,64] are an extension of the π-calculus inspired by biological phenomena. This calculus is based on the concept of *bio-process*, a box with some sites (*beta-binders*) to express the interaction capabilities of the element, in which π-calculus-like processes (*pi-processes*) are encapsulated. Beta-binders enrich the π-calculus with some constructs that allow us to represent biological features, such as the join between two bio-processes, the split of one bio-process into two, the change of the bio-process interface by hiding, unhiding and exposing a site. The Beta Workbench [64] is a collection of tools for the modelling, simulation and analysis of Beta-binders system. The BetaWB simulator is based on a variant of Gillespie's algorithm.

In most of the calculi considered it is not possible to represent all the features of biochemical networks. Generally the kinetic laws are assumed to be mass-action and reactions can have at most two reactants. Indeed these calculi refer to the standard Gillespie's algorithm for the analysis and this assumes elementary reactions (i.e. monomolecular or bimolecular) with constant rates. Furthermore, biological reactions are abstracted as communications/interactions between agents and in some process algebras such as π-calculus, CCS and Beta-binders, these actions are pairwise. Therefore multiple-reactant multiple-product reactions cannot be modelled in these calculi. In order to represent multiple-reactant multiple-product reactions, π-calculus and Beta-binders have been enriched with transactions [24,25].

A first proposal to deal with general kinetic laws has been shown in [9]. The authors present a stochastic extension of Concurrent Constraint Programming (CCP) and show how to apply it to biological systems. Here each species is represented by a variable and the reactions are expressed by constraints on these variables. The domain of application is extended to any kind of reactions and the rate can be expressed by a generic function.

The possibility of representing general kinetic laws is also offered by BIOCHAM [20], a programming environment for modelling biochemical systems, which supports making simulations and querying the model in temporal logic. This language is not a process algebra, but it is based on a rule-based language for modelling biochemical systems, in which species are expressed by objects and reactions by reaction rules.

A similar approach is taken in the κ-calculus [27], based on the description of protein interactions. Processes describe proteins and their compounds. A set of processes model solutions and protein behaviour is given by a set of rewriting rules, driven by suitable side-conditions. The two main rules concern activation and complexation. A stochastic simulator for κ-calculus is described in [30]. A few applications are reported, as in [29].

Finally, some calculi have been defined to model compartments and membranes. Here we briefly describe Bio-ambients [19] and Brane calculi [18]. Bio-ambients are centered on *ambients,* bounded places where processes are contained and where communication may happen. Ambients can be nested and organised in a hierarchy. This hierarchy may be modified by suitable operations that have a biological interpretation. It is possible to have *enter* and *exit* primitives to move an ambient into or out of another ambient or a *merge* for merging two ambients together. Ambients contain compounds that interact via communication. Bio-ambients have been used to model compartments in *BIOSPI* [6]. A stochastic semantics for Bio-ambients has been formalized in [10]. There have been some applications, for instance [3].

In Brane calculi [18] a system consists of nested membranes, which are collections of actions. Membranes may shift, merge, break apart and may be replenished, leading to very expressive models, in which actions occur on membranes. Membranes may be seen as oriented objects that must obey some restrictions on orientation. In particular they must preserve *bitonality,* which requires nested membranes to have opposite orientations.

2.4   PEPA and Biological Systems

Performance Evaluation Process Algebra (PEPA) is a SPA originally defined for the performance modelling of systems with concurrent behaviour [42]. In PEPA each action is assumed to have a duration, represented by a random variable with a negative exponential distribution. We informally introduce the syntax of the language below. For more details see [42].

Prefix. The basic term is the *prefix combinator* $(\alpha, r).S$. It denotes a component which has action of type α and an exponentially distributed duration with parameter r (mean duration $1/r$), and it subsequently behaves as S.

Choice. The component $S + R$ represents a system which may behave either as S or as R. The activities of both S and R are enabled. The first activity to complete distinguishes one of them and the other is discarded.

Constant. Constants are components whose meaning is given by a defining equation $C \stackrel{def}{=} S$. They allow us to assign names to patterns of behaviour associated with components.

Hiding. In $S/\mathcal{H}$ the set $\mathcal{H}$ identifies those activities which can be considered internal or private to the component S.

Cooperation. The term $P \bowtie_{\mathcal{L}} Q$ denotes cooperation between P and Q over the cooperation set $\mathcal{L}$, that determines those activities on which the cooperands are forced to synchronise. PEPA supports *multiway synchronisation* between components: the result of synchronising on an activity α is thus another α, available for further synchronisation. For action types not in $\mathcal{L}$, the components proceed independently and concurrently with their enabled activities. In the context of performance evaluation the rate for the synchronised activities is the minimum of the rates of the synchronising activities.

Recently, PEPA has been applied to the modelling and analysis of signalling pathways. An initial study concerned the influence of the Raf Kinase Inhibitor Protein (RKIP) on the Extracellular signal Regulated Kinase (ERK) [14]. In [15] the PEPA representation of Schoeberl's model [32] involving the MAP kinase and EFG receptors is reported. The biological modelling in PEPA was motivated by a desire to experiment with more abstract modelling than that afforded by the *processes as molecules* mapping generally used in process algebra models. Indeed a *processes as species* mapping is applied instead. In [14] two different modelling styles were proposed, one based on the *reagent-centric view* and the other on the *pathway-centric view*. The former focuses on the variation in the concentrations of the reagents: the concentrations are discretized in levels, each level representing an interval of concentration values. The level l can assume values between 0 and N_{max} (maximum level). The pathway-centric style provides a different abstract view of the system and focuses on the subpathways. The two representations were shown to be equivalent [14]. In addition to the standard analysis offered by process algebras, in [13] a mapping from reagent-centric PEPA models to a system of ordinary differential equations (ODEs), has been proposed.

From the applications discussed above PEPA has been shown to be appropriate for the modelling of biological systems: it offers a high level of abstraction for the model and focuses on compositionality and on the interactions. Furthermore, by using PEPA as a modelling language it is possible to apply different kinds of analysis, not only stochastic simulation, but also differential equations and model checking.

However, not all the features of biochemical networks can be expressed using the present version of PEPA: general kinetic laws are not considered and stoichiometry is added by hand in the conversion of PEPA into ODEs. As observed above, with a few exceptions (e.g. [9]) and a few cases (dimerization), these features cannot be represented in other process algebras either. These and other problems motivated us to develop a new process algebra, Bio-PEPA, which is closely related to PEPA but better adapted to biological modelling.

3   Bio-PEPA: Definition of the Language

Our earlier experience using PEPA, and other stochastic process algebras, to model biochemical networks, developed insights which we then used in the definition of Bio-PEPA. We felt it was important to have a language which can represent all reactions in a straightforward way as well as handle stoichiometry and general kinetic laws. We retained the *reagent-centric view* previously used in PEPA models of biochemical pathways as this had been demonstrated to provide a flexible approach to modelling. For example, it is straightforward to capture reactions with any number of participants, something that is not readily captured in other process algebras such as the π-calculus. Moreover, once the model is constructed it is amenable to a variety of different analysis techniques.

We adopt a high level of abstraction similar to the one proposed in formalisms such as *SBML* [7], which have been widely adopted by biologists. Furthermore we make the following assumptions:

1. Compartments are *static*, i.e. compartments are not actively involved in the reactions — they are simply containers. The transport of a species from one compartment to another is modelled by introducing two distinct components for representing the species. The translocation is abstracted by a transformation of one species into another. Compartments are included in the definition of a Bio-PEPA system because the volume of the containing compartment can impact on reactions of a species.
2. Reactions are *irreversible reactions*. A reversible reaction is represented as a pair of irreversible reactions.

3.1   Discrete Concentrations and Granularity

Following the reagent-centric view, models are based not on individual molecules, but on discrete levels of concentration within a species: each component represents a species and it is parametric in terms of concentration level. Some advantages of this view are:

– It allows us to deal with uncertainty/incomplete information in the exact number of elements (semi-quantitative data);

- In a discrete state space representation the focus is on the concentration levels rather than the number of elements. This means that the state space is reduced as there are less states for each component.
- The population level view, in terms of continuously changing concentrations, and the individual level view, counting molecules, are both easily recovered from this abstract view.

This view was presented in [16]. The authors focused on the case of reactions with mass-action kinetics and stoichiometry equal to one for all the reactants and products. The granularity of the system has been expressed in terms of the number of levels, representing concentration intervals. Furthermore they considered the same step size h and the same maximum level N for all the species.

In Bio-PEPA we adapt this approach to general kinetic laws, stoichiometry greater than one and different numbers of levels for the species. The granularity of the system is defined in terms of the step size h of the concentration intervals instead of the number of levels. We define the same step size h for all the species[4]. This is motivated by the fact that, following the *law of conservation of mass*, there must be a "balance" between the concentrations consumed (reactants) and the ones created (products). In the case the stoichiometry is greater than one we need to consider concentration quantities proportional to stoichiometric coefficients. Given a species i, we can assume that it has a maximum finite concentration M_i. The number of levels for the species i is given by $N_i + 1$ where $N_i = \lceil \frac{M_i}{h} \rceil$ (the integer value greater than or equal to $\frac{M_i}{h}$). Each species can assume the discrete concentration levels from 0 (concentration null) to N_i (maximum concentration).

If l_i is the concentration level for the species i, the concentration is taken to be $x_i = l_i \times h$.

When a finite state space CTMC is to be generated, for numerical analysis or stochastic model checking, we must assume that there is a maximum concentration for each species. However, we can have a species without a limiting value: we use a maximum level to capture all values greater than a given (high) value.

3.2   The Syntax

The syntax of Bio-PEPA is similar to that of PEPA but with some important differences. As in PEPA a model is made up of a number of sequential components; here there is one sequential component for each species. As we will see, the syntax of Bio-PEPA is designed in order to collect the biological information that we need. For example, instead of a single prefix combinator there are a number of different operators which capture the role that the species plays with respect to this reaction.

---

[4] There can be some exceptions to this assumption: 1) since modifiers remain constant during reaction, we may define a different step size for each species which is only a modifier; 2) any species which is involved on in creation/degradation reactions may have a different step size.

$$S ::= (\alpha, \kappa) \text{ op } S \mid S + S \mid C \qquad P ::= P \underset{\mathcal{L}}{\bowtie} P \mid S(l)$$

where $\text{op} = \downarrow \mid \uparrow \mid \oplus \mid \ominus \mid \odot$.

The component S is called *sequential component* (or *species component*) and represents the species. The component P, called a *model component*, describes the system and the interactions among components. We suppose a countable set of sequential components $\mathcal{C}$ and a countable set of action types $\mathcal{A}$. The parameter $l \in \mathbb{N}$ represents the discrete level of concentration. The prefix term, $(\alpha, \kappa) \text{ op } S$, contains information about the role of the species in the reaction associated with the action type α:

- (α, κ) is the *activity* or *reaction*, where $\alpha \in \mathcal{A}$ is the *action type* and κ is the *stoichiometric coefficient* of the species in that reaction; information about the rate of the reaction is defined elsewhere (in contrast to PEPA);
- the *prefix combinator* "op" represents the role of the element in the reaction. Specifically, $\downarrow$ indicates a *reactant*, $\uparrow$ a *product*, $\oplus$ an *activator*, $\ominus$ an *inhibitor* and $\odot$ a generic *modifier*.

The choice operator, cooperation and definition of constant are unchanged. In contrast to PEPA the hiding operator is omitted.

In order to fully describe a biochemical network in Bio-PEPA we need to define structures that collect information about the compartments, the maximum concentrations, number of levels for all the species, the constant parameters and the functional rates which specify the rates of reactions. In the following the function *name* returns the names of the elements of a given Bio-PEPA component.

First of all we define the set of compartments.

Definition 1. *Each compartment is described by "V: v unit", where V is the compartment name, "v" is a positive real number expressing the compartment size and the (optional) "unit" denotes the unit associated with the compartment size. The set of compartments is denoted $\mathcal{V}$.*

In Bio-PEPA compartments are static and they cannot change their structure/size. The set of compartments must contain at least one element. When we have no information about compartments we add a default compartment whose size is 1 and whose unit depends on the model.

Definition 2. *For each species we define the element $C : H, N, M_0, M, V$, where:*

- *C is the species component name,*
- *$H \in \mathbb{N}$ is the step size,*
- *$N \in \mathbb{N}$ is the maximum level,*
- *$M_0 \in \mathbb{R}^+ \cup \{\_\}$ is the initial concentration,*
- *$M \in \mathbb{R}^+ \cup \{\_\}$ is the maximum concentration,*
- *$V \in name(\mathcal{V}) \cup \{\_\}$ is the name of the enclosing compartment.*

The set of all the elements $C : H, N, M_0, M, V$ is denoted $\mathcal{N}$.

In the definition the symbol "_" denotes the empty string, indicating that the last three components are optional. The initial concentration may added when we want to compare our model results with the results in the literature. The maximum concentration is used in the definition of the number of levels, but generally it can be derived from the step size and the maximum number of levels. Finally, if there is only one compartment for all the species in the model we can omit it in the definition of $\mathcal{N}$.

In order to specify the dynamics of the system we associate a functional rate f_{α_j} with each action α_j. This function represents the kinetic law of the associated reaction. For the definition of functional rates we consider mathematical expressions with simple operations and operators involving constant parameters and components. All the kinetic laws proposed in the book by Segel [65] can be defined in this way. In addition, for convenience, we include some predefined functions to express the most commonly used kinetic laws.

The predefined kinetic laws considered are mass-action (fMA), Michaelis-Menten (fMM) and Hill kinetics (fH). They depend only on some parameters; the components/species are derived from the context[5]. The functional rates are defined externally to the components and are evaluated when the system is derived. They are used to derive the transition rates of the system. In the functional rates some parameter constants can be used. These must be defined in the model by means of the set of parameter definitions $\mathcal{K}$.

Definition 3. *Each parameter is defined by "k_{name} = value unit", where "k_{name}"$\notin C$ is the parameter name, "value" denotes a positive real number and the (optional) "unit" denotes the unit associated with the parameter. The set of the parameters is denoted $\mathcal{K}$.*

Finally, we have the following definition for the set of sequential components:

Definition 4. *The set $Comp$ of sequential components is defined as*

$$Comp ::= \{C \stackrel{\text{def}}{=} S, \text{ where } S \text{ is a sequential component }\}$$

We can define a Bio-PEPA system in the following way:

Definition 5. *A Bio-PEPA system $\mathcal{P}$ is a 6-uple $\langle \mathcal{V}, \mathcal{N}, \mathcal{K}, \mathcal{F}_R, Comp, P \rangle$, where:*

- $\mathcal{V}$ *is the set of compartments;*
- $\mathcal{N}$ *is the set of quantities describing each species;*

---

[5] In the case of mass-action, the function $fMA(r)$ is $r \times \prod_{i=1}^{n_j}(C_i)^{\kappa_i}$, where C_i $i = 1, ..., n_j$ are the n_j distinct reactants involved in the reaction and κ_i is the associated stoichiometric coefficients. The information about the reactants are derived from the Bio-PEPA specifications of the system. In the case of Michaelis-Menten, the function $fMM(v_M, K_M)$ is $v_M \times E \times S/(K_M + S)$, where E is the concentration of the enzyme and S the concentration of the substrate. Also in this case E and S are derived from the Bio-PEPA specifications. In the case of Hill kinetics, the function $fH(v, K, n)$ is $v \times C^n/(K + C^n)$, where C is the concentration of the element involved in the reaction.

- $\mathcal{K}$ is the set of parameter definitions;
- $\mathcal{F}_R$ is the set of functional rate definitions;
- Comp is the set of definitions of sequential components;
- P is the model component describing the system.

In a *well-defined* Bio-PEPA system each element has to satisfy some (reasonable) conditions. Details can be found in [23]. In the remainder of the chapter we consider only well-defined Bio-PEPA systems. The set of such systems is denoted $\tilde{\mathcal{P}}$.

3.3 The Semantics

The semantics of Bio-PEPA is defined in terms of an operational semantics. We define two relations over the processes. The former, called the *capability relation*, supports the derivation of quantitative information and it is auxiliary to the latter which is called the *stochastic relation*. The stochastic relation gives us the rates associated with each action. The rates are obtained by evaluating the functional rate corresponding to the action, divided by the step size of the species involved, using quantitative information derived from the capability relation.

The capability relation is $\to_c \subseteq \mathcal{C} \times \Theta \times \mathcal{C}$, where the label $\theta \in \Theta$ contains the quantitative information needed to evaluate the functional rate. We define the labels θ as:

$$\theta := (\alpha, w)$$

where w is defined as $w ::= [S : op(l, \kappa)] \mid w :: w$, with $S \in \mathcal{C}$, l the level and κ the stoichiometric coefficient of the components. The order of the components is not important. The rules governing the behaviour of components are presented in the structured operational style [57] in Table 1. The rules should be read as follows: if the transition above the line can be inferred then the transition below the line can be deduced. The relation $\to_c$ is defined as the minimum relation satisfying the rules reported in Table 1.

The first three axioms describe the behaviour of the three different prefix terms. In the case of a reactant, the level decreases; in the case of a product, the level increases; whereas in the case of modifiers, the level remains the same. For reactants and products, the number of levels increment or decrement depends on the stoichiometric coefficient κ. This expresses the degree to which a species (reactant or product) participates in a reaction. Therefore some side conditions concerning the present concentration level must be added to the rules. Specifically, for the reactants the level has to be greater than or equal to κ, whereas for the products the level has to be less than or equal to $(N - \kappa)$, where N is the maximum level. The modifiers can have any possible value between 0 and N. In all three cases the label θ records the level and the stoichiometry of the associated component. The rules choice1 and choice2 have the usual meaning, but note that choices only occur within a species component so both alternatives are associated with the same level. The rule constant is used to define the behaviour of the constant term, defined by one or more prefix terms in summation. The label contains the information about the level and the stoichiometric coefficient related to the action α. The last three rules report the case of cooperation.

Table 1. Axioms and rules for Bio-PEPA

prefixReac $\quad ((\alpha,\kappa)\downarrow S)(l) \xrightarrow{(\alpha,[S:\downarrow(l,\kappa)])}_c S(l-\kappa) \quad \kappa \le l \le N$

prefixProd $\quad ((\alpha,\kappa)\uparrow S)(l) \xrightarrow{(\alpha,[S:\uparrow(l,\kappa)])}_c S(l+\kappa) \quad 0 \le l \le (N-\kappa)$

prefixMod $\quad ((\alpha,\kappa)\,op\,S)(l) \xrightarrow{(\alpha,[S:op(l,\kappa)])}_c S(l) \quad$ with $op = \odot,\oplus,\ominus$ and $0 \le l \le N$

choice1 $\quad \dfrac{S_1(l) \xrightarrow{(\alpha,w)}_c S_1'(l')}{(S_1+S_2)(l) \xrightarrow{(\alpha,w)}_c S_1'(l')}$ $\qquad$ choice2 $\quad \dfrac{S_2(l) \xrightarrow{(\alpha,w)}_c S_2'(l')}{(S_1+S_2)(l) \xrightarrow{(\alpha,w)}_c S_2'(l')}$

constant $\quad \dfrac{S(l) \xrightarrow{(\alpha,S':[op(l,\kappa)])}_c S'(l')}{C(l) \xrightarrow{(\alpha,C:[op(l,\kappa)])}_c S'(l')} \quad$ with $C \stackrel{def}{=} S$

coop1 $\quad \dfrac{P_1 \xrightarrow{(\alpha,w)}_c P_1'}{P_1 \bowtie_{\mathcal{L}} P_2 \xrightarrow{(\alpha,w)}_c P_1' \bowtie_{\mathcal{L}} P_2} \quad$ with $\alpha \notin \mathcal{L}$

coop2 $\quad \dfrac{P_2 \xrightarrow{(\alpha,w)}_c P_2'}{P_1 \bowtie_{\mathcal{L}} P_2 \xrightarrow{(\alpha,w)}_c P_1 \bowtie_{\mathcal{L}} P_2'} \quad$ with $\alpha \notin \mathcal{L}$

coop3 $\quad \dfrac{P_1 \xrightarrow{(\alpha,w_1)}_c P_1' \quad P_2 \xrightarrow{(\alpha,w_2)}_c P_2'}{P_1 \bowtie_{\mathcal{L}} P_2 \xrightarrow{(\alpha,w_1@w_2)}_c P_1' \bowtie_{\mathcal{L}} P_2'} \quad$ with $\alpha \in \mathcal{L}$

The rules coop1 and coop2 concern the case when the action enabled does not belong to the cooperation set. In this case the label in the conclusion contains only the information about the component that fires the action. The rule coop3 describes the case in which the two components synchronize and the label reports the information from both the components. The concatenation operator of lists @ is used for this purpose.

In order to associate the rates with the transitions we introduce the stochastic relation $\rightarrow_s \subseteq \tilde{\mathcal{P}} \times \Gamma \times \tilde{\mathcal{P}}$, where the label $\gamma \in \Gamma$ is defined as $\gamma := (\alpha, r_\alpha)$, with $r_\alpha \in \mathbb{R}^+$. In this definition r_α represents the parameter of a negative exponential distribution. The dynamic behaviour of processes is determined by a *race condition*: all activities enabled attempt to proceed but only the fastest succeeds.

The relation $\rightarrow_s$ is defined as the minimal relation satisfying the rule

Final $\quad \dfrac{P \xrightarrow{(\alpha_j,w)}_c P'}{\langle \mathcal{V},\mathcal{N},\mathcal{K},\mathcal{F},Comp,P\rangle \xrightarrow{(\alpha_j,r_\alpha[w,\mathcal{N},\mathcal{K}])}_s \langle \mathcal{V},\mathcal{N},\mathcal{K},\mathcal{F},Comp,P'\rangle}$

The second component in the label of the conclusion represents the rate associated with the transition. The rate is calculated from the functional rate f_α in the following way:

$$r_\alpha[w, \mathcal{N}, \mathcal{K}] = \frac{f_\alpha[w, \mathcal{N}, \mathcal{K}]}{h}$$

where h is the step size and $f_\alpha[w, \mathcal{N}, \mathcal{K}]$ denotes the function f_α is evaluated over w, $\mathcal{N}$ and $\mathcal{K}$. Specifically, for each component C_i we derive the concentration as $l_i \times h$. Then we replace each free occurrence of C_i by $(l_i \times h)^{\kappa_{ij}}$, where κ_{ij} is the stoichiometric coefficient of the species i with respect to the reaction R_j. The derivation of rates is discussed in some more detail later.

A *Stochastic Labelled Transition System* can be defined for a Bio-PEPA system.

Definition 6. *The Stochastic Labelled Transition System (SLTS) for a Bio-PEPA system is $(\tilde{\mathcal{P}}, \Gamma, \rightarrow_s)$, where $\rightarrow_s$ is the minimal relation satisfying the rule* **Final**.

The states of *SLTS* are defined in terms of the concentration levels of the species components and the transitions from one state to another represent reactions that cause changes in the concentration levels of some components.

Note that using the relation $\rightarrow_c$ it is possible to define another labelled transition system (*LTS*) as $(\mathcal{C}, \Theta, \rightarrow_c)$ which differs only in the transition labels.

Derivation of Rates. In the *SLTS* the states represent *levels of concentration* and the transitions cause a change in these levels for one or more species. As we have seen the number of levels depends on the stoichiometric coefficients of the species involved.

Consider a reaction j described by a *kinetic law* f_j and with all stoichiometric coefficients equal to one. Following [16], we can define the transition rate as $(\Delta t)^{-1}$, where Δt is the time to have a variation in the concentration of one step for both the reactants and the products of the reaction. Let y be a variable describing one product of the reaction. We can consider the rate equation for that species with respect to the given reaction. This is $dy/dt = f_j(\bar{x}(t))$, where $\bar{x}$ is the set (or a subset) of the reactants/modifiers of the reaction. We can apply the *Taylor expansion* up to the second term and we obtain

$$y_{n+1} \approx y_n + f(\bar{x}_n) \times (t_{n+1} - t_n)$$

Now we can fix $y_{n+1} - y_n = h$ and then derive the time interval $(t_{n+1} - t_n) = \Delta t$ as $\Delta t \approx h/f(\bar{x}_n)$. From this we obtain the transition rate as $f(\bar{x}_n)/h$.

When the reaction has stoichiometric coefficients different from one, we can consider an approach similar to the one above. However, in this case, we assume mass action kinetics as this is generally the case for stoichiometric coefficient greater than one. Let y be a product of the reaction. The approximation gives:

$$y_{n+1} \approx y_n + r \times \kappa \times \prod_{i=1}^{n_r} x_{i,n}^{\kappa_i} \times (t_{n+1} - t_n)$$

where r is the reaction constant rate, κ is stoichiometric coefficient of the product y, x_i $i = 1, ..., n_r$ are the reactants of the reaction, κ_i $i = 1, ..., n_r$ are the associated stoichiometric coefficients, n_r is the number of distinct reactants.

Now we can fix $y_{n+1} - y_n = \kappa \times h$ and then derive the respective $(t_{n+1} - t_n) = \Delta t$ as $\Delta t \approx h/(r \times \prod_{i=1}^{n_r} x_{i,n}^{\kappa_i})$. From this expression we can derive the rate as usual.

Note that this approach is based on an *approximation*, the accuracy of which will depend on the time/concentration steps used.

From Biochemical Networks to Bio-PEPA. We define a translation, tr_BM_BP, from a biochemical network $\mathcal{M}$ to a Bio-PEPA system $\mathcal{P} = \langle \mathcal{V}, \mathcal{N},$ $\mathcal{K}, \mathcal{F}_R, Comp, P \rangle$, based on the following abstraction:

1. Each compartment is defined in the set $\mathcal{V}$ in terms of a name and an associated volume. Recall that currently in Bio-PEPA, compartments are not involved actively in the reactions and therefore are not represented by processes.
2. Each species i in the network is described by a constant component $C_i \in Comp$. The constant component C_i is defined by the "sum" of *elementary components* describing the interaction capabilities of the species. We suppose that there is at most one term in each species component with an action of type α. A single definition can express the behaviour of the species at any level.
3. Each reaction j is associated with an action type α_j and its dynamics is described by a specific function $f_{\alpha_j} \in \mathcal{F}_R$. The constant parameters used in the function can be defined in $\mathcal{K}$.
4. The model P is defined as the cooperation of the different components C_i.

3.4   Some Examples

Now we present some simple examples in order to show how Bio-PEPA can be used to capture some biological situations.

Example 1: Mass-action Kinetics. Consider the reaction $2X + Y \xrightarrow{-;f_M} 3Z$, described by the mass-action kinetic law $f_M = r \times X^2 \times Y$. The three species can be specified by the syntax:

$$X \stackrel{def}{=} (\alpha, 2){\downarrow}X \quad Y \stackrel{def}{=} (\alpha, 1){\downarrow}Y \quad Z \stackrel{def}{=} (\alpha, 3){\uparrow}Z$$

The system is described by $(X(l_{X0}) \underset{\{\alpha\}}{\bowtie} Y(l_{Y0})) \underset{\{\alpha\}}{\bowtie} Z(l_{Z0})$, where l_{X0}, l_{Y0} and l_{Z0} denote the initial concentration level of the three components. The functional rate is $f_\alpha = fMA(r)$. The rate associated with a transition is given by:

$$r_\alpha = \frac{r \times (l_X \times h)^2 \times (l_Y \times h)}{h}$$

where l_X, l_Y are the concentration levels for the species X and Y in a given state and h is the step size of all the species. The reaction can happen only if we have at least 3 levels $(0, 1, 2)$ for X, 2 levels for Y $(0, 1)$ and 4 levels $(0, 1, 2, 3)$ for Z.

Example 2: Michaelis-Menten Kinetics. One of the most commonly used kinetic laws is Michaelis-Menten. It describes a basic enzymatic reaction from the substrate S to the product P and is written as $S\xrightarrow{E;f_E}P$, where E is the enzyme involved in the reaction. This reaction is an approximation of a sequence of two reactions, under the quasi-steady state assumption (QSSA). The whole sequence of reactions is described by the kinetic law $f_E = \frac{v_M \times E \times S}{(K_M + S)}$. For more details about the derivation of this kinetic law and the meaning of parameters see [65].

The three species can be specified in Bio-PEPA by the following components:

$$S \stackrel{def}{=} (\alpha, 1)\downarrow S \quad P \stackrel{def}{=} (\alpha, 1)\uparrow P \quad E \stackrel{def}{=} (\alpha, 1) \oplus E$$

The system is described by $(S(l_{S0}) \underset{\{\alpha\}}{\bowtie} E(l_{E0})) \underset{\{\alpha\}}{\bowtie} P(l_{P0})$ and the functional rate is

$f_\alpha = fMM(v_M, K_M)$.

The transition rate is given by:

$$r_\alpha = \frac{v_M \times (l_S \times h) \times (l_E \times h)}{(K_M + l_S \times h)} \times \frac{1}{h}$$

where l_S, l_E are the concentration levels for the species S and E in a given state and h is the step size of all the species. The reaction can happen only if we have at least 2 levels $(0, 1)$ for all the species involved.

Example 3: Competitive Inhibition. Competitive inhibition is a form of enzyme inhibition where binding of the inhibitor to the enzyme prevents binding of the substrate and vice versa. In classical competitive inhibition, the inhibitor binds to the same active site as the normal enzyme substrate, without undergoing a reaction. The substrate molecule cannot enter the active site while the inhibitor is there, and the inhibitor cannot enter the site when the substrate is there. This reaction is described as:

$$S + E \longleftrightarrow SE$$
$$SE \longrightarrow P + E$$
$$E + I \longleftrightarrow EI$$

where S is the substrate, E the enzyme, I the inhibitor and P the product. Under QSSA the intermediate species SE and EI are constant and we can approximate the reactions above by a unique reaction $S\xrightarrow{E,I:f_I}P$, with rate $f_I = \dfrac{v_c \times S \times E}{S + K_M(1 + \frac{I}{K_I})}$, where v_c is the the turnover number (catalytic constant), K_M is the Michaelis-constant and K_I is the inhibition constant.

The specification in Bio-PEPA is:

$$S \stackrel{def}{=} (\alpha, 1)\downarrow S \quad P \stackrel{def}{=} (\alpha, 1)\uparrow P \quad E \stackrel{def}{=} (\alpha, 1) \oplus E \quad I \stackrel{def}{=} (\alpha, 1) \ominus I$$

The system is described by $((S(l_{S0}) \bowtie_{\{\alpha\}} E(l_{E0})) \bowtie_{\{\alpha\}} I(l_{I0})) \bowtie_{\{\alpha\}} P(l_{P0})$ with functional rate

$$f_\alpha = f_{CI}((v_c, K_M, K_I), S, E, I) = \frac{v_c \times S \times E}{S + K_M(1 + \frac{I}{K_I})}.$$

The transition rate is given by:

$$r_\alpha = \frac{v_c \times (l_S \times h) \times (l_E \times h)}{(l_S \times h + K_M(1 + \frac{l_I \times h}{K_I}))} \times \frac{1}{h}$$

where l_S, l_E, l_I are the concentration levels for the species S, E, I in a given state and h is the step size of all the species. The reaction can happen only if we have at least 2 levels (0, 1) for all the species involved.

Example 4: Degradation and Synthesis of a Species. Two particular reactions are those which describe the degradation and the creation of a species. In order to model these reactions we need to add two auxiliary species components to represent respectively the *residue (Res)* of the reaction and the *creation factor (CF)*, i.e. genes or DNA.

Let us consider the degradation reaction $A \rightarrow \emptyset$. We describe this reaction in Bio-PEPA by introducing the component *Res* as the residue/product of the reaction. The two species A and *Res* are defined as:

$$A \stackrel{def}{=} (\alpha, 1) \downarrow A \qquad Res \stackrel{def}{=} (\alpha, 1) \odot Res$$

The component *Res* is described by one or more sub-terms each of which describes a different degradation reaction.

In contrast the synthesis of a species $\emptyset \rightarrow A$ is described by a new component CF. The two species A and CF are described by:

$$A \stackrel{def}{=} (\alpha, 1) \uparrow A \qquad CF \stackrel{def}{=} (\alpha, 1) \odot CF$$

In the definitions of the components *Res* and *CF* we use the symbol $\odot$ to indicate that they do not change with the reaction.

3.5   Equivalences

It is sometimes useful to consider *equivalences* between models in order to determine whether the systems represented are in some sense the "same". In this section we discuss some notions of equivalence for Bio-PEPA. We consider two styles of equivalence which are commonly considered for process algebras: *isomorphism*, a structural equivalence, and *bisimulation*, a behavioural equivalence. Some characteristics of the language impact on the definitions of equivalence and we start by highlighting those. Firstly, there is no hiding operator or τ actions. Therefore, in Bio-PEPA we do not have weaker forms of equivalence based on abstracting τ actions. Secondly, in well-defined systems we have at most one action of a given type in each sequential term and each component describes the behaviour of a single species. So we cannot have processes of the form "$S + S$" and terms such as "$A = a.C$" (where A and C differ). Thirdly, if we have two transitions between the processes P and P', they involve different action types and they represent similar reactions that differ only in the kind/number of modifiers. Finally, we have defined two relations within the semantics. In one case the labels contain the information about the action type and about the elements involved. This is used as an auxiliary relation for the derivation of the second one, in which the labels contain the information about the action type and the rate (similarly to PEPA activity). Thus we have a choice of which relation on which to base each notion of equivalence.

Recall that in Bio-PEPA we make a distinction between systems and model components. However note that the only element that is modified by the transitions of a Bio-PEPA system is the model component. All the other components remain unchanged. Thus we define equivalences for the Bio-PEPA systems in terms of equivalences for the model components. Specifically, we say that two Bio-PEPA systems $\mathcal{P}_1$ and $\mathcal{P}_2$ are equivalent if their respective model components are equivalent.

Auxiliary Definitions. Before we proceed it will be useful to make some auxiliary definitions. Firstly we consider the derivative of a component, the derivative set and the derivative graph. We refer to the relation $\rightarrow_s$, the case of $\rightarrow_c$ is analogous, the only differences are in the label and in the fact that the former relation refers to Bio-PEPA systems and the latter refers to model components.

Definition 7. *If $\mathcal{P} \xrightarrow{(\alpha,r)}_s \mathcal{P}'$ then $\mathcal{P}'$ is a one-step $\rightarrow_s$ system derivative of $\mathcal{P}$. If $\mathcal{P} \xrightarrow{(\alpha_1,r_1)}_s \mathcal{P}_1 \xrightarrow{(\alpha_2,r_2)}_s .... \xrightarrow{(\alpha_n,r_n)}_s \mathcal{P}'$ then $\mathcal{P}'$ is a system derivative of $\mathcal{P}$.*

We can indicate the sequence $\xrightarrow{\gamma_1}_s \xrightarrow{\gamma_2}_s .... \xrightarrow{\gamma_n}_s$ with $\xrightarrow{\mu}_s$, where μ denotes the sequence $\gamma_1 \gamma_2, ... \gamma_n$ (possibly empty).

Definition 8. *A system α-derivative of $\mathcal{P}$ is a system $\mathcal{P}'$ such that $\mathcal{P} \xrightarrow{(\alpha,r)}_s \mathcal{P}'$. For each $\alpha \in \mathcal{A}$ we have at most one system α-derivative of a system $\mathcal{P}$.*

Definition 9. *The system derivative set $ds(\mathcal{P})$ is the smallest set such that:*

- *$\mathcal{P} \in ds(\mathcal{P})$;*
- *if $\mathcal{P}' \in ds(\mathcal{P})$ and there exists $\alpha \in \mathcal{A}(\mathcal{P}')$ such that $\mathcal{P}' \xrightarrow{(\alpha,r)}_s \mathcal{P}''$ then $\mathcal{P}'' \in ds(\mathcal{P})$, where $\mathcal{A}(\mathcal{P}')$ is the set of action types currently enabled in the system derivative $\mathcal{P}'$.*

Definition 10. *The system derivative graph $\mathcal{D}(\mathcal{P})$ is the labelled directed multigraph whose set of nodes is $ds(\mathcal{P})$ and whose multi-set of arcs are elements in $ds(\mathcal{P}) \times ds(\mathcal{P}) \times \Gamma$.*

Note that in well-defined Bio-PEPA components the multiplicity of $\langle \mathcal{P}_i, \mathcal{P}_j, \gamma \rangle$ is always one.

The definitions above refer to Bio-PEPA systems. The only components of the system $\mathcal{P} = \langle \mathcal{V}, \mathcal{N}, \mathcal{K}, \mathcal{F}, Comp, P \rangle$ that evolves is the model component P. The other components collect information about the compartments, the species, the rates and report the definition of the species components. They remain unchanged in the evolution of the system. In some cases it can be useful (and simpler) to focus on the model component instead of considering the whole system and use the other components for the derivation of the rates. We define a function $\pi_P(\mathcal{P}) = P$, that, given a Bio-PEPA system returns the model component. Then we define a *(component) derivative* of P by considering the model component P' of the system derivative of $\mathcal{P}$. Similarly, we define a *(component) α-derivative* of P, *(component) derivative set* $ds(P)$ and the *(component) derivative graph* $\mathcal{D}(P)$ starting from the definitions for the associated system $\mathcal{P}$.

In the derivation of the CTMC (see Section 3.6) we need to identify the actions describing the interactions from one state to another.

Definition 11. *Let $\mathcal{P}$ be a Bio-PEPA system and let $P = \pi_P(\mathcal{P})$. Let P_u, P_v be two derivatives of a model component P with P_v a one-step derivative of P_u. The set of action types associated with the transitions from the process P_u to the process P_v is denoted $\mathcal{A}(P_u | P_v)$.*

The next definition concerns the *complete action type set* of a system $\mathcal{P}$ and a component P.

Definition 12. *The complete action type set of a system $\mathcal{P}$ is defined as:*

$$\bar{\mathcal{A}} = \cup_{\mathcal{P}_i \in ds(\mathcal{P})} \mathcal{A}(\mathcal{P}_i)$$

The complete action type set of a component P is defined similarly.

Other useful definitions are the ones concerning the exit rate and transition rates. In the following we report the definition for the model components, but a similar definition can be used for Bio-PEPA systems.

Definition 13. *Let us consider a Bio-PEPA system $\mathcal{P} = \langle \mathcal{V}, \mathcal{N}, \mathcal{K}, \mathcal{F}, Comp, P \rangle$ and let $P_1, P_2 \in ds(P)$. The exit rate of a process P_1 is defined as:*

$$rate(P_1) = \sum_{\{\alpha | \exists \mathcal{P}_2 . \mathcal{P}_1 \xrightarrow{(\alpha, r_\alpha[w, \mathcal{N}, \mathcal{K}])}_s \mathcal{P}_2,\, P_1 = \pi_P(\mathcal{P}_1)\}} r_\alpha[w, \mathcal{N}, \mathcal{K}]$$

Similarly, the transition rate is defined as:

$$rate(P_1 \mid P_2) = \sum_{\{\alpha | \mathcal{P}_1 \xrightarrow{(\alpha, r_\alpha[w, \mathcal{N}, \mathcal{K}])}_s \mathcal{P}_2,\, P_1 = \pi_P(\mathcal{P}_1),\, P_2 = \pi_P(\mathcal{P}_2)\}} r_\alpha[w, \mathcal{N}, \mathcal{K}]$$

For the label γ in the stochastic relation, the function $action(\gamma) = \alpha$ extracts the first component of the pair (i.e. the action type) and the function $rate(\gamma) = r \in \mathbb{R}$ returns the second component (i.e. the rate).

In the following we use the same symbol to denote equivalences for both the system and the corresponding model component. In this section we present definitions of isomorphism and strong bisimulation which are similar to the relations defined for PEPA in [42]. Furthermore we show some relationships between the defined equivalences.

Isomorphism. *Isomorphism* is a strong notion of equivalence based on the derivation graph of the components (systems). Broadly speaking, two components (systems) are isomorphic if they generate derivation graphs with the same structure and capable of carrying out exactly the same activities.

We have the following definition of isomorphism based on the capability relation:

Definition 14. *Let P_1, P_2 be two Bio-PEPA systems whose model components are P and Q, respectively. A function $\mathcal{F}$: $ds(P) \rightarrow ds(Q)$ is a component isomorphism between P and Q, with respect to $\rightarrow_c$, if $\mathcal{F}$ is an injective function and for any component $P' \in ds(P)$, $\mathcal{A}(P') = \mathcal{A}(\mathcal{F}(P'))$, with $r_\alpha[w, \mathcal{N}, \mathcal{K}] = r'_\alpha[\mathcal{F}(w), \mathcal{N}', \mathcal{K}']$ for each $\alpha \in \mathcal{A}(P)$, where $\mathcal{F}(w)$ is defined component-wise over the list w, and for all $\alpha \in \mathcal{A}$ the set of α-derivatives of $\mathcal{F}(P')$ is the same as the set of $\mathcal{F}-$images of the α-derivatives of P', with respect to $\rightarrow_c$.*

This is a very strong relation because the labels associated with the capability relation contain a lot of information, all of which must be matched. Formally, we can define isomorphic components in the following way:

Definition 15. *Let P_1, P_2 be two Bio-PEPA systems whose model components are P and Q. P and Q are isomorphic with respect to $\rightarrow_c$ (denoted $P =_c Q$), if there exists a component isomorphism $\mathcal{F}$ between them such that $\mathcal{D}(\mathcal{F}(P)) = \mathcal{D}(Q)$, where $\mathcal{D}$ denotes the derivative graph.*

We can now define when two Bio-PEPA systems are isomorphic.

Definition 16. *Let P_1, P_2 be two Bio-PEPA systems whose model components are P and Q. P_1 and P_2 are isomorphic with respect to $\rightarrow_c$ (denoted $P_1 =_c P_2$), if $P =_c Q$.*

A similar structural relation based on the stochastic relation can also be defined and used to characterise another form of isomorphism between systems (components) $=_s$ (see [23] for details). Both isomorphisms, $=_c$ and $=_s$ are equivalence relations, and congruences with respect to the combinators of Bio-PEPA. In both cases they retain enough information about the structure and behaviour of the isomorphic components to ensure that they give rise to identical underlying Markov processes. However, $=_c$ is more strict than $=_s$, i.e. there will be pairs of systems (components) which satisfy $=_s$ but do not satisfy $=_c$.

Equational Laws. Once an equivalence relation has been defined it can be used to establish equational laws which may be used to manipulate models and recognise equivalent terms. In the following the symbol "$=$" denotes either $=_c$ or $=_s$. The proof of the laws follow from the definition of isomorphism and the semantic rules.

Choice

1. $(P + Q) \bowtie_{\mathcal{L}} S = (Q + P) \bowtie_{\mathcal{L}} S$

2. $(P + (Q + R)) \bowtie_{\mathcal{L}} S = ((P + Q) + R) \bowtie_{\mathcal{L}} S$

Cooperation

1. $P \bowtie_{\mathcal{L}} Q = Q \bowtie_{\mathcal{L}} P$

2. $P \bowtie_{\mathcal{L}} (Q \bowtie_{\mathcal{L}} R) = (P \bowtie_{\mathcal{L}} Q) \bowtie_{\mathcal{L}} R$

3. $P \bowtie_{\mathcal{K}} Q = P \bowtie_{\mathcal{L}} Q$ if $\mathcal{K} \cap (\bar{\mathcal{A}}(P) \cup \bar{\mathcal{A}}(Q)) = \mathcal{L}$

4. $(P \bowtie_{\mathcal{L}} Q) \bowtie_{\mathcal{K}} R = \begin{cases} P \bowtie_{\mathcal{L}} (Q \bowtie_{\mathcal{K}} R) \text{ if } \bar{\mathcal{A}}(R) \cap (\mathcal{L} \backslash \mathcal{K}) = \emptyset \wedge \bar{\mathcal{A}}(P) \cap (\mathcal{K} \backslash \mathcal{L}) = \emptyset \\ Q \bowtie_{\mathcal{L}} (P \bowtie_{\mathcal{K}} R) \text{ if } \bar{\mathcal{A}}(R) \cap (\mathcal{L} \backslash \mathcal{K}) = \emptyset \wedge \bar{\mathcal{A}}(Q) \cap (\mathcal{K} \backslash \mathcal{L}) = \emptyset \end{cases}$

Constant If $A \stackrel{def}{=} P$ then $A = P$

Bio-PEPA systems

Let $\mathcal{P}_1$ and $\mathcal{P}_2$ be two Bio-PEPA systems, with $P = \pi_P(\mathcal{P}_1)$ and $Q = \pi_P(\mathcal{P}_2)$. If $P = Q$ then $\mathcal{P}_1 = \mathcal{P}_2$.

Strong Bisimulation. The definition of bisimulation is based on the *labelled transition system*. Strong bisimulation captures the idea that bisimilar components (systems) are able to perform the same actions with same rates resulting in derivatives that are themselves bisimilar. This makes the components (systems) indistinguishable to an external observer. As with isomorphism we can develop two definitions based on the two semantic relations. This time for illustration we present the definitions based on the stochastic relation. The strong capability bisimulation, $\sim_c$, is defined similarly (see [23] for details).

Definition 17. *A binary relation $\mathcal{R} \subseteq \tilde{\mathcal{P}} \times \tilde{\mathcal{P}}$ is a strong stochastic bisimulation, if $(\mathcal{P}_1, \mathcal{P}_2) \in \mathcal{R}$ implies for all $\alpha \in \mathcal{A}$:*

- *if $\mathcal{P}_1 \stackrel{\gamma}{\rightarrow}_s \mathcal{P'}_1$ then there exists $\mathcal{P'}_2$ such that $\mathcal{P}_2 \stackrel{\gamma}{\rightarrow}_s \mathcal{P'}_2$ with $(\mathcal{P'}_1, \mathcal{P'}_2) \in \mathcal{R}$.*
- *if $\mathcal{P}_2 \stackrel{\gamma}{\rightarrow}_s \mathcal{P'}_2$ then there exists $\mathcal{P'}_1$ such that $\mathcal{P}_1 \stackrel{\gamma}{\rightarrow}_s \mathcal{P'}_1$ with $(\mathcal{P'}_1, \mathcal{P'}_2) \in \mathcal{R}$.*

Definition 18. *Let $\mathcal{P}_1$, $\mathcal{P}_2$ be two Bio-PEPA systems whose model components are P and Q, respectively. P and Q are strong stochastic bisimilar, written $P \sim_s Q$, if $(\mathcal{P}_1, \mathcal{P}_2) \in \mathcal{R}$ for some strong stochastic bisimulation $\mathcal{R}$.*

Definition 19. *Let $\mathcal{P}_1$, $\mathcal{P}_2$ be two Bio-PEPA systems whose model components are P and Q, respectively. $\mathcal{P}_1$, $\mathcal{P}_2$ are strong stochastic bisimilar, written $\mathcal{P}_1 \sim_s \mathcal{P}_2$, if $P \sim_s Q$.*

Both $\sim_c$ and $\sim_s$ are equivalence relations and congruences with respect to the combinators of Bio-PEPA. Moreover it is straightforward to see that isomorphism implies strong bisimulation in both cases.

Example. Consider the following systems representing two biological systems. The former system $\mathcal{P}_1$ represents a system described by an enzymatic reaction with kinetic law $\dfrac{v_1 \times E \times S}{K_1 + S}$, where S is the substrate and E the enzyme. We have that the set $\mathcal{N}$ is defined as $\{S \colon h, N_S;\ P \colon h, N_P;\ E \colon 1, 1\}$ for some step size h and maximum levels N_S and N_P. The component and the model components are defined as:

$$S \overset{def}{=} (\alpha, 1){\downarrow}S \quad E \overset{def}{=} (\alpha, 1) \oplus E \quad P \overset{def}{=} (\alpha, 1){\uparrow}P$$

The model component P_1 is $(S(l_{S0}) \underset{\{\alpha\}}{\bowtie} E(1)) \underset{\{\alpha\}}{\bowtie} P(l_{P0})$. The functional rate is $f_\alpha = fMM(v_1, K_1)$.

The second system $\mathcal{P}_2$ describes an enzymatic reaction where the enzyme is left implicit (it is constant). The rate is given by $\dfrac{v_1 \times S'}{K_1 + S'}$, where S' is the substrate.

We have that the set $\mathcal{N}$ is defined as $\{S' \colon h, N_{S'};\ P' \colon h, N_{P'}\}$.

The components are defined as $S' \overset{def}{=} (\alpha, 1){\downarrow}S'$ and $P' \overset{def}{=} (\alpha, 1){\uparrow}P'$ and the model component $P2$ is $S'(l_{S0}) \underset{\{\alpha\}}{\bowtie} P'(l_{P0})$. In this case $f_\alpha = fMM'((v_1, K_1), S') = \dfrac{v_1 \times S'}{K_1 + S'}$ and the component S' and P' have the same number of levels/maximum concentration of S and P.

We have that $P_1 \sim_s P_2$, but $P_1 \not\approx_c P_2$, because the number of enzymes is different. The same relations are valid if the systems rather than the model components are considered.

3.6   Analysis

A Bio-PEPA system is an *intermediate, formal, compositional* representation of the biological model. Based on this representation we can perform different kinds of analysis. In this section we discuss briefly how to use a Bio-PEPA system to derive a *CTMC with levels*, a set of *Ordinary Differential Equations (ODEs)*, a *Gillespie simulation* and a *PRISM* model.

From Bio-PEPA to a CTMC. As for the reagent-centric view of PEPA, the CTMC associated with the system refers to the concentration levels of the species components. Specifically, the states of the CTMC are defined in terms of concentration levels and the transitions from one state to the other capture some variations in these levels. Hereafter we call the CTMC derived from a Bio-PEPA system (or from a PEPA reagent-centric view system) *CTMC with levels*.

Theorem 1. *For any finite Bio-PEPA system $\mathcal{P} = \langle \mathcal{V}, \mathcal{N}, \mathcal{K}, \mathcal{F}_R, Comp, P \rangle$, if we define the stochastic process $X(t)$ such that $X(t) = P_i$ indicates that the system behaves as the component P_i at time t, then $X(t)$ is a Markov Process.*

The proof is not reproduced here but it is analogous the one presented for PEPA [42]. Instead of the PEPA activity we consider the label γ and the rate is obtained by evaluating the functional rate in the system. We consider finite models to ensure that a solution for the CTMC is at least theoretically feasible (in practice the size of the state space may make the model intractable). The finiteness assumption is equivalent to supposing that each species in the model has a maximum level of concentration.

Theorem 2. *Given* $(\tilde{\mathcal{P}}, \Gamma, \rightarrow_s)$, *let* $\mathcal{P}$ *be a Bio-PEPA system, with model component P. Let $n_c = |ds(P)|$, where $ds(P)$ is the derivative set of P. Then the infinitesimal generator matrix of the CTMC for $\mathcal{P}$ is a square matrix Q $(n_c \times n_c)$ whose elements $q_{u,v}$ are defined as*

$$q_{u,v} = \sum_{\alpha_j \in \mathcal{A}(P_u|P_v)} r_{\alpha_j} \quad if\ u \neq v \qquad q_{u,u} = -\sum_{u \neq v} q_{u,v} \quad otherwise.$$

where P_u, P_v are two derivatives of P.

It is worth noting that the states of the CTMC are defined in terms of the derivatives of the model component. These derivatives are uniquely identified by the levels of species components in the system, so we can give the following definition of the CTMC states:

Definition 20. *The CTMC states derived from a Bio-PEPA system can be defined as vectors of levels $\sigma = (l_1, l_2, ..., l_n)$, where l_i, for $i = 1, 2, ..., n$ is the level of the species i and n is the total number of species.*

Note that we can avoid consideration of the two levels for *Res* and *CF* as they are always constant.

From this we can deduce that if two transitions are possible between a pair of states, the actions involved are different and they represent reactions that differ only in the modifiers and/or the number of enzymes used. The former point follows from the definition of well-defined Bio-PEPA system. The second point follows because the only possibility of having two transitions between two given states is that the associated reactions have the same reactants and products. We can see this by observing that the states depend on the levels and the reactions cause some changes in these levels. The only elements that do not change during a reaction are the modifiers.

The objective in forming the CTMC with levels is to generate a discrete state space model for which the state space is not prohibitively large. Such a model can then be subjected to numerical analysis, deriving the transient or steady state probability distribution over the states of the model. This form of analysis simultaneously considers all possible behaviours of the model. This is quite distinct from stochastic simulation, also based on a CTMC, which only considers a single trajectory over the state space of the model in each run, i.e. each run captures only one possible behaviour of the model.

From Bio-PEPA to ODEs. The translation into ODEs is similar to the method proposed for PEPA (reagent-centric view) [13]. It is based on the syntactic presentation of the model and on the derivation of the stoichiometry matrix

$D = \{d_{ij}\}$ from the definition of the components. The entries of the matrix are the stoichiometric coefficients of the reactions and are obtained in the following way: for each component C_i consider the prefix subterms C_{ij} representing the contribution of the species i to the reaction j. If the term represents a reactant we write the corresponding stoichiometry κ_{ij} as $-\kappa_{ij}$ in the entry d_{ij}. For a product we write $+\kappa_{ij}$ in the entry d_{ij}. All other cases are null.

Let t_{ODE} denote the mapping of a Bio-PEPA system $\mathcal{P}$ into a set of ODEs. This mapping is based on the following steps:

1. Definition of the stoichiometry $(n \times m)$ matrix D, where n is the number of species and m is the number of molecules;
2. Definition of the *kinetic law vector* $(m \times 1)$ v_{KL} containing the kinetic laws of each reaction;
3. Association of the variable x_i with each component C_i and definition of the vector $(n \times 1)$ $\bar{x}$.

The ODE system is then obtained as:

$$\frac{d\bar{x}}{dt} = D \times v_{KL}$$

with initial concentrations $x_{i0} = l_{i0} \times h$, for $i = 1, ..., n$.

The following property holds:

Property 1. For a biochemical network $\mathcal{M}$ and a Bio-PEPA system $\mathcal{P} = tr\_BM\_BP(\mathcal{M})$, we have that $t_{ODE}(\mathcal{P}) = t_{BODE}(\mathcal{M})$, where t_{ODE} and t_{BODE} are the translation functions from Bio-PEPA and the biological system into ODEs, respectively.

The ODE system derived from a Bio-PEPA system $\mathcal{P}$ is "equal" to the one obtained directly from the biological network itself. This means that in the translation into Bio-PEPA no information for the derivation of ODEs is lost. This result is unsurprising since in both cases the construction of the ODEs is based on stoichiometric matrix. However the Bio-PEPA model can generally collect more information than the respective ODEs. This can been seen by considering examples which give rise to the same set of ODEs but which differ in their Bio-PEPA representation. For example consider the Bio-PEPA models corresponding to the following sets of reactions:

$$\{A \xrightarrow{r} B + C; \ A \xrightarrow{r} B; \ A \xrightarrow{r} C + D\}$$

and

$$\{A \xrightarrow{2r} B + C; \ A \xrightarrow{r} D\}.$$

The two Bio-PEPA models are different, but the ODE systems that we derive from them coincide.

From Bio-PEPA to Stochastic Simulation. Gillespie's stochastic simulation algorithm [36] is a widely-used method for the simulation of biochemical reactions. It applies to homogeneous, well-stirred systems in thermal equilibrium and constant volume, composed of n different species that interact through m reactions. Broadly speaking, the goal is to describe the evolution of the system $\mathbf{X}(t)$, described in terms of the number of elements of each species, starting from an initial state. Every reaction is characterised by a stochastic rate constant c_j, termed the *basal rate* (derived from the constant rate r by means of some simple relations proposed in [36,68]). Using this it is possible to calculate the *actual rate* $a_j(\mathbf{X}(t))$ of the reaction, that is the probability of the reaction R_j occurring in time $(t, t + \Delta t)$ given that the system is in a specific state.

The algorithm is based on the following two steps:

– Calculation of the next reaction to occur in the system;
– Calculation of the time at which that reaction occurs.

The calculations are based on two conditional density functions:

$$p(j \mid \mathbf{X}(t)) = a_j(\mathbf{X}(t))/a_0,$$

that is, the probability that the next reaction is R_j and

$$p(\tau \mid \mathbf{X}(t)) = a_0 e^{a_0 \mathbf{X}(t)\tau},$$

the probability that the next reaction occurs in $[t + \tau, t + \tau + d\tau]$, where $a_0 = \sum_{v=1}^{m} a_v(\mathbf{X}(t))$.

The translation of a Bio-PEPA model to a simulation model amenable to Gillespie's algorithm is similar to the approach proposed for ODEs. The main drawbacks are the definition of the rates and the correctness of the approach in the case of general kinetic laws. Indeed Gillespie's stochastic simulation algorithm supposes elementary reactions and constant rates (mass-action kinetics). If the model contains only this kind of reactions the translation is straightforward. If there are non-elementary reactions and general kinetic laws, a widely-used approach is to consider them translated directly into a stochastic context. This is not always valid and some counterexamples have been demonstrated [11]. The authors of [11] showed that when Gillespie's algorithm is applied to Hill kinetics in the context of the transcription initiation of autoregulated genes, the magnitude of fluctuations is overestimated. The application of Gillespie's algorithm in the case of general kinetics laws is discussed by several authors [1,17]. Rao and Arkin [1] show that this approach is valid in the case of some specific kinetic laws, such as Michaelis-Menten and inhibition. However, it is important to remember that these laws are approximations, based on some assumptions that specific conditions (such as "$S \gg E$" in the case of Michaelis-Menten) hold. The approach we advocate is as in [47]: we apply Gillespie's algorithm, but particular attention must be paid to the interpretation of the simulation results and to their validity.

The definition of a Gillespie model is based on:

- Definition of the state vector $\bar{X}$. It is composed of n components X_i, representing the number of elements for each species i.
- Definition of the initial condition $\bar{X}_0$. The values are given by:

$$X_{i0} = l_{i0} \times h \times N_A \times v_i \text{ molecules}$$

where N_A is the Avogadro number, i.e. the number of molecules in a mole of a substance, and v_i is the volume of the containing compartment V_i.
- Definition of the actual rate for each reaction. We have two cases:
  1. Reactions described by the mass-action law and with constant rate r_j. The actual rate for the reaction is:

$$a_j(\bar{X}_j) = c_j \times f_h(\bar{X}_j)$$

where c_j is the stochastic rate constant, f_h is a function that gives the number of distinct combinations of reactant molecules and $\bar{X}_j$ are the species involved in the reaction j. The stochastic rate constant is defined in [68] as:

$$c_j = \frac{r_j}{(N_A \times v)^{n_{tot}-1}} \times \prod_{u=1}^{n_j} \kappa_{uj}!$$

where n_j is the number of distinct reactants in the reaction j, r_j is the rate of the reaction and $n_{tot} = \sum_{u=1}^{n_j} \kappa_{uj}$ is the total number of reactants[6].

Finally, the number of possible combinations of reactants is defined as

$$f_h((\bar{X}_j) = \prod_{u=1}^{n_j} \binom{X_{p(u,j)}}{\kappa_{uj}} \sim \frac{\prod_{u=1}^{n_j} (X_{p(u,j)})^{\kappa_{uj}}}{\prod_{u=1}^{n_j} \kappa_{uj}!}$$

  2. Reactions with general kinetic laws $f_{\alpha_j}(\bar{k}, \bar{C})$. The actual rate is:

$$a_j(\bar{X}_j) = f_{\alpha_j}(\bar{k}, \bar{X}_j)$$

From Bio-PEPA to PRISM. PRISM [61] is a probabilistic model checker, a tool for the formal modelling and analysis of systems which exhibit random or probabilistic behaviour. PRISM has been used to analyse systems from a wide range of application domains. Models are described using the PRISM language, a simple state-based language and it is possible to specify quantitative properties of the system using a temporal logic, called *CSL* [2] (Continuous Stochastic

---

[6] We assume that all the species that are involved in the reaction as reactants are inside the same compartment with volume v.

Logic). For our purposes the underlying mathematical model of a PRISM model is a CTMC and the PRISM models we generate from Bio-PEPA correspond to the CTMCs with levels. However we present the translation separately as the models are specified in the PRISM language.

The PRISM language is composed of *modules* and *variables*. A model is composed of a number of modules which can interact with each other. A module contains a number of local variables. The values of these variables at any given time constitute the state of the module. The global state of the whole model is determined by the local state of all modules. The behaviour of each module is described by a set of commands. Each update describes a transition which the module can make if the guard is true. A transition is specified by giving the new values of the variables in the module, possibly as a function of other variables. Each update is also assigned a probability (or in some cases a rate) which will be assigned to the corresponding transition. It is straightforward to translate a Bio-PEPA system into a PRISM model. We have the following correspondences:

- The model is defined as **stochastic** (this term is used in PRISM for CTMC).
- Each element in the set of parameters $\mathcal{K}$ is defined as a *global constant*.
- The maximum levels, the concentration steps and the volume sizes are defined as *global constants*.
- Each species component is represented by a *PRISM module*. The species component concentration is represented by a *local variable* and it can (generally) assume values between 0 and N_i. For each sub-term (i.e. reaction where the species is involved) we have a definition of a *command*. The name of the command is related to the action α (and then to the associated reaction). The guards and the change in levels are defined according to whether the element is a reactant, a product or a modifier of the reactions.
- The functional rates are defined inside an auxiliary module.
- In PRISM the rate associated with an action is the *product* of the rates of the commands in the different modules that cooperate. For each reaction, we give the value "1" to the rate of each command involved in the reaction, with the exception of the command in the module containing the functional rates. In this case the rate is the functional rate f, expressing the kinetic law. The rate associated with a reaction is given by $1 \times 1 \times \ldots \times f = f$, as desired.

4   Examples

This section reports the translation of two biological models into Bio-PEPA and some analysis results. The first example is taken from [37] and describes a minimal model for the cascade of post-translational modifications that modulate the activity of cdc2 kinase during the cell cycle. The second example is the repressilator [33], a synthetic genetic network with an oscillating behaviour.

In the present work the stochastic and deterministic simulations are obtained exporting the Bio-PEPA system by means of the derivations described in Section 3.6. An automatic translation is under implementation.

4.1   The Goldbeter's Model

In the following we show the translation of the Goldbeter's model presented in [37] into Bio-PEPA and we discuss the kinds of analysis that are possible for it. Broadly speaking, the model describes the activity of the *protein cyclin* in the cell cycle. The cyclin promotes the activation of a *cdk* (*cdc2*) which in turn activates a *cyclin protease*. This protease promotes cyclin degradation, and thus a negative feedback loop is obtained.

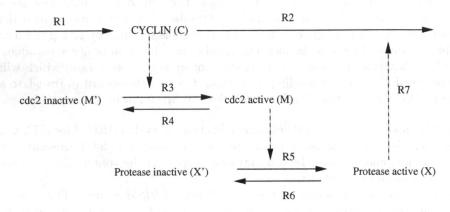

Fig. 2. Goldbeter's model

The Biological Model. A schema of the model is shown in Fig. 2. There are three distinct species involved:

- *cyclin*, the protein protagonist of the cycle, represented by variable C;
- *cdc2 kinase*, in both active (i.e. dephosphorylated) and inactive form (i.e. phosphorylated). The variables used to represent them are M and M', respectively;
- *cyclin protease*, in both active (i.e. phosphorylated) and inactive form (i.e. dephosphorylated). The variables are X and X'.

A detailed list of reactions is reported in Table 2. The first two reactions are the creation of cyclin and its degradation. The reactions *R3-R6* are enzymatic reactions describing the activation/deactivation of the biological species cdc2 and protease. These reactions are activated through phosphorylation/dephosphorylation. The last reaction is the degradation of the cyclin triggered by the protease.

Concerning the kinetic laws, the first two reactions have mass-action kinetics, whereas the others all have Michaelis-Menten kinetics. We have some kinetic laws in which the enzyme is explicit (reactions 3, 5), other ones in which it is implicit (reactions 4, 6) as it is constant and abstracted within the Michaelis-Menten parameter V_i.

Table 2. Goldbeter model. The list of reactions.

id	name	react.	prod.	mod.	kinetic laws
R1	creation of cyclin	-	C	-	v_i
R2	degradation of cyclin	C	-	-	$k_d \times C$
R3	activation of cdc2 kinase	M'	M	C	$\dfrac{C \times V_1}{(K_c + C)} \dfrac{M'}{(K_1 + M')}$
R4	deactivation of cdc2 kinase	M	M'	-	$\dfrac{M \times V_2}{(K_2 + M)}$
R5	activation of cyclin protease	X'	X	M	$\dfrac{X' \times M \times V_3}{(K_3 + X')}$
R6	deactivation of cyclin protease	X	X'	-	$\dfrac{X \times V_4}{K_4 + X}$
R7	degradation of cyclin triggered by protease	C	-	X	$\dfrac{C \times V_d \times X}{C + K_d}$

The Bio-PEPA System. The translation of the Goldbeter's model into Bio-PEPA is achieved in the following steps.

- *Definition of the list $\mathcal{V}$.* In the model compartments are not considered. Here we add the default compartment:

$$cell : \ 1.0 \times 10^{-14} \ \text{litre}$$

- *Definition of the set $\mathcal{N}$.* This is defined as:

$C : h, N_C, 0.01, 0.6, cell;$ $M' : h, N_{M'}, 0.99, 1, cell;$ $\ M : h, N_M, 0.01, 0.7, cell;$
$X' : h, N_{X'}, 0.99, 1, cell;$ $\ X : h, N_X, 0.01, 0.65, cell;$
$Res : 1, 1, \_, \_, cell;$ $\qquad CF : 1, 1, \_, \_, cell;$

The components Res and CF are added to represent degradation reactions and the synthesis of the cyclin, respectively. The information about the initial and the maximum concentrations are derived from Goldbeter's paper. We can fix the step size as 0.05. In this case the maximum levels are: $N_C = 12$, $N_M = 14$, $N_X = 13$, $N_{M'} = N_{X'} = 20$. If we wanted to consider the finer granularity $h = 0.01$ (corresponding to the initial concentration of some of the species) we would have $N_C = 60$, $N_M = 70$, $N_X = 65$, $N_{M'} = N_{X'} = 100$.

- *Definition of functional rates ($\mathcal{F}_R$) and parameters ($\mathcal{K}$).* The functional rates are:

$f_{\alpha_1} = fMA(v_i);$ $\qquad f_{\alpha_2} = fMA(k_d);$ $\qquad f_{\alpha_4} = fMM(V_2, K_2);$
$f_{\alpha_5} = fMM(V_3, K_3);$ $\ f_{\alpha_6} = fMM(V_4, K_4);$ $\ f_{\alpha_7} = fMM(V_d, K_d);$

$$f_{\alpha_3} = fMM'((V_1, K_c, K_1), M', C) = \frac{V_1 \times C}{K_c + C} \frac{M'}{K_1 + M'};$$

The parameters are those reported in the original paper and we have:

$$
\begin{aligned}
&v_i = 0.025\ \mu M.min^{-1}; \quad k_d = 0.01\ min^{-1}; \quad V_1 = 12\ \mu M.min^{-1}; \quad K_1 = 0.02\ \mu M;\\
&V_2 = 1.5\ \mu M.min^{-1}; \quad K_2 = 0.02\ \mu M; \quad V_3 = 12\ min^{-1}; \quad K_3 = 0.02\ \mu M;\\
&V_d = 0.0625\ \mu M.min^{-1}; \quad V_4 = 2\ \mu M.min^{-1}; \quad K_4 = 0.02\ \mu M; \quad K_d = 0.02\ \mu M;\\
&K_c = 0.5\ \mu M
\end{aligned}
$$

$-$ *Definition of species components (Comp) and of the model component (P).*

$$
C \stackrel{def}{=} (\alpha_1, 1)\uparrow C + (\alpha_2, 1)\downarrow C + (\alpha_7, 1)\downarrow C + (\alpha_3, 1) \oplus C;
$$
$$
M' \stackrel{def}{=} (\alpha_4, 1)\uparrow M' + (\alpha_3, 1)\downarrow M';
$$
$$
M \stackrel{def}{=} (\alpha_3, 1)\uparrow M + (\alpha_4, 1)\downarrow M + (\alpha_5, 1) \oplus M;
$$
$$
X' \stackrel{def}{=} (\alpha_6, 1)\uparrow X' + (\alpha_5, 1)\downarrow X';
$$
$$
X \stackrel{def}{=} (\alpha_5, 1)\uparrow X + (\alpha_6, 1)\downarrow X + (\alpha_7, 1) \oplus X;
$$
$$
Res \stackrel{def}{=} (\alpha_2, 1) \odot Res;
$$
$$
CF \stackrel{def}{=} (\alpha_1, 1) \odot CF;
$$

$$
C(l_{0C}) \underset{\{\alpha_3\}}{\bowtie} M(l_{0M}) \underset{\{\alpha_3,\alpha_4\}}{\bowtie} M'(l_{0M'}) \underset{\{\alpha_5,\alpha_7\}}{\bowtie} X(l_{0X}) \underset{\{\alpha_5,\alpha_6\}}{\bowtie} X'(l_{0X'}) \underset{\{\alpha_2\}}{\bowtie} Res(0) \underset{\{\alpha_1\}}{\bowtie} CF(1)
$$

The levels are chosen to reflect the initial values of the species and are set to $l_{0C} = l_{0M} = l_{0X} = 0$ and $l_{0M'} = l_{0X'} = 20$.

Analysis. In the following we report some observations about the analysis of the Bio-PEPA system.

SLTS and CTMC By considering the step size $h = 0.05$ and the number of levels given in the Bio-PEPA system we obtain a CTMC with 52 states and 185 transitions. The states are described by the vector:

$$
(C(l_C), M'(l_{M'}), M(l_M), X'(l_{X'}), X(l_X))
$$

where the different components can assume different values according to the possible number of levels for each species. This CTMC is not depicted.

Instead, for illustrative purposes, we present a simpler CTMC for our model, obtained assuming $h = 1$ and considering only two levels for each species. The vector $\mathcal{N}$ is modified accordingly. We show how to define the states and the transition rates of this CTMC starting from the Bio-PEPA system and the associated transition system. The initial situation is with C, M and X absent (0) and the other elements present (1). The initial state is $(C(0), M'(1), M(0), X'(1), X(0))$. Figure 3 reports the stochastic transition system in this simplified case.

The numbers indicate the different transitions. Each transition is characterized by a label γ_i containing the information about the action type and the rate.

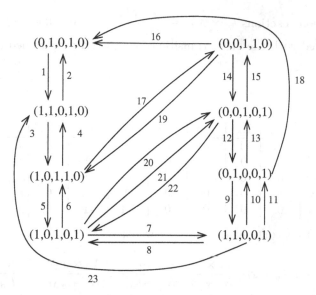

Fig. 3. The transition system for the Goldbeter's model in the case of two levels

We have:

$$\gamma_1 = (\alpha_1, r_1) \quad \gamma_2 = (\alpha_2, r_2) \quad \gamma_3 = (\alpha_3, r_3) \quad \gamma_4 = (\alpha_4, r_4)$$
$$\gamma_5 = (\alpha_5, r_5) \quad \gamma_6 = (\alpha_6, r_6) \quad \gamma_7 = (\alpha_4, r_7) \quad \gamma_8 = (\alpha_3, r_8)$$
$$\gamma_9 = (\alpha_1, r_9) \quad \gamma_{10} = (\alpha_2, r_{10}) \quad \gamma_{11} = (\alpha_7, r_{11}) \quad \gamma_{12} = (\alpha_4, r_{12})$$
$$\gamma_{13} = (\alpha_3, r_{13}) \quad \gamma_{14} = (\alpha_5, r_{14}) \quad \gamma_{15} = (\alpha_6, r_{15}) \quad \gamma_{16} = (\alpha_4, r_{16})$$
$$\gamma_{17} = (\alpha_2, r_{17}) \quad \gamma_{18} = (\alpha_6, r_{18}) \quad \gamma_{19} = (\alpha_1, r_{19}) \quad \gamma_{20} = (\alpha_2, r_{20})$$
$$\gamma_{21} = (\alpha_7, r_{21}) \quad \gamma_{22} = (\alpha_1, r_{22}) \quad \gamma_{23} = (\alpha_6, r_{23})$$

where

$$r_1 = r_9 = r_{19} = r_{22} = v_i = 0.025, \qquad r_2 = r_{10} = r_{20} = r_{17} = k_d \times C = 0.0001,$$

$$r_3 = r_{13} = \frac{V_1 * C}{K_c + C} \frac{M'}{(K_1 + M')} = 0.23, \quad r_4 = r_7 = r_{12} = r_{16} = \frac{V_2 \times M}{(K_2 + M)} = 2.66,$$

$$r_5 = r_{14} = \frac{V_3 \times M \times X'}{(K_3 + X')} = 0.117, \qquad r_6 = r_{15} = r_{23} = r_{18} = \frac{V_4 \times X}{(K_4 + X)} = 2.66,$$

$$r_{11} = r_{21} = \frac{V_d \times C \times X}{(K_d + C)} = 0.00086$$

The states and transitions of the CTMC correspond directly to those of the SLTS with the exception of the case when there are multiple transitions between the same two states. In this example we have only two transitions in the CTMC whose rate is the sum of the rates of two single transitions in the SLTS. In the graph above these cases correspond to the degradation of cyclin, that can happen both with and without the protease. In the CTMC the rate associated with the transition between the states $(1,0,1,0,1)$ and $(0,0,1,0,1)$ and between $(1,1,0,0,1)$ and $(0,1,0,0,1)$ is given by the sum of the rates of the two degradation reactions $k_d \times M_C + \dfrac{V_d \times C \times X}{(K_d + C)} = 0.00096\ \mu M.min^{-1}$. The rates associated with the other transitions are the ones contained in the labels γ_i above.

ODEs. The stoichiometry matrix D associated with the Bio-PEPA system above is

	R1	R2	R3	R4	R5	R6	R7	
C	+1	-1	0	0	0	0	-1	x_C
M'	0	0	-1	+1	0	0	0	$x_{M'}$
M	0	0	+1	-1	0	0	0	x_M
X'	0	0	0	0	-1	+1	0	$x_{X'}$
X	0	0	0	0	+1	-1	0	x_X

The vector that contains the kinetic laws is:

$$v_{KL}^T = \left(v_i \times 1, k_d \times x_C, \frac{V_1 \times x_C}{K_c + x_C}\frac{x_{M'}}{(K_1 + x_{M'})}, \frac{V_2 \times x_M}{(K_2 + x_M)}, \frac{V_3 \times x_M \times x_{X'}}{(K_3 + x_{X'})}, \right.$$

$$\left. \frac{V_4 \times x_X}{(K_4 + x_X)}, \frac{V_d \times x_C \times x_X}{(K_d + x_C)} \right)$$

where "T" indicates the transpose of the vector. The system of ODEs is obtained as $\frac{d\bar{x}}{dt} = D \times v_{KL}$, with $\bar{x}^T := (x_C, x_{M'}, x_M, x_{X'}, x_X)$, the vector of the species variables:

$$\frac{dx_C}{dt} = v_i \times 1 - k_d \times x_C - \frac{V_d \times x_C \times x_X}{(K_d + x_C)};$$

$$\frac{dx_{M'}}{dt} = -\frac{V_1 \times x_C}{K_c + x_C} \times \frac{x_{M'}}{(K_1 + x_{M'})} + \frac{V_2 \times x_M}{(K_2 + x_M)};$$

$$\frac{dx_M}{dt} = \frac{V_1 \times x_C}{K_c + x_C} \times \frac{x_{M'}}{(K_1 + x_{M'})} - \frac{V_2 \times x_M}{(K_2 + x_M)};$$

$$\frac{dx_{X'}}{dt} = -\frac{V_3 \times x_M \times x_{X'}}{(K_3 + x_{X'})} + \frac{V_4 \times x_X}{(K_4 + x_X)};$$

$$\frac{dx_X}{dt} = \frac{V_3 \times x_M \times x_{X'}}{(K_3 + x_{X'})} - \frac{V_4 \times x_X}{(K_4 + x_X)};$$

The initial conditions are the ones reported in the set $\mathcal{N}$. It is worth noting that the system is equivalent, after some arithmetic manipulations, to the ODE model presented in [37]. The analysis of the model using ODEs is reported in Figure 8. The graphs coincide with results in the original paper.

PRISM. The full translation of the model into PRISM is reported in the Appendix A. The number of levels, the maximum concentrations and the parameters used in the kinetic laws are expressed using global constants. For each species a module is constructed. The module representing the cyclin is:

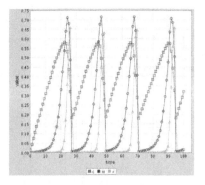 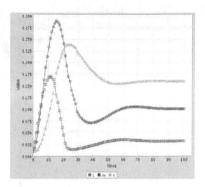

Fig. 4. ODE simulation results for two different instantiations of the model. The two instantiations differ only in the values of the Michaelis-Menten constants. For K_i $i = 1, 2, 3, 4$ we have that $K_i = 0.02$ μM for the graph on the left and $K_i = 40$ μM for the graph on the right. The initial concentrations are those reported in the Goldbeter's original paper: 0.01 μM for C, X and M. The simulation time is 100 minutes. In first instantiation of the model, depicted in the figure on the left, we have sustained oscillations whereas in the second, depicted in the figure on the right, we have no oscillations.

> **module cyclin**
> $cyclin : [0..Nc]$ **init** 0;
> $[creationC]\ cyclin < Nc \rightarrow (cyclin' = cyclin + 1);$
> $[degradationC]\ cyclin > 0 \rightarrow (cyclin' = cyclin - 1);$
> $[activationM]\ cyclin > 0 \rightarrow (cyclin' = cyclin);$
> $[degradationCX]\ cyclin > 0 \rightarrow (cyclin' = cyclin - 1);$
> **endmodule**

The variable cyclin is *local* and represents the species "cyclin". The possible values are $[0..Nc]$ (where Nc is the maximum level for cyclin) and the initial value is set to 0. Cyclin is involved in four different reactions represented by four commands. The name in the square brackets denotes the reaction. The *guards* are defined according to whether cyclin is a reactant, product or modifier of the reaction (this can be derived from the Bio-PEPA specification of the model). The rate associated with each command is "1" with the exception of the command in the module describing the functional rates. The functional rates are defined in a specific module.

Extension of the Model with a Control Mechanism Based on Inhibition. The authors of [34] proposed an extension of Goldbeter's model in order to represent a control mechanism for the cell division cycle (CDC). Their approach is based on the introduction of a protein that binds to and inhibits one of the proteins involved in the CDC. This influences the initiation and the conclusion of cell division and modulates the frequency of oscillations. Their approach is based on the basic biochemical network of the CDC oscillations and not on the details of the model so that it may work for other models of this kind. One possible extension for Goldbeter's model is reported in Figure 5.

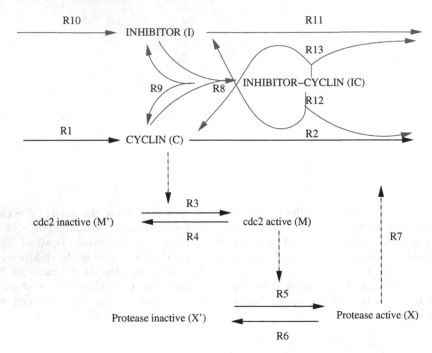

Fig. 5. Extension of the Goldbeter's model. An inhibitor is added.

Generally speaking, given a general CDC model with l proteins $U_1, U_2, ..., U_l$, Gardner *et al.* show that the ODE model is modified in the following way (see [34] for details):

$$\frac{dU_1}{dt} = f_1(U_1, U_2, \cdots, U_l) - a_1 \times U_1 \times Y + (a_2 + \theta \times d_1);$$

$$\frac{dU_2}{dt} = f_2(U_1, U_2, \cdots, U_l);$$

$$\vdots$$

$$\frac{dU_l}{dt} = f_l(U_1, U_2, \cdots, U_l);$$

$$\frac{dY}{dt} = v_s - d_1 \times Y - a_1 \times U_1 \times Y + (a_2 + \theta \times k_d) \times Z;$$

$$\frac{dZ}{dt} = a_1 \times U_1 \times Y - (a_2 + \theta \times d_1 + \theta \times k_d) \times Z;$$

where:

- $f_i(U_1, U_2, ...)$ with $i = 1, 2, ..., l$ are the functions of the standard model;
- U_1 is the concentration of the target protein of the inhibitor, Y is the inhibitor and Z denotes the concentration of the inhibition-target complex. $U_2, ..., U_l$ are the other proteins involved in the cycle;
- a_1 and a_2 are the constant rates for the binding and for the release;

- v_s and d_1 are the rate for the inhibitor synthesis and degradation;
- $\theta < 1$ is the fraction of the degradation rates for the complex Z.

In the following we show how to modify the Bio-PEPA system in order to capture the new reactions and species. Bio-PEPA offers a *compositional approach*: it is possible to compose the whole system by defining the simple subcomponents that compose it. As observed in Section 1, compositionality is one of the main properties of process algebras, that makes them particularly useful for capturing of complex models. In our example, the new reactions and species can indeed be added in a straightforward way, with minor modifications of the system specification. Broadly speaking, we need to define components for the new species, some new terms to describe the new reactions and new functional rates. Finally, the new components are added to the system component.

Here we consider $l = 3$, $U_1 = C$, $U_2 = M$ and $U_3 = X$. The inhibition-target complex Z is thus IC in this case. This complex may dissociate in three distinct ways ($R9, R12$ and $R13$ in Figure 5) since each of I and C may be degraded during the dissociation. Note that we could obtain modulation of CDC frequency by using an inhibitor of any of the proteins, so alternative models could be formed with $U_1 = M$ or $U_1 = X$.

We need to extend the Bio-PEPA model in the following way:

$$C \stackrel{def}{=} \cdots + (\alpha_8, 1){\downarrow}C + (\alpha_9, 1){\uparrow}C + (\alpha_{12}, 1){\uparrow}C;$$

$$\vdots \quad \vdots$$

$$Res \stackrel{def}{=} \cdots + (\alpha_{11}, 1) \odot Res;$$

$$CF \stackrel{def}{=} \cdots + (\alpha_{10}, 1) \odot CF;$$

$$I \stackrel{def}{=} (\alpha_8, 1){\downarrow}I + (\alpha_9, 1){\uparrow}I + (\alpha_{10}, 1){\uparrow}I + (\alpha_{11}, 1){\downarrow}I + (\alpha_{13}, 1){\uparrow}I;$$

$$IC \stackrel{def}{=} (\alpha_8, 1){\uparrow}IC + (\alpha_9, 1){\downarrow}IC + (\alpha_{12}, 1){\downarrow}IC + (\alpha_{13}, 1){\downarrow}IC;$$

where I stands for the inhibitor and IC for the inhibitor-cyclin complex in Figure 5. The new functional rates, all described by mass-action kinetics:

$$\begin{aligned}
f_{\alpha_8} &= v_s; & f_{\alpha_9} &= fMA(d_1); & f_{\alpha_{10}} &= fMA(a_1); \\
f_{\alpha_{11}} &= fMA(a_2); & f_{\alpha_{12}} &= fMA(\theta \times d_1); & f_{\alpha_{13}} &= fMA(\theta \times k_d)
\end{aligned}$$

The list of parameters must also be extended to reflect the new elements. Finally the Bio-PEPA model is:

$$C(l_{0C}) \underset{\{\alpha_3\}}{\bowtie} M(l_{0M}) \underset{\{\alpha_3,\alpha_4\}}{\bowtie} M'(l_{0M'}) \underset{\{\alpha_5,\alpha_7\}}{\bowtie} X(l_{0X}) \underset{\{\alpha_5,\alpha_6\}}{\bowtie} X'(l_{0X'})$$

$$\underset{\{\alpha_2\}}{\bowtie} Res(0) \underset{\{\alpha_1\}}{\bowtie} CF(1) \underset{\{\alpha_8,\alpha_9,\alpha_{10},\alpha_{11}\}}{\bowtie} I(l_{0I}) \underset{\{\alpha_8,\alpha_9,\alpha_{12},\alpha_{13}\}}{\bowtie} IC(l_{0IC})$$

The results of the ODE simulations corresponding to the new model are reported in Fig. 6.

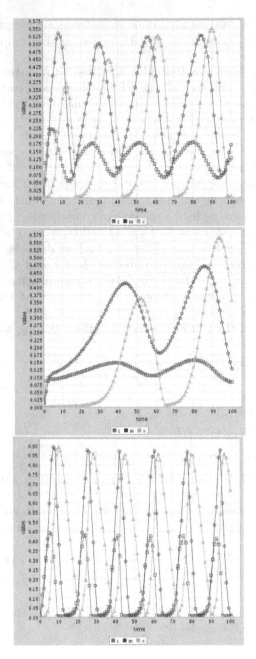

Fig. 6. ODE simulation results for the extended model. The parameters of Goldbeter's model are as before. For the new parameters, in all the graphs $d_1 = 0.05$, $\theta = 0.1$ and $K_{diss} = \frac{a_1}{a_2} = 1$. The top graph corresponds to $a_1 = a_2 = 0.3$ and $v_s = 0.6$, the middle graph to $a_1 = a_2 = 0.7$ and $v_s = 1.4$ and the lower graph to $a_1 = a_2 = 0.05$ and $v_s = 0.1$. The initial values of C, X, M and I are $0.01\mu M$. Simulation time is 100 minutes.

4.2   The Repressilator

The *repressilator* is a synthetic genetic regulatory network with oscillating behaviour reported in [33]. The repressilator consists of three genes connected in
a *feedback loop*, such that the transcription of a gene is inhibited by one of the
other proteins. In the following we present the translation of the original model
into Bio-PEPA and we report some analysis results.

The Biological Model. A schema of network is reported in Figure 7.

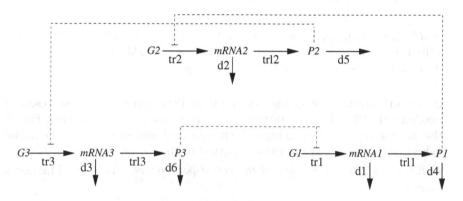

Fig. 7. Repressilator model

The species involved are:

-   Three kinds of genes, hereafter denoted *G1, G2, G3*. These represent the
    genes *lacl, tetR* and *cI*, respectively.
-   The mRNAs transcribed from the three genes, hereafter denoted *mRNA1,
    mRNA2, mRNA3,* respectively.
-   The proteins corresponding to the three genes, denoted *P1, P2, P3,* respec-
    tively. These represent the proteins associated with the previous genes i.e.
    Lacl, TetR, CI.

The reactions are:

-   The *transcription* of the three mRNAs with inhibition by one of the proteins.
    These reactions are indicated as *tr1, tr2, tr3*. The genes are constant and
    are kept implicit;
-   The *translation* of mRNAs into the proteins, indicated as *trl1, trl2, trl3*;
-   *Degradation* of both mRNAs and proteins, indicated as d_i with $i = 1, ..., 6$.

The transcription reactions are described by Hill kinetics, while the other reactions have mass-action kinetic laws.

The Bio-PEPA System. The definition of the Bio-PEPA corresponding to the repressilator model is reported below. The parameters and the initial concentrations are one of the possibilities defined in the paper [33].

- *Definition of compartments.* There are no compartments defined explicitly in the model. We consider the default compartment:

$$v_{Cell} : 1;$$

- *Definition of the set $\mathcal{N}$* It is defined as:

$$mRNA1 : 1, 1, 0, \_, v_{Cell}; \; mRNA2 : 1, 1, 0, \_, v_{Cell}; \; mRNA3 : 1, 1, 0, \_, v_{Cell};$$
$$P1 : 1, 1, 5, \_, v_{Cell}; \qquad P2 : 1, 1, 0, \_, v_{Cell}; \qquad P3 : 1, 1, 15, \_, v_{Cell};$$
$$Res : 1, 1, \_, \_, v_{Cell}; \qquad CF : 1, 1, \_, \_, v_{Cell};$$

It is worth noting that in the original model the genes are not represented explicitly. In Bio-PEPA we introduce CF to define the transcription. For all the species we consider two levels (*high* and *low*) and step $h = 1$. The initial values (third elements) are those reported in the paper.

- *Definition of the set $\mathcal{F}_R$ and of the set of parameters.* The set of functional rates is:

$$f_{tr1} = fI((\alpha, \alpha 0), P3, 2) = \frac{\alpha}{1 + P3^2} + \alpha 0;$$
$$f_{tr2} = fI((\alpha, \alpha 0), P1, 2) = \frac{\alpha}{1 + P1^2} + \alpha 0;$$
$$f_{tr3} = fI((\alpha, \alpha 0), P2, 2) = \frac{\alpha}{1 + P2^2} + \alpha 0;$$
$$f_{trl1} = fMA(\beta);$$
$$f_{trl2} = fMA(\beta);$$
$$f_{trl3} = fMA(\beta);$$
$$f_{di} = fMA(1) \; i = 1, 2, 3, 4, 5, 6;$$

All the three repressors have same behaviour except for their DNA-binding specificities. We assume that all the degradation reactions have rate 1. The other parameters are: $\alpha = 250; \quad \alpha 0 = 0; \quad \beta = 5.$

These parameters have the following meaning:

- $\alpha 0$ is the number of protein copies per cell produced from a given promoter type during growth in the presence of saturing amounts of the repressor. In the case of the absence of the repressor this number is $\alpha 0 + \alpha$;
- β is the ratio of the protein decay rate to the mRNA decay rate.

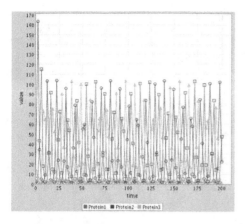 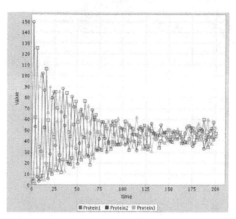

Fig. 8. Analysis of the model: ODE solution is depicted on the left and stochastic simulation results (averaged over 100 runs) are depicted on the right. The parameters are as reported in the text.

- *Definition of the species components.* The species components are:

$$mRNA1 \stackrel{def}{=} (d1,1){\downarrow}mRNA1 + (tr1,1){\uparrow}mRNA1 + (trl1,1) \oplus mRNA1;$$
$$mRNA2 \stackrel{def}{=} (d2,1){\downarrow}mRNA2 + (tr2,1){\uparrow}mRNA2 + (trl2,1) \oplus mRNA2;$$
$$mRNA3 \stackrel{def}{=} (d3,1){\downarrow}mRNA3 + (tr3,1){\uparrow}mRNA3 + (trl3,1) \oplus mRNA3;$$
$$P1 \stackrel{def}{=} (d4,1){\downarrow}P1 + (trl1,1){\uparrow}P1 + (tr3,1) \ominus P1;$$
$$P2 \stackrel{def}{=} (d5,1){\downarrow}P2 + (trl2,1){\uparrow}P2 + (tr1,1) \ominus P2;$$
$$P3 \stackrel{def}{=} (d6,1){\downarrow}P3 + (trl3,1){\uparrow}P3 + (tr2,1) \ominus P3;$$
$$CF \stackrel{def}{=} (tr1,1) \odot CF + (tr2,1) \odot CF + (tr3,1) \odot CF;$$
$$Res \stackrel{def}{=} (d1,1) \odot Res + (d2,1) \odot Res + (d3,1) \odot Res$$
$$+ (d4,1) \odot Res + (d5,1) \odot Res + (d6,1) \odot Res;$$

- *Definition of the model component.* The model is defined as:

$$\left(\left(\left(\left(\left((M1(l_{M10}) <> M2(l_{M20})) \bowtie M3(l_{M30})\right) \underset{\{trl1,tr3\}}{\bowtie} P1(l_{P10})\right) \underset{\{trl2,tr1\}}{\bowtie} P2(l_{P20})\right) \underset{\{trl3,tr2\}}{\bowtie}\right.$$
$$\left.P3(l_{P30})\right) \underset{\{tr1,tr2,tr3\}}{\bowtie} CF(1)\right) \underset{\{d1,d2,d3,d4,d5,d6\}}{\bowtie} Res(0)$$

The initial levels are defined according to the initial values of the model.

Analysis. We consider analysis based on both ODEs and stochastic simulation. The analysis results are reported in Figures 8 and 9. In Figure 8 we have used the parameters reported in the original paper. On the left, the ODE simulation results are reported. An oscillating behaviour is shown by all three proteins. On the right the results of stochastic simulation, averaged over 100 runs, are

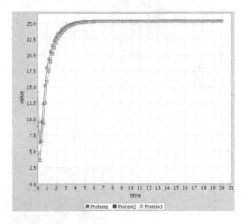 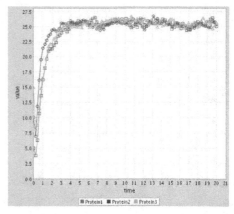

Fig. 9. Analysis of the model: as previously the ODE solution is depicted on the left and the stochastic simulation results (averaged over 100 runs) are depicted on the right. In this case the parameters differ from those reported in the text: $\alpha 0$ is 25 and the initial values are $P1 = 5$, $P2 = 10$ and $P3 = 15$.

reported. In this case the average oscillating behaviour becomes weaker after some time. This is probably due to the slight difference in phase in the 100 runs so that the averaged behaviour no longer shows oscillatory behaviour after some time. Note that varying the values of α and β for the different elements we obtain different amplitudes for the oscillations. In the case of Figure 9, the three proteins reach a steady state, with both ODE and stochastic simulation.

5   Conclusions and Future Perspectives

In this chapter we have introduced systems biology modelling based on process algebra, particularly focussing on Bio-PEPA. This new formalism is a modification of the process algebra PEPA and is designed specifically for the modelling and the analysis of biochemical networks. Bio-PEPA allows explicit representation of some features of biochemical networks, such as stoichiometry and general kinetic laws which are not readily captured in other process algebra based formalisms. Thus not only elementary reactions with constant rates, but also complex reactions described by general kinetic laws can be considered. Each reaction in the model is associated with an action type and a functional rate. The potential to consider various kinds of kinetic laws permits us to model a vast number of biochemical networks. Indeed complex reactions are frequently found in biologists' models as abstractions of sequences of elementary steps and reducing these to elementary reactions is often undesirable, or even impossible.

Some notions of equivalence have been developed for Bio-PEPA and we have shown how these may be used to compare models. In particular we presented definitions of isomorphism and strong bisimulation which are similar to the relations defined for PEPA in [42]. These equivalences are motivated by the semantics of the language, in that they are standard notions of equivalence in process algebra, and turn out to be quite strict with respect to the biological systems. In future work we intend to investigate alternative forms of equivalence, motivated more by the biological domain with the aim of finding equivalences which may be used to manipulate and simplify models.

A principal feature of Bio-PEPA is the possibility of mapping the system to different kinds of analysis. A single system description may be interpreted in a number of ways, giving rise to ODEs for a population view of the system, a stochastic simulation for an individuals-based view of the system, or a CTMC with levels for a more abstract view of the system. Of course stochastic simulation is also a CTMC-based representation of the system but the focus on individual molecules means that such a CTMC is only amenable to analysis by simulation. The advantage of the CTMC with levels is that it may have a state space small enough to be tackled by numerical analysis, meaning that a different set of analysis techniques may be used. In particular the numerical solution of a CTMC captures all possible behaviours of the model, whereas each run of a simulation only captures one trajectory through the state space, i.e. one possible behaviour.

Currently, a tool for the analysis of biochemical networks using Bio-PEPA is under implementation and a translation from SBML into Bio-PEPA is planned.

References

1. Arkin, A.P., Rao, C.V.: Stochastic chemical kinetics and the quasi-steady-state assumption: application to the Gillespie algorithm. Journal of Chemical Physics 11, 4999–5010 (2003)
2. Aziz, A., Kanwal, K., Singhal, V., Brayton, V.: Verifying continuous time Markov chains. Proc. 8th International Conference on Computer Aided Verification (CAV 1996). In: Alur, R., Henzinger, T.A. (eds.) CAV 1996. LNCS, vol. 1102, pp. 269–276. Springer, Heidelberg (1996)
3. van Bakel, S., Kahn, I., Vigliotti, M., Heath, J.: Modelling intracellular fate of FGF receptors with Bio-Ambients. In: Sixth Workshop on Quantitative Aspects of Programming Languages (QAPL 2008). Electronic Notes in Theoretical Computer Science (to appear, 2008)
4. Bernardo, M., Gorrieri, R., Donatiello, L.: MPA: A Stochastic Process Algebra. Technical report UBLCS-94-10, Laboratory of Computer Science, University of Bologna (1994)
5. Bernardo, M., Gorrieri, R.: A tutorial on EMPA: a theory of concurrent processes with nondeterminism, priorities, probabilities and time. Theoretical Computer Science 202, 1–54 (1998)
6. The BIOSPI Project, http://www.wisdom.weizmann.ac.il/~biospi/
7. Bornstein, B.J., Doyle, J.C., Finney, A., Funahashi, A., Hucka, M., Keating, S.M., Kitano, H., Kovitz, B.L., Matthews, J., Shapiro, B.E., Schilstra, M.J.: Evolving a Lingua Franca and Associated Software Infrastructure for Computational Systems Biology: The Systems Biology Markup Language (SBML) Project. Systems Biology 1, 41–53 (2004)
8. BioModels Database, http://www.ebi.ac.uk/biomodels/
9. Bortolussi, L., Policriti, A.: Modeling Biological Systems in Stochastic Concurrent Constraint Programming. In: Proc. of WCB 2006 (2006)

10. Brodo, L., Degano, P., Priami, C.: A Stochastic Semantics for Bio-Ambients. In: Malyshkin, V.E. (ed.) PaCT 2007. LNCS, vol. 4671, pp. 22–34. Springer, Heidelberg (2007)
11. Bundschuh, R., Hayot, F., Jayaprakash, C.: Fluctuations and Slow Variables in Genetic Networks. Biophys. J. 84, 1606–1615 (2003)
12. Busi, N., Zandron, C.: Modeling and analysis of biological processes by membrane calculi and systems. In: Proc. of the Winter Simulation Conference (WSC 2006) (2006)
13. Calder, M., Gilmore, S., Hillston, J.: Automatically deriving ODEs from process algebra models of signalling pathways. In: Proc. of CMSB 2005, pp. 204–215 (2005)
14. Calder, M., Gilmore, S., Hillston, J.: Modelling the influence of RKIP on the ERK signalling pathway using the stochastic process algebra PEPA. In: Priami, C., Ingólfsdóttir, A., Mishra, B., Riis Nielson, H. (eds.) Transactions on Computational Systems Biology VII. LNCS (LNBI), vol. 4230, pp. 1–23. Springer, Heidelberg (2006)
15. Calder, M., Duguid, A., Gilmore, S., Hillston, J.: Stronger computational modelling of signalling pathways using both continuous and discrete-space methods. In: Priami, C. (ed.) CMSB 2006. LNCS (LNBI), vol. 4210, pp. 63–77. Springer, Heidelberg (2006)
16. Calder, M., Vyshemirsky, V., Gilbert, D., Orton, R.: Analysis of Signalling Pathways using Continuous Time Markov Chains. In: Priami, C., Plotkin, G. (eds.) Transactions on Computational Systems Biology VI. LNCS (LNBI), vol. 4220, pp. 44–67. Springer, Heidelberg (2006)
17. Cao, Y., Gillespie, D.T., Petzold, L.: Accelerated Stochastic Simulation of the Stiff Enzyme-Substrate Reaction. J. Chem. Phys. 123(14), 144917–144929 (2005)
18. Cardelli, L.: Brane Calculi - Interactions of Biological Membranes. In: Danos, V., Schachter, V. (eds.) CMSB 2004. LNCS (LNBI), vol. 3082, pp. 257–278. Springer, Heidelberg (2005)
19. Cardelli, L., Panina, E.M., Regev, A., Shapiro, E., Silverman, W.: BioAmbients: An Abstraction for Biological Compartments. Theoretical Computer Science 325(1), 141–167 (2004)
20. Chabrier-Rivier, N., Fages, F., Soliman, S.: Modelling and querying interaction networks in the biochemical abstract machine BIOCHAM. Journal of Biological Physics and Chemistry 4, 64–73 (2004)
21. Chiarugi, D., Degano, P., Marangoni, R.: A Computational Approach to the Functional Screening of Genomes. PLOS Comput. Biol. 9, 1801–1806 (2007)
22. Ciocchetta, F., Hillston, J.: Bio-PEPA: an extension of the process algebra PEPA for biochemical networks. In: Proc. of FBTC 2007. Electronic Notes in Theoretical Computer Science, vol. 194(3), pp. 103–117 (2008)
23. Ciocchetta, F., Hillston, J.: Bio-PEPA: a framework for the modelling and analysis of biological systems. Technical Report of the School of Informatics, University of Edinburgh, EDI-INF-RR-1231 (2008)
24. Ciocchetta, F., Priami, C.: Biological transactions for quantitative models. In: Proc. of MeCBIC 2006. Electronic Notes in Theoretical Computer Science, vol. 171(2), pp. 55–67 (2007)
25. Ciocchetta, F., Priami, C.: Beta-binders with Biological Transactions. Technical report TR-10-2006, The Microsoft Research-University of Trento Centre for Computational and Systems Biology (2006)
26. Costantin, G., Laudanna, C., Lecca, P., Priami, C., Quaglia, P., Rossi, B.: Language modeling and simulation of autoreactive lymphocytes recruitment in inflamed brain vessels. SIMULATION: Transactions of the Society for Modeling and Simulation International 80, 273–288 (2003)

27. Danos, V., Laneve, C.: Formal molecular biology. Theoretical Computer Science 325(1), 69–110 (2004)
28. Danos, V., Krivine, J.: Formal molecular biology done in CCS-R. In: Proc. of Workshop on Concurrent Models in Molecular Biology (BioConcur 2003) (2003)
29. Danos, V., Feret, J., Fontana, W., Harmer, R., Krivine, J.: Ruled-based modelling of cellular signalling. In: Caires, L., Vasconcelos, V.T. (eds.) CONCUR. LNCS, vol. 4703, Springer, Heidelberg (2007)
30. Danos, V., Feret, J., Fontana, W., Krivine, J.: Scalable simulation of cellular signalling networks. In: Shao, Z. (ed.) APLAS 2007. LNCS, vol. 4807, Springer, Heidelberg (2007)
31. Danos, V., Krivine, J.: Reversible Communicating Systems. In: Gardner, P., Yoshida, N. (eds.) CONCUR 2004. LNCS, vol. 3170, pp. 292–307. Springer, Heidelberg (2004)
32. Eichler-Jonsson, C., Gilles, E.D., Muller, G., Schoeberl, B.: Computational modeling of the dynamics of the MAP kinase cascade activated by surface and internalized EGF receptors. Nature Biotechnology 20, 370–375 (2002)
33. Elowitz, M.B., Leibler, S.: A synthetic oscillatory network of transcriptional regulators. Nature 403(6767), 335–338 (2000)
34. Gardner, T.S., Dolnik, M., Collins, J.J.: A theory for controlling cell cycle dynamics using a reversibly binding inhibitor. Proc. Nat. Acad. Sci. USA 95, 14190–14195 (1998)
35. Geisweiller, N., Hillston, J., Stenico, M.: Relating continuous and discrete PEPA models of signalling pathways. Theoretical Computer Science (to appear, 2007)
36. Gillespie, D.T.: Exact stochastic simulation of coupled chemical reactions. Journal of Physical Chemistry 81, 2340–2361 (1977)
37. Goldbeter, A.: A Minimal Cascade Model for the Mitotic Oscillator Involving Cyclin and Cdc2 kinase. Proc. Nat. Acad. Sci. 8, 9107–9111 (1991)
38. Götz, N., Herzog, U., Rettelbach, M.: TIPP—a language for timed processes and performance evaluation. Technical report 4/92, IMMD7, University of Erlangen-Nürnberg, Germany (1992)
39. Haseltine, E.L., Rawlings, J.B.: Approximate simulation of coupled fast and slow reactions for stochastic chemical kinetics. J. Chem. Phys. 117, 6959–6969 (2006)
40. Heath, J., Kwiatkowska, M., Norman, G., Parker, D., Tymchyshyn, O.: Probabilistic Model Checking of Complex Biological Pathways. Theoretical Computer Science (2007) (Special Issue on Converging Sciences: Informatics and Biology)
41. Hermanns, H.: Interactive Markov Chains. LNCS, vol. 2428. Springer, Heidelberg (2002)
42. Hillston, J.: A Compositional Approach to Performance Modelling. Cambridge University Press, Cambridge (1996)
43. Hoare, C.A.R.: Communicating sequential processes. International Series in Computer Science. Prentice Hall, Englewood Cliffs (1985)
44. Jou, C.C., Smolka, S.: Equivalences, Congruences and Complete Axiomatizations of Probabilistic Processes. In: Baeten, J.C.M., Klop, J.W. (eds.) CONCUR 1990. LNCS, vol. 458, pp. 367–383. Springer, Heidelberg (1990)
45. Kanehisa, M.: A database for post-genome analysis. Trends Genet 13, 375–376 (1997)
46. KEGG home page http://sbml.org/kegg2sbml.html.
47. Kierzek, A.M., Puchalka, J.: Bridging the gap between stochastic and deterministic regimes in the kinetic simulations of the biochemical reaction networks. BIOPHYS J 86, 1357–1372 (2004)
48. Kuttler, C., Lhoussaine, C., Niehren, J.: A Stochastic Pi Calculus for Concurrent Objects. Technical report RR-6076 INRIA (2006)

49. Kuttler, C., Niehren, J.: Gene regulation in the π-calculus: simulating cooperativity at the lambda switch. In: Priami, C., Ingólfsdóttir, A., Mishra, B., Riis Nielson, H. (eds.) Transactions on Computational Systems Biology VII. LNCS (LNBI), vol. 4230, pp. 24–55. Springer, Heidelberg (2006)

50. Lecca, P., Priami, C.: Cell Cycle control in Eukaryotes: a BioSpi model. In: Proc. of Bioconcur 2003 (2003)

51. Milner, R.: Communication and Concurrency. International Series in Computer Science. Prentice Hall, Englewood Cliffs (1989)

52. Milner, R.: Communicating and mobile systems: the π-calculus. Cambridge University Press, Cambridge (1999)

53. Moller, F., Tofts, C.: A Temporal Calculus for Communicating Systems. In: Baeten, J.C.M., Klop, J.W. (eds.) CONCUR 1990. LNCS, vol. 458, pp. 401–415. Springer, Heidelberg (1990)

54. Nicollin, X., Sifakis, J.: An Overview and Synthesis on Timed Process Algebras. In: Huizing, C., de Bakker, J.W., Rozenberg, G., de Roever, W.-P. (eds.) REX 1991. LNCS, vol. 600, pp. 526–548. Springer, Heidelberg (1992)

55. NuMSV model checker, http://nusmv.irst.itc.it

56. Le Novére, N., Bornstein, B., Broicher, A., Courtot, M., Donizelli, M., Dharuri, H., Li, L., Sauro, H., Schilstra, M., Shapiro, B., Snoep, J.L., Hucka, M.: BioModels Database: a Free, Centralized Database of Curated, Published, Quantitative Kinetic Models of Biochemical and Cellular Systems. Nucleic Acids Research 34, D689–D691 (2006)

57. Plotkin, G.D.: A Structural Approach to Operational Semantics. Technical report DAIMI FM-19, Computer Science Department, Aarhus University (1981)

58. Priami, C., Quaglia, P.: Beta-binders for biological interactions. In: Danos, V., Schachter, V. (eds.) CMSB 2004. LNCS (LNBI), vol. 3082, pp. 20–33. Springer, Heidelberg (2005)

59. Priami, C.: Stochastic π-calculus. The Computer Journal 38(6), 578–589 (1995)

60. Priami, C., Regev, A., Silverman, W., Shapiro, E.: Application of a stochastic name-passing calculus to representation and simulation of molecular processes. Information Processing Letters 80, 25–31 (2001)

61. Prism web site, http://www.prismmodelchecker.org/

62. Regev, A.: Representation and simulation of molecular pathways in the stochastic π-calculus. In: Proc. of the 2nd workshop on Computation of Biochemical Pathways and Genetic Networks (2001)

63. Regev, A., Shapiro, E.: Cells as computation. Nature 419, 343 (2002)

64. Romanel, A., Dematté, L., Priami, C.: The Beta Workbench. Technical report TR-03-2007, The Microsoft Research-University of Trento Centre for Computational and Systems Biology (2007)

65. Segel, I.H.: Enzyme Kinetics: Behaviour and Analysis of Rapid Equilibrium and Steady-State Enzyme Systems. Wiley-Interscience, New York (1993)

66. SPIM, The stochastic Pi-Machine, www.doc.ic.ac.uk/$\sim$anp/spim/

67. Strulo, B.: Process Algebra for Discrete Event Simulation. PhD Thesis, Imperial College (1993)

68. Wolkenhauer, O., Ullah, M., Kolch, W., Cho, K.H.: Modelling and Simulation of IntraCellular Dynamics: Choosing an Appropriate Framework. IEEE Transactions on NanoBioScience 3, 200–207 (2004)

69. Versari, C., Busi, N.: Efficient stochastic simulation of biological systems with multiple variable volumes. In: Proc. of FBTC 2007. Electronic Notes in Theoretical Computer Science, vol. 194(3) (2008)

A   Appendix A: PRISM Specification of the Goldbeter's Model

```
//Kind of model
stochastic

//Volume
const double cell = 1;

// Levels
const int Nc = 1;
const int Nm = 1;
const int Nx = 1;
const int Nxi = 1;
const int Nmi = 1;

//Steps
const double Hc = 0.01;
const double Hm = 0.01;
const double Hx = 0.01;
const double Hxi = 0.01;
const double Hmi = 0.01;

//Parameters
const double vi = 0.05;
const double vd = 0.025;
const double kd = 0.01;
const double Kc = 0.5;
const double V1 = 3;
const double V3 = 1;
const double Kd = 0.2;
const double V2 = 1.5;
const double V4 = 0.5;
const double K1 = 0.005;
const double K2 = 0.005;
const double K3 = 0.005;
const double K4 = 0.005;

//Modules

//module Cyclin
module cyclin
cyclin : [0..Nc] init 0;
[creationC] cyclin<Nc --> 1: (cyclin' = cyclin+1);
[degradationC] cyclin>0 --> 1: (cyclin' = cyclin-1);
[activationM] cyclin>0 --> 1: (cyclin' = cyclin);
[degradationCX] cyclin>0 --> 1:  (cyclin' = cyclin-1);
endmodule

//module kinase inactive
```

```
module kinasei
kinasei : [0..Nmi] init  1;
[activationM] kinasei>0 --> 1: (kinasei' = kinasei-1);
[deactivationM] kinasei<Nmi --> 1: (kinasei'= kinasei+1);
endmodule

//module kinase active
module kinase
kinase : [0..Nm] init 0;
[activationM] kinase<Nm --> 1: (kinase'= kinase+1);
[deactivationM] kinase>0 --> 1: (kinase' = kinase-1);
[activationX] kinase>0 --> 1: (kinase' = kinase);
endmodule

//module protease inactive
module proteasei
proteasei : [0..Nxi] init 1;
[activationX] proteasei>0 --> 1: (proteasei'= proteasei-1);
[deactivationX] proteasei<Nxi --> 1: (proteasei'= proteasei+1);
endmodule

//module protease active
module protease
protease : [0..Nx] init 0;
[activationX] protease<Nx  --> 1: (protease' = protease+1);
[deactivationX] protease>0 --> 1: (protease' = protease-1);
[degradationCX] protease>0 --> 1: (protease' = protease);
endmodule

module Functional_rates
dummy: bool init true;
[creationC] cyclin<Nc --> vi/Hc: (dummy'=dummy);
[degradationC] cyclin<Nc --> (kd*cyclin*Hc)/Hc: (dummy'=dummy);
[activationM] cyclin>0 & kinasei>0 -->
   ((cyclin*Hc*V1 )/(Kc + cyclin*Hc))*((kinasei*Hmi)/(K1+kinasei*Hmi))
   *(1/Hmi): (dummy'=dummy);
[activationX] kinase>0 & proteasei>0 -->
   (kinase*Hm*proteasei*Hxi*V3/(K3+proteasei*Hxi))*(1/Hxi):
   (dummy'=dummy);
[deactivationM] kinase>0 --> ((kinase*Hm*V2)/(K2 +kinase*Hm))*(1/Hm):
   (dummy'=dummy);
[deactivationX] protease>0 --> (protease*Hx*V4/(K4 + protease*Hx))
   *(1/Hx): (dummy'=dummy);
[degradationCX] cyclin>0 & protease>0 -->
   ((cyclin*Hc*vd *protease*Hx)/(cyclin*Hc + Kd))*(1/Hc): (dummy'=dummy);
endmodule
```

The BlenX Language: A Tutorial

L. Dematté[1,2], C. Priami[1,2], and A. Romanel[1,2]

[1] CoSBi, Trento, Italy
[2] Dipartimento di Ingegneria e Scienza dell'Informazione,
Università di Trento, Italy
{dematte,priami,romanel}@cosbi.eu

Abstract. This paper presents a new programming language, BlenX. BlenX is inspired to the process calculus Beta-binders and it is intended for modelling any system whose basic step of computation is an interaction between sub-components. The original development was thought for biological systems. Therefore this tutorial exemplifies BlenX features on biology-related systems.

1 Introduction

In recent times a large effort has been devoted to the application of computer science formal specification approaches in the realm of biological modelling, simulation and analysis. A successful strand of these activities is related to the use of process calculi: simple formalisms made up of a very limited set of operators to describe interaction-driven computations and originated from the CCS [18] and CSP [15] precursors.

Process calculi are usually based on the notion of communication described through a set of actions and reactions (complementary actions, or simply co-actions), temporally ordered. To denote such a chain of events, the action prefix operator is used, which is written as an infix dot. For instance, $a!.b?.P$ denotes a process that may offer a, then offers b, and then behaves as process P. The behaviour of the process consists of sending a signal over a channel named a ($a!$) and waiting for a reply over a channel named b ($b?$). Parallel composition (denoted by the infix operator "|", as in $P|Q$) allows the description of processes which may run independently in parallel and also synchronize on complementary actions (a send and a receive over the same channel). Communication is binary and synchronous. If we have more than one process willing to send a signal over a channel, but only one process willing to receive a signal on the same channel we will select non deterministically the pair of processes that synchronize. Since non deterministic behaviour is inherent to concurrent systems where we cannot make any assumption on the relative speed of processes, we also introduce the summation operator to specify non deterministic behaviour. The process $P + Q$ behaves either as P or as Q. The selection of an alternative discards the other forever. Note that instead parallel composition is such that the non moving process is unaffected and it is still available after the move of the other. To

M. Bernardo, P. Degano, and G. Zavattaro (Eds.): SFM 2008, LNCS 5016, pp. 313–365, 2008.

represent a deadlock situation, where the process is unable to perform any sort of action or co-action, the *nil* operator is used.

The behavior of a system is given by the ordered sequence of actions and reactions that a system can perform. Despite of its simplicity, the language contains the crucial ingredients for the description of concurrent and cooperating systems. Actions and co-actions, that are usually seen as input and output activities, can be the abstract view of any sort of complementarities. Actions could well correspond to the abstract view of requests sent by an operating system to a printer manager, or the conformational changes that take place in a receptor protein in response to its binding with the signal molecule. What is crucial to notice here is that, whichever is the level of abstraction considered, by its own nature a process algebra describes a system in terms of what its subcomponents can do rather than of what they are.

The first process calculus applied to biological problems has been the stochastic π-calculus [20] for which run-time supports that allow for the simulation of the models have implemented [19], then followed by other calculi as BioAmbients [24], Brane Calculi [2], CCS-R [4], k-calculus [3], PEPA [14]. For a general introduction to the use of process calculi in biology see [8, 23]. The experience done with the stochastic π-calculus to model biological systems shows limitations of the classical process calculi approach for life science modelling. The main drawbacks are two:

1. the modularity (encapsulation) features needed to limit complexity and for fostering scalability and incremental model building that is implemented through the restriction or scope operator;
2. key-lock mechanism of communication. Two processes can synchronize only if the share exactly the same channel name. The biological situation is quite different. In fact two molecules interact if they have a certain degree of affinity or sensitivity which usually is different from exact complementarity of their structure.

An attempt to overcome the above limits has been done through the definition of the calculus Beta-binders [21]. The novelty of this calculus is given by the introduction of *boxes* with interfaces identified by unique identifiers that express the interaction capabilities of the processes encapsulated into the boxes.

Boxes can be interpreted as *biological entities*, i.e. components that interact in a model to accomplish some biological function: proteins, enzymes, organic or inorganic compounds as well as cells or tissues. The interaction sites on boxes are called *binders*; as for biological entities, a box has an interface (its set of binders) and an internal structure that drives its behaviour (see Fig. 1). For example, when a box is used to model a protein domain, binders can be used to represent *sensing domains* and *effecting domains*. Sensing domains are the places where the protein receives signals, effecting domains are the places that a protein uses for propagating signals, and the *internal structure* codifies for the mechanism that transforms an input signal into a protein conformational change, which can result in the activation or deactivation of another domain.

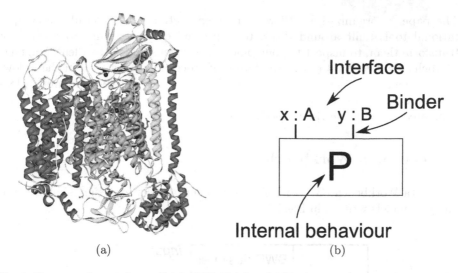

Fig. 1. Boxes as abstractions of biological entities. Active sites, or *domains*, in a protein are represented as binders on the box interface.

This is inspired by the available knowledge of protein structure and function (see for example [27]).

Signals are represented as messages exchanged over communication channels. Consider the pairs $x : A$ on a binder (see Fig. 1(b)): the binder name x is the name used by the internal process to perform input/output actions, while the binder identifier A expresses the interaction capabilities at x. When composing different boxes together, we use the binder identifier A to express the possible interactions between boxes; in other words, two boxes with binder identifiers A and C can interact only if A is *affine* to C.

Starting from this basic idea we moved from process calculi toward programming languages with run-time stochastic support. In this paper we present an introduction to the BlenX language and to its supporting modelling, analysis and visualization tools. The requirements we followed in the definition of BlenX and that now are the distinguishing features of BlenX are:

- dynamically varying interfaces of biological components;
- sensitivity-based interaction;
- one-to-one correspondence between biological components and boxes specified in the model;
- description of complexes an dynamic generation of complexes;
- spatial information;
- hybrid parameter specification;
- de-coupling of qualitative description from the quantities needed to drive execution;
- events;
- Markov chain generation;
- biochemical reactions generation.

The paper is organized as follows. The next section briefly recall the computational tools built around BlenX to write and edit programs, to execute or transform them, to inspect the outcome of executions. Since the BlenX language is stochastic, Section 3 recalls the basics of stochasticity we need in the following development. Section 4 introduces the primitives and programming ideas of BlenX. Section 5 reports some biological examples modelled in BlenX and simulated through the Beta Workbench.

2   The Beta Workbench

The Beta Workbench (BWB for short), is a set of tools to design, simulate and analyse models written in BlenX[1].

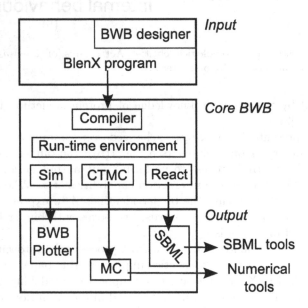

Fig. 2. The logical strucure of BWB

The core of BWB is a command-line application (core BWB) that hosts three tools: the BWB *simulator*, the BWB *CTMC generator* and the BWB *reactions generator*. These three tools share the BlenX *compiler* and the BlenX *runtime environment*. The core BWB takes as input the text files that represent a BlenX program (see Sec. 4), passes them to the *compiler* that translates these files into a runtime representation that is then stored into the *runtime environment*. The logical arrangement of the computational blocks above is depicted in Fig. 2.

The BWB *simulator* is a *stochastic simulation engine*. The *runtime environment* provides the *stochastic simulation engine* with primitives for checking the

---

[1] BWB is available at http://www.cosbi.eu/Rpty_Soft_BetaWB.php

current state of the system and for modifying it. The *stochastic simulation engine* drives the simulation handling the time evolution of the environment in a stochastic way and preserving the semantics of the language. The stochastic simulation engine implements an efficient variant of the Gillespie's algorithms described in [12, 13].

When rates are drawn from an exponential distribution (see Sec. 3) and models are finite-state, a BlenX program give rise to a continuous-time Markov process (CTMC). The BWB *CTMC generator* adds to the core blocks a set of *iterators* to exhaustively traverse the whole state space of a BlenX program. The *CTMC generator* also labels all the transitions between states with their exponential rate.

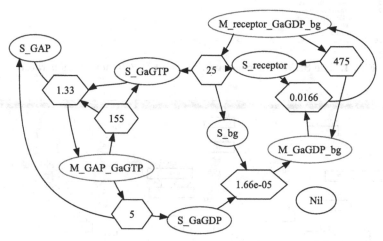

Fig. 3. The graph of all the reactions generated by the BWB Reactions generator

The BWB *reactions generator* identifies state changes that can be performed by *entities* and *complexes* generated by the execution of a BlenX program and produces a description of the system as a list of *species* and a list of chemical reactions in which species are involved. These lists are abstracted as a digraph in which nodes represent species and edges represent reactions (see Fig. 3). This graph can be reduced to avoid presence of reactions with infinite rate. The final result is an SBML description of the original BlenX program (Fig. 4).

The core BWB is enriched by two tools for input/output operations: the BWB designer and the BWB plotter.

The BWB designer is a tool that allows to write BlenX programs both in a textual and in a graphical way. The two representations are interchangeable: the tool can parse and generate the graphical representation from any valid BlenX program, and generate the textual representation from the graphical form (see the upper left and the bottom left parts of Fig. 5). In particular, it is possible to draw boxes, pi-processes, interactions, events and to form complexes using graphs (see Figures 5 and 6). The textual representation can then be used as input to the core BWB.

```
1   <?xml version="1.0" encoding="UTF-8"?>
2   <sbml xmlns="http://www.sbml.org/sbml/level1" level="1" version="1">
3     <model name="SBMLmodel">
4       <listOfSpecies>
5         <specie name="S_GAP" compartment="compartment" initialAmount="206"/>
6         <specie name="S_GaGTP" compartment="compartment" initialAmount="600"/>
7         <specie name="S_GaGDP" compartment="compartment" initialAmount="600"/>
8         <specie name="S_bg" compartment="compartment" initialAmount="1500"/>
9         <specie name="S_receptor" compartment="compartment" initialAmount="313"/>
10        <specie name="M_receptor_GaGDP_bg" compartment="compartment" initialAmount="0"/>
11        <specie name="M_GaGDP_bg" compartment="compartment" initialAmount="1100"/>
12        <specie name="M_GAP_GaGTP" compartment="compartment" initialAmount="0"/>
13      </listOfSpecies>
14      <listOfReactions>
15        <reaction name="R0" reversible="false">
16          <listOfReactants>
17            <specieReference specie="M_GAP_GaGTP"/>
18          </listOfReactants>
19          <listOfProducts>
20            <specieReference specie="S_GAP"/>
21            <specieReference specie="S_GaGTP"/>
22          </listOfProducts>
23          <kineticLaw formula="M_GAP_GaGTP * c0">
24            <listOfParameters>
25              <parameter name="c0" value="155"/>
26            </listOfParameters>
27          </kineticLaw>
28        </reaction>
29        <reaction name="R1" reversible="false">
```

Fig. 4. The SBML file generated by the BWB Reactions generator

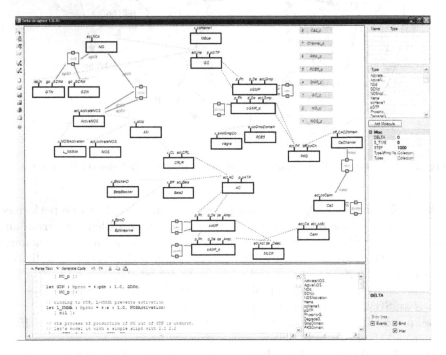

Fig. 5. The model of a complex pathway in the designer

The BWB plotter is a graphical tool that parses and display simulation outputs as changes in concentrations (Fig. 7), graphs of the reactions executed by the simulator (Fig. 8) and other views of the relations between entities and reactions. The BWB plotter provides to the user a picture of the dynamic behaviour of a simulated model and the topology of the network that originated that behaviour.

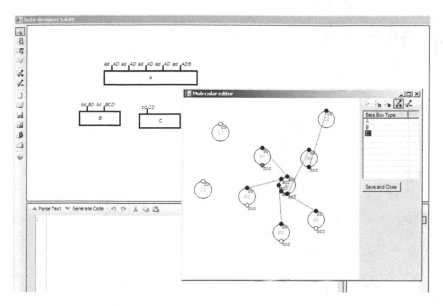

Fig. 6. Definition of a complex through the Designer interface

3 Stochastic Rates

The *stochastic approach* to chemical kinetics has been proved to be grounded on a physical base; early experimental studies (see as e.g. [26], [25]) have demonstrated that stochastic effects can be significant in cellular reactions. More recent experimental studies show the importance of noise in gene regulation:

> *The proliferation of both noise and noise reduction systems is a hallmark of organismal evolution* – Federoff et al. [6]

> *Transcription in higher eukaryotes occurs with a relatively low frequency in biologic time and is regulated in a probabilistic manner* – Hume [16]

> *Gene regulation is a noisy business* – Mcadams et al. [17]

These studies, together with the success of Monte Carlo stochastic simulation techniques in the quantum physics simulation, have ignited widespread interest in stochastic simulation techniques for biochemical networks.

The stochastic approach to chemical kinetics was first employed by Delbruck in the '40s. The basic assumptions of this approach are that a chemical reaction occurs when two (or more) molecules of the right type collide in an appropriate way, and that these collisions in a system of molecules in thermal equilibrium are *random*.

Moreover, Gillespie in [10, 11] makes some simplifying assumptions to avoid difficulties generated by the usual procedure of estimating the collision volume for each particle; he assumes that the system is in thermal equilibrium.

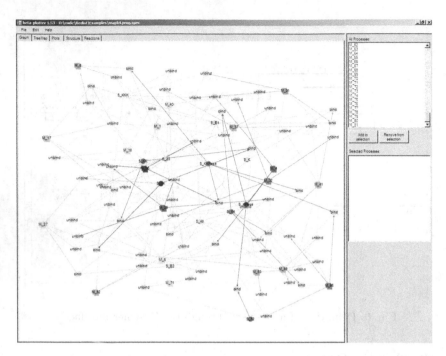

Fig. 7. The Plotter displaying the result of a simulation of the MAPK cascade with the BWB simulator

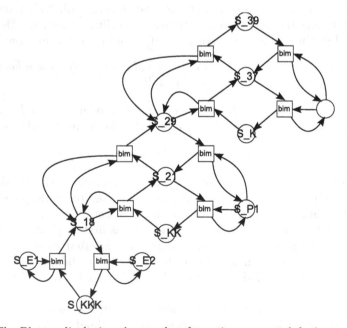

Fig. 8. The Plotter displaying the graphs of reactions executed during a simulation

This assumption means that the considered system is a well-stirred mixture of molecules. Furthermore, the assumption that the number of non-reactive collisions is much higher than the number of chemical reactions makes it possible to state that the molecules are randomly and uniformly distributed at all times.

All stochastic methods rely on these assumptions; furthermore, we can observe that biological systems can be modeled on different levels of abstraction, but models at each level follow the same pattern:

- pairs *entity type, quantity*;
- interactions between the entities.

For example, in the case of biochemical models *entities* are molecules and *interactions* are coupled chemical reactions.

Therefore we can reduce the parameters needed to describe a system to:

- the *entities*, usually referred to as *species*, present in the system $S_1, ..., S_N$;
- the number and type of *interactions*, called *reaction channels*, through which the molecules interact $R_1, ..., R_M$;
- the state vector $\mathbf{X}(t)$ of the system at time t , where $X_i(t)$ is the number of molecules of species S_i present at time t.

The state vector $\mathbf{X}(t)$ is a vector of random variables, that does not permit to track the position and velocity of the single molecules.

3.1   Base Rate and Actual Rate

For each reaction channel R_j a function a_j, called the *propensity function* for R_j, is defined as:

$$a_\mu = h_\mu c_\mu \text{ for } \mu = 1, \ldots, M \tag{1}$$

such that h_μ is the number of distinct reactant combinations for reaction R_μ and c_μ is a constant depending on physical properties of the reactants and

$$a_0 = \sum_{\mu=1}^{M} a_\mu$$

The c_μ constant is usually called *base rate*, or simply *rate* of an action, while the value of the function a_μ is called the *actual rate*.

Gillespie derives a physical correct *Chemical Master Equation* (CME) from the above representation of biochemical interactions. Intuitively, this equation shows the stochastic evolution of the system over time, which is indeed a Markov process.

Gillespie also presented in [11] an exact procedure, called *exact stochastic simulation*, to numerically simulate the stochastic time evolution of a biochemical system, thus generating one single trajectory. The procedure is based on the *reaction probability density function* $P(\tau, \mu)$, which specifies the probability that the next reaction is an R_μ reaction and that it occours at time τ. The analytical expression for $P(\tau, \mu)$ is:

$$P(\tau, \mu) = \begin{cases} a_\mu \exp(-a_0\tau) & \text{if } 0 \leq \tau < \infty \text{ and } \mu = 1, \ldots, M \\ 0 & \text{otherwise} \end{cases}$$

where a_μ is the *propensity function*.

The *reaction probability density function* is used in a stochastic framework to compute the probablility of an action to occour. The way of computing the combinations h_μ, and consequentely the *actual rate* a_μ, varies with the different kind of reactions we consider.

Rate of a *monomolecular* Reaction: the simplest kind of reactions we can encounter are first-order reactions, usually referred to as *monomolecular reactions*, that take the form:

$$S_1 \rightarrow S_2...S_n$$

In this case, the number of combinations h_μ is equal to n, where n is the number of entities (the *cardinality*) of S_1.

Rate of a *bimolecular* Reaction: second-order reactions, usually referred to as *bimolecular reactions*, take the form:

$$S_1 + S_2 \rightarrow S_3...S_n \text{ or } S_1 + S_1 \rightarrow S_2...S_n$$

The second case explicitly consider the fact that the two elements reacting are indeed of the same species, as in homodimerization reactions.

To obtain h_μ, we have to compute the number of all possible interactions that can take place between elemets of the first species and elements of the second species. Let n be the *cardinality* of the species S_1, and m the cardinality of the species S_2.

In the former case, the number of combinations h_μ is equal to $n \cdot m$, while in the latter the number of combinations h_μ is equal to $\frac{n \cdot (n-1)}{2}$.

Constant Rates: constant rates are used when the number of combinations h_μ is not meaningful; in this case $h_\mu = 1$, so the base rate constant c_μ is directly used as the exponent of the exponential distribution form which a time of execution will be sampled.

Rate Functions: the computation of the *reaction probability density function* has been proved by Gillespie to be *exact*, in the sense that a Monte Carlo simulation of the method represents a random walk that is an unbiased realization of the master equation.

However, when a specie represents a higher aggregation entity (e.g. a cell) then the input-output relation can exhibit a non-linear behaviour (e.g. sigmoidal dose-responses for signaling molecules). In this case, we let the user specify a *rate functions*, that is used in place of the Gillespie method to compute the propensity function.

Note that in this case the proof that the method, and so the algorithm, is *exact* does not hold anymore. It is up to the user that choose a rate function demonstrate that the assumptions he/she made are realistic and that the produced results are correct. We are only providing the BlenX programmer with the highest flexibility in specifying the quantitative parameters that drive the simulation engine.

4   The Language

A BlenX program is made of an optional *declaration* file for the declaration of user-defined constants and functions, a *binder definition* file that associates unique identifiers to binders of entities used by the program and a *program* file, that contains the program structure.

All the BlenX files share the syntax definition of identifiers, numbers and rates as reported below:

$$
\begin{array}{ll}
Letter & ::= [a-zA-Z] \\
Digit & ::= [0-9] \\
Exp & ::= [Ee][+]?\{Digit\} \\
real1 & ::= \{Digit\}^+\{Exp\} \\
real2 & ::= \{Digit\}^* \cdots Digit^+(\{Exp\})? \\
real3 & ::= \{Digit\}^+ \cdots Digit^*(\{Exp\})? \\
\\
Real & ::= real1 \mid real2 \mid real3 \\
Decimal & ::= \{Digit\}^+ \\
Id & ::= (\{Letter\}|\_)(\{Letter\}|\{Digit\}|\_)^* \\
\\
number & := Real \mid Decimal \\
\\
rate & := number \mid \textbf{rate} \ (\ Id\ ) \mid \textbf{inf}
\end{array}
$$

Note that in the following sections, during the description of the programming constructs, we prefix qualifying words to Id in order to clarify the kind of identifier that can occour in a given position. We will write $boxId$, $binderId$, $funcId$ and $varId$ to specify identifiers referring to boxes, binders, functions and variables respectively. Syntactically, they are all equal to Id; the disambiguation is done by the BlenX compiler using a symbol table. For examples, if an identifier Id is used in a function declaration, it will be stored as a $funcId$ in the symbol table.

4.1   The Declaration File

A declaration file is a file with *.decl* extension that contains the definition of variables, constants and functions. Since these constructs are optional, it is possible to skip the definition of the whole file. The declaration file has the following syntax:

$declarations$ ::=
    $decList$

$decList$ ::=
    dec
    | $dec\ decList$

dec ::=
    let Id : **function** $= exp$;
    | **let** Id : **var** $= exp$;
    | **let** Id : **var** $= exp$ **init** $number$;
    | **let** Id ($number$) : **var** $= exp$;
    | **let** Id : **const** $= exp$;

exp ::=
    $number$
    | Id
    | $|\ Id\ |$
    | **log** (exp)
    | **sqrt** (exp)
    | **exp** (exp)
    | **pow** (exp , exp)
    | $exp + exp$
    | $exp - exp$
    | $exp * exp$
    | $exp\ /\ exp$
    | $-exp$
    | $+exp$
    | (exp)

An *expression* is made up of operators and operands. The syntax for the expression exp and the possible algebraic operators that can be used is given in the previous table. Operator precedence follows the common rules found in every programming language. $+$ and $-$ have the precedence when used as unary operators, while $\times$ and $/$ have the precedence w.r.t. $+$ and $-$ when used as binary operators.

A *state variable* or simply *variable* is an identifier that can assume real modifiable values (Real value). The content of a variable is automatically updated when the defining expression exp changes; The content of the variable can also be changed by an **update** event (see Sec. 4.7). In this case, the function associated with the event is evaluated and the variable is updated with the resulting value. After the variable identifier and the **var** keyword, the user has to specify the expression used to control the value of the variable and an optional initial value after the **init** keyword. Examples of variable declarations follows:

```
let v1 : var = 10 * |A|;
let mCycB : var = 2 * |X| * log(v1) init 0.1;
```

In addition, we define another type of variables, called *continuous variables*. These variables depend on *time* and their value is still determined by an expression. Consider for example the following equation, commonly used to express the growth of mass in a cell-cycle model:

$$\frac{\delta m}{\delta t} = \mu \cdot m$$

This equation expresses the continuous variation of mass during time. If we discretize it we obtain:

$$\frac{\Delta m}{\Delta t} = \mu \cdot m \quad \rightarrow \quad \Delta m = \mu \cdot m \cdot \Delta t$$

To update the m variable every Δt, we can write the following expression:

$$m_{t(i)} = m_{t(i-1)} + \Delta m \quad \rightarrow \quad m_{t(i)} = m_{t(i-1)} + (\mu \cdot m \cdot \Delta t)$$

The syntax to write the previous equation, given a Δt of 0.1, is:

```
let m(0.1): var = mu * m init 0.2;
```

More generally, in a *continuous variable* declaration the user has to specify the Id of the variable, immediately followed by the Δt value. The expression after the = sign is used to compute the delta value, with Δt implicit. Therefore, the declaration `let v(t): var = exp;` corresponds to the differential equation $\frac{\delta v}{\delta t} = exp$.

A *constant* is an identifier that assumes a value that cannot be changed at run-time and specified through a constant expression (an expression that does not rely on any variable or concentration $|Id|$ to be evaluated). As an extension, BlenX allows the use of *constant expressions*. Examples of constant declarations and of constant expressions follow:

```
let c1 : const = 1.0;
let pi : const = 3.14;
let c2 : const = (2.5 + 1) / (2.5 - 1);
let c3 : const = (4.0/3.0) * pi * pow(c1, 3);
let e: const = exp(1.0);
```

In the current version of BlenX, *functions* are parameterless and always return a Real value. As is, a function is only a named expression that can be used to evaluate a rate or to update the content of a state variable. An example of function definition follows:

```
let f1 : function =
   (k5s / alpha) / (pow( (J5 / (m * alpha * |X|) ) , 4) + 1);
```

Notice that when a program contains continuous variables, then the CTMC generation is not allowed.

4.2   The Binder Definition File

The binder definition file is a file with *.types* extension that stores all the binder identifiers that can be used in the declaration of binders (see Sec. 4.4) and the affinities between binders associated with a particular identifier.

Affinities are a peculiar feature of BlenX. The interaction mechanism of many biological modelling languages is based on the notion of exact complement of communication channel names, as in computer science modelling where two programs can interact only if they know the exact address of the interacting partners. In BlenX instead interactions are guided by affinities between a pair of binder identifiers. There are three advantages in this approach: it allows us to avoid any global policy on the usage of names in order to make components interact; it relaxes the exact, or *key-lock*, style of interaction of exact name pairing; it permits a better separation of concerns, as it allows us to put interaction information in a separate file that can be modified or substituted without altering the program. The usage of affinities in a separate file is comparable to program interactions guided by *contracts* or service definitions, like in some web-service models (see [1]).

affinities   ::=
> { *binderIdList* }
> | { *binderIdList* }%%{ *affinityList* }

binderIdList :
> *binderId*
> | *binderId*, *binderIdList*

affinity   ::=
> (*binderId*, *binderId*, *rate*)
> | (*binderId*, *binderId*, *funcId*)
> | (*binderId*, *binderId*, *rate*, *rate*, *rate*)

affinityList   :=
> *affinity*
> | *affinity*, *affinityList*

An *affinity* is a tuple of three or five elements. The first two elements are binder identifiers declared in the *binderIdList*, while the other elements can either be rate values or a single function identifier. If the affinity tuple contains a single rate value, then the value is interpreted as the base rate of *inter-communication* (Sec. 4.5) between binders with identifier equal to the first and second *binderId* respectively.

If the affinity tuple contains three rate values, these values are interpreted as the base rate for *complex, decomplex* (see Sec. 4.6 for the definition of complexes) and *inter-complex communication* between binders with identifier equal to the first and second *binderId* respectively.

When the element after the two *binderId*s is a function identifier, the expression associated to the function will be evaluated to yield a value, then interpreted as the rate of *inter-communication*.

4.3   The Program File

The central part of a BlenX program is the program file. The program file has a *.prog* extension; it is generated by the following BNF grammar:

$$program ::=$$

$$info \langle\langle \ rateDec \ \rangle\rangle \ decList \ \textbf{run} \ bp$$
$$| \quad info \ decList \ \textbf{run} \ bp$$

$$info \qquad ::=$$

$$[\ \textbf{steps} = decimal\ ]$$
$$| \quad [\ \textbf{steps} = decimal, \ \textbf{delta} = number\ ]$$
$$| \quad [\ \textbf{time} = number\ ]$$

$$rateDec ::=$$

$$Id : rate$$
$$| \quad \textbf{CHANGE} : rate$$
$$| \quad \textbf{EXPOSE} : rate$$
$$| \quad \textbf{UNHIDE} : rate$$
$$| \quad \textbf{HIDE} : rate$$
$$| \quad \textbf{BASERATE} : rate$$
$$| \quad rateDec, rateDec$$

$$decList \quad ::=$$

$$dec$$
$$| \quad dec \ decList$$

$$dec \qquad ::=$$

$$\textbf{let} \ Id : \textbf{pproc} = process \ ;$$
$$| \quad \textbf{let} \ Id : \textbf{bproc} = box \ ;$$
$$| \quad \textbf{let} \ Id : \textbf{complex} = complex \ ;$$
$$| \quad \textbf{let} \ Id : \textbf{prefix} = actSeq \ ;$$
$$| \quad \textbf{let} \ Id : \textbf{bproc} = Id \ \langle\langle \ invTempList \ \rangle\rangle \ ;$$
$$| \quad \textbf{when} \ (\ cond\ ) \ verb \ ;$$
$$| \quad \textbf{template} \ Id : \textbf{pproc} \ \langle\langle \ decTempList \ \rangle\rangle = process \ ;$$
$$| \quad \textbf{template} \ Id : \textbf{bproc} \ \langle\langle \ decTempList \ \rangle\rangle = box \ ;$$

$$bp \qquad ::=$$

$$Decimal \ Id$$
$$| \quad Decimal \ Id \ \langle\langle \ invTempList \ \rangle\rangle$$
$$| \quad bp \ || \ bp$$

A *prog* file is made up of an header *info*, an optional list of rate declarations (*rateDec*), a list of declarations *decList*, the keyword **run** and a list of starting entities *bp*.

The *info* header contains information used by the BWB simulator that will execute the program. A stochastic simulation can be considered as a succession of timestamped steps that are executed sequentially, in non-decreasing time order. Thus, the duration of a simulation can be specified as a **time**, intended as the maximum timestamp value that the simulation clock will reach, or as a number of **steps** that the simulator will schedule and execute. The **delta** parameter can be optionally specified to instruct the simulator to record events only at a certain frequency (and not every time and event is simulated).

A BlenX program is a stochastic program: every single step that the program can perform has a *rate* associated to it, representing the frequency at which that step can, or is expected to, occur. The *rateDec* specifies the global rate associations for individual channel names or for four particular *classes* of actions that a program can perform. In addition, a special class **BASERATE** can be used to set a common basic rate for all the actions that do not have an explicit rate set. The explicit declaration of a rate in the definition of an *action* has the precedence on this global association (see Sec. 4.4).

The list of declarations *decList* follows. Each declaration is a small, self-contained piece of code ended by a ';'. A declaration can be named, e.g. it can have an *Id* that designates uniquely the declaration unit in the program, or it can be nameless. Declarations of boxes, processes, sequences of prefixes and complexes must be named[2], while events are *nameless*.

4.4   Processes and Boxes

Boxes are generated by the following BNF grammar:

$$
\begin{array}{ll}
box & ::= \\
 & binders \ [\ process\ ] \\[6pt]
binders & ::= \\
 & \#\ (\ Id\ :\ rate,\ Id\ ) \\
 & |\quad \#\ (\ Id,\ Id\ ) \\
 & |\quad \#\mathbf{h}\ (\ Id\ :\ rate,\ Id\ ) \\
 & |\quad \#\mathbf{h}\ (\ Id,\ Id\ ) \\
 & |\quad binders,\ binders \\[6pt]
process & ::= \\
 & par \\
 & |\quad sum
\end{array}
$$

The intuition is that a box represents an autonomous biological entity that has its own control mechanism (the *process*) and some interaction capabilities expressed by the *binders*.

A *binders* list is made up of a non empty list of *elementary binders* of the form $\#(Id : rate, Id)$ (active with rate), $\#(Id, Id)$ (active without rate), $\#\mathbf{h}(Id : rate, Id)$ (inactive with rate), $\#\mathbf{h}(Id, Id)$ (inactive without rate), where the first *Id* is the *subject* of the binder, *rate* is the stochastic parameter that quantitatively drives the activities involving the binder (hereafter, stochastic rate) and the second *Id* represents the identifier of the binder. Binder identifiers cannot occur in processes while subjects of binders can. The subject of an elementary beta binder is a binding occurrence that binds all the free occurrences of it in the process inside the box to which the binder belongs. Hidden binders

---

[2] Note that some language constructs, i.e. processes and sequences, can appear throughout a program without a name; they must be named only when they appear as a declaration.

are useful to model interaction sites that are not available for interaction although their status can vary dynamically. For instance a receptor that is hidden by the shape of a molecule and that becomes available if the molecule interacts with/binds to other molecules. Given a list of binders, we denote the set of all its subjects with *sub(binders)*. A box is considered *well-formed* if the list of binders has subjects and identifiers all distinct. Well-formedness of each box defined in a BlenX program is checked statically at compile-time. Moreover, well-formedness is preserved during the program execution. The BlenX graphical representation of a box is:

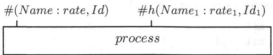

Boxes are generated by the following BNF grammar:

$$process ::=$$
$$par$$
$$|\quad sum$$

$$par \quad ::=$$
$$parElem$$
$$|\quad sum \mid sum$$
$$|\quad sum \mid par$$
$$|\quad par \mid sum$$
$$|\quad par \mid par$$
$$|\quad (\,par\,)$$

$$sum \quad ::=$$
$$sumElem$$
$$|\quad sum + sum$$
$$|\quad (\,sum\,)$$

$$sumElem ::=$$
$$\textbf{nil}$$
$$|\quad seq$$
$$|\quad \textbf{if } condexp \textbf{ then } sum \textbf{ endif}$$

$$parElem \quad ::=$$
$$Id$$
$$|\quad Id \,\langle\langle\, invTempList \,\rangle\rangle$$
$$|\quad \textbf{rep } action \,.\, process$$
$$|\quad \textbf{if } condexp \textbf{ then } par \textbf{ endif}$$

$$seq \quad ::=$$
$$action$$
$$|\quad action \,.\, process$$
$$|\quad Id \,.\, process$$

A process can be a *par* or a *sum*. The non-terminal symbol *par* composes through the binary operator | two processes that can concurrently, while the non-terminal symbol *sum* of the productions of *process* is used to introduce guarded choices of processes, composed with the operator +. The + operator act intuitively as an *or* operator, meaning that at a certain step a process offers a choice of different possible actions such that the execution of each of them eliminates the others. By the contrary, the | operator act intuitively as an *and* operator, meaning that processes composed by | run effectively in parallel.

Notice that we can put in parallel processes also with the constructs *Id* and *Id* ⟨⟨ *invTempList* ⟩⟩, meaning that we are instantiating a template (see Section 4.9) or an occurrence of a process previously defined. As an example, consider the following sequence of processes definition:

```
let p1 : pproc = nil ;
let p2 : pproc = nil | p1 ;
```

Process *p2* is defined as a parallel composition of the **nil** process and an instance of the *p1* process. In BlenX the definition of a process can only rely on identifiers of previously defined processes. Mechanisms of recursive definitions and mutual recursive definitions are not admitted.

The **rep** operator is used to replicate copies of the process passed as argument. Note that we use only guarded replication, i.e. the process argument of the **rep** must have a prefix *action* that forbids any other action of the process until it has been consumed. The **nil** process does nothing (it is a deadlocked process), while the **if-then** statement allows the user to control, through an *expression*, the execution of a *process*. The non-terminal symbol *seq* identifies an action, a process prefixed by an action and a process prefixed by an *Id*. When in a program we have a process defined using the statement *Id.process* we statically check that the *Id* corresponds to a previously defined sequence of prefixes.

4.5   Actions

The actions that a process can perform are described by the syntactic category *action*.

$$action ::=$$

$$\quad Id\,!\,(\,Id\,)$$
$$| \quad Id\,!\,()$$
$$| \quad Id\,?\,(\,Id\,)$$
$$| \quad Id\,?\,()$$
$$| \quad \textbf{delay}\,(\,rate\,)$$
$$| \quad \textbf{expose}\,(\,Id:rate\,,\,Id\,)$$
$$| \quad \textbf{hide}\,(\,Id\,)$$
$$| \quad \textbf{unhide}\,(\,Id\,)$$
$$| \quad \textbf{ch}\,(\,Id,\,Id\,)$$
$$| \quad \textbf{expose}\,(\,rate,\,Id:rate,\,Id\,)$$
$$| \quad \textbf{hide}\,(\,rate,\,Id\,)$$
$$| \quad \textbf{unhide}\,(\,rate,\,Id\,)$$
$$| \quad \textbf{ch}\,(\,rate,\,Id,\,Id\,)$$

The first four actions are common to most process calculi. The first pair of actions represent an output/send of a value on a channel, while the second pair represent the input/reception of value or a signal on a channel. The remaining actions are peculiar of the BlenX language. The definition of *free names* for processes is obtained by stipulating that $Id?(Id').process$ is a binder for Id' in *process* and that **expose**$(Id : rate, Id).process$ and **expose**$(rate, Id : rate, Id).process$ are binders for Id in *process*. The definitions of *bound names* and of *name substitution* are extended consequently. The definition of free and bound names for boxes is obtained by specifying that the set of free names of a box *binders*[*process*] is the set of free names of the *process* minus the set *sub*(*binders*) of subjects of the binders. Moreover, as usual two processes *process* and *process'* are α-equivalent if *process'* can be obtained from *process* by renaming one or more bound names in *process*, and vice versa. As usual renaming avoids name clashes, i.e. a free name never becomes bound after the renaming. More details of this definitions can be found in [22, 5].

Species: In BlenX species are defined as classes of boxes which are *structurally congruent*. The structural congruence for boxes, denoted with $\equiv$, is the smallest relation which satisfies the following laws:

- $process \equiv process'$, if *process* and *process'* are α-equivalent
- $process \mid \mathbf{nil} \equiv process$
- $process_1 \mid (process_2 \mid process_3) \equiv (process_1 \mid process_2) \mid process_3$
- $process_1 \mid process_2 \equiv process_2 \mid process_1$
- $sum \mid \mathbf{nil} \equiv sum$
- $sum_1 \mid (sum_2 \mid sum_3) \equiv (sum_1 \mid sum_2) \mid sum_3$
- $sum_1 \mid sum_2 \equiv sum_2 \mid sum_1$
- $!action.process \equiv action.(process \mid !action.process)$
- $binders[process] \equiv binders[process']$, if $process \equiv process'$
- $binders, binders'[process] \equiv binders', binders[process]$
- $\#(Id : rate, Id_1), binders[process] \equiv \#(Id' : rate', Id_1), binders[process\{^{Id'}/_{Id}\}]$
  if $Id' \notin sub(binders)$
- $\#(Id, Id_1), binders[process] \equiv \#(Id', Id_1), binders[process\{^{Id'}/_{Id}\}]$
  if $Id' \notin sub(binders)$
- $\#\mathbf{h}(Id : rate, Id_1), binders[process] \equiv \#\mathbf{h}(Id' : rate', Id_1), binders[process\{^{Id'}/_{Id}\}]$
  if $Id' \notin sub(binders)$
- $\#\mathbf{h}(Id, Id_1), binders[process] \equiv \#\mathbf{h}(Id', Id_1), binders[process\{^{Id'}/_{Id}\}]$
  if $Id' \notin sub(binders)$

Consider for example the program:

```
...
let b1 : bproc = #(x:1,A)
   [ ( x!().nil + z?(w).w!().nil ) | x!(z).nil ];
...
let b2 : bproc = #(y:1,A)
   [ y!(z).nil | ( z?(t).t!().nil + y!().nil ) ];
...
```

In the example we have $b1 \equiv b2$, hence the boxes belong to the same species. Notice that if we have multiple definition of boxes that represent the same species, then at run-time they are collected together and the species name is taken from the first definition (e.g. in the example the name of the corresponding species is $b1$). Hereafter, when we say that in a particular state of execution of a program the cardinality of a box species $b1$ is n we mean that in that state of execution the number of boxes structurally congruent to $b1$ is n.

Intra-communication: consider the following piece of code:

```
let p : pproc =
  x!(m).nil + y?(z).z?().nil + y?().nil ;

let b1 : bproc = #(x:1,A),#h(m,B)
  [ p | x?(z).z!(c).nil + x?().nil + y!().nil ];
```

Box $b1$ has a binder $\#(x : 1, A)$ and an internal process defined as a parallel composition of the *sum* process p and the *sum* process $x?(z).z!(c).nil + y!().nil$. Each *sum* composes processes guarded by input or output actions. Parallel processes that perform complementary actions on the same channel inside the same box can synchronize and eventually exchange a message, generating an *intra-communication*. In the example, several intra-communications can be performed. Indeed, each output in the first *sum* can synchronize with an input on the same channel in the other *sum*, and vice-versa. Consider the input/output pair:

```
x!(m).nil + ... | x?(z).z!(c).nil + ...
```

$x?(z)$ represents an input/reception of something that will instantiate the placeholder z over channel x, while $x!(m)$ represent an output/send of a value m over channel x. The placeholder z in the input is a binding occurrence that binds all the free occurrences of z in the scope of the prefix $x?(z)$ (in this case in $z!(c).nil$). Sometimes the channel name x is called the subject and the placeholder/value z is called the object of the prefix. The execution of the intra-communication consumes the input and output prefixes and the object m of the output flows from the process performing the output to the one performing the input:

```
nil | m!(c).nil
```

The flow of information affects the future behavior of the system because all the free occurrences bound by the input placeholder are replaced in the receiving process by the actual value sent by the output (in the example z is substituted by m). The graphical representation of the intra-communication is

$$\#(x : 1, A) \ \#(m, B) \qquad\qquad \#(x : 1, A) \ \#(m, B)$$

$$\boxed{x!(m).nil + ...|x?(z).z!(c).nil + ...} \ \rightarrow \ \boxed{nil \mid m!(c).nil}$$

If an input has no object and it is involved in a intra-communication:

```
x!(m).nil + ... | x?().nil + ...
```

then the two prefixes are consumed and no substitution is performed:

```
nil | nil
```

If an output has no object and is involved in an intra-communication:

```
... + y?(z).z?().nil + ... | ... + y!().nil + ...
```

then the two prefixes are consumed and the substitution in the process prefixed by the input is performed by using a reserved string *$emp* on which no further intra-communication is allowed.

```
$emp?().nil | nil
```

Notice that the string *$emp* cannot be generated by the regular expression defining the *Id* (see Section 4).

If object-free outputs and inputs synchronize in an intra-communication:

```
... + y?().nil + ... | ... + y!().nil + ...
```

then the two prefixes are consumed, generating the process:

```
nil | nil
```

The stochastic nature of BlenX emerges in the above examples through the rates associated to the input/output channels. In particular, if the channel is bound to a binder, the rate is specified in the binder definition; if the binder is $\#(x : 1, A)$ (or $\#h(x : 1, A)$) the rate associated to an intra-communication over channel x is 1, while if the binder is $\#(x, A)$ (or $\#h(x, A)$) the associated rate is assumed to be 0 and hence no intra-communications over channel x can happen.

If the channel is not bound to a binder, then the rate has to be defined in the global *rateDec*. In particular, if *rateDec* is:

```
<< ... , x : 2.5 , ... >>
```

the rate associated to an intra-communication over channel x is 2.5. Instead, if no specific x rate definition appears in the *rateDec* list, then the **BASERATE** definition is used. If also no **BASERATE** definition appears in the *rateDec* list, then a compile time error is generated. In the example, intra-communications over channel y need a specific definition or the **BASERATE** in the *rateDec* list.

Since to each communication channel in a box we can associate an unique rate r, then the overall propensity of performing an intra-communication on a channel x is given by the following formula:

$$r \times ((In(x) \times Out(x)) - Mix(x))$$

where $In(x)$ identifies all the enabled input on x, $Out(x)$ the enabled output on x and $Mix(x)$ all the possible combinations of input/output within the same *sum*. As an example, consider the box:

```
let b1 : bproc = #(x,A),#h(m,B)
   [ x?().nil + x!().nil + x!().nil |
      x?().nil + x!().nil + x!().nil ]
```

Let the rate associated to x be 3, the overall propensity associated to an intra-communication on the channel x is calculated using the previous formula obtaining:

$$3 \times ((2 \times 4) - 4) = 12$$

where term (2×4) represents all the combinations of input/output and the last 4 represents the combinations contained in the same *sum* and hence the ones that cannot give raise to an inter-communication.

Notice that multiplying 12 by the cardinality of the species $b1$ we obtain the overall propensity that a box of that species performs an intra-communication on channel x.

Hide: consider the following box:

```
let b1 : bproc = #(x:1,A)
  [ hide(2,x).nil + hide(x).nil ]
```

Box $b1$ can perform two *hide* actions. The execution of both actions cause the modification of the box interface hiding the binder $\#(x:1,A)$. The graphical representation of the actions is

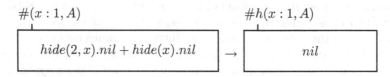

The only difference between the actions is the stochastic rate association. Indeed, the first action specifies its own rate and hence is performed with a rate of value 2. For the second action, a rate has to be defined in the global *rateDec*. In particular, if *rateDec* is:

```
<< ... , HIDE : 4 , ... >>
```

the rate associated to the all hide actions is 4. Instead, if no specific **HIDE** rate definition appears in the *rateDec* list, then the **BASERATE** definition is used. If also no **BASERATE** definition appears in the *rateDec* list, then a compile-time error is generated.

To compute the overall propensity associated to *hide* actions performed by boxes of a given species, we need to calculate all the possible combinations. This combination is obtained by multiplying the number of all the enabled hide actions $hide(r, x)$ on the same binder with the same rate r and the number of all the enabled hide actions $hide(x)$ on the same binder by the corresponding base rates. The overall propensity is then obtained by multiplying this combination with the cardinality of the species.

Notice that an hide action on an binder which is already hide is not enabled. A definition of an hide action on a name which is not a binder is not enabled and generates a compile-time warning.

Unhide: consider the following box:

```
let b1 : bproc = #h(x:1,A)
   [ unhide(2,x).nil + unhide(x).nil ]
```

Box $b1$ can perform two *unhide* actions. The execution of both actions cause the modification of the box interface unhiding the binder $\#h(x : 1, A)$. The graphical representation of the actions is

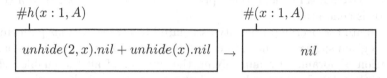

The only difference between the actions is the stochastic rate association. Indeed, the first action specifies its own rate and hence is performed with a rate of value 2. For the second action, a rate has to be defined in the global *rateDec*. In particular, if *rateDec* is:

```
<< ... , UNHIDE : 4 , ... >>
```

the rate associated to the hide action is 4. Instead, if no specific **UNHIDE** rate definition appears in the *rateDec* list, then the **BASERATE** definition is used. If also no **BASERATE** definition appears in the *rateDec* list, then a compile time error is generated.

To compute the overall propensity associated to *unhide* actions performed by boxes of a given species, we need to calculate all the possible combinations. This combination is obtained by multiplying the number of all the enabled unhide actions $unhide(r, x)$ on the same binder with the same rate r and the number of all the enabled unhide actions $unhide(x)$ on the same binder by the corresponding base rates. The overall propensity is then obtained by multiplying this combination with the cardinality of the species.

Notice that an unhide action on an binder which is already unhidden is not enabled and that a definition of an unhide action on a name which is not a binder is not enabled and generates a compile-time warning.

Change: consider the following box:

```
let b1 : bproc = #(x:1,A)
   [ ch(2,x,D).nil + ch(x,D).nil ]
```

Box $b1$ can perform two *change* actions. The execution of both actions cause the modification of the box interface changing the value A of the binder $\#(x : 1, A)$ into D. The graphical representation of the actions is

$$\#(x : 1, A)$$

$$\boxed{ch(2, x, D).nil + ch(x, D).nil} \quad \rightarrow \quad \#(x : 1, D)$$

$$\boxed{nil}$$

The first action specifies its own rate and hence is performed with a rate of value 2. For the second action, a rate has to be defined in the global *rateDec*. In particular, if *rateDec* is:

```
<< ... , CHANGE : 4 , ... >>
```

the rate associated to the hide action is 4. Instead, if no specific **CHANGE** rate definition appears in the *rateDec* list, then the **BASERATE** definition is used. If also no **BASERATE** definition appears in the *rateDec* list, then a compile time error is generated.

To compute the overall propensity associated to *change* actions performed by boxes of a given species, we need to calculate all the possible combinations. This combination is obtained by multiplying the number of all the enabled change actions $ch(r, x, D)$ on same values and the number of all the enabled change actions $ch(x, D)$ on same binders and with equal substituting types by the corresponding base rates. The overall propensity is then obtained by multiplying this combination with the cardinality of the species.

Die: consider the following box:

```
let b1 : bproc = #(x:1,A)
   [ die(2).nil ]
```

Box *b1* can perform a *die* action. The execution of the action eliminates the related box. The graphical representation of the action is

$$\#(x : 1, A)$$

$$\boxed{die(2).nil} \rightarrow \text{Nil}$$

The action is executed with the specified rate of value 2. To compute the overall propensity associated to *die* actions we calculate the number of all the enabled die actions $die(r)$ on same rates and multiply this values by the corresponding base rates and by the cardinality of the species.

Delay: consider the following box:

```
let b1 : bproc = #(x:1,A)
   [ delay(2).nil ]
```

Box *b1* can perform a *delay* action. The execution of the action allows the box to evolve internally. The graphical representation of the action is

The action is executed with the specified rate of value 2. Moreover, Nil is used to identify a deadlocked box which does nothing. To compute the overall propensity associated to $delay$ actions we calculate the number of all the enabled delay actions $delay(r)$ on same rates and multiply this values by the corresponding base rates and by the cardinality of the species.

Expose: consider the following box:

```
let b1 : bproc = #(x:1,A)
   [ expose(2,x:3,B).x!() + expose(x:3,B).x!() ]
```

Box $b1$ can perform two $expose$ actions. The execution of both actions add a new binder $\#(y : 3, B)$ to the interface, by renaming the subject into a new name to avoid clashes of names (x renamed into y with all the occurrences bound by the subject in the expose). The graphical representation of the actions is

$$\#(x : 1, A) \qquad\qquad\qquad\qquad\qquad \#(x : 1, A) \#(y : 3, B)$$

$$\boxed{expose(2, x : 3, B).x!() + expose(x : 3, B).x!()} \quad \rightarrow \quad \boxed{y!()}$$

The first action specifies its own rate and hence is performed with a rate of value 2. For the second action, a rate has to be defined in the global $rateDec$. In particular, if $rateDec$ is

```
<< ... , EXPOSE : 4 , ... >>
```

the rate associated to the hide action is 4. Instead, if no specific **EXPOSE** rate definition appears in the $rateDec$ list, then the **BASERATE** definition is used. If also no **BASERATE** definition appears in the $rateDec$ list, then a compile-time error is generated. Expose actions are considered separately and hence the overall propensity that a box species perform an expose action is calculated multiplying the rate associated to the action by the action rates and by the cardinality of the box species performing the action.

Notice that an expose action of a binder identifier which is already present in the set binders of the box is not enabled.

If-then Statement: consider the following box:

```
let b1 : bproc = #(x:1,A)
   [ if (x,unhidden) and (x,A) then x!().nil ]
```

Box $b1$ can perform the output action $x!()$ only if the conditional expression is satisfied by the actual configuration of the binders of the box containing the if-then statement. In this example if the binder with subject x is unhidden and its binder identifier is A, then the output can be executed. The general form of the conditional expressions of if-then statements are generated by the following BNF grammar:

$$condexp ::=$$
$$atom$$
$$| \quad condexp \text{ and } condexp$$
$$| \quad condexp \text{ or } condexp$$
$$| \quad \textbf{not } condexp$$
$$| \quad (\text{ } condexp \text{ })$$

$$atom \quad ::=$$
$$(\text{ } Id, \text{ } Id \text{ })$$
$$| \quad (\text{ } Id, \textbf{ hidden })$$
$$| \quad (\text{ } Id, \textbf{ unhidden })$$
$$| \quad (\text{ } Id, \textbf{ bound })$$
$$| \quad (\text{ } Id, \text{ } Id, \textbf{ hidden })$$
$$| \quad (\text{ } Id, \text{ } Id, \textbf{unhidden })$$
$$| \quad (\text{ } Id, \text{ } Id, \textbf{ bound })$$

Conditional expressions are logical formulas built atoms (conditions on binder states) connected by classical binary logical operators (and, or, not). In the atoms the first Id identifies the subject of a binder, while the second Id (if present) identifies the binder identifier. The keywords $hidden$, $unhidden$ and $bound$ identify the three states in which a binder can be. As an example, the conditional expression:

`(x,A) and ( not(y,B,hidden) or (z,bound) )`

is satisfied only if the box has a binder with subject x of type A and has a binder with subject y which is not hidden and with type different from B or has a bound binder with subject z (see Section 4.6). Notice that boxes of the form:

```
let b1 : bproc = #(x:1,A)
  [ if (y,unhidden) and (x,A) then x!().nil ]

let b1 : bproc = #(x:1,A)
  [ y?(x).if (x,unhidden) and (x,A) then x!().nil ]
```

generates compile-time warnings. Indeed, in the first case the $(y, unhidden)$ do not refer to any binder of the box, while in the second case the atom $(x, unhidden)$ is bound by the input $y?(x)$ and not by the subject of the binder. In general, at run-time atoms on binders which are not present are evaluated as false value.

Inter-communication: processes in different boxes can perform an *inter- communication* (distinct from the *intra-communication* described above) if one sends a value y over a link x that is bound to an active binder of the box $\#(x : r, A)$ and a process in another box is willing to receive a value from a *compatible* binder $\#(y : s, B)$ through the action $y!(z)$. The two corresponding binders are compatible if a *compatibility* value (i.e. a stochastic rate) greater than zero is specified in the binder declaration file

```
{...,A,...,B,...}
%%
{ ... , (A,B,2.5), ... }
```

Note that intra-communications occur on perfectly symmetric input/output pairs that share the same subject, while inter-communication can occur between primitives that have different subjects provided that their binder identifiers are compatible. This new notion of communication is particularly relevant in biology where interactions occur on the basis of sensitivity or affinity which is usually not exact complementarity of molecular structures. The same substance can interact with many other in the same context, although with different levels of affinity expressed through different properties.

The graphical representation of an inter-communication is:

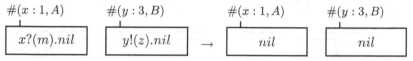

If the compatibility is specified by a stochastic rate, the overall propensity of the inter-communication is computed as bimolecular rate (see Section 3), considering all the possible combinations of inputs on channel x in the first box and outputs on y in the second box and multiplying this value with the product of the cardinality of the box species in the system. As an example consider the program:

```
...
let b1 : bproc = #(x:1,A)
  [ x!().nil + x!().nil | x!().nil ];
...
let b2 : bproc = #(y:3,B)
  [ y?().nil | y?().nil ];
...
let b3 : bproc = #(z:2,C)
  [ z?().nil ];
run 10 A || 20 B || 5 b3
```

Assuming boxes $b1$ and $b2$ defines two different species, the overall propensity of the inter-communication on boxes species A and B is

$$(2.5 \times (3 \times 2)) \times (10 \times 20)$$

where 2.5 is the basal rate, (3×2) is the number of combinations of inputs and outputs and (10×20) is the product of the cardinality of the two box species.

If the compatibility is expressed by a function defined in the declaration file:

```
{...,A,...,B,...}
%%
{ ..., (A,B,f1), ... }
```

then the overall propensity of the inter-communication is computed as a *rate function* (see Section 3) and therefore it does not depend directly on the cardinality of the involved species. In the example, if the function $f1$ is as:

```
...
let f1 : function = 2 * pow(|b3|,2);
...
```

the overall propensity of the inter-communication has value 50.

Notice that in an inter-communication, values corresponding to binder subjects cannot be sent.

4.6   Complexes

A complex is a graph-like structure where boxes are nodes and dedicated communication bindings are edges. Figure 9 report an example is reported, where $b_0 = \#(x : r_0, A_0)$ and $b_1 = \#(y : r_1, A_1)$. In BlenX, complexes are not defined

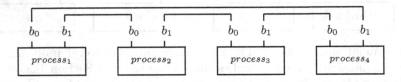

Fig. 9. Example of complex

as *species*, but as graph-like structures of box species. Complexes can be created automatically during the program execution or they can be instantiated also in the initial program. A complex can be defined using the following BNF grammar:

complex	::=	
		{ (*edgeList*) ; *nodeList* }
edgeList	::=	
		edge
	|	*edge, edgeList*
edge	::=	
		(*Id, Id, Id, Id*)
nodeList	::=	
		node
	|	*node nodeList*
node	::=	
		Id : *Id* = (*complBinderList*) ;
	|	*Id* = *Id* ;
complBinderList	::=	
		Id
	|	*Id, complBinderList*

A complex is created by specifying the list of edges (*edgeList*) and the list of nodes (*nodeList*). Each *edge* is a composition of 4 *Ids*. The first and the third identifiers represent node names, while the others represent subject names. Each *node* in the *nodeList* associates to a node name the corresponding box name and specifies the subjects of the bound binders. As an example, consider the program:

```
...
let b1 : bproc = #(x:r0,A0),#(y:r1,A1)
  [ x!().nil ];
...
let b2 : bproc = #(x:r0,A0),#(y:r1,A1)
  [ y!().nil ];
...
let C : complex =
{
  (
    (Box0,y,Box1,x),(Box1,y,Box2,x),
    (Box2,y,Box3,x),(Box3,y,Box0,x)
  );
  Box0:b1=(x,y);
  Box1:b2=(x,y);
  Box2=Box0;
  Box3=Box1;
}
...
```

The complex C defines a complex with a structure equivalent to the one reported in Figure 9. A complex can also be generated automatically at run-time thorough a set of primitives for complexation and decomplexation. The ability of two boxes to form and break complexes is defined in the bind declaration file by specifying for pairs of binder identifiers triples of stochastic rates:

```
{...,A,...,B,...}
%%
{ ..., (A,B,1.5,2.5,10), ... }
```

Complex and *decomplex* operations create and delete dedicated communication bindings between boxes. The biological counterpart of this construct is the binding of a ligand to a receptor, or of an enzyme to a substrate through an active domain. Given two boxes with binder with identifiers A and B respectively, the *complex* operation creates, with rate 1.5, a dedicated communication binding:

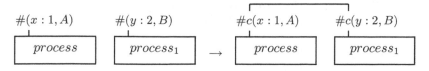

while the *decomplex* operation deletes, with rate 2.5, an already existing binding:

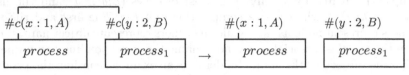

Finally, the *inter-complex communication* operation enables, with rate 10, a communication between complexed boxes through the complexed binders:

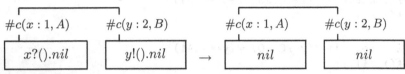

Notice that a binder in *bound* status is identified by $\#c(y : B)_s$ where c means that the corresponding box is part of a complex. It is important to underline that, although the bound status cannot be explicitly specified trough the syntax of the language and is used only as an internal representation, a binder in bound status is different from a hidden or unhidden binder and hence the structural congruence definition has to be extended accordingly:

– $\#\mathbf{c}(Id : rate, Id_1), binders[process] \equiv \#\mathbf{c}(Id' : rate', Id_1), binders[process\{^{Id'}/_{Id}\}]$
   if $Id' \notin sub(binders)$
– $\#\mathbf{c}(Id, Id_1), binders[process] \equiv \#\mathbf{c}(Id', Id_1), binders[process\{^{Id'}/_{Id}\}]$
   if $Id' \notin sub(binders)$

4.7 Events

Events specify statements, or *verbs*, to be executed with a specified rate and/or when some conditions are satisfied. A single *event* is the composition of a condition *cond* and an action *verb* (recall the syntax of declarations in Sect. 4.3).

$$dec ::=$$
$$| \quad \ldots$$
$$| \quad \mathbf{when} \; (\; cond \;) \; verb \; ;$$
$$| \quad \ldots$$

Conditions. Events are used to express actions that are enabled by global conditions, expressed by *cond*. Conditions are used to trigger the execution of an event when some elements are present in the system, when a particular condition is met, with a given rate, or at a precise simulation time or simulation step.

$$cond ::=$$
$$\quad\quad entityList \; : \; EvExpr \; : \; rate$$
$$\quad | \quad entityList \; : \; EvExpr \; : \; funcId$$
$$\quad | \quad entityList \; : \; EvExpr \; :$$
$$\quad | \quad entityList \; :: \; rate$$
$$\quad | \quad entityList \; :: \; funcId$$
$$\quad | \quad : \; EvExpr \; :$$

$$entityList ::=$$
$$boxId$$
$$|\quad boxId,\ entityList$$

$$EvAtom ::=$$
$$|\ Id\ | = Decimal$$
$$|\quad |\ Id\ | < Decimal$$
$$|\quad |\ Id\ | > Decimal$$
$$|\quad |\ Id\ | ! = Decimal$$
$$|\quad \textbf{time} = Real$$
$$|\quad \textbf{steps} = Decimal$$
$$|\quad stateOpList$$

$$EvExpr ::=$$
$$EvAtom$$
$$|\quad EvExpr\ \textbf{and}\ EvExpr$$
$$|\quad EvExpr\ \textbf{or}\ EvExpr$$
$$|\quad \textbf{not}\ EvExpr$$
$$|\quad (\ EvExpr\ )$$

More precisely, a condition *cond* consists of three parts: *entityList*, a list of boxes present in the system; an expression used to enable or disable the event; a *rate* or rate function, used to stochastically select and include them in the set of standard interaction-enabled actions.

EvExpr can be combined through logical operators starting from atoms; furthermore, a condition can specify both an *EvExpr* and a rate (see definition of *cond*), so that we can simultaneously address rates and conditions (e.g. on structures and concentrations of species). As an example, consider the following event:

```
when(A, B : (|A| > 2 and |B| > 2) : rate(r1)) join (C);
```

The entities involved in the event are A and B, as they appear in the *entityList*; moreover, the *EvExpr* requires the cardinality of both the species identified by boxes A and B to be greater than two, so the event will fire only when there are at least two A and two B in the system. When the condition is satisfied, the event will fire with rate $r1$.

The *EvAtoms* evaluate to the boolean values *true* and *false*, and can be used to express conditions over concentrations of species identified by an *Id* ($|\ Id\ |\ op\ Decimal$, where $op \in <, >, =, ! =$) or over simulation time or simulation steps.

A condition on *simulation time* will be satisfied as soon as the simulation clock is greater or equal to the specified time; a conditions on *simulation steps* will be satisfied as soon as the step count will exceed the number specified in the *EvAtom*. In both cases, the condition will remain *true* until the event is fired. So, events for which the only condition specified is the number of steps or the execution time are guaranteed to fire exactly once. For example, the event:

```
when(A : time = 3.0 : inf) delete;
```

will fire as soon as the simulation clock reaches 3.0, removing one A form the system.

It is important to make a remark: *Ids* that can appear in the *EvExpr* must be entities that appear in the *entityList*. The following code:

```
when(A, B : (|C| > 2) : rate(r1)) join (C);
```

will produce a compilation error. The only exception is when the *entityList* is empty (the sixth case in the BNF declaration of *cond*). In this case, the *Ids* in the expression can be chosen among all the *betaIds* or *varIds* already declared, with no restrictions.

If more complex expressions are needed (i.e. for expressing conditions on more species in the system) it is possible to use a *rate function* instead (see Sect. 4.1).

Note that the number of *Ids* specified in the *entityList* depends on the event verb that is used for the current event. See the next section for more details on this point.

Events, like all the other actions that can trigger an execution in a BlenX program, can have an associated rate. It is possible to specify both rate constants (form 1, 4 in the BNF specification of *cond*) or rate functions (form 2, 5 in the BNF specification of *cond*). The rate constants are treated differently in the case of events with or without explicit *EvExprs*. When there is no *EvExpr*, the rate is computed as a monomolecular or bimolecular rate, using the concepts introduced in Sec. 3. In the monomolecular case, the number h_μ of reactant combinations is equal to the cardinality of the species designated by the unique box in the *entityList*, in the bimolecular case the number h_μ of reactant combinations is the product of the cardinalities of the species designated by the first and second box in the *entityList*.

When a condition is present, the rate is a *constant rate* (see Sec. 3.1). This is to avoid the case in which a decimal value used in a comparison operation in a *EvAtom* can influence the rate of that action. Consider the two following pieces of code:

```
when (A : |A| > 2 : r) delete(2);
```

and

```
when (A : |A| > 10 : r) delete(2);
```

The second event will be triggered when there is an higher concentrations of boxes of species A, ten in this case. If we use the monomulecular way of computing the actual rate, the second event will be triggered with an higher rate than the first one, as monomolecular rates are proportional to the reactants concentration. What we intuitively expect, however, is that the two actions will take place with the same *actual rate*, hence the event rate is considered as a constant rate. Consider also the following example:

```
when (A : |A| = 0 : r) new;
```

Intuitively, this event introduces a box of species A with a given rate when there are no such entities in the system. If we compute the rate in the usual way, the event will be never executed (which is clearly different form what we expect).

For the case in which rates are specified as functions (form 2, 5 in the BNF specification of *cond*), the function is evaluated and the resulting value is used directly to compute the propensity function (see Sec. 3.1).

Verbs. Events can split an entity into two entities, join two entities into a single one, inject or remove entities into/from the system. Events are feature is essential to program perturbation of the systems triggered by particular conditions emerging during simulation and to observe how the overall behaviour is affected. An example could be the knock-out of a gene at a given time.

$$
\begin{aligned}
verb ::= \quad & \\
& \textbf{split} \ (\ boxId, \ boxId\ ) \\
| \ & \textbf{join} \ (\ boxId\ ) \\
| \ & \textbf{new} \ (\ Decimal\ ) \\
| \ & \textbf{delete} \ (\ Decimal\ ) \\
| \ & \textbf{new} \\
| \ & \textbf{delete} \\
| \ & \textbf{update} \ (\ varId, \ funcId\ )
\end{aligned}
$$

Verbs and conditions have some dependencies: not all verbs can apply to all conditions. The *entityList* in *cond* is used by the event to understand which species the event will modify; at the same time, the *verb* dictates which action will take place. Indeed, a *verb* specify how many entities will be present in the *entityList*:

- the **split** verb requires exactly one entity to be specified in the condition list;
- the **join** verb requires exactly two entities to be specified in the condition list;
- the **new** and **delete** verbs requires exactly one entities to be specified in the condition list;
- the **update** verb requires that the condition list is empty (form 6 in the BNF specification of *cond*).

The **split** verb removes one box of the specified species from the system, and substitutes it with the two other entities specified in the (*boxId, boxId*) pair. In the following piece of code:

```
when(A :: r) split(B, C);
```

One A will be substituted by one B and one C, leading to the following behaviour:

The **join** verb removes two boxes, one for each of the species specified in the list, from the system, and introduces on box of the species specified in its (*boxId*) argument:

```
when(A, B :: r) join(C);
```

One A and one B will be joined in one C, leading to the following behaviour:

$$\#(x, A) \qquad \#(x, B) \qquad \#(x, C)$$

$$\boxed{P_A} \quad \boxed{P_B} \quad \rightarrow \quad \boxed{P_C}$$

The target of the join, i.e. the box specified as argument, is optional:

```
when(A, B :: r) join;
```

If no box is specified, a new box, automatically generated form two originating boxes, will be introduced into the system:

$$\#(x, A) \qquad \#(x, B) \qquad \#(x, A) \quad \#(x, B)$$

$$\boxed{P_A} \quad \boxed{P_B} \quad \rightarrow \quad \boxed{P_A \mid P_B}$$

The new box will have as the interface the union of the interfaces of boxes A and B, and as its internal process the parallel composition of the internal processes of A and B.

The **new** and **delete** verbs introduce and remove boxes. **New** will introduce into the system one copy (in its parameterless variant) or n copies (in its second variant) of the single entity present in the event list. As for the other events, the event is triggered with a certain rate and/or with a condition expression is met. The behaviour of **delete** is complementary: it will remove one or more boxes from the system when its *cond* triggers the event. Note that in the case of **delete** a box of the species specified in the entity list must be present:

```
when(A : |A| = 0 : inf) delete;
when(A : |A| = 0 : inf) new(2);
```

The first event will never fire, while the second one will fire as soon as there are no more boxes of species A in the system. Other examples of valid events are:

```
when(A : (|A| > 1 and |A| < 10)  : inf) new(100);
when(A :: r) delete;
when(A : (|A| = 2) and (steps = 3000) : inf) delete(2);
```

This set of event will produce oscillations of the concentrations of A, by introducing some boxes when the concentrations falls under a threshold and deleting them with a *decay* of rate r, until the simulation reaches 3000 steps; after that, all *A*s are deleted from the system and no further evolution is possible.

The **update** verb is used to modify the value of a variable in the system. When the event is fired, the function *funcId* and the resulting value is assigned to the variable *varId*. Functions and variables are explained in greater detail in Sec. 4.1; here it is sufficient to know that variables are global *Ids* bound to real values, and that functions are mathematical expressions on variables and cardinality of entities that evaluate to a real value.

The condition of an **update** event has no entities in its *entityList*, and no rate or rate function in its *rate* part: the event is triggered as soon as its *EvExpr* evaluates to *true*. Jointly to an **update** event it is possible to use a particular kind of condition, based on the traversal of successive states.

$$statOpList :$$
$$stateOp$$
$$| \; stateOp, stateOpList$$

$$statOp \quad :$$
$$Id \leftarrow Real$$
$$| \; Id \rightarrow Real$$

The list of states to be traversed are expressed in a *stateOpList*; each *stateOp* element in the list expresses a condition on the quantity of an *Id* (i.e. cardinality of boxes for *boxId* or the *value* bound to a variable for *varId*).

StateOps are examined in sequence, one after the other. We say that a *stateOp* becomes *valid* when the condition on its *Id* is met for the first time. The '$\rightarrow$' operator recognizes when the quantity bound to *Id* becomes greater than the specified real value, while the '$\leftarrow$' operator recognizes when the quantity bound to *Id* becomes smaller than the specified real value.

When a *stateOp* becomes valid, the *EvExpr* passes to the evaluation of the following *stateOp* of the list. As soon as the last state in the *stateOpList* becomes valid, the *EvExpr* evaluates to *true*, so the event (update, in this case) can be fired. Once fired, the *EvExpr* restart its evaluation from the beginning of the *stateOpList*, waiting for the first *stateOp* to become valid again.

For instance, to recognize the oscillatory behaviour in Fig. 10, we can use the following piece of BlenX code:

```
let n : var = 1;
let f : function = n + 1;
...
when (: A -> 20, A <- 20 :) update (n, f);
```

This code updates the variable n, also depicted in the figure, by incrementing it at every oscillation.

The concatenation of an arbitrary succession of states allows to overcome possible limitations that are often encountered when dealing with a stochastic

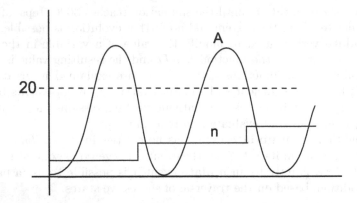

Fig. 10. The species A exhibits an oscillating behaviour, captured by a state-list condition. n is a variable that "counts" the number of oscillations.

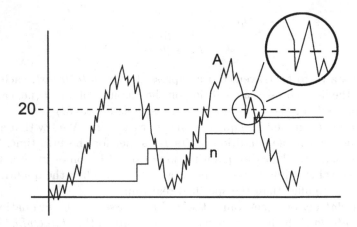

Fig. 11. The species A exhibits an oscillating behaviour, but data has some noise: the state-list condition cannot capture it and n is updated in a wrong way

approach, mainly noise. As an example, look at Fig. 11: the simple state list just introduced is not enough to capture the correct period of oscillations, as highlighted in the upper-right corner of the figure.

It is easy to solve this issues adding more states to the *stateOpList*:

```
let n : var = 1;
let f : function = n + 1;
...
when (:A -> 10, A -> 20, A <- 20, A <- 10:) update (n, f);
```

This event can capture correctly the behaviour of the noisy oscillating system, as depicted in Fig. 12.

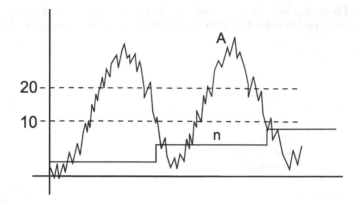

Fig. 12. The new state-list condition is able to capture the oscillations correctly

4.8   Prefixes

Prefixes are generated by the following BNF grammar:

$$dec \quad ::=$$
$$...$$
$$| \quad \textbf{let } Id : \textbf{prefix} = actSeq \; ;$$

$$actSeq ::=$$
$$action$$
$$| \quad action \, . \, prefix$$

In other words, a *prefix* is an object bound to a sequence of actions. Prefixes are used exclusively in templates (see Sec. 4.9). Templates can contain variable parts; among these parts, it is possible to specify a variable *prefix* that can be substituted with a custom sequence of actions when instantiated. An example of the usage of prefixes for easing template definitions is given in the next Section.

4.9   Templates

Templates, often referred to as *generics* or *parametric processes*, are a feature of many programming languages that allows code in an extended grammar in which code can contain variable parts that are then instantiated later by the compiler with respect to the base grammar.

In BlenX template code is *specialized* and *instantiated* at compile time using binder identifiers, code or names that are passed as template arguments. Therefore, BlenX provides a grammar for defining templates and code to instantiate and use them.

Template Declaration. It is possible to define templates for processes, boxes and sequences. The BNF for template declaration and definition is the following:

$$
\begin{array}{lll}
dec & ::= \\
& & ... \\
& \mid & \textbf{template } Id : \textbf{pproc } \langle\langle\ formList\ \rangle\rangle = piProcess\ ; \\
& \mid & \textbf{template } Id : \textbf{bproc } \langle\langle\ formList\ \rangle\rangle = betaProcess\ ; \\
form & ::= \\
& & \textbf{name } Id \\
& \mid & \textbf{pproc } Id \\
& \mid & \textbf{binder } Id \\
& \mid & \textbf{prefix } Id \\
\\
formList & ::= \\
& & form \\
& \mid & form,\ formList
\end{array}
$$

The declaration of a template **bproc** or **pproc** follows closely the declaration of their standard counterparts, with the **let** keyword substituted by **template**, and an additional list of template formal parameters enclosed by double angular parenthesis.

The template parameter *formList* is a comma-separated list of *form*s; each *form* declares a template argument made up of a keyword among name, pproc, binder, prefix followed by an Id. The Id will be added to the environment of the object being defined, acting as a placeholder for the object that will be used during parameter instantiation. For example, in the following code:

```
template P : pproc<<pproc P1, name N1, name N2, binder T1>> =
   x?().N1!().ch(N2, T1).P1;
```

we do not have to define the pproc $P1$, nor we have to insert the binder identifier $T1$ into the type file: this piece of code will compile without errors, as the process $P1$ and the binder identifier $T1$ are inserted into P's environment as template arguments. P will be treated by the compiler as pproc with four template arguments: a process, two names and a binder identifier. Note that the notion of "name" is pretty general: it can be any name appearing into the template, being it a channel name, an action argument or a binder name.

Template Instantiation. A declared template (pproc or bproc) is held by the compiler in its symbol-table in order to satisfy following *invocations* or *instantiations* of that template. Template instantiation is the compile time procedure that substitute the template formal parameters with the actual parameter with which the template object will be used. For example, the following code is a possible instantiation of the previous pproc template:

```
let NilProc : pproc = nil;
let B : bbproc  = #(z, Z)
   [ P<<NilProc, y, z, Z2>> | y?().nil ];
```

The code generate by the compiler as the result of this instantiation is equivalent to the following hand-written code:

```
let NilProc : pproc = nil;
let B : bbproc  = #(z, Z)
    [ x?().y!().ch(z, Z2).NilProc | y?().nil ];
```

More precisely, a template is instantiated by using the Id of the template (pproc or bproc) and providing it with a list *invTempList* of comma-separated template invocations *invTempElem*s, whose kind has to match the kind of the template formal parameters.

$$invTempElem ::=$$
$$Id$$
$$| \quad Id \langle\langle\ invTempList\ \rangle\rangle$$
$$| \quad (\ Id,\ \textbf{unhidden}\ )$$
$$| \quad (\ Id,\ \textbf{hidden}\ )$$

$$invTempList \ ::=$$
$$invTcmpElem$$
$$| \quad invTempElem,\ invTempList$$

$$bp \qquad\qquad ::=$$
$$\dots$$
$$| \quad Decimal \langle\langle\ invTempList\ \rangle\rangle$$

Note that templates do not increase the expressive power of the language, they only make it easier to write generic and reusable code. Consider the following code:

```
template rep : pproc<<name x, pproc P>> = !x?().(P.nil);

template detach : pproc<<name x, prefix P, binder T, name y>> =
    x?().P.ch(x, UN).hide(x).ch(x, T).unhide(x).y!().nil;
```

The first template is the general pattern of a replicating process, that performs some actions and then gets back to its original state. The second template is the general pattern of an entity that waits for a signal on a binder, responds by performing some action and then forces an unbind.

Enzymes that catalyse a reaction with a substrate and then detach from it can then be written as follows:

```
let E1p : prefix = delay(rate).p!(). ... ;
let E1p : prefix =  ... ;

let E1 : bproc = #(p, TyrDomain) =
    [ rep<<y, detach<<p, E1p, TyrDomain, y>> >> ];
let E2 : bproc = #(q, XYDomain) =
    [ rep<<r, detach<<q, E2p, XYDomain, r>> >> ];
```

The programmer has only to define the prefix that codifies for the response ($E1p$ and $E2p$), without having to worry how to write code for forcing the detachment of the substrate.

5   Examples

This section reports some classical examples inspired by biology and it shows how BlenX can easily used to model them.

5.1   Enzymatic Reactions

Most of the chemical reactions that happen in living organism are very slow, even when thermodynamically favored. The common way to speed up a reaction is to add a *catalyst* to the reaction itself; in cells, enzymes play the role of catalysts.

Enzyme - Substrate: a simplistic mechanism for the catalysis of a product P from a substrate S is the following:

$$E + S \xrightarrow{k} E + P$$

This very simple bimolecular reaction can be modelled using an *inter* communication between the box representing the enzyme E and the box representing the substrate S. Basically, the E box outputs a message through its binder, while the S box waits an input on its binder. When an input is received, S reacts by changing its structure or interface (the identifier of its binder, for example) and becomes a new species codifying for the product P:

```
[steps = 1000]
<<BASERATE:inf>>

let Enzyme : bproc = #(x,DE)
    [ rep x!().nil ];

let S : bproc = #(y,DS)
    [ y?().ch(y, DP).nil ];

run 1 Enzyme || 100 S
```

Complementary shape of molecules domains are responsible for enzymes selectivity. In our model, domains are represented as binders and their specificity is represented by the affinity between the binder identifiers DE and DS. Hence, the affinity drives the ability of the *Enzyme* to interact with the *Substrate*. We want the enzyme E to catalyse the product P with rate k, so the identifier of the binder DE on E is set to have an affinity k with the identifier DS of the binder on S:

```
{ DE, DS, DP }
%%
{ DE, DS, k }
```

where k is a Real value or *inf*.

Michaelis-Menten: the mechanism just introduced is too simplistic and do not approximate well the dynamics of enzymatic reactions. Realistically, the substrate must somehow bind to the enzyme before the enzyme can do its work:

$$E + S \underset{k_{-1}}{\overset{k_1}{\rightleftharpoons}} ES \overset{k_2}{\longrightarrow} E + P$$

where ES is an enzyme-substrate complex. This behaviour is captured by the *Michaelis-Menten kinetics*, one of the most important chemical reaction mechanisms in biochemistry used to describe the catalysis of biological chemical reactions. The most convenient derivation of the Michaelis-Menten equation is based on the *quasi steady state* approximation, where it is assumed that the concentration of the substrate-bound enzyme (and hence also the unbound enzyme) change much more slowly than those of the product and substrate.

Due to this assumption, it is possible to express the relationship between the substrate concentration and the bound and unbound enzyme concentrations in terms of the various rate constants:

$$v = \frac{v_{max}[S]}{K_m + [S]}$$

where the Michaelis constant K_m is defined as $\frac{k_{-1}+k_2}{k_1}$.

As introduced in Sec. 4.1, BleX allows programmers to define the affinity between binder identifiers using a triple of values or a function. The previous example can be easily changed to use Michaelis-Menten kinetics instead of the standard mass-action law, by changing the type file:

```
{ DE, DS, DP }
%%
{ DE, DS, f1 }
```

where $f1$ is defined in the declaration file as:

```
let VMax : const = 100;
let Km : const = 1.0;
let f1: function = VMax * (|S| / (Km + |S|));
```

Michaelis-Menten with Inhibitor: enzyme inhibitors are molecules that bind to an enzyme, blocking or decreasing enzymatic activity. Since this way of regulating the enzymatic activity is easy to obtain and can correct a metabolic imbalance, many drugs are enzyme inhibitors.

There are several possibilities for an inhibitor I to interfere with enzymatic reactions: the binding of an inhibitor can stop a substrate from entering the enzyme's active site, or alternatively hinder the enzyme from catalysing its reaction:

$$E + I \underset{k'_{-1}}{\overset{k'_1}{\rightleftharpoons}} EI$$

$$ES + I \underset{k''_{-1}}{\overset{k''_1}{\rightleftharpoons}} ES + I$$

In the second case, the inhibitor binds to the enzyme-substrate complex and alters the action of the enzyme on the substrate. The derivation of the Michaelis-Menten equation is the same as for the uninhibited mechanism except for an additional term in the expression for the total enzyme concentration and a new transient, EI. The derived equation is:

$$v = \frac{v_{max}[S]}{K_m + [S] + K_m \frac{k'_{-1}}{k'_1}[I]}$$

Note how even in this case the concentration of intermediate complexes EI and ES, along with the concentration of product P, are not present in the final equation. It is straightforward to modify our BlenX model to introduce the inhibitor, by changing the $f1$ function.

```
let ki1 : const = ... ;
let ki2 : const = ... ;
let f1 : function = (VMax * |S|)/(Km + |S| + Km * (ki1/ki2) * Ci);
```

where Ci is the constant concentration of the inhibitor I and $ki1$ and $ki2$ are the constants of dissociation and association of the enzyme E with the inhibitor I. The simulated system exhibits the dynamic behaviour of Fig. 13(a).

Enzyme with Inhibitor - Detailed Model: consider again the bio-chemical representation of an enzymatic reaction, adding a little more detail:

$$E + S \underset{K_{ES}^{-1}}{\overset{K_{ES}}{\rightleftharpoons}} ES \overset{K_{EP}}{\rightharpoonup} EP \overset{K_P}{\rightharpoonup} E + P$$

We consider every intermediate complex and conformation in this model. As before, we define boxes for the enzyme and the substrate:

```
[steps = 1000]
<< BASERATE:inf >>

let E : bproc = #(x,DE)[ rep x!().nil ];
let S : bproc = #(y,DS)[ y?().ch(y,P).nil ];

run 1 E || 100 S
```

and we set their interaction capabilities and affinities in the corresponding *type* file:

```
{ DS, DP, DE }
%%
{ (DS, DE, 1.0, 1.0, 1.0),
  (DP, DE, 0.0, 1.0, 0.0) }
```

We set the affinity between DE and DS as $(K_{ES}, K_{ES}^{-1}, K_{EP})$, as they represent respectively the rate of binding, unbinding and communication between E and S; in the same way, we define the affinity between DE and Dp as $(0, K_P, 0)$, as the enzyme E and the product P can only dissociate.

This very simple and short program is able to reproduce the desired dynamic behaviour. Let us consider an enzyme E and a substrate S in their initial configuration:

The enzyme E and the substrate S can complex together with rate K_{ES}:

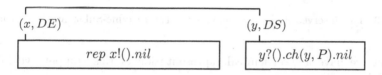

and consume an *inter-communication* through the dedicated connection. After the communication, the substrate S consume immediately the action ch because its rate is infinite[3] and the pi-process of the enzyme E is replicated. The resulting system is:

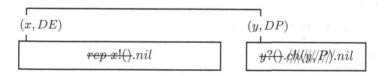

Now the two entities will decomplex with rate K_P, because of the affinity between DE and DP, by producing the two boxes:

The substrate S has been converted to the product P in the resulting system.

This representation of the enzymatic reaction mechanism is pretty accurate, as we do not make any assumption on the relative speed of each reaction. Furthermore, it is trivial to modify the system to introduce competitive inhibition.

---

[3] Since no rate is associated to the change operation, we consider the BASERATE.

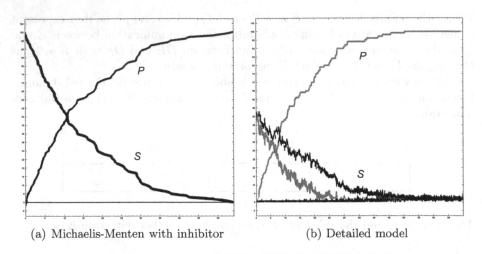

(a) Michaelis-Menten with inhibitor   (b) Detailed model

Fig. 13. The observed dynamic behaviour of the Enzyme-Substrate-Inhibitor system

Assume we have a bio-chemical representation of this competitive inhibition mechanism:

$$EI + S \overset{K_{EI}^{-1}}{\underset{K_{EI}}{\rightleftharpoons}} I + E + S \overset{K_{ES}}{\underset{K_{ES}^{-1}}{\rightleftharpoons}} ES + I \overset{K_{EP}}{\rightharpoonup} EP + I \overset{K_P}{\rightharpoonup} E + P + I$$

this mechanism can be obtained by adding to the previous **BlenX** program a box representing the inhibitor, putting it in parallel with the existing enzymes and substrates.

```
let I : bproc = #(z,DI)[ nil ];
```

```
run 10 E || 100 S || 10 I
```

We also have to update the *type* file with affinity information:

```
{ ... , DI }
%%
{ ... ,
(DE,DI,1.,1.,0.) }
```

As the affinity between DI and DE is equal to $(K_{EI}, K_{EI}^{-1}, 0)$, we have that the enzyme E can bind with the substrate S or with the inhibitor I:

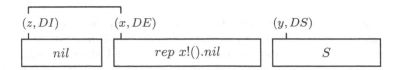

Since a binder can be complexed with only another binder at a time, the resulting behaviour is exactly the one of the competitive inhibition. The dynamics of this system are reported in Fig. 13.

It is straightforward to see how it is possible to construct and modify in a compositional way complicated scenarios in which we have multi-substrate and multi-products reactions with competitive inhibition mechanisms.

5.2   Oscillatory Behaviour

Many biological and ecological systems exhibit an oscillatory behaviour: the circadian rhythm, a roughly-24-hour cycle in the physiological processes of living beings; gene regulation networks; activator/inhibitor systems with feedback loops; Lotka-Volterra dynamics. Here we show with two simple examples how to codify these mechanisms in BlenX.

Repressilator: the *repressilator* is a synthetic genetic regulatory network, designed specifically to exhibit a stable oscillation which is reported via the expression of a protein [7]. It acts like a clock but resembles no known natural clock. The network was implemented in Escherichia coli using standard molecular biology methods, and observations were performed that verify that the engineered colonies do indeed exhibit the desired oscillatory behavior.

The repressilator consists of three genes connected in a feedback loop, such that each gene represses the next gene in the loop, and is repressed by the previous gene (see the left part of Fig. 14).

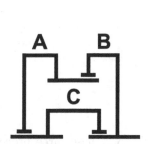
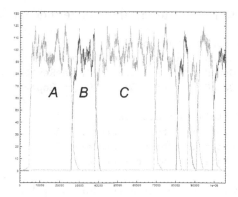

Fig. 14. Left: the structure of the *Repressilator* oscillatory network. Right: the observed time course of a stochastic simulation of the network.

The repressilator can be easily codified in BlenX using a process for each of the genes, a process for each of the proteins and events for transcription of a gene and the following production of a protein. Even better, as the high level behaviour of the three proteins and of the three genes is the same, it is possible to create a template for them

```
[steps = 20000]
<< BASERATE : inf >>

// Process definitions
let geneProc : pproc =
    delay(0.1).nil +                  //transcribe
    signal?().delay(0.0001).rec!(); //a protein attaches

let proteinProc : pproc =
    die(0.001) +              //decay (be degraded)
    signal!().rec!() ;        //attach to a gene

// Template for a recurring pproc
template repp : pproc <<pproc P>> =
    ((rep rec?().P) | P);

let geneRep : pproc = repp<<geneProc>>;
let proteinRep : pproc = repp<<proteinProc>>;

//The process that represent a transcribed strand of DNA
let nilProc : pproc = (rep rec?().geneProc);

// Genes and Proteins templates
template Gene : bproc <<binder T,pproc P>> = #(signal:inf,T)
  [ P ];
template Protein : bproc <<binder T>> = #(signal:inf,T)
  [ proteinRep ];
```

and to instantiate the appropriate code for the three copies:

```
// Genes definitions
let GeneA : bproc = Gene<<GA,geneRep>>;
let GeneB : bproc = Gene<<GB,geneRep>>;
let GeneC : bproc = Gene<<GC,geneRep>>;

// Proteins definitions
let ProteinA : bproc = Protein<<A>>;
let ProteinB : bproc = Protein<<B>>;
let ProteinC : bproc = Protein<<C>>;
```

As a commodity, we also define three boxes *ExpressN*. These three processes define species that are structurally congruent to intermediate states of *GeneN* boxes, representing "ready for transcription" states. The *ExpressN* boxes are not used in the program; they unique purpose is to capture a particular state of genes and trigger an event:

```
let ExpressA : bproc = Gene<<GA,nilProc>>;
let ExpressB : bproc = Gene<<GB,nilProc>>;
let ExpressC : bproc = Gene<<GC,nilProc>>;
```

Events can now be easily defined:

```
// Genes expressions definitions
when ( ExpressA :: inf ) split ( GeneA , ProteinA ) ;
when ( ExpressB :: inf ) split ( GeneB , ProteinB ) ;
when ( ExpressC :: inf ) split ( GeneC , ProteinC ) ;
```

The *prog* file is completed with the set-up of the initial conditions:

```
// Init
run 1 GeneA || 1 GeneB || 1 GeneC
```

The behaviour of the simulated system is the cyclical behaviour depicted on the right side of Fig. 14.

Cell-cycle: The cell cycle is a complex network of biochemical phenomena that controls the duplication of the cell. The cycle is usually subdivided into four phases (*G*1, *S*, *G*2, *M*). The transition between them is driven by cyclin-dependent protein kinases (Cdks) that, when bound to a cyclin partner, are able to make cells to progress along their cycle. A simple model of this mechanism can be obtained just by studing the hysteresis loop that derives from the fundamental antagonistic relationship between the APC (Anaphase Promotig Complex) and cyclin/Cdk dimers: APC (with two auxiliary proteins Cdc20 and Cdh1) extinguishes Cdk activity by destroying its cyclin partners, whereas cyclin/Cdk dimers inhibit APC activity by phosporylating Cdh1. This antagonism creates two stable steady states: a *G*1 state with low cyclin/Cdk activity and an high Cdh1/APC activity, and a *S*-*G*2-*M* state with the opposite configuration.

The following code represent a simplified model of this biochemical system:

```
[steps = 2000, delta = 0.2]

let X : bproc = #(x:0,X)[ nil ];
when(X :: X_synthesis) new(1);
when(X :: X_self_degradation ) delete(1);
when(X :: X_degraded_by_Y ) delete(1);

let Y : bproc = #(y:0,Y)[ nil ];
let Y_IN : bproc = #(y_in:0,Y_IN) [ nil ];
when( Y_IN :: Y_self_activation ) split(Nil, Y);
when( Y_IN :: Y_activation_with_A ) split(Nil, Y);
when( Y :: Y_deactivation ) split(Nil, Y_IN);

let A : bproc = #(a:0,A)[ nil ];
when(A :: A_synthesis ) new(1);
when(A :: A_collaborate_M_X ) new(1);
when(A :: A_self_degradation ) delete(1);

when ( : mCycB -> 0.2, mCycB <- 0.1 : ) update (m, mass_div);

run 4 X || 424 Y || 424 A
```

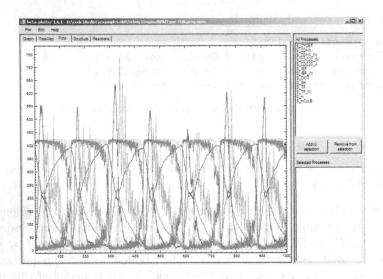

Fig. 15. The observed dynamic behaviour of the Cell-Cycle system

In this code, X and Y are representing the cyclin/Cdk dimer and the active Cdh1/APC complex respectively, and A is an activator (Cdc14) that is activated indirectly by a complex pathway that involves the activation of Cdc20.

Events are used together with functions to obtain a high-level model that is the straightforward translation of the ODE model found in biological textbooks, for example in Chapter 10 of [9]. **Split** events with rate functions are used to model Michaelis-Menten reaction kinetics, while synthesis of new compounds is modelled using **new** events and degradation using **delete** events.

The *func* file holds the constant definitions:

```
let mu  :  const = 0.005 ;
let k1  : const = 0.04;
let k2p : const  = 0.04;
let k2s : const = 1;
let J3  : const = 0.04;
let k3p : const = 1;
let k3s : const = 10;
let k4  : const = 35;
let J4  : const = 0.04;
let k5p : const = 0.005;
let k5s : const = 0.2;
let J5  : const = 0.3;
let k6  : const = 0.1;
let mstar : const = 10;
let alpha : const = 0.00236012;
let n : const = 4;
```

and also the definition of functions used by the events in the main *prog* file:

```
let m(0.1): var = mu * m * (1 - m/mstar) init 0.45;
let mass_div : function = m / 2;
let mCycB : var = m * |X| * alpha;

let X_synthesis: function = k1 / alpha ;
let X_self_degradation : function = k2p * |X|;
let X_degraded_by_Y : function = k2s * alpha * |X| * |Y|;

let Y_self_activation : function =
   (k3p * |Y_IN|) / (J3 + alpha * |Y_IN|) ;
let Y_activation_with_A : function =
   (k3s * alpha * |A| * |Y_IN|) / (J3 + alpha * |Y_IN|);
let Y_deactivation : function =
   (k4 * m * alpha * |X| * |Y|) / (J4 + alpha * |Y|);

let A_synthesis : function = k5p / alpha ;
let A_collaborate_M_X : function =
   (k5s / alpha) / (pow( (J5 / (m * alpha * |X|) ) , 4) + 1);
let A_self_degradation : function = k6 * |A|;
```

The mass is considered in our model as a time-dependent variable, which is involved in the calculations of some of the rate functions and which is driven by a specific ODE. Mass halving due to cell division is controlled by a condition on the concentration of a specific variable (e.g. mCycB, somehow related to the concentration of X); an *update* event controls the value of the mass, adjusting it whenever the concentration of mCycB cross above a threshold level and then drops below another threshold. This mechanism is described in detail in Sec. 4.7.

5.3 Self-assembly

Self-assembly is a process in which a disordered system of components forms an organized structure as a consequence of specific, local interactions among the components themselves, without an external coordination. In this example we consider a population of boxes that through complexation and decomplexation primitives and a communicating protocol organize themselves to form *binary balanced trees*. We consider a tree structure to be balanced if all the leaves in the tree are at the same depth w.r.t the root node. An initial system is a composition of boxes called *Initiators* and boxes called *Nodes*. *Initiators* start the construction of trees; they complex to *Nodes* which, after an exchange of signals at infinite rates, become *Roots* of different trees.

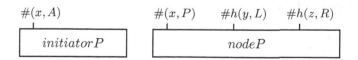

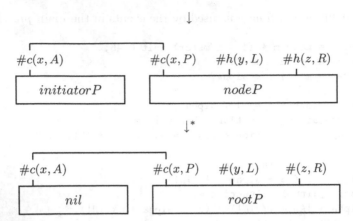

When activated, a *Root* can bind with other *Nodes* on the previously hidden binders $\#(b : L)_0$ and $\#(c : R)_0$. Now, all the *Nodes* that perform a complexation with the *Root* are activated as *Child* boxes. The internal behaviour of a *Root* is defined by the process

```
let rootP : pproc = rep y?().z?().y!(node).z!(node).nil;
```

meaning that recursively a *Root* waits for signals from all his children and then propagates to them a signal with object *node*. The internal behaviour of a *Child* is defined by the process

```
let childP : pproc = rep y?().z?().x!().x?(m).y!(m).z!(m).nil;
```

meaning that recursively a *Child* waits for signals from all his children, then sends a signal to his parent, waits for a signal from his parent and finally propagates that signal to his child. The local behaviours of *Roots* and *Child* generates, in combination with the ability of boxes to bind together, a *global* behaviour which results in the creation of binary balanced trees. In general, starting with a population of *Initiators* and *Nodes* a simulation generates populations of trees as those reported in Figure 16.

Notice that given a tree of depth level n, the depth level $n - 1$ is always complete. Moreover, notice that when the missing *Node* binds to the tree, then signals from all the *Child* nodes are propagated recursively to the *Root* which propagates the acknowledgment with subject *node* till to the leaves, which finally become *Child* and hence active. The complete code of the example is:

```
[ steps = 100 ]

<< BASERATE:inf >>

// Initiator Definition
let I : bproc = #(x,I)
  [ x?().x!(root).nil ];

// Node Definition
let rootP : pproc =
  rep y?().z?().y!(node).z!(node).nil ;
```

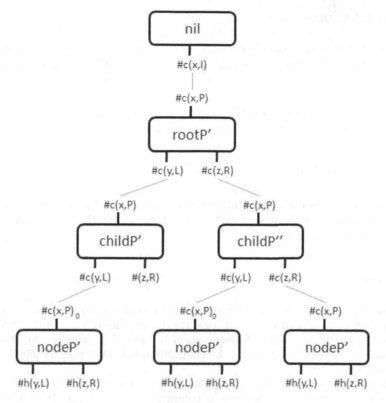

Fig. 16. Example of generated tree

```
let childP : pproc =
  rep y?().z?().x!().x?(m).y!(m).z!(m).nil ;

let nodeP : pproc =
  x!().x?(t).( t!() | (
    node?().unhide(y).unhide(z).childP +
    root?().unhide(y).unhide(z).rootP
  ) );

let Node : bproc = #(x,P),#h(y,L),#h(z,R)
  [ nodeP ];

// Init
run 2 I || 10 Node
```

where the corresponding *type* file is:

```
{P,L,R,I}
%%
{(I,P,100,0,inf),(L,P,1,0,inf),(R,P,1,0,inf)}
```

6   Conclusions

We presented the basic primitives and components of the new biology-inspired language BlenX. We then showed the usability of BlenX reporting some models of biological examples. We also briefly described the input/output supporting tools of BlenX. The BlenX environment is under further development to address relevant (biological) questions like spatial modelling and simulation as well as multi-level, multi-scale modelling of large systems.

Acknowledgments

We would like to thank Alida Palmisano for the insightful discussions and the Cell Cycle BlenX model as well as Roberto Larcher for the part regarding the BWB reaction generator.

References

1. Bravetti, M., Zavattaro, G.: Service oriented computing from a process algebraic perspective. Journal of Logic and Algebraic Programming 70(1), 3–14 (2007)
2. Cardelli, L.: Brane Calculi - Interactions of B iological Membranes. In: Danos, V., Schachter, V. (eds.) CMSB 2004. LNCS (LNBI), vol. 3082, pp. 257–278. Springer, Heidelberg (2005)
3. Danos, V., Laneve, C.: Formal molecular biology. In: TCS (2004)
4. Danos, V., Krivine, J.: Reversible communicating systems. In: Gardner, P., Yoshida, N. (eds.) CONCUR 2004. LNCS, vol. 3170, pp. 292–307. Springer, Heidelberg (2004)
5. Degano, P., Prandi, D., Priami, C., Quaglia, P.: Beta-binders for Biological Quantitative Experiments. In: Proc. of the 4th International Workshop on Quantitative Aspects of Programming Languages (QAPL 2006). ENTCS, vol. 164, pp. 101–117. Elsevier, Amsterdam (2006)
6. Elowitz, M., Levine, A., Siggia, E., Swain, P.: Stochastic gene expression in a single cell. Science 297, 1183–1186 (2002)
7. Elowitz, M.B., Leibler, S.: A synthetic oscillatory network of transcriptional regulators. Nature 403(20), 335–338 (2000)
8. Errampalli, D., Priami, C., Quaglia, P.: A formal language for computational systems biology. OMICS: A Journal of Integrative Biology 8(4), 370–380 (2004)
9. Fall, C.P., Marland, E.S., Wagner, J.M., Tyson, J.J.: Computational Cell Biology. Springer, Heidelberg (2002)
10. Gillespie, D.T.: A general method for numerically simulating the stochastic time evolution of coupled chemical reactions. The Journal of Computational Physics 22(4), 403–434 (1976)
11. Gillespie, D.T.: Exact stochastic simulation of coupled chemical reactions. The Journal of Chemical Physics 81, 2340–2361 (1977)
12. Gillespie, D.T.: A general method for numerically simulating the stochastic time evolution of coupled chemical reactions. J. Phys. Chem. 22, 403–434 (1976)
13. Gillespie, D.T.: Exact stochastic simulation of coupled chemical reactions. J. Phys. Chem. 81(25), 2340–2361 (1977)

14. Gilmore, S., Hillston, J.: The PEPA Workbench: A Tool to Support a Process Algebra-based Approach to Performance Modelling. LNCS, vol. 794, pp. 353–368. Springer, Heidelberg (1994)
15. Hoare, C.A.R.: A calculus of total correctness for communicating processes. Science of Computer Programming 1(1-2), 49–72 (1981)
16. Hume, D.: Probability in transcriptional regulation and its implications for leukocyte differentiation and inducible gene expression. Blood 96, 2323–2328 (2000)
17. McAdams, H.H.: It is a noisy business! genetic regulation at the nanomolar scale. Trends Genet 15, 65–69 (1999)
18. Milner, R.: Communication and Concurrency. Prentice-Hall, Inc., Englewood Cliffs (1989)
19. Phillips, A., Cardelli, L.: A correct abstract machine for the stochastic pi-calculus. In: Bioconcur 2004, ENTCS (August 2004)
20. Priami, C.: The stochastic π-calculus. The Computer Journal (38), 578–589 (1995)
21. Priami, C., Quaglia, P.: Beta binders for biological interactions. In: CMSB, pp. 20–33 (2004)
22. Priami, C., Quaglia, P.: Beta binders for biological interactions. In: Danos, V., Schachter, V. (eds.) CMSB 2004. LNCS (LNBI), vol. 3082, pp. 20–33. Springer, Heidelberg (2005)
23. Priami, C., Quaglia, P.: Modeling the dynamics of bio-systems. Briefings in Bioinformatics 5(3), 259–269 (2004)
24. Regev, A., Panina, E.M., Silverman, W., Cardelli, L., Shapiro, E.: Bioambients: an abstraction for biological compartments. Theor. Comput. Sci. 325(1), 141–167 (2004)
25. Ross, I., Browne, C., Hume, D.: Transcription of individual genes in eukaryotic cells occurs randomly and infrequently. In: Immunol Cell Biol. (1994)
26. Spudich, J., Koshland, D.E.J.: Non-genetic individuality: Chance in the single cell. Nature (1976)
27. Stock, A.M., Robinson, V.L., Goudreau, P.N.: Two-component signal transduction. Annu. Rev. Biochem. (69), 183–215 (2000)

Cells *in Silico*: A Holistic Approach

D. Chiarugi[1], P. Degano[2], J. B. Van Klinken[1],
and R. Marangoni[2,3]

[1] Dipartimento di Scienze Matematiche e Informatiche,
Università di Siena
[2] Dipartimento di Informatica, Università di Pisa
[3] Istituto di Biofisica - CNR, Pisa
{chiarugi3,vanklinken}@unisi.it, {degano,marangon}@di.unipi.it

Abstract. This paper reports on our experience in modelling whole cells with process calculi. We followed a holistic approach, aiming at investigating the behaviour of biological objects at the system level, in particular of a hypothetical and a of real prokaryote. These cells, namely VICE and *Escherichia coli*, have been specified through the π-calculus, endowed with a stochastic semantics. We describe a couple of variants of the π-calculus and briefly survey three interpreters of it, with increasing efficiency. We show how the usage of tools based on process calculi greatly helped us in designing the virtual cell VICE, and in comparing it with other prposals. The main properties of the *in silico* experiments on VICE and on *Escherichia coli* are then discussed and shown in agreement with those of real prokaryoptes acting *in vivo/vitro*.

1 Introduction

The outstanding improvement of wet-lab techniques have strongly influenced experimental biology in the last few years. In particular, high-throughput techniques are rapidly making available a large amount of biological data, while novel or enhanced analytical methods (e.g. NMR, MS, etc.) permit to obtain more accurate measures and to detect very small amount of substances in a single cell, e.g. the concentration of metabolites. Even though the knowledge about the structure and the components list of many living organisms are quickly growing, understanding the dynamics underlying the biological machinery is a task far from being accomplished. In other words, the knowledge we lack in the post-genomic era of biology regards the *functioning* of living organisms more than their structure.

To reconstruct the functioning of a living cell is the main goal of molecular biologists, who have embraced a holistic point of view to finalize their research. The same point of view is shared by the recent field of synthetic biology, where the main goal is to synthesise a whole organism completely *de novo*. A preliminary global design of the wanted organism is obviously mandatory, before starting its synthesis.

M. Bernardo, P. Degano, and G. Zavattaro (Eds.): SFM 2008, LNCS 5016, pp. 366–386, 2008.

In representing a cell as a whole, the crucial point is again acquiring information about the function played by its different molecular entities (genes, proteins, metabolites, etc.) and about their mutual interactions. Estabilising these relationships between biological molecules and their function however is absolutely non trivial in most of the cases. The most relevant difficulties arise in the investigation of emergent properties, that come into play only when the parts composing the whole system interact [24]. Living organisms tipically act as complex systems and so most of their relevant properties are indeed emergent. Using the words of Schrödinger: *"Life is an emergent rather than an immanent or inherent property of matter"*.

Presently, experimental wet-lab approaches are scarcely adequate to cope with this kind of global problems: even the so-called -*omic* techniques seem able to provide only some snapshots of the complete movie.

Instead, *in silico* methods are a promising alternative to address these problems at the system level. These methods offer advantages both from a practical and from a theorethical point of view. On the one hand, it is possible to use technologies less expensive and time demanding with respect to wet-lab ones. On the other hand, theorethical computer science offers challenging, new ways of looking at living matter. Indeed computer science not only provides us with algorithms to describe, store and analyze huge quantities of data, but it is also possible to interpret biological facts computationally. The best examples of this are perhaps the *"cells-as-computation"* or the *"molecules-as-computation"* approaches [31] described in more detail in Section 2.

Generally speaking, *in silico* methods consist in describing the object of interest through a formal language and in rendering this description executable. Such a formal executable model can be exercised to give rise to computer-based simulations, the results of which are then analyzed to acquire knowledge about the investigated phenomena.

Ordinary or Stochastic Differential Equations are possibly the most used such formalisms, upon which powerful *in silico* techniques have been developped, e.g. Flux Balance Analysis, Metabolic Control Analysis or Metabolic Flux Analysis (see [29,9] for a comprehensive review). These methods have been successfully used to investigate properties of biological systems [10], although they seem to be hard to compose and modify, and often require close acquaintance with them to be used efficiently.

Also process calculi offer features for describing biological systems. This kind of formal languages have been developped to specify and reason about concurrent systems, i.e. systems made of a huge number of autonomous entities, geographically distributed and capable of exchanging information through communication channels and of cooperating to achieve common goals. Biological systems clearly fit this description and can therefore be described in terms of process calculi. An advantage of these formalisms is compositionality. This feature allows the user to describe a given system simply by putting together the specifications of its sub-systems, so facilitating the study of various biological phenomena, e.g. the cross-talk among signal transduction pathways or the evolution of biochemical pathways[32]. Moreover, compositionality helps in integrating existent and new knowledge into a coherent framework. Indeed, as the information on the studied phenomenon eventually grows, the correspondent specification can be updated, by just adding the formal descriptions of the new elements. Furthermore, perturbative "what-if" experiments can be performed by acting locally, i.e. by varying the selected parameters in a single point of the description, with no need of changing the whole specification.

These characteristics helped us to realize and study large scale models of biological systems, such as whole cell specifications of ideal and real prokaryotes. In this way we have been able to investigate the properties of biological objects at the system level, following a holistic approach. This approach is particularly interesting for biologists, because each subpart of the described object can be studied when embedded in its context. Indeed, as we have verified in our experimentation, the properties exhibited by a biological entity in isolation can significantly differ if the same entity is observed when interacts with other parts of the system.

We used the π-calculus to model biological systems, actually some stochastic variants of it. In the following section we will detail some technical aspects of the calculus and in particular of the abstract machines that we have implemented to run the specifications of our virtual cells. Section 3 will present our two case studies. We shall first report on VICE, a VIrtual simplified prokaryotic CEll possessing a minimal genome, yet exhibiting those properties necessary for an organism to live. Subsequently, we shall discuss some results drawn from the formal description of the metabolic pathways of the real prokaryote *Escherichia coli*, in particular due to gene knock-out and enzyme inhibition.

2   Modelling Biological Systems with the π-Calculus

We assume the reader familiar with process calculi, so in this section we shall briefly survey how to use the π-calculus for representing the behaviour of living matter. We shall then report on our own experience with a couple of variants of the π-calculus and on the abstract machines used to run the specifications of the virtual cells we wrote using them.

We follow the already mentioned approach of "cells as computation" [31], that takes as starting point the observation that there is "a strong correspondence between the syntax of the π-calculus and the biochemical networks" and that "biologists typically characterize molecules by *what they can do*." Indeed, Regev and Shapiro realized that there is little difference between a network of autonomously computing and interacting agents, geographically dispersed, and a biological network, in particular at the bio-chemical level. E.g., a metabolic pathway has a number of reactants floating in a solution, pairs of which interact through their active sites according to reaction rules, governed by stochastic laws. Each reactant can be represented by a π-process and interaction sites by complementary communication channels. The occurrence of a reaction on a site between two reactants is then interpreted as the occurrence of a transition, that embodies the communication between the corresponding processes possessing the channel associated with that interaction site.

A delicate point concerns the stochastic behaviour of living matter, as the π-calculus has a non-deterministic semantics. To account for that, the π-calculus has been extended with a quantitative, stochastic semantics in [28], that builds upon [27]. Roughly speaking, each channel is associated with a specific rate r, the parameter of an exponential distribution related to the stochastic behaviour of the inputs and outputs along that channel. The bio-chemical counterpart of r is the *specific rate constant* (aka *microscopic rate constant*) of the described chemical reaction. Determining the rates of transitions is a very hard task — as well as finding those of the real biochemical reactions! A commonly accepted way of computing the actual rates of transitions relies on embedding in the semantics of the stochastic π-calculus the Stochastic Simulation Algorithm (SSA), proposed by Gillespie [16,15] and proved to correctly approximate the chemical master equation [17]. We refer the reader to [17] for a survey of this MonteCarlo algorithm and of some variants of it. Here we only recall that it numerically simulates the time evolution of a chemically reacting system, taking into account the randomness in chemical systems. As a matter of fact, the actual rate of a transition is computed starting from (two random numbers,) the number of the reactants/processes which could have generated the same molecular collision and the so-called basal rate b (unfortunately not easy to obtain from the kinetic constants).

Needless to say, the important point is that a computation of a network of processes can now be interpreted as a *virtual experiment* over the modelled biological system. Standard tools can then be used to statistically analyse these experiments, to perform markovian analysis on the whole stochastic behaviour, to model-check logical properties of the system, or to translate the obtained results in the more traditional continuous representations.

2.1 The Enhanced π-Calculus

Our first approach [4] to the specification of a whole cell begun with using a very expressive operational semantics of the full π-calculus, called Enhanced Operational Semantics (EOS) [7]. The main motivation was to exploit the features that EOS offers for deriving in a mechanical way various aspects of process computations. We were particularly interested in expressing *causal* dependencies between transitions, so expressing, e.g., the need of some bio-chemical reactions to occur before a selected one [6]. Also, we were unaware of Gillespie's work at that time, and we had already used EOS for deriving stochastic information and making markovian analyses on the system activities. Our approach was succesfully applied to study the performance of systems [26].

Intuitively we assigned a rate to a π-calculus transition as follows. We considered first the execution of an action on a dedicated machine that has only to perform it, and we estimated the corresponding "primary" rate r. Then, we took into account the syntactic context in which the action is placed. Indeed, the context represents the environment in which the corresponding communication occurs. The actual rate of a transition was finally given by a suitable combination of the estimate of the action performed, of the quantities of the reactants involved, and of the effects due to the operators of the context — a sort of home-made SSA.

A crucial point was determining the primary rates. As reported in sub-sections 3.1 and 3.2, we mainly investigated VICE metabolome and we found it more adequate to slightly deviate from the usage of channels to represent interaction sites. Instead, channels stood for the enzymes that catalyse a reaction. We therefore defined primary rates in agreement with some biological considerations on the kinetical and thermodynamical aspects of the described biochemical reaction, linking each reaction rate to a measurable biological parameter. In brief, for the kinetic parameters we considered the constants K_M of Michaelis-Menten [14,20]. For thermodynamical constraints, since we considered VICE at its steady-state, we could split the relevant biochemical reactions in two classes:

- *near-equilibrium* reactions, where r is close to the equilibrium constant, and the rates of a reaction and of its reverse are close; or
- *non-equilibrium* reactions, where rates of direct and reverse reactions greatly differ.

According to Metabolic Control Theory [13], the choice above reflected the *control strength* of the enzymes involved in a pathway. This quantifies the impact of the activity of an enzyme on the overall flux of a pathway: the greater the control strength, the more perturbated the flux when the enzyme is inhibited [12,13].

Due to the rich and expressive semantic machinery, the abstract machine running the EOS specification of VICE was rather inefficient. E.g., it took about 8 hours to carry on a simulation, i.e. a virtual experiment involving about 10^3 metabolites/processes and consisting of 4×10^4 reactions/transitions. Actually, most of the time was spent in mechanically deriving the rates, according to the EOS rules. Additionally, we realised that only a fragment of the π-calculus was actually needed for specifying the virtual cells of interest. A simplification was then in order.

2.2   A Simplified Calculus

Even though we firstly exploited the full π-calculus, we found it sufficient a small subset of it for specifying biochemical pathways of prokaryote-like virtual cells. This subset is very similar to the Chemical Ground Form proposed by Cardelli in [2]. Indeed, no message passing was actually needed, as synchronization suffices. Moreover, restriction ν was useless, because we were not interested in modelling intracellular compartments that prokaryotes do not possess. Additionally, we only had stochastic guarded choices. As usual, we associated each channel a, representing an enzyme, with a corresponding reaction rate, written $rate(a)$. The actual rate of a transition/reaction, is computed using Gillespie's SSA, slightly modified. Indeed, we imposed an upper bound to the rate of channels, called "top-rate," and the actual rate of a transition cannot exceed the top-rate of the involved channel. In this way, we described *saturation*, a typical feature of reactions catalysed by enzymes, like those occurring in metabolic pathways. Actually, the capability of an enzyme to catalyse a reaction grows up until it reaches its maximum value, usually known as V_{max}.

More formally, let $Chan = \{a, b, \ldots\}$ be a set of communication channels and $Hid = \{\tau_1, \tau_2, \ldots\}$ be a set of hidden, internal channels, with $Chan \cap Hid = \emptyset$. Let $rate, top\_rate : Chan \cup Hid \to \Re^+$ be the functions associating channels with their *basal* and *top-rate* respectively, with the condition:

$$\forall x \in Chan \cup Hid \qquad 0 < rate(x) \le top\_rate(x)$$

Finally, given the set of *constant names* $\{A, B, \ldots\}$, the set $\mathcal{P}$ of *processes* $P, Q, \ldots$ are defined by the following BNF-like grammar:

$$P ::= Nil \mid \pi.A \mid P|Q \mid \sum_{i \in I} \pi_i.A$$

where:

- π is a prefix of the form a, $\bar{a}$ for an input or output on a, and τ for a silent move;
- each constant A has a unique defining equation $A \triangleq P$.

As usual the operational semantic comprises the standard structural congruence $\equiv$, i.e. the minimal congruence such that both $(\mathcal{P}_{/\equiv}, +, Nil)$ and $(\mathcal{P}_{/\equiv}, |, Nil)$ are abelian monoids and $P + P \equiv P$. The inference rules defining the dynamics of our tiny calculus are in Table 1. The definition is layered: the final step only computes the actual rate $g(P, Q, r)$ of the transition P to Q through a call to the function g that implements our slight refinement of Gillespie's SSA.

Table 1. Inference rules

$$(a.A + \textstyle\sum_i P_i)|(\bar{a}.B + \textstyle\sum_j Q_j) \xrightarrow{r} A|B \qquad \text{where } r = rate(a)$$

$$\frac{P \xrightarrow{r} Q}{P|R \xrightarrow{r} Q|R} \qquad\qquad \frac{P \xrightarrow{r} Q}{A \xrightarrow{r} Q} A \triangleq P$$

$$\frac{P \xrightarrow{r} Q}{P \xRightarrow{q} Q} \qquad \text{where } q = g(P, Q, r)$$

We designed and built an abstract machine, called BEAST, that implements the operational semantics defined above [5]. Its design is rather classical, and has been greatly inspired by SPiM [3]. Just to give a rough idea of the computational performance of BEAST, consider a system made of about 2×10^6 processes, each with 10 stochastic choices in average. On an AMD Athlon 1.5 GHz duo with 1 Gb of RAM, the simulation of about 3×10^4 transitions took about 10 hours — much better than the EOS machine, but not yet enough for our desiderata.

We took then further advantage from the relative simplicity of the π-calculus fragment we tailored to model biochemical pathways. The next sub-section describes a very efficient interpreter of it, that we used to perform large-scale simulations.

2.3   Towards a Matrix-Based Interpreter

Here we shall present a representation of (stochastic) π-processes exploiting stoichiometric matrices. Through it, we could implement a quite efficient interpreter of the ν-free fragment of the π-calculus, and slightly extend Cardelli's observation that reducing the π-calculus to the Chemical Ground Form allows for a direct translation of it into matrix representation [2]. Also, such representation enabled us to slightly extend the binary communication primitive of the π-calculus to allow more than two processes to interact. Of course, the new communication required us to also extended the quantitative part of the semantics that dictates the rate, taking into account all the processes involved.

This feature turns out to help in specifying more naturally biochemical pathways, since biochemists often happen to use reactions involving more than two reactants. These type of reactions do not actually take place in nature, but they are widely used, because they greatly simplify the description of biochemical systems. Indeed, biochemists use to coalesce a set of coupled reactions into a single *generalised reaction*, obtained by neglecting intermediate products.

For example, consider the biochemical system containing the following reversible, enzymatically catalysed reactions

$$\mathrm{E} + \mathrm{S} \underset{k_{-1}}{\overset{k_1}{\rightleftharpoons}} \mathrm{ES} \underset{k_{-2}}{\overset{k_2}{\rightleftharpoons}} \mathrm{E} + \mathrm{P}$$

where E is the enzyme, S is the substrate, P is the product, ES is the enzyme-substrate complex, and the k's are the reaction rate coefficients. As said, it is very common to neglect the production of the complex ES and to describe the above as a single reversible reaction. This system is compactly represented by the following matrices, which express all the details given by the equation above and at the same time they are closer to the generalised reaction biochemists would use:

$$\mathbf{k} = \begin{pmatrix} k_1 \\ k_{-1} \\ k_2 \\ k_{-2} \end{pmatrix} \quad \mathbf{R} = \begin{pmatrix} 1\,0\,0\,0 \\ 0\,0\,0\,1 \\ 1\,0\,0\,1 \\ 0\,1\,1\,0 \end{pmatrix} \quad \mathbf{\Sigma} = \begin{pmatrix} -1 +1 & 0 & 0 \\ 0 & 0 +1 -1 \\ -1 +1 +1 -1 \\ +1 -1 -1 +1 \end{pmatrix}$$

where $\mathbf{k}$ is the vector containing the kinetic coefficients, $\mathbf{R}$ is the reactant matrix and $\boldsymbol{\Sigma}$ is the stoichiometric matrix, where the rows are indexed by the reactants (in our case S, P, E and ES in the order), the columns by the reactions, and the entries say which reactants disappear and which are produced (in our case, the first column says that one element of S and of E are consumed producing a new copy of ES). [1]

This representation allows to efficiently compute the reaction rates $\mathbf{v}$ of elementary reactions through matrix operations, yielding the complete set of ordinary differential equations:

$$\begin{cases} \mathbf{v} = \mathrm{diag}(\mathbf{k}) \; e^{(\mathbf{R}^{\mathrm{T}} \; \log(\mathbf{x}))} \\ d\mathbf{x}/dt = \boldsymbol{\Sigma}\mathbf{v} \end{cases}$$

where $\mathrm{diag}(\mathbf{k})$ is the matrix containing the kinetic parameters at its diagonal, $\mathbf{v}$ is the vector with reaction rates and $\mathbf{x}$ is the vector of the substance concentrations

$$\mathbf{v} = \begin{pmatrix} v_1 \\ v_{-1} \\ v_2 \\ v_{-2} \end{pmatrix} \qquad \mathbf{x} = \begin{pmatrix} [S] \\ [P] \\ [E] \\ [ES] \end{pmatrix}$$

A direct benefit of the matrix representation approach is that we could implement a fast interpreter for the subset of the π-calculus we choose, and even in presence of name-passing, i.e. for the full π-calculus except for restriction ν. All we had to do was building a front-end translator from the π-calculus processes to their representation as matrices. We then simply exploited the environment MATLAB that offers powerful and very efficient built-in routines for matrix computations. Note that the matrices $\mathrm{diag}(\mathbf{k})$, $\mathbf{R}$ and $\boldsymbol{\Sigma}$ are all sparse, and thus they require little storage. More importantly, computations run very quickly because of this.

Efficiency was our main target, because we had to perform large simulations in order to obtain sensible statistical results. Our longest experiments where made of 10^8 transitions and involved 10^7 processes. Just to compare the matrix-based interpreter with those of the previous sub-sections, consider one such simulation took only a few minutes on the same machine mentioned at the end of sub-section 2.2.

3   Modelling Whole-Cell Systems

As already mentioned in the introduction, we are interested in investigating biological phenomena at the system level. In the following sub-sections we report on our efforts in projecting, building and simulating whole-cell scale formal

---

[1] The stoichiometric matrix $\boldsymbol{\Sigma}$ alone might seem to suffice because the reactant matrix $\mathbf{R}$ can be deduced from $\boldsymbol{\Sigma}$ by only considering the negative elements. However, the reactant matrix is needed in the inside loop of the Gillespie algorithm, so it would be inefficient to recalculate $\mathbf{R}$ from $\boldsymbol{\Sigma}$ each time. Additionally, in generalised reactions a substance may occur both as reactant and as product, thereby being cancelled out in $\boldsymbol{\Sigma}$, which shows $\mathbf{R}$ indispensable.

models. First we will describe how we designed the genome of VICE, our ideal prokaryote. Then we will discuss our steps towards building up and simulating the description of all the constitutive metabolic pathways of a real prokaryote, namely *Escherichia coli*.

3.1   From the Minimal Gene Set to VICE

In [4] we specified a hypothetical prokaryote with a very basic structure, yet significantly close to a real cell. Our starting point was the Minimal Gene Set (MGS) proposed by Mushegian and Koonin ([25]), composed by 237 genes. The authors obtained this minimal genome by intersecting the complete genomes of *Haemophilus influenzae* and *Mycoplasma genitalium* and manually eliminating all the functionally redundant elements.

We specified in the π-calculus the whole set of pathways composed by the enzymes encoded by the 237 genes and the corresponding substrate and products. In particular the "MGS-prokaryote" possess:

- the Glycolytic Pathway;
- the Pentose Phosphate Pathway;
- pathways involved in nucleotyde, aminoacids, coenzyme, lipids and glycerol metabolism;
- a set of membrane carriers for metabolite uptake, including the PTS carrier.

To study the characteristics of the MGS-prokaryote, we run simulations using the interpreter for the enhanced π-calculus mentioned in 2.1. Simulations play the role of "virtual experiments" and have been performed considering an optimal virtual environment, characterized by the following conditions:

- the physical and chemical conditions of the external medium are ideal: pressure, temperature, pH and total ion activity are supposed not to request any adaptive response from the cell;
- the essential metabolites are present in the external medium in non-limiting concentration, e.g. the needed nutrients among which glucose;
- the external environment is shaped to remove all the potentially toxic catabolites;
- biological competitors are completely banned.

These assumptions reflect the typical conditions of the so-called continuous culture *in vitro*, in which bacteria are artificially grown in a medium that is continuously refreshed.

The input file contains the definitions of all the metabolites inside the cell, the initial intracellular concentrations of metabolites and the rates of enzymatic activities, derived from the available real experimental data and determined from the Michaelis-Menten kinetics, as described in Section 2.1. At the end of each virual experiment, we determined the time course of the concentration of any virtual metabolite and we inspected the usage rate of the enzymes specified in the definitions. Using these data, it is possible to evaluate the functionality of the specified

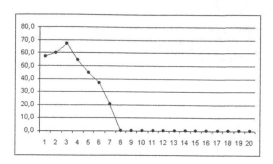

Fig. 1. Time course of ATP in the MGS-prokaryote . The concentration of metabolites (in arbtrary units) is plotted vs the number of transitions.

metabolic pathways and therefore to test the presence of "broken pipes", i.e. if there were enough genes in the MGS to encode all the necessary enzymes.

A large number of simulations had been run, differing in the initial values of some parameters such as the time interval of the observation (roughly, the total number of transitions) and the amount of glucose in the extracellular environment. We then inspected the output of the computations, and we found that in all the studied cases, the MGS-prokayiote could not reach a steady state: indeed the amount of most of the essential metabolites fell to zero in a short period, as clearly shown in Figure 1 that display the time course of ATP a typical element to monitor.

To make sure that this negative result was not influenced by stochastic fluctuations, we also inspected the list of the transition executed during the simulation runs. We found that all the computations resulted to be qualitatively "similar" i.e. composed by the same kind of transitions. Thus the studied metabolite was not produced because of "structural" reasons (e.g. a broken pipe), so we could say that the MGS-prokaryote does not possess enough components to achieve homeostasis which is a fundamental capability of living organisms: a cell with such a genome is not able to live, at least *in silico*.

We then approached the problem to establish which genes present in the MGS were really necessary and which were missing for this cell to live. We manually inspected all the metabolic pathways examining all the possible situations of missing or duplicated functions. In the case of a suspect functional deletion or duplication, we modified the MGS adding genes pertaining to *Mycoplasma genitalium* or *Haemophilus influenzae* or deleting one of the duplicated elements according a case-by-case criterion.

Once a modification had been made, we iteratively performed several simulations on the newly proposed genome and we evaluated the time-course of the metabolites. Finally, our efforts converged to the hypothetical genome of VICE. This virtual prokaryote is able to reach, after a while, a steady state in all its metabolites and additionally it exhibits the required capabilities of producing biomass. As an example of time course approaching the steady state, see Figure 2 that shows the plot of ATP vs. time.

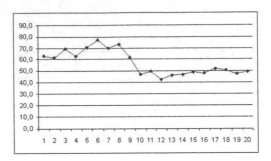

Fig. 2. Time course of ATP in VICE. The concentration of metabolites (in arbtrary units) is plotted vs the number of transitions.

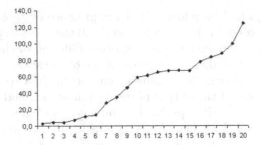

Fig. 3. Time course of Phosphatydil ethanolamine in VICE. The concentration of metabolites (in arbtrary units) is plotted vs the number of transitions.

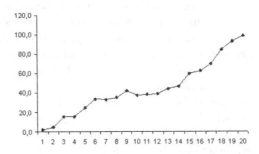

Fig. 4. Time course of Phospatydil glicerol in VICE. The concentration of metabolites (in arbtrary units) is plotted vs the number of transitions.

Figures 4, 3 and 5 display the time courses of Phosphatydil ethanolamine, Phospatydil glicerol and of the total protein quantity as representative of the overall trend of the biomass. These three plots show the concentration of the three metabolites growing with time suggesting that the biomass produced by VICE increases over time, similarly to what happens to real prokaryotes.

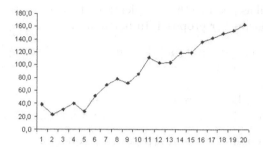

Fig. 5. Time course of the total amount of proteins in VICE. The concentration of metabolites (in arbtrary units) is plotted vs the number of transitions.

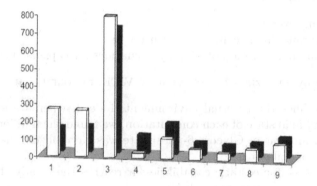

Fig. 6. Metabolites along the glycolitic pathway of VICE (foreground) and of real prokaryotes (bacground)

Moreover, when we computed the relative proportions of the amount of metabolites along the glycolitic pathway of VICE, it turned out that the obtained values are compatible to that of a real prokaryote, as shown in fig. 6.

To verify whether the trend of metabolites time course reached the steady state (i.e. it approached a constant value) we performed a regression analysis that confirmed our claim. Moreover, we exhaustively searched the computations and we found that all the pathways have been followed with almost the same probability. This means that VICE endows sufficient components in its genome. Also, all the components of VICE turned out to be necessary as each of them has been used during some computations.

Comparing the genome of VICE with MGS, we note that the most important difference is due to the insertion in VICE of 7 genes which play fundamental roles and the deletion of 76 genes present in the MGS. At the end of all these refinements, VICE resulted to be equipped by: Glycolytic pathway, pathways for Pyruvate metabolism, for Reduced-NAD oxidation and ATP synthesis, for lipid metabolism, for DNA/RNA synthesis, salvage pathways for nucleotyde synthesis, systems for metabolites uptake.

To keep as small as possible the specification of our virtual cell, we introduced some simplifications in our proposal. In particular:

- we grouped in a single entity all the multi-enzymatic complexes (such as the Pyruvate-Dehydrogenase-complex, the ATP-syntase complex and the trans-membrane ion carriers) when they act as a single cluster;
- we used a "black-box" representation for those pathways leading to the synthesis of macromolecules such as DNA, RNA and proteins.

Furthermore, we did not specify control mechanisms like gene transcription regulation or signalling pathways, because we were designing an autonomous cell, living in an optimal environment. Finally, we did not endow our "minimal" prokaryote with the structural elements necessary to sustain other biological function, such as:

- protein turnover;
- cell-membrane lipidic components turnover;
- production and secretion of exopolysaccharides for capsular formation.

Summing up by analyzing the behaviour of VICE, we found that:

- VICE modifies the external environment. Indeed, when we examined the initial and final state of each computation, we found them different, because a certain amount of Glucose-6-phosphate was catabolized, yielding energy and other metabolites;
- VICE possess homeostatic capabilities: it reaches the steady state, starting from an non-steady state condition;
- VICE biomass increase with time;
- all VICE components are necessary and sufficient;
- at the steady state, the distribution of the amount of VICE metabolites along glycolitic pathway is similar to that of real prokaryotes.

This clearly supports our claim that, at least *in silico*, VICE behaves as a living cell acting *in vivo* in similar circumstancies.

The fact that the designed genome is minimal is further supported by the comparison of our results with those obtained by some authors that recently used a wet-lab approach to characterize the minimal gene set necessary to sustain bacterial life [18]. Their study involved *Mycoplasma genitalium*, whose genome was supposed to be a close approximation of a minimal one. The experimentation consisted of knocking-out *Mycoplasma genitalium* genes through global transposon mutagenesis. The resulting viable mutant strains were isolated and their genome analyzed to identify the distrupted genes. These genes was assumed to be dispensable for bacterial life. Below we compare the results of [18] with ours. The diagram depicted in Figure 7 shows the relationships between the set of genes considered not dispensable in [18] (call it R-genome), the MGS and the genome of VICE.

The intersection between the three sets contains 169 elements. Because these genes resulted not dispensable according to all the three approaches, they are

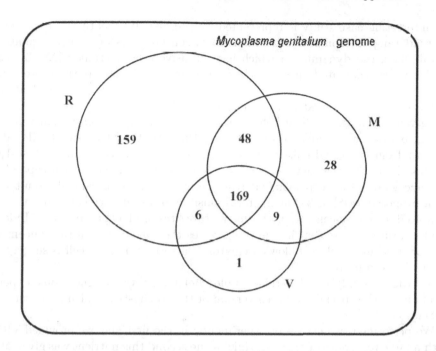

Fig. 7. Relationships between the set of genes considered not dispensable in [18] (R), those included in the MGS (M) and those composing the genome of VICE (V)

likely to be necessary for a minimal bacterium. Note that these genes represents the 90% (169/187) of VICE's genome. This can be seen as an argument for supporting the validity of our method, and more generally of the techniques *in silico*. Moreover, consider that all but one the genes of VICE (i.e. 186/187) are included also in R-genome or in MGS. In other words the probability of obtaining a false positive (i.e. a necessary gene that resulted to be not dispensable according to the last two approaches) is 1/187. Additionally, if we assume not dispensable all the genes contained in the intersection of R-genome with MGS (namely 169 + 48), the probability of obtaining a false negative, i.e. the probability of considering dispensable an essential gene, is 48/187. Summing up and referring again to Figure 7, it results that:

- the genes in VICE are 187 and all are essential;
- the genes present in VICE and in MGS and in R-Genome are 169;
- only one gene is in VICE but not in R-genome or MGS (1/187 false positives);
- the genes included in R-genome and in MGS but not in VICE are 48 (48/187 false negatives)

3.2   Regulation Mechanisms in VICE

In a second experimental series we focused our attention on those aspects of VICE concerning the regulation of metabolite flux through metabolic pathways.

An interesting case study is represented by the glycolytic pathway. It presents a broad range of complex interactions between enzymes and their regulatory metabolites, the dynamics of which has intensively been studied [22]. In particular we concentrated on feedback control circuits. To this purpose, we compositionally added a feedback circuit to VICE. Specifically, we modelled the regulatory circuit related to the phosphofruttokinase (PFK), a key enzyme of the glycolytic pathway. The behaviour of bacterial PFK is particularly interesting, because it is regulated by ADP and Phospho-Enol-Pyruvate (PEP), differently from the usual eukaryotic regulation, based on ATP and fructose-1,6-bisphosphate [8]. ADP acts on the enzyme enhancing its catalytical capability and accelerates the correspondent reaction. PFK feedback control circuit has been proposed in [8] to be the main responsible for oscillatory behaviour that is exhibited in the concentration of some metabolites of glycolitic pathway. Indeed the literature reports that in real prokaryotes the time course of the concentration of these metabolites follows oscillatory patterns when the cell is subject to particular feeding rates.

In order to study *in silico* this complex behaviour, we designed some experiments using the specially tailored version of the stochastic π-calculus, described in Section 2.2.

We performed two classes of experiments: in the first one, we provided VICE with a large reservoire of glucose, while in the second this nutrient was given at a constant rate. The first feeding regimen is intended to check whether the new implementation of VICE still has the homeostatic properties described in Section 3.1. The second regimen is used to detect the emergence of oscillatory patterns in presence of the PFK feedback control circuit. Again, all our tests have been carried on assuming that the virtual cell acts in the ideal environment discussed in Section 3.1.

It turned out that, when fed with a large amount of glucose, VICE reaches its steady state after a certain initial period of time, as shown in Figure 8. It depicts the time course distribution of the concentrations of three selected metabolites, namely pyruvate, diacilglycerol and phosphoribosylpyrophosphate. These metabolites represents critical nodes in the entire metabolic network, so their behaviour gives a sketch of the overall trend of VICE. The distributions displayed in Figure 8 are affected by white gaussian noise. This is because BEAST is indeed stochastic, due to Gillespie's SSA it embodies.

We also compared some aspects of the behaviour of the cell with that of real prokaryotes acting *in vivo* in similar circumstances [20]. In particular, we examined the time course distribution of certain metabolites concentration that are representative of the modelled pathways. We computed ATP vs. ADP and NAD vs. ATP. These ratios express a measure of the cellular energy content in two different ways. We also computed the ratio glucose-6-phosphate vs. fructose-1,6-bisphosphate, giving the trend of metabolic flux along glycolisis. Table 3 shows that the selected ratios significantly match those of real organisms, we computed from the values of [1], obtained *in vivo*.

These results confirm that the VICE still exhibits some capability of "living" *in silico*, also enriched with a regulatory mechanism.

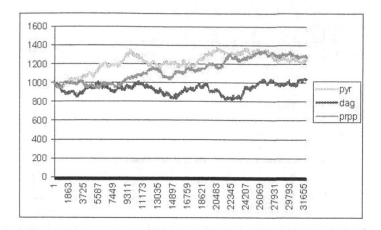

Fig. 8. Time course distribution of pyruvate (pyr), diacilglycerol (dag), phosphoribo-sylpyrophosphate (prpp). The concentration of metabolites is plotted vs the number of transitions.

Table 2. Metabolites Ratio Comparison

	ATP/ADP	glu6p/fru16bp	NAD/ATP
Real	0.775	0.067	11.452
Virtual	0.697	0.053	10.348

We then ran BEAST (see Section 2.2) simulating the condition of continue glucose feeding. It turned out that sustained oscillations emerged, for certain feeding rates within a range compatible with that established through experiments *in vivo*. Figure 9 displays the oscillations of fructose-6-phosphate and of fructose-1,6-bisphosphate. In spite of white gaussian noise, the two plots have a clear constant period and amplitude. We confirmed this assessment through a χ^2-test, that compared the above experimental distributions against sinusoidal model curves. Our experimental, virtual data significantly approach the correspondent values on the model curve. The reader may be interested in comparing Figure 9 with Figure 10, that shows the oscillations of the same metabolites in experiments carried on *in vivo*.

An interesting side result derives by simulating the glycolitic pathway in a stand-alone configuration (extracted from VICE). It turned out that the oscillatory pattern emerges both in the stand alone and in the whole-cell glycolisis, but the oscillation amplitude is significantly different. This suggests us that simulating a *whole* cell could lead to more realistic models, whereas single circuits can generate metabolites, whose concentration varies over a too wide range, because of a relative lacking of constraints. In our view, this confirms that the holistic approach is worth pursuing.

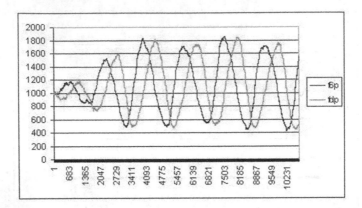

Fig. 9. *In silico* oscillations of fructose-6-phosphate (f6p) and fructose-1,6-bisphosphate (fdp) in the glycolysis

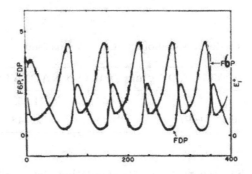

Fig. 10. *In vivo* oscillations of fructose-6-phosphate (f6p) and fructose-1,6-bisphosphate (fdp) in the glycolysis. Adapted from [22]

3.3 *Escherichia Coli*

Here we discuss our work in formally describing and simulating a real prokaryote through the stochastic π-calculus discussed in sub-section 2.3. We chosed to describe *Escherichia coli*, a prokaryote that has been largely investigated, both with molecular biology techniques and *in silico* (see e.g. [10,21]). Indeed, *Escherichia coli* has an average complexity, and it has been explored at a very fine detail, making it one of the most known organisms in the world. We considered the set of the energetic and biosynthetic metabolic pathways of *Escherichia coli* defined in [11,30]. We specified all the pathways in this set, except for a few of those needed for using some carbohydrates as carbon and energy sources. It was particularly difficult to estimate the kinetic parameters of the involved reactions. We determined satisfactory approximations of them relying on the so-called Quasi Steady State Assumption, that gives a safe estimate of the actual reaction rates.

Table 3. Metabolites ratio obtained *in silico* and reported in the literature

	Ratio reported in the literature	Ratio obtained in silico
ATP/ADP	3.2	4.1
NAD/NADH	19	17.1
NADP/NADPH	1.2	1.9

We also took into account the Gibbs free energy of formation of metabolites [21], and a fuzzy measure of the activation energy of each biochemical reaction.

We first performed *in silico* experiments to confirm that our proposal was safe, checking in particular that it shows the basic property of homeostasis. For this pourpose, we studied the behaviour of *Escherichia coli* in interphase by repeatedly running its specification. Since ours is a genome-scale model of a whole cell, we are able to simultaneously examine *all* its metabolic pathways, as well as their interactions. In particular we checked whether our virtual *Escherichia coli* was able to "survive" in an "ideal" environment with enough nutrients and in which chemical and physical paramenters are kept constant. These are the typical conditions of the continuous culture *in vitro*.

We ran some hundred simulations, using the interpreter described in subsection 2.3. We were interested in observing whether the time course distribution of metabolites reaches a plateau, i.e. whether the virtual cell reaches its steady state after a certain initial period of time. Indeed, the plot of this time course clearly approaches a constant value. A linear regression analysis confirmed that the distribution of metabolites concentration is fitted by a horizontal line.

We then compared the distributions coming out from our simulations with those of the real *Escherichia coli* at the steady state. To do that, we computed the ratio between physiologically related pairs of metabolites, becausethese ratios give indications about physiological parameters of the organism. For example, the ratio ATP/ADP measures the energetic level of the cell. The values obtained in this way are close to those measured *in vivo* [21], as shown in Table 3.

These findings represent a clue that both our description and the chosen parameters are adequate to represent the behaviour of *Escherichia coli* in the given conditions. Anyway, deeper analysis need to be performed in order to support the claim that our proposal is safe.

A particular attention has to be dedicated to the problem of *stiffness*. Indeed the biochemical reactions considered in our model are characterized by reaction rates spanning over six to seven orders of magnitude. Under these conditions, it may happen that Gillespie's SSA spends all the simulation time to execute only the fastest reactions. Therefore the amount of processes involved in the slowest reactions do not change over time, because these reactions are never selected. So the simulation of a stiff system may show a plateau because the system has

Table 4. Metabolites produced per unit of glucose consumed

	Succinate in vivo / in silico	Lactate in vivo / in silico	Formate in vivo / in silico
wild type	.10 / .31	.09 / .13	.40 / .62
null *ppc* mutant	.03 / .06	.21 / .24	.35 / .50

reached a steady state, but also because the observed reactions never occur and so the plot shows a "flat line."

To further validate our model, we performed some perturbative experiments. We "knocked-out" three selected genes, namely the *ppc*, the *pgi* and *zwf* genes, similarly to what done *in vivo* [19,23]. *In silico* this corresponds to rule out from the specification the enzymes encoded by the selected genes. This experimentation is at avery preliminar stage and the results need to be validated properly. Below, we will present some results showing the agreement betwen *in silico* and *in vitro* results, at least at a qualitative level.

Knockout of ppc *gene.* This gene encodes for the enzyme Phosphoenolpyruvate Carboxylase, an enzyme belonging to the glycolytic pathway. *In vivo* knock-out are performed in an anaerobic glucose-limited environment [19]. We mimicked this condition by removing the processes corresponding to oxigen from the extra-cellular environment, and by providing a limited reservoir of glucose. The results *in vivo* and ours are in Table 4 — we display the amount of metabolite produced per unit of glucose consumed. Although there are some differennces in the two cases, the behavioural trend after the knock-out of the gene is similar: succinate and formate production result lowered, while lactate production increased with a similar rate.

Knockout of pgi *and* zwf *genes.* These genes encode for Phosphoglucose isomerase (an enzyme of glycolytic pathway) and Glucose-6-phosphate dehydrogenase (the first enzyme of Penthose Phosphate Pathway), respectively. The experiments *in vivo* have been carried on in glucose or ammonia limited cultures [23]. In our simulations we modelled these constraints, by providing a limited reservoir of extracellular glucose or ammonia. We do not report here the results of our simulations, mainly beacause for glucose limited cultures, the data in the real case are below the detection limits. Anyway, the quantities measured *in silico* and *in vivo* differ, but there is a qualitative agreement in the behaviour of the real and virtual *Escherichia coli*. Indeed, in both prokaryotes, the production rates of acetate and pyruvate are low in glucose limited condition and increase in ammonia limited condition, both for mutants and wild types. Furthermore, in the ammonia limited condition, the rate of production of acetate and pyruvate per unit of ammonia consumed is the highest for *zfw* mutants and the lowest for *pgi* mutants.

Acknowledgements. This research has been partially supported by MIUR PRIN Bisca, and by EU-FET Global Computing Project IST-2005-16004 Sensoria (Software Engineering for Service-Oriented Overlay Computers). Pierpaolo Degano has been also partially supported by the Microsoft Research – University of Trento Centre for Computational and Systems Biology (CoSBi).

References

1. Buchholz, A., Takors, R., Wandrey, C.: Quantification of intracellular metabolites in escherichia coli k12 using liquid chromatographic-electrospray ionization tandem mass spectrometric techniques. Analytical Biochemistry 295, 129–137 (2001)
2. Cardelli, L.: From processes to odes by chemistry, draft (2006)
3. Cardelli, L., Phillips, A.: A correct abstract machine for stochastic *pi*-calculus. In: Procs. BioConcur (2004)
4. Chiarugi, D., Curti, M., Degano, P., Marangoni, R.: ViCe: a VIrtual CEll. In: Danos, V., Schachter, V. (eds.) CMSB 2004. LNCS (LNBI), vol. 3082, Springer, Heidelberg (2005)
5. Curti, M., Degano, P., Baldari, C.T.: Causal π-calculus for biochemical modelling. In: Priami, C. (ed.) CMSB 2003. LNCS, vol. 2602, Springer, Heidelberg (2003)
6. Curti, M., Degano, P., Priami, C., Baldari, C.T.: Modelling biochemical pathways through enhanced π-calculus. Theoretical Computer Science 325/1, 111–140 (2004)
7. Degano, P., Priami, C.: Enhanced operational semantics. ACM Computing Surveys 28(2), 352–354 (1996)
8. Diaz Ricci, J.C.: Adp modulates the dynamic behavior of the glycolytic pathway of *Escherichia coli*. Biochemical and Biophysical Research Communications 271(1), 244–249 (2000)
9. Edwards, J.S., Cover, M., Palsson, B.O.: Metabolic modelling of microbes: the flux-balance approach. Env. Microbiol. 4, 133–140 (2002)
10. Edwards, J.S., Ibarra, R.U., Palsson, B.O.: In silico predictions of escherichia coli metabolic capabilities are consistent with experimental data. predictions of *escherichia coli* metabolic capabilities are consistent with experimental data 19, 125–130 (2001)
11. Edwards, J.S., Palsson, B.O.: The *escherichia coli* mg1655 *in silico* metabolic genotype: its definition, characteristics and capabilities. Proc. Natl. Acad. Sci. USA 97, 5528–5533 (2000)
12. Devlin, T.M., et al.: Textbook of Biochemistry, 5th edn. Wiley and Sons, Inc, Chichester (2002)
13. Fell, D.A.: Understanding the control of metabolism. Portland Press, London, United Kingdom (1997)
14. Fersht, A.: Structure and Mechanism in Protein Science: A Guide to Enzyme Catalysis and Protein Folding. Freeman, New York (1999)
15. Gillespie, D.T.: Concerning the validity of the stochastic approach to chemical kinetics. Journal of Statistical Physics 3, 311–318 (1977)
16. Gillespie, D.T.: Exact stochastic simulation of coupled chemical reactions. Journal of Physical Chemistry 81(25), 2340–2361 (1977)
17. Gillespie, D.T.: Stochastic simulation of chemical kinetics. Annu. Rev. Phys. Chem. 58, 35–55 (2007)
18. Glass, J., Assad-Garcia, N., Alperovich, N.: Essential genes of a minimal bacterium. PNAS 103, 425–430 (2006)

19. Gokarn, R.R., Eiteman, M.A., Altman, A.: Metabolic analysis of *escherichia coli* in the presence and absence of the carboxylating enzymes phosphoenolpyruvate carboxylase and pyruvate carboxylase. App. Env. Microbiol. 66, 1844–1850 (2000)

20. Hammes, G.G., Shimmel, P.R.: The Enzymes, P.D. Boyer, vol. 2. New York Academic Press, London (1970)

21. Henry, C.S., Broadbelt, L.J., Hatzimanikatis, V.: Thermodynamics-based metabolic flux analysis. Biophys. J. 92, 1792–1805 (2007)

22. Higgins, J.: A chemical mechanism for oscillation of glycolytic intermediates in yeast cell. Proceeding of National Academy Science USA 51, 989–994 (1964)

23. Hua, Q., Yang, C., Baba, T., Mori, H., Shimizu, K.: Responses of the central metabolism in *escherichia coli* to phosphoglucose isomerase and glucose-6-phosphate dehydrogenase knockouts. J. Bacteriol. 185, 7053–7067 (2003)

24. Kitano, H.: Foundations of System Biology. MIT Press, Cambridge (2002)

25. Mushegian, A.R., Koonin, E.V.: A minimal gene set fir cellular life derived by comparison of complete bacterial genome. Proceedings of National Academy of Science USA 93, 10268–10273 (1996)

26. Nottegar, C., Priami, C., Degano, P.: Performance evaluation of mobile processes via abstract machines. IEEE Transactions on Software Engineering 10, 867–889 (2001)

27. Priami, C.: Stochastic π-calculus. The Computer Journal 38(6), 578–589 (1995)

28. Priami, C., Regev, A., Silverman, W., Shapiro, E.: Application of a stochastic passing-name calculus to representation and simulation of molecular processes. Information Processing Letters 80, 25–31 (2001)

29. Reed, J.L., Palsson, B.O.: Thirteen years of building constraint-based in silico models of escherichia coli. J. Bacteriol. 185, 2692–2699 (2003)

30. Reed, J.L., Vo, T.D., Schilling, C.H., Palsson, B.O.: An expanded genome-scale model of *escherichia coli* k-12 (ijr904 gsm/gpr). Genome Biol R54.1–R54.12 (2000)

31. Regev, A., Silverman, W., Shapiro, E.: Representation and simulation of biochemical processes using the π-calculus process algebra. In: Pacific Symposium of Biocomputing (PSB 2001), pp. 459–470 (2001)

32. Soyer, O.S., Pfeiffer, T., Bonhoeffer, S.: Simulating the evolution of signal transduction pathways. Journal of theoretical biology 241, 223–232 (2006)

The Calculus of Looping Sequences

Roberto Barbuti, Giulio Caravagna, Andrea Maggiolo–Schettini,
Paolo Milazzo, and Giovanni Pardini

Dipartimento di Informatica, Università di Pisa
Largo B. Pontecorvo 3, 56127 Pisa, Italy
{barbuti,caravagn,maggiolo,milazzo,pardinig}@di.unipi.it

Abstract. We describe the Calculus of Looping Sequences (CLS) which
is suitable for modeling microbiological systems and their evolution. We
present two extensions, CLS with links (LCLS) and Stochastic CLS.
LCLS simplifies the description of protein interaction at a lower level of
abstraction, namely at the domain level. Stochastic CLS allows us to describe quantitative aspects of the modeled systems, such as the frequency
of chemical reactions. As examples of application to real biological systems, we show the simulation of the activity of the lactose operon in
E. coli and the quorum sensing process in *P. aeruginosa*, both described
with Stochastic CLS.

1 Introduction

Cell biology, the study of the morphological and functional organization of cells,
is now an established field in biochemical research. Computer Science can help
research in cell biology in several ways. For instance, it can provide biologists
with models and formalisms capable of describing and analyzing complex systems such as cells. In the last few years many formalisms originally developed by
computer scientists to model systems of interacting components have been applied to Biology. Among these, there are Petri Nets [29], Hybrid Systems [1], and
the π-calculus [15,42]. Moreover, new formalisms have been defined for describing biomolecular and membrane interactions [4,11,13,17,36,40]. Others, such as
P Systems [31,32], have been proposed as biologically inspired computational
models and have been later applied to the description of biological systems.

The π–calculus and new calculi based on it [36,40] have been successful in the
description of biological systems, as they allow systems to be described in a compositional way. However, these calculi offer very low–level interaction primitives,
causing models to become very large and difficult to understand. Calculi such as
those proposed in [11,13,17] give a more abstract description of systems and offer special biologically motivated operators. However, they are often specialized
to the description of some particular kinds of phenomena such as membrane or
protein interactions. Finally, P Systems have a simple notation and are not specialized to the description of a particular class of systems, but they are still not
completely general. For instance, it is possible to describe biological membranes
and the movement of molecules across membranes, and there are some variants

M. Bernardo, P. Degano, and G. Zavattaro (Eds.): SFM 2008, LNCS 5016, pp. 387–423, 2008.
© Springer-Verlag Berlin Heidelberg 2008

able to describe also more complex membrane activities. However, the formalism is not flexible enough to allow an easy description of new activities observed on membranes without extending the formalism itself.

Therefore, the need has arisen for a formalism with a simple notation, having the ability of describing biological systems at different levels of abstraction, having some notions of compositionality and being flexible enough to allow the description of new kinds of phenomena, without being specialized to the description of a particular class of systems. For this reason in [7] we have introduced the Calculus of Looping Sequences (CLS).

CLS is a formalism based on term rewriting with some features, such as a commutative parallel composition operator, and some semantic means, such as bisimulations, which are common in process calculi. All this permits us to combine the simplicity of notation of rewriting systems with the advantage of a form of compositionality.

Given an alphabet of symbols representing basic biological entities, such as genes, proteins and other macro–molecules, CLS terms are constructed by applying to these symbols operators of sequencing, looping, containment and parallel composition. Terms constructed by means of these operators represent biological structures such as DNA sequences and membranes. Rewrite rules can be used to model biological events that permit the system to evolve. In particular, they can be used to model biochemical reactions and structure rearragements such as membrane fusion and dissolution.

Some variants of CLS have been defined in [30]. Moreover, in [5,6], two extensions have been introduced. The first, CLS with links (LCLS), allows the description of protein interaction at a lower level of abstraction, namely at the domain level. The second, Stochastic CLS, allows the description of quantitative aspects of the modeled systems such as the frequency of chemical reactions. For Stochastic CLS a simulator has been developed [14] that allows simulating the evolution of biological systems over time.

In [8,9] we have defined bisimulations for CLS. Bisimulations may be used to compare the behaviour of two systems and as an alternative technique to verify a property of a system. This can be done by assessing the bisimilarity of a system with a system one knows to enjoy that property.

In this paper, we describe CLS and its two extensions, and we show two examples of application to real biological systems. While the formulations of CLS and LCLS differ slightly from those given in [7,5], the present formulation of Stochastic CLS is new and is more convenient than the one in [6] when dealing with biochemical systems. As examples of application to real biological systems, we show the simulation of the activity of the lactose operon in *E.coli* and the quorum sensing process in *P.aeruginosa*, both described with Stochastic CLS.

2   Setting the Context

Both the qualitative and the quantitative aspects of biological systems are interesting. The former are related to *state dependent properties*, such as reachability of states or existence of equilibria and stable states; the latter are related to *time and probability dependent properties*, like the time needed to reach a certain state and the probability of reaching a certain state in a given time or in any time. We briefly describe some notable examples of formalisms that have been used in the last few years for modeling both aspects.

As regards qualitative aspects of biological systems, Lindenmayer systems (or L systems) [38] are one of the oldest formalisms. An L system is a formal grammar most famously used to model the growth processes of plant development.

In the tradition of automata and formal language theory, more recently Paun has proposed P Systems [31,32]. P Systems introduce the idea of membrane computing in the subject of natural computing. They represent a new computational paradigm which allows NP-complete problems to be solved in polynomial time (but in exponential space), have originated a huge amount of work and recently have been also applied to the description of biological systems (see [39] for a complete list of references).

A pioneering formalism for the description of biological systems is the κ–calculus of Danos and Laneve [17]. It is a formal language for protein interactions, is enriched with a very intuitive visual notation and has been encoded into the π–calculus. The κ–calculus idealizes protein-protein interactions, essentially as a particular restricted kind of graph–rewriting operating on graphs with sites. A formal protein is a node with a fixed number of sites, and a complex (i.e. a bundle of proteins connected together by low energy bounds) is a connected graph built over such nodes, in which connections are established between sites. The κ–calculus has been recently extended to model also membranes [28].

An example of direct application of a model for concurrency to biochemical systems has been shown by Regev and Shapiro in [41] and by Regev, Silverman and Shapiro in [42]. Their idea is to describe biomolecular pathways as π–calculus processes. Chemical reactions between biological components are modeled as communications on channels whose names can be passed and sharing names of private channels allows the description of biological compartments. Regev, Panina, Silverman, Cardelli and Shapiro in [40] defined the BioAmbients calculus, a model inspired by both the π–calculus and the Mobile Ambients calculus [12], which can be used to describe biochemical systems with a notion of compartments (as, for instance, membranes). An extension of the π–calculus for the description of membranes and of biological interfaces is the Beta–binders calculus defined by Priami and Quaglia in [36]. More details of membrane interactions have been considered by Cardelli in the definition of Brane Calculi [11], which are elegant formalisms for describing intricate biological processes involving membranes. A refinement of Brane Calculi has been introduced by Danos and Pradalier in [18].

We mention also some works by Harel [23] and Kam et al.[26], in which the challenging idea is introduced of modelling a full multi–cellular animal as a reactive system. The multi–cellular animal should be, specifically, the *C.elegans* nematode worm, which is complex, but well defined in terms of anatomy and genetics. Moreover, Harel proposes to use the languages of Statecharts [22] and Live

Sequence Charts (LSC) [16], which are visual notations with a formal semantics and are commonly adopted in the specification of software projects. Harel et al. apply the same formalisms also to cellular and multi–cellular systems related to the immune systems of living organisms in [25] and [21].

As regards quantitative aspects of biological systems, they are usually described by biologists by means of differential equations. Each equation gives the transformation rate of one of the components of the described system. Hence, the dynamics of the system can be studied analitically and simulations can be performed by using a computer tool for solving differential equations. This technique has been successfully used in a huge number of cases, but it suffers from the following drawbacks: (i) the solution of a set of differential equations gives a unique "average" behavior of the system, and does not model stochastic fluctuations of the quantities of the involved components; (ii) when the size and the complexity of the modeled system increases, differential equations become difficult to manage; (iii) the approach assumes quantities to be expressed as continuous values, and this could lead to erroneous approximations, in particular when the number of components of the system is very small.

An alternative approach to the simulation of biological systems is the use of stochastic simulators. This kind of tools are usually based on simulation algorithms proved to be correct with respect to the kinetic theory of chemical reactions. The most used and well–established of such algorithms is the one introduced by Gillespie in [24]. In his paper, Gillespie shows that the quantity of time spent between the occurrences of two chemical reactions is exponentially distributed, with the sum of the kinetic rates of the possible reactions as the parameter of the exponential distribution. This allows him to give a very simple and exact stochastic algorithm for simulating chemical reactions.

Gillespie's algorithm is the *trait–d'union* between simulation of biological systems and stochastic process algebras, and permits the latter to be easily applied to the description of biological systems. In particular, the *stochastic π–calculus* [35,37] has been successfully applied to the (quantitative) modeling of biological systems. In this extension of the π–calculus, kinetic constants are associated with communication channels and determine the stochastic behaviour of the model, in terms of communications, as in Gillespie's algorithm they determine occurrences of chemical reactions. Analogous stochastic extensions have been proposed for other formalisms such as P Systems [34], BioAmbients [10] and Beta–binders [19], and simulation tools have been developed.

The transition system obtained by the semantics of a stochastic formalism may be transformed into a Continuous Time Markov Chain (CTMC). If the set of states of the CTMC is manageable, a standard probabilistic model checker (such as PRISM [27]) can be used to verify properties of the described system.

3   The Calculus of Looping Sequences (CLS)

In the next sections we introduce the Calculus of Looping Sequences (CLS) and two variants, CLS with links (LCLS) and Stochastic CLS. The former is a variant to model protein interaction at the domain level. The latter, equipped with a stochastic semantics, permits the description of quantitative aspects of biological systems. For all the formalisms presented here we show the modeling of some real biological systems.

3.1   The Basic Formalism

CLS is based on term rewriting, hence a CLS model consists of a term and a set of rewrite rules. The term is intended to represent the structure of the modeled system, and the rewrite rules to represent the events that may cause the system to evolve.

We start with defining the syntax of terms. We assume a possibly infinite alphabet $\mathcal{E}$ of symbols ranged over by $a, b, c, \ldots$.

Definition 1 (Terms). *Terms T and sequences S are given by the following grammar:*

$$T ::= S \quad | \quad (T)^L \rfloor T \quad | \quad T \,|\, T$$
$$S ::= \epsilon \quad | \quad a \quad | \quad S \cdot S$$

where a is a generic element of $\mathcal{E}$, and ϵ represents the empty sequence. We denote with $\mathcal{T}$ the infinite set of terms, and with $\mathcal{S}$ the infinite set of sequences.

In CLS we have a sequencing operator $\_ \cdot \_$, a parallel composition operator $\_ \,|\, \_$, a looping operator $(\_)^L$ and a containment operator $\_ \rfloor \_$. Sequencing can be used to concatenate elements of the alphabet $\mathcal{E}$. The empty sequence ϵ denotes the concatenation of zero symbols. By definition, looping and containment are always applied together, hence we can consider them as a single binary operator $(\_)^L \rfloor \_$. Brackets can be used to indicate the order of application of the operators, and we assume $(\_)^L \rfloor \_$ to have precedence over $\_ \,|\, \_$.

The biological interpretation of the operators is the following: the main entities which occur in cells are DNA and RNA strands, proteins, membranes, and other macro–molecules. DNA strands (and similarly RNA strands) are sequences of nucleic acids, but they can be seen also at a higher level of abstraction as sequences of genes. Proteins are sequence of amino acids which usually have a very complex three–dimensional structure. In a protein there are usually (relatively) few subsequences, called domains, which actually are able to interact with other entities by means of chemical reactions. CLS sequences can model DNA/RNA strands and proteins by describing each gene or each domain with a symbol of the alphabet. Membranes are closed surfaces, often interspersed with proteins, which may have a content. Looping and containment allow the representation of membranes with their contents. For example, the term $(a \,|\, b)^L \rfloor c$ represents a membrane with the elements a and b on its surface and containing the element c. Other macro–molecules can be modeled as single alphabet symbols, or as short sequences. Finally, juxtaposition of entities can be described by the parallel composition of their representations.

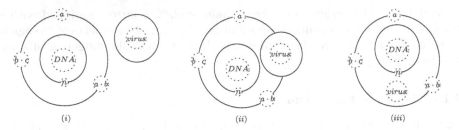

Fig. 1. A visual representation of some examples of CLS terms

In Figure 1 we show the visual representation of some examples of CLS terms. Term (i), $(\epsilon)^L \rfloor virus \mid (a \mid b \cdot c \mid a \cdot b)^L \rfloor (n)^L \rfloor DNA$, represents an environment where there exist a virus, represented by $(\epsilon)^L \rfloor virus$, and a cell represented by $(a \mid b \cdot c \mid a \cdot b)^L \rfloor (n)^L \rfloor DNA$. The cell has three proteins on its external membrane, represented by the sequences a, $b \cdot c$ and $a \cdot b$, and contains a membrane with surface n, representing the nucleus and containing a DNA strand, represented by the sequence DNA. Term (ii), $(a \mid b \cdot c \mid a \cdot b \mid (\epsilon)^L \rfloor virus)^L \rfloor (n)^L \rfloor DNA$, represents the same cell of term (i) but with the virus attached to the surface of its external membrane. Finally, term (iii), $(a \mid b \cdot c \mid a \cdot b)^L \rfloor (virus \mid (n)^L \rfloor DNA)$, represents the state in which the virus, dissolving its external membrane, has entered the cell.

In CLS we may have syntactically different terms representing the same structure. We introduce a structural congruence relation to identify such terms.

Definition 2 (Structural Congruence). *The structural congruence relations $\equiv_S$ and $\equiv$ are the least congruence relations on sequences and on terms, respectively, satisfying the following rules:*

$$S_1 \cdot (S_2 \cdot S_3) \equiv_S (S_1 \cdot S_2) \cdot S_3 \qquad S \cdot \epsilon \equiv_S \epsilon \cdot S \equiv_S S$$

$$S_1 \equiv_S S_2 \; implies \; S_1 \equiv S_2$$

$$T_1 \mid T_2 \equiv T_2 \mid T_1 \qquad T_1 \mid (T_2 \mid T_3) \equiv (T_1 \mid T_2) \mid T_3$$

$$T \mid \epsilon \equiv T \qquad (\epsilon)^L \rfloor \epsilon \equiv \epsilon$$

Rules of the structural congruence state the associativity of $\cdot$ and $\mid$, the commutativity of the latter and the neutral role of ϵ.

Note that there exist variants of the CLS formalism having a different syntax of terms and a different structural congruence relation. Among these variants it is worth mentioning those defined in [8] and in [30]. In the former, the looping operator can be applied only to a single sequence of alphabet symbols, and such a sequence can rotate by applying an axiom of the structural congruence. In the latter, called CLS+, the looping operator can be applied to a parallel composition of sequences, but not to other loopings.

Rewrite rules will be defined essentially as pairs of terms, with the first term describing the portion of the system in which the event modeled by the rule may occur, and the second term describing how that portion of the system changes when the event occurs. In the terms of a rewrite rule we allow the use of variables. As a consequence, a rule will be applicable to all terms which can be obtained by properly instantiating its variables. Variables can be of three kinds: two of these are associated with the two different syntactic categories of terms and sequences, and one is associated with single alphabet elements. We assume a set of term variables TV ranged over by $X, Y, Z, \ldots$, a set of sequence variables SV ranged over by $\widetilde{x}, \widetilde{y}, \widetilde{z}, \ldots$, and a set of element variables $\mathcal{X}$ ranged over by $x, y, z, \ldots$. All these sets are possibly infinite and pairwise disjoint. We denote by $\mathcal{V}$ the set of all variables, $\mathcal{V} = TV \cup SV \cup \mathcal{X}$, and with ρ a generic variable of $\mathcal{V}$. Hence, a pattern is a term that may include variables.

Definition 3 (Patterns). *Patterns P and sequence patterns SP of CLS are given by the following grammar:*

$$P ::= SP \mid (P)^L \rfloor P \mid P \mid P \mid X$$
$$SP ::= \epsilon \mid a \mid SP \cdot SP \mid \widetilde{x} \mid x$$

where a is a generic element of $\mathcal{E}$, and $X, \widetilde{x}$ and x are generic elements of TV, SV and $\mathcal{X}$, respectively. We denote with $\mathcal{P}$ the infinite set of patterns.

We assume the structural congruence relation to be trivially extended to patterns. An *instantiation* is a partial function $\sigma : \mathcal{V} \to \mathcal{T}$. An instantiation must preserve the type of variables, thus for $X \in TV, \widetilde{x} \in SV$ and $x \in \mathcal{X}$ we have $\sigma(X) \in \mathcal{T}, \sigma(\widetilde{x}) \in \mathcal{S}$ and $\sigma(x) \in \mathcal{E}$, respectively. Given $P \in \mathcal{P}$, with $P\sigma$ we denote the term obtained by replacing each occurrence of each variable $\rho \in \mathcal{V}$ appearing in P with the corresponding term $\sigma(\rho)$. With Σ we denote the set of all the possible instantiations and, given $P \in \mathcal{P}$, with $Var(P)$ we denote the set of variables appearing in P. We can now define rewrite rules.

Definition 4 (Rewrite Rules). *A rewrite rule is a pair of patterns (P_1, P_2), denoted with $P_1 \mapsto P_2$, where $P_1, P_2 \in \mathcal{P}$, $P_1 \not\equiv \epsilon$ and such that $Var(P_2) \subseteq Var(P_1)$. We denote with $\mathfrak{R}$ the infinite set of all the possible rewrite rules.*

A rewrite rule $P_1 \mapsto P_2$ states that a term $P_1\sigma$, obtained by instantiating variables in P_1 by some instantiation function σ, can be transformed into the term $P_2\sigma$. For instance, the rule $a \cdot b \mid b \cdot \widetilde{x} \mapsto c \cdot \widetilde{x}$ prescribes the replacement, with respect to an instantiation function σ, of a sequence $a \cdot b$ and a sequence $b \cdot \sigma(\widetilde{x})$ with a sequence $c \cdot \sigma(\widetilde{x})$. If the term to which the rule is applied is $a \cdot b \mid b \cdot a \cdot b \mid c$, and we assume an instantiation function $\sigma = \{(\widetilde{x}, a \cdot b)\}$, the result of applying the rule to the term is $c \cdot a \cdot b \mid c$. The rule $p \mid (m \mid Y)^L \rfloor X \mapsto (m \mid Y \mid p)^L \rfloor X$ could describe the attachment of element p to a membrane containing on its surface at least an element m. As in the previous example, the membrane to which the element p gets attached, depends on the instantiation of variables X and Y.

With reference to Figure 1, the rewrite rule that transforms the state represented by term (i) into the state represented by term (ii) could be $(\epsilon)^L \rfloor virus \mid (X)^L \rfloor (Y \mid (n)^L \rfloor DNA) \mapsto (X \mid (\epsilon)^L \rfloor virus)^L \rfloor (Y \mid (n)^L \rfloor DNA)$. Analogously, the rule which transforms the state represented by term (ii) into the state

represented by term (iii) could be $\left(X \mid (\epsilon)^L \rfloor virus\right)^L \rfloor \left(Y \mid (n)^L \rfloor DNA\right) \mapsto$
$(X)^L \rfloor \left(Y \mid virus \mid (n)^L \rfloor DNA\right)$.

We now define the semantics of CLS as a transition system in which states correspond to terms and transitions correspond to rule applications.

Definition 5 (Semantics). *Given a finite set of rewrite rules $\mathcal{R} \subseteq \mathfrak{R}$, the semantics of CLS is the least transition relation $\rightarrow$ on terms closed under structural congruence $\equiv$ and satisfying the following inference rules:*

$$\frac{P_1 \mapsto P_2 \in \mathcal{R} \quad P_1\sigma \not\equiv \epsilon \quad \sigma \in \Sigma}{P_1\sigma \rightarrow P_2\sigma} \qquad \frac{T_1 \rightarrow T_2}{T \mid T_1 \rightarrow T \mid T_2}$$

$$\frac{T_1 \rightarrow T_2}{(T)^L \rfloor T_1 \rightarrow (T)^L \rfloor T_2} \qquad \frac{T_1 \rightarrow T_2}{(T_1)^L \rfloor T \rightarrow (T_2)^L \rfloor T}$$

Note that, by the definition of the semantics, a rule cannot be applied to a portion of a sequence. This means that a rule such as $b \mapsto d$ cannot be applied to $a \cdot b \cdot c$ (so to obtain $a \cdot d \cdot c$). This constraint is necessary because the application of a rule to a portion of a sequence could lead to syntactically wrong terms. For instance, if it would be possible to apply $b \mapsto d \mid e$ to $a \cdot b \cdot c$, one would obtain $a \cdot (d \mid e) \cdot c$ as a result which is not a valid term. However, the constraint does not reduce the expressiveness of the formalism because, in order to modify a portion of a system, one can replace any rule such as $b \mapsto d$ with $\widetilde{x} \cdot b \cdot \widetilde{y} \mapsto \widetilde{x} \cdot d \cdot \widetilde{y}$.

Finally, a *model* in CLS is given by a term describing the initial state of the system and by a set of rewrite rules describing all the events that may occur.

Examples. A well–known example of biomolecular system is the epidermal growth factor (EGF) signal transduction pathway [44,33]. If EGF proteins are present in the environment of a cell, they should be interpreted as a proliferation signal from the environment, and hence the cell should react by synthesizing proteins which stimulate its proliferation. A cell recognizes the EGF signal because it has on its membrane some EGF receptor proteins (EGFR), which are transmembrane proteins (they have some intra–cellular and some extra–cellular domains). One of the extra–cellular domains binds to one EGF protein in the environment, forming a signal–receptor complex on the membrane. This causes a conformational change on the receptor protein that enables it to bind to another signal–receptor complex. The formation of the binding of the two signal–receptor complexes (called dimerization) causes the phosphorylation of some intra–cellular domains of the dimer. This, in turn, causes the internal domains of the dimer to be recognized by a protein that is inside the cell (in the cytoplasm), called SHC. The protein SHC binds to the dimer, enabling a long chain of protein–protein interactions, which finally activate some proteins, such as one called ERK, which bind to the DNA and stimulate synthesis of proteins for cell proliferation.

Now, we use CLS to build a model of the first steps of the EGF signaling pathway up to the binding of the signal-receptor dimer to the SHC protein.

We model the EGFR,EGF and SHC proteins as the alphabet symbols $EGFR$, EGF and SHC, respectively. The cell is modeled as a looping applied to a parallel composition of sequences (representing the external membrane) initially composed only by symbols $EGFR$, containing symbols SHC and surrounded by symbols EGF. The rewrite rules modeling the first steps of the pathway are the following:

$$EGF \mid (EGFR \mid Y)^L \rfloor X \ \mapsto \ (CPL \mid Y)^L \rfloor X \qquad (R1)$$

$$(CPL \mid CPL \mid Y)^L \rfloor X \ \mapsto \ (CPL \cdot CPL \mid Y)^L \rfloor X \qquad (R2)$$

$$(CPL \cdot CPL \mid Y)^L \rfloor X \ \mapsto \ (CPLp \cdot CPLp \mid Y)^L \rfloor X \qquad (R3)$$

$$(CPLp \cdot CPLp \mid Y)^L \rfloor (SHC \mid X) \mapsto (CPLp \cdot CPLp \cdot SHC \mid Y)^L \rfloor X \quad (R4)$$

Rule R1 describes the binding of a EGF protein to a EGFR receptor protein on the membrane surface. The result of the binding is a signal-receptor complex denoted CPL. Rule R2 describes the dimerization of two signal-receptor complexes, the result is a sequence of two signal-receptor CPL symbols. Rule R3 describes the phosphorylation (and activation) of a signal-receptor dimer, that is the replacement of a $CPL \cdot CPL$ sequence with $CPLp \cdot CPLp$. Finally, rule R4 describes the binding of an active dimer $CPLp \cdot CPLp$ to a SHC protein contained in the cytoplasm. The result is a $CPLp \cdot CPLp \cdot SHC$ sequence placed on the membrane surface.

A possible initial term for the model in this example is given by a membrane having, on its surface, a parallel composition of symbols $EGFR$ and, inside, some symbols SHC and, outside, some symbols EGF. A possible evolution of such a term by means of application of the given rewrite rules is the following (we write on each transition the name of the applied rewrite rule):

$$EGF \mid EGF \mid (EGFR \mid EGFR \mid EGFR \mid EGFR)^L \rfloor (SHC \mid SHC)$$

$$\xrightarrow{(R1)} EGF \mid (EGFR \mid CPL \mid EGFR \mid EGFR)^L \rfloor (SHC \mid SHC)$$

$$\xrightarrow{(R1)} (EGFR \mid CPL \mid EGFR \mid CPL)^L \rfloor (SHC \mid SHC)$$

$$\xrightarrow{(R2)} (EGFR \mid CPL \cdot CPL \mid EGFR)^L \rfloor (SHC \mid SHC)$$

$$\xrightarrow{(R3)} (EGFR \mid CPLp \cdot CPLp \mid EGFR)^L \rfloor (SHC \mid SHC)$$

$$\xrightarrow{(R4)} (EGFR \mid CPLp \cdot CPLp \cdot SHC \mid EGFR)^L \rfloor SHC$$

We show another example of modeling of a biomolecular system with CLS, that is the modeling of a simple gene regulation process. This kind of processes are essential for cell life as they allow a cell to regulate the production of proteins that may have important roles, for instance in metabolism, growth, proliferation and differentiation.

The example we consider is as follows: we have a simple DNA fragment consisting of a sequence of three genes. The first, denoted p, is called *promoter* and is the place where a *RNA polymerase* enzyme (responsible for translation of DNA into RNA) binds to the DNA. The second, denoted o, is called *operator* and it is the place where a *repressor* protein (responsible for regulating the activity of the RNA polymerase) binds to the DNA. The third, denoted g, is the gene that encodes for the protein whose production is regulated by this process.

When the repressor is not bound to the DNA, the RNA polymerase can scan the sequence of genes and transcribe gene g into a piece of RNA that will be later translated into the protein encoded by g. When the repressor is bound to the DNA, it becomes an obstacle for the RNA polymerase that cannot scan anymore the sequence of genes.

The CLS model of this simple regulation process is a follows. The sequence of genes is represented as the CLS sequence $p \cdot o \cdot g$, the RNA polymerase enzyme as *polym*, the repressor protein as *repr*, and the piece of RNA obtained by the translation of gene g as *rna*. The rewrite rules describing the process are the following:

$$polym \mid p \cdot \widetilde{x} \; \mapsto \; pp \cdot \widetilde{x} \tag{R1}$$

$$repr \mid \widetilde{x} \cdot o \cdot \widetilde{y} \; \mapsto \; \widetilde{x} \cdot ro \cdot \widetilde{y} \tag{R2}$$

$$pp \cdot o \cdot \widetilde{x} \; \mapsto \; p \cdot po \cdot \widetilde{x} \tag{R3}$$

$$\widetilde{x} \cdot po \cdot g \; \mapsto \; \widetilde{x} \cdot o \cdot pg \tag{R4}$$

$$\widetilde{x} \cdot pg \; \mapsto \; polym \mid rna \mid \widetilde{x} \cdot g \tag{R5}$$

Rules R1 and R2 describe the binding of the RNA polymerase and of the repressor to the corresponding genes in the DNA sequences. The results of these bindings are that the symbols representing the two genes are replaced by pp and ro, respectively. Rules R3, R4 and R5 describe the activity of the RNA polymerase enzyme in the absence of the repressor: it moves from gene p to gene o in rule R3, then it moves from gene o to gene g in rule R4, and finally it produces the RNA fragment and leaves the DNA in rule R5. Note that, in order to apply rule R3, the repressor must not be bound to the DNA.

The only possible evolution of a term representing an initial situation in which no repressors are present is

$$polym \mid p \cdot o \cdot g \; \xrightarrow{(R1)} \; pp \cdot o \cdot g \; \xrightarrow{(R3)} \; p \cdot po \cdot g$$
$$\xrightarrow{(R4)} \; p \cdot o \cdot pg \; \xrightarrow{(R5)} \; polym \mid rna \mid p \cdot o \cdot g$$

that represents the case in which the RNA polymerase enzyme can scan the DNA sequence and transcribe gene g into a piece of RNA. When the repressor is present, instead, a possible evolution is

$$repr \mid polym \mid p \cdot o \cdot g \; \xrightarrow{(R1)} \; repr \mid pp \cdot o \cdot g \; \xrightarrow{(R2)} \; pp \cdot ro \cdot g$$

that corresponds to a situation in which the repressor stops the transcription of the gene by hampering the activity of the RNA polymerase.

3.2   An Extension for the Modeling of Protein Interaction at the Domain Level

To model a protein at the domain level in CLS it would be natural to use a sequence with one symbol for each domain. However, the binding between two domains of two different proteins, that is the linking between two elements of two different sequences, cannot be expressed in CLS. To represent this, CLS has been extended in [5] by labels on basic symbols. If in a term two symbols have the same label, we intend that they represent domains that are bound to each other. If in a term there is a single symbol with a certain label, we intend that the term represents only a part of a system we model, and that the symbol will be linked to another symbol in another part of the term representing the full model.

As membranes create compartments, elements inside a looping sequence cannot be linked to elements outside. Elements inside a membrane can be linked either to other elements inside the membrane or to elements of the membrane itself. An element can be linked at most to another element. The partner to which an element is bound can be different at different times, and a domain able to bind to multiple partners simultaneously could be described by using more elements instead of a single one.

For the sake of simplicity, the syntax of terms of the CLS with links (LCLS) is defined as in [5], namely the looping operator can be applied only to a single sequence rather than a LCLS term.

Definition 6 (Terms). *Terms T and sequences S of LCLS are given by the following grammar:*

$$T ::= S \mid (S)^L \, \rfloor \, T \mid T \mid T$$
$$S ::= \epsilon \mid a \mid a^n \mid S \cdot S$$

where a is a generic element of $\mathcal{E}$, and n is a natural number. We denote with $\mathcal{T}$ the infinite set of terms, and with $\mathcal{S}$ the infinite set of sequences.

Definition 7 (Structural Congruence). *The structural congruence relations $\equiv_S$ and $\equiv$ are the least congruence relations on sequences and on terms, respectively, satisfying the following rules:*

$$S_1 \cdot (S_2 \cdot S_3) \equiv_S (S_1 \cdot S_2) \cdot S_3 \qquad S \cdot \epsilon \equiv_S \epsilon \cdot S \equiv_S S$$

$$S_1 \equiv_S S_2 \text{ implies } S_1 \equiv S_2 \text{ and } (S_1)^L \, \rfloor \, T \equiv (S_2)^L \, \rfloor \, T$$
$$T_1 \mid T_2 \equiv T_2 \mid T_1 \qquad T_1 \mid (T_2 \mid T_3) \equiv (T_1 \mid T_2) \mid T_3 \qquad T \mid \epsilon \equiv T$$
$$(\epsilon)^L \, \rfloor \, \epsilon \equiv \epsilon \qquad (S_1 \cdot S_2)^L \, \rfloor \, T \equiv (S_2 \cdot S_1)^L \, \rfloor \, T$$

Note that, differently from the structural congruence relation of CLS, in this case the sequence to which the looping operator is applied can be rotated by axiom $(S_1 \cdot S_2)^L \, \rfloor \, T \equiv (S_2 \cdot S_1)^L \, \rfloor \, T$. For instance, the sequence $(a \cdot b^3 \cdot c)^L \, \rfloor \, d$ is equivalent to the sequence $(b^3 \cdot c \cdot a)^L \, \rfloor \, d$ and to the sequence $(c \cdot a \cdot b^3)^L \, \rfloor \, d$.

Patterns of LCLS are similar to those of CLS, with the addition of the labels.

Definition 8 (Patterns). *Patterns P and sequence patterns SP of LCLS are given by the following grammar:*

$$P ::= SP \mid (SP)^L \, \rfloor \, P \mid P \mid P \mid X$$
$$SP ::= \epsilon \mid a \mid a^n \mid SP \cdot SP \mid \tilde{x} \mid x \mid x^n$$

where a is an element of $\mathcal{E}$, n is a natural number and $X, \tilde{x}$ and x are elements of TV, SV and $\mathcal{X}$, respectively. We denote with $\mathcal{P}$ the infinite set of patterns.

Note that an LCLS term is also an LCLS pattern; everything we define for patterns will be immediately defined also for terms. Moreover, in what follows, we will often use the notions of *compartment* and of *top–level compartment* of a pattern. A compartment is a subpattern that is the second operand of a containment operator and in which the contents of inner containment operators are not considered. The top–level compartment is the portion of the pattern that is not the content of any containment operator. For instance, the top–level compartment of a pattern $P = a \mid (b)^{L} \rfloor c \mid (d)^{L} \rfloor (X \mid (e)^{L} \rfloor f)$ is $a \mid (b)^{L} \rfloor \epsilon \mid (d)^{L} \rfloor \epsilon$. Other compartments in P are c, $X \mid (e)^{L} \rfloor \epsilon$, and f.

An LCLS pattern is well–formed if and only if a label occurs no more than twice, and two occurrences of a label are always in the same compartment. The following type system will be used for deriving the well–formedness of patterns.

In each inference rule the conclusion has the form $(N, N') \models P$, where N and N' are sets of natural numbers with N the set of labels used twice and N' the set of labels used only once in the top–level compartment of P.

Definition 9 (Type System). *The typing algorithm for LCLS patterns is defined by the following inference rules:*

$$1.\ (\varnothing, \varnothing) \models \epsilon \qquad 2.\ (\varnothing, \varnothing) \models a \qquad 3.\ (\varnothing, \{n\}) \models a^{n}$$

$$4.\ (\varnothing, \varnothing) \models x \qquad 5.\ (\varnothing, \{n\}) \models x^{n} \qquad 6.\ (\varnothing, \varnothing) \models \tilde{x} \qquad 7.\ (\varnothing, \varnothing) \models X$$

$$8.\ \frac{(N_1, N_1') \models SP_1 \quad (N_2, N_2') \models SP_2 \quad N_1 \cap N_2 = N_1' \cap N_2 = N_1 \cap N_2' = \varnothing}{(N_1 \cup N_2 \cup (N_1' \cap N_2')), (N_1' \cup N_2') \setminus (N_1' \cap N_2')) \models SP_1 \cdot SP_2}$$

$$9.\ \frac{(N_1, N_1') \models P_1 \quad (N_2, N_2') \models P_2 \quad N_1 \cap N_2 = N_1' \cap N_2 = N_1 \cap N_2' = \varnothing}{(N_1 \cup N_2 \cup (N_1' \cap N_2')), (N_1' \cup N_2') \setminus (N_1' \cap N_2')) \models P_1 \mid P_2}$$

$$10.\ \frac{(N_1, N_1') \models SP \quad (N_2, N_2') \models P \quad N_1 \cap N_2 = N_1' \cap N_2 = N_1 \cap N_2' = \varnothing \quad N_2' \subseteq N_1'}{(N_1 \cup N_2', N_1' \setminus N_2') \models (SP)^{L} \rfloor P}$$

where a is a generic element of $\mathcal{E}$, n is a natural number, and $X, \tilde{x}$ and x are generic elements of TV, SV and $\mathcal{X}$, respectively. We write $\models P$ if there exist $N, N' \subset \mathbb{N}$ such that $(N, N') \models P$, and $\not\models P$ otherwise.

Rules 1–7 are self explanatory. Rule 8 states that a sequence pattern $SP_1 \cdot SP_2$ is well–typed if there are no labels occurring either four times ($N_1 \cap N_2 = \varnothing$) or three times ($N_1' \cap N_2 = N_1 \cap N_2' = \varnothing$). Labels occurring twice in $SP_1 \cdot SP_2$ are those which occur twice either in SP_1 or in SP_2 together with labels occurring once both in SP_1 and in SP_2. Rule 9 for the parallel composition is analogous to rule 8. Rule 10 states that the only labels which can be used for typing $(SP)^{L} \rfloor P$ must be different from those used for typing P. Moreover the labels used once in P must be used once in SP, that is these labels are used to bind elements inside the membrane to elements on the membrane itself. As an example, the pattern

$P \equiv a^1 \mid \left(b^1 \cdot b^2\right)^L \rfloor c \cdot c^2 \cdot c$ can be typed as follows.

$$(\emptyset, \{1\}) \models a^1 \qquad \text{(by rule 3)}$$
$$(\emptyset, \{1, 2\}) \models b^1 \cdot b^2 \qquad \text{(by rules 3 and 8)}$$
$$(\emptyset, \{2\}) \models c \cdot c^2 \cdot c \qquad \text{(by rules 2, 3 and 8)}$$
$$(\{2\}, \{1\}) \models \left(b^1 \cdot b^2\right)^L \rfloor c \cdot c^2 \cdot c \qquad \text{(by rule 10)}$$
$$(\{1, 2\}, \emptyset) \models P \qquad \text{(by rule 9)}$$

On the contrary, the pattern $a^1 \mid (b)^L \rfloor c^1$ cannot be typed because the premise $N_2' \subseteq N_1'$ of rule 10 of the type system is not satisfied. Similarly, $\not\models a^1 \mid b^1 \mid c^1$ and $\not\models a^1 \mid (b^1)^L \rfloor c^1$ hold since the premises of rules 9 and 10, respectively, are not satisfied.

The type system can be used to introduce a concept of well–formedness.

Definition 10 (Well–Formedness of Patterns). *A pattern P is* well–formed *if and only if $\models P$ holds.*

The use of labels to represent links is not new. In [17] well–formedness of terms is given by a concept of graph–likeness. We notice that in our case membranes, which are not present in the formalism of [17], make the treatment more complicated. In [28], where the concept of membrane is introduced, well–formedness of terms is given intuitively and not formally defined.

In the following we shall use a notion of multiset of labels and set of links of a pattern. The former represents the multiset of all the labels appearing in the top level compartment of a pattern, the latter represents the set of labels that occur twice in the top–level compartment of a pattern. We shall denote with $\#(e, M)$ the number of occurrences of element e in the multiset M.

Definition 11. *The* multiset of labels *of a pattern P is $L_M(P)$ where:*

$$L_M(\epsilon) = \varnothing \qquad L_M(\nu) = \varnothing \qquad L_M(\nu^n) = \{n\} \qquad L_M(\widetilde{x}) = \varnothing$$
$$L_M(SP_1 \cdot SP_2) = L_M(SP_1) \cup L_M(SP_2) \qquad L_M(P_1 \mid P_2) = L_M(P_1) \cup L_M(P_2)$$
$$L_M((SP)^L \rfloor P) = L_M(SP) \cup (L_M(SP) \cap L_M(P)) \qquad L_M(X) = \varnothing$$

where $\nu \in \mathcal{E} \cup EV$, $n \in \mathbb{N}$, P_1, P_2 are any pattern, SP is any sequence pattern.

Definition 12. *The* set of links *of a pattern P is $L(P) = \{n \mid \#(n, L_M(P)) = 2\}$,*

As an example, given pattern $P \equiv a^1 \mid \left(b^1 \cdot b^2\right)^L \rfloor c \cdot c^2 \cdot c^3 \mid a^3$, we have that $L_M(P) = \{1\} \cup \{1, 2\} \cup (\{1, 2\} \cap \{2, 3\}) = \{1, 1, 2, 2\}$ and, consequently, $L(P) = \{1, 2\}$ because link labeled by number 3 is not in the top–level compartment of P. If P is a well–formed pattern, there exists $N \subset \mathbb{N}$ such that $(L(P), N) \models P$.

Let $\mathcal{A}$ be the set of all total injective functions $\alpha : \mathbb{N} \rightarrow \mathbb{N}$. Given $\alpha \in \mathcal{A}$, the α–renaming of an LCLS pattern P is the pattern $P\alpha$ obtained by replacing every label n in P by $\alpha(n)$. For example, let P be $a^1 \mid (b^2)^L \rfloor c^2$ and α be such that $\alpha(n) = n + 1$. We have that $P\alpha \equiv a^2 \mid \left(b^3\right)^L \rfloor c^3$. It is easy to note that, since α is injective, the application of α–renaming to well–formed patterns preserves the well-formedness.

Links in a term are placeholders: the natural number used in the two labels of a link has not a particular meaning. Hence, we can consider as equivalent patterns which differ only in the values of their links. This equivalence is formally defined as follows.

Definition 13 (α–equivalence). *The α–equivalence relation $=_\alpha$ on LCLS patterns is the least equivalence relation which satisfies the following rules:*

1. $\dfrac{P_1 \equiv P_2}{P_1 =_\alpha P_2}$

2. $\dfrac{ni \notin L_M(SP_j) \quad i = 1,2 \quad j = 1,2,3}{SP_1 \cdot \nu^{n1} \cdot SP_2 \cdot \mu^{n1} \cdot SP_3 =_\alpha SP_1 \cdot \nu^{n2} \cdot SP_2 \cdot \mu^{n2} \cdot SP_3}$

3. $\dfrac{ni \notin L_M(SP_j) \quad i = 1,2 \quad j = 1,2,3,4}{SP_1 \cdot \nu^{n1} \cdot SP_2 \mid SP_3 \cdot \mu^{n1} \cdot SP_4 =_\alpha SP_1 \cdot \nu^{n2} \cdot SP_2 \mid SP_3 \cdot \mu^{n2} \cdot SP_4}$

4. $\dfrac{ni \notin L_M(SP_j) \cup L_M(P) \quad i = 1,2 \quad j = 1,2,3,4}{\left(SP_1 \cdot \nu^{n1} \cdot SP_2\right)^L \rfloor (SP_3 \cdot \mu^{n1} \cdot SP_4 \mid P) =_\alpha}$
$$\left(SP_1 \cdot \nu^{n2} \cdot SP_2\right)^L \rfloor (SP_3 \cdot \mu^{n2} \cdot SP_4 \mid P)$$

5. $\dfrac{ni \notin L_M(SP_j) \cup L_M(P) \quad i = 1,2 \quad j = 1,2,3,4}{SP_1 \cdot \mu^{n1} \cdot SP_2 \mid \left(SP_3 \cdot \nu^{n1} \cdot SP_4\right)^L \rfloor P =_\alpha}$
$$SP_1 \cdot \mu^{n2} \cdot SP_2 \mid \left(SP_3 \cdot \nu^{n2} \cdot SP_4\right)^L \rfloor P$$

6. $\dfrac{ni \notin L_M(SP_j) \cup L_M(P_k) \quad i = 1,2 \quad j = 1,2,3,4 \quad k = 1,2}{\left(SP_1 \cdot \mu^{n1} \cdot SP_2\right)^L \rfloor P_1 \mid \left(SP_3 \cdot \nu^{n1} \cdot SP_4\right)^L \rfloor P_2 =_\alpha}$
$$\left(SP_1 \cdot \mu^{n2} \cdot SP_2\right)^L \rfloor P_1 \mid \left(SP_3 \cdot \nu^{n2} \cdot SP_4\right)^L \rfloor P_2$$

7. $\dfrac{ni \notin L_M(SP_j) \cup L_M(P_k) \quad i = 1,2 \quad j = 1,2,3,4 \quad k = 1,2}{\left(SP_1 \cdot \mu^{n1} \cdot SP_2\right)^L \rfloor (P_1 \mid \left(SP_3 \cdot \nu^{n1} \cdot SP_4\right)^L \rfloor P_2) =_\alpha}$
$$\left(SP_1 \cdot \mu^{n2} \cdot SP_2\right)^L \rfloor (P_1 \mid \left(SP_3 \cdot \nu^{n2} \cdot SP_4\right)^L \rfloor P_2)$$

8. $\dfrac{\begin{array}{c} P_1 =_\alpha P_2 \quad P_3 =_\alpha P_4 \\ L_M(P_1) \cap L(P_3) = L(P_1) \cap L_M(P_3) = \varnothing \\ L_M(P_2) \cap L(P_4) = L(P_2) \cap L_M(P_4) = \varnothing \end{array}}{P_1 \mid P_3 =_\alpha P_2 \mid P_4}$

9. $\dfrac{\begin{array}{c} SP_1 =_\alpha SP_2 \quad P_1 =_\alpha P_2 \\ L_M(SP_1) \cap L(P_1) = L(SP_1) \cap L_M(P_1) = \varnothing \\ L_M(SP_2) \cap L(P_2) = L(SP_2) \cap L_M(P_2) = \varnothing \end{array}}{\left(SP_1\right)^L \rfloor P_1 =_\alpha \left(SP_2\right)^L \rfloor P_2}$

where $\nu, \mu \in \mathcal{E} \cup EV$, $n1, n2 \in \mathbb{N}$, P_1, P_2, P_3, P_4 are any pattern, SP_1, SP_2, SP_3, SP_4 are any sequence pattern.

Rule 1 says that structurally congruent patterns are also α–equivalent. rules from 2 to 7 describe the ridenomination of the two labels of a link with fresh labels. Each rule deals with a possible situation in which a link may occur. Rule 2 deals with links between two elements of the same sequence, rule 3 with links between two elements of two sequences composed in parallel, and so on. Rules 8 and 9 describe the closure of the relation with respect to parallel composition and containment.

As an example, the term $a^1 \cdot b^2 \cdot c^1 \cdot d \mid \left(e^2 \cdot f^3 \cdot g\right)^L \rfloor h^3 \cdot i$ is α–equivalent to the term $a^4 \cdot b^5 \cdot c^4 \cdot d \mid \left(e^5 \cdot f^6 \cdot g\right)^L \rfloor h^6 \cdot i$ as rules 2 and 8 can be used to replace link 1 with link 4, rules 5 and 8 to replace link 2 with link 5 and rules 4 and 8 to replace link 3 with link 6.

Note that the labels occurring only once in a pattern P are not renamed by the α–equivalence relation. Instead, the application of an α–renaming function to P may change these labels. Moreover, labels which occur twice in more than one compartment of the pattern can be renamed differently in each compartment by the α–equivalence relation, while they are all renamed by the same value by applying some α–renaming function.

As in CLS, rewrite rules in LCLS are pairs of patterns, but in this case we require that the two patterns are well–formed.

Definition 14 (Rewrite Rules). *A rewrite rule is a pair of well–formed patterns* (P_1, P_2), *denoted with* $P_1 \mapsto P_2$, *where* $P_1, P_2 \in \mathcal{P}$, $P_1 \not\equiv \epsilon$, *and such that* $Var(P_2) \subseteq Var(P_1)$. *We denote with* $\Re$ *the infinite set of all the possible rewrite rules.*

Now, we can define the semantics of LCLS.

Definition 15 (Semantics). *Given a set of rewrite rules* $\mathcal{R} \subseteq \Re$, *the semantics of LCLS is the least transition relation* $\rightarrow$ *on well–formed terms closed under* $\equiv$ *and* $=_\alpha$, *and satisfying the following inference rules:*

$$(app) \quad \frac{P_1 \mapsto P_2 \in \mathcal{R} \quad P_1\sigma \not\equiv \epsilon \quad \sigma \in \Sigma \quad \alpha \in \mathcal{A}}{P_1\alpha\sigma \rightarrow P_2\alpha\sigma}$$

$$(par) \quad \frac{T_1 \rightarrow T_1' \quad L(T_1) \cap L(T_2) = \{n_1, \ldots, n_M\} \quad n_1', \ldots, n_M' \; fresh}{T_1 \mid T_2 \rightarrow T_1'\{n_1', \ldots, n_M'/n_1, \ldots, n_M\} \mid T_2}$$

$$(cont) \quad \frac{T \rightarrow T' \quad L(S) \cap L(T') = \{n_1, \ldots, n_M\} \quad n_1', \ldots, n_M' \; fresh}{(S)^L \rfloor T \rightarrow (S)^L \rfloor T'\{n_1', \ldots, n_M'/n_1, \ldots, n_M\}}$$

where the symmetric rule for the parallel composition is omitted.

Rule *(app)* says that a rewrite rule $P_1 \mapsto P_2$ can be applied to a term that can be obtained from P_1 by some renaming α and instantiation σ. The result of the application is P_2 renamed and instantiated in the same manner. Rule *(par)* describes the derivation of a transition from a state represented by a parallel composition of terms. In such a state, for the set of links $\{n_1, \ldots, n_M\}$ of both T_1 and T_2, a set of fresh links $\{n_1', \ldots, n_M'\}$ is assumed. The fresh links substitute in T_1' the links with the same name T_1 and T_2. Rule *(cont)* describes the derivation of a transition from a state given by a looping. Also in this case fresh links are assumed and substituted into the term which describes the new content of the membrane T'. It is worth noting that, as the semantics is defined over well–formed terms, no transitions can be derived that lead to non well–formed terms. As a consequence, rewrite rules cannot be applied if they transform a term into another which is not well–formed. For instance, rewrite rule $a^1 \mapsto a$ cannot be applied to $(c)^L \rfloor (a^1 \mid b^1 \cdot b)$ as it would result in $(c)^L \rfloor (a \mid b^1 \cdot b)$ that is not well–formed. We have introduced this restriction on the the domain of the semantics for the sake of simplicity. In [5] we have given a more complex semantics which preserves well–formedness without the need of this restriction.

Example. We model in LCLS the steps of the EGF pathway (see example in Section 3.1) up to the binding of the protein SHC to the dimer. We model the EGFR protein as the sequence $R_{E1} \cdot R_{E2} \cdot R_{I1} \cdot R_{I2}$, where R_{E1} and R_{E2} are two extra–cellular domains and R_{I1} and R_{I2} are two intra–cellular domains. The membrane of the cell is modeled as a looping sequence which could contain EGFR proteins. Outside the looping sequence (i.e. in the environment) there could be EGF proteins, and inside (i.e. in the cytoplasm) there could be SHC proteins. The rewrite rules modeling the pathway are the following:

$$EGF \mid \left(R_{E1} \cdot \widetilde{x}\right)^L \rfloor X \;\; \mapsto \;\; \left(SR_{E1} \cdot \widetilde{x}\right)^L \rfloor X \tag{R1}$$

$$\left(SR_{E1} \cdot R_{E2} \cdot R_{I1} \cdot R_{I2} \cdot \widetilde{x} \cdot SR_{E1} \cdot R_{E2} \cdot R_{I1} \cdot R_{I2} \cdot \widetilde{y}\right)^L \rfloor X \;\; \mapsto$$
$$\left(SR_{E1} \cdot R_{E2}^1 \cdot R_{I1} \cdot R_{I2} \cdot SR_{E1} \cdot R_{E2}^1 \cdot R_{I1} \cdot R_{I2} \cdot \widetilde{x} \cdot \widetilde{y}\right)^L \rfloor X \tag{R2}$$

$$\left(R_{E2}^1 \cdot R_{I1} \cdot \widetilde{x} \cdot R_{E2}^1 \cdot R_{I1} \cdot \widetilde{y}\right)^L \rfloor X \;\; \mapsto \;\; \left(R_{E2}^1 \cdot PR_{I1} \cdot \widetilde{x} \cdot R_{E2}^1 \cdot R_{I1} \cdot \widetilde{y}\right)^L \rfloor X \tag{R3}$$

$$\left(R_{E2}^1 \cdot PR_{I1} \cdot \widetilde{x} \cdot R_{E2}^1 \cdot R_{I1} \cdot \widetilde{y}\right)^L \rfloor X \;\; \mapsto \;\; \left(R_{E2}^1 \cdot PR_{I1} \cdot \widetilde{x} \cdot R_{E2}^1 \cdot PR_{I1} \cdot \widetilde{y}\right)^L \rfloor X \tag{R4}$$

$$\left(R_{E2}^1 \cdot PR_{I1} \cdot R_{I2} \cdot \widetilde{x} \cdot R_{E2}^1 \cdot PR_{I1} \cdot R_{I2} \cdot \widetilde{y}\right)^L \rfloor (SHC \mid X) \;\; \mapsto$$
$$\left(R_{E2}^1 \cdot PR_{I1} \cdot R_{I2}^2 \cdot \widetilde{x} \cdot R_{E2}^1 \cdot PR_{I1} \cdot R_{I2} \cdot \widetilde{y}\right)^L \rfloor (SHC^2 \mid X) \tag{R5}$$

Rule R1 represents the binding of the EGF protein to the receptor domain R_{E1} with SR_{E1} as a result. Rule R2 represents that when two EGFR proteins activated by proteins EGF occur on the membrane, they may bind to each other to form a dimer (shown by the link 1). Rule R3 represents the phosphorylation of one of the internal domains R_{I1} of the dimer, and rule R4 represents the phosphorylation of the other internal domain R_{I1} of the dimer. The result of each phosphorylation is PR_{I1}. Rule R5 represents the binding of the protein SHC in the cytoplasm to an internal domain R_{I2} of the dimer. Remark that the binding of SHC to the dimer is represented by the link 2, allowing the protein SHC to continue the interactions to stimulate cell proliferation.

Let us denote the $R_{E1} \cdot R_{E2} \cdot R_{I1} \cdot R_{I2}$ by EGFR. By starting from a cell with some EGFR proteins on its membrane, some SHC proteins in the cytoplasm and some EGF proteins in the environment, a possible evolution is the following (we write on each transition the name of the rewrite rule applied):

$$EGF \mid EGF \mid (EGFR \cdot EGFR \cdot EGFR \cdot EGFR)^L \; \rfloor \; (SHC \mid SHC)$$

$$\xrightarrow{(R1)} EGF \mid (SR_{E1} \cdot R_{E2} \cdot R_{I1} \cdot R_{I2} \cdot EGFR \cdot EGFR \cdot EGFR)^L \; \rfloor \; (SHC \mid SHC)$$

$$\xrightarrow{(R1)} (SR_{E1} \cdot R_{E2} \cdot R_{I1} \cdot R_{I2} \cdot EGFR \cdot SR_{E1} \cdot R_{E2} \cdot R_{I1} \cdot R_{I2} \cdot EGFR)^L \; \rfloor \; (SHC \mid SHC)$$

$$\xrightarrow{(R2)} (SR_{E1} \cdot R_{E2}^1 \cdot R_{I1} \cdot R_{I2} \cdot SR_{E1} \cdot R_{E2}^1 \cdot R_{I1} \cdot R_{I2} \cdot EGFR \cdot EGFR)^L \; \rfloor \; (SHC \mid SHC)$$

$$\xrightarrow{(R3)} (SR_{E1} \cdot R_{E2}^1 \cdot PR_{I1} \cdot R_{I2} \cdot SR_{E1} \cdot R_{E2}^1 \cdot R_{I1} \cdot R_{I2} \cdot EGFR \cdot EGFR)^L \; \rfloor \; (SHC \mid SHC)$$

$$\xrightarrow{(R4)} (SR_{E1} \cdot R_{E2}^1 \cdot PR_{I1} \cdot R_{I2} \cdot SR_{E1} \cdot R_{E2}^1 \cdot PR_{I1} \cdot R_{I2} \cdot EGFR \cdot EGFR)^L \; \rfloor \; (SHC \mid SHC)$$

$$\xrightarrow{(R5)} (SR_{E1} \cdot R_{E2}^1 \cdot PR_{I1} \cdot R_{I2}^2 \cdot SR_{E1} \cdot R_{E2}^1 \cdot PR_{I1} \cdot R_{I2} \cdot EGFR \cdot EGFR)^L \; \rfloor \; (SHC^2 \mid SHC)$$

3.3 A Stochastic Extension

In CLS only qualitative aspects of biological systems are considered, such as their structure and the presence (or the absence) of certain molecules. As a consequence, on CLS models it is only possible to verify properties such as the reachability of particular states or causality relationships between events. It would be interesting to verify also properties such as the time spent to reach a particular state, or the probability of reaching it. To face this problem, in [6] we have developed a stochastic extension of CLS, called *Stochastic CLS*, in which quantitative aspects, such as time and probability, are taken into account.

The standard way of extending a formalism to model quantitative aspects of biological systems is by incorporating the stochastic framework developed by Gillespie with its simulation algorithm for chemical reactions [24] in the semantics of the formalism. This has been done, for instance, for the π–calculus [35,37]. The idea of Gillespie's algorithm is that a rate constant is associated with each chemical reaction that may occur in the system. Such a constant is obtained by multiplying the kinetic constant of the reaction by the number of possible combinations of reactants that may occur in the system. The resulting rate constant is then used as the parameter of an exponential distribution modeling the time spent between two occurrences of the considered chemical reaction.

The use of exponential distributions to represent the (stochastic) time spent between two occurrences of chemical reactions allows the description of the system as a Continuous Time Markov Chain (CTMC), and consequently it allows the verification of properties of the described system by means of analytic tools and by means of stochastic model checkers.

In Stochastic CLS, the incorporation of Gillespie's stochastic framework is not a simple exercise. The main difficulty is counting the number of possible reactant combinations of the chemical reaction described by a rewrite rule. Reactants are given by the left pattern in a rewrite rule, which may contain variables. A rewrite rule can be applied in different positions of the term which describes the state of the system. In order to compute the rate of application of the rule we have to count the number of different positions where the rewrite rule can be applied, by taking into account instantiation of variables.

We have defined the Stochastic CLS in [6], and showed how to derive a CTMC from the semantics of a system modeled in the formalism. This allows performing simulation and verification of properties of the described systems, for instance by using stochastic model checkers, such as PRISM [27].

In the present work the semantics given in [6] is slightly revised. In particular, the rewrite rules defined in [6] are enriched, with respect to those of CLS, with a rate function while, here, they are enriched with a kinetic constant. Rate functions, built over the domain of the instantiation functions σ, were assumed to be defined in order to correctly compute the rate of the modeled chemical reaction. Intuitively, a rule with left hand side $a \mid (c \mid X)^L \rfloor \epsilon$ modeling a reaction with reactants a and c, where c is placed on the surface of a membrane, should have a rate which depends on the number of c appearing on the surface itself, that is on the instantiation of X. In the semantics of [6], the computation of the number of c appearing at in the term $\sigma(X)$ is assumed to be done by the rate function associated with the rule. Differently, the semantics we define here, embeds such a computation. Obviously, the version of Stochastic CLS of [6] is more general as any function can be associated with a rule to specify how the rule rate has to be computed. However, the restrictions we introduce here simplify the modeling of biochemical systems.

Now we can define Stochastic CLS. The syntax of terms and the structural congruence relations are the same as those of CLS defined in Section 3.1.

As regards patterns, in Stochastic CLS we distinguish between the patterns that will be used on the left hand side of rewrite rules (called *left patterns*) and those that will be used on the right hand side of rewrite rules (called *right patterns*). In particular, we will impose restrictions on the use of term variables of left patterns in order to simplify the definition of the stochastic semantics.

Definition 16 (Patterns). Left patterns P_L and right patterns P_R of Stochastic CLS are given by the following grammar:

$$
\begin{aligned}
P_L &::= SP \mid \left(P_X\right)^L \rfloor P_X \mid P_L \mid P_L \\
P_X &::= P_L \mid P_L \mid X \\
P_R &::= SP \mid \left(P_R\right)^L \rfloor P_R \mid P_R \mid P_R \mid X \\
SP &::= \epsilon \mid a \mid SP \cdot SP \mid \tilde{x} \mid x
\end{aligned}
$$

where $X, \tilde{x}$ and x are generic elements of TV, SV and $\mathcal{X}$, respectively. The sets of all left and right patterns are denoted with $\mathcal{P}_L$ and $\mathcal{P}_R$, respectively.

We assume the structural congruence relation to be trivially extended to patterns. Furthermore, note that right patterns P_R are exactly the same as CLS patterns (see Definition 3) while left patterns P_L contain the following restrictions:

- term variables cannot appear in a parallel composition at the top–level of the pattern. In other words, they must always appear in an operand of some looping and containment operator. For example, $a \cdot b \mid X$ is not a syntactically correct left pattern, whereas $\left(a\right)^L \rfloor (a \cdot b \mid X)$ and $\left(a \cdot b \mid X\right)^L \rfloor a$ are correct;

– a parallel composition cannot have among its components more than one term variable which is not involved in the application of some looping and containment operator. For example, $(a)^L \rfloor (a{\cdot}b \mid X \mid Y)$ is not a syntactically correct term, whereas $(a)^L \rfloor (a \cdot b \mid X \mid (Y)^L \rfloor Z)$ is correct.

These restrictions simplify the definition of the stochastic semantics and the development of a simulator of Stochastic CLS models. In fact, the restrictions allow us to prove that for all $P \in \mathcal{P}_L$ and $\sigma, \sigma' \in \Sigma$, $P\sigma \equiv P\sigma'$ implies that for all $X \in TV$ it holds $\sigma(X) \equiv \sigma'(X)$. This means that the instantiation of term variables in the application of a rewrite rule to a specific portion of a term is always unique. This result is important in the definition of the stochastic semantics because, as we shall see, to compute the application rate of a rule we will need to count the number of occurrences of some sequences in the instantiation of the term variables of the rule.

The restrictions we impose do not reduce significantly the expressiveness of the formalism in the modeling of biological systems. As regards the use of term variables at top–level of a left pattern of a rule, by the definition of the semantics, such a rule could rewrite any portion of the term representing the state of the system. From a biological perspective, this would correspond to modeling a reaction with an uncertain number of reactants. Analogously, two term variables inside a looping or a containment operator of a rule could be instantiated in many different ways correspondingly to different partitions of the term. From a biological perspective, this would represent a reaction between, for instance, two arbitrary portions of the content of a membrane. Consequently, as chemical reactions happen usually between a fixed and small number of reactants, the restriction appears to be reasonable.

We now introduce stochastic rewrite rules.

Definition 17 (Stochastic Rewrite Rules). *A stochastic rewrite rule is a pair of patterns and a kinetic constant (P_1, P_2, k), denoted with $P_1 \xmapsto{k} P_2$, where $P_1 \in \mathcal{P}_L$, $P_2 \in \mathcal{P}_R$, $P_1 \not\equiv \epsilon$, $k \in \mathbb{R}$ and such that $Var(P_2) \subseteq Var(P_1)$. We denote with $\mathfrak{R}$ the infinite set of all the possible rewrite rules.*

As said above, we distinguish between the patterns on the left and on the right hand sides of a (stochastic) rewrite rule, and we assume some restrictions on the use of term variables on the left hand side. As examples of forbidden rules, consider $a \mid X \mapsto a$ and $(b)^L \rfloor (X \mid Y) \mapsto (b)^L \rfloor X$. The former removes from the term to which it is applied an arbitrary number of components of a parallel composition where a appears. The latter removes an arbitrary portion of the content of any $(b)^L$ occurring in the term to which it is applied. The left hand sides of both of these rules violate the restrictions we have imposed on left patterns.

Stochastic rewrite rules will be applied with a frequency that corresponds to the rate of occurrence of chemical reactions computed by Gillespie's algorithm [24]. This means that a rule such as $a \mid b \xmapsto{k} c$, modeling the formation of a complex c as result of the binding of two molecules a and b, will be applied with a frequency proportional to k and to the number of possible combinations of elements a and b in the term to which the rule is applied. For instance, if the rule is applied to term $a \mid a \mid b \mid b \mid b$, then its application rate will be $6k$. Instead, if the rule is applied to $a \mid a \mid b \mid (c)^L \rfloor (a \mid a \mid b \mid b)$, then its application rate will be $2k$ if the rule is applied to a pair a, b at the top–level of the term, and will be $4k$ if the rule is applied to a pair a, b contained in the looping.

More complex is the case of a rule such as $a \mid (b{\cdot}\widetilde{x} \mid X)^L \rfloor Y \overset{k}{\mapsto} (c{\cdot}\widetilde{x} \mid X)^L \rfloor Y$, modeling the binding of a molecule a with a portion b of a molecule on the surface of some membrane. In this case, the frequency of application of the rule should be proportional to the number of symbols a in the term and to the number of sequences starting with b in the instantiation of X plus one (the instantiation of $b{\cdot}\widetilde{x}$). For instance, the rate of application of the rule to the term $a \mid a \mid a \mid (b \cdot a \mid b \cdot a)^L \rfloor c$ should be $6k$.

The application rate of a rewrite rule will be computed by the semantics of Stochastic CLS. Before defining it, we need to introduce some auxiliary functions. Let $\mathbf{n} : \mathcal{T} \times \mathcal{T} \to \mathbb{N}$ be a function such that $\mathbf{n}(T, T')$ computes the *number of occurrences* of the term T', assumed either to be a sequence or to have the form $(T_1)^L \rfloor T_2$, as a component of the parallel composition at the top–level of T. Formally,

$$\mathbf{n}(T_1 \mid T_2, T') = \mathbf{n}(T_1, T') + \mathbf{n}(T_2, T')$$

$$\mathbf{n}(S, S') = \begin{cases} 1, & \text{if } S \equiv S' \\ 0, & \text{otherwise} \end{cases}$$

$$\mathbf{n}((T_1)^L \rfloor T_2, (T'_1)^L \rfloor T'_2) = \begin{cases} 1, & \text{if } T_1 \equiv T'_1 \text{ and } T_2 \equiv T'_2 \\ 0, & \text{otherwise} \end{cases}$$

For instance, $\mathbf{n}(a \cdot b \mid a \cdot b, a \cdot b) = 2$ and $\mathbf{n}((m)^L \rfloor a \mid (m)^L \rfloor b, (m)^L \rfloor a) = 1$. Furthermore, let us denote with $\overline{T}$ the set containing all the sequences and all the membranes (with their content) appearing at top–level in T. For instance, if $T \equiv a \mid a \mid (a)^L \rfloor b \mid (a \mid a)^L \rfloor b$, then $\overline{T} = \{a, (a)^L \rfloor b, (a \mid a)^L \rfloor b\}$. Let $comb : \mathcal{P}_L \times \Sigma \to \mathbb{N}$ be a function which, given a left pattern P_L and an instantiation function σ, computes the number of *combinations of reactants* of P_L in $P_L \sigma$. The function $comb$ can be recursively defined as follows:

$$comb(SP, \sigma) = 1$$

$$comb(P_{L1} \mid P_{L2}, \sigma) = comb(P_{L1}, \sigma) \cdot comb(P_{L2}, \sigma)$$

$$comb((P_{X1})^L \rfloor P_{X2}, \sigma) = comb'(P_{X1}, \sigma) \cdot comb'(P_{X2}, \sigma)$$

where $comb'$ is defined as follows:

$$comb'(P_L, \sigma) = comb(P_L, \sigma)$$

$$comb'(P_L \mid X, \sigma) = \prod_{T \in \overline{P_L \sigma}} \binom{\mathbf{n}(P_L \sigma \mid \sigma(X), T)}{\mathbf{n}(P_L \sigma, T)} \cdot comb(P_L, \sigma).$$

The reactants of a left pattern are the sequence patterns it contains. As a consequence, for a single sequence pattern, *comb* is 1. For the parallel composition of two left patterns *comb* is the product of the values of *comb* for the two components. For looping and containment of two patterns, note that the restriction we have imposed on left patterns ensures that in each pattern there may be at most one term variable. Therefore, one must count the occurrences of reactant combinations in the instantiations of such variables. This implies the computation of a binomial coefficient for each distinct reactant, and the result of this computation is given by *comb'*. If in the considered pattern there are no term variables, then *comb'* is equal to *comb*. If a term variable is present, then *comb'* gives the product of all binomial coefficients for each distinct reactant, namely for each element of the set $P_L\sigma$, multiplied by the number of combinations of reactants which may result from P_L.

For instance, given $\sigma = \{(X, b \mid c), (Y, a \mid c \mid c)\}$ and $P_L \equiv a \mid a \mid (b \mid X)^L \rfloor (c \mid Y)$, we have $comb(P_L, \sigma) = 1 \cdot 1 \cdot comb'(b \mid X, \sigma) \cdot comb'(c \mid Y, \sigma) = 2 \cdot 3 = 6$.

Now we must also take into account the fact that in the context in which a rewrite rule applies there may be other reactants, and therefore the rate of application of the rule should be consequentially increased.

If we have a rewrite rule $P_L \overset{k}{\mapsto} P_R$, we have seen that we can compute the number of combinations of reactants of such a rule in $P_L\sigma$ as $comb(P_L, \sigma)$. However, if the term to which the rule is applied is $P_L\sigma \mid T$, then the number of combinations of reactans should become

$$comb(P_L, \sigma) \cdot \prod_{T' \in \overline{P_L\sigma}} \binom{\mathbf{n}(P_L\sigma \mid T, T')}{\mathbf{n}(P_L\sigma, T')}.$$

In fact, $\prod_{T' \in \overline{P_L\sigma}} \binom{\mathbf{n}(P_L\sigma \mid T, T')}{\mathbf{n}(P_L\sigma, T')}$ is the number of combinations of components of $P_L\sigma$ in the extended term $P_L\sigma \mid T$, that is the number of positions in $P_L\sigma \mid T$ where a rule with left hand side P_L can be applied.

As an example, if $P_L \equiv (a)^L \rfloor (b \mid X), \sigma(X) = b$ and $T \equiv (a)^L \rfloor (b \mid b) \mid c$, then $P_L\sigma \mid T$ is $(a)^L \rfloor (b \mid b) \mid (a)^L \rfloor (b \mid b) \mid c$ and the number of combinations of reactants of P_L in $P_L\sigma \mid T$ is $comb(P_L, \sigma) \cdot \prod_{T' \in \overline{P_L\sigma}} \binom{\mathbf{n}(P_L\sigma \mid T, T')}{\mathbf{n}(P_L\sigma, T')} = 2 \cdot \binom{2}{1} = 4$. In fact, in $P_L \mid T$ there are four pairs of reactants a and b to which a rule with P_L on the left hand side could be applied.

Our aim is to compute compositionally this increase of the rate of application of a rule due to some reactant that is in the context of the portion of the term to which the rule applies. To this purpose we define, as follows, an auxiliary function $binom : \mathcal{T} \times \mathcal{T} \times \mathcal{T} \to \mathbb{Q}$:

$$binom(T_1, T_2, T_3) = \prod_{T \in \overline{T_1}} \prod_{i=1}^{\mathbf{n}(T_3, T)} \frac{\mathbf{n}(T_2, T) + i}{\mathbf{n}(T_2, T) - \mathbf{n}(T_1, T) + i}.$$

The following two propositions show that *binom* can be used to compute the increase of the application rate we are interested in, and that such and increase can be computed compositionally.

Proposition 1. *Given* $P_L \in \mathcal{P}_L, T \in \mathcal{T}$ *and* $\sigma \in \Sigma$ *it holds*

$$binom(P_L\sigma, P_L\sigma, T) = \prod_{T' \in \overline{P_L\sigma}} \binom{\mathbf{n}(P_L\sigma \mid T, T')}{\mathbf{n}(P_L\sigma, T')}.$$

Proof. By the definition of *binom* it follows

$$binom(P_L\sigma, P_L\sigma, T) = \prod_{T' \in \overline{P_L\sigma}} \prod_{i=1}^{\mathbf{n}(T,T')} \frac{\mathbf{n}(P_L\sigma, T') + i}{\mathbf{n}(P_L\sigma, T') - \mathbf{n}(P_L\sigma, T) + i} =$$

$$= \prod_{T' \in \overline{P_L\sigma}} \frac{(\mathbf{n}(P\sigma, T') + \mathbf{n}(T, T')) \cdot (\mathbf{n}(P\sigma, T') + \mathbf{n}(T, T') - 1) \cdots (\mathbf{n}(P\sigma, T') + 1)}{\mathbf{n}(T, T')!}$$

since $\mathbf{n}(P_L\sigma, T') + \mathbf{n}(T, T') = \mathbf{n}(P_L\sigma \mid T, T')$ this is equal to

$$\prod_{T' \in \overline{P_L\sigma}} \frac{\mathbf{n}(P_L\sigma \mid T, T') \cdot (\mathbf{n}(P_L\sigma \mid T, T') - 1) \cdots (\mathbf{n}(P_L\sigma \mid T, T') - \mathbf{n}(T, T') + 1)}{\mathbf{n}(T, T')!} =$$

$$= \prod_{T' \in \overline{P_L\sigma}} \frac{\mathbf{n}(P_L\sigma \mid T, T')!}{\mathbf{n}(T, T')! \cdot (\mathbf{n}(P_L\sigma \mid T, T') - \mathbf{n}(T, T'))!} = \prod_{T' \in \overline{P_L\sigma}} \binom{\mathbf{n}(P_L\sigma \mid T, T')}{\mathbf{n}(T, T')}$$

and, by the well-known property of binomial coefficients such that $\binom{n}{k} = \binom{n}{n-k}$, this is equal to

$$\prod_{T' \in \overline{P_L\sigma}} \binom{\mathbf{n}(P_L\sigma \mid T, T')}{\mathbf{n}(P_L\sigma, T')}.$$

$\square$

Proposition 2. *Given* $P_L \in \mathcal{P}_L, T_1, T_2 \in \mathcal{T}$ *and* $\sigma \in \Sigma$ *it holds*

$$binom(P_L\sigma, P_L\sigma, T_1 \mid T_2) = binom(P_L\sigma, P_L\sigma, T_1) \cdot binom(P_L\sigma, P_L\sigma \mid T_1, T_2).$$

Proof. By Proposition 1 the property we have to prove can be rewritten as

$$\prod_{T \in \overline{P_L\sigma}} \binom{\mathbf{n}(P_L\sigma \mid T_1 \mid T_2, T)}{\mathbf{n}(P_L\sigma, T)} = \prod_{T \in \overline{P_L\sigma}} \binom{\mathbf{n}(P_L\sigma \mid T_1, T)}{\mathbf{n}(P_L\sigma, T)} \cdot binom(P_L\sigma, P_L\sigma \mid T_1, T_2) =$$

$$= \prod_{T \in \overline{P_L\sigma}} \binom{\mathbf{n}(P_L\sigma \mid T_1, T)}{\mathbf{n}(P_L\sigma, T)} \cdot \prod_{T \in \overline{P_L\sigma \mid T_1}} \prod_{i=1}^{\mathbf{n}(T_2, T)} \frac{\mathbf{n}(P_L\sigma \mid T_1, T) + i}{\mathbf{n}(P_L\sigma \mid T_1, T) - \mathbf{n}(P_L\sigma, T) + i}$$

Now, let $n, m, k \in \mathbb{N}$ be such that $k \leq n$. The following equation holds:

$$\binom{n+m}{k} = \frac{(n+m)!}{k!(n+m-k)!} = \frac{(n+m)\cdots(n+1) \cdot n \cdots (k+1)}{(n+m-k)!} =$$

$$= \frac{(n+m)\cdots(n+1)}{(n+m-k)\cdots(n+1-k)} \cdot \frac{n \cdots (k+1)}{(n-k)!} = \left(\prod_{i=1}^{m} \frac{n+i}{n+i-k}\right) \cdot \binom{n}{k}.$$

This resuls and the fact that $\mathbf{n}(P_L\sigma \mid T_1 \mid T_2, P_L\sigma) = \mathbf{n}(P_L\sigma \mid T_1, P_L\sigma) + \mathbf{n}(T_2, P_L\sigma)$, are used in what follows:

$$\prod_{T \in \overline{P_L\sigma}} \binom{\mathbf{n}(P_L\sigma \mid T_1 \mid T_2, T)}{\mathbf{n}(P_L\sigma, T)} = \prod_{T \in \overline{P_L\sigma}} \binom{\mathbf{n}(P_L\sigma \mid T_1, T) + \mathbf{n}(T_2, T)}{\mathbf{n}(P_L\sigma, T)} =$$

$$= \prod_{T \in \overline{P_L\sigma}} \left(\binom{\mathbf{n}(P_L\sigma \mid T_1, T)}{\mathbf{n}(P_L\sigma, T)} \cdot \prod_{i=1}^{\mathbf{n}(T_2,T)} \frac{\mathbf{n}(P_L\sigma \mid T_1, T) + i}{\mathbf{n}(P_L\sigma \mid T_1, T) - \mathbf{n}(P_L\sigma, T) + i} \right) =$$

$$= \left(\prod_{T \in \overline{P_L\sigma}} \binom{\mathbf{n}(P_L\sigma \mid T_1, T)}{\mathbf{n}(P_L\sigma, T)} \right) \cdot \left(\prod_{T \in \overline{P_L\sigma}} \prod_{i=1}^{\mathbf{n}(T_2,T)} \frac{\mathbf{n}(P_L\sigma \mid T_1, T) + i}{\mathbf{n}(P_L\sigma \mid T_1, T) - \mathbf{n}(P_L\sigma, T) + i} \right) =$$

$$= \left(\prod_{T \in \overline{P_L\sigma}} \binom{\mathbf{n}(P_L\sigma \mid T_1, T)}{\mathbf{n}(P_L\sigma, T)} \right) \cdot binom(P_L\sigma, P_L\sigma \mid T_1, T_2).$$

$\square$

As an example, if we assume $P_L \equiv a \mid b$ and $\sigma = \varnothing$, we have $comb(P_L, \sigma) = 1$. Let us consider the terms $T_1 = a \mid c$ and $T_2 = a \mid b$. We have that the number of combinations of reactants of P_L in $P_L\sigma \mid T_1 \mid T_2$ is $comb(P_L, \sigma) \cdot \prod_{T \in \{a,b\}} \binom{\mathbf{n}(a\mid b\mid a\mid c\mid a\mid b, T)}{\mathbf{n}(a\mid b, T)} = \binom{3}{1}\binom{2}{1} = 6$. By applying $binom$ compositionally, we obtain $comb(P_L, \sigma) \cdot binom(a \mid b, a \mid b, a \mid c) \cdot binom(a \mid b, a \mid b \mid a \mid c, a \mid b) = 1 \cdot 2 \cdot 3 = 6$.

The stochastic semantics of Stochastic CLS can be defined as follows.

Definition 18 (Semantics). *Given a finite set of stochastic rewrite rules $\mathcal{R}$, let $\xrightarrow{R,T,r,b}$, with $R \in \mathcal{R}, T \in \mathcal{T}, r \in \mathcal{R}$ and $b \in \mathbb{Q}$, be the least labeled transition relation on terms closed with respect to $\equiv$ and satisfying the following inference rules:*

$$1. \quad \frac{R : P_L \xmapsto{k} P_R \in \mathcal{R} \quad \sigma \in \Sigma \quad P_L\sigma \not\equiv P_R\sigma}{P_L\sigma \xrightarrow{R, P_L\sigma, k \cdot comb(P_L,\sigma), 1} P_R\sigma}$$

$$2. \quad \frac{T_1 \xrightarrow{R,T,r,b} T_2}{T_1 \mid T_3 \xrightarrow{R,T,r,b \cdot binom(T, T_1, T_3)} T_2 \mid T_3}$$

$$3. \quad \frac{T_1 \xrightarrow{R,T,r,b} T_2}{\left(T_1\right)^L \rfloor T_3 \xrightarrow{R, \left(T_1\right)^L \rfloor T_3, r \cdot b, 1} \left(T_2\right)^L \rfloor T_3}$$

$$4. \quad \frac{T_1 \xrightarrow{R,T,r,b} T_2}{\left(T_3\right)^L \rfloor T_1 \xrightarrow{R, \left(T_3\right)^L \rfloor T_1, r \cdot b, 1} \left(T_3\right)^L \rfloor T_2}$$

The semantics of Stochastic CLS is the least labeled transition relation on terms $\xrightarrow{R,r}$, with $R \in \mathcal{R}$ and $r \in \mathbb{R}$, satisfying

$$\frac{T_1 \xrightarrow{R,T,r,b} T_2}{T_1 \xrightarrow{R, r \cdot b} T_2}$$

The semantics is defined as a labeled transition system where each transition $T_1 \xrightarrow{R,r} T_2$ represents the application of the stochastic rewrite rule R to a subterm of T_1 yielding term T_2, and where $r \in \mathbb{R}$ specifies the application rate.

The definition uses an auxiliary transition relation, whose transitions are of the form $T_1 \xrightarrow{R,T,r,b} T_2$. The following labels appear on transitions:

- R, that is the rewrite rule applied and which is used to distinguish between two transitions corresponding to the application of different rules, which have the same application rate and take to the same result;
- T, that is either the instantiation of the left hand side of rule R or a term consisting of a looping and containment operator applied to a term which contains the instantiation of the left hand side of R;
- r, that is the application rate of R to T;
- b, that is the number of occurrences of T in the term which is transformed, with the exclusion of occurrences inside looping and containment operators.

The auxiliary transition relation $\xrightarrow{R,T,r,b}$ is defined by four inference rules. Rule 1 allows to derive a transition corresponding to the instantiation of a rewrite rule. Its rate is obtained by multiplying the kinetic constant of the rule, k, with the number of different reactant combinations appearing in the instantiation of the left pattern, namely the result of applying the function *comb*. Transitions which correspond to rule applications that do not modify terms are excluded by the condition $P_L\sigma \neq P_R\sigma$. Rule 2 uses the function *binom* to compute the number of different reactant combinations for the state $T_1 \mid T_3$, by assuming that b is the number of different reactant combinations for the only term T_1. Finally, rules 3 and 4 deal with looping and containment. In both the rules, the second label of the premises, namely T, is substituted by the label $(T_1)^L \rfloor T_3$ or $(T_3)^L \rfloor T_1$, respectively. This because, if the term is furtherly composed in parallel with other terms, *bisim* should count the occurrences of $(T_1)^L \rfloor T_3$ or $(T_3)^L \rfloor T_1$ rather than of the sole T.

The main transition relation $\xrightarrow{R,r}$ of the semantics is obtained by from the auxiliary relation by removing from all transitions the second label T, used only to compositionally compute the application rate of the rule, and by multiplying, and by multiplying their third and fourth labels r and b, so to obtain the total application rate.

As a simple example of application of the semantics, let us consider a Stochastic CLS model consisting of the term

$$T \equiv (m)^L \rfloor (a \mid a) \mid (m)^L \rfloor (a \mid a) \mid a \cdot b \mid a$$

and of the rewrite rules

$$R_1 : (m)^L \rfloor X \xrightarrow{k_1} \epsilon \qquad R_2; a \cdot b \cdot \widetilde{x} \xrightarrow{k_2} a \mid b \mid \widetilde{x} \qquad R_3 : a \xrightarrow{k_3} b.$$

As regards rule R_1, it is possible to derive, given an instantiation function $\sigma = \{(X, a \mid a)\}$, the following transition of the auxiliary relation of the semantics:

$$\dfrac{\dfrac{\dfrac{R_1 : (m)^L \rfloor X \overset{k_1}{\mapsto} \epsilon \quad \sigma = \{(X, a \mid a)\}}{(m)^L \rfloor (a \mid a) \xrightarrow{R_1, (m)^L \rfloor (a \mid a), k_1, 1} \epsilon}}{T \xrightarrow{R_1, (m)^L \rfloor (a \mid a), k_1, 2} (m)^L \rfloor (a \mid a) \mid a \cdot b \mid a}}{}$$

Note that the transition from state T has the forth label equal to 2 because $binom((m)^L \rfloor (a \mid a), (m)^L \rfloor (a \mid a), (m)^L \rfloor (a \mid a) \mid a \cdot b \mid a) = 2$.

Finally, the corresponding main transition is

$$T \xrightarrow{R_1, 2 \cdot k_1} (m)^L \rfloor (a \mid a) \mid a \cdot b \mid a.$$

Note that, as term T contains two occurrences of $(m)^L \rfloor (a \mid a)$, then the rule is correctly applied with rate $2 \cdot k_1$.

Differently, as regards rule R_2, given an instantiation function $\sigma = \{(\widetilde{x}, \epsilon)\}$, it is possible to derive, after the application of the auxiliary transition relation $\xrightarrow{R, T, r, b}$, the transition

$$T \xrightarrow{R_2, k_2} (m)^L \rfloor (a \mid a) \mid (m)^L \rfloor (a \mid a) \mid a \mid b \mid a.$$

Also in this case the value computed as rate is correct because T contains just one sequence $a \cdot b$.

Finally, as regards rule R_3, it is possible to derive the following transition:

$$\dfrac{\dfrac{\dfrac{\dfrac{R_3 : a \overset{k_3}{\mapsto} b \quad \sigma = \emptyset}{a \xrightarrow{R_3, a, k_3, 1} b}}{a \mid a \xrightarrow{R_3, a, k_3, 2} a \mid b}}{(m)^L \rfloor (a \mid a) \xrightarrow{R_3, (m)^L \rfloor (a \mid a), 2 \cdot k_3, 1} (m)^L \rfloor (a \mid b)}}{T \xrightarrow{R_3, (m)^L \rfloor (a \mid a), 2 \cdot k_3, 2} (m)^L \rfloor (a \mid b) \mid (m)^L \rfloor (a \mid a) \mid a \cdot b \mid a}$$

As expected, the semantics of Stochastic CLS gives the transition

$$T \xrightarrow{R_3, 4 \cdot k_3} (m)^L \rfloor (a \mid b) \mid (m)^L \rfloor (a \mid a) \mid a \cdot b \mid a$$

where the rate is $4 \cdot k_3$ because there are 4 different sequences a to which the rule R_3 can be applied.

Example. Let us consider the simple regulation process we modeled with CLS in Section 3.1. We now extend the CLS model by including a kinetic constant in each rewrite rule. The result is a Stochastic CLS model. In order to make the

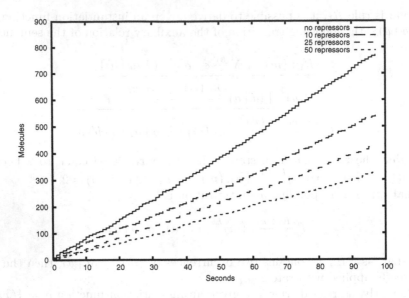

Fig. 2. Simulation result of the regulation process: number of RNA molecules over time

model a little more realistic we add two rewrite rules describing the unbinding of the RNA polymerase and of the repressor from the DNA. Hence, the rewrite rules of the Stochastic CLS model are the following:

$$polym \mid p \cdot \widetilde{x} \xmapsto{0.1} pp \cdot \widetilde{x} \qquad (R1)$$

$$pp \cdot \widetilde{x} \xmapsto{2} polym \mid p \cdot \widetilde{x} \qquad (R1')$$

$$repr \mid \widetilde{x} \cdot o \cdot \widetilde{y} \xmapsto{1} \widetilde{x} \cdot ro \cdot \widetilde{y} \qquad (R2)$$

$$\widetilde{x} \cdot ro \cdot \widetilde{y} \xmapsto{10} repr \mid \widetilde{x} \cdot o \cdot \widetilde{y} \qquad (R2')$$

$$pp \cdot o \cdot \widetilde{x} \xmapsto{100} p \cdot po \cdot \widetilde{x} \qquad (R3)$$

$$\widetilde{x} \cdot po \cdot g \xmapsto{100} \widetilde{x} \cdot o \cdot pg \qquad (R4)$$

$$\widetilde{x} \cdot pg \xmapsto{30} polym \mid rna \mid \widetilde{x} \cdot g \qquad (R5)$$

We have developed a simulator based on Stochastic CLS, and we used it to study the behaviour of the regulation process. In particular, we performed simulations by varying the quantity of repressors and we observed the production of RNA fragments in each case. The initial configuration of the system is given by the following term

$$\underbrace{repr \mid \ldots \mid repr}_{n} \mid \underbrace{polym \mid \ldots \mid polym}_{100} \mid p \cdot o \cdot g$$

and we performed simulations with $n = 0, 10, 25$ and 50. The results of the simulations are shown in Figure 2. By varying the number of repressors from 0 to 50 the rate of transcription of the DNA into RNA molecules decreases.

4   Application Examples

We present two biological systems modeled with Stochastic CLS. The first describes the regulation process of the lactose operon in *Escherichia coli*. The second describes an example of *quorum sensing*, namely the ability of bacteria of monitoring their population density and modulating their gene expressions according to this density. We show the results of simulations of both models.

4.1   Application to the Modeling of Metabolic Pathways

We give a Stochastic CLS model of the well–known regulation process of the lactose operon in *Escherichia coli*.

The lactose operon is a sequence of genes that are responsible for producing three enzymes for lactose degradation, namely the *lactose permease*, which is incorporated in the membrane of the bacterium and actively transports the sugar into the cell, the *beta galactosidase*, which splits lactose into glucose and galactose, and the *transacetylase*, whose role is marginal.

The first three genes of the operon (i,p,o) regulate the production of the enzymes, and the last three (z, y, a), called *structural genes*, are transcribed (when allowed) into the mRNA for beta galactosidase, lactose permease and transacetylase, respectively.

The regulation process is as follows (see Figure 3): gene i encodes the *lac Repressor*, which, in the absence of lactose, binds to gene o (the *operator*). Transcription of structural genes into mRNA is performed by the RNA polymerase enzyme, which usually binds to gene p (the *promoter*) and scans the operon from left to right by transcribing the three structural genes z, y and a into a single mRNA fragment. When the lac Repressor is bound to gene o, it becomes an obstacle for the RNA polymerase, and transcription of the structural genes is not performed. On the other hand, when lactose is present inside the bacterium, it binds to the Repressor and this cannot stop anymore the activity of the RNA

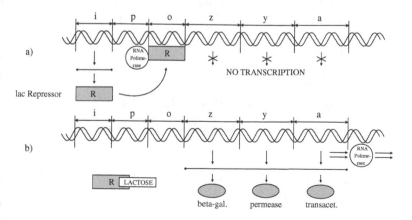

Fig. 3. The regulation process in the Lac Operon

polymerase. In this case the transcription is performed and the three enzymes for lactose degradation are synthesized.

A detailed mathematical model of the regulation process can be found in [46]. It includes information on the influence of lactose degradation on the growth of the bacterium.

We give a Stochastic CLS model of the gene regulation process, with stochastic rates taken from [45]. We model the membrane of the bacterium as the looping sequence $(m)^L$, where the alphabet symbol m generically denotes the whole membrane surface in normal conditions. Moreover, we model the lactose operon as the sequence $lacI \cdot lacP \cdot lacO \cdot lacZ \cdot lacY \cdot lacA$ ($lacI–A$ for short), in which each symbol corresponds to a gene. We replace $lacO$ with RO in the sequence when the lac Repressor is bound to gene o, and $lacP$ with PP when the RNA polymerase is bound to gene p. When the lac Repressor and the RNA polymerase are unbound, they are modeled by the symbols $repr$ and $polym$, respectively. We model the mRNA of the lac Repressor as the symbol $Irna$, a molecule of lactose as the symbol $LACT$, and beta galactosidase, lactose permease and transacetylase enzymes as symbols $betagal, perm$ and $transac$, respectively. Finally, since the three structural genes are transcribed into a single mRNA fragment, we model such mRNA as a single symbol Rna.

The initial state of the bacterium when no lactose is present in the environment and when 100 molecules of lactose are present are modeled by the following terms (where $n \times T$ stands for a parallel composition $T \mid \ldots \mid T$ of length n):

$$Ecoli ::= (m)^L \rfloor (lacI–A \mid 30 \times polym \mid 100 \times repr) \tag{1}$$

$$EcoliLact ::= Ecoli \mid 100 \times LACT \tag{2}$$

The transcription of the DNA, the binding of the lac Repressor to gene o, and the interaction between lactose and the lac Repressor are modeled by the following set of rules:

$$lacI \cdot \widetilde{x} \overset{0.02}{\longmapsto} lacI \cdot \widetilde{x} \mid Irna \tag{S1}$$

$$Irna \overset{0.1}{\longmapsto} Irna \mid repr \tag{S2}$$

$$polym \mid \widetilde{x} \cdot lacP \cdot \widetilde{y} \overset{0.1}{\longmapsto} \widetilde{x} \cdot PP \cdot \widetilde{y} \tag{S3}$$

$$\widetilde{x} \cdot PP \cdot \widetilde{y} \overset{0.01}{\longmapsto} polym \mid \widetilde{x} \cdot lacP \cdot \widetilde{y} \tag{S4}$$

$$\widetilde{x} \cdot PP \cdot lacO \cdot \widetilde{y} \overset{20.0}{\longmapsto} polym \mid Rna \mid \widetilde{x} \cdot lacP \cdot lacO \cdot \widetilde{y} \tag{S5}$$

$$Rna \overset{0.1}{\longmapsto} Rna \mid betagal \mid perm \mid transac \tag{S6}$$

$$repr \mid \widetilde{x} \cdot lacO \cdot \widetilde{y} \overset{1.0}{\longmapsto} \widetilde{x} \cdot RO \cdot \widetilde{y} \tag{S7}$$

$$\widetilde{x} \cdot RO \cdot \widetilde{y} \overset{0.01}{\longmapsto} repr \mid \widetilde{x} \cdot lacO \cdot \widetilde{y} \tag{S8}$$

$$repr \mid LACT \overset{0.005}{\longmapsto} RLACT \tag{S9}$$

$$RLACT \overset{0.1}{\longmapsto} repr \mid LACT \tag{S10}$$

Rules (S1) and (S2) describe the transcription and translation of gene i into the lac Repressor (assumed for simplicity to be performed without the intervention of the RNA polymerase). Rules (S3) and (S4) describe binding and unbinding of the RNA polymerase to gene p. Rules (S5) and (S6) describe the transcription and translation of the three structural genes. Transcription of such genes can be performed only when the sequence contains $lacO$ instead of RO, that is when the lac Repressor is not bound to gene o. Rules (S7) and (S8) describe binding and unbinding of the lac Repressor to gene o. Finally, rules (S9) and (S10) describe the binding and unbinding, respectively, of the lactose to the lac Repressor. The following rules describe the behaviour of the three enzymes for lactose degradation:

$$\left(X \right)^{L} \rfloor \left(perm \mid Y \right) \overset{0.1}{\mapsto} \left(perm \mid X \right)^{L} \rfloor Y \qquad (S11)$$

$$LACT \mid \left(perm \mid X \right)^{L} \rfloor Y \overset{0.001}{\mapsto} \left(perm \mid X \right)^{L} \rfloor \left(LACT \mid Y \right) \qquad (S12)$$

$$betagal \mid LACT \overset{0.001}{\mapsto} betagal \mid GLU \mid GAL \qquad (S13)$$

Rule (S11) describes the incorporation of the lactose permease in the membrane of the bacterium, rule (S12) the transportation of lactose from the environment to the interior performed by the lactose permease, and rule (S13) the decomposition of the lactose into glucose (denoted GLU) and galactose (denoted GAL) performed by the beta galactosidase. The following rules describe

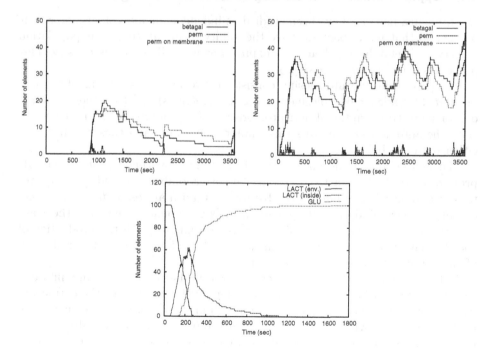

Fig. 4. Simulation results: production of enzymes in the absence (left) and presence (center) of lactose, and degradation of lactose into glucose (right)

the degradation of all the proteins and pieces of mRNA involved in the process:

$$perm \overset{0.001}{\mapsto} \epsilon \qquad lrna \overset{0.001}{\mapsto} \epsilon \qquad transac \overset{0.001}{\mapsto} \epsilon \qquad \text{(S14-S16)}$$

$$repr \overset{0.002}{\mapsto} \epsilon \qquad betagal \overset{0.01}{\mapsto} \epsilon \qquad Rna \overset{0.01}{\mapsto} \epsilon \qquad \text{(S17-S19)}$$

$$RLACT \overset{0.002}{\mapsto} LACT \qquad\qquad \text{(S20)}$$

We have simulated the evolution of the bacterium in the absence of lactose (modeled by the term $Ecoli$ of Eq. (1)) and in the presence of 100 molecules of lactose in the environment (modeled by the term $EcoliLact$ of Eq. (2)).

In Figure 4 we show the results of the two simulations. The first graph shows that in the absence of lactose the production of the beta galactosidase and lactose permease enzymes starts after more than 750 seconds, and that the number of such enzymes is always smaller than 20. The amount of time elapsed before the production of these enzymes does not depend on the presence of the lactose in the environment, as the lactose cannot enter the bacterium until some molecules of permease have joint the membrane. Once some molecules of lactose permease join the membrane, the lactose starts entering the bacterium and being transformed into glucose (see the third graph).

4.2 Application to the Modeling of Quorum Sensing

Traditionally, bacteria have been studied as independent individuals. Now, it is recognised that many bacteria have the ability of monitoring their population density and modulating their gene expressions according to this density. This process is called *quorum sensing.*

The process of quorum sensing consists in two activities, one involving one or more diffusible small molecules (called *autoinducers*) and the other involving one or more transcriptional activator proteins (*R-proteins*) located within the cell. The autoinducer can cross the cellular membrane, and thus it can diffuse either out or in bacteria.

The production of the autoinducer is regulated by the R-protein. The R-protein by itself is not active without the corresponding autoinducer. The autoinducer molecule can bind to the R-protein to form an *autoinducer/R-protein* complex, which binds to a target of the DNA sequence enhancing the transcription of specific genes. Usually, these genes regulate both the production of specific behavioural traits (as we will show in the following) and the production of the autoinducer and of the R-protein.

At low cell density, the autoinducer is synthesized at basal levels and diffuse in the environment where it is diluted. With high cell density both the extracellular and intracellular concentrations of the autoinducer increase until they reach thresholds beyond which the autoinducer is produced autocatalytically. The autocatalytic production results in a dramatic increase of product concentration.

Quorum sensing behaviour is very widespread in bacteria. An example is the regulation the bioluminescence in the symbiotic marine bacterium *Vibrio*

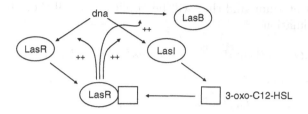

Fig. 5. A schematic description of the las system in *P. aeruginosa*.

fischeri, which colonizes the light organs of marine fishes and squids. The bacteria only luminesce when they are found in high concentrations in the light organs, while they do not emit light when they are free swimming [43]. Another example is given by the bacterium *Pseudomonas aeruginosa*, a prevalent human pathogen [20]. The ability of *P. aeruginosa* to infect a host mainly is based on controlling its virulence by quorum sensing. The level of virulence expressed by isolated bacteria is very low, thus avoiding host response. When a colony has reached a certain density, the production of virulence factors is autoinduced by quorum sensing, and it is generally sufficient to overcome the defenses of the host.

The quorum sensing system of *P. aeruginosa* has two regulatory systems. In this paper we are interested in the one regulating the expression of elastase LasB, named the *las* system. The two enzymes, LasB elastase and LasA elastase, are responsible for pulmonary hemorrhages associated with *P. aeruginosa* infections.

A schematic description of the *las system* is shown in Fig.5. The autoinducer 3-oxo-C12-HSL and the transcriptional activator protein LasR are produced at basal rates. The LasR/3-oxo-C12-HSL dimer is the activated form of LasR. It promotes the production of itself, of the autoinducer and of the LasB enzyme. The formation of the dimer is controlled mainly by the concentration of the autoinducer, which is influenced by the number of bacteria.

We now give the Stochastic CLS model of the quorum sensing process. We do not model the production of the LasB as it has no active role in the regulation process. The initial state of each bacterium is:

$$Bact ::= (m)^{L} \rfloor (lasO \cdot lasR \cdot lasI)$$

where the looping sequence $(m)^{L}$ represents the bacterium membrane, $lasO$ the target of the DNA sequence where LasR/3-oxo-C12-HSL complex binds to for promoting DNA transcription, and $lasR$ and $lasI$ the genes that encode $LasR$ and the autoinducer, respectively.

This model shows one of the advantages of using terms for describing the structure of biological systems in Stochastic CLS. In fact, in order to model a population of n bacteria we have to describe only one bacterium, and then compose n copies of such a description by using the parallel composition operator. In other words, we model a population of n bacteria simply as $n \times Bact$.

We now give the rewrite rules describing the protein/protein and protein/ DNA interactions in the described systems. Again, we have only to give the rules for one bacterium, and they will be applicable in all the n bacteria of the considered population.

$$lasO \cdot lasR \cdot lasI \xmapsto{20} lasO \cdot lasR \cdot lasI \mid LasR \qquad (S1)$$

$$lasO \cdot lasR \cdot lasI \xmapsto{5} lasO \cdot lasR \cdot lasI \mid LasI \qquad (S2)$$

$$LasI \xmapsto{8} LasI \mid 3oxo \qquad (S3)$$

$$3oxo \mid LasR \xmapsto{0.25} 3R \qquad (S4)$$

$$3R \xmapsto{400} 3oxo \mid LasR \qquad (S5)$$

$$3R \mid lasO \cdot lasR \cdot lasI \xmapsto{0.25} 3RO \cdot lasR \cdot lasI \qquad (S6)$$

$$3RO \cdot lasR \cdot lasI \xmapsto{10} 3R \mid lasO \cdot lasR \cdot lasI \qquad (S7)$$

$$3RO \cdot lasR \cdot lasI \xmapsto{1200} 3RO \cdot lasR \cdot lasI \mid LasR \qquad (S8)$$

$$3RO \cdot lasR \cdot lasI \xmapsto{300} 3RO \cdot lasR \cdot lasI \mid LasI \qquad (S9)$$

$$(m)^L \rfloor (3oxo \mid X) \xmapsto{30} 3oxo \mid (m)^L \rfloor X \qquad (S10)$$

$$3oxo \mid (m)^L \rfloor X \xmapsto{1} (m)^L \rfloor (3oxo \mid X) \qquad (S11)$$

$$LasI \xmapsto{1} \epsilon \qquad LasR \xmapsto{1} \epsilon \qquad 3oxo \xmapsto{1} \epsilon \qquad (S12 - S14)$$

Rules (S1) and (S2) describe the production from the DNA of proteins LasR and LasI, respectively. For the sake of simplicity we do not model the transcription of the DNA into mRNA. Rule (S3) describes the production of the autoinducer 3-oxo-C12-HSL, denoted $3oxo$, performed by the LasI enzyme. Rules (S4) and (S5) describe the complexation and decomplexation of the autoinducer and the LasR protein, where the complex is denoted $3R$. Rules from (S7) to (S9) describe the binding of the activated autoinducer to the DNA and its influence in the production of LasR and LasI. Rules (S10) and (S11) describe the autoinducer exiting and entering the bacterium. The kinetic constants associated with these two rules give a measure of the autoinducer dilution. Finally, rules from (S12) to (S14) describe the degradation of proteins.

We have simulated the behavior of a population of *P. aeruginosa* by varying the number of individuals. In Figure 6 we show how the concentration of the autoinducer varies inside bacteria when the population is composed by one, five and twenty individuals. In the last two cases we show the autoinducer concentration inside one only bacterium (the concentrations inside the others are analogous).

When the number of bacteria increases, also the concentration of the autoinducer in the extracellular space increases. As a consequence the concentration of the autoinducer in the intracellular spaces increases as well and the quorum sensing process starts. Note that the kinetic constants of rules (S10) and (S11) regulating the autoinducer exiting and entering the membrane cause the bacteria to maintain the autoinducer production mostly at a basal rate when the population size is one or five. When the population size is twenty the quorum sensing

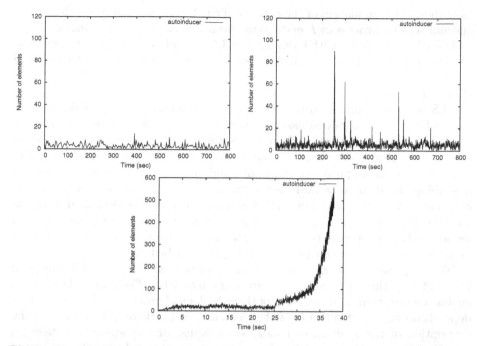

Fig. 6. Simulation results: quantity of autoinducer inside one bacterium in a population of one (left), five (center) and twenty (right) bacteria

starts after a few seconds thus causing a very high autocatalytic autoinducer production. Increasing the ratio between kinetic constants of (S10) and (S11) would cause the quorum sensing to be triggered when the number of individuals is bigger.

5   Conclusion and Future Perspectives

We have presented the Calculus of Looping Sequences (CLS) suitable to describe microbiological systems and their evolution. Terms of the calculus are constructed by basic constituent elements and operators of sequencing, looping, containment and parallel composition. The looping operator, together with the containment one, permits the description of arbitrarily nested membranes and of sequences on the surface and inside the membranes themselves. The evolution of a term is modeled by a set of rewrite rules and the semantics is a transition system, in which states correspond to terms, and transitions correspond to rules applications. We have presented two extensions, CLS with links (LCLS) and Stochastic CLS. LCLS allows the description of protein interaction at a lower level of abstraction, namely at the domain level. Stochastic CLS allows the description of quantitative aspects of the modeled systems, such as the frequency of chemical reactions. As examples of application to real biological systems, we have shown the simulation of the activity of the lactose operon in *E.coli* and the quorum sensing process in *P.aeruginosa*, both described with Stochastic CLS.

The CLS formalism, with its extensions LCLS and Stochastic CLS, fulfill the wanted request of having a simple notation, having the ability of describing biolgical systems at different abstraction levels, and being flexible enough to allow the description of new kinds of phenomena. In fact rewrite rules as those of CLS are more similar to the reaction notation employed by biologists and a model may be understood easier than models based, for instance, on process calculi. CLS basic elements and operators allow us to choose the level of detail of a model. As an example a cell may be described either as a single alphabet symbol or as the application of looping and containment operator to a term describing the membrane and to a term describing the cell content. Another example may be the model of a DNA strand which can be described either as a single alphabet symbol or as a sequence of symbols representing genes or as a sequence of symbols representing nucleic acids. Finally, the absence of constraints on rewrite rules allows new phenomena to be described easily.

We are presently working on another extension of CLS, called Topological CLS (TCLS), that integrates space and time into CLS. The aim of TCLS is to enable a more accurate description of those biological processes whose behaviour depends on the exact position of the elements. In particular, TCLS allows the description of the position of biological elements, and of space they take up in a 2D/3D space. The elements may move autonomously during the passage of time, and may interact when constraints on their positions are met. In particular, rewrite rules are extended with a function that constrains application of the rule depending on the exact positions of the elements involved. Similarly to Stochastic CLS, rewrite rules are also endowed with a reaction rate. Moreover, we model the space occupied by each object as a hard sphere, hence space conflicts may arise during the evolution. These conflicts are resolved by an appropriate algorithm, which rearranges the position of the elements by assuming that they push each other when they are too close.

The development of a simulator based on the Stochastic CLS has suggested the introduction of an intermediate language for the simulation of biological systems. Such a language, the Stochastic String MultiSet Rewriting (sSMSR) [2,3], is based on multiset rewriting. Multiset elements are strings built over a given alphabet and the state of a sSMSR system is represented by a multiset of strings. The evolution of a multiset is modeled by rewrite rules which rewrite multisets. Rules may contain variables that can be used to match either individual symbols or portions of the strings which are involved in the application of a rule. Furthermore rules can contain two different maching operators. The first allows a rule to be applicable to a multiset of strings only if such a multiset contains a single string with a certain prefix (unique matching), the second applies only if all the strings with the same given prefix are involved in the rule application (maximal matching). Finally, we have that fresh symbols, namely symbols that are present neither in the multiset of strings to which the rule is applied nor in the applied rewrite rule, can be generated when a rewrite rule is applied.

The use of strings as multiset elements and of operations on strings in rewrite rules allows the development of a simulator for sSMSR based on efficient data structures and pattern matching algoritms. The features of sSMSR can ease the translation of high level languages. In [3] we defined both the encoding of the Stochastic CLS and of the stochastic π-calculus into sSMSR.

References

1. Alur, R., Belta, C., Ivancic, F., Kumar, V., Mintz, M., Pappas, G., Rubin, H., Schug, J.: Hybrid modeling and simulation of biomolecular networks. In: Di Benedetto, M.D., Sangiovanni-Vincentelli, A.L. (eds.) HSCC 2001. LNCS, vol. 2034, pp. 19–32. Springer, Heidelberg (2001)
2. Barbuti, R., Caravagna, G., Maggiolo-Schettini, A., Milazzo, P.: An intermediate language for the simulation of biological systems. In: From Biology to Concurrency and Back (FBTC'07). ENTCS, vol. 194, pp. 19–34. Elsevier, Amsterdam (2007)
3. Barbuti, R., Caravagna, G., Maggiolo-Schettini, A., Milazzo, P.: An intermediate language for the stochastic simulation of biological systems. In: Submitted for publication (2008), http://www.di.unipi.it/$\sim$milazzo/
4. Barbuti, R., Cataudella, S., Maggiolo-Schettini, A., Milazzo, P., Troina, A.: A probabilistic model for molecular systems. Fundamenta Informaticae 67, 13–27 (2005)
5. Barbuti, R., Maggiolo-Schettini, A., Milazzo, P.: Extending the calculus of looping sequences to model protein interaction at the domain level. In: Măndoiu, I.I., Zelikovsky, A. (eds.) ISBRA 2007. LNCS (LNBI), vol. 4463, pp. 638–649. Springer, Heidelberg (2007)
6. Barbuti, R., Maggiolo-Schettini, A., Milazzo, P., Tiberi, P., Troina, A.: Stochastic cls for the modeling and simulation of biological systems. In: Submitted for publication (2008), http://www.di.unipi.it/$\sim$milazzo/
7. Barbuti, R., Maggiolo-Schettini, A., Milazzo, P., Troina, A.: A calculus of looping sequences for modelling microbiological systems. Fundamenta Informaticae 72, 21–35 (2006)
8. Barbuti, R., Maggiolo-Schettini, A., Milazzo, P., Troina, A.: Bisimulation congruences in the calculus of looping sequences. In: Barkaoui, K., Cavalcanti, A., Cerone, A. (eds.) ICTAC 2006. LNCS, vol. 4281, pp. 93–107. Springer, Heidelberg (2006)
9. Barbuti, R., Maggiolo-Schettini, A., Milazzo, P., Troina, A.: Bisimulations in Calculi Modelling Membranes. In: Formal Aspects of Computing (in press)
10. Brodo, L., Degano, P., Priami, C.: A stochastic semantics for bioambients. In: Malyshkin, V.E. (ed.) PaCT 2007. LNCS, vol. 4671, pp. 22–34. Springer, Heidelberg (2007)
11. Cardelli, L.: Brane calculi. interactions of biological membranes. In: Danos, V., Schachter, V. (eds.) CMSB 2004. LNCS (LNBI), vol. 3082, pp. 257–280. Springer, Heidelberg (2005)
12. Cardelli, L., Gordon, A.: Mobile ambients. Theoretical Compututer Scence 240(1), 177–213 (2000)
13. Chabrier-Rivier, N., Chiaverini, M., Danos, V., Fages, F., Schachter, V.: Modeling and querying biomolecular interaction networks. Theoretical Computer Science 325(1), 25–44 (2004)
14. CLSm: simulation tool (web page), http://www.di.unipi.it/~milazzo/biosims/

422   R. Barbuti et al.

15. Curti, M., Degano, P., Priami, C., Baldari, C.: Modelling biochemical pathways through enhanced pi-calculus. Theoretical Computer Science 325(1), 111–140 (2004)
16. Damm, W., Harel, D.: LSCs: Breathing life into message sequence charts. Formal Methods in System Design 19(1) (2001)
17. Danos, V., Laneve, C.: Formal molecular biology. Theoretical Computer Science 325(1), 69–110 (2004)
18. Danos, V., Pradalier, S.: Projective brane calculus. In: Danos, V., Schachter, V. (eds.) CMSB 2004. LNCS (LNBI), vol. 3082, pp. 134–148. Springer, Heidelberg (2005)
19. Degano, P., Prandi, D., Priami, C., Quaglia, P.: Beta-binders for biological quantitative experiments. In: Quantitative Aspects of Programming Languages (QAPL 2006). ENTCS, vol. 164, pp. 101–117. Elsevier, Amsterdam (2006)
20. Delden, C.V., Iglewski, B.: Cell-to-cell signaling and Pseudomonas aeruginosa infections. Emerg. Infect. Dis. 4, 551–560 (1998)
21. Efroni, S., Choen, I., Harel, D.: Toward rigorous comprehension of biological complexity: Modeling, execution and visualization of thymic t–cell maturation. Genome Research 13, 2485–2497 (2003)
22. Harel, D.: Statecharts: A visual formalism for complex systems. Science of Computer Programming 8(3), 231–274 (1987)
23. Harel, D.: A grand challenge: Full reactive modeling of a multi-cellular animal. Bulletin of the EATCS 81, 226–235 (2003)
24. Gillespie, D.: Exact stochastic simulation of coupled chemical reactions. Journal of Physical Chemistry 81, 2340–2361 (1977)
25. Kam, N., Cohen, I., Harel, D.: The immune system as a reactive system: Modeling t–cell activation with Statecharts. In: Symposia on Human Centric Computing Languages and Environments (HCC 2001), vol. 15, IEEE Computer Society, Los Alamitos (2001)
26. Kam, N., Harel, D., Kugler, H., Marelly, R., Pnueli, A., Hubbard, E., Stern, M.: Formal modeling of c. elegans development: A scenario-based approach. In: Priami, C. (ed.) CMSB 2003. LNCS, vol. 2602, pp. 4–20. Springer, Heidelberg (2003)
27. Kwiatkowska, M., Norman, G., Parker, D.: Probabilistic symbolic model checking with prism: a hybrid approach. Int. Journal on Software Tools for Technology Transfer 6(2), 128–142 (2004)
28. Laneve, C., Tarissan, F.: A simple calculus for proteins and cells. In: Membrane Computing and Biological Inspired Process Calculi (MeCBIC'06). ENTCS, vol. 171, pp. 139–154. Elsevier, Amsterdam (2007)
29. Matsuno, H., Doi, A., Nagasaki, M., Miyano, S.: Hybrid petri net representation of gene regulatory network. In: Pacific Symposium on Biocomputing, pp. 341–352. World Scientific Press, Singapore (2000)
30. Milazzo, P.: Qualitative and Quantitative Formal Modeling of Biological Systems. PhD thesis, Università di Pisa (2007)
31. Păun, G.: Computing with membranes. Journal of Computer and System Sciences 61(1), 108–143 (2000)
32. Păun, G.: Membrane Computing. An Introduction. Springer, Heidelberg (2002)
33. Pérez-Jiménez, M., Romero-Campero, F.: A study of the robustness of the egfr signalling cascade using continuous membrane systems. In: Mira, J., Álvarez, J.R. (eds.) IWINAC 2005. LNCS, vol. 3561, pp. 268–278. Springer, Heidelberg (2005)

34. Pérez-Jiménez, M., Romero-Campero, F.: P systems, a new computational modelling tool for systems biology. In: Priami, C., Plotkin, G. (eds.) Transactions on Computational Systems Biology VI. LNCS (LNBI), vol. 4220, pp. 176–197. Springer, Heidelberg (2006)

35. Priami, C.: Stochastic π–calculus. The Computer Journal 38(7), 578–589 (1995)

36. Priami, C., Quaglia, P.: Beta binders for biological interactions. In: Danos, V., Schachter, V. (eds.) CMSB 2004. LNCS (LNBI), vol. 3082, pp. 20–33. Springer, Heidelberg (2005)

37. Priami, C., Regev, A., Silverman, W., Shapiro, E.: Application of a stochastic name–passing calculus to representation and simulation of molecular processes. Information Processing Letters 80, 25–31 (2001)

38. Prusinkiewicz, P., Lindenmayer, A.: The Algorithmic Beauty of Plants. Springer, Heidelberg (1990)

39. P Systems: web page, http://psystems.disco.unimib.it/

40. Regev, A., Panina, E., Silverman, W., Cardelli, L., Shapiro, E.: Bioambients: An abstraction for biological compartments. Theoretical Computer Science 325(1), 141–167 (2004)

41. Regev, A., Shapiro, E.: Cells as computation. Nature 419, 343 (2002)

42. Regev, A., Silverman, W., Shapiro, E.: Representation and simulation of biochemical processes using the pi-calculus process algebra. In: Pacific Symposium on Biocomputing, pp. 459–470. World Scientific Press, Singapore (2001)

43. Stevens, A., Greenberg, E.: Quorum sensing in Vibrio fischeri: essential elements for activation of the luminescence genes. J. of Bacteriology 179, 557–562 (1997)

44. Wiley, H., Shvartsman, S., Lauffenburger, D.: Computational modeling of the egf–receptor system: a paradigm for systems biology. Trends in Cell Biology 13(1), 43–50 (2003)

45. Wilkinson, D.: Stochastic Modelling for Systems Biology. Chapman and Hall, Boca Raton (2006)

46. Wong, P., Gladney, S., Keasling, J.: Mathematical model of the lac operon: Inducer exclusion, catabolite repression, and diauxic growth on glucose and lactose. Biotechnology Progress 13, 132–143 (1997)

Hybrid Systems and Biology
Continuous and Discrete Modeling for Systems Biology

Luca Bortolussi[1] and Alberto Policriti[2,3]

[1] Department of Mathematics and Informatics, University of Trieste
luca.bortolussi@.units.it
[2] Department of Mathematics and Informatics, University of Udine
[3] Istituto di Genomica Applicata (IGA)
alberto.policriti@appliedgenomics.org

Abstract. Hybrid Systems are dynamical systems presenting both discrete and continuous evolution. Hybrid Automata are a formal model for hybrid systems, originally proposed to study embedded systems, where a discrete control acts on a continuously changing environment.

The presence of both discrete and continuous dynamics makes this formalism appealing also for modeling biological systems. However, the situation in this case is subtler, as there is no natural separation into discrete and continuous components. No surprise, then, that hybrid automata have been used in systems biology in rather different ways. Some approaches, like the description of biological switches, concentrate on the use of model-checking routines. Other applications, like the switching between continuous and discrete/stochastic simulation, focus on the exploitation of the interplay between discreteness and continuity in order to reduce the computational burden of numerical simulation, yet maintaining an acceptable precision.

We will survey the use of hybrid automata in systems biology, through a series of cases studies that we deem interesting and paradigmatic.

Introduction

In this survey we will discuss some aspects of the interplay between discreteness and continuity in the context of biological modeling. Biological models can be formalized in many ways and, common to most of such many formalisms, is the attempt of the proposed tools of favoring the isolation and study of system's properties: properties pertaining to a system as such, in opposition to properties readable and explainable as a (linear/simple) combinations of properties of its parts. We believe that, in order to give a contribution towards the understanding of systems's properties, we must come to terms with our, often limited, capabilities of combining mathematical tools of (very) different computational nature. In particular we see as major bottlenecks along the way the combination of discrete and continuous modeling tools/ideas and the computational limitations imposed by the use of fully stochastic methods.

Given the above premises, we decided to concentrate on the use of the so-called *hybrid automata*: formal tools designed to combine a collection of dynamical

M. Bernardo, P. Degano, and G. Zavattaro (Eds.): SFM 2008, LNCS 5016, pp. 424–448, 2008.

systems into a network allowing a discrete control on the evolution of fluxes. Researchers have used the potential of hybrid automata to study important biological applications. We will briefly report on examples—specifically genetic regulatory networks and bacterial chemotaxis—trying to show how Nature is much more easily mimicked using a mix of discrete and continuous ingredients.

Even though important, the faithfulness in modeling will not be our only aim. As a matter of fact, what we believe is the most intriguing use of hybrid automata, is in the attempt to tackle *computational* problems arising in modeling biological systems. If, on the one hand, a discrete and stochastic approach to biological modeling is by far the methodology having firmer physical bases, on the other hand a sort of *original sin* of such an approach imposes high (often unbearably) computational costs. We will review two—in a sense "non standard"—uses of hybrid automata consisting in employing the discrete control as a means to switch among possible modeling methods in the attempt to adapt to the most precise/economic available computational technique. In such example we will come across a view—extremely inspiring and popular—that calls *communication* and *concurrency* into play. In fact, the vision of computation as an emergent property of the process of communication, a property strictly pertaining to the system of interacting agents as such, resembles closely the idea that high level cellular processes emerge from complex patterns of low-level interactions. Therefore, modeling biological phenomena can be seen as the activity of modeling a complex communication network—at different levels of details. In fact, the stochastic ingredient is much more elegantly entered into the picture whenever communication provides the background machinery (*stochastic process algebras*). In our opinion this is a deep and important point, having to do with the correct choice of the computation model when modeling biological phenomena. Our examples touch upon this point and try to illustrate how introducing a limited amount of continuity in a discrete and stochastic system is a delicate issue. An important ingredient to tackle this problem is the use of formal languages like process algebras to describe biological systems. In fact, this modeling paradigm, matching interactions with communications, requires the modeler to focus deeply on the logical structure of interactions going on in the system. This effort, in turn, allows to identify those components that are inherently discrete and those amenable of continuous approximation.

It goes without saying that we will not be neither fully updated nor complete in our quotations and choices: we apologize for that. The reader should consider the reported examples and experiences as a (biased) collection of cases allowing us to illustrate our general considerations on the subject.

Basics

We begin with an informal definition of hybrid automata. Hybrid automata are collections of dynamical systems on the same set of (continuous) variables linked by a finite network controlling discrete jumps in the evolution. A set of variables

evolving continuously in time is fixed, and discrete *control* events are allowed
to happen. When discrete events happen the automaton enters its next *mode*,
where the laws governing the flow of continuous variables may change.

Formally, a hybrid automaton is a tuple

$$H = \langle Z, \mathcal{V}, \mathcal{E}, Inv, Dyn, Act, Reset \rangle,$$

where:

- $Z = \{Z_1, \ldots, Z_n\}$ is a finite set of real-valued variables (the time derivative
  of Z_j is denoted by $\dot{Z}_j$, while the value of Z_j after either a time step or a
  change of *mode* is indicated by Z_j').
- $\mathcal{G} = \langle \mathcal{V}, \mathcal{E} \rangle$ is a finite labeled graph, called *control graph*. Vertices $v \in \mathcal{V}$
  are the *(control) modes*, while edges $e \in \mathcal{E}$ are called *(control) switches* and
  model the happening of a discrete event.
- Associated with each vertex $v \in \mathcal{V}$ there is a formula *intensionally* defining
  the set of tuples admissible within mode v, that is $Inv(v)[Z]$. Such formula,
  also called *invariant condition*, must be true during the continuous evolution
  of variables in mode v and forces a change of mode to happen when is
  violated.
- $Dyn(v)[Z]$ is a set of (ordinary) differential equations associated to $v \in \mathcal{V}$
  and specifying the *dynamics* of the variables within mode $v \in \mathcal{V}$.
- Edges $e \in \mathcal{E}$ of the control graph are labeled by $Act(e)[Z]$, a formula on
  Z stating for what values of variables transition (switch) e is active: the
  so-called *activation region*.
- $Reset(e)[Z, Z']$ is a formula on $Z \cup Z'$ specifying the change of the variables'
  values after transition e has taken place.

Non-determinism is intrinsically captured by the above definition. If one
thinks of *traces* of the system, namely the time traces of the continuous variables, the activation conditions are, in general, non-deterministic (as well as resets). Hence, there will be different traces depending upon the non-deterministic
choices made at activation and reset stages.

The above informal description of hybrid automaton can, obviously, be formalized. Such a formalization would need to specify more precisely what kind
of systems of differential equations are admitted as dynamics. Below we do give
a formal definition, but taking a different position allowing us not to enter into
analysis technicalities and to comment on decidability issues related with hybrid
automata.

The idea is to fix a logical language $\mathcal{L}$ and a model $\mathcal{M}$ for such language,
require all formulæ to be written in $\mathcal{L}$ and give the definition of hybrid automata
as parametric on $\mathcal{M}$. The advantage will be that, for sufficiently expressive
$\mathcal{L}$, the dynamics will still be expressible but, moreover, if the decidability of
$\mathcal{M}$-satisfiability can be proved for $\mathcal{L}$-formulae, most of the properties of the
corresponding hybrid automata are guaranteed.

Definition 1 (Hybrid Automaton). *Let $\mathcal{L}$ be a first-order language over the reals, $\mathcal{M}$ be a model of $\mathcal{L}$, and Inv, Dyn, Act and Reset be formulæ of $\mathcal{L}$. A hybrid automaton (of dimension k) $H = \langle Z, Z', \mathcal{V}, \mathcal{E}, Inv, Dyn, Act, Reset \rangle$ over $\mathcal{M}$, consists of the following components:*

1. *$Z = \{Z_1, \ldots, Z_k\}$ and $Z' = \{Z'_1, \ldots, Z'_k\}$ are two sets of variables ranging over the reals;*

2. *$\langle \mathcal{V}, \mathcal{E} \rangle$ is a finite directed graph; the vertices of $\mathcal{V}$ are called* locations, *or* control modes, *the directed edges in $\mathcal{E}$ are sometimes called* control switches;

3. *Each $v \in \mathcal{V}$ is labeled by the two formulæ $Inv(v)[Z]$ and $Dyn(v)[Z, Z', T]$ such that if $Inv(v)[p]$ holds in $\mathcal{M}$, then $Dyn(v)[p, p, 0]$ holds as well;*

4. *Each $e \in \mathcal{E}$ is labeled by the formulæ $Act(e)[Z]$ and $Reset(e)[Z, Z']$.*

The key feature in the above definition is the use of formulæ to define flows *in place* of differential equations: if $Dyn(v)[Z, Z', T]$ holds, then Z' can be reached from Z in T units of time. This approach is extremely general: we admit an *infinite number of flows possibly self-intersecting*, freely governed by the formula *Dyn* (belonging to a decidable class). The merits of this approach are fully discussed in [PAM+05]. The key point is that when dynamics are given in *explicit* form (i.e. by differential equations), using the first few terms of their Taylor expansion formulae, a fully symbolic computation method can be applied to study traces of hybrid automata. The advantages are manyfold: On the one hand, since a numerical approximation of solutions of differential equation is—in general—necessary, the symbolic approach allows a sort of built-in (symbolic) approximation, whose error is explicitly tied with computational costs. On the other hand, the approach consents the study of situations in which no explicit form for the dynamics is available: an interesting situation of this kind is presented in Section (3).

The key to guarantee decidability when working with the above definition is to consider, given a formula $\psi[Z]$ and a model $\mathcal{M}$, the set of tuples of values satisfying ψ in $\mathcal{M}$ as $Sat(\mathcal{M}, \psi)$, i.e., $Sat(\mathcal{M}, \psi) \overset{\text{def}}{=} \{p \mid \mathcal{M} \models \psi[p]\}$. When $\mathcal{M}$ is clear from the context we will simply write $Sat(\psi)$. The decidability of $Sat(Inv(v))$, $Sat(Act(e))$, and $Sat(Reset(e))$, is a prerequisite to decide properties of the hybrid automata. Moreover, from the basic formulæ involved in the definition of hybrid automata other formulæ can be introduced. For example, define the formula $\overline{Reset}(e)[Z] \overset{\text{def}}{=} \exists Z' \, Inv(v)[Z'] \wedge Act(e)[Z'] \wedge Reset(e)[Z', Z] \wedge Inv(u)[Z]$, where $e = \langle v, u \rangle$, expressing the set of states reachable by edge e. The decidability of $Sat(\overline{Reset}(e))$ will be a further issue when studying computational issues on hybrid automata.

The above approach is similar to the one followed in [BMRT04], based on o-minimal hybrid automata. Note particularly that o-minimal hybrid automata [LPS00, BMRT04] are a special case of our hybrid automata and rectangular hybrid automata [PV94, HK96, Kop96] can be easily mapped into a subclass of the above definition

1   Hybrid Automata and Genetic Regulatory Networks

In this section we present the basic ideas behind what can be argued to be one of the most simple and natural uses of hybrid automata: a formalism to computationally study collections of continuous trajectories representing concentrations.

In particular, we will describe a use of hybrid automata to model *genetic regulatory networks*, thinking of "quantities" as values for gene expressions. Our reference work for this line of research is [BB06], a paper whose main tools (*transition systems*) can be easily recast into the hybrid automata formalism, giving us the possibility to exemplify on various aspects of the potential and specificities of their use.

A set of variables $X = \{X_1, \ldots, X_n\}$ will describe the *state* of a *genes' network*, as an n-tuple of real values associated to the concentration of the n genes' products of the network. It is rather natural to assume a minimum (equal to 0) and a maximum (equal to a fixed parameter M_i) for each gene's product concentration. From this assumption it follows that the entire states' space is, in fact, a fairly simple geometrical object: a cartesian product of intervals, also called a *hyper-rectangular polytope*. Assuming the same structure also for a set P of unknown quantities (the *parameters* of our network) we can formally speak of the following two spaces:

$$\mathcal{X} = \Pi_{i=1}^{n}[0, M_i], \qquad \mathcal{P} = \Pi_{j=1}^{p}[m_{p_j}, M_{p_j}].$$

The analysis of the temporal evolution of X is the first objective of the study but, equivalently important, is the ability to tune up parameters—analyzing the parameters' space $\mathcal{P}$—in order to guarantee "expected behaviors" within the model. A key preliminary point to perform an objective analysis of both $\mathcal{X}$ and $\mathcal{P}$ is a precise definition of "expected (unwanted) behaviors". To this end it is customary to introduce a *logic* allowing us to express properties and measure our ability to computationally decide the satisfiability of sentences (formulae). Such logic can be exemplified by one of the most celebrated temporal logic formalism, the so called *Linear Time Temporal Logic* (*LTL*, a classic in the field of verification), whose definition can be given as follows:

Definition 2. *An LTL-formula is either an atomic formula A chosen in a finite alphabet $\mathcal{AP}$ of atomic propositions, or is a boolean combination of LTL-formulae, or is obtained using the (modal) connectives $\mathbf{X}$ (neXt) or $\mathbf{U}$ (Until) as $\mathbf{X}\phi$ or $\psi\mathbf{U}\phi$, respectively, with ϕ and ψ LTL-formulae.*

The semantics of *LTL*-formulæ is natural: a discrete time is assumed and the truth of $\mathbf{X}\phi$ is defined as the truth of ϕ at the next time instant, while $\psi\mathbf{U}\phi$ is true if and only if ψ is true for all time instants preceding the first time instant at which ϕ is true. Many variants of the above outlined definition are available in the literature and we refer the reader to [Eme90] for a complete survey of such variants and for references relative to the actual expressive power of the (at first sight minimal) syntactic tool-set defining *LTL*. The most important issues for us here are the following:

- truth of LTL-formulæ is to be referred to LTL-*structures*;
- all important questions on LTL-formulæ (i.e. satisfiability, validity, model-checking, etc.) can be computationally decided—often, practically, even efficiently—on *finite LTL-structures*.

In view of the above two points, it turns out natural to ask whether is possible to define finite LTL-structures in which deciding (at least) LTL-formulae, relative to genetic regulatory networks.

Such structures can be defined starting from hybrid automata specifying the dynamics of our vectors X and P.

As the reader can imagine, it is natural to proceed by first giving a general format to the dynamics of values and parameters vectors, and then restricting the mathematical nature of functions expressing the dynamics, in order to guarantee computability. The computability constraint must come to term with a further constraint crucial for biological applications: the class of dynamics that can be specified using the chosen functions must be sufficiently expressive.

In the case under study, X is assumed to vary satisfying, for $i \in \{1, \ldots, n\}$,

$$\dot{X}_i = f_i(X, P) = Prod_i(X, P) - Deg_i(X, P)X_i, \tag{1}$$

and the functions $Prod_i(X, P)$ and $Deg_i(X, P)$—expressing production and degradation of each gene—are required to be *piecewise multi-affine* functions, that is multi-variables polynomials of degree at most 1 in each of the variables. As regulation is traditionally represented by a non-linear sigmoidal functions, piecewise multi-affine function turn out to be well suited for genetic regulatory networks (sigmoidal functions can be approximated by *ramp* functions, expressible as piecewise multi-affine).

The mathematical characterizations of production and degradation functions given above is one among many possible and is introduced in order to guarantee computability. Such computability begins with a discretisation of the states' space, as a preliminary step in the construction of the finite LTL-structures on which the analysis will be performed. This discretisation can be described in two steps: first a hybrid automata is produced and then a finite LTL-structure *similar* (in a formal sense) is introduced, allowing an effective control on LTL-properties of the given regulatory network. The authors of [BB06], for example, perform the first discretisation step, by exploiting a simple observation relative to the syntactic structure of LTL-formulae and functions' dynamics: the relevant values of each gene's product concentration are, essentially, the constants involved in (atomic) LTL-formulæ (plus its maximum value) and the threshold constants appearing in the dynamics. Such an observation allows to break the variability's range of each component of X in a finite number of intervals and, consequently, the entire states' space in a finite number of hyper-rectangles. This defines a cellular decomposition of the initial hyper-rectangle containing variability's values for gene's products concentrations. Formally we have:

$$R_c = \{x \in \mathcal{X} \mid \forall i \in \{1, \ldots, n\}(\lambda_i^{c_i} < X_i < \lambda_i^{c_i+1})\},$$

where $c = \{c_1, \ldots, c_n\}$ consists of one of the relevant variables' values (the λ's) for each of the genes. The condition $\lambda_i^{c_i} < X_i < \lambda_i^{c_i+1}$ expresses the constraint on the i-*th* gene to belong to one of its variability regions.

On the ground of the above cellular decomposition of the states' space, a partial definition of hybrid automata can be given very naturally:

- the invariant regions corresponds the hyper-rectangles R_c's and, therefore, can be easily expressed as conjunction of inequalities;
- continuous dynamics can be expressed simply requiring the existence of a solution for the system of differential equations (1) connecting two states in the same hyper-rectangle.

What is missing here, in order to complete the definition of hybrid automata, are the activation and reset conditions, as well as the entire discrete part of the automata. Activation and reset conditions are simple: the former correspond to boundaries and latter are identities.

The discrete part of the automata (the graph $\langle \mathcal{V}, \mathcal{E} \rangle$) is, in principle, also easy to determine:

- locations (nodes in $\mathcal{V}$) are hyper-rectangles R_c's;
- a transition between two locations R_c and $R_{c'}$ is introduced, whenever R_c and $R_{c'}$ are adjacent or equal, and a continuous trace ξ—solution of (1)— allows to move from $x \in R_c$ to $x' \in R_{c'}$ in a time interval $\tau \in \Re^+$: $\xi(0) = x$ and $\xi(\tau) = x'$.

This is in fact what can be done starting from the definition, given in [BB06], of *Embedding Transition Systems*, which are, essentially, hybrid automata with understood activation and reset conditions.

As a matter of fact, the discrete part of the automata is the more interesting one. On the one hand, it can be determined exploiting results on values of multi-affine functions on hyper-rectangular polytopes: any value of a multi-affine function f on a hyper-rectangular polytope P can be obtained as a linear combination of values of f on the vertices of P: this feature, ultimately, guarantees computability. On the other hand it can be seen as a quotient of the continuous states' space whose equivalence classes are the hyper-rectangles. Such quotient is in fact a (finite) LTL-structure, sufficient to *simulate* the continuous dynamics of the automaton in the following sense: any continuous time evolution of the hybrid automaton leaves a "blueprint"—sometimes called the *correspondig path*—on the LTL-structure. Even though the converse of this property is, obviously, false, the study of LTL-formula satisfiability/validity on this discrete structure can be carried out effectively.

Summarizing, three key ingredients of the technique are the following:

- the existence of a class of mathematical functions (multi-affine) with nice mathematical properties and sufficient expressive power to be used as approximations of real concentration's fluxes;
- the possibility of carrying out a syntactic analysis of LTL-formulae and dynamics' functions, allowing to produce a finite set of vertices representing regions of the states' space, homogeneous with respect to LTL-satisfiability;

– a theoretical result on values of multi-affine functions allowing us to draw edges faithfully representing dynamics among the regions produced as above.

As we said, the finite graph built using the above ingredients is the LTL-structure on which the computational study can be performed.

Summarizing, the technique shows how to use, in place of a non-linear mathematical description of a genetic regulatory network, a controlled net of local descriptions given in simpler mathematical terms.

The real power of such a study comes at this point and it is based on the following two features:

1. piecewise multi-affine function are well-suited for simulating gene's expression, maintaining the possibility of computing an LTL-structure on which performing a simulation analysis;
2. a thorough analysis of the parameters' space can be carried out, addressing, in addition, such issues as system's robustness with respect to parameters' variation and—most important—*synthesis* of parameters' values guaranteeing given properties.

The method presented is implemented in the RoVerGeNe (Robust Verification of Genetic Networks), interfaced with teh NuSMV model checker for LTL-analysis. . Further applications and refinements of the technique can be found in [BBW07]. A literature review on Genetic Regulatory Networks can be found in [dJ02].

We conclude this part pointing out that the above casting of the results of [BB06] in a hybrid automata perspective can be argued to add an unnecessary overload of formalism. The more minimalist approach of [BB06] is preferable, introducing only what is sufficient for the application. From an engineering point of view this is true and is it ultimately due to the fact that the collection of continuous traces under study is essentially "well-behaving": traces are (non intersecting) solutions of differential equations, there is no independent discrete control superimposed to the continuous evolutions, and discreteness is introduced using a very simple equivalence relation partitioning the states' space guided by the constants appearing directly in the formulæ to be analyzed.

Technically speaking, the last point is the crucial one and sheds some light on the difficulties involved in more advanced decidability results related to hybrid automata. In such more complex cases, as the ones we will overview below, the discrete control is somehow independent from the continuous part of the automaton. During the discretisation activity, the control and the quotienting step interact in a loop that produces much more complicate (in general not even finite) discrete structures. Keeping the size and the effectiveness of the construction of such structures under control, is *the* challenge.

2   Hybrid Automata and Bacterial Chemotaxis

In this section we illustrate a use of hybrid automata differing from the one presented in the previous section mainly in the following two points:

- instead of employing hybrid automata only to reason on a mathematical representation—families of fluxes on a discrete grid of geometrically characterized regions—they are used as a means to formally render continuous evolutions paired with a discrete control, found in Nature;
- the formal machinery that turns out necessary to solve decidability issues in this context, is a generalization of the situation we found in Section (1)— essentially, very similar to the case of *timed* automata (see [AD94])—and will allow us to illustrate important issues related with decidability on hybrid automata analysis.

We begin with the second of the above two points, considering the possible reasons for undecidability in hybrid automata theory. There is one main reason that—in most of the cases—is responsible for undecidability: the dynamics within a region R, associated to a node of the discrete part of the automaton, forces a partition of regions R' reachable from R, which triggers an infinite partitioning process not allowing a finite discretisation of the states' space. If this turns out to be the case, decidability is in danger, even though there are cases in which decidability can be lost even if a finite discretisation is possible.

The above observation is, ultimately, as to say that a finite *(bi)simulation quotient cannot* be produced for the automaton under study.

It is not surprising that whenever some basic level of decidability is guaranteed (e.g. the decidability of the class of formulæ defining invariants, for example), the role played by resets is crucial in proving effectiveness of methods on classes of hybrid automata.

Consider, as an example is the class of order-minimal hybrid automata defined as follows:

Definition 3 (O-Minimal Theory). *Let $\mathcal{L}$ be a first-order language whose set of relational symbols includes a binary symbol $\leq$ and let $\mathcal{M}$ be a model of $\mathcal{L}$ in which $\leq$ is interpreted as a linear order. The theory $T(\mathcal{M})$ is order minimal, or simply* o-minimal, *if every set definable in $T(\mathcal{M})$ is a finite union of points and intervals (with respect to $\leq$).*

Definition 4. *Let $T(\mathcal{M})$ be a decidable o-minimal theory (over the reals). An hybrid automaton H over $\mathcal{M}$ is an* o-minimal *hybrid automaton, if for each $v \in \mathcal{V}, e \in \mathcal{E}$, the formulæ $Dyn(v)$, $Inv(v)$, $Act(e)$, $Reset(e)$ are formulæ of $T(\mathcal{M})$.*

On the ground of the above definition it can be shown that *constant reset* o-minimal hybrid automata whose dynamics are smooth solutions of vectorial fields, have all temporal logic properties (e.g. reachability and model-checking) decidable (see [BMRT04]). This can is proved through a quotient by bisimulation that reduces to a finite number of cases the temporal analysis of the entire states' space.

Moreover, *constant reset* o-minimal hybrid automata with no further constraint on dynamics are decidable, even though in that case the bisimulation quotient is not finite (see [CPM05]).

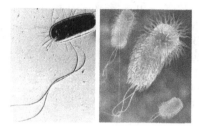

Fig. 1. Escherichia coli

It is clear that applications to systems biology must face the problem of what can be modeled with decidable hybrid automata (such as the o-minimal ones). Moreover, both the level of expressiveness of languages chosen for biological modeling, and the decidability issue for those languages, must be taken into account.

Our reference paper in this section is [CMPM05], where a very natural extension of the class of o-minimal hybrid automata is proved decidable and shown to be useful (in a sort of paradigmatic way) with respect to biological modeling. The authors of [CMPM05] start from the consideration that in biological modeling *identity reset* are crucial in order to model quantities variable in time, but maintaining their value across changes of modes. As a matter of fact this is a very natural statement: resetting every value to a constat after each mode's change is a very strong and un-natural constraint. The definition of *Independent Dynamics Hybrid Automata*, therefore, states that the variables of the automaton are divided into two groups: *independent* and *dependent* variables, respectively. The former are subject to a dynamics that is mode-independent (as in initialized rectangular automata [HHK95], [HK96]), while the latter are free to vary according to a standard dynamics and are subject to the constant reset requirement. Moreover, a constant amount of time is required to be spent in each mode.

O-minimal IDA-reachability over bounded time intervals is decidable. This is proved by showing that only finite length walks over the discrete part of the automaton are possible and, therefore, a decidability procedure checking all such paths can be designed.

Escherichia coli provides an example of mechanism for movement (bacterial chemotaxis) that can be modeled within the framework of hybrid automata as defined in [CMPM05]. The strategy has the goal of responding to a chemical gradient in its environment by detecting the concentration of ligands through a number of receptors. After sensing the environment, the reaction is a driving of "flagella motors" in one of two ways:

- "runs" – moves in a straight line by moving its flagella counterclockwise (CCW), or
- "tumbles" – randomly changes its heading by moving its flagella clockwise (CW).

The variables involved are the following (see Figure 2):

Y_P: CheY in phosphorylated form;
Y_0: CheY in un-phosphorylated form;
B_P: CheB in phosphorylated form;
B_0: CheB in un-phosphorylated form;
Z: CheZ in un-phosphorylated form;
LT: bound receptors;
T: un-bound receptors;
w: angular velocity of flagella.

The response is mediated through the molecular concentration of CheY in a phosphorylated form, which in turn is determined by the ligands bound (in more possible forms) at the receptors. The ratio of $y = Y_P/Y_0$ determines a bias with an associated probability that flagella will exert a CW rotation. The most important output variable is the angular velocity w that takes discrete values $+1$ for CW and -1 for CCW. The full pathway involves other molecules: CheB and CheZ (Z) whose continuous evolution is determined by a set of differential algebraic equations derived through kinetic mass action formulation.

The model in the above example captures the essence of how an *E. coli* cell performs a biased random walk by transiently decreasing its tumbling frequency to move towards a region with greater ligand concentration. This use of the discrete part of the automata to mimic stochastic behavior is interesting and, as stochastic simulation is computationally demanding, shows the potential of hybrid automata. We will come back on this points in the following two sections.

The authors of [CMPM05] mention the fact that model in the above example is also sensible more to concentration gradients than to absolute concentrations. This is in accordance with observations as, in fact, *E. coli* adapts quickly as it compares its environment during the immediate past to what existed a little earlier.

As opposed to the case of Section (1), the use of hybrid automata presented in this section illustrates the potential of the formal tool in combining discrete and continuous aspects of modeling. If in the case of genetic regulatory network

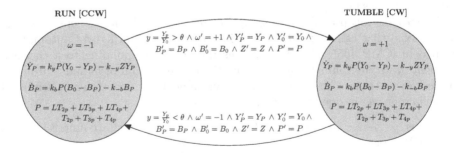

Fig. 2. An IDA capturing the run-tumble mechanism of *E. coli*.

discreteness was only employed to prove that a computational analysis of a collection of continuous traces was possible, in this case a discrete control is integral part of the construction and has a direct correspondence in the biological situation under study. The technical aspects involved in maintaining decidability in the bacterial chemotaxis example are a sort of "ground" decidability relative to the basic formulæ of the language—decidability of o-minimal theory in the example above—, and a finite partitioning of the states' space performed using the discrete control as guide—reducing the reachability issue to a finite number of verifications.

3   Switching between Simulation Techniques

In this section we discuss a inherently different use of the formalism of hybrid automata, consisting in their exploitation as a switch between two different simulation techniques for the same phenomenon. The general theme is the choice between a discrete-stochastic methodology and a continuous-deterministic one. In general terms, the issue of choosing between these two approaches reaches back in years and spans across many disciplines. From a computational point of view—as well as for further reasons that will become apparent in the following—a crucial contribution on this subject was given by D. Gillespie in the seventies (see [Gil76] and [Gil77]). What is known today as the *Gillespie algorithm* was proposed in those years as a stochastic simulation method to numerically simulating a mixture of interacting molecular species. Even though a completely continuous-deterministic approach, based on ordinary differential equations, could be taken to tackle this problem, Gillespie started from two crucial observations:

- a discrete-stochastic modeling approach has much firmer physical basis than the continuous-deterministic one;
- when small numbers of molecules are present and fluctuations play a central role, the deterministic-stochastic approach captures behaviors that are lost by the continuous deterministic one.

Starting from such observations and trying to avoid the mathematical complications involved in an attempt to analytically solve the Master equation defined by the discrete-stochastic approach, Gillespie came out with his elegant and extremely effective alternative numerical algorithms.

The situation is therefore the following: given a physical (biological) phenomenon two possible simulation techniques are available,

1. a continuous-deterministic one, involving variables regulated by differential equations;
2. a discrete-stochastic one, involving the use of Gillespie algorithm to determine the sequence of reactions taking place.

The idea is to use hybrid automata to combine within a single framework the two methods, switching between the two when system's variables satisfy a suitable condition, for instance when a variable reaches a certain threshold.

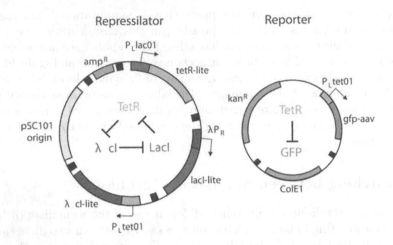

Fig. 3. The Repressilator

Our reference paper for this section is [ABI01], where the example chosen to illustrate the technique is a "classic" called *Repressilator* (see [EL00]). The Repressilator is a synthetic network of three genes expressing proteins repressing each other in cycle (see Figure 1).

The Repressilator can be simulated using the following differential equations defined as acting on variables $P_{LacI}, P_{TetR}, P_{cI}$, representing the concentration of three kind of modeled proteins, and by three additional variables $M_{LacI}, M_{TetR}, M_{cI}$, representing the three mRNA's concentrations.

$$\begin{cases} \dot{P}_{LacI} = -\beta(P_{LacI} - M_{LacI}); & \dot{M}_{LacI} = -M_{LacI} + \frac{\alpha}{1+P_{cI}^n} + \alpha_0; \\ \dot{P}_{TetR} = -\beta(P_{TetR} - M_{TetR}); & \dot{M}_{TetR} = -M_{TetR} + \frac{\alpha}{1+P_{LacI}^n} + \alpha_0; \quad (2) \\ \dot{P}_{cI} = -\beta(P_{cI} - M_{cI}); & \dot{M}_{cI} = -M_{cI} + \frac{\alpha}{1+P_{TetR}^n} + \alpha_0; \end{cases}$$

where α, α_0 and β are parameters and n is a Hill's coefficient. More specifically, β is the ratio of protein decay rate and mRNA decay rate, α_0 is the rate of transcription when the repressor is bound (i.e., a measure of the "leakage" of the repressor), and $\alpha+\alpha_0$ is the rate of transcription when the repressor is not bound. Protein concentration is measured in units of K_m, the number of repressors necessary to half-maximally repress a promoter, while mRNA concentration is re-scaled by the average number of proteins produced per mRNA molecule. The repression is modeled by Hill's equations with exponent $n = 2$ (or greater); this indicates a cooperative effect among repressors in the inhibition of the gene transcription. In [EL00], the authors discuss the properties of the phase space: there is a unique steady state which is stable for some parameter's values and becomes unstable for others, generating a stable limit cycle (see Figure 4 for an example of oscillations). In particular, the size of the unstable region, in which the solution of the equations oscillates, increases proportionally with the

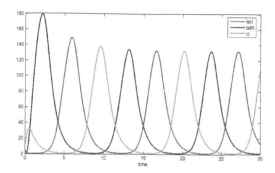

Fig. 4. The oscillating behavior of Repressilator for parameters'values $\alpha = 250$, $\beta = 5$, $\alpha_0 = 0$

Hill's coefficient n, and inversely with the leakage rate α_0. This means that the cooperative effect of binding stabilizes the oscillatory behavior of the system. Interestingly, in the stable region near the stability border, the steady state is reached through dumping oscillations (an example is given in Figure 5).

The corresponding hybrid automaton consists of two modes only, corresponding to the two simulating techniques available for Repressilator:

1. the first mode has six continuous variables and a dynamics consisting of the differential equations 2;
2. The second mode should specify the stochastic dynamics. In order to avoid the explicit introduction of stochastic evolution within the framework of hybrid automata (obtaining the so-called Stochastic Hybrid Automata [BL04]), the dynamics can be non-deterministically approximated using suitable formulae. For instance, the invariant region could be defined as a tube containing the limit cycle, while the discrete dynamics can be rendered using looping edges with appropriate activation and resets.

A delicate issue of this alternation is the fact that, ultimately, the switch imposes a transition from a Hill type equation description to a stochastic mass action description. Consequently, kinetic parameters are different between the two models.

In [ABI01] the switch between modes is regulated simply by monitoring the amount of different types of $mRNA$ molecules and proteins in the system: whenever one such value drops below a certain threshold, a switch from continuous-deterministic to discrete-stochastic behavior takes place. We believe that a more careful study of this kind of switch is necessary: looking at Figure 4, where an oscillatory solution of the ODE is shown, we can see that, if the switching thresholds is just slightly above the minimum concentration of proteins, then the switching condition would always be true! An alternative choice for the mechanism governing the switch could be, for example, monitoring the distance of mRNA or protein concentrations from their steady state value: whenever such value drops below a given threshold (say half the minimum distance of the limit cycle), a switch from continuous-deterministic to discrete-stochastic behavior takes place.

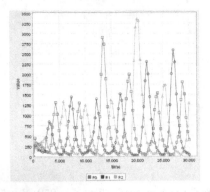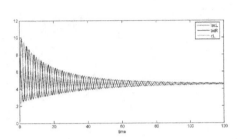

Fig. 5. Dumping oscillations of a continuous-deterministic model of Repressilator (parameters are $\alpha = 100$, $\beta = 200$, and $\alpha_0 = 0$) and stochastic oscillation behavior for the corresponding discrete-stochastic model

Moreover, the use of a non-deterministic approximation of stochastic dynamics within hybrid automata may introduce spurious behaviors (i.e. traces having extremely low probability of being observed in the stochastic system).

Actually, the reader can check how the system of ODE is sensitive to parameters' change. In fact, for a large number of combination of parameters' values, the oscillating behavior can either be not present at all, or asymptotically disappearing in time through dumping oscillations (see Figure 5). The introduction of the above control switch, therefore, can be seen as a means to guarantee a higher overall level of robustness to the network.

Hybrid automata used as illustrated above are, again, a tool to formalize and model situations that need to have some kind of switch between continuous and discrete. The limit of the Repressilator example is the fact that there is no real discrete control coupled with the system of differential equation describing the behavior: in one of the two modes the dynamics is fully governed by a single system of differential equations, while in the other is entirely governed stochastically (or by a non-deterministic approximation). No additional discrete control is present in either case. Actually, instead of globally switching the dynamics from continuous to discrete/stochastic, one can imagine to use the control structure of hybrid automata to perform this switch *locally*, in order to govern discretely *only* those variables having sufficiently low concentration. To the best of our knowledge the applications of this technique have not been exemplified in such more interesting cases in the literature.

4   Governing the Discrete and Continuous Parts

In this section we briefly discuss a recently proposed methodology investigating the possibility to pass from a stochastic process algebra model to a hybrid automaton, in which the degree of continuity can be tunable by the user.

Table 1. Syntax of restricted sCCP

$$
\begin{array}{ll}
Prog = D.N & D = \varepsilon \mid D.D \mid p : -A \\
\pi = [g(X) \rightarrow u(X, X')]_\lambda & M = \pi.G \mid M + M \\
G = \mathbf{0} \mid p \mid M & A = \mathbf{0} \mid M \\
N = A \mid A \parallel N
\end{array}
$$

In order to clarify the approach we need to introduce a simple stochastic process algebra suitable for programming and based on the *Concurrent Constraint* paradigm [Sar93]. Our reference papers for this section will be [BP08a, BP08b].

A *stochastic Concurrent Constraint* program consists of a set of agents interacting via a *shared store*, containing a finite set of variables $X = \{X_1, \ldots, X_n\}$, usually taking integer values. A configuration c of the store is a "snapshot" of the variables' values. The basic action π executable by agents is a *guarded update* of some variables. In addition, the language has all the basic constructs of process algebras: non-deterministic choice, parallel composition, and recursive calls.

The characteristic feature of sCCP is the fact that each action π is given a *stochastic duration* by associating to it an exponentially distributed random variable. Moreover, the rate of stochastic durations depends on the state of the system through a function $\lambda : X \rightarrow \mathbb{R}^+$. Therefore, durations are sensitive to the overall status of the system and this allows to reflect locally (on communications) global properties of the model. Stochastic actions, denoted by $[\pi]_\lambda$, permit to define a structural operational semantic [Bor06] by a transition relation, from which a Continuous Time Markov Chain [Wil06] can be inferred.

More precisely, a sCCP program is a tuple $\mathcal{N} = (Prog, X, init(X))$, where

1. $Prog$ is defined according to the grammar of Table 1;
2. X is the set of variables of the store (with global scope);
3. $init(X)$ is a predicate on X of the form $X = x_0$, assigning an *initial value* to store variables.

Analyzing the syntactic structure of sCCP programs, it can be proved that one such program is always a parallel composition of a finite and constant (at run time) number of *sequential components*, i.e. of agents not containing any occurrence of the parallel operator. Moreover, the number of different *states* (disregarding the value of variables) of each sequential agent is *finite*, so that its *transition system* is a finite labeled multi-graph.[1]

As a first step to move from from stochastic process algebras to hybrid automata, we observe that we can define a *fluid-flow approximation* [Hil05] of the *entire* sCCP program, by treating variables as continuous and describing their time-evolution by means of ODEs [Bor07, BP07].

---

[1] The CTMC can, however, have an infinite number of states, because the *configurations* of a sCCP program, i.e. the state of agents plus the value of variables, are generally infinite.

Starting from a sCCP network $\mathcal{N}$, consider the transition system associated to each sequential component A_i in $\mathcal{N}$ and associate a *fresh continuous variable* to each different state. Such variables, together with all variables X of the store, will be governed by differential equations.

Differential equations can be introduced defining an *interaction matrix I* of the sCCP-network. This matrix captures the effect of each action of a sequential agent (i.e. of each edge in the transition systems) on system's variables: it has as many rows as system's variables and as many columns as the edges in the transition systems of all components, each entry $I[X, e]$ storing the neat variation on the variable X caused by the update of edge e. In order to write the ODEs, we simply need to store in a vector r the (functional) *rates* of each transition, following the same order used in the interaction matrix, and compute the product $I \cdot r$.

The above technique discusses the construction of a system of differential equations governing the entire network. The crucial point in using hybrid automata is, instead, to use different systems of differential equations depending on the state in which each sequential agent is on. More specifically, the translation of a sCCP network $\mathcal{N}$ to a hybrid automaton proceeds in two phases: first, each sequential component A_i of $\mathcal{N}$ is converted into a hybrid automaton, then these hybrid automata are "glued" together using a suitable *product of automata* construction.

The first part of the construction, namely the definition of hybrid automata associated to sequential components of the network, is more or less direct: the control graph coincides with the transition system of the component, after removing all looping edges. Flows, instead, are obtained by localizing the general technique to a single state of a sequential component, considering only edges of the transition system looping in that state. The net effect will be a reduction of the hybrid automata variables to the variables of the constraint store. The delicate point in this phase is the definition of activation conditions on edges, in order to capture the timing of the associated events. Activation conditions are defined introducing one variable Y_e for each edge e, whose purpose is to control time varying rates $\lambda = \lambda(t)$.[2] The crucial observation is the fact that every transition, when isolated from the context, constitute a *non-homogeneous Poisson process* [Ros96]. Thus, we can define the *cumulative rate function*

$$\Lambda(t) = \int_{t_0}^{t} \lambda(s)ds,$$

which is a monotone function of t and use the fact, following from the theory of non-homogeneous Poisson processes, that the number of firings at time t behaves like a Poisson variable with rate equal to $\Lambda(t)$. Hence, *the average number of firings of the transition at time t equals $\Lambda(t)$.* Therefore, we may activate the transition whenever $\Lambda(t) \geq 1$, corresponding to the happening of at least one

---

[2] Rates depend on store variables, which vary continuously over time. Hence, also rates are time-varying functions.

firing on average. This condition is expressed in the hybrid automaton as $Y_e \geq 1$, with the associated transition variable Y_e evolving according to

$$\dot{Y}_e = \frac{d\Lambda(t)}{dt} = \lambda(X). \tag{3}$$

The above point is the kernel of the construction: in order to properly define activation conditions reflecting stochastic behavior in a given interval of time, it is sufficient to control cumulative rate functions.

The above discussion can be synthesized in a definition of hybrid automata associated to a given sequential component, which can be summarized as follows. Let A be a sCCP sequential agent operating on store variables X. The hybrid automaton $H(A) = (\mathcal{V}, \mathcal{E}, Z, Dyn, Inv, Act, Reset)$ associated to A is defined by

1. the control graph $\langle \mathcal{V}, \mathcal{E} \rangle$ is the transition system associated to A, with looping edges removed;
2. the variables are $Z = X \cup \{Y_e \mid e \in \mathcal{E}\}$;
3. for each $v \in \mathcal{V}$, the dynamics is governed by the equations induced by the interaction matrix of component A or by (3);
4. $Inv(v) = true$ for each $v \in \mathcal{V}$;
5. $Act(e)$ is true if $Y_e \geq 1$ and the guard of $e \in \mathcal{E}$ holds;
6. $Reset(e)$ resets variables according to the update of e and sets Y_e to 0 for each $e \in \mathcal{E}$.

To complete the construction, hybrid automata associated to sequential components have to be combined together to form the hybrid automaton of the network. The key point is that the same variable of the store must be allowed to be modified by several agents concurrently. Hence, the product automaton must superimpose fluxes, adding the right-hand side of the differential equations of each component for all shared variables. An almost classical product of two hybrid automata can be carried out (see [Hen96]), with the only difference of a special treatment of fluxes for variables shared among the factors.

Modes of the automaton $H(\mathcal{N})$ are the combination of modes of the sequential components; in total, $H(\mathcal{N})$ has $|\mathcal{V}(A_1)| \times \ldots \times |\mathcal{V}(A_n)|$ states. In addition, the variables of $H(\mathcal{N})$ are the store variables X of the system, shared by all components, for which fluxes are added, and the variables involved in the activation conditions of transitions, which are local within each component.

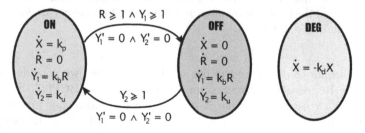

Fig. 6. Hybrid automaton associated to the sCCP program $G_f(X,Y)$ (left) and $Deg(X)$ (right)

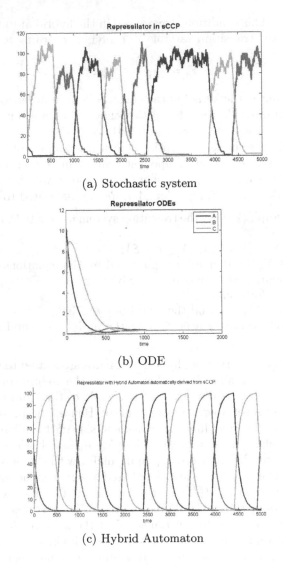

(a) Stochastic system

(b) ODE

(c) Hybrid Automaton

Fig. 7. Numerical simulation of Repressilator for the stochastic model (7(a)), the ODE model (7(b)), and the hybrid automaton model (7(c)). Parameters are $k_p = 1$, $k_b = 1$, $k_u = 0.0001$, and $k_d = 0.001$.

As an example to illustrate the use of this technique, we consider a simpler model of the Repressilator (see Section 3), presented in [BCP06]. Each gene is modeled as a two-state machine: it can be active, producing proteins, or re-pressed, producing nothing. Inhibition of a gene is caused by the binding of a single repressor, hence no cooperativity is assumed. Moreover, the transcription and translation are condensed in a single step. In sCCP, the formal model of the gene is

$$G_f(X,Y):\text{-}[* \to X' = X + 1]_{k_p}.G_f(X,Y) + [Y \geq 1 \to *]_{k_b Y}.G_b(X,Y)$$
$$G_b(X,Y):\text{-}[* \to *]_{k_u}.G_f(X,Y)$$
$$Deg(X):\text{-}[X \geq 1 \to X' = X - 1]_{k_d X}.Deg(X),$$

where Deg implements the first-order degradation of the protein, G_f and G_b are the free and repressed states of the gene, respectively, X is the protein produced by the gene and Y is the repressor. Henceforth, the complete model of repressilator is

$$G_f(A,C) \parallel G_f(B,A) \parallel G_f(C,B) \parallel Deg(A) \parallel Deg(B) \parallel Deg(C).$$

In Figure 6 we show the hybrid automata associated to $G_f(X,Y)$ and $Deg(X)$. The automaton of the entire Repressilator, obtainable by the product construction, has 8 states in total, one for each possible combination of states of the three composing genes.

Figure 7 compares the dynamics of the stochastic model, of the associated ODE, and of the hybrid automaton. As we can see, the oscillatory behavior is manifest in the stochastic and hybrid systems, but absent in the differential one. This difference is caused by the fact that in the ODE the state of each gene is represented by a continuous variable taking values in $[0, 1]$, thus leveling out the discrete switching dynamics of gene activation and deactivation. As a matter of fact, it is this switching dynamics that induces the oscillatory pattern in the stochastic and hybrid systems.

The mapping from sCCP to hybrid automata presented above introduces a fixed degree of continuity depending on the structure of agents: all store variables are approximated as continuous, even if they represent molecules present in a low number of copies in the system. An higher degree of tunability can be achieved by parameterizing the transformation w.r.t. the actions treated as continuous and the ones kept discrete. We explain this concept with an example. Consider the simple procaryote genetic network depicted in Figure 8: there is one single

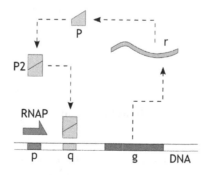

Fig. 8. Diagram of a simple self-repressing genetic network of a procaryote

gene, whose product, as a dimer, represses its own production. We can describe this network by the following list of reactions:

$$G_f + P_2 \to_{k_b} G_b; \quad G_b \to_{k_u} G_f + P_2; \quad G_f \to_{k_p} G_f + r; \quad r \to_{k_{d_1}} \emptyset; \qquad (4)$$
$$r \to_{k_t} r + P; \quad P \to_{k_{dim_1}} P_2; \quad P_2 \to_{k_{dim_2}} P; \quad P \to_{k_{d_2}} \emptyset.$$

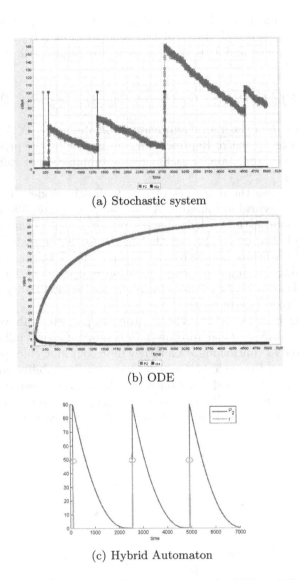

(a) Stochastic system

(b) ODE

(c) Hybrid Automaton

Fig. 9. Numerical simulation of simple genetic network of Figure8 for the stochastic model (9(a)), the ODE model (9(b)), and the hybrid automaton model (9(c)). Parameters are $k_p = 0.01$, $k_b = 1$, $k_u = 10$, $k_t = 10$, $k_{dim_1} = 1$, $k_{dim_2} = 1$, $k_{d_1} = 0.1$, and $k_{d_2} = 0.01$.

This example is taken from [Wil06], where it is modeled using Stochastic Petri Nets [HR04]. The example was intended to show how the behavior of stochastic and deterministic mass action models can differ (see Figure 9). In fact, the stochastic simulation of the network of Figure 9(a) shows a typical pattern of expression in "bursts", caused by the small half-life of mRNA w.r.t. gene transcription rate. The mass action ODE obtained from reactions (4), instead, exhibit a milder behavior, asymptotically converging to a steady state (Figure 9(b)). As a matter of fact, the amount of mRNA molecules is very low, usually alternating between 0 and 1. Therefore, approximating this quantity as continuous creates a divergent behavior from the stochastic model. In the associated hybrid automata, we can choose to treat as continuous only the last four reactions of (4), keeping discrete the first four, i.e. all those concerning the repression of the gene and the production and degradation of mRNA. In terms of the mapping previously defined, this corresponds in maintaining some looping edges of the transition system as edges of the hybrid automaton. In general, the previous mapping can be generalized by partitioning the set of edges of the transition system in two sets: those treated as discrete and those treated as continuous. The simulation of the hybrid automaton obtained from reactions (4) is shown in Figure 9(c): it presents a pattern of expression closer to the original stochastic system, the only difference being the regularity of the period of proteins' bursts.

The approach presented here is in line with the spirit of Section 3. The crucial difference, however, is that continuous and discrete dynamics can be mixed, exploiting the discrete control of hybrid automata. Moreover, the tunability of the degree of continuity provides a framework to study the interplay of continuous and discrete evolution in the light of systemic behaviors. This approach can be further extended introducing also the stochastic ingredient, ending up in using the so called stochastic hybrid automata [BL04]. This would add a further degree of tunability, involving the level of stochasticity of the model. Within this more general framework, hybrid stochastic simulation algorithms like [Neo04] can be easily described, showing that hybrid automata can also help in reducing the computational burden in the analysis of models.

5 Conclusion

In this survey we reviewed, from a personal perspective, a few issues related with the use of hybrid systems for biological modeling. Our starting point was the observation that, instrumental to the ultimate goal of Systems Biology— i.e. the isolation and study of systemic properties of biological networks—, is the set up of a formalism allowing to reason on both continuous and discrete aspects of the dynamics of biological systems. In this respect the proposal of modeling biological systems as hybrid systems and formalize their study by hybrid automata, is somehow natural. However, we must keep in mind that hybrid automata were born to combine continuous evolution and discrete control. In this respect they were directed more toward an attempt to provide the correct framework for *designing* a discrete control interacting with a continuous environment. Biological system are much less "artificial", as they do not provide any clear-cut view on the discrete control present in the system under study. As a matter of fact, the modeler usually only "feels" the presence of a discrete control over a continuous environment, while in reality things can be described in an entirely different manner. Consider, for example, the general fact that in, in biological systems, the dynamics of the environment is, ultimately, a discrete and stochastic sequence of events. At the same time the kind of control that can be distilled from available data on biological networks, is only a *partial* view on the functionalities of the system. All in all, a much more complex situation than the one that has to be faced in studying embedded systems!

Nevertheless we believe the use of hybrid automata has a great potential in biological modeling. We tried to exemplify on the variants of this potential by providing examples of definition and uses of hybrid automata in modeling biologically significant scenarios. Such scenarios provided also us the possibility to show the various level of complexity (sometimes given in very precise decidability terms) of the implementation machinery required.

Very effective methods to analyze, control, and synthesize Genetic Regulatory Networks can be cast into hybrid automata formalism to illustrate a basic level of logical complexity. The discrete part of the automata, in these cases, is suggested by a syntactic analysis of the query language and of the mathematical specification of dynamics. The implementation complexities in these cases do not stem from the logic but from the mathematics of the formalism. This part of our study was presented in Section (1).

In Section (2) a deeper level in control-analysis is illustrated, by showing how to model a discrete control in Bacterial Chemotaxis and how to constrain the logical format of dynamics in order to maintain decidability. Decidability issues related with the logical formulæ employed in the dynamics'definition are taken into account here. A higher level of logical complexity is involved, witness the fact that *reachability* becomes the crucial implementation issue.

In Section (3) and Section (4), instead, a different level of interaction between control and dynamics is illustrated. In the first case the possibility is mentioned to switch between continuous-deterministic and discrete-stochastic simulation modes. This is obtained by using the discrete-control capabilities of hybrid automata. In the last section it is shown how, using a stochastic process algebra simulation method as starting point, different levels of continuous/discrete subdivisions can be envisaged in designing the corresponding hybrid automata.

Continuous and discrete aspects of (biological) modeling drive researchers quickly into deep considerations concerning non-determinism, stochastic dynamics, and time ontology. Perhaps more important than this—from an Informatics[3] point of view—is the fact that the design and analysis of proper means for

---

[3] We prefer the term *Informatics* to *Computer Science*, as it clearly point at the difficulties to be faced in properly treating transfer and storage of *information*.

dealing with continuous and discrete aspects of modeling, is a kernel problem in the computational treatment of mathematical language.

References

[ABI01]   Alur, R., Belta, C., Ivančić, F.: Hybrid modeling and simulation of biomolecular networks. In: Di Benedetto, M.D., Sangiovanni-Vincentelli, A.L. (eds.) HSCC 2001. LNCS, vol. 2034, pp. 19–32. Springer, Heidelberg (2001)

[AD94]   Alur, R., Dill, D.L.: A theory of timed automata. Theoretical Computer Science 126(2), 183–235 (1994)

[BB06]   Batt, G., Belta, C.: Model checking genetic regulatory networks with applications to synthetic biology. Technical Report 2006-IR-0030, CISE Tech. Rep., Boston University (2006)

[BBW07]   Batt, G., Belta, C., Weiss, R.: Model checking liveness properties of genetic regulatory networks. In: Proceedings of TACAS, pp. 323–338 (2007)

[BCP06]   Blossey, R., Cardelli, L., Phillips, A.: A compositional approach to the stochastic dynamics of gene networks. T. Comp. Sys. Biology, pp. 99–122 (2006)

[BL04]   Bujorianu, M.L., Lygeros, J.: General stochastic hybrid systems: Modeling and optimal control. In: Proceedings of 43rd IEEE Conference on Decision and Control (CDC 2004), pp. 182–187 (2004)

[BMRT04]   Brihaye, T., Michaux, C., Rivière, C., Troestler, C.: On O-Minimal Hybrid Systems. In: Alur, R., Pappas, G.J. (eds.) HSCC 2004. LNCS, vol. 2993, pp. 219–233. Springer, Heidelberg (2004)

[Bor06]   Bortolussi, L.: Stochastic concurrent constraint programming. In: Proceedings of 4th International Workshop on Quantitative Aspects of Programming Languages, QAPL 2006. ENTCS, vol. 164, pp. 65–80 (2006)

[Bor07]   Bortolussi, L.: Constraint-based approaches to stochastic dynamics of biological systems. PhD thesis, PhD in Computer Science, University of Udine (preparation 2007)

[BP07]   Bortolussi, L., Policriti, A.: Stochastic concurrent constraint programming and differential equations. In: Proceedings of QAPL 2007 (2007)

[BP08a]   Bortolussi, L., Policriti, A.: Hybrid approximation of stochastic concurrent constraint programming. In: IFAC 2008 (2008)

[BP08b]   Bortolussi, L., Policriti, A.: Modeling biological systems in stochastic concurrent constraint programming. Constraints 13(1) (2008)

[CMPM05]   Casagrande, A., Mysore, V., Piazza, C., Mishra, B.: Independent dynamics hybrid automata in systems biology. In: Proceedings of the First International Conference on Algebraic Biology (AB 2005), November 2005, pp. 61–73. Universal Academy Press, Inc, Tokyo, Japan (2005)

[CPM05]   Casagrande, A., Piazza, C., Mishra, B.: Semi-Algebraic Constant Reset Hybrid Automata - SACoRe. In: Proceedings of the 44rd Conference on Decision and Control and European Control Conference (CDC-ECC 2005), Seville, Spain, December 2005, pp. 678–683. IEEE Computer Society Press, Los Alamitos (2005)

[dJ02]   de Jong, H.: Modeling and simulation of genetic regulatory systems: a literature review. J. Comput. Biol. 9(1), 67–103 (2002)

[EL00]   Elowitz, M.B., Leibler, S.: A syntetic oscillatory network of transcriptional
             regulators. Nature 403, 335–338 (2000)
[Eme90]   Emerson, E.A.: Temporal and Modal Logic. In: van Leeuwen, J. (ed.)
             Handbook of Theoretical Computer Science, vol. B, pp. 995–1072 (1990)
[Gil76]   Gillespie, D.T.: A general method for numerically simulating the stochas-
             tic time evolution of coupled chemical reactions. J. of Computational
             Physics 22 (1976)
[Gil77]   Gillespie, D.T.: Exact stochastic simulation of coupled chemical reactions.
             J. of Physical Chemistry 81(25) (1977)
[Hen96]   Henzinger, T.A.: The theory of hybrid automata. In: LICS 1996: Proceed-
             ings of the 11th Annual IEEE Symposium on Logic in Computer Science
             (1996)
[HHK95]   Henzinger, M.R., Henzinger, T.A., Kopke, P.W.: Computing simulations
             on finite and infinite graphs. In: Proceedings of the Thirty-Sixth Annual
             Symposium on Foundations of Computer Science (FOCS 1995), Washing-
             ton, DC, USA, p. 453 (1995)
[Hil05]   Hillston, J.: Fluid flow approximation of pepa models. In: Proceedings of
             the Second International Conference on the Quantitative Evaluation of
             Systems (QEST 2005) (2005)
[HK96]   Henzinger, T.A., Kopke, P.W.: State Equivalences for Rectangular Hybrid
             Automata. In: Montanari, U., Sassone, V. (eds.) Proc. of Int. Conference
             on Concurrency Theory (Concur 1996), vol. 1119, pp. 530–545 (1996)
[HR04]   Hardy, S., Robillard, P.N.: Modeling and simulation of molecular biology
             systems using petri nets: Modeling goals of various approaches. Journal
             of Bioinformatics and Computational Biology 2(4), 619–637 (2004)
[Kop96]   Kopke, P.W.: The Theory of Rectangular Hybrid Automata. PhD thesis,
             Faculty of the Graduate School, Cornell University, Advisor - T. A. Hen-
             zinger (1996)
[LPS00]   Lafferriere, G., Pappas, G.J., Sastry, S.: O-Minimal Hybrid Systems.
             Mathematics of Control, Signals, and Systems 13, 1–21 (2000)
[Neo04]   Neogi, N.A.: Dynamic partitioning of large discrete event biological sys-
             tems for hybrid simulation and analysis. In: Alur, R., Pappas, G.J. (eds.)
             HSCC 2004. LNCS, vol. 2993, pp. 463–476. Springer, Heidelberg (2004)
[PAM+05]   Piazza, C., Antoniotti, M., Mysore, V., Policriti, A., Winkler, F., Mishra,
             B.: Algorithmic algebraic model checking i: Challenges from systems biol-
             ogy. In: Etessami, K., Rajamani, S.K. (eds.) CAV 2005. LNCS, vol. 3576,
             pp. 5–19. Springer, Heidelberg (2005)
[PV94]   Puri, A., Varaiya, P.: Decidability of hybrid systems with rectangular
             differential inclusions. In: Dill, D.L. (ed.) CAV 1994. LNCS, vol. 818, pp.
             95–104. Springer, Heidelberg (1994)
[Ros96]   Ross, S.M.: Stochastic Processes. Wiley, New York (1996)
[Sar93]   Saraswat, V.A.: Concurrent Constraint Programming. MIT Press, Cam-
             bridge (1993)
[Wil06]   Wilkinson, D.J.: Stochastic Modelling for Systems Biology. Chapman and
             Hall, Boca Raton (2006)

π@: A π-Based Process Calculus for the Implementation of Compartmentalised Bio-inspired Calculi*

Cristian Versari and Roberto Gorrieri

Università di Bologna, Dipartimento di Scienze dell'Informazione
Mura Anteo Zamboni 7, 40127 Bologna, Italy
{versari,gorrieri}@cs.unibo.it

Abstract. The modelling of biological systems led to the explicit introduction of compartments in several bio-oriented process calculi. In this tutorial we show how different compartment semantics can be obtained by means of a simple and conservative extension of the standard pi-calculus, the pi@ calculus. Significant examples are given through the encoding of two well known bio-inspired process calculi: BioAmbients and Brane Calculi.

Keywords: pi-calculus, priority, polyadic synchronisation, BioAmbients, Brane Calculi.

1 Introduction

There is an increasing awareness that complex biological systems can be better understood and studied at a system level, where a network of biochemical cells can be seen as a computing machinery, made of processing agents which interact and cooperate to achieve a common goal. This informal description applies to concurrent system as well, hence it is natural to use techniques from the global computing field to study the behaviour of biological cells. Particularly promising is the use of process calculi, which are formalisms used to describe concurrent and mobile systems. Process calculi are equipped with a formal semantics describing their behaviour, and plenty of tools for the static and dynamic analysis of systems have been produced, in particular simulators. These tools can be therefore used in the field of biological organisms, as well, to analyse and possibly predict their behavior. The pioneering work on modelling biochemical systems with a calculus is the work by Fontana and Buss [1] where a version of the lambda-calculus is used. A better account of pathways descriptions is proposed in [2] by Regev, Silverman and Shapiro, who use the π-calculus [3], a well-known formalism for mobility.

---

* This work has been partially sponsored by the PRIN 2006 Project BISCA – Sistemi e calcoli di ispirazione biologica e loro applicazioni.

M. Bernardo, P. Degano, and G. Zavattaro (Eds.): SFM 2008, LNCS 5016, pp. 449–506, 2008.

This first case-study on the use of π-calculus for the modeling of biological processes raised an enormous interest for the potential application of process calculi techniques to Systems Biology. The direct employment of π-Calculus allowed the formalisation of several biological mechanisms, and even more by means of its variants and extensions [4,5,6] that permitted the representation or analysis *in silico* of complex cellular processes [7,8]. Nonetheless, π-calculus is not the ultimate answer: it is difficult to model some other aspects of biological systems that cannot be ignored, if one wishes to obtain descriptions at a higher abstraction level and with higher biological faithfulness. A basic missing abstraction is the notion of *compartment*: a cell is composed of different materials that are confined in different areas of the cell (the compartments), usually separated by suitable *membranes* (i.e., semi-permeable barriers), ensuring that certain substances always stay into the compartment while other substances stay out of it. Similarly, any non-trivial biological system is a construct in which various components in different compartments execute different "computations", and the results of these computations can be communicated among the components through the compartments.

To this aim, more complex calculi have been proposed, such as Brane Calculi [9] and its variants [10], Bioambients [11], Beta binders [12,13], the K-calculus [14], BioK [15] which are based on or get inspiration from π-calculus, enriched with some powerful mechanisms for compartmentalised computation. Even if they present many common features, each calculus focuses its attention on particular biological entities or mechanisms. Their similarity induces the interest for a parallel analysis, but their specialisation does not allow a direct comparison. Moreover, there is a lack of techniques and tool support for these calculi, because the added features are often radically new and the existing theories and tools cannot be adapted easily.

In this paper, we propose a novel calculus, called $\pi@$ (to be pronounced as the French word "paillette"), designed specifically to overcome the problems singled out above. It is a simple, conservative and powerful extension to π-calculus, with two new basic mechanisms: polyadic synchronisation and prioritised communication. In particular, polyadic synchronisation [16] allows for the modeling of compartments in a natural way, but still in the classic message-passing flavour typical of π-calculus.; priority instead is extremely useful for implementing transactional mechanisms that are essential when dealing with compartment operations (e.g., dissolution of a membrane) that involve many components that are to be updated consequently. Its simple syntax and semantics, very close to π-calculus, allow a natural extension of many properties and results already stated for standard π-calculus, thus facilitating $\pi@$ theoretical analysis. On the other hand, it is so powerful that it can be used with a pivotal role for comparing the various compartment-based formalisms. In this sense, we claim that $\pi@$ is the right compromise between the simple and elegant theory of π-calculus and the biological needs for modeling compartmentalised behavior. In order to match these expectations even more strikingly, we define a simpler sublanguage, called *core-$\pi@$*, where polyadic synchronisation is limited to its simplest form (two names at most are used in a channel name) and priority levels can only be two, and we show its great flexibility in modelling biological systems.

In this paper we show π@ and core-π@ at work by encoding two well-known compartment-based formalisms: BioAmbients and Brane Calculi. Their straightforward embedding in the same language allows to understand clearly their structural/semantical common points and differences and provides their ready-to-run implementation on top of a common platform. For the second language we show both encodings in π@ and core-π@, the former being more easily understandable, but the latter justifying our claim that, for systems biology modelling, core-π@ is enough.

The paper is organised as follows. Section 2 is a gentle introduction to the basic features of the π-calculus, in particular of its syntax and reduction semantics via a structural congruence. It also comprises a non-trivial example of a biological system modelled in π-calculus: the insuline secretion process of a pancreatic β cell in response to a rise of glucose in the blood. We discuss the limitations of this representation, in particular for the difficulties in handling properly the surrogate of compartments that π-calculus is able to express and for the lack of transactional mechanisms. For these reasons, Section 2.3 introduces polyadic synchronisation and Section 2.4 a form of prioritised communication, which constitute the basic ingredients added to π-calculus to obtain the language π@. This language is described in Section 3, with its syntax and reduction semantics. Moreover, the same biological case-study of the insuline secretion process is now modeled in π@, showing that the new representation is much more faithful. Section 3 ends with the presentation of core-π@, the minimal subcalculus of π@ that we claim is powerful enough to model complex biological systems. Section 4 is devoted to present the encodings of BioAmbents and Brane Calculi into π@ (and for the second language also in core-π@). Finally, Section 5 reports some related work, further research and conclusive remarks.

2   Setting the Context

2.1   The π-Calculus

The π-Calculus [17,18] is a derivation of CCS [19] where parallel processes interact through synchronisation over named channels, with the capability of receiving new channels and subsequently using them for the interaction with other processes, in order to model mobility.

Names constitute the basic entities of the calculus. Each name represents a channel which can be used for synchronisation by parallel processes. For example, the system

$$a(x).P \mid \overline{a}\langle z \rangle.Q \tag{1}$$

represents two parallel processes $a(x).P$ and $\overline{a}\langle z \rangle.Q$, the first one ready to receive some datum (whose local name is x) over the channel a, the second one ready to send some datum z over the same channel a. The datum z represents in turn another channel, which can be used by the first process for subsequent communications.

If $\overline{a}\langle z\rangle.Q$ sends z to $a(x).P$, then the subsequent behaviour of the two processes is specified by the expressions Q and P respectively. More precisely, we write that the system of Expr. (1) may evolve in the following way:

$$a(x).P \mid \overline{a}\langle z\rangle.Q \quad \rightarrow \quad P\{z/x\} \mid Q \tag{2}$$

where $P\{z/x\}$ represents the process P where all the occurrences of the place-holder x have been replaced by z. Here, x is said to be a *bound name*, in opposition to a which is *free*.

The *transition* of the system $a(x).P \mid \overline{a}\langle z\rangle.Q$ to the system $P\{z/x\} \mid Q$ is governed by to *reduction relation* "$\rightarrow$", which states that two processes may exchange data if they are ready to perform input/output respectively over the same channel.

The *nondeterministic choice* between two (or more) possible transitions is denoted by the *choice operator* "$+$". For example, in the system

$$a(x).P' + b(y).P'' \mid \overline{a}\langle z\rangle.Q \mid \overline{b}\langle w\rangle.R$$

the first process may undergo two different, equally possible transitions, caused by a synchronisation with the second process or the third one, respectively. The first transition can be written as

$$a(x).P' + b(y).P'' \mid \overline{a}\langle z\rangle.Q \mid \overline{b}\langle w\rangle.R \quad \rightarrow \quad P'\{z/x\} \mid Q \mid \overline{b}\langle w\rangle.R$$

while the second as

$$a(x).P' + b(y).P'' \mid \overline{a}\langle z\rangle.Q \mid \overline{b}\langle w\rangle.R \quad \rightarrow \quad P''\{w/y\} \mid \overline{a}\langle z\rangle.Q \mid R$$

Depending on the occurring transition, the future behaviour of the first process is denoted by $P'\{z/x\}$ or $P''\{w/y\}$ respectively.

Since the order used for enumerating the possible choices is meaningless, i.e. the choice operator is commutative (and associative), we write that

$$a(x).P' + b(y).P'' \quad \equiv \quad b(y).P'' + a(x).P'$$

where "$\equiv$" represents a *congruence relation* between processes that are meant to be characterised by the same behaviour.

Anyway, the choice operator is not the first cause of nondeterminism. As usual for concurrent calculi, the parallelism of the system can produce nondeterministic behaviour. For example, the system

$$a(x).P \mid \overline{a}\langle z\rangle.Q \mid \overline{a}\langle w\rangle.R$$

is subjected to two transitions, depending on the process that will actually perform the output operation on channel a:

$$a(x).P \mid \overline{a}\langle z\rangle.Q \mid \overline{a}\langle w\rangle.R \quad \rightarrow \quad P\{z/x\} \mid Q \mid \overline{a}\langle w\rangle.R$$
$$a(x).P \mid \overline{a}\langle z\rangle.Q \mid \overline{a}\langle w\rangle.R \quad \rightarrow \quad P\{w/x\} \mid \overline{a}\langle z\rangle.Q \mid R$$

It is possible to prevent unwanted interactions between processes by limiting the scope of a name:

$$(\nu\,a)\big(a(x).P \mid \overline{a}\langle z\rangle.Q\big) \mid \overline{a}\langle w\rangle.R \tag{3}$$

Thanks to the restriction operator "ν", the name a in the first two processes represents a private channel between them. Even if the same name a occurs also in the third process, it constitutes a completely different communication channel. Any renaming of the restricted channels (as well as bound names, by a procedure called alpha-conversion) has no effect on the behaviour of the systems. In fact the following expression

$$(\nu\,b)\big(b(x).P \mid \overline{b}\langle z\rangle.Q\big) \mid \overline{a}\langle w\rangle.R$$

is equivalent to Expr. 3, since $b(x).P$ and $\overline{b}\langle z\rangle.Q$ are able to exchange data exactly as before.

In order to model recursive behaviour, an operator of *replication* is introduced in the language. A process P preceded by "!" is thought as being replicated an unlimited number of times. That is

$$!\,P \equiv P \mid P \mid \cdots$$

The formal definition of π-Calculus grammar follows.

Definition 1. *Let*

$\mathcal{N}$ *be a set of names on a finite alphabet,* $x, y, z, \ldots \in \mathcal{N}$ *;*
$\overline{\mathcal{N}} = \{\overline{x} \mid x \in \mathcal{N}\}$

The syntax of π-Calculus is defined in terms of the following grammar:

$$P \quad ::= \quad \mathbf{0} \;\; \Big| \;\; \sum_{i \in I} \pi_i.P_i \;\; \Big| \;\; P \mid Q \;\; \Big| \;\; !\,P \;\; \Big| \;\; (\nu\,x)P$$

$$\pi \quad ::= \quad \tau \;\; \Big| \;\; x(y) \;\; \Big| \;\; \overline{x}\langle y\rangle$$

where

- $\mathbf{0}$ represents the null process;
- $x(y)$ expresses the capability of performing an input on the channel x and receiving a datum which is then bound to the name y;
- $\overline{x}\langle y\rangle$ expresses the capability of sending the name y on the channel x;
- τ is the invisible, uncontrollable action;
- $P \mid Q$ represents the parallel composition of processes;
- $!\,P$ stands for the unlimited replication of process P;
- $\sum_{i \in I} \pi_i.P_i$ represents the nondeterministic choice between several input/output communication capabilities, denoted also as $\pi_1.P_1 + \pi_2.P_2 + \ldots$;
- $(\nu\,x)P$ represents the scope restriction of the name x to process P.

The full definition of the congruence relation $\equiv$ follows. It depends in turn on the function $\mathrm{fn}(P)$ which returns the set of free names occurring in P.

Definition 2. *The congruence relation $\equiv$ is defined as the least congruence satisfying alpha conversion, the commutative monoidal laws with respect to both $(\mid ,0)$ and $(+,0)$ and the following axioms:*

$$(\nu\, x)P \mid Q \equiv (\nu\, x)(P \mid Q) \qquad\qquad if\ x \notin fn(Q)$$
$$(\nu\, x)P \equiv P \qquad\qquad if\ x \notin fn(P)$$
$$!\,P \equiv\ !\,P \mid P$$

where the function fn *is defined as*

$$\mathrm{fn}(\tau) \stackrel{def}{=} \emptyset \qquad\qquad \mathrm{fn}(x(y)) \stackrel{def}{=} \{x\}$$
$$\mathrm{fn}(\overline{x}\langle y\rangle) \stackrel{def}{=} \{x,y\} \qquad\qquad \mathrm{fn}(0) \stackrel{def}{=} \emptyset$$
$$\mathrm{fn}(\pi.P) \stackrel{def}{=} \mathrm{fn}(\pi) \cup \mathrm{fn}(P) \qquad \mathrm{fn}(\textstyle\sum_{i\in I} \pi_i.P_i) \stackrel{def}{=} \bigcup_i \mathrm{fn}(\pi_i.P_i)$$
$$\mathrm{fn}(P \mid Q) \stackrel{def}{=} \mathrm{fn}(P) \cup \mathrm{fn}(Q) \qquad \mathrm{fn}(!\,P) \stackrel{def}{=} \mathrm{fn}(P)$$
$$\mathrm{fn}((\nu\, x)P) \stackrel{def}{=} \mathrm{fn}(P) \setminus \{x\}$$

The relation describing the possible transitions of a process is defined in terms of few simple reduction rules, which exploit the congruence relation previously given.

Definition 3. *π-Calculus semantics is given in terms of the reduction system described by the following rules:*

$$TAU:\ \frac{}{\tau.P\ \rightarrow\ P} \qquad\qquad COMM:\ \frac{}{(\mu(y).P + M) \mid (\overline{\mu}\langle z\rangle.Q + N)\ \rightarrow\ P\{z/y\} \mid Q}$$

$$PAR:\ \frac{P\ \rightarrow\ P'}{P \mid Q\ \rightarrow\ P' \mid Q} \qquad\qquad RES:\ \frac{P\ \rightarrow\ P'}{(\nu\, x)P\ \rightarrow\ (\nu\, x)P'}$$

$$STRUCT:\ \frac{P \equiv Q\quad P\ \rightarrow\ P'\quad P' \equiv Q'}{Q\ \rightarrow\ Q'}$$

The TAU rule represents an internal, unobservable change of state of some process P. The transition of Expr. (2) is formalised by rule COMM. The PAR rule describes the meaning of the parallel operator: each process capable of some internal transition, can evolve even when put in parallel with other processes. The RES rule allows transition of processes in presence of restricted names. The key role of restriction (as well as the semantics of the replication) is hidden by rule STRUCT, which states that if two processes are structurally congruent, then they can perform the same transitions. For an extended treatment of the π-Calculus we refer to [17,18,20,21].

The key idea behind the modelling of biological systems by means of the π-Calculus is that biochemical elements can be seen as parallel processes, and their interaction as communication. In particular, each *molecule* of the system can be represented by a process and its *reaction* with other molecules can be modelled as a communication over a fixed channel. For example, the chemical reaction

$$R:\quad R_1 + R_2\ \rightarrow\ P_1 + P_2$$

where the molecules R_1 and R_2 react according to reaction R, and release P_1 and P_2 as products of the reaction, can be modelled in π-Calculus as

$$R_1 \triangleq r.P_1 \qquad R_2 \triangleq \bar{r}.P_2 \qquad\qquad R_1 \mid R_2 \quad \rightarrow \quad P_1 \mid P_2$$

where each process is named as the corresponding molecule, and reaction R is associated with channel r.

Furthermore, the communication of restricted names between π-Calculus processes can be exploited for the modelling of local bounds between molecules. If M_1 and M_2 represent two molecules ready to bind, the corresponding expression in π-Calculus is

$$M_1 \triangleq (\nu\, b)(\overline{bind}\langle b\rangle.M_1') \qquad M_2 \triangleq bind(x).M_2'$$
$$M_1 \mid M_2 \quad \rightarrow \quad (\nu\, b)(M_1' \mid M_2'\{b/x\}) \qquad\qquad (b \notin \mathrm{fn}(M_2'))$$

where M_1' and $M_2'\{b/x\}$ (and no other process) share the name b after their reaction.

Restriction may be also exploited in order to model *compartments*. A compartment can be thought as a box separating the external environment from its content. A typical biological example is the cell: its external membrane protects from the dispersion of cell material and regulates the exchange of substances. From an external point of view, the content of the compartment is completely hidden by the compartment itself. Hence we may represent in π-Calculus the compartment C as

$$(\nu\, c_1,\ldots,c_k)(M_1 \mid \cdots \mid M_l \mid P_1 \mid \cdots \mid P_n)$$

where the compartment C is represented by a set of restricted names $c_1,\ldots,c_k$, the content of C is constituted by $P_1,\ldots,P_n$ under the hypothesis that

$$\mathrm{fn}(P_1 \mid \cdots \mid P_n) \subseteq \{c_1,\ldots,c_k\}$$

i.e. the direct interaction of such elements with some external process is prevented by restricting all their channels. The set of processes $M_1 \mid \cdots \mid M_l$ constitutes an interface of the compartment to the external world, that is, in the case of a cell, the membrane itself (and in particular all the transmembrane channels and proteins). These would constitute the only processes enabled to interact with the outer environment.

2.2   Modelling Biological Systems in π-Calculus

We can now try to model in π-Calculus the simple biological system drawn in Fig. 1. The figure sketches the insuline secretion process of a pancreatic β cell in response to a rise in glucose in the blood. The glucose is transported inside the cell by a transmembrane channel protein, $GLUT2$. Here it undergoes glycolysis, which leads to the production of pyruvate and ATP. The rise in ATP concentration inhibits the action of K^+ channels, which in turn causes a rise

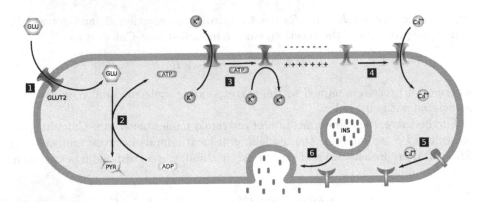

Fig. 1. Insuline secretion in pancreatic β cells in response to a rise in glucose concentration. (1) The rise in glucose concentration of the blood is reflected by a rise in glucose inside the cell, as a consequence of the action of $GLUT2$ glucose transporter. (2) The rise of glucose accelerates the conversion of ADP into ATP, with consequent rise in intracellular ATP concentration. (3) ATP inhibits the action of ATP-sensitive K^+ channels, which reduce the expulsion rate of K^+ ions from the cell. (4) The increasing presence of K^+ depolarises the membrane and triggers the opening of voltage-sensitive Ca^{2+} channels. (5) Fusion proteins are activated by Ca^{2+} ions and (6) trigger the exocytosis of secretory vesicles containing insuline.

in K^+ ions near the membrane and consequently its depolarisation. Voltage-sensitive Ca^{2+} channels are therefore activated and allow the entry of Ca^{2+} ions, which activate the fusion of the insuline-containing vesicles with the cell membrane (exocytosis), with subsequent dumping of insuline molecules into the blood.

The corresponding π-Calculus system will be composed of a compartment C representing the cell, with the shape

$$(\nu\, c_1, \ldots, c_k)(CHAN_1 \mid \cdots \mid CHAN_l$$
$$\mid MOL_1 \mid \cdots \mid MOL_n$$
$$\mid VES \mid \cdots \mid VES)$$

where membrane channels $CHAN_i$ are the only processes aware of names external to the cell itself, unlike the molecules MOL_i and the insuline vesicles VES.

The first elements to model are the glucose molecule and the glucose channel. The entry of glucose inside the cell can be modelled as an interaction between the process representing the glucose molecule and that representing the glucose channel. If the glucose molecule is represented by the process GLU, since its interaction with processes external to the cell must be prevented after its entry, it is worth substituting all the channels of GLU with new restricted names. Furthermore, the GLU process must exhibit some sort of recursive behaviour, because it must be able to synchronise at any time with some glucose channel and then be ready again for the other chemical interactions. Such recursive behaviour may be captured by an expression like

$$GLU \triangleq glutrans.GLU + \overline{glureact}.PYR$$

where the channel $glutrans$ carries the interaction with the glucose channel, while a synchronisation over $glureact$ triggers the glycolysis of GLU with consequent production of pyruvate PYR. The recursive behaviour would be obtained by direct recursion (after the transportation, indicated by the synchronisation over $glutrans$, the process becomes GLU again), but since it is not allowed in the version of the π-Calculus considered here, it must be encoded by combining replication and restriction, in the following way:

$$GLU \triangleq (\nu\, g)(\overline{g} \mid\ !\, g.(glutrans.\overline{g} + \overline{glureact}.PYR))$$

The internal synchronisation over g allows to spawn a new subprocess

$$(glutrans.\overline{g} + \overline{glureact}.PYR)$$

able to interact nondeterministically either over $glureact$ and generate PYR, or synchronise over $glutrans$ and then produce another coin $\overline{g}$, thus returning in its initial state. The above formalisation still lacks a significant detail: after the interaction over $glutrans$ and the entry in the cell, the process GLU must own a new set of restricted names. Such names must be received by GLU during the interaction with the glucose transporter:

$$GLU(glutrans, glureact) \triangleq$$
$$(\nu\, g)(\overline{g}\langle glutrans, glureact\rangle \mid\ !\, g(t,r).(t\langle nt, nr\rangle.\overline{g}\langle nt, nr\rangle + \overline{r}.PYR)) \quad (4)$$

Now the internal synchronisation over g spawns a new subprocess $GLUSUB$

$$GLU(glutrans, glureact) \quad \rightarrow$$
$$(\nu\, g)(GLUSUB \mid\ !\, g(t,r).(t\langle nt, nr\rangle.\overline{g}\langle nt, nr\rangle + \overline{r}.PYR))$$

with

$$GLUSUB \triangleq glutrans(nt, nr).\overline{g}\langle nt, nr\rangle + \overline{glureact}.PYR$$

where the placeholders t, r have been replaced by $glutrans, glureact$ respectively in consequence of the input/output operation. $GLUSUB$ is ready to react over $glureact$ or to trigger the simulated movement of GLU inside some other compartment whose respective names for the reaction and transportation of glucose are received as nr and nt by GLU at the time of the transportation itself.

The glucose transporter $GLUT2$, represented by the process $GLUCHAN$, can be easily modelled as

$$GLUCHAN(gt_{out}, gt_{in}, gr_{in}) \triangleq\ !\, \overline{gt_{out}}\langle gt_{in}, gr_{in}\rangle$$

where gt_{out} is the channel for glucose transportation *outside the cell*, gt_{in} is the name used for the same purpose but *inside the cell*, and gr_{in} is the channel for the glycolysis of GLU inside the cell. As previously noticed, $GLUCHAN$ is a cross-compartment process, since it must be aware of channels both inside and outside the cell.

The effect of glycolysis is the conversion of ADP into ATP. Even if such process involves several other chemical components, for sake of simplicity it can be easily modelled as direct interaction between the ADP and GLU molecules. For the same reason, the inhibition of K^+ channel proteins by ATP can be modelled as direct interaction between the ATP molecule and the K^+ channel proteins, over some name $inhk$:

$$ADP(glureact, inhk) \triangleq \overline{glureact}.ATP(inhk)$$
$$ATP(inhk) \triangleq \overline{inhk}$$

Since the consequent behaviour of the ATP molecule is not relevant for the present purposes, the corresponding process lacks any recursive formalisation.

In order to model the potassium molecule and channel protein, similar considerations can be applied. In particular, the potassium molecule K may be represented as

$$K(ktrans, kreact) \triangleq$$
$$(\nu \, k)(\overline{k}\langle ktrans, kreact \rangle \mid !\, k(t, r).(t\langle nt, nr \rangle.\overline{k}\langle nt, nr \rangle + \overline{r}))$$

Despite of their similarity, the processes GLU and K differ in the product of their reactions: GLU reduces to PYR, while in the current formalisation K reduces to the null process.

The expression of the K^+ channel protein, $KCHAN$, is a little more complex than the corresponding process $GLUCHAN$. In fact, $KCHAN$ can be inhibited in consequence of ATP binding. In other words, its recursive behaviour shall be interrupted after an interaction over the $inhk$ channel. This effect can be achieved by a slight modification of the recursion used for GLU:

$$KCHAN(kt_{in}, kt_{out}, kr_{out}, inhk) \triangleq$$
$$(\nu \, kc)(\overline{kc} \mid !\, kc.(inhk + \overline{kt_{in}}\langle kt_{out}, kr_{out} \rangle.\overline{kc}))$$

After the interaction over $inhk$, the coin $\overline{kc}$ is not replicated and any further action of the process $KCHAN$ is prevented.

The polarisation of the membrane caused by the rise in K^+ concentration after the inhibition of K^+ channels can be modelled by a fictitious process POL triggered by K^+ ions, which then activates the Ca^{2+} channels:

$$POL(kreact, caact) \triangleq kreact.\overline{caact}$$

The Ca^{2+} channel protein is formalised as the process $CACHAN$, which closely resembles $GLUCHAN$:

$$CACHAN(cat_{out}, cat_{in}, car_{in}, caact) \triangleq caact.!\, \overline{cat_{out}}\langle cat_{in}, car_{in} \rangle$$

The channel is activated only after interaction over *caact*, as required. The calcium process CA is defined exactly as K:

$$CA(catrans, careact) \triangleq$$

$$(\nu\ c)\big(\overline{c}\langle catrans, careact\rangle\ \big|\ !\ c(t, r).(t(nt, nr).\overline{c}\langle nt, nr\rangle + \overline{r})\big)$$

The stimulation of the exocytosis by the rise in Ca^{2+} concentration can be modelled as mediated by a docking protein $DOCKP$ which is activated by Ca^{2+} ions and trigger the expulsion of the insuline molecules INS contained in the vesicle VES:

$$DOCKP(careact, dockves, ins_{out}) \triangleq careact.\overline{dockves}\langle ins_{out}\rangle$$

Since the vesicle VES (as well as all the INS molecules inside it) is completely embedded inside the cell, the $DOCKP$ process must also communicate to VES the external name(s) ins_{out} which enables the communication of the processes INS with the environment surrounding the cell.

$$VES(dockves) \triangleq \quad (\nu\ ins_{in})\big(dockves(ins_{out}).!\ ins_{in}.INS(ins_{out})$$
$$\big|\ INS(ins_{in})\ \big|\ \cdots\ \big|\ INS(ins_{in})\big)$$

The process VES represents another compartment, where all the names of the embedded processes (INS) are restricted, while only one cross-compartment process filters their interaction with the external environment. In this very simple model, the INS processes are formalised as

$$INS(ins) \triangleq \overline{ins}$$

Finally, the whole system can be summarised as

$$SYS \triangleq \quad GLU(gt_{out}, gr_{out})\ \big|\ K(kt_{out}, kr_{out})\ \big|\ Ca(cat_{out}, car_{out})\ \big|$$
$$(\nu\ gt_{in}, gr_{in}, kt_{in}, kr_{in}, cat_{in}, car_{in}, inhk, caact, dockves, ins_{in})$$
$$\Big(GLU(gt_{in}, gr_{in})\ \big|\ GLUCHAN(gt_{out}, gt_{in}, gr_{in})$$
$$\big|\ K(kt_{in}, kr_{in})\ \big|\ KCHAN(kt_{out}, kt_{in}, kr_{in}, inhk)\ \big|$$
$$\big|\ ADP(gr_{in}, inhk)\ \big|\ ATP(inhk)\ \big|\ POL(kr_{in}, caact)$$
$$\big|\ Ca(cat_{in}, car_{in})\ \big|\ CACHAN(cat_{out}, cat_{in}, car_{in}, caact)$$
$$\big|\ DOCKP(car_{in}, dockves, ins_{out})\ \big|\ VES(dockves)\Big)$$

This modelling approach in π-Calculus allows to express somehow the idea of compartments, but reveals several drawbacks.

The most evident is the need to encode compartment scoping by restricting *all* the free names of the enclosed processes. As even worse consequence we have that cross-compartment processes must handle all the names of the interacting processes, taking care of the correspondence between distinct names representing the same channel inside different compartments. The model becomes even more complicated when such processes need to create new restricted names and communicate them externally. If we then require compartment operations which affect their nesting structure (merging, splitting, creation, movement of whole compartments) the above approach becomes practically unfeasible, both for the difficulties in name handling and the impossibility of ensuring atomicity of such complex operations without a purely centralised implementation.

Such issues can be overcome by the simple extensions that are presented in the next subsections.

2.3　Polyadic Synchronisation

In the π-Calculus, channels and transmitted names are usually synonyms. Polyadic synchronisation [16] consists in giving *structure* to channels: each channel is composed of one or more names and identified by all of them in relation to the exact sequence of their occurrence. For example, an email address is usually written in the form *username@domain*, where *username* and *domain* are two strings – two names – both necessary to identify the given email address. Moreover, their order is crucial since *domain@username* specifies another, likely nonexistent, address. Similarly, polyadic synchronisation (in its simplest form) provides the capability of writing channels as $name_1@name_2$. In other words, a channel is indicated by a vector of two names $(name_1, name_2)$ and communication between two processes may happen only if they are pursuing a synchronisation along channels denoted by the same names.

Apart from this, communication happens in the same way as in the π-Calculus. For example, the transition

$$\overline{polyadic@comm}\langle d\rangle.P \mid polyadic@comm(x).Q \quad \rightarrow \quad P \mid Q\{d/x\}$$

produces the same renaming effect of a π-Calculus transition, but with one difference: in the π-Calculus, the transmission of a name always stands for the transmission of a channel, while in the above example the transmitted name constitutes only one component of it.

An extended form of polyadic synchronisation allows for the use of more than two names for each channels, like in the following example:

$$\overline{@c_1@c_2@c_3}\langle d\rangle.P \mid c_1@c_2@c_3(x).Q \quad \rightarrow \quad P \mid Q\{d/x\}$$

In general, there is no limit to the length of the vector of names representing a channel.

For concision and readability, polyadic synchronisation is often used also in conjunction with polyadic communication:

$$\overline{polyadic@comm}\langle a, b, c\rangle.P \mid polyadic@comm(x, y, z).Q \quad \rightarrow$$
$$P \mid Q\{a/x, b/y, c/z\}$$

The benefits in terms of simplicity of biological modellings are immediate in presence of compartments. For example, if the π-calculus process

$$M(m_1, \ldots, m_n) \triangleq \pi.M' + \ldots$$

is a molecule subjected to movement across the cellular membrane (like the *GLU* process of Expr. (4)), all of its channels must be restricted after its conveyance into the cell:

$$M(m_1^{out}, \ldots, m_n^{out}) \mid (\nu\, m_1^{in}, \ldots, m_n^{in}, \ldots)(M(m_1^{in}, \ldots, m_n^{in}) \mid \cdots)$$

In particular, any channel protein able to convey the above molecule across different compartments should be aware of all the names $m_1^{out}, \ldots, m_n^{out}, m_1^{in}, \ldots, m_n^{in}$. Polyadic synchronisation allows to model the compartment just as *one* restricted name. For example, the above system may be converted as

$$M(m_1, \ldots, m_n, c_{out}) \mid (\nu\, c_{in}, \ldots)(M(m_1, \ldots, m_n, c_{in}) \mid \cdots)$$

where each input or output action $\pi.M'$ inside M has been encoded as $\pi@c.M'$, and c represents the compartment M lies in (c_{out} or c_{in} in the above example). In this way, only one restricted name is needed to formalise a new compartment, regardless of all the channels the enclosed processes may use. This substantial simplification affects also the formalisation of cross-compartment processes: they need to handle only one additional name for each compartment they partially reside in.

2.4 Priority

The idea behind the notion of priority applied here to the π-Calculus [22] is very similar to the mechanisms adopted for the implementation of schedulers which allow to give processes several levels of priority, in dependence of their requirements (responsiveness, cpu load, real-time constraints, etc) for the task they accomplish.

In this paper we consider a particular kind of priority characterised by global, immediate preemption: each process denoted by high priority holds the central processing unit and executes its job before any low priority process may perform some other task. In π-Calculus setting, this is equivalent to force high priority synchronisations or communications to happen before any low priority action. A high priority action is indicated by underlining the name of the channel. For example, the expression

$$\bar{l}\langle a \rangle.P \mid \underline{\bar{h}}\langle b \rangle.Q$$

contains two processes with different, increasing priority. In the above situation, both are blocked: in fact, no other process is ready to receive over the channel l or h. In presence of some process listening on channel l, the first process may react in the following way:

$$\bar{l}\langle a \rangle.P \mid l(x).P' \mid \underline{\bar{h}}\langle b \rangle.Q \quad \rightarrow \quad P \mid P'\{a/x\} \mid \underline{\bar{h}}\langle b \rangle.Q$$

In fact, this would be the only possible transition since no other reduction is available. Conversely, when both high and low priority actions are enabled, low-priority synchronisations can occur only after high-priority ones:

$$l\langle w\rangle \mid l(x).P \mid \overline{\underline{h}}\langle y\rangle \mid \underline{h}(z).Q \quad \nrightarrow \quad \mathbf{0} \mid P\{w/x\} \mid \overline{\underline{h}}\langle y\rangle \mid \underline{h}(z).Q$$

$$l\langle w\rangle \mid l(x).P \mid \overline{\underline{h}}\langle y\rangle \mid \underline{h}(z).Q \quad \rightarrow \quad l\langle w\rangle \mid l(x).P \mid \mathbf{0} \mid Q\{y/z\} \quad \rightarrow$$
$$\mathbf{0} \mid P\{w/x\} \mid \mathbf{0} \mid Q\{y/z\}$$

The first of the two transitions is not allowed because interactions on low-priority channel l may happen only after the high-priority communication on channel $\underline{h}$.

For sake of clarity, communications between channels with the same name but different priorities are forbidden. For example, in the following system there are no possible reductions:

$$\overline{c}\langle a\rangle.P \mid c(x).Q$$

An additional level of priority can be denoted by double underlining a channel name:

$$l\langle a\rangle.P \mid \overline{\underline{h}}\langle b\rangle.Q \mid \underline{\underline{u}}\langle c\rangle.R$$

If any reduction is available over the $\underline{\underline{u}}$ channel, it preempts any reduction over $\underline{h}$ and l. Additional levels of priority require the introduction of integer numbers as labels added to each input/output operation. For this reason the above expression may be also written as follows:

$$\overline{2:l}\langle a\rangle.P \mid \overline{1:h}\langle b\rangle.Q \mid \overline{0:u}\langle c\rangle.R$$

where 0 denotes the highest level of priority. The choice of identifying higher priority levels with decreasing integer numbers is arbitrary and does not affect the semantics or expressiveness of the language.

Since three levels of priority suffice for the purposes of this paper, only the first of these two syntaxes will be used in the encodings and modelling examples, for its conciseness and readability.

For a detailed survey of priority in process algebras, we refer to [22].

At first sight, the idea of priority seems foreign and unnecessary for biological modelling purposes. Anyway, the complexity of this realm makes almost impossible the design of a suitable and complete modelling language. The presence of several priority levels for operations allows to compose high-level, complex operations as sequences of several simple, low-level steps (transitions) by avoiding any interference of external processes with the involved elements. Such low-level transitions can be composed in different ways, depending on the abstraction adopted to formalise the system of interest. This effect can be achieved by encoding each high-level operation as a list of high priority actions, preceded by a single low priority operation which act as a *guard*. For example, if the processes P_1, P_2, P_3, P_4 represents four proteins which can bind together and form a new complex C, they can be modelled in π-Calculus by exploiting the restriction operator and representing the binding as the sharing of a private name:

$$(\nu\, b)P_1 \mid P_2 \mid P_3 \mid P_4 \quad \rightarrow \quad \cdots \quad \rightarrow \quad (\nu\, b)(P_1' \mid P_2' \mid P_3' \mid P_4')$$

Since more than one transition is needed to accomplish the whole process, if one of the requirements is its atomicity (this is often necessary when the modelled processes may meanwhile interact with other elements and give rise to undesirable situations not pertaining to the original model) then there is no way to obtain a satisfactory modelling in π-Calculus. Priority instead allows to ensure that no other process can interfere during the formation of the above complex. The four molecules can be formalised as

$$P_1 \triangleq \bar{l}\langle b \rangle.\overline{\underline{h_1}}\langle b \rangle.\overline{\underline{h_2}}\langle b \rangle.P_1' \qquad\qquad P_2 \triangleq l(x).P_2'$$
$$P_3 \triangleq \underline{h_1}(x).P_3' \qquad\qquad\qquad P_4 \triangleq \underline{h_2}(x).P_4'$$

so that after the first synchronisation of P_1 and P_2 over the low priority channel l, a sequence of (two) high priority communications between P_1 and P_3, P_4 is triggered and cannot be interrupted by any other process. In fact, the possibility of performing the initial low priority action over l guarantees that any other high priority operation occasionally available in the system has been previously consumed.

3   Description of the Formalism

3.1   The π@ Language

The π@ language joins the expressiveness of polyadic communication and priority in order to model both localisation of processes inside compartments and atomicity of complex operations that require more than one reduction step for their completion. Thanks to the simplicity of such extensions, π@ is very close to the π-Calculus: from a syntactical point of view the only difference is the structure of channels, composed of multiple names and tagged by the priority of the action. We use μ to denote a vector of names $x_1, \ldots, x_n$ and $k : \mu$ to denote a channel, that is a natural number k specifying the priority level followed by a vector of names μ. In particular, $\overline{k : \mu}$ represents an output operation along channel $k : \mu$, while $k : \alpha$ stands for a generic input, output or silent action τ of priority level k.

Definition 4. *Let*

$\mathcal{N}$ *be a set of names on finite alphabet,* $x, y, z, \ldots \in \mathcal{N}$;
$\mathcal{N}^+ = \bigcup_{i>0} \mathcal{N}^i$, $\mu \in \mathcal{N}^+$;
$\overline{\mathcal{N}}^+ = \{ \overline{\mu} \mid \mu \in \mathcal{N}^+ \}$;
$\alpha \in \left(\overline{\mathcal{N}}^+ \cup \mathcal{N}^+ \cup \{\tau\} \right)$;

The syntax of π@ *defined in terms of the following grammar:*

$$P \quad ::= \quad \mathbf{0} \ \Bigg| \ \sum_{i \in I} \pi_i.P_i \ \Bigg| \ P \mid Q \ \Bigg| \ !P \ \Bigg| \ (\nu\, x)P$$

$$\pi \quad ::= \quad k \,\mathbf{:}\, \tau \ \Bigg| \ k \,\mathbf{:}\, \mu(x) \ \Bigg| \ \overline{k \,\mathbf{:}\, \mu}\langle x \rangle$$

As previously introduced, the following abbreviations are used for readability:

$$\mu(x) = 2\!:\!\mu(x) \qquad\qquad \overline{\mu}\langle x\rangle = \overline{2\!:\!\mu}\langle x\rangle$$
$$\underline{\mu}(x) = 1\!:\!\mu(x) \qquad\qquad \underline{\overline{\mu}}\langle x\rangle = \overline{1\!:\!\mu}\langle x\rangle$$
$$\underline{\mu}(x) = 0\!:\!\mu(x) \qquad\qquad \underline{\overline{\mu}}\langle x\rangle = \overline{0\!:\!\mu}\langle x\rangle$$

The definition for structural congruence $\equiv$ is exactly the same as given for π-Calculus, where the function fn is naturally extended to the $\pi@$ syntax, that is

$$\mathrm{fn}(k : \mu(y)) \overset{def}{=} \{\mu_1,\ldots,\mu_n\}$$
$$\mathrm{fn}(\overline{k : \mu}\langle y\rangle) \overset{def}{=} \{\mu_1,\ldots,\mu_n, y\}$$

where $\mu = \mu_1@\cdots@\mu_n$. The reduction semantics is very similar, but defined in terms of an auxiliary function $I^k(P)$, representing the set of actions of priority k which the process P may immediately execute. For example, if

$$P = a.Q \mid \underline{b} \mid \underline{\overline{c}}.R \mid \underline{\overline{d}} + \underline{e}.S \mid \overline{a}.T$$

then $I^0(P) = \{\overline{c}, e\}$, $I^1(P) = \{b, \overline{d}\}$, $I^2(P) = \{a, \overline{a}, \tau\}$, where the availability of τ action derives from the interaction of the first and last process.

Definition 5. *Let $I^k(P)$ be*

$$I^k\Big(\sum_i l_i\!:\!\alpha_i.P_i\Big) = \{\alpha_i \mid l_i = k\};$$

$$I^k((\nu\, y)\, P) = I^k(P) \setminus \{\alpha \mid y \in \{x_1,\ldots,x_n\} \wedge$$
$$(\alpha = x_1@\ldots@x_n \ \vee \ \alpha = \overline{x_1@\ldots@x_n})\};$$

$$I^k(!P) = I^k(P \mid P);$$

$$I^k(P \mid Q) = I^k(P) \cup I^k(Q) \cup \{\tau \mid I^k(P) \cap \overline{I^k(Q)} \neq \emptyset\},$$
$$\overline{I^k(Q)} = \{\overline{\alpha} \mid \alpha \in I^k(Q)\}$$

$\pi@$ semantics is given in terms of the following reduction system:

$$\frac{\tau \notin \bigcup_{i<k} I^i(M)}{k\!:\!\tau.P + M \ \to_k\ P} \qquad\qquad \frac{P \ \to_k\ P'}{(\nu\, x)P \ \to_k\ (\nu\, x)P'}$$

$$\frac{\tau \notin \bigcup_{i<k} I^i(M \mid N)}{(k\!:\!\mu(y).P + M) \mid (\overline{k\!:\!\mu}\langle z\rangle.Q + N) \ \to_k\ P\{z/y\} \mid Q}$$

$$\frac{P \ \to_k\ P' \qquad \tau \notin \bigcup_{i<k} I^i(P \mid Q)}{P \mid Q \ \to_k\ P' \mid Q} \qquad\qquad \frac{P \equiv Q \quad P \ \to_k\ P' \quad P' \equiv Q'}{Q \ \to_k\ Q'}$$

$\pi@$ reduction rules are exactly the same of π-Calculus, except for the additional condition $\tau \notin \bigcup_{i<k} I^i(\ldots)$ which avoids the execution of low priority actions if higher priority communications (represented by τ actions) are immediately available.

3.2   Modelling the Insuline Example in π@

The benefits deriving from polyadic synchronisation and priority for biological modellings can be noticed as soon as even very simple systems are formalised, like the one in Fig. 1 already described into the π-Calculus. We have previously discussed why a faithful description of a compartment in π-Calculus implies that all the names of the enclosed processes are restricted, in order to prevent their interaction with the external environment. On the contrary, π@ allows to characterise each compartment by means of a single restricted name, as shown in Sect. 2.3. Therefore, the shape of the system of Fig. 1 becomes

$$(\nu \, c_{in})(CHAN_1 \mid \cdots \mid CHAN_l$$
$$\mid MOL_1 \mid \cdots \mid MOL_n$$
$$\mid VES \mid \cdots \mid VES)$$

where the cell is represented by the restricted name c_{in}, the cross-compartment processes $CHAN_1, \ldots, CHAN_l$ communicate to the external environment by a corresponding name c_{out}, and the set of free names of the processes $MOL_1, \ldots, MOL_n, VES$ is irrelevant for their confinement inside the compartment, as soon as c_{out} does not appear in such set and c_{in} constitutes one of the names which identify each channel.

Therefore, the GLU process of Expr. (4) may be translated as follows:

$$GLU(comp, gt, gr) \triangleq (\nu \, g)$$
$$(\overline{g}\langle comp \rangle \mid \; ! \, g(c).(gt@c(c_{new}).\overline{g}\langle c_{new} \rangle + \overline{gr@c}.PYR)) \tag{5}$$

The behaviour of the process is almost the same: replication is exploited for encoding the recursive behaviour of the molecule, which is always ready either to react or to be moved into another compartment. These two capabilities are formalised by an interaction over $gr@c$ and $gt@c$ respectively, where c represents the name of the compartment the molecule lies in. The movement of the molecule to another compartment is reflected by receiving a new compartment name and forgetting the previous one. Since such name appears in all the channels that allow the molecule to interact with the other processes, GLU can interact only with elements enclosed in its same compartment. The simplification of Expr. (4) w.r.t. Expr. (5) is minimal for the reason that the description of the GLU molecule includes only two public channels, but it becomes significant as soon as their number grows.

It is worth remarking that the current semantics of GLU may not correspond to the intended behaviour of the glucose molecule in the original biological model: if it requires the movement of the molecule across compartments to be instantaneous, then Expr. (5) does not constitute a correct formalisation because of the additional internal step needed to spawn the molecule inside the target compartment. Priority addresses exactly this very common modelling problem: it is possible to use high priority reductions to model all the operations that in the original model are purely atomic or not present at all:

$$GLU(comp, gt, gr) \triangleq (\nu\, g)$$
$$(\overline{g}\langle comp\rangle \mid \; ! \, \underline{g}(c).(gt@c(c_{new}).\overline{g}\langle c_{new}\rangle + \overline{gr@c}.PYR)) \tag{6}$$

The corresponding expression of the $GLUT2$ glucose transporter can be slightly simplified as well:

$$GLUCHAN(c_{out}, c_{in}, gt) \triangleq \; ! \, \overline{gt@c_{out}}\langle c_{in}\rangle$$

Now, the channel process does not need to know all the names of the transported molecule. This is a very valuable property, since it means that there is no need to change the expression of the glucose transporter each time the formalisation of GLU changes, for example after the addition of new reaction capabilities. As previously discussed, $GLUCHAN$ is characterised by the presence of two compartment names, for the reason that it represents a cross-compartment molecule.

The processes representing ADP and ATP are almost unchanged:

$$ADP(glureact, inhk, c) \triangleq \; \overline{glureact@c}.ATP(inhk, c)$$
$$ATP(inhk, c) \triangleq \; \overline{inhk@c}$$

In this case the use of polyadic synchronisation seems to make more complicated the expression of the above molecules, but the benefit will appear after the formalisation of the whole cell.

For the description of the potassium molecule K the same principles leading to Expr. (6) can be applied:

$$K(kt, kr, comp) \triangleq$$
$$(\nu\, k)(\overline{k}\langle comp\rangle \mid \; ! \, \underline{k}(c).(kt@c(c_{new}).\overline{k}\langle c_{new}\rangle + \overline{kr@c}))$$

Even in this case the high priority of internal reductions can provide a more faithful modelling, like for the potassium channel $KCHAN$:

$$KCHAN(c_{in}, c_{out}, inhk) \triangleq$$
$$(\nu\, kc)(\overline{kc} \mid \; ! \, \underline{kc}.(inhk + \overline{kt@c_{in}}\langle c_{out}\rangle.\overline{kc}))$$

The remaining processes can be translated in the same way:

$$POL(c, kreact, caact) \triangleq \; \overline{kreact@c}.\overline{caact@c}$$
$$CACHAN(c_{out}, c_{in}, cat, caact) \triangleq \; \overline{caact@c_{in}}.! \, \overline{cat@c_{out}}\langle c_{in}\rangle$$
$$CA(comp, cat, car) \triangleq \; (\nu\, ca)(\overline{ca}\langle comp\rangle \mid$$
$$! \, \underline{ca}(c).(cat@c(c_{new}).\overline{ca}\langle c_{new}\rangle + \overline{car@c}))$$
$$DOCKP(c_{in}, car, dockves, c_{out}) \triangleq \; \overline{car@c_{in}}.\overline{dockves@c_{in}}\langle c_{out}\rangle$$
$$INS(c, ins) \triangleq \; \overline{ins@c}$$

Since the vesicle VES constitutes another, nested compartment inside the cell, it can be as well represented by a new restricted name:

$$VES(c_{out}, dv, ins) \triangleq \; (\nu\, vc_{in})(dv@c_{out}(c_{ext}).! \, ins@vc_{in}.INS(c_{ext}, ins)$$
$$\mid INS(vc_{in}, ins) \mid \cdots \mid INS(vc_{in}, ins))$$

The internal compartment name for VES is vc_{in}, while c_{out} stands for the name corresponding to the cell compartment. c_{ext} will be bound to the name of the compartment surrounding the cell, where the insuline molecules will be dumped after the exocytosis of the vesicle VES.

If the process of exocytosis is abstracted as a single, atomic operation, then priority can be used for the loop of the process expelling all the insuline molecules. It may be modified as follows:

$$dv@c_{out}(c_{ext}).!\ \underline{ins@vc_{in}}.INS(c_{ext}, ins)$$

and the INS molecules accordingly:

$$INS(c, ins) \triangleq \overline{\underline{ins@c}}$$

In this way any sequence of movement of INS molecules would appear as atomic. The presence of the high priority action immediately after the replication constitutes a very dangerous operation: a high priority loop of this kind may block the whole system if there is no guaranty on its termination. In the case of the VES process the finite number of INS molecules guarantees such termination.

Finally, the whole system is represented as follows:

$$
\begin{aligned}
SYS \triangleq \ & GLU(c_{out}, gt, gr) \mid K(c_{out}, kt, kr) \mid Ca(c_{out}, cat, car) \mid \\
& (\nu\ c_{in}) \\
& \Big(GLU(c_{in}, gt, gr) \mid GLUCHAN(c_{out}, c_{in}, gt) \\
& \mid K(kt, kr, c_{in}) \mid KCHAN(c_{in}, c_{out}, inhk) \mid \\
& \mid ADP(gr, inhk, c_{in}) \mid ATP(inhk, c_{in}) \mid POL(c_{in}, kr, caact) \\
& \mid Ca(c_{in}, cat, car) \mid CACHAN(c_{out}, c_{in}, cat, caact) \\
& \mid DOCKP(c_{in}, car, dockves, c_{out}) \mid VES(c_{out}, dockves, ins) \Big)
\end{aligned}
$$

Like the VES compartment, the β cell is denoted by only one restricted name, c_{in}.

3.3   The Core-π@ Language

The π@ language is characterised by the capability of using an unbounded number of names for channels and of priority levels for reductions. The writing of complex encoding like those presented in Sect. 4.5 and 4.8 can be significantly simplified by such flexibility. Anyway, two levels of priority and two names for each channel are sufficient for most of the purposes, like the modelling examples previously shown. For this reason we introduce a subcalculus of π@, denoted as *core-π@*, characterised by only two levels of priority (i.e. normal actions and prioriotised actions) and two names for each channel. A valuable property of this core-π@ is its straighforward mapping into its stochastic counterpart Sπ@ [23,24].

We introduce three distinct sets of names $\mathcal{N}, \mathcal{P}, \mathcal{C}$ denoting respectively unprioritised actions, prioritised actions and compartments. Each channel $x@a$ is denoted by an action name and a compartment name. In order to keep notation simple, compartment names may be omitted when superfluous.

Definition 6. *Let N, P, C be distinct sets of names on finite alphabet, with m, n ranging over N, p, q over P, a, b over C and x, y over $X = N \cup P \cup C$. The syntax of the core-π@ language is defined as*

$$P \quad ::= \quad \mathbf{0} \quad \Big| \quad \sum_{i \in I} \pi_i . P_i \quad \Big| \quad P \mid Q \quad \Big| \quad !\,\pi . P \quad \Big| \quad (\nu\, x) P$$

$$\pi \quad ::= \quad \tau \quad \Big| \quad n@a(\mathbf{x}) \quad \Big| \quad \overline{n}@a\langle\mathbf{x}\rangle \quad \Big| \quad \underline{\tau} \quad \Big| \quad \underline{p}@a(\mathbf{x}) \quad \Big| \quad \overline{\underline{p}}@a\langle\mathbf{x}\rangle$$

where $\mathbf{x}$ represents one or more names $x_1, \dots, x_i$ ranging over X.

Like for π@, the semantics of this core-π@ is given by means of a reduction system based on the following congruence relation.

Definition 7. *The congruence relation $\equiv$ is defined as the least congruence satisfying alpha conversion, the commutative monoidal laws with respect to both $(\mid, \mathbf{0})$ and $(+, \mathbf{0})$ and the following axioms:*

$$(\nu\, x) P \mid Q \equiv (\nu\, x)(P \mid Q) \qquad\qquad \text{if } x \notin \text{fn}(Q)$$
$$(\nu\, x) P \equiv P \qquad\qquad \text{if } x \notin \text{fn}(P)$$
$$!\,\pi . P \equiv \pi.(!\,\pi . P \mid P)$$

where the function fn *is defined as*

$$\text{fn}(\tau) \triangleq \emptyset \qquad\qquad \text{fn}(\underline{\tau}) \triangleq \emptyset$$
$$\text{fn}(n@a(\mathbf{x})) \triangleq \{n, a\} \qquad \text{fn}(\overline{n}@a\langle\mathbf{x}\rangle) \triangleq \{n, a, \mathbf{x}\}$$
$$\text{fn}(\underline{p}@a(\mathbf{x})) \triangleq \{p, a\} \qquad \text{fn}(\overline{\underline{p}}@a\langle\mathbf{x}\rangle) \triangleq \{p, a, \mathbf{x}\}$$
$$\text{fn}(\mathbf{0}) \triangleq \emptyset \qquad\qquad \text{fn}((\nu\, x) P) \triangleq \text{fn}(P) \setminus \{x\}$$
$$\text{fn}(\pi . P) \triangleq \text{fn}(\pi) \cup \text{fn}(P) \qquad \text{fn}\Big(\sum_{i \in I} \pi_i . P_i\Big) \triangleq \bigcup_i \text{fn}(\pi_i . P_i)$$
$$\text{fn}(P \mid Q) \triangleq \text{fn}(P) \cup \text{fn}(Q) \qquad \text{fn}(!\,\pi . P) \triangleq \text{fn}(\pi . P)$$

Definition 8. *Core-π@ semantics is given in terms of the following reduction system:*

$$\frac{}{\underline{\tau}.P + M \,\twoheadrightarrow\, P} \qquad \frac{M \,\not\twoheadrightarrow\, M'}{\tau.P + M \,\mapsto\, P} \qquad \frac{P \,\twoheadrightarrow\, P'}{(\nu\, x)P \,\twoheadrightarrow\, (\nu\, x)P'} \qquad \frac{P \,\mapsto\, P'}{(\nu\, x)P \,\mapsto\, (\nu\, x)P'}$$

$$\frac{}{(\underline{p}@a(\mathbf{x}).P + M) \mid (\overline{\underline{p}}@a\langle\mathbf{y}\rangle.Q + N) \,\twoheadrightarrow\, P\{\mathbf{y}/\mathbf{x}\} \mid Q}$$

$$\frac{M \mid N \,\not\twoheadrightarrow\, R}{(n@a(\mathbf{x}).P + M) \mid (\overline{n}@a\langle\mathbf{y}\rangle.Q + N) \,\mapsto\, P\{\mathbf{y}/\mathbf{x}\} \mid Q}$$

$$\frac{P \,\twoheadrightarrow\, P'}{P \mid Q \,\twoheadrightarrow\, P' \mid Q} \qquad \frac{P \,\mapsto\, P' \quad P \mid Q \,\not\twoheadrightarrow\, R}{P \mid Q \,\mapsto\, P' \mid Q}$$

$$\frac{P \equiv Q \quad P \,\twoheadrightarrow\, P' \quad P' \equiv Q'}{Q \,\twoheadrightarrow\, Q'} \qquad \frac{P \equiv Q \quad P \,\mapsto\, P' \quad P' \equiv Q'}{Q \,\mapsto\, Q'}$$

The presence of only one additional level of priority allows to avoid the definition of the $I^k()$ function of Def. 5. On the other hand, the definition of the reduction relation requires two rules for each corresponding rule of π@ semantics.

4   Application Examples

The key feature which differentiates many recent bio-inspired calculi from the π-Calculus is the explicit formalisation of compartments. BioAmbients is a modified version of the Ambient calculus [25,26], where compartments are represented by *ambients*, a sort of boxes containing processes or other nested boxes. In Brane compartments are bounded by membranes, on the surface of which processes compute. Both ambients and membranes are organised in a tree structure, both can dinamically modify this structure by performing for example *merge*, *enter/exit* or *exo* operations. The central issue is *how* they modify this structure: the most observable difference is the bitonality preserved by brane semantics and totally absent in BioAmbients, which corresponds to the preservation of the parity of the nesting level of processes. As remarked in [9], this peculiarity is enough to preclude an immediate embedding of one language into the other.

Consequently, on the one hand they gain faithfulness because of their additional primitives designed to model the addressed biological phenomena, on the other their specialisation does not allow to mutually translate the models expressed in each language. Furthermore, the high abstraction level of such primitives hides the mechanisms underlying the idea of compartment, whose unfolding can reveal their strong resemblance.

π@ features were chosen to overcome all these issues: the lack of a predefined semantics for compartments together with the possibility of expressing localisation by means of polyadic synchronisation and complex atomic operations by means of priority place π@ one abstraction level underneath, as a sort of *assembly* language for compartmentalised formalisms. As previously discussed, it allows to simplify consistently w.r.t. the π-Calculus the formalisation of biological models which embed the notion of compartment. In this section we show that π@ is also able to supply the same high level features offered by bio-oriented languages like BioAmbients and Brane calculi. In particular, we show how both of them can be encoded directly into π@, by unfolding the basic functioning of compartment semantics and providing a common platform for their direct comparison and implementation.

4.1   Basic Ideas

Compartment and their nesting are very intuitive abstractions: the simple statement that an object is enclosed in a box suggests that it is someway isolated from the external context; putting one box into another means that, after the operation, the inner box *with all its content* are located inside the outer one; merging the content of two boxes implies putting in the same box *all the enclosed objects*.

To obtain this behaviour in $\pi@$ we must recognise the exact meaning of every operation on compartments and reproduce step by step the same semantics.

The first concept to unfold is nesting: compartments compose a dynamical tree structure which must be encoded in $\pi@$. As suggested in [21], these kind of structures can be represented as a set of processes linked by the share of private channels between parent and child nodes. The encoding of the insuline secretion process is a simple example of this situation: the cell and the insuline vesicles define the boundaries of compartments linked by the presence of cross-compartment processes (like cross-membrane molecular channels) which are able to interact with elements located in both compartments. Like in [2], the scoping of private names represents the boundaries of such compartments, but thanks to polyadic synchronisation each private name may represent an unlimited number of private communication channels, as discussed during the modelling of the insuline example. If each node is supplied with one distinctive name, the simplest way to encode the tree is by ensuring that each node knows the name identifying its parent compartment.

Therefore, trivial changes in the tree structure may affect an unlimited number of processes: the simple disclosure of a compartment implies that all contained processes must be notified of their new parent compartment name. The same situation occurs when splitting or merging the content of two compartments, like in BioAmbients $merge+$ /$merge-$ and Brane $exo/exo^\perp$ operations. In $\pi@$ this turns out to be a sort of *multicast* communication, where specific groups of nodes – that is sibling and child processes – must receive on the proper channel a new compartment name. This result is achieved by a smart use of priority levels: a high priority loop notifies in turn all the interested processes and ends when such processes do not exist anymore. By a single line of code, we obtain in $\pi@$ the same mechanism typical of broadcast communication:

$$BCAST \quad \triangleq \quad !\ \underline{bcast}(x,y).(\underline{\tau} + \underline{x}\langle y\rangle.\underline{bcast}\langle x,y\rangle)$$

The above process can be triggered by an output operation $\overline{bcast}\langle chn, newchn\rangle$ and terminate when no high priority synchronisations are available, leaving no residual terms. Obviously, a high priority complementary output loop $!\ \overline{bcast}\langle chn, newchn\rangle$ would cause the system to hang, since it prevents any other computation with normal priority. The avoidance of such high priority and non-terminating loops is often not trivial. In particular, an homomorphic translation of the replication operator would immediately cause them to appear, as we will discuss in the following encodings. This is one of the most difficult translation issues and will force us to represent *indirectly* the encoded replicated processes, by keeping explicit track of each replicated instance in our encoding functions.

4.2   Requirements

The fundamental criterion guiding any encoding is the preservation of some addressed semantics. According to [27], this often means that the encoding function

$[\![\,\cdot\,]\!]$ must at least fulfill the notion of *operational correspondence*, characterised by two complementary properties: completeness and soundness. The first means that every possible execution of the source language may be simulated by its translation, the second ensures that all the states reached by the translation correspond to some state of the source. Since all the languages we consider are Turing-complete (even Brane [28], despite of its simplicity), as usual for concurrent languages we require some additional criteria. As remarked in [29], a *reasonable* encoding should also preserve the degree of distribution of the source language (i.e. homomorphism w.r.t. parallel composition) and should not depend on the channel (or compartment) names of the term to be encoded. This also implies a very valuable property, that is modular compilation, as discussed in [30]. In addition to the cited criteria, we also require the encoding to preserve the termination or diverging behaviour of the translated term, in order to obtain a totally faithful encoding function. The following definition formalises the notion of *reasonable encoding* used in this paper.

Definition 9. *An encoding $[\![\,\cdot\,]\!]$ is reasonable if it enjoys the following properties:*

1. *homomorphism w.r.t. parallel composition:*

$$[\![\, P_1 \mid P_2 \,]\!] = [\![\, P_1 \,]\!] \mid [\![\, P_2 \,]\!]$$

2. *renaming preserving: for any permutation of the source names θ,*

$$[\![\, \theta(P) \,]\!] = \theta([\![\, P \,]\!])$$

3. *termination invariance:*

$$P\!\Downarrow \iff [\![\, P \,]\!]\!\Downarrow \qquad\qquad P\!\Uparrow \iff [\![\, P \,]\!]\!\Uparrow$$

4. *operational correspondence:*

   (a) *if $P \to P'$ then $[\![\, P \,]\!] \to^* [\![\, P' \,]\!]$,*

   (b) *if $[\![\, P \,]\!] \to^* Q$ then $\exists P' : P \to^* P' \wedge Q \to^* [\![\, P' \,]\!]$.*

4.3   BioAmbients

The BioAmbient calculus rises as an enhancement of the π-Calculus in order to overcome the same technical difficulties we encountered during the modelling example of insuline secretion in β cells. More precisely, BioAmbients joins the communication power of the π-Calculus and the compartment abstraction given by the Ambient calculus [25,26]. Compartments are represented by ambients, denoted by square brackets:

$$Sys \triangleq [P \mid Q \mid [R]]$$

The above system Sys is composed of one root ambient containing three elements: the processes P and Q, and another nested ambient $[R]$, which in turns contains another process R.

Processes can communicate in the style of the π-Calculus, but communication capabilities are extended to fit the needs of the new setting denoted by ambients. Processes can interact if they lie in the same ambient or in *nearby* ambients, where two ambients are nearby if one of them is directly nested into the other or they are children of the same parent ambient. Therefore, four directions of communications are introduced:

- intra-ambient, for processes inside the same ambient;
- sibling-to-sibling, when processes lie in compartments children of the same parent ambient;
- child-to-parent, for a process willing to communicate with a process located in the parent ambient;
- parent-to-child, representing the counterpart of the previous one.

Intra-ambient communication is denoted by the prefix *local*:

$$Sys \triangleq [local\ chan!\{d\}.P \mid local\ chan?\{x\}.Q \mid [R]]$$

The process $local\ chan!\{d\}.P$ is ready to send some datum d over the channel $chan$ to some process which must be located into same ambient. $local\ chan?\{x\}.Q$ is a candidate for such synchronisation, since it is listening on the same channel inside the same ambient. For these reason, the above system can reduce in the following way:

$$Sys \triangleq [local\ chan!\{d\}.P \mid local\ chan?\{x\}.Q \mid [R]] \quad \rightarrow$$
$$[P \mid Q\{d/x\} \mid [R]]$$

The effect of the communication is the same as for the π-Calculus: the name d is received and substituted for the local placeholder x in Q.

Sibling-to-sibling communication is denoted by the prefix $s2s$:

$$Sys \triangleq [[s2s\ chan!\{d\}.P \mid Q] \mid [s2s\ chan?\{x\}.R \mid S]] \quad \rightarrow$$
$$[[P \mid Q] \mid [R\{d/x\} \mid S]]$$

Parent-to-child and child-to-parent are complementary, denoted by $c2p$ and $p2c$ prefixes, and permit both the input/output directions:

$$Sys_1 \triangleq [[c2p\ chan!\{d\}.P \mid Q] \mid p2c\ chan?\{x\}.R \mid S] \quad \rightarrow$$
$$[[P \mid Q] \mid R\{d/x\} \mid S]$$
$$Sys_2 \triangleq [[c2p\ chan?\{x\}.P \mid Q] \mid p2c\ chan!\{d\}.R \mid S] \quad \rightarrow$$
$$[[P\{d/x\} \mid Q] \mid R \mid S]$$

In Sys_1 the outer process R receives the datum, while in Sys_2 it sends the datum to the inner process P.

In addition to the above communications, BioAmbients inherits from Mobile Ambients the operations needed to change dynamically the structure of nesting of ambients. Such operations are called *capabilities*. Processes cause the movement of whole ambients across the nesting tree, in agreement with the basic intuitions behind compartment semantics. For example, it is possible to cause the merging of two sibling ambients (children of the same parent ambient) in the following way:

$$[[merge+n.P \mid Q] \mid [merge-n.R \mid S] \mid T] \quad \rightarrow$$
$$[[P \mid Q \mid R \mid S] \mid T]$$

The *merge+* and *merge−* capabilities are complementary and can be triggered only if the name n matches.

Ambients can also enter some other sibling ambient

$$[[enter\ n.P \mid Q] \mid [accept\ n.R \mid S] \mid T] \quad \rightarrow$$
$$[[[P \mid Q] \mid R \mid S] \mid T]$$

or exit their own parent ambient

$$[[[exit\ n.P \mid Q] \mid expel\ n.R \mid S] \mid T] \quad \rightarrow$$
$$[[[P \mid Q] \mid [R \mid S] \mid T]$$

by additional complementary capabilities, *enter/accept* and *exit/expel*.

We now give the definitions for the syntax, structural congruence and reduction semantics of BioAmbients, in the same style of π-Calculus and π@ semantics. For further details we refer to [11].

Definition 10. *Let $\mathcal{N}$ be a set of names on a finite alphabet, $n, m, p, \ldots \in \mathcal{N}$. The syntax of BioAmbients is defined as*

$$\pi \quad ::= \quad \$n!\{m\} \quad \mid \quad \$n?\{m\}$$

$$\$ \quad ::= \quad local \quad \mid \quad s2s \quad \mid \quad p2c \quad \mid \quad c2p$$

$$M, N \quad ::= \quad enter\ n \quad \mid \quad accept\ n \quad \mid \quad exit\ n \quad \mid \quad expel\ n \quad \mid \quad merge+n \quad \mid \quad merge-n$$

$$P, Q \quad ::= \quad (new\ n)P \quad \mid \quad P \mid Q \quad \mid \quad !P \quad \mid \quad [P] \quad \mid \quad \sum_{i \in I} \pi_i.P_i \quad \mid \quad \sum_{i \in I} M_i.P_i$$

Definition 11. *The congruence relation $\equiv$ is defined as the least congruence satisfying the following rules:*

$$P|Q \equiv Q|P \qquad\qquad (P|Q)|R \equiv P|(Q|R)$$
$$P|0 \equiv P \qquad\qquad [0] \equiv 0$$
$$!0 \equiv 0 \qquad\qquad !P \equiv P|!P$$
$$(new\ n)0 \equiv 0 \qquad\qquad (new\ n)(new\ m)P \equiv (new\ m)(new\ n)P$$
$$(new\ n)(P|Q) \equiv P|(new\ n)Q \qquad if\ n \notin fn(P)$$
$$(new\ n)[P] \equiv [(new\ n)P]$$
$$\$n?\{m\}.P \equiv \$n?\{p\}.P\{p/m\} \qquad if\ p \notin fn(P)$$
$$(new\ n)P \equiv (new\ m)P\{m/n\} \qquad if\ m \notin fn(P)$$

where fn(P) *is naturally extended to BioAmbients processes.*

Definition 12. *BioAmbients semantics is given in terms of the reduction system described by the following rules:*

$$[(T + enter\ n.P)|Q]|[T' + accept\ n.R)|S] \rightarrow [[P|Q]|R|S]$$
$$[[(T + exit\ n.P)|Q]|(T' + expel\ n.R)|S] \rightarrow [P|Q]|[R|S]$$
$$[(T + merge+\ n.P)|(Q]|[T' + merge-\ n.R)|S] \rightarrow [P|Q|R|S]$$
$$(T + local\ n!\{m\}.P)|(local\ n?\{p\}.Q + T') \rightarrow P|Q\{m/p\}$$
$$(T + p2c\ n!\{m\}.P)|[(c2p\ n?\{p\}.Q + T')|R] \rightarrow P|[Q\{m/p\}|R]$$
$$[R|(T + c2p\ n!\{m\}.P)]|(p2c\ n?\{p\}.Q + T') \rightarrow [R|P]|Q\{m/p\}$$
$$[R|(T + s2s\ n!\{m\}.P)]|[(s2s\ n?\{p\}.Q + T')|S] \rightarrow [R|P]|[Q\{m/p\}|S]$$

$$\frac{P \rightarrow Q}{(\nu\ n)P \rightarrow (\nu\ n)Q} \quad \frac{P \rightarrow Q}{[P] \rightarrow [Q]} \quad \frac{P \rightarrow Q}{P|R \rightarrow Q|R} \quad \frac{P \equiv P' \quad P \rightarrow Q \quad Q \equiv Q'}{P' \rightarrow Q'}$$

4.4 Modelling the Insuline Example in BioAmbients

The example of Fig. 1 can be exploited again to explain the basic modelling ideas which may be applied in BioAmbients.

Since BioAmbients embeds directly the π-Calculus (we can obtain a straightforward translation just by substituting each π input/output operation with a *local* communication) we may start sketching the modelling of the *GLU* molecule of Expr. (4) in the following way:

$$GLU(\ldots) \triangleq \quad (\nu\ g)(local\ g!\{\ldots\}\ |\ !\ local\ g?\{\ldots\}.GLU'(g,\ldots))$$

GLU' should both listen for a possible transportation of the molecule into another compartment and communicate its ability of reacting as glucose. We may then try to take advantage of the multiple directions of communication of BioAmbients and use just a unique name *glu* in the *local* direction for reacting, and in the *c2p* and *p2c* directions for modelling the movement to a new compartment:

$$GLU'(g, glu, \ldots) \quad \triangleq \quad local\ glu!\{\}.PYR(\ldots) +$$
$$p2c\ glu?\{g', glu', \ldots\} +$$
$$c2p\ glu?\{g', glu', \ldots\}$$

Unfortunately, in this way we cannot exploit at all the abstraction of ambient and neither the directions of communication, because we are still modelling the localisation of processes by means of names: even if *GLU'* receives some new set of names after the *p2c* or *c2p* communication, it is not able to change ambient without some *exit* or *enter* capability. Consequently, in order to take some advantage from the novel primitives introduced in BioAmbients, we must forget the idea of name as means to model mobility or localisation, and leave this job to ambients: even a simple molecule like *GLU* should be modelled as an ambient on its own. Furthermore it may be possible to exploit the way ambients move as a whole in order to simplify the expression for *GLU*:

$$GLU \triangleq \quad [!\ enter\ glu\ |\ !\ exit\ glu\ |\ c2p\ glu?\{\}.PYR]$$

The above formalisation embeds the idea that the movement into a new ambient and the chemical reactivity are completely orthogonal and independent. The *exit glu* capability is superfluous, since in the simple model of the system we are considering the glucose molecules are not going to leave the cell once they entered, but it is valid in general for any molecule or element undergoing some sort of "passive" conveyance into other compartments without knowledge of its direction. The movement of the ambient as a whole preserves the integrity of the process even if composed of several parallel subprocesses, but the previous expression does not describe correctly the real behaviour of the glucose molecule: in fact, after its degradation into *PYR*, the *GLU* process is still able to be transported across compartments, even if the molecule itself may not exist anymore. Consequently we are forced to exploit the same expedient used for π-Calculus and π@ modelling, even in presence of ambients:

$$GLU \triangleq \quad [local\ glu!\{\}\ |\ !\ local\ glu?\{\}.(enter\ glu.local\ glu!\{\}\ +$$
$$exit\ glu.local\ glu!\{\}\ +$$
$$c2p\ glu?.PYR)]$$

Now the movement of the molecule is allowed in either direction and disabled after its degratation. It is worth noticing how the introduction of multiple communication directions (*local*, *s2s*, *p2c*, *c2p*) and capabilities (*merge*, *enter/accept*, *exit/expel*) reduces the number of channel names needed: each name embeds in fact seven distinct interactions. The scoping induced by ambients allows also to avoid the use of restriction, at least in this simple case.

The corresponding expression for the glucose channel becomes very simple:

$$GLUCHAN \triangleq \quad !\ accept\ glu$$

Even if the previous expression of *GLU* is correct intuitively, the mixing of communications and capabilities is not allowed in BioAmbients. A slight correction allows to overcome this issue:

$$GLU \triangleq \quad [local\ glu!\{\}\ |\ !\ local\ glu?\{\}.(s2s\ gludock!\{\}.enter\ glu.local\ glu!\{\}+$$
$$c2p\ gludock!\{\}.exit\ glu.local\ glu!\{\}+$$
$$c2p\ glu!.PYR)]$$

and *GLUCHAN* must be corrected accordingly:

$$GLUCHAN \triangleq \quad !\ s2s\ gludock?\{\}.accept\ glu$$

The direction *s2s* is justified by the structure of the system: the *GLU* molecule external to the cell is an ambient sibling of the ambient represented by the cell itself, where the process *GLUCHAN* resides.

The formalisation of GLU as an ambient affects the expression of ADP. The *local* reaction (inside the cell) of glycolysis becomes a inter-ambient communication, reflected by the $p2c$ direction:

$$ADP \triangleq \quad p2c \ glu?\{\}.ATP$$

The interaction of ATP can be instead considered *local*, as soon as the potassium channel is not modelled as an ambient:

$$ATP \triangleq \quad local \ inhk!\{\}$$

Under this hypothesis, the process $KCHAN$ is not substantially different from the corresponding π-Calculus expression:

$$KCHAN \triangleq \quad (\nu \ kc)(local \ kc!\{\} \mid \ ! \ local \ kc?\{\}.(local \ inhk?\{\}$$
$$+ \ p2c \ kdock!\{\}.expel \ k\{\}.local \ kc!\{\}))$$

The loop which spawns a new $KCHAN$ subprocess is disabled after the inhibition by the ATP molecule. The expulsion of potassium K from the current ambient is modelled in agreement with the previous considerations about the molecule GLU:

$$K \triangleq \quad [local \ k!\{\} \mid \ ! \ local \ k?\{\}.(s2s \ kdock!\{\}.enter \ k.local \ k!\{\}+$$
$$c2p \ kdock!\{\}.exit \ k.local \ k!\{\}+$$
$$c2p \ k!)]$$

The other processes can be encoded by following similar considerations:

$$POL \triangleq \quad p2c \ k?\{\}.local \ act!\{\}$$
$$CACHAN \triangleq \quad local \ act?\{\}.! \ s2s \ cadock!\{\}.accept \ ca$$
$$CA \triangleq \quad [local \ ca!\{\} \mid \ ! \ local \ ca?\{\}.$$
$$(s2s \ cadock!\{\}.enter \ ca.local \ ca!\{\}+$$
$$c2p \ cadock!\{\}.exit \ ca.local \ ca!\{\}+$$
$$c2p \ ca!\{\})]$$
$$DOCKP \triangleq \quad p2c \ ca?\{\}.expel \ dockves$$

The encoding of the vesicle VES requires more attention. In the biological model, the insuline molecules do *never* lie inside the cell. Therefore, if in BioAmbients VES is represented by an ambient, one way to carry the operation would be to make the VES ambient exit the cell and afterwards dump all the insuline molecules INS in the blood:

$$VES \triangleq \quad [exit \ dockves.! \ expel \ ins \mid [exit \ ins.INS] \mid \ \cdots \mid [exit \ ins.INS]]$$

Anyway, this encoding does not exploit the expressive power of ambients. A smarter approach would merge the content of VES with the ambient corresponding to the blood vessel after the expulsion of the vesicle from the cell:

$$VES \triangleq \quad [exit \ dockves.merge+ \ insves \mid [INS] \mid \ \cdots \mid [INS]]$$

This encoding requires that some complementary process is ready for the merge operation in the parent ambient of the cell:

$$VESMERGE \triangleq \ !\,merge-\ insves$$

It is worth remarking that in both cases the exocytosis process is *not modelled atomically*. Finally, the system is given by the following expression:

$$SYS \triangleq \ GLU \mid K \mid CA \mid VESMERGE \mid$$
$$[GLU \mid GLUCHAN \mid K \mid KCHAN \mid ADP \mid ATP \mid POL \mid$$
$$CA \mid CACHAN \mid DOCKP \mid VES]$$

Thanks to the introduction of ambients, there is no need to keep explicit trace of the free names of each process. Unfortunately, possible problems emerging from the need of atomicity for complex operations are not resolved, exactly like in π-Calculus.

After this short introduction to BioAmbients modelling, we are now able to grasp the key ideas which allow to encode BioAmbients into the $\pi@$ calculus.

4.5   Encoding BioAmbients into $\pi@$

As we have just seen, ambients are containers organised in a tree structure: running processes and nested sub-ambients are located inside them. If each node of the tree represents an ambient, nodes are complex structures: each node may contain zero or more parallel processes and may interact with zero or more nested sub-ambients. Consequently, for the implementation of this tree structure into $\pi@$, each encoded BioAmbients process must be aware of the name of its containing (immediate) ambient, but also of the name indicating the parent of its immediate ambient. In other words, the encoding function $[\![\ \cdot\ ]\!]^{\alpha}$ from BioAmbients processes to $\pi@$ processes which we are now ready to formalise requires the (bound) names a and pa, representing the immediate ambient and the parent ambient of each BioAmbients process respectively. This is in accordance with the modelling of cross-compartment objects in $\pi@$ (like ion channels) previously shown: in fact, every BioAmbients process may likely interact with some other process placed in some child or parent or sibling ambient, that is every BioAmbients process is a potential cross-compartment element.

The similarity between the basic π-Calculus operators and the corresponding operators inherited by Bioambients allows to encode some of them homomorphycally in $\pi@$. This is the case of parallel composition and restriction:

$$[\![\, P \mid Q \,]\!]^{\alpha}_{a,pa} \ \triangleq \ [\![\, P \,]\!]^{\alpha}_{a,pa} \mid [\![\, Q \,]\!]^{\alpha}_{a,pa}$$
$$[\![\, (new\ n)P \,]\!]^{\alpha}_{a,pa} \ \triangleq \ (\nu\ n)[\![\, P \,]\!]^{\alpha}_{a,pa}$$

According to the previous considerations, the encoding function is decorated with two names representing the ambient a where the encoded process resides and the outer ambient pa. The name a of the ambient can be used for *local* communication directions: [1]

$$\llbracket\ local\ n!\{m\}.P\ \rrbracket_{a,pa}^{\alpha*} \triangleq \overline{local@n@a}\langle m\rangle.(\llbracket\ P\ \rrbracket_{a,pa}^{\alpha})$$

$$\llbracket\ local\ n?\{m\}.P\ \rrbracket_{a,pa}^{\alpha*} \triangleq local@n@a(m).(\llbracket\ P\ \rrbracket_{a,pa}^{\alpha})$$

The name pa of the parent ambient can be exploited for any $s2s, c2p/p2c$ or ambient capability (*merge, exit/expel, enter/accept*). For example, the $s2s$ communication can be encoded in the following way:

$$\llbracket\ s2s\ n!\{m\}.P\ \rrbracket_{a,pa}^{\alpha*} \triangleq \overline{s2s@n@pa}\langle m\rangle.(\llbracket\ P\ \rrbracket_{a,pa}^{\alpha})$$

$$\llbracket\ s2s\ n?\{m\}.P\ \rrbracket_{a,pa}^{\alpha*} \triangleq s2s@n@pa(m).(\llbracket\ P\ \rrbracket_{a,pa}^{\alpha})$$

This encoding explains *where* such sibling-to-sibling communication is reasonably happening, that is inside the only compartment known by both processes: their parent ambient. Nevertheless, the effect of the communication is limited to the substitution of a name in the scope of the receiving process $\llbracket\ P\ \rrbracket_{a,pa}^{\alpha}$. The possibility of exploiting an unbounded number of names (three in this case) for each $\pi@$ channel allows to model easily the "triple matching" typical of BioAmbients actions: in fact, in addition to their "proximity" (i.e. the localisation in the same ambient or parent ambient), the interaction between two processes can happen only if both the direction (*local, c2p/p2c* or $s2s$) and the name n match.

The same considerations hold for $c2p/p2c$ communication:

$$\llbracket\ p2c\ n!\{m\}.P\ \rrbracket_{a,pa}^{\alpha*} \triangleq \overline{p2c@n@a}\langle m\rangle.(\llbracket\ P\ \rrbracket_{a,pa}^{\alpha})$$

$$\llbracket\ c2p\ n?\{m\}.P\ \rrbracket_{a,pa}^{\alpha*} \triangleq p2c@n@pa(m).(\llbracket\ P\ \rrbracket_{a,pa}^{\alpha})$$

While two processes able to perform a *local* or $s2s$ communication lie in a symmetrical position, the $c2p/p2c$ operation introduces asymmetry in the system, since one process must be located in the parent ambient of the other. This is reflected by the compartment names used in the $\pi@$ encoding: the outer process uses its ambient name a to communicate, while the inner process its parent ambient name pa. There would be no way to make such operation happen inside the child ambient, since the outer $\pi@$ process does not know (and *must* not know, in agreement with the abstraction of compartment scoping previously discussed) any name associated with the inner ambients.

The correspondence between ambient and parent ambient names of nested compartments is stated by the encoding of the compartment operator $[\cdot]$:

$$\llbracket\ [P]\ \rrbracket_{a,pa}^{\alpha} \triangleq (\nu\ c)\llbracket\ P\ \rrbracket_{c,a}^{\alpha}$$

At first sight it corresponds to the encoding of the restriction operator of BioAmbients. The substantial difference can be devised in the names appearing as parameters of the encoding function in the right-hand side of the expression: the

---

[1] The difference between the two mutually recursive encoding functions $\llbracket\ \rrbracket_{a,pa}^{\alpha}$ and $\llbracket\ \rrbracket_{a,pa}^{\alpha*}$ will be clarified later on.

restricted name c represents the new ambient of the process P, while a represents both the ambient of $[\,P\,]$ and the parent ambient of P.

So far, all the problems deriving from the introduction of compartments have been solved by the only use of polyadic synchronisation. The atomicity-related problems noticed during the formalisation of compartments in the π-Calculus would emerge now in the attempt of encoding BioAmbients capabilities in $\pi@$. Consider for example the simple *merge* capability:

$$[merge+.P \mid Q_1 \mid \cdots \mid Q_n] \mid [merge-.R \mid S_1 \mid \cdots \mid S_m] \quad \rightarrow$$

$$[P \mid Q_1 \mid \cdots \mid Q_n \mid R \mid S_1 \mid \cdots \mid S_m]$$

(7)

The encoding in $\pi@$ of the above system before the reduction would require two distinct restricted names corresponding to each of the ambients ready to be merged. After their merging, only one of such names must be present. This means that either $n+1$ or $m+1$ $\pi@$ processes must have replaced the name corresponding to their current ambient. Furthermore, BioAmbients semantics requires that all of these $n+1$ or $m+1$ changes in the structure of the system happen instantaneously, that is no other communication or capability can be executed meanwhile. The only way to grant this constraint in the standard π-Calculus (without introducing some divergent behaviour) would be to put as guard some *centralised monitor process* which enables the occurrence of one operation at a time, with the consequence of excluding any concurrent feature from the encoded system.

The presence of priority in $\pi@$ allows instead to overcome easily such kind of issues without any explicit centralised mechanism. The occurrence of the above *merge* synchronisation can be followed by a *sequence of high priority synchronisations* which notify all the involved processes of their new ambient (or parent ambient) name. This sequence of high priority operation is actually a *loop* which must terminate when all the addressed processes have received the desired data. A remarkable feature of such loop is that for any compartment-related operation of BioAmbients (but also of Brane) *all these processes reside in the same compartment*. This peculiarity allows to express the loop in a very general way:

$$BCAST \quad \triangleq \quad !\,\underline{bcast}(x,y,z).(\overline{x@y}\langle z\rangle.\overline{\underline{bcast}}\langle x,y,z\rangle + \underline{\tau})$$

The $BCAST$ process implements a loop triggered by the receiving of three names: the first two names are used to identify the channel $x@y$ over which the communication loop will be executed. The third name is a datum which is sent to all the processes listening on $x@y$, representing the name of some ambient where some group of processes is going to move. The use of two levels of (high) priority (denoted by single or double-underlined actions, corresponding to integer levels 1 and 0 respectively) provides two very important properties:

- once triggered, the loop will execute entirely before the occurrence of any other encoded BioAmbients operation, since all such operations – both communications, as we have showed, and capabilities, as we will show – are

guarded by an initial *low priority* (integer level 2 of priority, corresponding to no underline) actions;
- the loop will end without leaving any "garbage" which may interfere with the system later on.

The first property is granted by the high priority of the replicated *bcast* input. After the communication of the datum z over the channel $x@y$, the process spawns another copy of itself by means of the same expedient previously showed for the encoding of recursive behaviour by exploitation of replication. The presence of the τ action with an intermediate prioritised level allows to terminate the loop when all the processes listening on $x@y$ have actually received the datum z, so that the remainder of the *BCAST* process disappears completely *before* any other communication or capability may be performed.

Consequently, the implementation in $\pi@$ of the *merge* capability requires to trigger the *BCAST* loop with the correct parameters. First, we need to understand *where* two processes performing a *merge+/merge−* capability are located: by checking the semantic rules of Def. 12 we can see that such processes must be located in sibling ambients (ambients that are children of the same outer ambient), i.e. the corresponding synchronisation in $\pi@$ happens in the parent ambient, exactly as showed for the *s2s* communication. Second, the communication must carry on the name associated with one of the two ambients, so that the receiving process can use it as new compartment name for all of its subsequent synchronisations and forward it to all the other processes affected by the structural change in the ambient tree. Since the merging of two ambients is a symmetrical operation, the choice of the name to be communicated is arbitrary. Here we choose to keep the name associated with the ambient of the process exhibiting the *merge+* capability:

$$ [\![\, merge+\ n.P \,]\!]_{a,pa}^{\alpha *} \ \triangleq\ \overline{merge@n@pa}\langle a\rangle.([\![\, P \,]\!]_{a,pa}^{\alpha}) $$

In agreeement with the above considerations, the encoding of *merge+* is located in the parent ambient pa and communicates the name a of its ambient to the process ready for the complementary *merge−*:

$$ [\![\, merge-\ n.P \,]\!]_{a,pa}^{\alpha *} \ \triangleq\ merge@n@pa(x). $$
$$ \overline{bcast}\langle merge, a, x\rangle.([\![\, P \,]\!]_{x,pa}^{\alpha}) $$

The *merge−* operation implies the receiving of some name to be substituted for the placeholder x which will be used as new ambient in ($[\![\, P \,]\!]_{x,pa}^{\alpha}$), while the parent ambient pa remains unchanged exactly like in the original BioAmbients system. The subterm $\overline{bcast}\langle merge, a, x\rangle$ triggers the *BCAST* loop which in turn notifies all the sibling processes (represented by the siblings $S_1, \ldots, S_m$ of R in Expr. (7)) of their new ambient x (which, again, at this time has been replaced by the name of the ambient sent by the process performing the complementary *merge+* capability). The name *merge* used to denote the channels $merge@n@a$ and $merge@n@pa$ is completely arbitrary and allows to distinguish this broadcast-like communication occurring after the merging of compartments from the other broadcast-like loops that are triggered by the translation of the other BioAmbients capabilities.

Similar considerations lead to the encoding of the *enter/accept* and *exit/expel* capabilities. Their partial asymmetry requires to bring attention to the names transmitted during the reduction and the way they are used afterwards.

The *enter/accept* reduction is triggered by two processes whose localisation is symmetrical w.r.t. the global tree structure of the system: they are inside ambients children of the same parent ambient, exactly like in the case of the *merge* operation. After the reduction, anyway, their situation is asymmetrical since their respective ambients are one the child of the other. Consequently, the process performing the *accept* capability is not going to change location but must communicate the name corresponding to its ambient to the process ready for the *enter* capability, which will use such name to denote its new parent ambient:

$$[\![\ accept\ n.P\ ]\!]_{a,pa}^{\alpha*} \triangleq \overline{enter@n@pa}\langle a \rangle.([\![\ P\ ]\!]_{a,pa}^{\alpha})$$

$$[\![\ enter\ n.P\ ]\!]_{a,pa}^{\alpha*} \triangleq enter@n@pa(x).\overline{bcast}\langle pa,a,x \rangle.([\![\ P\ ]\!]_{a,x}^{\alpha})$$

As for the *merge−* operation, the encoding of the *enter* capability triggers the *BCAST* loop which notifies all the involved processes of their new parent ambient.

The *exit/expel* reduction is the converse of the previous one: the two processes performing it lie in an asymmetrical position and end to be symmetrically distributed w.r.t. the ambient tree. In this case the process exhibiting the *exit* capability and all of its siblings must be notified of their new parent ambient, represented by the name of the parent ambient of the process performing the complementary *expel*:

$$[\![\ expel\ n.P\ ]\!]_{a,pa}^{\alpha*} \triangleq \overline{expel@n@a}\langle pa \rangle.([\![\ P\ ]\!]_{a,pa}^{\alpha})$$

$$[\![\ exit\ n.P\ ]\!]_{a,pa}^{\alpha*} \triangleq expel@n@pa(x).\overline{bcast}\langle pa,a,x \rangle.([\![\ P\ ]\!]_{a,x}^{\alpha})$$

The *enter/accept* and *exit/expel* capabilities differ from *merge+ /merge−* for a subtle particular: in the *merge−* operation the name *merge* was sent as first parameter to *BCAST*, while in the other two the name *pa* was used. We may have used two distinct names *enter, exit* for indicating the change of the name of the parent compartment in consequence of each of such capabilities, but their effect is actually the same, so they can be condensed in the simple idea of "substitution of parent compartment name". Similar reasoning can be argued for the encoding of Brane actions.

A substantial consequence of the above encodings of BioAmbients capabilities is the silent assumption that *all the encoded processes are always listening on the right channels for possible changes of their ambient or parent ambient names*, independently of the other actions they are ready to perform. Furthermore, *after the receiving of a new ambient or parent ambient name in consequence of the triggering of the BCAST loop, each notified process must return exactly in its previous state*, except for the substitution of the old ambient or parent ambient name with the new one just received. As an example, consider again the situation of Expr. (7): the $\pi@$ processes corresponding to $S_1, \ldots, S_m$ are going to change their ambient name after the *BCAST* loop triggered by P and R. This means that each of those m processes is listening on some channel $merge@a$, with a representing their current ambient name. More exactly, each of them is listening simultaneously on

- $merge@a$ in order to be notified of the merging of their ambient,
- $merge@pa$ for the merging of their parent ambient, and
- $pa@a$ for the change of the name of their parent ambient in consequence of an *exit* or an *accept* operation.

In order to denote concisely this property, we may say that the $\pi@$ encoding of each BioAmbients communication or capability is put in nondeterministic choice with the three options expressed by the following process:

$$TREE(b, a, pa) \quad \triangleq \quad \underline{pa@a(x).\overline{\underline{b}}\langle a, x\rangle} + \underline{merge@pa(x).\overline{\underline{b}}\langle a, x\rangle} + \underline{merge@a(x).\overline{\underline{b}}\langle x, pa\rangle} \tag{8}$$

The three expressions with shape $\overline{\underline{b}}\langle a, x\rangle$ or $\overline{\underline{b}}\langle x, pa\rangle$, as we will see later on, spawn another copy of the original process which will use the first received name as ambient and the second one as parent ambient. It is worth noticing the use of the received name x after each choice branch:

- the name received over $pa@a$ is used as new parent ambient name, as required by the *exit* and *enter* capabilities;
- the name received over $merge@a$ is used as new ambient name, when the merging operation affects the local ambient;
- the name received over $merge@pa$ is used as new parent ambient name, when the merging operation affects the parent ambient.

After the execution of the *BCAST* loop, all the notified processes return to their previous state, that is they are ready again to behave as $S_1, \ldots, S_m$ in the case of Expr. (7), even if they are located in a new compartment. In other words, *the encoding of each communication or capability is represented by a loop which allows the process to return in its previous state after receiving some new ambient or parent ambient name*. With a slight abuse of notation we may then write that each communication or capability choice of BioAmbients can be encoded as follows:

$$\left[\!\!\left[\sum_{i \in I,\, I \neq \emptyset} \xi_i.P_i \right]\!\!\right]^{\alpha}_{a, pa} \quad \triangleq$$
$$(\nu\, s)(\overline{\underline{s}}\langle a, pa\rangle \mid\, !\, \underline{s}(na, npa).SUBSUM(s, na, npa)) \tag{9}$$

where *SUBSUM* is just a shorthand for the following expression (since its definition does not depend only on the names s, na, npa but also on the branches of the choice $\sum_i \xi_i.P_i$):

$$SUBSUM(s, na, npa) \quad \triangleq$$

$$\sum_{i \in I, \, I \neq \emptyset} [\![\, \xi_i.P_i \,]\!]_{na,npa}^{\alpha*} \quad + \quad TREE(s, na, npa) \tag{10}$$

Here, replication is exploited as usual for the modelling of recursive behaviour, which is needed in order to make each process return to the original state after the interaction with some triggered $BCAST$ loop. The presence of the $TREE$ process as part of the choice grants that each encoded process is listening on the right channels and ready to "be passively moved" inside some new ambient or parent ambient in consequence of the structural change in the nesting tree that has been triggered by another pair of processes. $\sum \xi_i.P_i$ represents either a choice between capabilities or between communications, since they are kept distinct in the definition of BioAmbients grammar. In the particular case of a single-branched choice in the form $\pi.P$ or $M.P$ the encoding is the same even if the choice operator is not written explicitly, because we still need to preserve the implicit choice branches with recursive behaviour expressed by $TREE$. The function $[\![\, \cdot \,]\!]^{\alpha*}$ decorated with an additional star denotes the encoding of each communication or capability, in order to distinguish it from the encoding of single-branched choices.

This $\pi@$ encoding of the choice operator determines severe consequences on the expression of BioAmbients replication. If we consider the following example

$$[\,!\, merge+n.P \mid Q\,] \mid [merge-.R \mid S\,] \quad \longrightarrow$$

$$[\,!\, merge+n.P \mid P \mid Q \mid R \mid S\,] \tag{11}$$

then we may suppose to encode the replication homomorphically:

$$[\![\, !\,P \,]\!]_{a,pa}^{\alpha} \quad \triangleq \quad !\, [\![\, P \,]\!]_{a,pa}^{\alpha} \tag{12}$$

Unfortunately this would cause a high priority loop without termination in Expr. (9). In fact, each encoded process $[\![\sum \xi_i.P_i]\!]_{a,pa}^{\alpha}$ undergoes an internal, high priority reduction on the private channel s which spawns a new copy of a subprocess $SUBSUM(s, a, pa)$. Consequently, a direct replication of Expr. (9) by Expr. (12) would cause an unbounded number of such reductions to happen immediately. Their high priority level would hang the entire system. It would be possible to overcome the problem by correcting the encoding of the choice in the following way:

$$[\![\, \sum_{i \in I, \, I \neq \emptyset} \xi_i.P_i \,]\!]_{a,pa}^{\alpha} \quad \triangleq$$

$$(\nu\, s)(SUBSUM(s, a, pa) \mid !\, \underline{s}(na, npa).SUBSUM(s, na, npa)) \tag{13}$$

with $SUBSUM$ corresponding to Expr. (10). The internal high priority reduction is eliminated because the spawned term $SUBSUM(s, a, pa)$ is now explicitly written in the encoding. The replication of Expr. (13) by Expr. (12) now can successfully translate the BioAmbients system of Expr. (11). In fact, after the first reduction on $merge@n@pa$, a copy of $[\![\, P\,]\!]^{\alpha}$ is spawned while the original $[\![\, !\, merge+\, n.P\,]\!]^{\alpha}$ is kept and ready to execute another $merge+$ reduction, in accordance with the right-hand side of Expr. (11).

Anyway, Expr. (12) is far from being correct. In fact, if we consider the following system

$$[merge+.P \mid Q] \mid [merge-.R \mid \,!\, S] \quad \rightarrow$$

$$[P \mid Q \mid R \mid \,!\, S] \tag{14}$$

where the replication acts on the process S which is sibling of the process undergoing the $merge-$ reduction, we may immediately notice the presence of another high priority non-terminating loop, even without unfolding the encoding of the whole system. We just need to recall the meaning of "replication of S" as "an unbounded number of copies of S":

$$!\, S \;\equiv\; !\, S \mid S \;\equiv\; !\, S \mid S \mid S \;\equiv\; !\, S \mid S \mid S \mid S \mid \;\cdots$$

The encoding of replication of Expr. (12) would require *each of the copies of* $[\![\, S\,]\!]^{\alpha}$ *represented by* $!\, [\![\, S\,]\!]^{\alpha}$ *to be notified of the change of compartment name* triggered by the $merge$ operation. Since such number of copies is unbounded and the loop is characterised by high priority, the system would hang immediately.

Consequently, we are forced to introduce an indirect encoding of BioAmbients replication by changing the intuitive abstraction of the replication operator itself. Even if $!\, P$ represents an unlimited number of copies of P, there is no need to unfold all of such copies. More precisely, we may think that there is no need to unfold more than just *one* copy of P at each time. In other words, we may represent $!\, P$ as $!\, P \mid P$ and consider to unfold a new copy of P only when its previous copy undergoes some reduction $P \rightarrow P'$. Actually this is equivalent to keep each replication in a sort of *normal form* where each replicated process is exactly unfolded once. Supposing that $P \rightarrow P'$, the reduction

$$!\, P \quad \rightarrow \quad !\, P \mid P'$$

would be then written as

$$!\, P \mid P \quad \rightarrow \quad !\, P \mid P \mid P'$$

where the copy of P in the right-hand side of the expression is unfolded from $!\, P$ only after the reduction of the first copy of P in the left-hand side to P'.

This behaviour can be straightforwardly obtained in $\pi@$ by encoding each BioAmbients replication as a loop where one copy of $[\![\, P\,]\!]^{\alpha}$ is always unfolded and undergoes the corresponding reductions of the BioAmbients process P. During any of such reductions, $[\![\, P\,]\!]^{\alpha}$ causes another copy of itself to spawn in order to grant that the semantics of $!\, P$ is preserved. Furthermore, the encoding of $!\, P$ must observe the same migration rules expressed by the $TREE$ process of Expr. (8). In order to allow $[\![\, P\,]\!]^{\alpha}$ to spawn a new copy of itself whenever it undergoes some reduction we must introduce a new parameter in the encoding function, which represents the private channel over which the spawning event will be communicated: this parameter is needed because the encoding of the action which causes P to reduce may be several nested calls later w.r.t. the recursive definition of $[\![\, !\, P\,]\!]^{\alpha}$. In fact, consider the following system:

$$ S \quad \triangleq \quad !\, (local\ n?.Q_1'\ |\ Q_2) $$

Its encoding in π@ requires three recursive calls of the encoding function $[\![\, \cdot\,]\!]^{\alpha}$, one for each of the following subsystems:

$$ S \triangleq\, !\, P \qquad\qquad P \triangleq Q_1\ |\ Q_2 \qquad\qquad Q_1 \triangleq local\ n?.Q_1' $$

By the previous considerations, we can keep one copy of P always unfolded and write S in the following way:

$$ S \quad \triangleq \quad !\, P\ |\ P $$

After the reduction of Q_1 to Q_1', the system should appear as

$$ S\ |\ local\ n!.0 \quad \rightarrow \quad !\, P\ |\ P\ |\ Q_1'\ |\ Q_2 $$

where one copy of P is still unfolded. The unfolding of the corresponding π@ process $[\![\, P\,]\!]^{\alpha}$ must be triggered by the $local\ n$ communication of $[\![\, Q_1\,]\!]^{\alpha}$. In other words, the π@ process $[\![\, Q_1\,]\!]^{\alpha}$ must cause $[\![\, !\, P\,]\!]^{\alpha}$ to spawn a new copy of $[\![\, P\,]\!]^{\alpha}$, even if $[\![\, !\, P\,]\!]^{\alpha}$ is defined recursively in function of $[\![\, P\,]\!]^{\alpha}$, in turn defined in function of $[\![\, Q_1\,]\!]^{\alpha}$. The only way to achieve this result is by introducing some new name k passed as parameter from $[\![\, !\, P\,]\!]^{\alpha}$ until the recursive call of the encoding function $[\![\, Q_1\,]\!]^{\alpha}$, which will use it to spawn a new copy of $[\![\, P\,]\!]^{\alpha}$ as soon as the $local\ n$ operation is executed. Hence, the encoding of the $local$ communication (and of all the other communications and capabilities) should be modified as follows:

$$ [\![\ local\ n?\{m\}.P\ ]\!]^{\alpha*}_{k,a,pa} \quad \triangleq \quad local@n@a(m).([\![\, P\,]\!]^{\alpha}_{a,pa}\ |\ \underline{unfold@k}) \tag{15} $$

$\underline{unfold@k}$ spawns a new copy of $[\![\, P\,]\!]^{\alpha}$ in the encoding of $!\, P$:

$$ [\![\, !\, P\,]\!]^{\alpha}_{a,pa} \quad \triangleq \quad (\nu\, k)(BANG(k,a,pa)\ |\ [\![\, P\,]\!]^{\alpha}_{k,a,pa}\ | $$
$$!\, \underline{new@k}(na,npa).[\![\, P\,]\!]^{\alpha}_{k,na,npa}) $$
$$ BANG(k,a,pa) \quad \triangleq \quad !\, \underline{k}(na,npa).SUBBANG(k,na,npa) $$
$$ |\ SUBBANG(k,a,pa) \tag{16} $$
$$ SUBBANG(k,na,npa) \quad \triangleq \quad unfold@k.\overline{new@k}\langle na,npa\rangle.\overline{k}\langle na,npa\rangle\, + $$
$$ TREE(k,na,npa) $$

The recursive call $[\![\, P \,]\!]^{\alpha}_{k,na,npa}$, together with the new encodings suggested by Expr.(15), ensures that each communication or capability appearing after the above replication will spawn a new copy of $[\![\, P \,]\!]^{\alpha}$ with a high priority reduction on the channel $unfold@k$. Such spawning is mediated by the $BANG$ subprocess, which regulates also the relocation of $[\![\, !\, P \,]\!]^{\alpha}_{a,pa}$ by direct embedding of the $TREE$ subprocess discussed previously. It is worth remarking that such relocation in practice affects only the subprocess $BANG$, which is the only process regulating $where$ (in terms of ambient and parent ambient) the following copies of $[\![\, P \,]\!]^{\alpha}$ will be spawned. In accordance with the previous considerations, one copy (at least one, more precisely) of $[\![\, P \,]\!]^{\alpha}$ is always kept unfolded. The relocation of this spawned copy into some new ambient or parent ambient after some $merge$ or $exit/expel$ or $enter/accept$ capability happens transparently, since it already embeds in the correct way the subprocess $TREE$ as part of each encoded choice.

Two remarks allow to refine Expr. (16), which is still not correct.

First, replications may be $nested$ and more than one unfolding may be needed after some reduction. As an example, consider the following system

$$S \triangleq !\, (\nu\, x)!\, local\ n?.R'$$

which we rewrite in terms of some additional shorthands:

$$S \triangleq !\, P \qquad P \triangleq (\nu\, x)Q \qquad Q \triangleq !\, R \qquad R \triangleq local\ n?.R'$$

The unfolding of one copy of each replicated process leads to the following expression:

$$S \ \equiv \ !\, P \mid (\nu\, x)(!\, R \mid R)$$

The reduction of R to R' requires $two\ unfoldings$: one of P and one of R, corresponding to $one\ unfolding\ for\ each\ replication\ appearing\ before\ the\ communication\ or\ capability$ (i.e. each replication appearing as ancestor not followed by choice in the syntactic tree generating the BioAmbients expression). Consequently, one name k as additional parameter in the corresponding $\pi@$ encoding is not enough if more than one nested replication is present in the BioAmbients process. Hence, the parameter k must be replaced by the set $K = \{k_1, k_2, \ldots, k_n\}$ containing one name for each encoded replication which must be unfolded. This set is added with a new name after the encoding of each replication and becomes empty after the encoding of any BioAmbients choice, since any subsequent reduction of R' does not affect the replication of P and R anymore.

Second, the constant unfolding of one copy of a replicated process is not sufficient to express its full behaviour. Consider for example the following system:

$$S \ \triangleq \ !\, P \qquad\qquad P \triangleq (local\ n?.P_1 + local\ n!.P_2)$$

If we unfold only one copy of P, we miss the reduction that may happen between two distinct copies of P themselves. In fact we have that

$$S \ \equiv \ !\, P \mid P \mid P \ \ \rightarrow \ \ !\, P \mid P_1 \mid P_2$$

where P_1 and P_2 follow the reduction over *local n*. Consequently, at least *two* copies of $[\![\, P \,]\!]^\alpha$ must be constantly kept unfolded in the corresponding encoded process.

Expr. (16) can be then modified as follows:

$$[\![\, !\, P \,]\!]^\alpha_{K,a,pa} \quad \triangleq \quad (\nu\, k)(BANG(k,a,pa)\, |$$
$$[\![\, P \,]\!]^\alpha_{K\cup\{k\},a,pa} \,|\, [\![\, P \,]\!]^\alpha_{K\cup\{k\},a,pa} \,|$$
$$!\, \underline{new@k}(na,npa).[\![\, P \,]\!]^\alpha_{K\cup\{k\},na,npa})$$

The encoding of communications and capabilities is updated accordingly:

$$[\![\, local\; n?\{m\}.P \,]\!]^{\alpha*}_{K,a,pa} \quad \triangleq \quad local@n@a(m).\Big([\![\, P \,]\!]^\alpha_{\emptyset,a,pa} \,|$$
$$\underline{unfold@k_1} \,|\, \cdots \,|\, \underline{unfold@k_n}\Big)$$

with $K = \{k_1,\dots,k_n\}$.

The full definition of $[\![\, \cdot \,]\!]^\alpha$ is given in Table 1 and Table 2. Here, the names oa and opa represent two fictitious names needed for the correct initialisation of the encoding function, and corresponding to the outermost ambient and parent ambient of the entire encoded system.

The encoding function $[\![\, \cdot \,]\!]^\alpha$ enjoys the requirements discussed in section 4.2, as stated by the following theorem.

Theorem 1. $[\![\, \cdot \,]\!]^\alpha$ *is a reasonable encoding (modulo structural congruence), that is: let* P, P_1, P_2 *be BioAmbients processes, let* Q *be a* π@ *process, then*

1. $[\![\, P_1 \,|\, P_2 \,]\!]^\alpha = [\![\, P_1 \,]\!]^\alpha \,|\, [\![\, P_2 \,]\!]^\alpha;$

2. *for any permutation of the source names* θ, $[\![\, \theta(P) \,]\!]^\alpha = \theta([\![\, P \,]\!]^\alpha);$

3. $P \Downarrow$ *iff* $[\![\, P \,]\!]^\alpha \Downarrow$, $P \Uparrow$ *iff* $[\![\, P \,]\!]^\alpha \Uparrow;$

4. (a) *if* $P \to P_1$ *then* $\exists P_2 : P_2 \equiv P_1 \wedge [\![\, P \,]\!]^\alpha \to^* [\![\, P_2 \,]\!]^\alpha;$

   (b) *if* $[\![\, P \,]\!]^\alpha \to^* Q$ *then* $\exists P_1 : P \to^* P_1 \wedge Q \to^* [\![\, P_1 \,]\!]^\alpha.$

4.6   Brane Calculi

The peculiar spatial rearrangement typical of biological membranes inspired the definition of Brane Calculi [9]. Here membranes constitute both the boundaries of compartments and the place where "computation" happens, that is where concurrent processes are thought to be located and to interact with the surrounding environment. Membranes are denoted by $(\!|\, \cdot\, |\!)$ and can be nested, exactly like ambients. In the following expression, the system S is composed of an outer membrane whose behaviour is specified by σ:

$$S \quad \triangleq \quad \sigma(\!|\, P \circ \rho(\!|\, Q \,|\!) \circ R \,|\!) \tag{17}$$

Table 1. Encoding of BioAmbients processes into $\pi@$

$$[\![\, 0\,]\!]^\alpha \;\triangleq\; 0$$

$$[\![\, P \mid Q\,]\!]^\alpha \;\triangleq\; [\![\, P\,]\!]^\alpha \mid [\![\, Q\,]\!]^\alpha$$

$$[\![\, (new\ n)P\,]\!]^\alpha \;\triangleq\; [\![\, (new\ n)P\,]\!]^\alpha_{\emptyset,oa,opa}$$

$$[\![\, [\,P\,]\,]\!]^\alpha \;\triangleq\; [\![\, [\,P\,]\,]\!]^\alpha_{\emptyset,oa,opa}$$

$$[\![\, !\,P\,]\!]^\alpha \;\triangleq\; [\![\, !\,P\,]\!]^\alpha_{\emptyset,oa,opa}$$

$$[\![\, 0\,]\!]^\alpha_{K,a,pa} \;\triangleq\; 0$$

$$[\![\, P \mid Q\,]\!]^\alpha_{K,a,pa} \;\triangleq\; [\![\, P\,]\!]^\alpha_{K,a,pa} \mid [\![\, Q\,]\!]^\alpha_{K,a,pa}$$

$$[\![\, (new\ n)P\,]\!]^\alpha_{K,a,pa} \;\triangleq\; \nu\, n [\![\, P\,]\!]^\alpha_{K,a,pa}$$

$$[\![\, [\,P\,]\,]\!]^\alpha_{K,a,pa} \;\triangleq\; \nu\, c [\![\, P\,]\!]^\alpha_{K,c,a}$$

$$[\![\, !\,P\,]\!]^\alpha_{K,a,pa} \;\triangleq\; (\nu\, b)(BANG(b,a,pa) \mid$$
$$[\![\, P\,]\!]^\alpha_{K\cup\{b\},a,pa} \mid [\![\, P\,]\!]^\alpha_{K\cup\{b\},a,pa} \mid$$
$$!\,\underline{new@b}(na,npa).[\![\, P\,]\!]^\alpha_{K\cup\{b\},na,npa})$$

$$\Big[\!\!\Big[\, \textstyle\sum_{i\in I,\ I\neq\emptyset} \xi_i.P_i\, \Big]\!\!\Big]^\alpha_{K,a,pa} \;\triangleq\; BCAST \mid \nu\, s(!\,\underline{s}(na,npa).$$
$$\Big(\textstyle\sum_{i\in I,\ I\neq\emptyset} [\![\, \xi_i.P_i\,]\!]^{\alpha*}_{K,na,npa}$$
$$+ TREE(s,na,npa)\Big) \mid$$
$$\textstyle\sum_{i\in I,\ I\neq\emptyset} [\![\, \xi_i.P_i\,]\!]^{\alpha*}_{K,a,pa} + TREE(s,a,pa))$$

$$BANG(b,a,pa) \;\triangleq\; !\,\underline{b}(na,npa).SUBBANG(b,na,npa)$$
$$\mid SUBBANG(b,a,pa)$$

$$SUBBANG(b,na,npa) \;\triangleq\; \underline{unfold@b}.\overline{new@b}\langle na,npa\rangle.\underline{b}\langle na,npa\rangle +$$
$$TREE(b,na,npa)$$

$$TREE(b,na,npa) \;\triangleq\; \underline{npa@na}(x).\underline{b}\langle na,x\rangle + \underline{merge@npa}(x).\underline{b}\langle na,x\rangle +$$
$$\underline{merge@na}(x).\underline{b}\langle x,npa\rangle$$

$$BCAST \;\triangleq\; !\,\underline{bcast}(x,y,z).(\overline{x@y}\langle z\rangle.\overline{bcast}\langle x,y,z\rangle + \tau)$$

The outer membrane contains another membrane, whose behaviour is specified by ρ and whose content is Q.

S, P, Q, R are called *systems*: each system represents a collection of zero or more membranes that may be nested as we have just seen or composed in parallel by means of the operator $\circ$, like the three systems P, $\rho(\!|\ Q\ |\!)$ and R. Systems

Table 2. Encoding of BioAmbients communications and capabilities into π@

$$[\![\ enter\ n.P\ ]\!]_{K,a,pa}^{\alpha*} \triangleq enter@n@pa(x).\overline{bcast}\langle pa,a,x\rangle.([\![\ P\ ]\!]_{\emptyset,a,x}^{\alpha} \mid \Pi_K)$$

$$[\![\ accept\ n.P\ ]\!]_{K,a,pa}^{\alpha*} \triangleq \overline{enter@n@pa}\langle a\rangle.([\![\ P\ ]\!]_{\emptyset,a,pa}^{\alpha} \mid \Pi_K)$$

$$[\![\ exit\ n.P\ ]\!]_{K,a,pa}^{\alpha*} \triangleq expel@n@pa(x).\overline{bcast}\langle pa,a,x\rangle.([\![\ P\ ]\!]_{\emptyset,a,x}^{\alpha} \mid \Pi_K)$$

$$[\![\ expel\ n.P\ ]\!]_{K,a,pa}^{\alpha*} \triangleq \overline{expel@n@a}\langle pa\rangle.([\![\ P\ ]\!]_{\emptyset,a,pa}^{\alpha} \mid \Pi_K)$$

$$[\![\ merge-\ n.P\ ]\!]_{K,a,pa}^{\alpha*} \triangleq merge@n@pa(x).$$

$$\overline{bcast}\langle merge,a,x\rangle.([\![\ P\ ]\!]_{\emptyset,x,pa}^{\alpha} \mid \Pi_K)$$

$$[\![\ merge+\ n.P\ ]\!]_{K,a,pa}^{\alpha*} \triangleq \overline{merge@n@pa}\langle a\rangle.([\![\ P\ ]\!]_{\emptyset,a,pa}^{\alpha} \mid \Pi_K)$$

$$[\![\ local\ n!\{m\}.P\ ]\!]_{K,a,pa}^{\alpha*} \triangleq \overline{local@n@a}\langle m\rangle.([\![\ P\ ]\!]_{\emptyset,a,pa}^{\alpha} \mid \Pi_K)$$

$$[\![\ local\ n?\{m\}.P\ ]\!]_{K,a,pa}^{\alpha*} \triangleq local@n@a(m).([\![\ P\ ]\!]_{\emptyset,a,pa}^{\alpha} \mid \Pi_K)$$

$$[\![\ s2s\ n!\{m\}.P\ ]\!]_{K,a,pa}^{\alpha*} \triangleq \overline{s2s@n@pa}\langle m\rangle.([\![\ P\ ]\!]_{\emptyset,a,pa}^{\alpha} \mid \Pi_K)$$

$$[\![\ s2s\ n?\{m\}.P\ ]\!]_{K,a,pa}^{\alpha*} \triangleq s2s@n@pa(m).([\![\ P\ ]\!]_{\emptyset,a,pa}^{\alpha} \mid \Pi_K)$$

$$[\![\ p2c\ n!\{m\}.P\ ]\!]_{K,a,pa}^{\alpha*} \triangleq \overline{p2c@n@a}\langle m\rangle.([\![\ P\ ]\!]_{\emptyset,a,pa}^{\alpha} \mid \Pi_K)$$

$$[\![\ c2p\ n?\{m\}.P\ ]\!]_{K,a,pa}^{\alpha*} \triangleq p2c@n@pa(m).([\![\ P\ ]\!]_{\emptyset,a,pa}^{\alpha} \mid \Pi_K)$$

$$[\![\ c2p\ n!\{m\}.P\ ]\!]_{K,a,pa}^{\alpha*} \triangleq \overline{c2p@n@pa}\langle m\rangle.([\![\ P\ ]\!]_{\emptyset,a,pa}^{\alpha} \mid \Pi_K)$$

$$[\![\ p2c\ n?\{m\}.P\ ]\!]_{K,a,pa}^{\alpha*} \triangleq c2p@n@a(m).([\![\ P\ ]\!]_{\emptyset,a,pa}^{\alpha} \mid \Pi_K)$$

$$\Pi_K \triangleq \overline{unfold@k_1} \mid \cdots \mid \overline{unfold@k_n} \quad ,$$

$$\text{with } K = \{k_1,\ldots,k_n\}$$

specify the global structure of each Brane expression, i.e. the shape of the tree of nested or sibling membranes.

σ and ρ are called *(mem)branes*: each brane specifies the behaviour of the membrane w.r.t. the other membranes, by indicating which type of *actions* may be performed. For example, if

$$\sigma \triangleq exo^\perp.\sigma' \qquad \rho \triangleq exo.\rho'$$

the system of Expr. (17) becomes

$$S \triangleq exo^\perp.\sigma'(\!|\ P \circ exo.\rho'(\!|\ Q\ |\!) \circ R\ |\!) \tag{18}$$

σ specifies that the outer membrane is ready to perform an $exo^\perp$ action, while ρ is ready to perform the complementary exo action. The $exo/exo^\perp$ reduction formalises exocytosis, corresponding to the same phenomenon described in the example of insuline secretion. In consequence of the exocytosis, the content Q of the inner membrane is expelled out of the external membrane, and the two membranes are merged together:

$$S \quad \rightarrow \quad S' \qquad\qquad S' \quad \triangleq \quad Q \circ \sigma'|\rho'(\!|\, P \circ R \,|\!) \qquad (19)$$

The expression $\sigma'|\rho'$ denotes the parallel composition of branes, where the '$|$' operator is kept distinct from the '$\circ$' operator for the parallel composition of systems. The peculiar behaviour of exocytosis preserves *bitonality*, that is the parity of the level of nesting of each Brane process w.r.t. the tree structure of membranes. In fact, consider the level of nesting of Q before and after the reduction: if we match such level with the number of membranes that surround a given process, then Q passes from level 2 to level 0 of nesting. Any $exo/exo^{\perp}$ operation will never move some process P from an odd level to an even one, or vice versa. This property is preserved not only by the $exo/exo^{\perp}$ action, but by all the actions of Brane.

The $phago/phago^{\perp}$ reduction causes the inverse effect of the exocytosis: an external process is engulfed by a sibling membrane by surrounding it with a portion of the membrane itself. For example, if

$$Q \quad \triangleq \quad phago.\gamma(\!|\, T \,|\!) \qquad\qquad \rho' \quad \triangleq \quad phago^{\perp}(\tau).\rho''$$

then the system S' of Expr. (19) becomes

$$S' \quad \triangleq \quad phago.\gamma(\!|\, T \,|\!) \circ \sigma'|phago^{\perp}(\tau).\rho''(\!|\, P \circ R \,|\!)$$

and can undergo the following reduction:

$$S' \quad \rightarrow \quad \sigma'|\rho''(\!|\, P \circ R \circ \tau(\!|\, \gamma(\!|\, T \,|\!) \,|\!) \,|\!)$$

The external system $\gamma(\!|T|\!)$ has been engulfed and surrounded by the membrane τ, which is thought as a portion of the original external membrane of S'.

The *pino* action is the simplest operation on membranes: it corresponds to the inward bending of a membrane which produces a new internal membrane without any content:

$$pino(\sigma).\rho(\!|\, P \,|\!) \quad \rightarrow \quad \rho(\!|\, P \circ \sigma(\!|\,\,|\!) \,|\!)$$

The *pino* action has no complementary $pino^{\perp}$ co-action.

In [9], two calculi are presented: the phago-exo-pino and the mate-bud-drip variants.

A study on the relative expressive power of the two variants is reported in [28], where it is shown that the phago-exo-pino calculus is strictly more expressive than the mate-bud-drip one. Therefore, only the phago-exo-pino variant is considered here.

The formal definition of Brane follows, given in terms of a reduction semantics exactly like for the previous calculi.

Definition 13. *Let $\mathcal{N}$ be a set of names on a finite alphabet, $n, m, p, \ldots \in \mathcal{N}$. The syntax of Brane is defined as*

$$P, Q \quad ::= \quad \diamond \mid P \circ Q \mid !P \mid \sigma(\!|P|\!)$$

$$\sigma, \tau \quad ::= \quad 0 \mid \sigma|\tau \mid !\sigma \mid a.\sigma$$

$$a \quad ::= \quad phago_n \mid phago_n^\perp(\sigma) \mid exo_n \mid exo_n^\perp \mid pino(\sigma)$$

Definition 14. *The congruence relation $\equiv$ is defined as the least congruence satisfying the following rules:*

$$P \circ Q \equiv Q \circ P \qquad\qquad \sigma|\tau \equiv \tau|\sigma$$
$$P \circ (Q \circ R) \equiv (P \circ Q) \circ R \qquad \sigma|(\tau|\rho) \equiv (\sigma|\tau)|\rho$$
$$P \circ \diamond \equiv P \qquad\qquad \sigma|0 \equiv \sigma$$
$$!\diamond \equiv \diamond \qquad\qquad !0 \equiv 0$$
$$!(P \circ Q) \equiv !P \circ !Q \qquad !(\sigma|\tau) \equiv !\sigma|!\tau$$
$$!!P \equiv !P \qquad\qquad !!\sigma \equiv !\sigma$$
$$!P \equiv P \circ !P \qquad\qquad !\sigma \equiv \sigma|!\sigma$$
$$0(\!|\diamond|\!) \equiv \diamond$$

$$P \equiv Q \implies P \circ R \equiv Q \circ R \qquad\qquad \sigma \equiv \tau \implies \sigma|\rho \equiv \tau|\rho$$
$$P \equiv Q \implies !P \equiv !Q \qquad\qquad\qquad \sigma \equiv \tau \implies !\sigma \equiv !\tau$$
$$P \equiv Q \wedge \sigma \equiv \tau \implies \sigma(\!|P|\!) \equiv \tau(\!|Q|\!) \qquad \sigma \equiv \tau \implies a.\sigma \equiv a.\tau$$

Definition 15. *Brane semantics is given in terms of the reduction system described by the following rules:*

$$\frac{P \to Q}{P \circ R \to Q \circ R} \qquad \frac{P \to Q}{\sigma(\!|P|\!) \to \sigma(\!|Q|\!)} \qquad \frac{Q \equiv P \quad P \to P' \quad P' \equiv Q'}{Q \to Q'}$$

$$phago_n.\sigma|\sigma_0(\!|P|\!) \circ phago_n^\perp(\rho).\tau|\tau_0(\!|Q|\!) \quad \to \quad \tau|\tau_0(\!|\rho(\!|\sigma|\sigma_0(\!|P|\!)|\!) \circ Q|\!)$$
$$exo_n^\perp.\tau|\tau_0(\!|exo_n.\sigma|\sigma_0(\!|P|\!) \circ Q|\!) \quad \to \quad P \circ \sigma|\sigma_0|\tau|\tau_0(\!|Q|\!)$$
$$pino(\rho).\sigma|\sigma_0(\!|P|\!) \quad \to \quad \sigma|\sigma_0(\!|\rho(\!|\diamond|\!) \circ P|\!)$$

For further details on Brane calculi we refer to [9].

4.7   Modelling the Insuline Example in Brane

In order to allow the reader to become a little familiar with the Brane language, we now show how the insuline secretion model can be expressed in this calculus. The explicit presence in the target model of molecules and molecule channels makes unfeasible its expression in the core phago-exo-pino variant of Brane that we formalised in the previous section.

Therefore we consider an additional class of actions which are proposed in [9] in order to handle explicitly sets of molecules, reactions and cross-membrane conveyance. The grammar of processes is then extended with molecules $m_1, \ldots, m_n$ and multisets of molecules

$$p, q \triangleq m_1 \circ \ldots \circ m_k$$

Multisets of molecules can be used to define *molecular reactions*, which constitute an additional class of Brane actions and have the following shape:

$$p_1(p_2) \rightrightarrows q_1(q_2)$$

with p_1, p_2, q_1, q_2 multisets of molecules. Like the other actions, molecular reactions are thought to be located on membranes and are part of branes. p_1 and p_2 represent the multisets of molecules which must be present outside and inside the membrane respectively, in order to allow the molecular reaction to occur. The multiset q_1 represents the molecules released outside the membrane after the reaction, while q_2 the molecules released inside it.

A cross-membrane channel like the calcium channel of Fig. 1 can be easily modelled as follows:

$$S \quad \triangleq \quad CA^{2+} \quad \circ \quad CA^{2+} \quad \circ \quad !CA^{2+}() \rightrightarrows (CA^{2+}) (\!| \; P \; |\!)$$

The molecular reaction $!CA^{2+}() \rightrightarrows (CA^{2+})$ is enabled independently of the molecules present inside the membrane, and requires (at least) one molecule of CA^{2+} to be located outside of it. After the reaction, the molecule is released inside the membrane while disappears outside of it:

$$S \quad \rightarrow \quad CA^{2+} \quad \circ \quad !CA^{2+}() \rightrightarrows (CA^{2+}) (\!| \; CA^{2+} \circ P \; |\!)$$

The chemical reaction

$$m_1 + m_2 \quad \rightarrow \quad m_3 + m_4$$

where the molecules m_1, m_2 appear as reactants and m_3, m_4 as products of the reaction, may be represented in Brane by the following action if we model the reaction as happening on the outer surface of the membrane:

$$m_1 \circ m_2() \rightrightarrows m_3 \circ m_4()$$

or

$$(m_1 \circ m_2) \rightrightarrows (m_3 \circ m_4)$$

if we want it to be located on the inner surface.

The explicit handling of molecular reactions in the calculus allows to model the processes GLU, ATP, ADP, PYR, CA, K and INS as simple molecules. Their behaviour is completely passive and specified by the molecular reactions present in the other processes.

The cross-membrane channel $GLUCHAN$, whose function is the conveyance of glucose inside the cell, is expressed straightforwardly:

$$GLUCHAN \triangleq \ !GLU() \rightrightarrows (GLU)$$

Glycolysis can be modelled as molecular reaction occurring inside the cell membrane:

$$GLYCOL \triangleq \ !(GLU \circ ADP) \rightrightarrows (ATP \circ PYR)$$

The encoding of the potassium channel requires it to be deactivated after its binding to some ATP molecule. The simplest way to obtain this behaviour with a single molecular reaction is the introduction of a fictitious catalyst $KCHANCAT$ present inside the cell, which allows the channel process $KCHAN$ to move the potassium ions across the membrane as soon as it does not disappear:

$$KCHAN \triangleq \ !(KCHANCAT \circ K) \rightrightarrows K(KCHANCAT)$$

Such catalyst disappears in consequence of the presence of ATP:

$$KCHANINH \triangleq \ !(KCHANACT, ATP) \rightrightarrows ()$$

The process of polarisation of the membrane POL can be modelled as molecular reaction as well:

$$POL \triangleq \ (K) \rightrightarrows (ACT)$$

ACT is another fictitious molecule which activates the calcium channel:

$$CACHAN \triangleq \ (ACT) \rightrightarrows ().!\,CA() \rightrightarrows (CA)$$

The exocytosis of the vesicles is now rendered straightforwardly by the $exo/exo^{\perp}$ reduction:

$$VES \triangleq \ exo(\!| \ INS \circ \cdots \circ INS |\!)$$

Obviously, on the external membrane there must be some process ready to execute the complementary action:

$$DOCKP \triangleq \ (CA) \rightrightarrows ().exo^{\perp}$$

Finally, the system can be expressed as follows:

$$SYS \triangleq \ GLU \circ K \circ CA \circ$$
$$\sigma(\!| \ KCHANACT \circ K \circ ADP \circ ATP \circ CA \circ VES |\!)$$

with

$$\sigma \triangleq \ GLUCHAN \mid GLYCOL \mid KCHAN \mid KCHANINH \mid$$
$$POL \mid CACHAN \mid DOCKP$$

The addition of molecular reactions makes Brane a powerful language for biological modelling. This is evident in the formalisation of the previous example, which perfectly suited the bitonal properties of Brane. Anyway, the expression of behaviours that are not included in the design of the calculus (like the calcium channel $CACHAN$, or other compartment-related operations which do not preserve bitonality) requires either the extension of the language with additional primitives or the introduction of intermediate, fictitious elements which may lead again to the same atomicity problems encountered during the modelling with π-Calculus or BioAmbients.

4.8   Encoding Brane into π@

Like ambients, membranes are organised in tree structures: each node of the tree may contain membrane processes or nested membranes. Unlike BioAmbients, Brane Calculi present two main entities: systems and branes. Their distinction implies slightly different translations, because the encoding function of systems needs only two parameters (K, the set corresponding to the bang operators in front of the system and pc, the name representing the parent compartment) while an additional parameter is needed for encoding branes (c, the name of the compartment where the brane process resides). In fact, branes represent the boundaries of compartments: each new membrane corresponds to the definition of a new compartment, i.e. the name of the immediate compartment where the associated π@ process is located. Consequently, the function $[\![\cdot]\!]^{\beta}$ from Brane to π@ has two formal parameters when applied to the parallel composition of systems

$$[\![P \circ Q]\!]^{\beta}_{K,pc} \triangleq [\![P]\!]^{\beta}_{K,pc} \mid [\![Q]\!]^{\beta}_{K,pc}$$

and three for the parallel composition of branes:

$$[\![\sigma \mid \rho]\!]^{\beta}_{K,c,pc} \triangleq [\![\sigma]\!]^{\beta}_{K,c,pc} \mid [\![\rho]\!]^{\beta}_{K,c,pc}$$

Their encoding is almost the same as the encoding of parallel composition of BioAmbients processes. The names c and pc play the same role of a and pa for the encoding function $[\![\cdot]\!]^{\alpha}$. The rise of the additional name c occurs after the first application of $[\![\cdot]\!]^{\beta}$ to branes:

$$[\![\sigma (\!|P|\!)]\!]^{\beta}_{K,pc} \triangleq (\nu\, c)([\![\sigma]\!]^{\beta}_{K,c,pc} \mid [\![P]\!]^{\beta}_{K,c})$$

The encoding of a membrane corresponds to the introduction of the new name c that is used as compartment for branes, and as parent compartment for the inner system P. Any encoded brane occurring in $[\![P]\!]^{\beta}_{K,c}$ will use the above name c as parent compartment and will be able to interact over it with the surrounding branes represented here by $[\![\sigma]\!]^{\beta}_{K,c,pc}$. The name pc of the parent compartment is known only by the branes placed in the outer membrane, in accordance with the same intuition of compartment nesting exploited for the encoding of ambients.

The basic actions $exo/exo^\perp$, $phago/phago^\perp$ and $pino$ are encoded almost like BioAmbients capabilities: each operation of the original language is translated with a synchronisation followed by a sequence of high priority actions which manage the reorganisation of the tree structure and the unfolding of replicated processes involved in the computation.

For example, the translation of the $exo/exo^\perp$ actions requires three names for each channel and triggers the $BCAST$ loop whose definition is exactly the same as for $[\![\ ]\!]^\alpha$:[2]

$$[\![\ exo_n.\sigma\ ]\!]^{\beta*}_{K,c,pc} \quad \triangleq \quad exo@n@pc(x).\overline{bcast}\langle exo, c, x\rangle.([\![\ \sigma\ ]\!]^\beta_{\emptyset,pc,x} \mid \Pi_K) \quad (20)$$

$$[\![\ exo^\perp_n.\sigma\ ]\!]^{\beta*}_{K,c,pc} \quad \triangleq \quad \overline{exo@n@c}\langle pc\rangle.([\![\ \sigma\ ]\!]^\beta_{\emptyset,c,pc} \mid \Pi_K) \quad (21)$$

The asymmetry of the situation reminds the encoding of the $exit/expel$ capability, since the internal process listens on the channel $exo@n@pc$ intuitively located in the parent compartment pc, while the external process is ready to send on the local channel $exo@n@c$. The main difference is in the choice and use of the transmitted name pc by the $TREE$ subprocess and in the compartment where the broadcast effect of $BCAST$ occurs. In order to understand the rearrangement of the membrane tree structure, consider the following example:

$$S \triangleq \cdots \circ \underbrace{\sigma(\!|\ \underbrace{\tau(\!|\ P\ |\!)}_{c_3}\ |\!)}_{c_1}^{c_2} \qquad \sigma \triangleq exo^\perp.\sigma'|\rho \qquad \tau \triangleq exo.\rho'|\gamma$$

c_1 represents the parent compartment of the whole system S, while c_2 is both the compartment of σ and the parent compartment of τ (and of the entire subsystem $\tau(\!|\ P\ |\!)$). The system S can reduce as follows:

$$S \quad \rightarrow \quad S' \qquad S' \triangleq \cdots \circ P \circ \underbrace{\sigma'|\rho|\rho'|\gamma(\!|\ \cdot\ |\!)}_{c_1}^{c_2}$$

Two kinds of structural changes can be noticed in the reduction from S to S'. First, the parent compartment of P after the reduction coincides with the parent compartment c_1 of S: this justifies the name pc transmitted by the encoded $exo^\perp$ process. Second, the branes ρ' and γ changed both their compartment and their parent compartment. In fact, before the reduction, they were respectively c_3 and c_2, while after the reduction they become c_2 and c_1. This means that the corresponding π@ processes must replace their previous compartment name c_3 by their parent compartment c_2, and use as new parent compartment the name c_1 sent by the process performing the $[\![\ exo^\perp\ ]\!]^\beta$ action. The recursive call $[\![\ \sigma\ ]\!]^\beta_{\emptyset,pc,x}$ of Expr. (20) reflects this behaviour, as well as the definition of the $TREE$ process:

---

[2] Also for this encoding, we use two mutually recursive functions $[\![\ ]\!]^\beta_{K,c,pc}$ and $[\![\ ]\!]^{\beta*}_{K,c,pc}$, whose precise role will be clear later on.

$$TREE(b, c, pc) \quad \triangleq \quad exo@pc(x).\underline{b}\langle c, x\rangle +$$
$$exo@c(x).\underline{b}\langle pc, x\rangle +$$
$$pc@c(x).\underline{b}\langle c, x\rangle$$

The first branch of the choice is followed, in the previous example, by the subsystem P which receives the name of its new parent compartment. The second branch is followed by the brane γ which receives the name of its new parent compartment but replace also the name of its immediate compartment by the name of the previous parent compartment.

The third branch is needed for the encoding of the $phago/phago^\perp$ reduction:

$$[\![\, phago_n.\sigma \,]\!]^{\beta*}_{K,c,pc} \quad \triangleq \quad phago@n@pc(x).\overline{bcast}\langle pc, c, x\rangle.([\![\, \sigma \,]\!]^{\beta}_{\emptyset,c,x} \mid \Pi_K)$$
$$[\![\, phago_n^\perp(\rho).\sigma \,]\!]^{\beta*}_{K,c,pc} \quad \triangleq \quad (\nu\, x)(\overline{phago@n@pc}\langle x\rangle.$$
$$([\![\, \sigma \,]\!]^{\beta}_{\emptyset,c,pc} \mid [\![\, \rho \,]\!]^{\beta}_{\emptyset,x,c} \mid \Pi_K))$$

In this case, the name transmitted by the $[\![\, phago^\perp \,]\!]^{\beta}$ process corresponds to the new created membrane that surrounds the engulfed process and is used as new parent compartment.

The $pino$ action has a similar, but simpler encoding:

$$[\![\, pino(\rho).\sigma \,]\!]^{\beta*}_{K,c,pc} \quad \triangleq \quad (\nu\, x)\tau.([\![\, \sigma \,]\!]^{\beta}_{\emptyset,c,pc} \mid [\![\, \rho \,]\!]^{\beta}_{\emptyset,x,c} \mid \Pi_K)$$

In the right-hand side of the encoding, the reduction τ represents an invisible $\pi@$ transition, and must not be confused with the notation used for branes. The lack of complementary action and the very localised effect allows to disregard any broadcast loop. The new created membrane is represented by a new restricted name x used as local compartment by $[\![\, \rho \,]\!]^{\beta}_{\emptyset,x,c}$, whose parent compartment coincides with the immediate compartment of the encoded process $[\![\, pino(\rho).\sigma \,]\!]^{\beta}_{K,c,pc}$.

The sequential composition of branes $\sigma.\sigma'$ is encoded exactly like the choice operator of BioAmbients, as a sort of single-branch choice:

$$[\![\, a.\sigma \,]\!]^{\beta}_{K,c,pc} \quad \triangleq \quad BCAST \mid \nu\, s(!\, \underline{s}(nc, npc).$$
$$([\![\, a.\sigma \,]\!]^{\beta*}_{K,nc,npc} + TREE(s, nc, npc)) \mid$$
$$[\![\, a.\sigma \,]\!]^{\beta*}_{K,c,pc} + TREE(s, c, pc))$$

The presence of two distinct replication operators in Brane leads to two slightly different encodings which reflect the fact that systems are only provided with parent compartment, while branes are also aware of their immediate compartment. The encoding of branes replication is the same as the one seen for BioAmbients replication:

$$[\![\, ! \, \sigma \,]\!]^{\beta}_{K,c,pc} \triangleq (\nu \, b)(BANG(b,c,pc) \, |$$

$$[\![\, \sigma \,]\!]^{\beta}_{K \cup \{b\},c,pc} \, | \, [\![\, \sigma \,]\!]^{\beta}_{K \cup \{b\},c,pc} \, |$$

$$! \, \underline{new@b}(nc,npc).[\![\, \sigma \,]\!]^{\beta}_{K \cup \{b\},nc,npc})$$

$$BANG(b,c,pc) \triangleq ! \, \underline{b}(nc,npc).SUBBANG(b,nc,npc) \, |$$

$$SUBBANG(b,c,pc)$$

$$SUBBANG(b,nc,npc) \triangleq unfold@b.\overline{new@b}\langle nc,npc\rangle.\overline{\underline{b}}\langle nc,npc\rangle +$$

$$TREE(b,nc,npc)$$

The encoding of systems replication is simplified by the absence of name for the immediate compartment, which allow to shrink the definition in the following way:

$$[\![\, ! \, P \,]\!]^{\beta}_{K,pc} \triangleq (\nu \, b)(BANG'(b,pc) \, |$$

$$[\![\, P \,]\!]^{\beta}_{K \cup \{b\},pc} \, | \, [\![\, P \,]\!]^{\beta}_{K \cup \{b\},pc} \, |$$

$$! \, \underline{new@b}(npc).[\![\, P \,]\!]^{\beta}_{K \cup \{b\},npc}$$

$$BANG'(b,npc) \triangleq ! \, \underline{b}(npc).SUBBANG'(b,npc) \, |$$

$$SUBBANG'(b,pc)$$

$$SUBBANG'(b,npc) \triangleq unfold@b.\overline{new@b}\langle npc\rangle.\overline{\underline{b}}\langle npc\rangle +$$

$$exo@npc(x).\overline{\underline{b}}\langle x\rangle$$

Instead of the three branches of the $TREE$ process, only one is present, since only one of those branches (triggered by a reduction over $exo@npc$) is related to changes of the parent compartment name.

The full definition of $[\![\cdot]\!]^{\beta}$ is given in Table (3) and Table (4). Similarly to BioAmbients encoding, oc and opc are placeholders standing for the compartment and parent compartment of the outermost processes. The non-trivial encoding in π@ of molecular reactions and other extensions proposed in [9] is not strictly related to compartment semantics, but is being considered due to its relevance in chemical modelling.

Also the encoding function $[\![\cdot]\!]^{\beta}$ enjoys the requirements discussed in section 4.2:

Theorem 2. $[\![\cdot]\!]^{\beta}$ *is a reasonable encoding (modulo structural congruence), that is: let P, P_1, P_2 and ρ_1, ρ_2 be respectively Brane systems and processes, let Q be a π@ process, then*

1. $[\![\, P_1 \circ P_2 \,]\!]^{\beta} = [\![\, P_1 \,]\!]^{\beta} \, | \, [\![\, P_2 \,]\!]^{\beta}$

$[\![\, \rho_1 \, | \, \rho_2 \,]\!]^{\beta} = [\![\, \rho_1 \,]\!]^{\beta} \, | \, [\![\, \rho_2 \,]\!]^{\beta}$

2. for any permutation of the source names θ, $[\![\, \theta(P) \,]\!]^{\beta} = \theta([\![\, P \,]\!]^{\beta})$;

Table 3. Encoding of Brane processes into $\pi@$

$$[\![\diamond]\!]^\beta \triangleq 0$$

$$[\![P \circ Q]\!]^\beta \triangleq [\![P]\!]^\beta \mid [\![Q]\!]^\beta$$

$$[\![!P]\!]^\beta \triangleq [\![!P]\!]^\beta_{\emptyset,oc}$$

$$[\![\sigma(\!|P|\!)]\!]^\beta \triangleq [\![\sigma(\!|P|\!)]\!]^\beta_{\emptyset,oc}$$

$$[\![\diamond]\!]^\beta_{K,pc} \triangleq 0$$

$$[\![P \circ Q]\!]^\beta_{K,pc} \triangleq [\![P]\!]^\beta_{K,pc} \mid [\![Q]\!]^\beta_{K,pc}$$

$$[\![\sigma(\!|P|\!)]\!]^\beta_{K,pc} \triangleq (\nu c)([\![\sigma]\!]^\beta_{K,c,pc} \mid [\![P]\!]^\beta_{K,c})$$

$$[\![0]\!]^\beta_{K,c,pc} \triangleq 0$$

$$[\![\sigma \mid \rho]\!]^\beta_{K,c,pc} \triangleq [\![\sigma]\!]^\beta_{K,c,pc} \mid [\![\rho]\!]^\beta_{K,c,pc}$$

$$[\![!P]\!]^\beta_{K,pc} \triangleq (\nu b)(BANG'(b,pc) \mid$$
$$[\![P]\!]^\beta_{K\cup\{b\},pc} \mid [\![P]\!]^\beta_{K\cup\{b\},pc} \mid$$
$$! \underline{new@b}(npc).[\![P]\!]^\beta_{K\cup\{b\},npc})$$

$$[\![!\sigma]\!]^\beta_{K,c,pc} \triangleq (\nu b)(BANG(b,c,pc) \mid$$
$$[\![\sigma]\!]^\beta_{K\cup\{b\},c,pc} \mid [\![\sigma]\!]^\beta_{K\cup\{b\},c,pc} \mid$$
$$! \underline{new@b}(nc,npc).[\![\sigma]\!]^\beta_{K\cup\{b\},nc,npc})$$

$$BANG(b,c,pc) \triangleq ! \underline{b}(nc,npc).SUBBANG(b,nc,npc) \mid$$
$$SUBBANG(b,c,pc)$$

$$BANG'(b,npc) \triangleq ! \underline{b}(npc).SUBBANG'(b,npc) \mid$$
$$SUBBANG'(b,pc)$$

$$SUBBANG(b,nc,npc) \triangleq \underline{unfold@b}.\overline{new@b}\langle nc,npc\rangle.\overline{\underline{b}}\langle nc,npc\rangle +$$
$$TREE(b,nc,npc)$$

$$SUBBANG'(b,npc) \triangleq \underline{unfold@b}.\overline{new@b}\langle npc\rangle.\overline{\underline{b}}\langle npc\rangle +$$
$$\underline{exo@npc}(x).\overline{\underline{b}}\langle x\rangle$$

$$TREE(b,nc,npc) \triangleq \underline{npc@nc}(x).\overline{\underline{b}}\langle nc,x\rangle + \underline{exo@npc}(x).\overline{\underline{b}}\langle nc,x\rangle +$$
$$\underline{exo@nc}(x).\overline{\underline{b}}\langle npc,x\rangle$$

---

3. $P \Downarrow$ iff $[\![P]\!]^\beta \Downarrow$, $P \Uparrow$ iff $[\![P]\!]^\beta \Uparrow$;

4. (a) if $P \rightarrow P_1$ then $\exists P_2 : P_2 \equiv P_1 \wedge [\![P]\!]^\beta \rightarrow^* [\![P_2]\!]^\beta$;

   (b) if $[\![P]\!]^\beta \rightarrow^* Q$ then $\exists P_1 : P \rightarrow^* P_1 \wedge Q \rightarrow^* [\![P_1]\!]^\beta$.

Table 4. Encoding of Brane actions into $\pi@$

$$[\![\, a.\sigma \,]\!]^{\beta}_{K,c,pc} \triangleq BCAST \mid (\nu\, s)(!\, \underline{s}(nc, npc).$$

$$([\![\, a.\sigma \,]\!]^{\beta*}_{K,nc,npc} + TREE(s, nc, npc)) \mid$$

$$[\![\, a.\sigma \,]\!]^{\beta*}_{K,c,pc} + TREE(s, c, pc))$$

$$[\![\, phago_n.\sigma \,]\!]^{\beta*}_{K,c,pc} \triangleq phago@n@pc(x).\overline{bcast}\langle pc, c, x\rangle.([\![\, \sigma \,]\!]^{\beta}_{\emptyset,c,x} \mid \Pi_K)$$

$$[\![\, phago_n^{\perp}(\rho).\sigma \,]\!]^{\beta*}_{K,c,pc} \triangleq (\nu\, x)(\overline{phago@n@pc}\langle x\rangle.([\![\, \sigma \,]\!]^{\beta}_{\emptyset,c,pc} \mid [\![\, \rho \,]\!]^{\beta}_{\emptyset,x,c} \mid \Pi_K))$$

$$[\![\, exo_n.\sigma \,]\!]^{\beta*}_{K,c,pc} \triangleq exo@n@pc(x).\overline{bcast}\langle exo, c, x\rangle.([\![\, \sigma \,]\!]^{\beta}_{\emptyset,pc,x} \mid \Pi_K)$$

$$[\![\, exo_n^{\perp}.\sigma \,]\!]^{\beta*}_{K,c,pc} \triangleq \overline{exo@n@c}\langle pc\rangle.([\![\, \sigma \,]\!]^{\beta}_{\emptyset,c,pc} \mid \Pi_K)$$

$$[\![\, pino(\rho).\sigma \,]\!]^{\beta*}_{K,c,pc} \triangleq (\nu\, x)\tau.([\![\, \sigma \,]\!]^{\beta}_{\emptyset,c,pc} \mid [\![\, \rho \,]\!]^{\beta}_{\emptyset,x,c} \mid \Pi_K)$$

$$\Pi_K \triangleq \overline{unfold@k_1} \mid \cdots \mid \overline{unfold@k_n}\ ,$$

$$K = \{k_1, \ldots, k_n\}$$

$$BCAST \triangleq\ !\,\underline{bcast}(x, y, z).(\overline{x@y}\langle z\rangle.\overline{bcast}\langle x, y, z\rangle + \underline{\tau})$$

4.9   Encoding Brane into Core-$\pi@$

In the encodings of BioAmbients and Brane previously defined, we used three priority levels and up to three names for each channel in $\pi@$. In order to provide similar encodings in core-$\pi@$, we need now to use not more than two names for channel and two priority levels.

The expedient for reducing the number of names needed for encoding capabilities and actions is very simple: for example, the $exo_n/exo_n^{\perp}$ action can be encoded with the only name exo_n (where the underscore character '$\_$' is used just for sake of clarity and is part of the string representing the name) instead of the two names exo and n joint by polyadic synchronisation as $exo@n$. Anyway, the (unique) consequence of this change in the encoding is the multiplication of the names needed for representing each private name in BioAmbients. In fact, each BioAmbients name n must now be translated as a vector

$$(enter\_n, expel\_n, merge\_n, local\_n, s2s\_n, p2c\_n, c2p\_n)$$

in order to allow each different communication or capability to operate independently. Since Brane lacks restriction and name passing, its encoding in $\pi@$ is not affected by such conversion.

The reduction of the number of levels of priority influences the encoding of both languages. In the definition of the previous encoding functions, one prioritised intermediate level was used to "garbage-collect", by means of a prioritised

τ action, the $BCAST$ processes which terminated the loop with broadcast-like effect. Here we recall the definition of $BCAST$:

$$BCAST \quad \triangleq \quad !\;\underline{bcast}(x,y,z).(\overline{x@y}\langle z\rangle.\overline{\underline{bcast}}\langle x,y,z\rangle + \underline{\tau})$$

A naive way to reduce the number of priority levels would be to decrease the priority level of both the τ transition (which would become a normal low priority transition) and all the other high priority reductions (which would still be prioritised). The definition of the $BCAST$ process would be consequently modified as follows:

$$BCAST \quad \triangleq \quad !\;bcast(x,y,z).(\overline{x@y}\langle z\rangle.\overline{bcast}\langle x,y,z\rangle + \tau)$$

The problem with this definition of $BCAST$ is that there is no way to know *when* the above τ transition will be executed and the loop will terminate its action. In principle this would not constitute an important issue, since the high priority of the reductions over $x@y$ and $bcast$ would force the loop to be interrupted when all the processes waiting for a possible broadcast on the corresponding channel have been notified of the new compartment or ambient name. Unfortunately, a spurious process

$$SP \quad \triangleq \quad \overline{x@y}\langle z\rangle.\overline{bcast}\langle x,y,z\rangle + \tau$$

would still be around, ready to interfere with the normal behaviour of the system over some channel $x@y$. Such interference may happen for example in the encoding of the following Brane system:

$$S \quad \triangleq \quad \overbrace{\underbrace{phago.\sigma|\sigma'(\!|\,P\,|\!)}_{c_2} \circ \underbrace{phago^{\perp}(exo.\gamma).exo^{\perp}.\rho(\!|\,Q\,|\!)}_{c_3}}^{c_1}$$

c_1 represents the name of the parent compartment of the whole system S, c_2 and c_3 are the names corresponding to the immediate compartments of its two subsystems. S undergoes the following reductions:

$$S \quad \rightarrow \quad S' \quad \rightarrow \quad S''$$

with

$$S' \quad \triangleq \quad exo^{\perp}.\rho(\!|\,exo.\gamma(\!|\,\overbrace{\underbrace{\sigma|\sigma'(\!|\,P\,|\!)}_{c_2}}^{c_4}\,|\!)\,|\!) \circ Q\,|\!)$$

and

$$S'' \quad \triangleq \quad \overbrace{\underbrace{\sigma|\sigma'(\!|\,P\,|\!)}_{c_2}}^{c_1} \circ \rho|\gamma(\!|\,Q\,|\!)$$

After the first reduction, a fresh membrane is represented by the name c_4 which is then lost after the following exo operation. The $BCAST$ loop triggered by the encoding of the first reduction would be spawned by the process performing the *phago* action with parameters c_1, c_2, c_4, in order to make all the branes in σ' replace their parent compartment c_1 by the fresh compartment c_4. Such $BCAST$ loop may leave the following spurious process:

$$SP \quad \triangleq \quad \overline{c_1 @ c_2} \langle c_4 \rangle . \overline{bcast} \langle c_1, c_2, c_4 \rangle + \tau$$

The use of three priority levels, with an intermediate prioritised level for τ, would have forced SP to disappear before the transition

$$[\![\, S' \,]\!]^{\beta} \; \rightarrow \; [\![\, S'' \,]\!]^{\beta}$$

while with only two levels it may be still present in parallel composition with $[\![\, S'' \,]\!]^{\beta}$. This means that the subprocess $[\![\, \sigma | \sigma' (\!| P |\!) \,]\!]^{\beta}$ of the encoded system S'' may be still subject to the effect of SP and be moved again into the parent compartment identified by c_4, even if such compartment is not present anymore in the original Brane process.

In order to avoid this annoying side effect, we must ensure that any residual SP process is totally isolated from the the system. This can be achieved by using two names c, c_b for each compartment, c for the low-priority synchronisation of processes corresponding to actions, communications and capabilities, while c_b for the high-priority sequence of broadcast actions. After each broadcast, the name c_b is forgotten completely by all the processes and replaced by a new name c_b' for the next broadcast. Consequently, each SP process remaining after the regular end of the broadcasting loop is not able to communicate with the system, so it is going to disappear spontaneously by executing the internal τ action after a while. If we denote any pair of names n, n_b as $\ddot{n}$, the new encoding functions $[\![\, \cdot \,]\!]^{\beta'}$ from Brane to core-π@ and $[\![\, \cdot \,]\!]^{\alpha'}$ from BioAmbients to core-π@ have almost the same shape as the previous functions $[\![\, \cdot \,]\!]^{\beta}$ and $[\![\, \cdot \,]\!]^{\alpha}$. For example, the parallel composition of Brane systems is encoded as

$$[\![\, P \circ Q \,]\!]^{\beta'}_{K, \ddot{pc}} \quad \triangleq \quad [\![\, P \,]\!]^{\beta'}_{K, \ddot{pc}} \;|\; [\![\, Q \,]\!]^{\beta'}_{K, \ddot{pc}}$$

with the only difference of the names of compartments which are now paired as discussed. The definition of the processes $TREE$ and $BCAST$ reveals how name pairs are handled:

$$BCAST \quad \triangleq \quad !\, \underline{bc} @ bcast(x, y, ny_b, \ddot{z}).$$
$$(\tau + \overline{x} @ y \langle ny_b, \ddot{z} \rangle . \overline{bc} @ bcast \langle x, y, ny_b, \ddot{z} \rangle)$$

$$TREE(b, \ddot{c}, \ddot{pc}) \quad \triangleq \quad \underline{pc} @ c_b(nc_b, \ddot{x}).\overline{cycle} @ b \langle c, nc_b, \ddot{x} \rangle +$$
$$\underline{exo} @ pc_b(npc_b, \ddot{x}).\overline{cycle} @ b \langle \ddot{c}, \ddot{x} \rangle +$$
$$\underline{exo} @ c_b(nc_b, \ddot{x}).\overline{cycle} @ b \langle \ddot{pc}, \ddot{x} \rangle$$

The presence of the names bc and $cycle$ is due to the definition of core-π@ grammar, which does not allow to denote channels by means of only one name.

The $BCAST$ process is not substantially changed, except for the number of names (five instead of three) handled during the loop: the first two identify the

Table 5. Encoding of Brane processes into core-π@

$$[\![\, \diamond \,]\!]^{\beta'} \triangleq \mathbf{0}$$

$$[\![\, P \circ Q \,]\!]^{\beta'} \triangleq [\![\, P \,]\!]^{\beta'} \mid [\![\, Q \,]\!]^{\beta'}$$

$$[\![\, !P \,]\!]^{\beta'} \triangleq [\![\, !P \,]\!]^{\beta'}_{\emptyset, \ddot{o}c}$$

$$[\![\, \sigma(\!|P|\!) \,]\!]^{\beta'} \triangleq [\![\, \sigma(\!|P|\!) \,]\!]^{\beta'}_{\emptyset, \ddot{o}c}$$

$$[\![\, \diamond \,]\!]^{\beta'}_{K, \ddot{p}c} \triangleq \mathbf{0}$$

$$[\![\, P \circ Q \,]\!]^{\beta'}_{K, \ddot{p}c} \triangleq [\![\, P \,]\!]^{\beta'}_{K, \ddot{p}c} \mid [\![\, Q \,]\!]^{\beta'}_{K, \ddot{p}c}$$

$$[\![\, \sigma(\!|P|\!) \,]\!]^{\beta'}_{K, \ddot{p}c} \triangleq (\nu\, \ddot{c})([\![\, \sigma \,]\!]^{\beta'}_{K, \ddot{c}, \ddot{p}c} \mid [\![\, P \,]\!]^{\beta'}_{K, \ddot{c}})$$

$$[\![\, 0 \,]\!]^{\beta'}_{K, \ddot{c}, \ddot{p}c} \triangleq \mathbf{0}$$

$$[\![\, \sigma \mid \rho \,]\!]^{\beta'}_{K, \ddot{c}, \ddot{p}c} \triangleq [\![\, \sigma \,]\!]^{\beta'}_{K, \ddot{c}, \ddot{p}c} \mid [\![\, \rho \,]\!]^{\beta'}_{K, \ddot{c}, \ddot{p}c}$$

$$[\![\, !P \,]\!]^{\beta'}_{K, \ddot{p}c} \triangleq (\nu\, b)\big(BANG'(b, \ddot{p}c) \mid$$
$$[\![\, P \,]\!]^{\beta'}_{K \cup \{b\}, \ddot{p}c} \mid [\![\, P \,]\!]^{\beta'}_{K \cup \{b\}, \ddot{p}c} \mid$$
$$!\,\underline{new}@b(n\ddot{p}c).[\![\, P \,]\!]^{\beta'}_{K \cup \{b\}, n\ddot{p}c}\big)$$

$$[\![\, !\sigma \,]\!]^{\beta'}_{K, \ddot{c}, \ddot{p}c} \triangleq (\nu\, b)\big(BANG(b, \ddot{c}, \ddot{p}c) \mid$$
$$[\![\, \sigma \,]\!]^{\beta'}_{K \cup \{b\}, \ddot{c}, \ddot{p}c} \mid [\![\, \sigma \,]\!]^{\beta'}_{K \cup \{b\}, \ddot{c}, \ddot{p}c} \mid$$
$$!\,\underline{new}@b(\ddot{n}c, n\ddot{p}c).[\![\, \sigma \,]\!]^{\beta'}_{K \cup \{b\}, \ddot{n}c, n\ddot{p}c}\big)$$

$$BANG(b, \ddot{c}, \ddot{p}c) \triangleq !\,\underline{cycle}@b(\ddot{n}c, n\ddot{p}c).SUBBANG(b, \ddot{n}c, n\ddot{p}c) \mid$$
$$SUBBANG(b, \ddot{c}, \ddot{p}c)$$

$$BANG'(b, n\ddot{p}c) \triangleq !\,\underline{cycle}@b(n\ddot{p}c).SUBBANG'(b, n\ddot{p}c) \mid$$
$$SUBBANG'(b, \ddot{p}c)$$

$$SUBBANG(b, \ddot{n}c, n\ddot{p}c) \triangleq \underline{unfold}@b().\overline{\underline{new}}@b\langle \ddot{n}c, n\ddot{p}c\rangle.\overline{\underline{cycle}}@b\langle \ddot{n}c, n\ddot{p}c\rangle +$$
$$TREE(b, \ddot{n}c, n\ddot{p}c)$$

$$SUBBANG'(b, n\ddot{p}c) \triangleq \underline{unfold}@b().\overline{\underline{new}}@b\langle n\ddot{p}c\rangle.\overline{\underline{cycle}}@b\langle n\ddot{p}c\rangle +$$
$$\underline{exo}@npc_b(nnpc_b, \ddot{x}).\overline{\underline{cycle}}@b\langle \ddot{x}\rangle$$

$$TREE(b, \ddot{n}c, n\ddot{p}c) \triangleq npc@nc_b(nnc_b, \ddot{x}).\overline{\underline{cycle}}@b\langle nc, nnc_b, \ddot{x}\rangle +$$
$$\underline{exo}@npc_b(nnpc_b, \ddot{x}).\overline{\underline{cycle}}@b\langle \ddot{n}c, \ddot{x}\rangle +$$
$$\underline{exo}@nc_b(nnc_b, \ddot{x}).\overline{\underline{cycle}}@b\langle n\ddot{p}c, \ddot{x}\rangle$$

Table 6. Encoding of Brane actions into core-π@

$$\llbracket a.\sigma \rrbracket_{K,\ddot{c},\ddot{p}c}^{\beta'} \triangleq BCAST \mid (\nu\, s)(!\, \underline{cycle}@s(\ddot{n}c, n\ddot{p}c).$$

$$(\llbracket a.\sigma \rrbracket_{K,\ddot{n}c,n\ddot{p}c}^{\beta'\,*} + TREE(s, \ddot{n}c, n\ddot{p}c)) \mid$$

$$\llbracket a.\sigma \rrbracket_{K,\ddot{c},\ddot{p}c}^{\beta'\,*} + TREE(s, \ddot{c}, \ddot{p}c))$$

$$\llbracket phago_n.\sigma \rrbracket_{K,\ddot{c},\ddot{p}c}^{\beta'\,*} \triangleq phago\_n@pc(\ddot{x}).$$

$$(\nu\, nc_b)(\overline{bc}@bcast\langle pc, c_b, nc_b, \ddot{x}\rangle.(\llbracket \sigma \rrbracket_{\emptyset,c,nc_b,\ddot{x}}^{\beta'} \mid \Pi_K)$$

$$\llbracket phago_n^\perp(\rho).\sigma \rrbracket_{K,\ddot{c},\ddot{p}c}^{\beta'\,*} \triangleq (\nu\, \ddot{x})(\overline{phago\_n}@pc\langle\ddot{x}\rangle.(\llbracket \sigma \rrbracket_{\emptyset,\ddot{c},\ddot{p}c}^{\beta'} \mid \llbracket \rho \rrbracket_{\emptyset,\ddot{x},\ddot{c}}^{\beta'} \mid \Pi_K)$$

$$\llbracket exo_n.\sigma \rrbracket_{K,\ddot{c},\ddot{p}c}^{\beta'\,*} \triangleq exo\_n@pc(\ddot{x}).$$

$$(\nu\, nc_b)(\, \overline{bc}@bcast\langle exo, c_b, nc_b, \ddot{x}\rangle.\llbracket \sigma \rrbracket_{\emptyset,\ddot{p}c,\ddot{x}}^{\beta'} \mid \Pi_K)$$

$$\llbracket exo_n^\perp.\sigma \rrbracket_{K,\ddot{c},\ddot{p}c}^{\beta'\,*} \triangleq \overline{exo\_n}@c\langle\ddot{p}c\rangle.(\llbracket \sigma \rrbracket_{\emptyset,\ddot{c},\ddot{p}c}^{\beta'} \mid \Pi_K)$$

$$\llbracket pino(\rho).\sigma \rrbracket_{K,\ddot{c},\ddot{p}c}^{\beta'\,*} \triangleq (\nu\, \ddot{x})\tau.(\llbracket \sigma \rrbracket_{\emptyset,\ddot{c},\ddot{p}c}^{\beta'} \mid \llbracket \rho \rrbracket_{\emptyset,\ddot{x},\ddot{c}}^{\beta'} \mid \Pi_K)$$

$$\Pi_K \triangleq \overline{unfold}@k_1\langle\rangle \mid \cdots \mid \overline{unfold}@k_n\langle\rangle$$

$$\text{with} \quad K = \{k_1,\ldots,k_n\}$$

$$BCAST \triangleq !\, \underline{bc}@bcast(x, y, ny_b, \ddot{z}).$$

$$(\tau + \underline{x}@y\langle ny_b, \ddot{z}\rangle.\overline{bc}@bcast\langle x, y, ny_b, \ddot{z}\rangle)$$

channel $x@y$ where the broadcast will occur, while $\ddot{z} = z, z_b$ denote the two names associated with the compartment undergoing some structural change. The name ny_b constitute the replacement of y for the next broadcast occurring in the related compartment.

Accordingly, the $TREE$ subprocess receives the three names $nc_b, \ddot{x}$ (with $\ddot{x} = x, x_b$) instead of only one. nc_b is used in the first branch of the choice as new broadcast name associated with c in substitution to c_b, in consistency with the encoded $phago$ operation which updates the names of the parent compartment pc for all the processes in c. The encoded exo action is characterised by the peculiar property of eliminating already the name of the inner compartment where the broadcast happens, so that the new name nc_b is useless in the second and third branch of the $TREE$ process (and in fact it disappears). The same would happen with BioAmbients $merge$ capability.

The encoding of actions should be consistently updated. The $phago^\perp$ co-action is not substantially changed:

$$\llbracket phago_n^\perp(\rho).\sigma \rrbracket_{K,\ddot{c},\ddot{p}c}^{\beta'\,*} \triangleq (\nu\, \ddot{x})(\overline{phago\_n}@pc\langle\ddot{x}\rangle.$$

$$(\llbracket \, \sigma \, \rrbracket_{\emptyset,\ddot{c},\ddot{p}c}^{\beta'} \mid \llbracket \, \rho \, \rrbracket_{\emptyset,\ddot{x},\ddot{c}}^{\beta'} \mid \varPi_K)$$

Each action which triggers a $BCAST$ process requires the creation of the new name nc_b previously discussed:

$$\llbracket \, phago_n.\sigma \, \rrbracket_{K,\ddot{c},\ddot{p}c}^{\beta'\,*} \quad \triangleq \quad phago\_n@pc(\ddot{x}).(\nu \ nc_b)$$

$$(\overline{bc}@bcast\langle pc, c_b, nc_b, \ddot{x}\rangle.(\llbracket \, \sigma \, \rrbracket_{\emptyset,c,nc_b,\ddot{x}}^{\beta'} \mid \varPi_K)$$

nc_b is substituted for c_b here as well, as we can notice from the parameters used in the recursive call of the encoding function.

In Table 5 and Table 6 the full encoding of Brane into core-π@ is reported. The encoding of BioAmbients is based on the same ideas and does not require further insights, so it is left as exercise to the reader.

5   Conclusion and Future Perspectives

The language π@ has been introduced with the aim to play a pivotal role in comparing the many compartment-based. bio-inspired process calculi. Its distinguishing features is that it is a plain, conservative extension to π-calculus with the additional features of polyadic synchronisation and prioritised communication. Our claim is substantiated by the encoding of two well-known such formalisms, BioAmbients and Brane Calculi, into π@, and this is even reinforced by a recent paper [31] offering an encoding into π@ of Beta-binders [12,13], another complex model for compartmentalised, bio-inspired behaviour.

The kernel language core-π@ is extremely interesting because it can be provided of a stochastic semantics in a very simple and clean way. In [23,24] the stochastic language Sπ@ (stochastic paillette) is proposed as a natural stochastic version of core-π@, and provided with a generalisation of Gillespie simulation algorithm [32] to multi-compartments. Its stochastic semantics is obtained by the simple addition of polyadic synchronisation to the stochastic π-Calculus, thanks to the possibility of exploiting infinite rate transitions as alternative definition of (one additional level of) priority.

This opens the way to multi-compartment simulation algorithms also for all the bio-inspired calculi that can be encoded faithfully into core-π@, such as Brane Calculi and BioAmbients. Higher level semantic features like those considered in [33] may constitute a valid mean to facilitate the organisation of the code and increase readability and usability of such encodings.

One of the two key features of π@ is priority. However, the power of the global preemption mechanism which it is based on seems to prevent the definition of encodings that are not centralised (i.e., such that the execution can be parallelised or distributed). This seems an obstacle that cannot be overcome. In [34] we have studied the expressive power of two forms of priority (i.e., global and local) and showed that they give to π-calculus a strict increase of expressiveness, so strong that it seems impossible to identify prioritised construct easier to implement in a parallel, if not distributed, framework.

References

1. Fontana, W., Buss, L.: The Barrier of Objects: From Dynamical Systems to Bounded Organizations. In: Casti, J., Karlqvist, A. (eds.) Boundaries and Barriers, pp. 56–116. Addison-Wesley, Reading (1996)
2. Regev, A., Silverman, W., Shapiro, E.Y.: Representation and simulation of biochemical processes using the pi-calculus process algebra. In: Pacific Symposium on Biocomputing, pp. 459–470 (2001)
3. Milner, R., Parrow, J., Walker, D.: A calculus of mobile processes, i and ii. Inf. Comput. 100(1), 1–77 (1992)
4. Priami, C.: Stochastic pi-calculus. Comput. J. 38(7), 578–589 (1995)
5. Priami, C., Regev, A., Shapiro, E.Y., Silverman, W.: Application of a stochastic name-passing calculus to representation and simulation of molecular processes. Inf. Process. Lett. 80(1), 25–31 (2001)
6. Curti, M., Degano, P., Priami, C., Baldari, C.T.: Modelling biochemical pathways through enhanced pi-calculus. Theor. Comput. Sci. 325(1), 111–140 (2004)
7. Lecca, P., Priami, C., Laudanna, C., Constantin, G.: Predicting cell adhesion probability via the biochemical stochastic pi-calculus. In: Haddad, H., Omicini, A., Wainwright, R.L., Liebrock, L.M. (eds.) Symposium on Applied Computing, pp. 211–212. ACM, New York (2004)
8. Chiarugi, D., Curti, M., Degano, P., Marangoni, R.: Vice: A virtual cell. In: [35], pp. 207–220 (2004)
9. Cardelli, L.: Brane calculi. In: [35], pp. 257–278 (2004)
10. Danos, V., Pradalier, S.: Projective brane calculus. In: [35], pp. 134–148 (2004)
11. Regev, A., Panina, E.M., Silverman, W., Cardelli, L., Shapiro, E.Y.: Bioambients: an abstraction for biological compartments. Theor. Comput. Sci. 325(1), 141–167 (2004)
12. Priami, C., Quaglia, P.: Beta binders for biological interactions. In: [35], pp. 20–33 (2004)
13. Degano, P., Prandi, D., Priami, C., Quaglia, P.: Beta-binders for Biological Quantitative Experiments. Electronic Notes in Theoretical Computer Science 164(3), 101–117 (2006)
14. Danos, V., Laneve, C.: Formal molecular biology. Theor. Comput. Sci. 325(1), 69–110 (2004)
15. Laneve, C., Tarissan, F.: A simple calculus for proteins and cells. Electr. Notes Theor. Comput. Sci. 171(2), 139–154 (2007)
16. Carbone, M., Maffeis, S.: On the expressive power of polyadic synchronisation in pi-calculus. Nord. J. Comput. 10(2), 70–98 (2003)
17. Milner, R., Parrow, J., Walker, D.: A calculus of mobile processes, i. Inf. Comput. 100(1), 1–40 (1992)
18. Milner, R., Parrow, J., Walker, D.: A calculus of mobile processes, ii. Inf. Comput. 100(1), 41–77 (1992)
19. Milner, R.: Communication and concurrency. Prentice-Hall, Inc, Englewood Cliffs (1989)
20. Milner, R.: The polyadic pi-calculus: a tutorial. In: Bauer, F.L., Brauer, W., Schwichtenberg, H. (eds.) Logic and Algebra of Specification, pp. 203–246. Springer, Heidelberg (1993)
21. Milner, R.: Communicating and mobile systems: the π-calculus. Cambridge University Press, New York (1999)

22. Cleaveland, R., Lüttgen, G., Natarajan, V.: Priority in process algebra. In: Bergstra, J., Ponse, A., Smolka, S. (eds.) Handbook of Process Algebra, pp. 711–765. Elsevier Science Publishers, Amsterdam (2001)
23. Versari, C., Busi, N.: Stochastic simulation of biological systems with dynamical compartment structure. In: Calder, M., Gilmore, S. (eds.) CMSB 2007. LNCS (LNBI), vol. 4695, pp. 80–95. Springer, Heidelberg (2007)
24. Versari, C., Busi, N.: Efficient Stochastic Simulation of Biological Systems with Multiple Variable Volumes. Electronic Notes in Theoretical Computer Science 194(3), 165–180 (2008)
25. Cardelli, L., Gordon, A.D.: Mobile ambients. In: Nivat, M. (ed.) ETAPS 1998 and FOSSACS 1998. LNCS, vol. 1378, pp. 140–155. Springer, Heidelberg (1998)
26. Cardelli, L., Gordon, A.D.: Mobile ambients. Theoretical Computer Science 240(1), 177–213 (2000)
27. Nestmann, U., Pierce, B.C.: Decoding choice encodings. Inf. Comput. 163(1), 1–59 (2000)
28. Busi, N., Gorrieri, R.: On the computational power of brane calculi. In: Priami, C., Plotkin, G. (eds.) Transactions on Computational Systems Biology VI. LNCS (LNBI), vol. 4220, pp. 16–43. Springer, Heidelberg (2006)
29. Palamidessi, C.: Comparing the expressive power of the synchronous and asynchronous pi-calculi. Mathematical Structures in Computer Science 13(5), 685–719 (2003)
30. de Boer, F.S., Palamidessi, C.: Embedding as a tool for language comparison. Inf. Comput. 108(1), 128–157 (1994)
31. Cappello, I., Quaglia, P.: A translation of beta-binders in a prioritized pi-calculus (to appear, 2008)
32. Gillespie, D.T.: Exact stochastic simulation of coupled chemical reactions. J. Phys. Chem. 81(25), 2340–2361 (1977)
33. Kuttler, C., Lhoussaine, C., Niehren, J.: A stochastic pi calculus for concurrent objects. In: Anai, H., Horimoto, K., Kutsia, T. (eds.) Ab 2007. LNCS, vol. 4545, pp. 232–246. Springer, Heidelberg (2007)
34. Versari, C., Busi, N., Gorrieri, R.: On the expressive power of global and local priority in process calculi. In: Caires, L., Vasconcelos, V.T. (eds.) CONCUR. LNCS, vol. 4703, pp. 241–255. Springer, Heidelberg (2007)
35. Danos, V., Schächter, V. (eds.): Computational Methods in Systems Biology, International Conference CMSB 2004. In: Danos, V., Schachter, V. (eds.) CMSB 2004. LNCS (LNBI), vol. 3082, Springer, Heidelberg (2005)

A Gentle Introduction to
Stochastic (Poly)Automata Collectives
and the (Bio)Chemical Ground Form⋆

Gianluigi Zavattaro

Dip. Scienze dell'Informazione, Università di Bologna, Italy.
zavattar@cs.unibo.it

Abstract. We present uniformly four related models for the representation of biochemical systems recently proposed in the literature in different publications. Namely, we consider Stochastic Automata Collectives (SAC) [2], Stochastic Polyautomata Collectives (SPC) [2], Chemical Ground Form (CGF) [3], and Biochemical Ground Form (BGF) [4].

1 Introduction

The aim of this paper is to provide a unified introduction to four related models for the representation of biochemical systems recently proposed in the literature in three different papers. Namely, we present Stochastic Automata Collectives (SAC) [2], Stochastic Polyautomata Collectives (SPC) [2], the Chemical Ground Form (CGF) [3], and the Biochemical Ground Form (BGF) [4]. The first pair of models are based on a graphical automata-based notation, while the second pair of models have been defined with a formal syntax and semantics similar to those of traditional (stochastic) process algebras.

We unify the presentation of the four models presenting for all of them both a graphical and a process algebraic notation. For the sake of readability, we do not report the definition of the formal semantics of the calculi that can be found in [4]. Moreover, we gently introduce the four models using several examples that allow us to focus on the specific differences and similarities among the four different models.

The remainder of the paper is divided in four Sections, one for each of the considered models.

2 Stochastic Automata Collectives

In this section we introduce Stochastic Automata Collectives (SAC), the notation for the representation of chemical systems presented in [2]. In that paper, SAC are

---

⋆ This paper is an introductory material to the lecture "Expressiveness Issues in Calculi for Artificial Biochemistry" given by the author at the summer school SFM-08:Bio. More precisely, the calculi considered in the lecture are gently and uniformly introduced.

M. Bernardo, P. Degano, and G. Zavattaro (Eds.): SFM 2008, LNCS 5016, pp. 507–523, 2008.

only informally presented. In order to equip this model with a formal semantics, we simply observe that this model is a fragment of CGF, a process algebra whose formal syntax and semantics have been defined in [3]. We characterize the precise fragment defining a syntax for SAC as a subset of the syntax of CGF. The reader interested in the definition of the formal semantics of SAC can then refer to [3] where the semantics of the whole CGF is reported.

Before presenting SAC, we introduce the running example for this section.

Example 1 (Two-stations rotaxane). We consider two-stations rotaxanes [10] (simply called rotaxanes in the following), which are supramolecular systems composed of an axle surrounded by a ring-type molecule. Bulky chemical moieties ("stoppers") are placed at the extremities of the axle to prevent the disassembly of the system. In rotaxanes containing two different recognition sites on the axle ("stations"), it is possible to switch the position of the ring between the two stations by an external energy input (called the "stimulus") as illustrated in Figure 1. The part (a) of the figure represents the structure of the rotaxane,

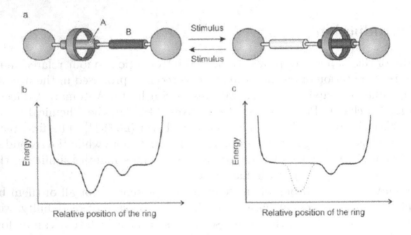

Fig. 1. Representation of a rotaxane with stations A and B (a) and its energy curves before (b) and after (c) the stimulus activating the ring movement from A to B

while in part (b) and (c) the energy curves before and after the stimulus are depicted: in the former the energy minimum corresponds to station A, while in the latter it corresponds to station B. For this reason, the stimulus triggers the shuttling of the ring from station A to station B.

It is worth mentioning that several rotaxanes of this kind, known as *molecular shuttles*, have been already developed (see [5] and the references therein) and used for building more complex systems [8,7,1].

We complete the example presenting a modeling of the behavior of the rotaxane given in chemical reaction style. We call the two stations of the rotaxane A and B, respectively, and we call S the species of the molecules that stimulates the movement of the ring from station A to station B. We consider four distinct species for the representation of the rotaxane: R^A (resp. R^B) representing the *nonstimulated* rotaxane with the ring in position A (resp. B), and R_s^A (resp. R_s^B) representing the *stimulated* rotaxane with the ring in position A (resp. B).

The chemical reactions are as follows (here we abstract away from the rates of the reactions that will be discussed in the next Example 2):

$$R^A + S \rightarrow R_s^A$$
$$R^B + S \rightarrow R_s^B$$
$$R_s^A \leftrightarrow R_s^B$$
$$R^A \leftrightarrow R^B$$

We consider two bi-molecular reactions and two mono-molecular invertible reactions. The first two represents the reaction between the stimulus and the rotaxane. As the rotaxane has two nonstimulated species R^A and R^B, we need to consider two distinct reactions, one for each of these species. The two monomolecular bidirectional reactions model the movement of the ring. We need to consider two distinct reactions because by Brownian motion we can assume that the ring can move from station A to station B, and vice versa, both when the rotaxane is stimulated and when it is not stimulated.

We now introduce SAC. It is an automata based notation in which each state of an automaton corresponds to a chemical species X, and each outgoing transition from state X represents one possible reaction in which the molecules of species X can be engaged. The transitions are labeled with one of three possible kinds of labels. The label $\tau_{(r)}$ indicates the possibility for one molecule to be engaged in a unary reaction with stochastic rate r. On the contrary, the transitions labeled with $?a_{(r)}$ and $!a_{(r)}$ models the complementary transitions executed by the two reacting molecules. The name a is a name used to identify the reaction, while r is a stochastic rate; both the name a and the rate r must match for the reaction to be enabled. For instance, if the states associated to the species X and Y have outgoing transitions labeled with $?a_{(r)}$ and $!a_{(r)}$, respectively, we have that one molecule of species X can react with one molecule of species Y, and the time needed for this reaction to occur is distributed according to exponential distribution with rate r. The target states of the transitions represent the species of the product of the reaction. For instance, if the two above transitions labeled with $?a_{(r)}$ and $!a_{(r)}$ have the species X' and Y' as target state, respectively, we have that the product of the reaction is given by two molecules, one of species X' and one of species Y'.

As a less trivial example of SAC, we model the rotaxane of the Example 1.

Example 2 (Modeling rotaxanes in SAC –graphical notation–). We present the modeling of rotaxanes in SAC. The main difference between this new modeling and the one proposed in the Example 1 is that it is molecular oriented instead of reaction oriented. In other words, the modeling approach of SAC is based on the description of the behavior of a molecule based on the sequence of reactions in which a molecule can be engaged during its lifetime. Such behavior is depicted in Figure 2. It is worth noting that the SAC modeling is based on two distinct

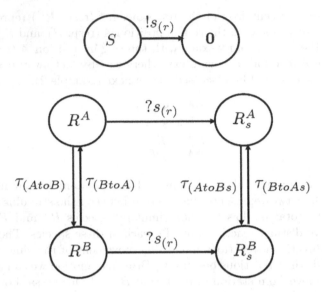

Fig. 2. Behavior of a rotaxane depicted as a stochastic automata collective

automata; one for the description of the behavior of the stimulus S, and one for
the behavior of the rotaxane. The stimulus can only be engaged in a reaction
(that we call a) in order to stimulate the rotaxane. After this reaction, the
molecule is "consumed" (i.e. it forms a complex with the rotaxane). Consumed
molecules, are modeled with a special species that we denote with **0**. On the
contrary, the modeling of the rotaxane includes bi-directional transitions for
the ring shuttling, and the complementary transitions for the reaction with the
stimulus.

We conclude this example reporting a discussion about the rates that are included in the SAC modeling as symbolic (i.e. we use names instead of positive real
numbers) subscripts of the transition labels. The rate r is the stochastic rate for
the bi-molecular reaction between the rotaxane and the stimulus. As far as the
ring shuttling is concerned, we recall that, by Brownian motion, we assume that
the ring can move from station A to station B, and vice versa, both when the
rotaxane is stimulated and when it is not stimulated. Different rates are considered for these movements: $AtoB$ (resp. $AtoBs$) for the movement from station
A to station B when the rotaxane is nonstimulated (resp. stimulated), $BtoA$
(resp. $BtoAs$) for the opposite movement. According to the energy minimum in
the two distributions in Figure 1 parts (b) and (c), we have that $AtoB < BtoA$
and $AtoBs > BtoAs$. Thus, according to the stochastic behavior of these monomolecular reactions, when the rotaxane is stimulated (resp. nonstimulated), the
sojourn time of the ring on station A (resp. B) is longer than the sojourn time
on station B (resp. A).

We complete this section describing a formal syntax for SAC. This is obtained
as a fragment of a process algebra, called Chemical Ground Form (CGF) defined

in [3]. According to this syntax, each species has an associated definition describing the possible actions for the molecules of that species. There are three kinds of actions that coincide with the possible labels for transitions in SAC. Namely, we have the action $\tau_{(r)}$ indicating the possibility for a molecule to be engaged in a unary reaction. For instance, the definition $A = \tau_{(r)}; B$ is used to specify the possibility for one molecule of species A to be engaged in a unary reaction that produces one molecule of species B. Binary reactions have two reactants. The two reactants perform two complementary actions $?a_{(r)}$ and $!a_{(r)}$, where a is a name used to identify the reaction; both the name a and the rate r must match for the reaction to be enabled. For instance, given the definitions $A = ?a_{(r)}; C$ and $B = !a_{(r)}; D$, we have that two molecules of species A and B can be engaged in a binary reaction that produces two molecules, one of species C and one of species D. If the molecules of one species can be engaged in several reactions, then the corresponding definition admits a choice among several actions. The syntax of choice is as follows: $A = \tau_{(r)}; B \oplus ?a_{(r')}; C$, meaning that molecules of species A can be engaged in either a unary reaction that produces a molecule of species B, or in a binary reaction with another molecule able to execute the complementary action $!a_{(r')}$. In the second case, the molecule of species A contributes to the reaction by producing a new molecule of species C.

We are now ready to define formally the syntax for Stochastic Automata Collectives.

Definition 1 (Stochastic Automata Collectives (SAC)). *Consider the following denumerable sets:* Species *ranged over by variables* $X, Y, \cdots$, Channels *ranged over by* $a, b, \cdots$, *Moreover, let* $r, s, \cdots$ *be rates (i.e. positive real numbers).*

The syntax of SAC *is as follows (where the big* | *separates syntactic alternatives while the small* | *denotes parallel composition):*

$$
\begin{array}{llll}
E & ::= & \mathbf{0} \mid X = M, E & \text{Reagents} \\
M & ::= & \mathbf{0} \mid \pi; X \oplus M & \text{Molecule} \\
P & ::= & \mathbf{0} \mid X \mid P & \text{Solution} \\
\pi & ::= & \tau_{(r)} \mid ?a_{(r)} \mid !a_{(r)} & \text{Internal, Input, Output prefix} \\
\text{SAC} & ::= & (E, P) & \text{Reagents and initial Solution}
\end{array}
$$

Given a SAC (E, P), *we assume that all variables occurring in* P *occur also in* E. *Moreover, for every variable* X *occurring in* E, *there is exactly one definition* $X = M$ *in* E.

In the following, trailing $\mathbf{0}$ are usually left implicit, and we use | also as an operator over the syntax: if P and P' are $\mathbf{0}$-terminated lists of variables, according to the syntax above, then $P|P'$ means appending the two lists into a single $\mathbf{0}$-terminated list. Therefore, if P is a solution, then $\mathbf{0}|P$, $P|\mathbf{0}$, and P are syntactically equal. Moreover, the solution composed of k instances of X is denoted with $\prod_k X$.

As an example of exploitation of the SAC syntax, we report the syntax for the modeling of the rotaxane graphically depicted in the Figure 2 and discussed in the Example 2.

Example 3 (Modeling rotaxanes in SAC –formal syntax–). We can consider the following definitions for the species R^A, R^B, R_s^A, R_s^B, and S used in the previous examples.

$$
\begin{aligned}
R^A &= \tau_{(AtoB)}; R^B \oplus ?s_{(r)}; R_s^A \\
R^B &= \tau_{(BtoA)}; R^A \oplus ?s_{(r)}; R_s^B \\
R_s^A &= \tau_{(AtoBs)}; R_s^B \\
R_s^B &= \tau_{(BtoAs)}; R_s^A \\
S &= !s_{(r)}; \mathbf{0}
\end{aligned}
$$

where $\mathbf{0}$ specifies reactions which have no product. Let E be the sequence of definitions of the species R^A, R^B, R_s^A, R_s^B, and S are defined above. A solution with one instance of non-stimulated rotaxane with the ring on station A and 2 instances of stimulus, is represented by the SAC $(E, R^A|S|S)$.

As already discussed, the syntax of SAC is obtained as a fragment of the process algebra CGF defined in [3]. More precisely, the fragment is simply obtained imposing that after an action π only one molecule can be produced, i.e. using the syntax $\pi; X$ instead of the more general syntax $\pi; (X_1|\cdots|X_n)$ of CGF. In [3] also the formal semantics for CGF is defined; here we simply recall how the semantics is defined without reporting the full definition (the interested reader can refer to [3]).

The semantics is obtained associating to each term of the process algebra a Continuous Time Markov Chain (CTMC). Such CTMC is obtained in two steps. First, a labeled transition graph (LTG) is defined which represents all possible actions that can be executed by the molecules in the considered solution. Second, a CTMC is extracted from such labeled transition graph by collapsing those transitions which share the same source and target solutions in one CTMC transition, whose rate is the sum of the rates of the collapsed transitions.

More precisely, the labeled transition graph is a labaled transition system among solutions that consider two possible kinds of labels: $i : r$ and $i, j : r$ representing, respectively, mono-molecular reactions with rate r involving the i-th molecule and bi-molecular reactions with rate r involving the i-th and the j-th molecules. As an example of labeled transition graph, we consider the SAC $(E, R^A|S|S)$ defined in the example 3.

Example 4 (LTG of a rotaxane). As an example of labeled transition graph, we show in Figure 3 the LTG of the SAC $(E, R^A|S|S)$ defined the Example 3. It is worth noting that due to the presence of two stimulating molecules there exist two pairs of transitions sharing the same source and target solutions.

As reported above, the extraction of the CTMC from one labeled transition graph simply requires the collapsing of those transitions which share the same source and target solutions in one CTMC transition, whose rate is the sum of the rates of the collapsed transitions. As an example, we discuss the CTMC of the solution considered in the Example 4.

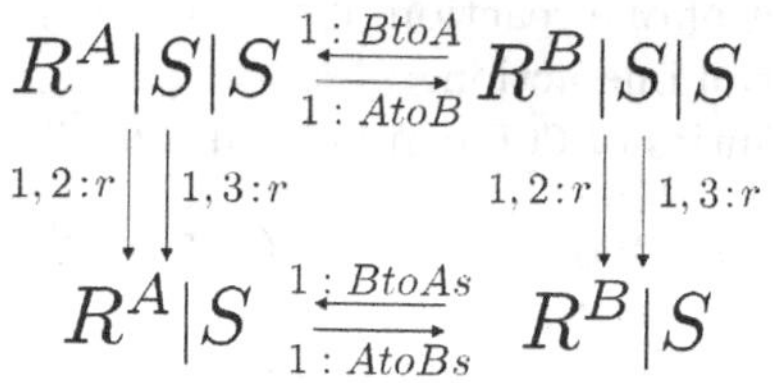

$$R^A|S|S \xrightleftharpoons[1:AtoB]{1:BtoA} R^B|S|S$$

$$1,2:r \quad \Big\downarrow 1,3:r \qquad\qquad 1,2:r \quad \Big\downarrow 1,3:r$$

$$R^A|S \xrightleftharpoons[1:AtoBs]{1:BtoAs} R^B|S$$

Fig. 3. Labeled Transition Graph of the SAC $(E, R^A|S|S)$

Example 5 (CTMC of a rotaxane). As an example of Continuous Time Markov Chain extracted from a Labeled Transition Graph, we show in Figure 4 the CTMC obtained from the LTG in Figure 3. It is worth noting that the CTMC

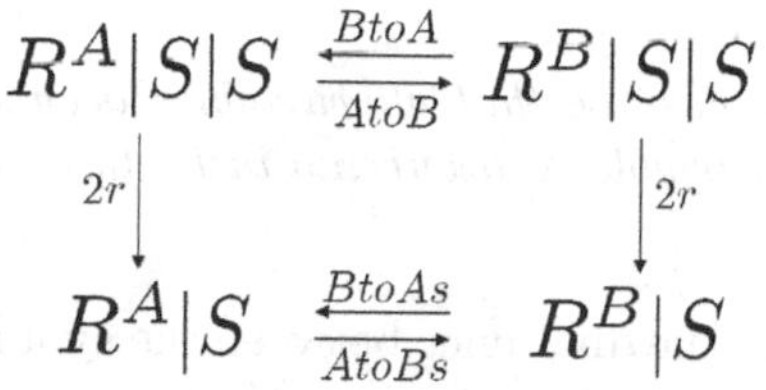

$$R^A|S|S \xrightleftharpoons[AtoB]{BtoA} R^B|S|S$$

$$2r \Big\downarrow \qquad\qquad\qquad \Big\downarrow 2r$$

$$R^A|S \xrightleftharpoons[AtoBs]{BtoAs} R^B|S$$

Fig. 4. Continuous Time Markov Chain of the SAC $(E, R^A|S|S)$

has the same states of the corresponding LTG. There are two differences: the transitions are labeled only with the stochastic rates, and the transitions sharing the same source and target solutions collapse in a unique transition, with rate equal to the sum of the rates of the collapsed transitions.

The CTMC semantics allows us to interpret the behavior of a SAC (E, P) as follows. Given any state T of the CTMC of (E, P), if it has n outgoing transitions labeled with $r_1, \cdots, r_n$, then the probability that the sojourn time in T is less than t is exponentially distributed with rate $\sum_i r_i$, i.e. *Prob*$\{delay < t\} = 1 - e^{-t \sum_i r_i}$, and the probability that the j-th transition is taken is $r_j/(\sum_i r_i)$.

3   Chemical Ground Form

One of the main feature of SAC is that the number of molecules in a modeled solution is an invariant, in fact when a molecule engage a reaction it produces exactly one new molecule. This is guaranteed by the syntax of molecule definitions $\pi; X$, according to which an actions π is always followed by one and only one species X. In [3], an extension of the model is considered in which the product can be a multiset of species, namely, the new syntax of action execution is $\pi; (X_1|\cdots|X_n)$. The new model is called Chemical Ground Form (CGF). The motivation for the definition of CGF is to obtain a process algebraic modeling of basic chemistry. As in basic chemistry there is no limitation to the number of molecules in the product of one reaction, it is necessary to admit more than one molecule as the product of one action.

The syntax and semantics of CGF can be found in [3]. We recall the syntax.

Definition 2 (Chemical Ground Form (CGF)). *Consider the following denumerable sets:* Species *ranged over by variables* X, Y, $\cdots$, Channels *ranged over by* a, b, $\cdots$, Moreover, *let* r, s, $\cdots$ *be rates (i.e. positive real numbers). The syntax of* CGF *is as follows:*

$$
\begin{array}{rcll}
E & ::= & \mathbf{0} \mid X = M, E & \text{Reagents} \\
M & ::= & \mathbf{0} \mid \pi; P \oplus M & \text{Molecule} \\
P & ::= & \mathbf{0} \mid X | P & \text{Solution} \\
\pi & ::= & \tau_{(r)} \mid ?a_{(r)} \mid !a_{(r)} & \text{Internal, Input, Output prefix} \\
\text{CGF} & ::= & (E, P) & \text{Reagents and initial Solution}
\end{array}
$$

Given a CGF (E, P), *we assume that all variables occurring in* P *occur also in* E. *Moreover, for every variable* X *occurring in* E, *there is exactly one definition* $X = M$ *in* E.

It is worth observing that the difference between the syntax of SAC and the syntax of CGF is that after the execution of one action π a solution, i.e. a multiset of molecules, can be specified as the product of the action. We call *molecule splitting* this possibility for one reactant to produce more than one molecule.

In [3] CGF is proved to be equivalent to basic chemistry both for discrete state and continuous state semantics. Discrete state semantics describe a solution as a multiset of molecules (i.e. for each molecule the exact number of instances is known) while continuous state semantics model a solution indicating the concentration of each species of interest (i.e. each species has an associated real number quantifying the concentration). By basic chemistry we mean systems modeled by a finite set of mono-molecular and bi-molecular reactions. To prove this equivalence result, CGF is equipped with both a discrete state semantics defined in terms of CTMC and a continuous state semantics defined in terms of ordinary differential equations. In this paper, we consider only the discrete state semantics.

We now present the running example for this section.

Example 6 (Counting the number of reactions). This example is not inspired by a specific chemical system, but it is proposed on purpose to focus on the increment of expressive power of CGF with respect to SAC. The idea is to consider two kinds of bi-molecular reactions, the first one called a and the second one called b. We present a system in which an arbitrary number of reactions of kind a are executed, and then a corresponding number of reactions of kind b occurs. In order to define such a system, we need the ability to "count" the number of occurrences of the reaction of kind a.

We can define such system in CGF considering two pairs of species: A and A' as the reactants of the reaction a and B and B' as the reactants of the reaction b:

$$A = \; !a_{(h)}; (A|B) \oplus \tau_{(l)}; B'$$
$$A' = \; ?a_{(h)}; A'$$
$$B = \; !b_{(h)}; \mathbf{0}$$
$$B' = \; ?b_{(h)}; B'$$

We assume that the rate h is greater than the rate l. We consider, as initial solution, one instance of species A and one of species A': formally, we consider the CGF $(E, A|A')$ where E includes the definitions of the species A, A', B, and B' as reported above.

As done in the previous section for SAC, we do not report the formal definition of the semantics that can be found in [3]. We simply recall that it is defined in terms of CTMCs obtained in two steps: first a labeled transition graph is associated to a CGF, then a CTMC is extracted from this labeled transition graph. As an example, we discuss the CTMC of the CGF $(E, A|A')$ defined in the Example 6.

Example 7. We present in Figure 5 the CTMC that, following the technique already described in the previous section (and formlized in [3]), is associated to the CGF $(E, A|A')$ of the Example 6. As we assume that the rate h is greater than

$$A|A' \xrightarrow{h} A|A'|B \xrightarrow{h} A|A'|B|B \xrightarrow{h} A|A'|B|B|B \xrightarrow{h} \ldots$$
$$\Big\downarrow l \qquad\qquad \Big\downarrow l \qquad\qquad\qquad \Big\downarrow l \qquad\qquad\qquad \Big\downarrow l$$
$$B'|A' \xleftarrow{h} B'|A'|B \xleftarrow{h} B'|A'|B|B \xleftarrow{h} B'|A'|B|B|B \xleftarrow{h} \ldots$$

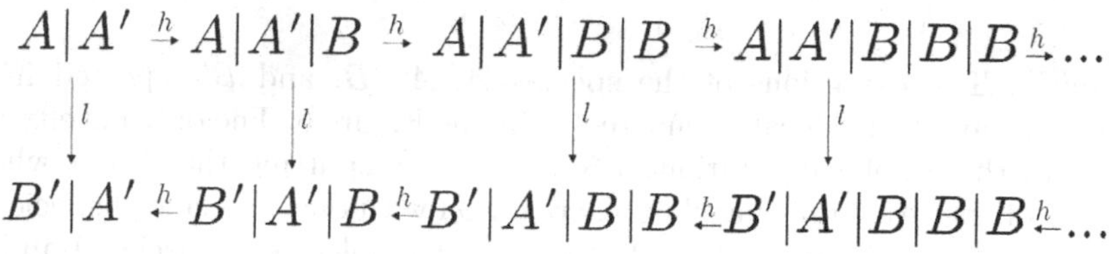

Fig. 5. Continuous Time Markov Chain of the CGF $(E, A|A')$

l, the initial solution more probably will select the reaction of kind a depicted horizontally in the Figure. Due to the fairness implicit in stochastic systems, the transition with the lower rate l cannot be delayed indefinitely, thus eventually one of the states of the second row will be reached with probability one. At this point of the computation, a number of transitions of kind b will be executed that coincides with the number of transitions of kind a already executed.

We complete the section showing how the graphical notation of SAC can be extended to cope also with molecule splitting of CGF. The idea is to separate, in case of splitting, the transitions in two parts adding an intermediary state. This new intermediary state is graphically represented with a line. We use one transition from the state representing the species of the reactant leading to the new intermediary transition. This transition is labeled with the executed action. Then, we use as many (unlabeled) transitions as the number of produced molecules. Each transition is from the new intermediary state to the state representing the species of one of the product. As an example, we show the graphical representation of the system described in the Example 6.

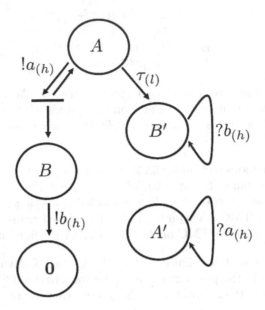

Fig. 6. Graphical representation of the CGF described in the Example 6

Example 8. The definitions of the species A, A', B, and B' reported in the Example 6 can be graphically rendered as in the Figure 6. The only novelty with respect to the graphical notation of SAC is in one splitting that occur when a molecule of species A is engaged in one reaction with one molecule of species A': in this case, the molecule splits and produces one molecule of species A and one of species B.

4   Stochastic Polyautomata Collectives

Stochastic Polyautomata Collectives (SPC) have been proosed in [2] as an extension of SAC able to capture the essential primitives of biochemistry. Biochemistry is obviously based on chemistry, and in principle one can always express the behavior of a biochemical systems by a collections chemical reactions. But there is a major practical problem with that approach: the collection of reactions for virtually all biochemical systems is an infinite one. For example, just to express the chemical reactions involved in linear polymerization, we need to have a different chemical species for each length n of polymer P_n, with reactions to grow the polymer: $P_n + M \rightarrow P_{n+1}$. While each polymer is finite, the set of possible polymerization reactions is infinite.

Nature adopts a more modular solution: the act of joining two molecules is called *complexation*, and polymers are made by iteratively complexing monomers. Each monomer obeys a *finite* simple set of rules that leads to the formation of polymers of any length; therefore, it seems that there should be a finite way of describing such systems. One can start by writing pseudo-reactions like $P + M \rightarrow P{:}M$, where $P : M$ is meant to represent a P(olymer) molecule attached to an extra M(onomer), yielding a longer polymer. However, there are in general many possible ways (that is, many different patches on the surface of a molecule) by which one molecule can exclusively form a complex with other molecules, and soon one needs to describe the *interface* of each molecule. This situation, while not commonly found in basic chemistry, is particularly acute in biochemistry, where virtually all reactions are governed by enzymes and molecular machines, which are themselves often built by complexation, and which usually operate by complexing with their reactants.

Both SAC and CGF have been extended to model also a minimalistic form of complexation. In this section we present Stochastic Polyautomata Collectives (SPC), the extension of the former with primitives for association (i.e. the creation of a complex) and dissociation (i.e. the separation of parts of the complex). This model has been presented in [2]. More precisely, two additional pairs of complementary prefixes, $\&?a_{(r)}, \&!a_{(r)}$ for association and $\%?a_{(r)}, \%!a_{(r)}$ for dissociation are added. Before presenting the formal syntax of SPC, we introduce the new primitives informally by means of examples. To simplify the notation, in the examples we abstract away from the stochastic rates, e.g., we write $\&?a$ instead of $\&?a_{(r)}$.

Example 9 (Linearly growing polymer). Each complexation event involves exactly two partners. We imagine that the partners have two complementary surface patches that can interlock. If c represents a surface shape (say, a paraboloid), then $!c$ indicates one of the two patches (say, the convex one) and $?c$ indicates the complementary patch (the concave one). Then, $\&!c$ is the action that presents the convex patch, and $\&?c$ is the action that presents the concave patch. When two such *association* actions meet, an actual complexation event can take place, joining the two complementary surfaces.

A linearly growing polymer could be represented as follows, using a seed S and a collection of equal monomers M. The seed starts the chain by presenting a concave patch $?c$: this is our initial, zero-length, polymer. Each monomer presents a convex patch $!c$, which can bind with an existing polymer on the complementary concave patch. After (and only after) such a binding, a bound monomer M' presents another concave patch $?c$, so that the polymer can keep growing. Both the seed and each monomer can have further behavior, S' and M''.

$$S = \&?c; S'$$
$$M = \&!c; M'$$
$$M' = \&?c; M''$$

Each complexation event creates a unique bond between exactly the two molecules that are joined to each other. This bond needs to be represented somehow, to make sure that a molecule can bind with only one other molecule at a time on any given patch. We represent such a bond as a unique key k that is shared by the two complexed molecules (think of k as a fresh number, or as a fresh channel in π-calculus [9]). Such unique keys, and related information, are collected in the *association history* of each molecule. So, the first interaction of an S with an M, which initially have empty association histories ($\mathbf{0}$), proceeds as follows:

$$S_0 \mid M_0 \rightarrow S'_{\langle ?c,k1 \rangle} \mid M'_{\langle !c,k1 \rangle}$$

Interaction with a second monomer then introduces a second fresh key in the histories:

$$S_0 \mid M_0 \mid M_0 \rightarrow S'_{\langle ?c,k1 \rangle} \mid M'_{\langle !c,k1 \rangle} \mid M_0 \rightarrow S'_{\langle ?c,k1 \rangle} \mid M''_{\langle ?c,k2 \rangle :: \langle !c,k1 \rangle} \mid M'_{\langle !c,k2 \rangle}$$

and so on. In any configuration, we can reconstruct from the association histories who is bound to whom, and on what surface the bond was formed. Note that the description of the system is finite (3 reagents, S, M, M'), but that polymers of any length can be assembled.

Example 10 (Branching polymer). After complexation, a molecule is still free to perform additional complexations or other interactions. That is, complexation places no restrictions on the behavior of the original molecules, except for the fact that new complexations cannot occur on surfaces that are already occupied, and that decomplexations must happen consistently with prior complexations (as we discuss shortly). To illustrate this freedom, let us modify the previous example and allow each bound monomer to offer a seed for growing a new polymer branch:

$$
\begin{aligned}
S &= \&?c; S' \\
M &= \&!c; M' \\
M' &= \&?c; S
\end{aligned}
$$

When an M' turns into a seed S, that is a seed with an non-empty association history that connects it to its current branch, but that can also start a new branch. If we do not wish to start a branch at every monomer, we can modify M' to something like $M' = \&?c; S \oplus \tau; M''$, so that an M' has a temporary potential to act as a seed, but after some delay (τ) it may change to an M'' that is not a seed. By adjusting the stochastic rates of the delay and of c, we can produce different (stochastic) branching factors.

Example 11 (Actin-like polymer). *Decomplexation* is the inverse of complexation, that is, two formerly joined molecules can dissociate. We indicate by $\%!c$ the attempt to dissociate from the convex side, and $\%?c$ the attempt to dissociate from the concave side. When two complexed molecules attempt complementary dissociations, an actual decomplexation event can take place. To illustrate this situation, we describe a different kind of linear polymer: one that can grow only at one end, and can shrink only at the other end. There are four molecular states for each monomer: M^f (free monomer), M^l (monomer bound on the left), M^r (monomer bound on the right), and M^b (monomer bound on both sides). Each monomer has a left convex surface and a complementary right concave surface. A polymer should associate (grow) only on the right and should dissociate (shrink) only on the left.

$$
\begin{aligned}
M^f &= \&!c; M^l \oplus \&?c; M^r \\
M^l &= \%!c; M^f \oplus \&?c; M^b \\
M^r &= \%?c; M^f \\
M^b &= \%!c; M^r
\end{aligned}
$$

A free monomer M^f can either associate on the left convex surface and become bound on the left, or associate on the right concave surface and become bound on the right. A monomer M^l bound only on the left can either dissociate on the left (if allowed by its partner, which must in fact be an M^r in this case) and return free, or associate on the right (with an M^f) and become bound on both sides. A monomer M^r bound only on the right can only dissociate on the right: that is, a polymer cannot grow on the left. A monomer M^b bound on both sides can only dissociate on the left (with an M^r): that is, a polymer cannot shrink on the right or break in the middle. These rules cover also the base cases when a polymer of length 2 initially forms or finally dissolves.

A decomplexation should succeed only between a pair of molecules that were actually complexed in their past history, and this can be checked by inspecting the unique keys introduced during complexation. For example let us consider two M^f molecules that complex and then immediately decomplex:

$$M_0^f \mid M_0^f \rightarrow M_{\langle !c,k \rangle}^l \mid M_{\langle ?c,k \rangle}^r \rightarrow M_0^f \mid M_0^f$$

The second transition is allowed to happen because M^l offers $\%!c$, M^r offers the complementary $\%?c$, and the same key k appears in both association histories on the c interface (and with the correct convexity). As a consequence of decomplexation, the keys are removed from the histories.

After this gentle introduction to SPC by means of examples, we present the formal definition of its syntax. The main novelty deals with the association histories which are added to each molecule to keep track of the association keys representing the bonds currently active between the molecule itself, and the other molecules to which it is complexed.

Definition 3 (Stochastic Polyautomata Collectives (SPC)). *Consider the following denumerable sets:* Species *ranged over by variables* X, Y, X^1, X^2, $\cdots$, Channels *ranged over by* a, b, $\cdots$, *a set of* Association keys *ranged over by* k, k', $\cdots$. *Moreover, let* r, s, $\cdots$ *be rates (i.e. positive real numbers).*
The syntax of SPC *is as follows:*

$$
\begin{aligned}
E &::= \mathbf{0} \mid X = M, E & &\text{\textit{Reagents}} \\
M &::= \mathbf{0} \mid \pi; X \oplus M & &\text{\textit{Molecule}} \\
\pi &::= \tau_{(r)} \mid ?a_{(r)} \mid !a_{(r)} & &\text{\textit{Internal, Input, Output prefix}} \\
&\quad \mid \&?a_{(r)} \mid \&!a_{(r)} & &\text{\textit{Association prefixes}} \\
&\quad \mid \%?a_{(r)} \mid \%!a_{(r)} & &\text{\textit{Dissociation prefixes}} \\
P &::= \mathbf{0} \mid X_H \mid P & &\text{\textit{Solution}} \\
H &::= \mathbf{0} \mid \langle ?a, k \rangle :: H \mid \langle !a, k \rangle :: H & &\text{\textit{Association history}} \\
\text{BGF} &::= (P, S) & &\text{\textit{Reagents and initial Solution}}
\end{aligned}
$$

Given a BGF (E, P), *we assume that all variables occurring in* P *occur also in* E. *Moreover, for every variable* X *occurring in* E, *there is exactly one definition*

$X = M$ in E. Moreover, each association key k in P, occur in exactly two complementary associations $\langle ?a, k \rangle$ and $\langle !a, k \rangle$, that appear in the association histories H and H' of two distinct molecules X_H and $X'_{H'}$.

The syntax of SPC has been obtained as a fragment of the Biological Ground Form (BGF), a process algebra defined in [4]. More precisely, SPC is as the fragment of BGF without molecule splitting. In [4], the formal semantics of BGF is defined; clearly, this applies also to its fragment SPC.

We complete the section presenting an example of graphical notation for SPC, depicting the representation of the actin-like polymer described in the Example 11.

Example 12 (Graphical representation of the actin-like polymer). The graphical representation of SPC simply includes four new labels for the new actions $\&?a_{(r)}$, $\&!a_{(r)}$, $\%?a_{(r)}$ and $\%!a_{(r)}$. As an example, we depict in the Figure 7 the representation of the behavior of an actin-like polymer as described in the Example 11 (as done in that example, we abstract away from the rates).

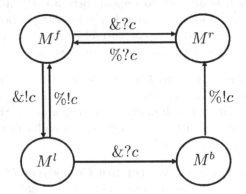

Fig. 7. Graphical representation of the actin-like polymer described in the Example 11

5   Biochemical Ground Form

We now move to the last model considered in this paper, the Biochemical Ground Form (BGF). This model includes all mechanisms discussed in this paper, both molecule splitting and complexation. The main technical problem deals with the specification of the distribution of the associations in the association history of one reactant over the different products of a splitting. In fact, in case a molecule forks it is necessary to specify how its associations are distributed over the produced molecules. This information is described by means of a new syntactic category called *association markers*. These are additional information associated to the produced molecule, that completely and uniquely define the distribution of associations, that is, all possible associations of one reactant should be reported in one and only one association marker of the product.

The formal syntax of BGF is defined as follows.

Definition 4 (Biochemical Ground Form (BGF)). *Consider the following denumerable sets:* Species *ranged over by variables* X, Y, X^1, X^2, $\cdots$, Channels *ranged over by* a, b, $\cdots$, *a totally ordered set of* Association keys *ranged over by* k, k', $\cdots$. *Moreover, let* r, s, $\cdots$ *be rates (i.e. positive real numbers). The syntax of BGF is as follows:*

$$
\begin{array}{lll}
E ::= \mathbf{0} \mid X = M, E & & \textit{Reagents} \\
M ::= \mathbf{0} \mid \pi; P \oplus M & & \textit{Molecule} \\
\pi ::= \tau_{(r)} \mid ?a_{(r)} \mid !a_{(r)} & & \textit{Internal, Input, Output prefix} \\
\quad \mid \&?a_{(r)} \mid \&!a_{(r)} & & \textit{Association prefixes} \\
\quad \mid \%?a_{(r)} \mid \%!a_{(r)} & & \textit{Dissociation prefixes} \\
P ::= \mathbf{0} \mid X_h \mid P & & \textit{Product} \\
h ::= \mathbf{0} \mid ?a :: h \mid !a :: h & & \textit{Association markers} \\
S ::= \mathbf{0} \mid X_H \mid S & & \textit{Solution} \\
H ::= \mathbf{0} \mid \langle ?a, k \rangle :: H \mid \langle !a, k \rangle :: H & & \textit{Association history} \\
\text{BGF} ::= (E, S) & & \textit{Reagents and initial Solution}
\end{array}
$$

Given a BGF (E, S), *we assume that all variables occurring in* S *occur also in* E. *Moreover, for every variable* X *occurring in* E, *there is exactly one definition* $X = M$ *in* E. *Moreover, each association key* k *in* P, *occur in exactly two complementary associations* $\langle ?a, k \rangle$ *and* $\langle !a, k \rangle$, *that appear in the association histories* H *and* H' *of two distinct molecules* X_H *and* $X'_{H'}$.

As discussed above, a well formed BGF should be defined in such a way that every time a molecule splits, it is always possible to define the way in which the associations in the history of the reactants are distributed over the products. The reader interested in the formalization of this notion of well formed CGF can refer to [4], where also the formal definition of the semantics can be found.

We complete this section with an extension of the example of the actin-like polymer discussed in the Example 11. The idea is to allow a fully bound monomer to split into two independent monomers, each one inheriting one of the two bonds. In this way, the polymer breaks in two new independent polymers.

Example 13 (Breaking polymer). To illustrate complexation in combination with molecule splitting, we describe a linearly growing polymer similar to the actin-like polymer of the Example 11 in which each monomer, once bound on both sides, is free to split into two new monomers each one inheriting one of the two bonds. The definition is as follows:

$$
\begin{array}{rcl}
M^f & = & \&!c; M^l \oplus \&?c; M^r \\
M^l & = & \%!c; M^f \oplus \&?c; M^b \\
M^r & = & \%?c; M^f \\
M^b & = & \%!c; M^r \oplus \tau; (M^l_{!c} \mid M^r_{?c})
\end{array}
$$

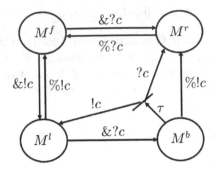

Fig. 8. Graphical representation of the breaking polymer described in the Example 13

It is worth observing that in case of splitting of the molecules of species M^b, it is necessary to indicate also how to split the associations among the two produced molecules of species M^l and M^r, respectively. This is obtained adding the association marker corresponding to the bonds to be split.

Also the graphical representation for CGF that we consider need to add graphical notation for dealing with association splitting. This is achieved adding the association markers as labels of the transitions incoming into the species of the products of a splitting reaction. As an example, we depict the graphical representation of the breaking polymer of the Example 13.

Example 14 (Graphical representation of the breaking polymer). The graphical representation of BGF simply combine those of CGF and SPC with the addition of association markers as labels for the transitions representing the target states in case of splitting. As an example, we depict in the Figure 8 the representation of the behavior of an breaking polymer as described in the Example 13 (as done in that example, we abstract away from the rates).

Acknowledgements. We thank Luca Cardelli for the discussions about the Chemical Ground Form and the association and dissociation mechanisms formalized in its extension Biochemical Ground Form. We thank also Alberto Credi, Marco Garavelli, Cosimo Laneve, Sylvain Pradalier, and Serena Silvi co-authors of the paper [6] from which the example of the rotaxane was taken.

References

1. Badjic, J.D., Balzani, V., Credi, A., Silvi, S., Stoddart, J.F.: A molecular elevator. Science 303, 1845–1849 (2004)
2. Cardelli, L.: Artificial Biochemistry (2007), http://lucacardelli.name
3. Cardelli, L.: On Process Rate Semantics. In: Theoretical Computer Science (in press, 2008), http://dx.doi.org/10.1016/j.tcs.2007.11.012
4. Cardelli, L., Zavattaro, G.: On the Computational Power of Biochemistry (2008), http://lucacardelli.name

5. Champin, B., Mobian, P., Sauvage, J.-P.: Transition metal complexes as molecular machine prototypes. Chemical Society Reviews 36(2), 358–366 (2006)
6. Credi, A., Garavelli, M., Laneve, C., Pradalier, S., Silvi, S., Zavattaro, G.: Modelization and Simulation of Nano Devices in nano-kappa Calculus. In: Calder, M., Gilmore, S. (eds.) CMSB 2007. LNCS (LNBI), vol. 4695, pp. 168–183. Springer, Heidelberg (2007)
7. Huang, T.-J., Brough, B., Ho, C.-M., Liu, Y., Flood, A.H., Bonvallet, P.A., Tseng, H.-R., Stoddart, J.F., Baller, M., Magonov, S.: A nanomechanical device based on linear molecular motors. Applied Physics Letters 85(22), 5391–5393 (2004)
8. Jimenez, M.C., Dietrich-Buchecker, C., Sauvage, J.-P.: Towards synthetic molecular muscles: Contraction and stretching of a linear rotaxane dimer. Angew. Chem. Int. Ed. 39(18), 3284–3287 (2000)
9. Milner, R.: Communication and Concurrency. Prentice-Hall, Englewood Cliffs (1989)
10. Sauvage, J.-P., Dietrich-Bucheker, C.O. (eds.): Molecular Catenanes, Rotaxanes and Knots. Wiley-VCH, Weinheim (1999)

Author Index

Lecture Notes in Computer Science

Sublibrary 2: Programming and Software Engineering

For information about Vols. 1– 4350
please contact your bookseller or Springer

Vol. 4716: B. Meyer, M. Joseph (Eds.), Software Engineering Approaches for Offshore and Outsourced Development. X, 201 pages. 2007.

Vol. 4709: F.S. de Boer, M.M. Bonsangue, S. Graf, W.-P. de Roever (Eds.), Formal Methods for Components and Objects. VIII, 297 pages. 2007.

Vol. 4680: F. Saglietti, N. Oster (Eds.), Computer Safety, Reliability, and Security. XV, 548 pages. 2007.

Vol. 4670: V. Dahl, I. Niemelä (Eds.), Logic Programming. XII, 470 pages. 2007.

Vol. 4652: D. Georgakopoulos, N. Ritter, B. Benatallah, C. Zirpins, G. Feuerlicht, M. Schoenherr, H.R. Motahari-Nezhad (Eds.), Service-Oriented Computing ICSOC 2006. XVI, 201 pages. 2007.

Vol. 4640: A. Rashid, M. Aksit (Eds.), Transactions on Aspect-Oriented Software Development IV. IX, 191 pages. 2007.

Vol. 4634: H. Riis Nielson, G. Filé (Eds.), Static Analysis. XI, 469 pages. 2007.

Vol. 4620: A. Rashid, M. Aksit (Eds.), Transactions on Aspect-Oriented Software Development III. IX, 201 pages. 2007.

Vol. 4615: R. de Lemos, C. Gacek, A. Romanovsky (Eds.), Architecting Dependable Systems IV. XIV, 435 pages. 2007.

Vol. 4610: B. Xiao, L.T. Yang, J. Ma, C. Muller-Schloer, Y. Hua (Eds.), Autonomic and Trusted Computing. XVIII, 571 pages. 2007.

Vol. 4609: E. Ernst (Ed.), ECOOP 2007 – Object-Oriented Programming. XIII, 625 pages. 2007.

Vol. 4608: H.W. Schmidt, I. Crnković, G.T. Heineman, J.A. Stafford (Eds.), Component-Based Software Engineering. XII, 283 pages. 2007.

Vol. 4591: J. Davies, J. Gibbons (Eds.), Integrated Formal Methods. IX, 660 pages. 2007.

Vol. 4589: J. Münch, P. Abrahamsson (Eds.), Product-Focused Software Process Improvement. XII, 414 pages. 2007.

Vol. 4574: J. Derrick, J. Vain (Eds.), Formal Techniques for Networked and Distributed Systems – FORTE 2007. XI, 375 pages. 2007.

Vol. 4556: C. Stephanidis (Ed.), Universal Access in Human-Computer Interaction, Part III. XXII, 1020 pages. 2007.

Vol. 4555: C. Stephanidis (Ed.), Universal Access in Human-Computer Interaction, Part II. XXII, 1066 pages. 2007.

Vol. 4554: C. Stephanidis (Ed.), Universal Acess in Human Computer Interaction, Part I. XXII, 1054 pages. 2007.

Vol. 4553: J.A. Jacko (Ed.), Human-Computer Interaction, Part IV. XXIV, 1225 pages. 2007.

Vol. 4552: J.A. Jacko (Ed.), Human-Computer Interaction, Part III. XXI, 1038 pages. 2007.

Vol. 4551: J.A. Jacko (Ed.), Human-Computer Interaction, Part II. XXIII, 1253 pages. 2007.

Vol. 4550: J.A. Jacko (Ed.), Human-Computer Interaction, Part I. XXIII, 1240 pages. 2007.

Vol. 4542: P. Sawyer, B. Paech, P. Heymans (Eds.), Requirements Engineering: Foundation for Software Quality. IX, 384 pages. 2007.

Vol. 4536: G. Concas, E. Damiani, M. Scotto, G. Succi (Eds.), Agile Processes in Software Engineering and Extreme Programming. XV, 276 pages. 2007.

Vol. 4530: D.H. Akehurst, R. Vogel, R.F. Paige (Eds.), Model Driven Architecture - Foundations and Applications. X, 219 pages. 2007.

Vol. 4523: Y.-H. Lee, H.-N. Kim, J. Kim, Y.W. Park, L.T. Yang, S.W. Kim (Eds.), Embedded Software and Systems. XIX, 829 pages. 2007.

Vol. 4498: N. Abdennahder, F. Kordon (Eds.), Reliable Software Technologies - Ada-Europe 2007. XII, 247 pages. 2007.

Vol. 4486: M. Bernardo, J. Hillston (Eds.), Formal Methods for Performance Evaluation. VII, 469 pages. 2007.

Vol. 4470: Q. Wang, D. Pfahl, D.M. Raffo (Eds.), Software Process Dynamics and Agility. XI, 346 pages. 2007.

Vol. 4468: M.M. Bonsangue, E.B. Johnsen (Eds.), Formal Methods for Open Object-Based Distributed Systems. X, 317 pages. 2007.

Vol. 4467: A.L. Murphy, J. Vitek (Eds.), Coordination Models and Languages. X, 325 pages. 2007.

Vol. 4454: Y. Gurevich, B. Meyer (Eds.), Tests and Proofs. IX, 217 pages. 2007.

Vol. 4444: T. Reps, M. Sagiv, J. Bauer (Eds.), Program Analysis and Compilation, Theory and Practice. X, 361 pages. 2007.

Vol. 4440: B. Liblit, Cooperative Bug Isolation. XV, 101 pages. 2007.

Vol. 4408: R. Choren, A. Garcia, H. Giese, H.-f. Leung, C. Lucena, A. Romanovsky (Eds.), Software Engineering for Multi-Agent Systems V. XII, 233 pages. 2007.

Vol. 4406: W. De Meuter (Ed.), Advances in Smalltalk. VII, 157 pages. 2007.

Vol. 4405: L. Padgham, F. Zambonelli (Eds.), Agent-Oriented Software Engineering VII. XII, 225 pages. 2007.

Vol. 4401: N. Guelfi, D. Buchs (Eds.), Rapid Integration of Software Engineering Techniques. IX, 177 pages. 2007.

Vol. 4385: K. Coninx, K. Luyten, K.A. Schneider (Eds.), Task Models and Diagrams for Users Interface Design. XI, 355 pages. 2007.

Vol. 4383: E. Bin, A. Ziv, S. Ur (Eds.), Hardware and Software, Verification and Testing. XII, 235 pages. 2007.

Vol. 4379: M. Südholt, C. Consel (Eds.), Object-Oriented Technology. VIII, 157 pages. 2007.

Vol. 4364: T. Kühne (Ed.), Models in Software Engineering. XI, 332 pages. 2007.

Vol. 4355: J. Julliand, O. Kouchnarenko (Eds.), B 2007: Formal Specification and Development in B. XIII, 293 pages. 2006.

Vol. 4354: M. Hanus (Ed.), Practical Aspects of Declarative Languages. X, 335 pages. 2006.